ETHICAL CHALLENGES TO BUSINESS AS USUAL

ETHICAL CHALLENGES TO BUSINESS AS USUAL

second edition

edited by

Shari Collins

broadview press

Broadview Press – www.broadviewpress.com
Peterborough, Ontario, Canada

Founded in 1985, Broadview Press remains a wholly independent publishing house. Broadview's focus is on academic publishing: our titles are accessible to university and college students as well as scholars and general readers. With over 800 titles in print, Broadview has become a leading international publisher in the humanities, with world-wide distribution. Broadview is committed to environmentally responsible publishing and fair business practices.

Library and Archives Canada Cataloguing in Publication

Title: Ethical challenges to business as usual / edited by Shari Collins.
Names: Collins, Shari. editor.
Description: Second edition. | Includes bibliographical references.
Identifiers: Canadiana (print) 20220227594 | Canadiana (ebook) 20220227713 | ISBN 9781554814510 (softcover) |
    ISBN 9781770488403 (PDF) | ISBN 9781460407875 (EPUB)
Subjects: LCSH: Business ethics. | LCSH: Social responsibility of business. | LCSH: International business
    enterprises—Developing countries. | LCSH: Industrial management—Environmental aspects. |
    LCSH: Industrial management—Moral and ethical aspects.
Classification: DDC 174/.4—dc23

Broadview Press handles its own distribution in North America:
PO Box 1243, Peterborough, Ontario, K9J 7H5, Canada
555 Riverwalk Parkway, Tonawanda, NY 14150, USA
Tel: (705) 743-8990; Fax: (705) 743-8353
email: customerservice@broadviewpress.com

For all territories outside of North America, distribution is handled by Eurospan Group.

Broadview Press acknowledges the financial support of the Government of Canada for our publishing activities. Canada

Copy-edited by Martin R. Boyne
Designed by George Kirkpatrick

PRINTED IN CANADA

Dedicated to my students—current and past—especially
Bryce Barraza, an exceptional student who embodies my hope for a
transformative future.

Contents

Preface

THE FIRST EDITION OF this anthology addressed a significant gap in the business ethics anthology texts in that it challenged the status quo rather than simply argued that the existing system needs some adjustments from fair competition to meritocratic access and opportunity. This edition continues in this vein, including challenging development, capitalism, environmental destruction, market appropriations, consumption, and human rights violations. As in the first edition, this one does not cordon off environmental issues as a subset of business ethics but rather integrates them throughout. Each and every action of business relies upon the Earth's *finite* resources, and any business analysis that omits this is incomplete.

The advantages of this anthology are at least threefold. First is its challenging the assumptions of the status quo, from development, to pollution, to white privilege, to consumption. Second is the unique combination of topical coverage, including human rights, corporate responsibility, transgenic biotechnology, development resistance, factory farming, and alternative economies. The third advantage is that I have retained enough classic selections so as to be familiar, yet I've also included new voices that pull the discussion firmly into the twenty-first century.

I would like to thank the following people who contributed to the first edition in myriad ways. They include Gloria Cuádraz, Alejandra Elenes, Donald Chobanian, Blake Chobanian, Gene Burgess, Mark Koan, Manny Avalos, Kristie Pinner, Karen Merry, Cat Lollis, Dennis Isbell, Kenneth Lux, Robert Heilbroner, Clive Ponting, Jean Blackstone, Deane Curtin, Christopher Stone, R. Edward Freeman, Arjun Makhijani, Peggy McIntosh, Paul W. Taylor, Rodger Field, Russell Mokhiber, Martha L. Crouch, Brian Tokar, Mark Sagoff, Sissela Bok, David C. Korten, Bill Smith, Jenny Dunhill, Carla Worner, Jessica Balch, and Ross Miller. For this edition I owe many thanks to Louis Mendoza for his comments on the manuscript, and to my editor, Stephen Latta, and the people at Broadview Press.

—Shari Collins

Chapter 1: Ethical and Economic Theoretical Grounding

Data for, and Values in, Ethics

BUSINESS ETHICS IS A branch of applied ethics. Applied ethics is the philosophical study of how one makes a moral judgment about how we should act regarding issues in public and private life. In applied ethics, ethical theories are put forward and applied to cases, and then an argument is advanced about what *ought to be* regarding a specific action or policy. In general, ethics is about what ought to be, as opposed to what is.

Facts about what is—that is, what exists in the world—are empirical issues. Many things exist and occur, including murder, philanthropy, poverty, and all kinds of harms and benefits. Since ethics concerns what ought to be, it is reflected in our laws, codes, religions, social roles, and intuitions.

Intuitions are gut feelings that we have that initially lead us to believe if something is right or wrong. They are important to applied ethics because they can help us to identify moral problems, and because they can give us insight into the ethical claims of what people actually believe. However, intuitions in and of themselves are merely a quick check and do not provide the kinds of reasons or arguments needed to answer ethical questions.

Likewise, laws, codes, and religion all give us rules to follow, with the underlying assumption that following these is what is morally right. However, following them without reflecting on their justification(s) may lead us to do what is morally wrong. Just because a law or a religious edict exists—for example, allowing human slavery—does not provide its moral justification. In order to provide a moral justification, an argument for those laws or codes must be given.

The purpose of studying applied ethics is to take an ethical stand on the issues, and this requires a reasoned argument as to what ought to be the case, not a mere appeal to what is the case, whether that be facts, laws, or religious belief. Many values enter into applied ethics, including autonomy, responsibility, justice, care, community, and empathy.

Autonomy is one's ability to make informed decisions for oneself, without coercion. Autonomy is a prerequisite for ethical responsibility, and we don't normally hold people fully ethically responsible for their actions if they lack autonomy. In the United States, the age of 18 is when we recognize people's legal autonomy for such things as sexual consent, voting, and being able to make most legal decisions for themselves. Up until that point, we normally hold people less than fully responsible for their actions, which is why minors are typically subject to different legal processes and punishments than adults. Likewise, we don't generally recognize full autonomy in severely mentally incompetent persons.

Responsibility is the ability to both see and accept the consequences of one's behavior. Autonomy is a prerequisite to responsibility, for if one cannot make decisions, one cannot be held responsible. Think of duress or coercion here. Suppose someone has a gun to another person's head. A gun to one's head is extreme coercion, and one cannot be held accountable when one is under such duress. In law, one can be at fault only if one is responsible, and one can be at fault either for intentionally bringing about a harm or for failing to do a duty (acting recklessly, for example) that results in harm.

Justice is where one gets one's due. This can either be a benefit or a punishment. Justice in the legal field is supposed to be impartial, absent of unfair privileges, such as those that fame or fortune might bring.

Care is a bit of a contrast to justice, as this value encourages one to act partially toward those in need, or to those with whom one has a relationship, such as a family member or friend. Care is reflected in laws such as those that require access for all people to buildings via ramps, automatic doors, and so forth. It is also reflected in the right not to testify against a spouse. In a business context, we might see the value of care reflected in the special responsibilities an employer has to employees.

Community as a value is the recognition that we don't achieve what we do in life alone: to use a cliché, it takes a village. Every aspect of our lives depends on a network of public services that act as infrastructure. Furthermore, taxes provide for the social welfare system that allows for such things such as education (whether it's fully or partially funded by government).

Empathy is the ability to put oneself in another's place. This is a crucial value in ethics, as so many issues are contentious and require an understanding of more than one side in order to take a reasoned position and put forth a strong argument. Empathy may also shift one's perspective on an issue.

Intuitions, laws, religion, and social roles provide data for applied ethics. They tell us what is, what people believe. Values are those things that we hold and try to reinforce in our laws and codes. Neither the data nor the values constitute ethical arguments on their own. We'll now look at a number of the major historical ethical theories that shape contemporary reasoning in applied ethics.

Ethical Theories

Aristotle's Nicomachean (aka "Virtue") Ethics

Aristotle (384–322 BCE) was a Greek philosopher who, at age 17, attended Plato's Academy of Athens as a student and then remained as a teacher until Plato's death in 348. In 335 he founded the Lyceum and taught there for twelve years, until political strife forced him to Euboea, where he died shortly thereafter.

Aristotle is the most famous advocate of virtue ethics, wherein developing the right character that exhibits virtues brings one the ability to make proper moral judgments. For Aristotle, virtues are "moral states" that we judge via praise or blame, good or evil. Aristotle holds *eudaimonia*, a Greek work that can be translated as happiness, or well-being, as the highest human good. This is not just any happiness but a happiness where one acts according to human virtues that are suited to the human soul and uses one's reason in developing proper, virtuous habits. When we choose virtuous behavior, a wisdom emerges that includes acting in accordance with justice. Virtues are not merely theoretical; they are applied, that is, put to practical use.

In acquiring a virtuous character, one must strive for the "mean." The mean is situated between two extremes of excess and deficiency. Aristotle writes,

> By the mean ... I understand that which is neither too much nor too little; but this is not one thing, nor is it the same for everybody ... *the right amount will vary with the individual.* This being so, everybody who understands his business avoids alike excess and deficiency; he seeks and chooses the mean, not the absolute mean, but the mean considered relatively to ourselves.... It is a mean state *firstly* as *lying* between two vices.[1]

For example, consider bravery. This falls in between cowardice and foolhardiness. Cowardice is the deficiency and foolhardiness is the excess. Bravery is the virtue here, and while it will vary somewhat between individuals, one must strive to be clear of the excess and the deficiency, or the vices. When one acts in accordance with vice, one is vicious and without moral merit.

Aristotle notes that this must be a choice. If someone is unable to act autonomously, or is acting in ignorance, they will not be held responsible. However, on the latter point, ignorance is not an excuse if the person could have reasonably known, or should have known, the nature of the act(s) in question.

Aristotle reiterates that our choices place us in circumstances where we are responsible for the character we acquire. If we wallow in licentious activities, such as drunkenness or wickedness, or if we envy or commit adultery, or anything along these lines, we set ourselves up not only for bad character but also to be judged as immoral. Virtue ethics, therefore, is a roadmap for developing good character that begets more good character, as well as a moral theory that can be applied to make judgments of both actions and character.

Immanuel Kant's Deontological Ethical Theory

Immanuel Kant (1724–1804) was a German philosopher and university professor in Königsberg, Prussia, known for his three "Critiques": the *Critique of Pure Reason* (1781), the *Critique of Practical Reason* (1788), and the *Critique of Judgment* (1790). Here the focus is on his writings in *The Groundwork of the Metaphysics of Morals* (1785).

Deontology is a branch of ethical theory that focuses on obligations and duty. Kant's approach to deontology assumes that we cannot control consequences but only our intention, and it is there that the morality of the action is judged. Kant put forth his deontological ethical theory with categorical imperatives (CI). *Categorical* means that it applies in all circumstances; it is universal. *Imperative* means that you must follow the categorical duties.

Kant's first formulation of the CI is that of the universalization of an act. Kant states, "act only in accordance with that maxim through which you can at the same time will that it become a universal law." Thus, when you are considering an action, you take that action and state it as a universal law that all rational agents follow as a law of nature. If this act, universalized, in a world of rational agents is acceptable, then the action is morally permissible.

Kant's second formulation of the CI has been called both the "Formula of Humanity" and the "Formula of the End in Itself." It states, "Act in such a way that you always treat humanity, whether in your own person or in the person of any other, never simply as a means but always at the same time as an end." Humans have intrinsic value, they are ends in themselves, and to treat them *merely* as means, as if they were a machine or instrument, is to deny their humanity and to violate their autonomy. This does not mean that we may not "use" others for things that we do, such as performing tasks or producing goods. However, when we rely on others, hire others, or need others, we should not see them as simple means to our ends but instead respect their intrinsic human value and honor that they are ends in themselves.

An application of Kant's CI can be seen via the act of telling a lie. Suppose your romantic partner asks you how they look in an outfit that you find unflattering, but you are tempted to lie about this.

First, apply the universalization CI. To do so, we ask what maxim we would be operating on if we decided to lie in this context. The maxim would be something along these lines: "It is permissible to lie when doing so protects another person from hurt feelings." Now imagine this maxim universalized. This would result in all people at all times being able to lie whenever doing so would protect others from hurt feelings. If everyone were to act in accordance with this maxim, we would no longer be able to trust other people's claims, as all people would be lying, and this would make the claims meaningless. Therefore, this maxim cannot be universalized. As it cannot be universalized, it is therefore immoral to act on this maxim. In addition, if you lie, you are violating the other person's autonomy because they need to have accurate information to be able to make decisions.

Second, if you apply the humanity CI to the act of a lie, you see that you are treating the other person merely as a means to your end. This is because you are trying to control the other person through misinformation. For example, suppose you lie to spare their feelings. Remember that consequences are not what you are responsible for; instead, you are responsible for your will and intent. This means

that you have tried to bring about a certain consequence, whether it is sparing their feelings, or preventing them from being angry, or avoiding conflict. That is using another person as a means to your end and denying their humanity. Therefore, both formulations of the CI show that lying to your partner would be immoral.

Remember that Kant is an absolutist, that is, one who asserts that moral laws are universal. There is only one morally correct answer. You might object that lying, especially "white lies," are needed to keep the peace in relationships. For Kant, that is dangerous ground, and also unethical, as you have led the other person to believe you and have given them false information. Remember that you have to raise the act to a universal law, and it is there that you can see the rational contradiction.

Kant also argues that our duty to follow the CI

> does not rest at all on feelings, impulses, or inclinations, but solely on the relation of rational beings to one another, a relation in which the will of a rational being must always be regarded as *legislative*, since otherwise it could not be conceived as *an end in itself*. Reason then refers to every maxim of the will, regarding it as legislating universally, to every other will and also to every action towards oneself ... from the idea of the *dignity* of a rational being, obeying no law but that which he himself also gives.[2]

John Stuart Mill's Utilitarianism

Another major theory, in contrast to deontology, is consequentialism. Utilitarianism is a form of consequentialism. Unlike deontology, utilitarianism assumes that what makes an action morally right or wrong are the consequences. It is further assumed, and logically necessary, that the actor has knowledge of the consequences the action will bring and can control bringing about that end.

Mill (1806–73) was an English social reformer, an empiricist philosopher who was influenced by Jeremy Bentham, among others. Bentham (1748–1832) coined the term *utilitarianism*, which he advanced regarding how to morally judge actions. For Bentham, what makes an action right is how it maximizes pleasure and minimizes pain among its recipients.

In 1863, Mill wrote *Utilitarianism*, which modified Bentham's work and made significant qualitative distinctions between pleasures. Mill rejected Bentham's notion of self-interest, as he found it less than adequate as a way to define moral goodness. Using "pleasures" as a moral measure risks reduction to hedonism. Hedonism in ethics is associated with the Cyrenaics (fourth century BCE) and is the position that happiness derived from pleasures is what humans should and do seek. For the Cyrenaics, this included both intellectual pleasures and the pleasures of our senses. Bentham's revival placed a quantitative emphasis on acquiring pleasures, and this is where Mill diverges.

Mill's hierarchy of "pleasures" places intellectual pursuits and other "higher" pleasures above "lower" pleasures. His famous quote "It is better to be a human being dissatisfied than a pig satisfied; better to be Socrates dissatisfied, than a fool satisfied" illustrates this well. Philosophy and other related pleasures are desired over physical, lower pleasures, and Mill's utilitarianism requires that we bring about the greatest overall good (higher pleasures) and minimize pain and suffering.

Importantly, Mill places the fundamental obligations of justice as the highest value/pleasure, in order to protect human rights and promote overall social utility, or the overall good. This distinguishes his form of utilitarianism from hedonistic and crude versions, which are questionable from an ethical standpoint. Justice is an important check on these versions, as utilitarianism is often misrepresented as a crude form of the tyranny of the majority. Tyranny of the majority (also known as tyranny of the masses) occurs when the majority places their interests above, and at the expense of, the minority or minorities.

In *Utilitarianism*, Mill states, "The creed which accepts as the foundation of morals 'utility' or the 'greatest happiness principle' holds that actions are right in proportion as they tend to promote happiness; wrong as they tend to produce the reverse of happiness."[3]

Mill explains that this is a "theory of life" which grounds such morality, "that pleasure and freedom from pain are the only things desirable as ends."[4] This does not reduce us to swine, and "the accusation supposes human beings to be capable of no pleasures except those of which swine are capable."[5]

In order to understand the ranking of pleasures, Mill argues that one must be acquainted with those under consideration. That is, one must be acquainted with both higher and lower pleasures in order to be capable of ranking them. He sees the following as an "unquestionable fact":

Those who are equally acquainted with and equally capable of appreciating and enjoying both do give a most marked preference to the manner of existence which employs their higher faculties. Few human creatures would consent to be changed into any of the lower animals for a promise for the fullest allowance of a beast's pleasures; no intelligent human being would consent to be a fool, no instructed person would be an ignoramus, no person of feeling and conscience would be selfish and base, even though they should be persuaded that the fool, the dunce, or the rascal is better satisfied with his lot than they are with theirs.[6]

Mill noted that sometimes those with knowledge of both pleasures will occasionally turn to the lower pleasures, either out of temptation for sensual indulgence, or from becoming indolent and selfish. Such actions may be at the expense of health—mental or physical—even though the person is aware of these costs. He provides further explanation:

> Capacity for the nobler feelings is in most natures a very tender plant, easily killed, not only by hostile influences, but by mere want of sustenance; and in the majority of young persons it speedily dies away if the occupations to which their position in life has devoted them, and the society into which it has thrown them are not favorable to keeping that higher capacity in exercise. Men lose their higher aspirations as they lose their intellectual tastes, because they have not time or opportunity for indulging them; and they addict themselves to inferior pleasures, not because they deliberately prefer them, but because they are either the only ones to which they have access or the only ones which they are any longer capable of enjoying.[7]

The "tender plant" is the ability to choose the higher pleasures, the ability to associate one's own pleasure with the overall good, with justice. Mill foresaw the possibility of the lack of higher pleasures being valued. These higher pleasures include critical thinking, consuming truth and knowledge, and seeing one's own well-being tied to that of others.

While Mill calls money a "heap of glittering pebbles," he notes,

> The love of money is not only one of the strongest moving forces of human life, but money is, in many cases, desired in and for itself; the desire to possess it is often stronger than the desire to use it, and goes on increasing when all the desires by which point to ends beyond it, to be compassed by it, are falling off ... it has come to be itself a principal ingredient of the individual's conception of happiness.[8]

While utilitarian theory must grapple with the human tendency to be subject to (base) hedonistic addictions, and the love of money (as well as fame and power), Mill asserts that if one does gravitate toward these lower pleasures, one is likely to be rendered "noxious to the other members of the society to which [one] belongs."[9]

For Mill, cultivating virtue via embracing the higher pleasures and seeing one's own life as connected to the common good are crucial to moral decision making. And insofar as turning away from the higher values leads to people being noxious to others in society, harm and suffering are not minimized, and justice, the highest pleasure/value, is not served.

Mill writes, "Justice remains the appropriate name for certain social utilities which are vastly more important, and therefore more absolute and imperative, than any others as a class."[10] He explains that justice presupposes two crucial elements: first, that this theory is intended only for the good of all humans; second, that rights play an important role, a check, on the behavior of others. For Mill, a right is "a valid claim on society to protect him in the possession of it, either by the force of law or by that of education and opinion."[11] Justice inherently involves people getting what they deserve, be that a benefit or a consequence for harming another. And as Mill makes clear, "To have a right, then, is, I conceive to have something which society ought to defend me in the possession of.... but security no human being can possibly do without on it we depend."[12] Further, Mill rightly notes that "physical nutriment" is the most basic need of all. Thus justice, rights, and meeting basic needs are indisputable aspects of utilitarianism.

To apply Mill's theory, consider the following example. A city has a certain amount of money that can be spent on operating a food bank for one year to meet the needs of hungry children and adults, on increasing a public library's collection, or toward building a sports stadium. Given the above theory, what is the answer to the city's dilemma?

First of all, the principle of minimizing harm and suffering comes in to play. Next, we must consider that physical nutriment is the most basic need of humans. While Mill argues that the higher pleasures include the intellect (and only those who have had experience with all of the options can judge), it seems that the food bank will minimize the most harm and therefore should be the utilitarian choice. Some might argue that the stadium would generate money and jobs, which could feed families who are hungry, so that should be the choice.

While both of these are utilitarian arguments, we know empirically that we have less control over actions that stretch into the future. Adults and children are hungry now, and hunger threatens health and life itself. Further in the future, a stadium might bring about economic and employment changes, but what should be done about the suffering now? The person arguing for the stadium might respond, "What will happen to the hungry when the food bank runs out? They will be the same and not have a way out that a stadium job could give them." Or one might argue that the library is a place to access the Internet and learn and could also lead to employment. And a library satisfies the intellect, is free, and provides other forms of assistance.

Regardless of how you run the utilitarian calculation regarding the city's choices, you must minimize harm, not violate justice or rights, and keep in mind that one's right to life requires food as a prerequisite. If you are hungry and cannot afford food, what does a right to life mean? If there is excess food, how is it just to let children go hungry? Utilitarianism requires us to take into account the empirical conditions and to apply the theory, keeping all of its facets in mind. How you answer the city's dilemma will depend on where in time you intend to minimize suffering. Regardless of the position you take, it is clear that utilitarianism is a theory that we utilize, on a regular basis in our daily lives, in everything from medical triage to economic decisions to personal relationships.

John Rawls, Justice, and Meritocracy

John Rawls (1921–2002) is a critic of utilitarianism who provides his theory of justice, a theory that justifies material inequality, and sets the criteria for a meritocracy. A meritocracy is a society in which the positions that people have are those that they have earned.

Rawls uses a thought exercise to establish his theory. First, one is required to go behind the "veil of ignorance" where one does not know what one's position in society will be ("the contingencies of social class and fortune"). We are asked to imagine that we do not know our own economic class, gender, race, education, or anything else that affects our position and ability to move in society. The reason for this is that Rawls wants to establish a "just" society, with principles that justify that society. If you are setting up a society, and you know these contingencies, Rawls assumes that you will set up the society to benefit yourself over others. Therefore, he asks us to imagine that we don't know where we stand as individuals.

Behind the veil of ignorance, Rawls considers two possible arrangements of society. The first is a society in which we have equality not only of liberty and rights but also of means (equality of material wealth). The resources in such a society would be distributed like an evenly cut pie, where everyone gets the same-sized piece. Rawls argues that in this society no one would be motivated to do work, as there is no larger piece of the pie for those who are industrious. That is, in this society hard work doesn't allow one to acquire more in the form of material benefits. Because this society lacks this form of incentive, Rawls asserts that this is not the kind of society people would choose.

The society with inequality seems to be better for those who are able to obtain a greater share of the wealth. However, we know that wealth inequalities are not merely the product of hard work; myriad other factors such as gender, race, birthplace, intelligence, and so forth have a bearing on wealth acquisition. Recall that Rawls requires a veil of ignorance so that we won't know these contingencies. Given this, why would we prefer a society in which material inequality is possible, if in doing so we risk being among the people who receive a smaller portion of the pie than others?

Rawls argues that we would accept the inequality if two principles of justice were operating. The first one is the liberty principle: "Each person engaged in an institution or affected by it has an equal right to the most extensive liberty with a like liberty for all."[13] That is to say, we have as broad a set of freedoms as is possible. This means that no one is stuck in a caste society, and that movement is possible.

The second principle is the difference principle. This principle has two parts, and it first requires that if there is material inequality, this inequality *must* work out—here he allows for two possible outcomes—either for everyone's or for the worst-off people's advantage. Suppose, for example, that the operations

of a business resulted in a great increase of wealth of the firm's senior management and shareholders, providing them with a disproportionate share of the pie. According to the first part of the difference principle, this would be unjust if it merely made the rich even richer without benefitting (at least) those who are worse off. In this scenario, the first part of the difference principle would be violated, and this arrangement would be unjust and therefore rejected.

However, if society were structured in such a way that the wealth gained by the firm's management and shareholders *increased* the wealth of (at least) those who are worse off—perhaps through substantial taxes then used to provide needed social programs and/or actual income increases—then Rawls would consider this inequality justified (as long as the second half of the difference principle were also satisfied).

The second part of the difference principle holds that all positions in society must be open to all; there must be equal access and opportunity. Behind the veil of ignorance, one would not accept losing equality of material goods by entering a society where one was worse off than under material equality and, in addition to this, frozen there as if in a caste society. Now, the poorest in this society can work hard, and if they have talents, they can move up. Furthermore, if there is "fair" competition for all positions, and access and opportunity, Rawls assumes that the most qualified will rise; this also raises society overall, through technological progress and other advances. That is, a meritocracy will result, the consequence of following the principles of justice.

Capitalism and Critique

Many ethical theories seek to describe virtues, rules, or principles that can be used to help structure a society in ways that promote harmony. Ethics, however, is not the only field interested in discovering the best ways for people to live together. Fields like political science, economics, and others have important things to say about the ways in which people interact to form government institutions, legal codes, social policy, and economic systems. In fact, for most of human history, these topics were not distinguished and separated into the distinct fields of inquiry that now delineate them. Though it can be useful to distinguish among these fields, it can also obscure the many connections among them. Drawing clear and rigid distinctions among ethics, political science, economics, sociology, and psychology—just to name a few—can sometimes be more difficult than it would first appear. Adam Smith, often regarded as one of the fathers of modern capitalism and perhaps best known for his book *Wealth of Nations*, was actually a philosophy professor who wrote and taught about a variety of topics, including ethics, natural theology, jurisprudence, and what is now called economics (this word had not yet been coined when Smith wrote).

In a business ethics anthology such as this one, it is important, then, to consider some of the other influences that are technically outside the realm of traditional moral philosophy but that bear on it in important ways. Of particular importance in considering business ethics is the influence of economic and political theory. As businesses are concerned, at least in part, with things like reducing costs and maximizing profits, it is important to consider the moral implications of actions taken by businesses and their agents. Moreover, it would be a mistake to assume that the economic and political structures within which they operate have no impact on the ways in which they conduct business.

Some of the dominant economic theories worth considering in this context are the values of capitalism and socialism and how they relate to things like business practices, employment policies, government interaction, private property, and so on. The following theorists look at the moral ramifications of various forms of governmental and economic policies and how they impact ethical considerations for businesses, individuals, and societies.

Adam Smith

Adam Smith (1723–90), a Scottish economist, is the father of "free market" economic theory. Though his book is one of the most important books ever written about economics, Smith's *An Inquiry Into the Nature and Causes of the Wealth of Nations* also has significant implications for the structures of society and government and, ultimately, ethics. In direct contrast to Kant, who holds that people cannot behave morally by following their inclinations, Smith argues that individuals should do exactly that and seek to promote their own self-interest. His claim is that if everyone behaves in this fashion, society will automatically find balance and harmony. As each individual pursues their goals, there will be positive, but unintended, consequences from those actions that will serve the greater good. He uses the famous "invisible hand" phrase to suggest the almost magical way in which individuals promoting their own agendas will actually have a beneficial effect on the society as a whole. This aligns with the concept of "laissez-faire" economics. Laissez-faire comes from the French phrase "laissez-nous faire," which means "let us do it." It is the idea that the state should leave business people to their own means without interference or regulation from the government.

The invisible hand relies on the predictability of human behavior that creates supply and demand. Paul Krugman uses the example of ride-sharing providers such as Uber or Lyft to illustrate the invisible hand. When the supply of drivers is relatively equal to the demand, prices will be lower than when demand is higher, such as at the airport or at an entertainment venue. With higher demand, prices rise and more drivers pursue those riders. Krugman concludes that this redistribution of wealth, from riders to drivers, creates wealth and allows for the overall good in society.[14]

Smith gives justice an important place in his system: "Every man, as long as he does not violate the laws of justice, is left perfectly free to pursue his own interests in his own way, and to bring both his industry and capital into competition with those of any other man, or order of men."[15] However, it is important to note Smith's concept of justice: "Justice is the infinite set of permissible actions remaining after specifying the finite limited set of prohibited actions and corresponding penalties."[16] This notion of justice more closely resembles liberty. Kenneth Lux challenges Smith's notion of the invisible hand, arguing that it entails a fundamental mistake.

Kenneth Lux

Kenneth Lux (1939–2016) was a social theorist and clinical psychologist who took issue with Adam Smith's explanation of human motivation and interaction. In *Adam Smith's Mistake: How a Moral Philosopher Invented Economics and Ended Morality*, Lux argues that Smith made a critically important error. He argues that Smith's position amounts to something like "selfish behavior is good behavior." He contends that there is a conflict between self-interest and benevolence in Smith's work and that eliminating things like benevolence, generosity, and honesty from the moral order creates serious ethical problems.

What social and ethical problems have the elimination of benevolence and the enshrinement of unrestrained selfishness given us? Selfishness and self-interest do not necessarily preclude deception, cheating, and eliminating competition. Consider our natural environment, as Lux writes:

> From the Industrial Revolution and continuing down into the present, self-interest has produced pollution, depletion, and the progressive destruction of the natural world. The evidence begins with the foul streets, sewers, and air of Adam Smith's London, and extends to the acid rain, ozone depletion, and "greenhouse effect" of today.[17]

Karl Marx's (1818–83) insight that "the only wheels which political economy sets in motion are *avarice* and the *war amongst the avaricious—competition*"[18] is most relevant here. Selfish self-interest is closely tied to greed, as well as penetrating political sources of power that further protect and grow more of the same. We see this with the "1%" in the wealth gap, we see it in special interest lobbying groups as well as in political "donations," and we see it with the environmental destruction that Lux describes.

Lux argues that Smith failed to recognize that self-interest should operate *in addition to* these other influences on human behavior. In the end, he suggests that Smith made what Lux calls a "transvaluation," by equating selfishness (something generally taken to be a social evil) with self-interest (which Smith holds up as a social good). If on one end of the continuum there is benevolence, and on the other is self-interest/selfishness, this is similar to Aristotle's virtue and vice, a classic choice between good and evil. Lux argues that Smith "reversed the poles of the continuum of motivation" and in effect claimed that what we would consider a private vice, selfishness, was in fact a public virtue. Lux compares this to doublespeak, and he quotes Confucius's "rectification of names." In this case, Confucius argued that when things are not referred to by their proper and correct names, and what is good is called bad and what is bad is called good, immorality flourishes.

Lux therefore concludes that "self-interest in essence means selfishness, and selfishness cannot produce the social good because in fact it is the very force that destroys the social good, despite the claim of economics to the contrary."[19] It is for these reasons, among others, that many see free-market, laissez-faire, invisible-hand capitalism as a destructive, inhumane, and failed system and argue instead for significant regulation and/or other options such as socialism.

Kai Nielsen

Kai Nielsen (1926–2021) was a moral philosopher who also took up the question of justice. In "A Moral Case for Socialism,"[20] he compares and contrasts the dominant political theories of capitalism and socialism and outlines some of the moral implications of each. Nielsen contends that capitalism, a system in which the means of production is held privately, requires a class-based society that has both a worker class and a capitalist-owner class. Socialism, on the other hand, is a system in which the means of production are owned publicly, therefore suggesting the possibility of a classless egalitarian society where everyone is a worker. He notes, however, that pure forms of capitalism and socialism are hard to find in the real world and that the forms we do find (corporate or monopoly capitalism and state bureaucratic socialism) are impure and should not be taken as paradigmatic. Nielsen notes that competitive capitalism (the pure form) and democratic socialism (the pure form) have likely never been actualized,

with Hong Kong coming closest to the former and various European countries closest to the latter.

Nielsen views each form from the perspective of some very important points, namely freedom, autonomy, democracy, rights, justice, and equality. Beginning with autonomy, Nielsen points out that under capitalism, workers' autonomy is determined on many levels, from whether they can work, what they do, how they work, the object of their labor, the working conditions, and the disposition of the object of their labor. As workers outnumber owners, this is a significant impact on human freedom and autonomy. As capitalism continues its unfettered course, we find that we have the domination of the many by the few, not to mention its focus on profit and growth with corresponding environmental destruction. In contrast, under democratic socialism, workers determine how and on what they work, the hours and conditions, what they will produce, and its disposition. Under this socialism, each person truly has a *right* to work, as well as the ability to acquire the needs for life.

Under capitalism, political democracy is possible, but we have seen that advanced capitalism has infiltrated the political and regulatory system through economic, media, and social media manipulation and rendered democracy nearly impotent. Under socialism, workplace democracy is possible and political democracy can be restored (with procedures and safeguards), with the protection and valuing of autonomy and equality.

Nielsen notes that while many—or most—people give lip service to the moral equality of humans, it is impossible to ignore the empirical evidence that shows the existence of the contrary. Minimal assurances of moral equality would include equal access and opportunity, meaningful work, equal education, nutrition, health care, secure housing, and to pretend that these exist for all is, as Nielsen says, "an obscene joke given the social realities of our lives."[21] In contrast, under democratic socialism, "There would be a commitment ... to attaining or at least approximating, as far as it is feasible, equality of condition: and this, where approximated, would help make for real equality of opportunity, making equal life chances something less utopian than it must be under capitalism."[22]

Socialism is a system whose rationale for existence is to meet human needs, to provide equality of condition (without which any moral claim to merit rings hollow), and therein it is clear that socialism produces more moral equality than capitalism does. This leads to the question of justice. As Nielsen illuminates, justice does not dwell in a society that undermines autonomy and democracy, a society that is inequitable and violates human rights. He concludes that on every moral human value we claim to respect, socialism actually presents a more appealing model than capitalism.

Robert Heilbroner

Robert Heilbroner (1919–2005) was an American economist. In "Some Reflections on the Triumph of Capitalism," Heilbroner examines the links between economic systems and their impact on society. He outlines a number of problems with capitalism and some concerns about the system, as noted by some of its most famous commentators, including Thomas Malthus (1766–1834), Smith, Mill, Marx, Alfred Marshall (1842–1924), John Maynard Keynes (1883–1946), and Joseph Schumpeter (1883–1950). Though he takes a somewhat different approach from Nielsen, Heilbroner also discusses some of the advantages of considering some socialistic restraints on unchecked capitalism. Important for his analysis is a critical distinction between the economic and political realms.

Heilbroner asserts that capitalism has triumphed, but he notes that whether it can work well enough to last is something else. Heilbroner describes capitalism as a "regime" and, like Nielsen, asserts that it is fundamentally a class-based system with businessmen as its representative "ruling class":

Capitalism['s] largely uncritical worship of the idea of economic growth is as central to its nature as the similar veneration of the idea of divine kingship or blue blood or doctrinal orthodoxy has been for other regimes.... It is this regime-like aspect of capitalism that ... makes the working class, far from the opposition that Marx hoped it would become, into stalwart supporters.[23]

While he sees two distinct realms—the economy and the government—he does foresee the (now) fait accompli of firms wielding more economic power than governments, and he notes the destabilizing power that would have. Heilbroner comes close but does not go as far as Thomas Jefferson (1743–1826), who wrote in 1816, "I hope we shall take warning ... and crush in its birth the aristocracy of our monied corporations which dare already to challenge our government to a trial of strength, and to bid defiance to the laws of their country."

In 2010, *Citizens United v. Federal Election Commission*, 558 U.S. 310, the Supreme Court ruled that corporations' expenditures for political campaigns and other communications could not be restricted by the government, citing the First Amendment's free speech clause. This ruling entrenched the entanglement with, and significant power that corporations now wield over, government and its legislative, judicial, and executive branches. Given Heilbroner's explanation of the poor and middle classes being capitalism's "stalwart supporters," the corporate economic creep into politics and government has proceeded at a rapid pace.

However, Heilbroner writes that socialism, especially democratic socialism, continues to hold sway with many, especially in addressing inequalities in the systems. Capitalism "triumphed," but as a regime—and regimes fall. He concludes by pointing to socialism's commitment to "social goals that have seemed incompatible with, or at least unattainable under, capitalism—above all, the moral, not just the material, elevation of mankind."[24]

Thomas Piketty

Thomas Piketty (b. 1971) is a French economist and the author of *Capital in the Twenty-First Century* (2013).[25] In this book, he addresses income and wealth concentration historically, from the eighteenth to the twenty-first centuries. Piketty is notable for focusing on both income and wealth, and the resulting inequalities. Piketty notes that rigid class structures were disrupted by World Wars I and II and resulted in a more egalitarian period. This was relatively short-lived, as we now find ourselves in the era of the 1%, and the 0.1% and 0.01%, with its accompanying income and wealth gaps.

Piketty defines capital as wealth, which is not distributed as labor income but rather held by the few and concentrated further in light of low to no taxation and inheritance. Piketty draws from extensive historical data to show that the economic return on capital is faster and higher than earned income, and by a significant margin. This wealth, he argues, will amass to amounts inconsistent with democracy and, certainly, social justice. He urges that this inequality should be addressed by taxation, not just on (high) income but also on wealth.

The central part of the moral myth of capitalism is that it rewards hard work. This myth is also wielded as a justification for the inequalities that exist, with blame directed in no small part at the unsuccessful and poor for their own circumstances. Inheritance of wealth is inconsistent with this moral myth, and if it is taken to the extreme (where we already find ourselves), it contains the seeds (now juvenile plants) of capitalism's undoing.

Piketty views the 2008 banking crash as a normal outcome of capitalism as it has progressed. He warns that without intervention, this will repeat. In order to avoid these outcomes, he proposes significantly taxing capital/wealth and high incomes. These are not inconsistent with capitalism, but they are radical in the face of the present. He notes that it is likely utopian. Utopia has come to mean an ideal society, but it translates into "nowhere" or "no place." It is unlikely, given the intermingling of those with wealth in the political and especially legislative and representative arenas, that we will see significant enough redistribution to address social justice and inequality in any voluntary manner.

Ultimately, the moral and economic theories outlined here represent major currents in Western thought over the past 2,500 years. Central to the discussions of ethics are questions about how people ought to conduct themselves, how societies ought to be arranged to ensure that important social and individual goods such as justice and autonomy can flourish, and how people can structure their personal lives, economic pursuits, and governmental systems to promote these ends. Thus, this has been a look at how various notable thinkers—past and present—have tried to approach these questions and how each theory might be applied in analyzing and reflecting upon the real-world challenges of business ethics.

Notes

1. Aristotle, "Selection from The Nicomachean Ethics," in *Nicomachean Ethics*, trans. J.E.C. Welldon (London: Macmillan, 1892).

2. Immanuel Kant, "Selection from *The Foundations of the Metaphysics of Morals*," in *Ethical Theory: A Concise Anthology*, ed. Heimir Geirsson and Margaret R. Holmgren (Peterborough, ON: Broadview Press, 2000), 127; original translation T.K. Abbott, 1873.

3. John Stuart Mill, *Utilitarianism*, ed. George Sher (Indianapolis, IN: Hackett, 1979), 8.

4. Ibid.

5. Ibid.

6. Ibid., 9.

7. Ibid., 10–11.

8. Ibid., 31.

9. Ibid., 32.

10. Ibid., 54.

11. Ibid., 45.

12. Ibid.

13. John Rawls, "Distributive Justice," in *Philosophy, Politics, and Society*, third series, ed. Peter Laslett et al. (Oxford: Blackwell, 1967), 134.

14. Paul Krugman, "What Is the Invisible Hand in Economics?" MasterClass, https://www.masterclass.com/articles/what-is-the-invisible-hand-in-economics.

15. Adam Smith, *The Wealth of Nations*, ed. Edwin Gannan (New York: Modern Library, 1937), 14.

16. Adam Smith, *The Theory of Moral Sentiments* (Indianapolis: Liberty Classics, 1976), 47.

17. Kenneth Lux, *Adam Smith's Mistake: How a Moral Philosopher Invented Economics and Ended Morality* (Boston: Shambhala, 1990), 49.

18. Karl Marx, "Estranged Labour," in *Economic and Philosophic Manuscripts* (1844).

19. Lux, *Adam Smith's Mistake*, 53.

20. Kai Nielsen, "A Moral Case for Socialism," *Critical Review* 3, no. 3–4 (1989): 542–53.

21. Ibid., 546.

22. Ibid., 548.

23. Robert Heilbroner, "Reflections on the Triumph of Capitalism," *The New Yorker* (June 23, 1989): 98.

24. Ibid.

25. Thomas Piketty, *Capital in the Twenty-First Century* (Cambridge, MA: Harvard University Press, 2013).

Chapter 2: Human Rights and Environmental Challenges to Development and Globalization

Introduction

"We must find new lands from which we can easily obtain raw materials and at the same time exploit the cheap slave labour that is available from the natives of colonies. The colonies would also provide a dumping ground for the surplus goods produced in our factories."[1]

THIS CHAPTER ADDRESSES HUMAN rights and corporate activity as they pertain to the firm's home country, internationally, and the closely related issues of "development" and globalization. The above quote reflects classic development, at least when development refers to actions in the "Third World," or an "Underdeveloped Country," a "Less Developed Country," or a "Developing Country."[2] How should firms proceed in their international activities of development? For whom is this development undertaken? Did those in the "underdeveloped country" consent to development? Once development proceeds, whose ethical responsibility (the government's, the firm's, or the people's) is it to protect human rights under these activities? Is it justified for a firm's activities, in any way, to contribute to the violation of human rights? These questions, as well as an historical overview of rights, are taken up in

this chapter. Before I turn to a discussion of human rights and firms, I briefly address two areas of controversy: the use of terms that signify a developing country and some of the debate on the legitimacy of human rights.

History and Usage of the Terms "Third World," "Underdeveloped," and "Developing"

The term *third world* is a controversial and problematic term, with multiple uses, including a reference to geographic areas and certain peoples. In addition, the terms *underdeveloped* and *developing* are also used somewhat interchangeably with *third world*. Gayatri Chakravorty Spivak recounts that *third world* was first used in 1955 at the Bandung Conference in Bandung, Indonesia.[3] The conference was attended by twenty-nine Asian and African nation representatives who came together "to promote economic and cultural cooperation and to oppose colonialism."[4] The term *third world* "was originally intended to distinguish the nonaligned nations that gained independence from colonial rule beginning after World War II from the Western nations and from those that formed the former Eastern bloc, and sometimes specifically from the United States and from the former Soviet Union (the first and second worlds, respectively)."[5]

Chandra Talpade Mohanty further elaborates on the controversy around the term:

> Terms such as *third* and *first world* are very problematical both in suggesting oversimplified similarities between and among countries labeled thus, and in implicitly reinforcing existing economic, cultural, and ideological hierarchies which are conjured up in using such terminology. I use the term *third world* with full awareness of its problems, only because this is the terminology available to us at the moment. The use of quotation marks is meant to suggest a continuous questioning of the designation. Even when I do not use quotation marks, I mean to use the term critically.[6]

Mohanty and her coeditors further clarify:

> While the term *third world* is a much maligned and contested one, we use it deliberately, preferring it to *postcolonial* or *developing countries*. *Third world* refers to the colonized, neocolonized, or decolonized countries (of Asia, Africa, and Latin America) whose economic and political structures have been deformed within the colonial process, and to black, Asian, Latino, and indigenous peoples in North America, Europe, and Australia. Thus, the term does not merely indicate a hierarchical cultural and economic relationship

between "first" and "third" world countries; it intentionally foregrounds a history of colonization and contemporary relationships of structural dominance between first and third world peoples. In drawing on histories of antiracist, anti-imperialist struggles around the world, the term *third world* is also a form of self-empowerment.[7]

I share Mohanty's perspective and most specifically find the term *developing* to be problematic due to its hierarchical nature and assumptions of "progress." While I acknowledge this dissent, I also use the terminology throughout this chapter and anthology, because all current terminology is problematic, and this terminology is the most pragmatically clear because of its wide recognition. In addition, the legitimacy of human rights is not without controversy.

Challenges to Human Rights Legitimacy/Justification

While human rights are broadly accepted and used both as a baseline and an ideal for human treatment, there is dissent regarding both the assumptions and legitimacy of individual human rights. For example, some authoritarian Asian governments claim that they should not be expected to protect all human rights—either individually, or to the same degree as Western advocates—due to "cultural relativism." In *The East Asian Challenge for Human Rights*,[8] authors respond to the rather vague cultural relativism defense, and they advance critical analyses of human rights. Much of the debate focuses on the individualistic notion of human rights, as well as the feasibility of actualizing human rights if a country cannot provide the economic means to do so. Charles Taylor summarizes some of the resistance to human rights as follows:

We can therefore see how resistance to the Western discourse of rights might occur on more than one level. Some governments might resist the enforcement of even widely accepted norms because they have an agenda that involves their violation (for example, the contemporary People's Republic of China). Others, however, are certainly ready, even eager to espouse some universal norms, but they are made uneasy by the underlying philosophy of the human person in society. This seems to give pride of place to autonomous individuals, determined to demand their rights, even (indeed especially) in the face of widespread social consensus.[9]

There are many competing conceptions to the (rather fictional) autonomous individual assumed as the recipient of human rights, from communitarian challenges in the West, to traditional and codified (cultural and religious) conceptions of the group/community/family/nation as the basic unit/recipient and receptacle of concern, rather than an individual human. Some, such as Joseph Chan, argue for a middle ground between the polar considerations of individual and group. Chan sees human rights as a "fall-back position" when traditional virtues of Confucianism, as espoused by Confucius (551–479 BCE) and Mencius (372–289 BCE), fail:

> The central elements in Confucianism—the emphasis on role-based ethics, the Confucian ideal of community, the respect for seniority and the elderly, and the preference for harmony rather than litigation—are all compatible with the idea of human rights. Moreover, the Confucian philosophy of *ren* would endorse human rights as an instrument to protect humanity and important human interests, although such an instrument should be

seen as primarily a fallback apparatus. On the Confucian view, we should strive to resolve conflicts first by means of education, mediation, and compromise in order to preserve the spirit of mutual caring and trust, but this should not mislead us to believing that the instrument of human rights is unimportant ... they require each other.[10]

Although a fuller debate concerning human rights is beyond the scope of this chapter and anthology, I mean to underscore the fact that even though the legitimacy of human rights is not without controversy, nonetheless many human rights provide a crucial moral minimum regarding the treatment of human beings.[11] However, this chapter emanates from the perspective that many human rights establish a minimum standard of humane treatment, and regardless of the existence of resistance and debate concerning the legitimacy of (mostly) the individualistic notion of human rights, this in no way provides a prima facie justification for their violation by firms.

Human Rights and Firms

In the 1980s, due to human rights violations, the United Nations began discussions of an international code of conduct concerning human rights for transnational corporate activity. However, with the rapidly increasing move toward globalization, discussions were thought unnecessary. This dismissal was due in part to the uncritical belief that globalization is a social good, a process by which economic development will be provided to the poor, human rights violations perpetrated by governments will end, and basic freedoms such as speech, expression, and equality will be disseminated. However, by the mid-1990s there was increasing exposure of human rights violations through both direct corporate action and corporate complicity in activities ranging from sweatshops to child labor, to not paying a living wage, to forbidding union formation, to displacement of Indigenous and other peoples. Public outcry in Europe, Canada, Asia, and the United States resulted in some corporations taking responsibility to change or minimize harmful practices, yet many human rights violations continue unchecked. Further, as illustrated in the *Human Development Report of 1999* (United Nations Development Program), transnational firms have played a significant role in increasing, not decreasing, the gap between rich and poor. This report has been challenged due to its focus on countries, and not individuals, a point that is salient if one considers that China and Grenada should not be given equal weight, as there are about 12,000 Chinese for every one Grenadan.[12] Further, it appears that a number of Chinese and Indians have benefited economically from globalization. Yet overall inequality has risen, and not all those affected have benefited from globalization; in fact, many have been harmed by it.[13]

However problematic different statistical approaches may be in measuring globalization's effects, human rights are meant to be universal. That is, human rights are meant to apply to each human being alive. Far too often, transnational firms have, rather than enabling free speech and expression, violently repressed union formation in sweatshop factories. Rather than providing development, firms "country-hop," looking for the cheapest labor, leaving a country no more "developed" than before they arrived. Therefore, globalization is far from delivering the goods promised, and an international call for a code of conduct for transnational corporate activity regarding human rights is under way again.[14]

This chapter provides a thorough grounding in human rights, explores their local relevance for firms, as well as the relevance for transnational cross-cultural global economic activity, and questions whether the *United Nations Declaration of Human Rights* is adequate to protect the most basic rights humans possess.

Human Rights: A Definition

Human rights are rights that humans possess by virtue of being human. Thus, human rights are universal in that they apply to every human and do not depend on any particular government, business, or group to recognize them for validity. This is in contrast to civil rights, which are rights that a government enumerates for those recognized as citizens only. While they are not always labeled "human rights," the concept of human rights can be found throughout history. The articulation of limitations on government, on other individuals, and of private property can be found in ancient law such as Babylon's Hammurabi Codes; in legal documents such as England's Magna Carta, the US Bill of Rights, and France's Declaration of the Rights of Man; and in limitations on war activity enumerated in the Geneva Convention of 1864 (to protect medical personnel), and the Hague Convention of 1899 (which established naval warfare rules). Further overlap with the concept of human rights can be seen in most religions, including Islamic, Buddhist, Christian, Confucian, Hindu, and Jewish traditions, as well as in writings by philosophers on natural law from St. Thomas Aquinas (1225–74) to John Locke (1632–1704).

More recognizable "rights language" can be seen in the Covenant of the League of Nations. In 1919, partially in order to address the use of violent warfare and poisonous gas in World War I, as well as various other human conditions, the League of Nations was formed. The League formed the 1920 International Labor Organizations to improve workplace conditions and obligated members to contribute to the development of people under the jurisdiction of the League. Lacking commitment and effectiveness, due in no small part to US non-ratification, the League disbanded, an event that was soon to be followed by World War II.

World War II left over 38 million dead, as well as millions hungry and homeless. The February 1945 Yalta Conference brought together British prime minister Winston Churchill, Soviet leader Joseph Stalin, and US president Franklin D. Roosevelt, who all discussed a desire for both peace and for better overall human conditions and sowed the seeds for what would become the United Nations. After the exposure of the genocidal,[15] nuclear, and other atrocities of World War II, a method of ensuring universal rights for all human beings, regardless of citizenship, war, or peace, was sought. *The United Nations Declaration of Human Rights* was unanimously[16] adopted by the member states of the United Nations on December 10, 1948. The Declaration appears in this chapter.

Although not without controversy (as discussed earlier), especially concerning the basis for, the individualistic nature of, as well as the scope and extent that rights should have, human rights are held by many to be foundational moral considerations. Some consider rights to be a sort of "trump card" (in Ronald Dworkin's language) that are brought to bear upon competing claims where an individual is protected in the exercise of their right. One competing claim concerns the right to free speech. Suppose the owners of a firm were offended by an employee's union's speech, that is, the union's position on an issue. The firm's owners' offense, under rights theory (remember these are thought to be universal, applying to all cultures), will not outweigh the individual's right to free speech. However, rights are not without limitations in their exercise.

Generally, rights are not thought justifiably overridden by any claim other than the exercise of a more fundamental right. This can be illustrated again using the right to free speech. The classic case of limiting, or overriding, the right to free speech is to prevent a person from exercising free speech by yelling "Fire!" in a crowded theater (when there is, in fact, no fire). The right to free speech is overridden here because yelling "Fire!" risks a resulting stampede wherein the more basic right of physical safety and right to life itself are threatened.

Another important issue concerning rights is the distinction between positive and negative rights, along with the corresponding debate. A positive right is a right that requires others to act in some way to ensure that the rights-holder can exercise their rights. A negative right is one that requires others to refrain from doing anything that could interfere with the rights-holder exercising their rights. Consider the right to life. If one had a "positive right" to life,[17] others—perhaps communities, citizens, governments, or employers—would have correlative duties to act in ways that ensure that the rights-holder could exercise their right to life. These "positive" duties could include providing food to someone who was too ill, young, or aged to provide for themself; paying a living wage to employees; or welfare programs such as food stamps for the unemployed. Each of the previous examples requires *an other* to "do something" that contributes to the exercise of the right. If one had a "negative right" to life, others would need only to refrain from acting in ways that violate that right, such as murdering or directly attacking the rights-holder. Given the economic and resource distribution issues facing humans today, many have argued that negative rights are meaningless. For example, if you are, through no fault of your own, unable to access what is needed to live, and you only have a negative right to life, what does your right to life mean? A negative right to life would imply no correlative duty to any person, firm, or government to provide access to any of the following: unemployment insurance, a living wage, food stamps, or medical care. Without access to what is necessary to live, a right to life is useless.

There are two final issues to consider regarding the positive/negative distinction. First, any action that interferes with a rightsholder exercising the right to life would be forbidden under the negative aspect of rights. That would include activities where, if individuals take more than they need, it results in others not having access to what they need; an example would be American citizens' consumption resulting in interference of the right to life of anyone or any group in the "Global Village." Therefore, a robust reading of negative rights, coupled with an understanding of the empirical conditions of this planet, illustrates that those who assume that they are not interfering in the right to life of others might, in fact, be doing just that, and at a minimum they would need to change their behavior. Second, a positive right does not imply that one is simply handed whatever is necessary to live but that one has access, such as through employment, to what is needed, and that access is assured by duties upon others.

Consider yet another issue regarding human rights. The human right to life makes sense only if there are, in fact, enough resources to provide the subsistence necessities for all humans to live. This condition is usually referred to as moderate scarcity. If scarcity becomes severe, and there are not enough resources to meet the *objective empirical requirements* for subsistence for all people's lives, a universal human right to life appears nonsensical. This is tied to an important tenet of ethics, of which human rights theory is a part. The tenet is "ought implies can." That

is, to claim that all humans *ought* to have their right to life respected implies that this *can* be done, that it is possible. If there are not enough resources to meet the subsistence necessities for life, then all humans cannot have their right to life respected. Most of the current empirical evidence points to the conclusion that there are enough resources to provide subsistence necessities for all humans. However, continued development and environmental destruction pose threats to the remaining resources. What kind of development, if any, would not harm the environment, or, more pointedly, what kind of development would ensure, as this chapter addresses, our environmental rights, is taken up in the reading selections.

Environmental considerations drastically change the common notions of development, growth, wealth, property, and human rights as they are broadly considered and discussed in the media, business, economic, and most other literature. Environmental challenges drastically change our measures of progress, such as the GNP, economic measures of a standard of living, and the deeply problematic "goal" to develop the world in our image. The earth's atmosphere and resources cannot sustain the world's population consuming at the level of the United States. Ecological limits and ecological scarcity—both real and created—will, despite technological optimism, have to be addressed. This can either be through a human rights approach, an ecological conscience, or methods yet to be determined.

Notes

1. Cecil Rhodes (1853–1902), "one of the driving forces behind the last period of British expansion in Africa," as quoted in Clive Ponting, *A Green History of the World: The Environment and the Collapse of Great Civilizations* (New York: Penguin Books, 1991), 221–22.

2. These terms are all problematic and are addressed below.

3. See *The Spivak Reader: Selected Works of Gayatri Chakravorty Spivak*, by Gayatri Chakravorty Spivak, edited by Donna Landry and Gerald MacLean (New York: Routledge, 1995), 270.

4. *The Columbia Encyclopedia*, 6th ed. (New York: Columbia University Press, 2002).

5. Ibid.

6. Chandra Talpade Mohanty, "Under Western Eyes," in *Third World Women and The Politics of Feminism* (Bloomington: Indiana University Press, 1991), 74–75.

7. *Third World Women and The Politics of Feminism* (Bloomington: Indiana University Press, 1991), ix–x.

8. *The East Asian Challenge for Human Rights*, edited by Joanne R. Bauer and Daniel A. Bell (Cambridge, UK: Cambridge University Press, 1999).

9. Charles Taylor, "Toward a More Inclusive Human Rights Regime," in ibid., 128.

10. Joseph Chan, "A Confucian Perspective on Human Rights for Contemporary China," in ibid., 237.

11. For more discussion on individualistic rights, see Claude Ake, "The African Context of Human Rights," *Africa Today*, 34, no. 142 (1987): 5–13. For a discussion of Islamic cultural clashes with human rights conceptions, see Abdullahi Ahmed An-Na'im, "Islam, Islamic Law, and the Dilemma of Cultural Legitimacy for Universal Human Rights," in *Asian Perspectives on Human Rights*, edited by Claude E. Welch, and Virginia Leary (Boulder, CO: Westview Press, 1990). For a feminist critique of human rights, see Charlotte Bunch, "Women's Rights as Human Rights: Toward a Re-Vision of Human Rights," *Human Rights Quarterly* 12, no. 4 (November 1990).

12. See Xavier Sala-i-Martin, "The Disturbing 'Rise' of Global Income Inequality," http://www.columbia.edu/~xs23/papers.

13. See William H. Meyer, *Human Rights and International Political Economy in Third World Nations: Multinational Corporations, Foreign Aid, and Repression* (London: Praeger Publishers, 1998); Richard Douthwaite, *The Growth Illusion: How Economic Growth Has Enriched the Few, Impoverished the Many, and Endangered the Planet* (Tulsa, OK: Council Oak Books, 1993); and Tina Rosenberg, "So Far Globalization Has Failed the World's Poor," *New York Times Magazine*, August 18, 2002.

14. See hrw.org/legacy. August 2002.

15. The term "genocide" was coined in the early 1940s by Raphael Lemkin, a Polish attorney.

16. Eight of the member nations abstained (Soviet bloc countries, Saudi Arabia, and South Africa), and two member nations were absent. The Commission's chairperson was Eleanor Roosevelt, who among other things, was successful in adding gender protection.

17. "Right to life" refers to the foundational right, not the appropriated use of "right to life" in the contentious abortion debate.

I. The United Nations Universal Declaration of Human Rights

THE SELECTIONS IN THIS chapter address human rights and set the stage for a discussion of business responsibilities in light of human rights; pieces were selected in part to reflect historical and contemporary debate. The first selection is the *United Nations Universal Declaration of Human Rights* (1948). The Declaration enumerates what were agreed to be all of the fundamental human rights a person should enjoy regardless of "race, color, sex, language, religion, political or other opinion, national or social origin, property, birth or other status." Member nations are bound—both by membership in the United Nations and by the ethical duty to carry out their contractual agreement—to respect and uphold these rights. These rights can be analyzed and classified according to categories of economic, political, social, and basic rights. They can be further analyzed for positive and negative duties each carries.

There is no exemption listed for corporations, transnational organizations, or employers to ignore or violate human rights. Neither is there any exemption listed that states once a human being becomes an employee, that individual's human rights are null and void while working. Perhaps the failure to recognize these obvious latter points led to the development of the next reading, the *Human Rights Principles and Responsibilities for Transnational Corporations and Other Business Enterprises.*

The United Nations Declaration of Human Rights (UNDHR)

Preamble

WHEREAS RECOGNITION OF THE inherent dignity and of the equal and inalienable rights of all members of the human family is the foundation of freedom, justice and peace in the world,

Whereas disregard and contempt for human rights have resulted in barbarous acts which have outraged the conscience of mankind, and the advent of a world in which human beings shall enjoy freedom of speech and belief and freedom from fear and want has been proclaimed as the highest aspiration of the common people,

Whereas it is essential, if man is not to be compelled to have recourse, as a last resort, to rebellion against tyranny and oppression, that human rights should be protected by the rule of law,

Whereas it is essential to promote the development of friendly relations between nations,

Whereas the peoples of the United Nations have in the Charter reaffirmed their faith in fundamental human rights, in the dignity and worth of the human person and in the equal rights of men and women and have determined to promote social progress and better standards of life in larger freedom,

Whereas Member States have pledged themselves to achieve, in co-operation with the United Nations, the promotion of universal respect for and observance of human rights and fundamental freedoms,

Whereas a common understanding of these rights and freedoms is of the greatest importance for the full realization of this pledge,

Now, Therefore THE GENERAL ASSEMBLY proclaims THIS UNIVERSAL DECLARATION OF HUMAN RIGHTS as a common standard of achievement for all peoples and all nations, to the end that every individual and every organ of society, keeping this Declaration constantly in mind, shall strive by teaching and education to promote respect for these rights and freedoms and by progressive measures, national and international, to secure their universal and effective recognition and observance, both among the peoples of Member States themselves and among the peoples of territories under their jurisdiction.

Article 1.
All human beings are born free and equal in dignity and rights. They are endowed with reason and conscience and should act towards one another in a spirit of brotherhood.

Article 2.
Everyone is entitled to all the rights and freedoms set forth in this Declaration, without distinction of any kind, such as race, colour, sex, language, religion, political or other opinion, national or social origin, property, birth or other status. Furthermore, no distinction shall be made on the basis of the political, jurisdictional or international status of the country or territory to which a person belongs, whether it be independent, trust, non-self-governing or under any other limitation of sovereignty.

Article 3.
Everyone has the right to life, liberty and security of person.

Article 4.
No one shall be held in slavery or servitude; slavery and the slave trade shall be prohibited in all their forms.

Article 5.
No one shall be subjected to torture or to cruel, inhuman or degrading treatment or punishment.

Article 6.
Everyone has the right to recognition everywhere as a person before the law.

Article 7.
All are equal before the law and are entitled without any discrimination to equal protection of the law. All are entitled to equal protection against any discrimination in

violation of this Declaration and against any incitement to such discrimination.

Article 8.

Everyone has the right to an effective remedy by the competent national tribunals for acts violating the fundamental rights granted him by the constitution or by law.

Article 9.

No one shall be subjected to arbitrary arrest, detention or exile.

Article 10.

Everyone is entitled in full equality to a fair and public hearing by an independent and impartial tribunal, in the determination of his rights and obligations and of any criminal charge against him.

Article 11.

(1) Everyone charged with a penal offence has the right to be presumed innocent until proved guilty according to law in a public trial at which he has had all the guarantees necessary for his defence.

(2) No one shall be held guilty of any penal offence on account of any act or omission which did not constitute a penal offence, under national or international law, at the time when it was committed. Nor shall a heavier penalty be imposed than the one that was applicable at the time the penal offence was committed.

Article 12.

No one shall be subjected to arbitrary interference with his privacy, family, home or correspondence, nor to attacks upon his honour and reputation. Everyone has the right to the protection of the law against such interference or attacks.

Article 13.

(1) Everyone has the right to freedom of movement and residence within the borders of each state.

(2) Everyone has the right to leave any country, including his own, and to return to his country.

Article 14.

(1) Everyone has the right to seek and to enjoy in other countries asylum from persecution.

(2) This right may not be invoked in the case of prosecutions genuinely arising from non-political crimes or from acts contrary to the purposes and principles of the United Nations.

Article 15.

(1) Everyone has the right to a nationality.

(2) No one shall be arbitrarily deprived of his nationality nor denied the right to change his nationality.

Article 16.

(1) Men and women of full age, without any limitation due to race, nationality or religion, have the right to marry and to found a family. They are entitled to equal rights as to marriage, during marriage and at its dissolution.

(2) Marriage shall be entered into only with the free and full consent of the intending spouses.

(3) The family is the natural and fundamental group unit of society and is entitled to protection by society and the State.

Article 17.

(1) Everyone has the right to own property alone as well as in association with others.

(2) No one shall be arbitrarily deprived of his property.

Article 18.

Everyone has the right to freedom of thought, conscience and religion; this right includes freedom to change his religion or belief, and freedom, either alone or in community with others and in public or private, to manifest his religion or belief in teaching, practice, worship and observance.

Article 19.

Everyone has the right to freedom of opinion and expression; this right includes freedom to hold opinions without interference and to seek, receive and impart information and ideas through any media and regardless of frontiers.

Article 20.

(1) Everyone has the right to freedom of peaceful assembly and association.
(2) No one may be compelled to belong to an association.

Article 21.

(1) Everyone has the right to take part in the government of his country, directly or through freely chosen representatives.
(2) Everyone has the right of equal access to public service in his country.
(3) The will of the people shall be the basis of the authority of government; this will shall be expressed in periodic and genuine elections which shall be by universal and equal suffrage and shall be held by secret vote or by equivalent free voting procedures.

Article 22.

Everyone, as a member of society, has the right to social security and is entitled to realization, through national effort and international co-operation and in accordance with the organization and resources of each State, of the economic, social and cultural rights indispensable for his dignity and the free development of his personality.

Article 23.

(1) Everyone has the right to work, to free choice of employment, to just and favourable conditions of work and to protection against unemployment.
(2) Everyone, without any discrimination, has the right to equal pay for equal work.
(3) Everyone who works has the right to just and favourable remuneration ensuring for himself and his family an existence worthy of human dignity, and supplemented, if necessary, by other means of social protection.
(4) Everyone has the right to form and to join trade unions for the protection of his interests.

Article 24.

Everyone has the right to rest and leisure, including reasonable limitation of working hours and periodic holidays with pay.

Article 25.

(1) Everyone has the right to a standard of living adequate for the health and well-being of himself and of his family, including food, clothing, housing and medical care and necessary social services, and the right to security in the event of unemployment, sickness, disability, widowhood, old age or other lack of livelihood in circumstances beyond his control.
(2) Motherhood and childhood are entitled to special care and assistance. All children, whether born in or out of wedlock, shall enjoy the same social protection.

Article 26.

(1) Everyone has the right to education. Education shall be free, at least in the elementary and fundamental stages. Elementary education shall be compulsory. Technical and professional education shall be made generally available and higher education shall be equally accessible to all on the basis of merit.
(2) Education shall be directed to the full

development of the human personality and to the strengthening of respect for human rights and fundamental freedoms. It shall promote understanding, tolerance and friendship among all nations, racial or religious groups, and shall further the activities of the United Nations for the maintenance of peace.

(3) Parents have a prior right to choose the kind of education that shall be given to their children.

Article 27.

(1) Everyone has the right freely to participate in the cultural life of the community, to enjoy the arts and to share in scientific advancement and its benefits.

(2) Everyone has the right to the protection of the moral and material interests resulting from any scientific, literary or artistic production of which he is the author.

Article 28.

Everyone is entitled to a social and international order in which the rights and freedoms set forth in this Declaration can be fully realized.

Article 29.

(1) Everyone has duties to the community in which alone the free and full development of his personality is possible.

(2) In the exercise of his rights and freedoms, everyone shall be subject only to such limitations as are determined by law solely for the purpose of securing due recognition and respect for the rights and freedoms of others and of meeting the just requirements of morality, public order and the general welfare in a democratic society.

(3) These rights and freedoms may in no case be exercised contrary to the purposes and principles of the United Nations.

Article 30.

Nothing in this Declaration may be interpreted as implying for any State, group or person any right to engage in any activity or to perform any act aimed at the destruction of any of the rights and freedoms set forth herein.

Questions

1. Which of the articles/human rights addresses the most basic human needs of life? What does this human right mean if a nation does not have the resources to meet this right?

2. The natural environment is not covered in this declaration. Why do you think it is absent? What representation should it be granted, given that it is the basis of all life and life activities?

3. Does Article 23 go far enough to protect workers? Why has this article not been respected by firms regarding livable and non-discriminatory wages?

2. The United Nations Declaration of Human Rights Principles and Responsibilities for Transnational Corporations and Other Business Enterprises[1]

THE *United Nations Declaration of Human Rights Principles and Responsibilities for Transnational Corporations and Other Business Enterprises*, 2002 (hereinafter *Responsibilities*) is the product of the United Nations Commission on Human Rights, the Sub-Commission on the Promotion and Protection of Human Rights, and the Sessional Working Group on the Working Methods and Activities of Transnational Corporations. *Responsibilities* states that "transnational corporations, as organs of society, are also responsible for promoting and securing the human rights set forth in the Universal Declaration." *Responsibilities* reminds transnational firms that they are obligated to recognize and uphold numerous other "treaties and international instruments," and it notes the increasing influence they have on most economies, the increasing reports of human rights violations, and the universality of human rights. The document reiterates categories of rights that transnational firms, and all businesses, have special duties to uphold, and it calls for periodic monitoring of all business activities. *Responsibilities* is (at the time of this writing) currently under discussion by the aforementioned groups.

Preamble

Bearing in mind the principles and obligations under the United Nations Charter, in particular the preamble and Articles 1, 2, and 55, *inter alia,* to promote universal respect for, and observance of, human rights and fundamental freedoms,

Recalling that the Universal Declaration of Human Rights proclaims a common standard of achievement for all peoples and all nations,

to the end that governments, other organs of society, and individuals shall strive by teaching and education to promote respect for human rights and freedoms and by progressive measures to secure their universal and effective recognition and observance,

Recognizing that even though States have the primary responsibility to promote and protect human rights, transnational corporations and other business enterprises, as organs of society, are also responsible for promoting and securing the human rights set forth in the Universal Declaration of Human Rights,

Realizing that transnational corporations and other business enterprises, their officers, and their workers are further obligated to respect generally recognized principles and norms in United Nations treaties and other international instruments such as the Convention on the Prevention and Punishment of Genocide; the International Convention Against Torture and Other Forms of Cruel, Inhuman or Degrading Treatment or Punishment; the Slavery Convention and the Supplementary Convention on the Abolition of Slavery, the Slave Trade, and Institutions and Practices Similar to Slavery; the International Convention on the Elimination of All Forms of Racial Discrimination; the Convention on the Elimination of All Forms of Discrimination Against Women; the International Covenant on Economic, Social and Cultural Rights; the International Covenant on Civil and Political Rights; the Convention on the Rights of the Child; the four Geneva Conventions and two Additional Protocols for the Protection of Victims of Armed Conflict; the Nuremberg Charter; the Declaration on the Right and Responsibility of Individuals, Groups and Organs of Society to Promote and Protect Universally Recognized Human Rights and Fundamental Freedoms; the Rome Statute of the International Criminal Court; the Convention Against Transnational Organized Crime; the Convention on Civil Liability for Oil Pollution Damage; the Convention on Civil Liability for Damage Resulting from Activities Dangerous to the Environment; the WHO International Code of Marketing of Breast-milk Substitutes and the Ethical Criteria for Medical Drug Promotion; the UNESCO Convention Against Discrimination in Education; ILO conventions and recommendations; the Convention and Protocol relating to the Status of Refugees; the African Charter on Human Rights and Peoples' Rights; the American Convention on Human Rights; the European Convention on Human Rights; the European Charter on Fundamental Rights; the OECD's Convention on Combating Bribery of Foreign Public Officials in International Business Transactions; and other instruments,

Taking into account the standards set forth in the International Labour Organization Tripartite Declaration of Principles Concerning Multinational Enterprises and Social Policy,

Aware of the Organisation for Economic Cooperation and Development Guidelines for Multinational Enterprises and its Committee on International Investment and Multinational Enterprises; the U.N. Global Compact initiative which challenges business leaders to "embrace and enact" nine basic principles with respect to human rights, including labour rights and the environment; and the ILO Declaration on Fundamental Principles and the Rights at Work,

Conscious of the efforts of the ILO Committee on Multinational Enterprises; the interpretation of standards by the ILO Committee on Multinational Enterprises, the ILO Committee of Experts, the Conference Committee on the Application of Standards, and the Declaration Expert-Advisors; as well as the ILO Committee on Freedom of Association which has named business enterprises implicated in States' failure to comply with ILO Conventions 87 and 98, and seeking to supplement and assist their efforts to encourage transnational corporations and other business enterprises to protect human rights,

Taking note of global trends which have increased the influence of transnational corporations and other business enterprises—and particularly transnational corporations—on the economies of most countries and in international economic relations; and the growing number of other business enterprises which operate across national boundaries in a variety of arrangements resulting in economic activities beyond the actual capacities of any one national system,

Noting that transnational corporations and other business enterprises have the capacity to foster economic well-being, development, technological improvement, and wealth as well as have the capacity to cause deleterious human rights impacts on the lives of individuals through their employment practices, environmental policies, relationships with suppliers and consumers, interactions with governments, and other activities,

Noting also that new international human rights issues and concerns are continually emerging and that transnational corporations and other business enterprises often are related to these issues and concerns, such that further standard-setting and implementation are required at this time and in future,

Acknowledging the universality, indivisibility, interdependence, and interrelatedness of human rights, including the right to development, that entitles every human person and all peoples to participate in; contribute to; and enjoy economic, social, cultural, and political development in which all human rights and fundamental freedoms can be fully realized,

Reaffirming that transnational corporations and other business enterprises, their officers, and their workers have human rights obligations and responsibilities and that these human rights principles will contribute to the making and development of international law as to their responsibilities and obligations,

Solemnly proclaims these Human Rights Principles and Responsibilities for Transnational Corporations and Other Business Enterprises and urges that every effort be made so that they become generally known and respected:

A. General Obligations

1. States have the primary responsibility to respect, ensure respect for, prevent abuses of, and promote human rights recognised in international as well as national law. Within their respective spheres of activity and influence, transnational corporations and other business enterprises have the obligation to respect, ensure respect for, prevent abuses of, and promote human rights recognized in international as well as national law.

B. Right to Equal Opportunity and Non-Discriminatory Treatment

2. Transnational corporations and other business enterprises shall ensure equality of opportunity and treatment, for the purpose of eliminating discrimination based on race, colour, sex, religion, political opinion, nationality, social origin, social status, indigenous status, disability, age (except for children who may be given greater protection), or other status of the individual unrelated to the individual's ability to perform his/her job.

C. Right to Security of Persons

3. Transnational corporations and other business enterprises shall not engage in nor benefit from war crimes, crimes against humanity, genocide, torture, forced disappearance, forced or compulsory labour, hostage-taking, other violations of humanitarian law, and other international crimes against the human person as defined by international law.

4. Security arrangements for transnational corporations and other business enterprises shall observe international human rights norms as well as the laws and professional standards of the country or countries in which they operate.

D. Rights of Workers

5. Transnational corporations and other business enterprises shall not use forced or compulsory labour as forbidden by the relevant international instruments and national legislation.

6. Transnational corporations and other business enterprises shall respect the rights of children to be protected from economic exploitation as forbidden by the relevant international instruments and national legislation.

7. Transnational corporations and other business enterprises shall provide a safe and healthy working environment as provided by the relevant international instruments and national legislation.

8. Transnational corporations and other business enterprises shall compensate workers with remuneration that ensures an adequate standard of living for them and their families. Such remuneration shall take due account of their needs for adequate living conditions with a view towards progressive improvement.

9. Transnational corporations and other business enterprises shall ensure the freedom of association and effective recognition of the right to collective bargaining by protecting the right to establish and, subject only to the rules of the organization concerned, to join organizations of their own choosing without distinction, previous authorization, or interference, for the protection of their employment interests and for other collective bargaining purposes as provided in the relevant ILO conventions.

E. Respect for National Sovereignty and Local Communities

10. Transnational corporations and other business enterprises shall recognize and respect applicable norms of international law; national laws; regulations; administrative practices; the rule of law; development objectives; social, economic, and cultural policies; and authority of the countries in which the enterprises operate.

11. Transnational corporations and other business enterprises shall not offer, promise, give, accept, condone, knowingly benefit from, or demand a bribe or other improper advantage. Nor shall they be solicited or expected to give a bribe or other improper advantage to any government, public official, candidate for elective post, or any other individual or organization.

12. Transnational corporations and other business enterprises shall respect civil, cultural, economic, political, and social rights, and contribute to their realization, in particular the rights to development; adequate food; adequate health; adequate housing; education; freedom of thought, conscience, and religion; and freedom of opinion and expression; and refrain from actions which obstruct the realization of those rights.

F. Obligations with regard to Consumer Protection

13. Transnational corporations and other business enterprises shall act in accordance with fair business, marketing, and advertising practices and shall take all necessary steps to ensure the safety and quality of the goods and services they provide. They shall not produce, distribute, market, or advertise potentially harmful or harmful products for use by consumers.

G. Obligations with regard to Environmental Protection

14. Transnational corporations and other business enterprises shall carry out their activities in accordance with national laws, regulations, administrative practices, and policies relating to the preservation of the environment of the countries in which they operate as well as in accordance with relevant international agreements, principles, objectives, and standards with regard to the environment as well as human rights, public health, and safety; and shall generally conduct their activities in a manner contributing to the wider goal of sustainable development.

H. General Provisions of Implementation

15. As an initial step towards compliance with these Principles, each transnational corporation or other business enterprise shall adopt, disseminate, and implement internal rules of operation consistent with these Principles. Further, they shall take other measures fully to implement these Principles and to provide at least for the prompt implementation of the protections set forth in these Principles.

16. Transnational corporations and other businesses enterprises shall be subject to periodic monitoring by national, international, governmental, and/or nongovernmental mechanisms regarding their application of the Principles. This monitoring shall be transparent, independent, and take into account input from relevant stakeholders. Further, transnational corporations and other businesses enterprises shall conduct periodic evaluations concerning the impact of their own activities on human rights under these Principles.

17. Transnational corporations and other business enterprises shall provide prompt, effective, and adequate reparation to those persons, entities, and communities who have been adversely affected by failures to comply with these Principles through restoring, replacing, or otherwise compensating for any damage done or property taken.

18. Nothing in these Principles shall be construed as diminishing, restricting, or adversely affecting the human rights obligations of States under national and international law. Nor shall they be construed as diminishing, or adversely affecting more protective human rights norms.

I. Definitions

19. (a). The term "transnational corporation" refers to a cluster of economic entities operating in two or more countries—whatever their legal form, whether in their home country or country of activity, and whether taken individually or collectively.

(b). The phrase "other business enterprise" includes any business entity, regardless of the international or domestic nature of its activities, including a transnational corporation; the corporate, partnership, or other legal form used to establish the business entity; and the nature of the ownership of the entity.

(c). The term "stakeholder" includes stockholders, other owners, workers, and their representatives, as well as any other individual or group that is affected by the activities of the business. The term "stakeholder" should be interpreted functionally in light of the objectives of these Principles and include indirect stakeholders when their interests are or will be substantially affected by the activities of the transnational corporation or business enterprise. In addition to parties directly affected by the activities of business enterprises, stakeholders can include parties which are indirectly affected by the activities of businesses such as consumer groups, customers, governments, neighboring communities, indigenous peoples and communities, NGOs, public and private lending institutions, suppliers, trade associations, and others.

(d). The terms "contractor," "subcontractor,"

"supplier," and "licensee" include any natural or legal person who enters into any agreement with the transnational corporation or business enterprise to accomplish the enterprise's activities.

(e). The phrases "internationally recognized human rights" and "international human rights" include civil, cultural, economic, political, and social rights, as set forth in the International Bill of Human Rights and other human rights treaties, as well as the right to development and rights recognized by international humanitarian law, international refugee law, international labour law, and other relevant instruments adopted within the United Nations system.

Questions

1. What is covered in this document that is not covered in the *United Nations Universal Declaration of Human Rights*? Should firms be held to these principles and responsibilities? Why or why not?

2. Does this document go far enough to protect those affected by transnational corporations? Are other protections needed?

3. Many transnational corporations wield more wealth and resources than many nations. Does this document protect nations sufficiently?

Note

1. Human Rights Principles and Responsibilities for Transnational Corporations and Other Business Enterprises, U.N. Doc. E/CN.4/Sub.2/2002/XX, E/CN.4/Sub.2/2002/WG.2/WP.1 (February 2002 for discussion in July/August 2002).

3. Moral Minimums for Multinationals[1]

Thomas Donaldson

PROVIDING A GROUNDBREAKING MODEL for determining when it would be ethically justified to do business abroad is Thomas Donaldson's "Moral Minimums for Multinationals." Donaldson argues for ten minimum human rights that a firm, when doing business abroad, should never violate. He provides a distinction between two types of ethical conflicts that can arise when doing business abroad. The first one, a type 1 conflict, is when there is a conflict between the norms of the home and host countries that arises out of the relative levels of economic development. In a type 1 conflict, the home country is the "developed" country and has "higher" standards for such things as environmental quality, whereas the host country is "developing" and willing to accept some trade-offs, such as some forms of pollution, in order to develop. A type 2 conflict is a conflict that is not due to issues of economic development, such as a cultural conflict.

In either type of conflict, Donaldson argues that a firm is justified in doing business abroad only if it does not violate the minimal rights and if the action in question passes additional tests, depending on the type of conflict in question. Donaldson's model is much more challenging to business as usual than it first appears. In arguing that a firm is not justified in doing business if it violates one of the ten minimum rights, he is stating that if a firm cannot operate without violations, it should not engage in the particular business in question, period. As Donaldson makes clear, his model will find resistance, yet even to adopt some of the ethical guidelines he advocates would have a dramatic effect on multinational business as currently practiced.

WHEN EXPLORING ISSUES OF international ethics, researchers frequently neglect multinational corporations. They are prone to forget that these commercial leviathans often rival nation-states in power and organizational skill, and that their remarkable powers imply nonlegal responsibilities. Critics and defenders agree on the enormity of corporate multinational power. Richard Barnet and Ronald Muller, well-known critics of multinationals, remark that the global corporation is the "most powerful human organization yet devised for colonizing the future."[2] The business analyst P.P. Gabriel, writing in the *Harvard Business Review*, characterizes the multinational as the "dominant institution" in a new era of world trade.[3] Indeed, with the exception of a handful of nation-states, multinationals are alone in possessing the size, technology, and economic reach necessary to influence human affairs on a global basis.

Ethical issues stemming from multinational

corporate activities often derive from a clash between the cultural attitudes in home and host countries. When standards for pollution, discrimination, and salary schedules appear lower in a multinational's host country than in the home country, should multinational managers always insist on home-country standards? Or does using home standards imply a failure to respect cultural diversity and national integrity? Is a factory worker in Mexico justified in complaining about being paid three dollars an hour for the same work a U.S. factory worker, employed by the same company, is paid ten dollars?[4] Is an asbestos worker in India justified in criticizing the lower standards for regulating in-plant asbestos pollution maintained by a British multinational relative to standards in Britain, when the standards in question fall within Indian government guidelines and, indeed, are stricter than the standards maintained by other Indian asbestos manufacturers? Furthermore, what obligations, if any, do multinationals have to the people they affect indirectly? If a company buys land from wealthy landowners and turns it to the production of a cash crop, should it ensure that displaced farmers will avoid malnutrition?

I

It is well to remember that multinational power is not a wholly new phenomenon. Hundreds of years ago, the East India Company deployed over 40 warships, possessed the largest standing army in the world, was lord and master of an entire subcontinent, had dominion over 250 million people, and even hired its own church bishops.[5] The modern multinational is a product of the post–World War II era, and its dramatic success has stemmed from, among other factors, spiraling labor costs in developed countries, increasing importance of economies of scale in manufacturing, better

communication systems, improved transportation, and increasing worldwide consumer demand for new products.[6] Never far from the evolution of the multinational has been a host of ethical issues, including bribery and corrupt payments, employment and personnel issues, marketing practices, impact on the economy and development of host countries, effects on the natural environment, cultural impacts of multinational operations, relations with host governments, and relations with the home countries.[7]

The formal responsibilities of multinationals as defined in domestic and international law, as well as in codes of conduct, are expanding dramatically. While many codes are nonbinding in the sense that noncompliance will fail to trigger sanctions, these principles, taken as a group, are coming to exert significant influence on multinational conduct. A number of specific reasons lie behind the present surge in international codes and regulations. To begin with, some of the same forces propelling domestic attempts to bring difficult-to-control activities under stricter supervision are influencing multinationals.[8] Consider, for example, hazardous technology, a threat which by its nature recognizes no national boundaries yet must be regulated in both domestic and foreign contexts. The pesticide industry, which relies on such hazardous technology (of which Union Carbide's Bhopal plant is one instance), in 1987 grossed over $13 billion a year and has been experiencing mushrooming growth, especially in the developing countries.[9] It is little surprise that the rapid spread of hazardous technology has prompted the emergence of international codes on hazardous technology, such as the various U.N. resolutions on the transfer of technology and the use of pesticides....

II

The growing tradition of international business codes and policies suggests that the investigation of ethical issues in international business is pressing and proper. But what issues deserve attention?

One key set of issues relates to business practices that clearly conflict with the moral attitudes of most multinationals' home countries. Consider, for example, the practice of child labor, which continues to plague developing countries. While not the worst example, Central America offers a sobering lesson. In dozens of interviews with workers throughout Central America conducted in the fall of 1987, most respondents said they started working between the ages of 12 and 14.[10] The work week lasts six days, and the median salary (for all workers including adults) is scarcely over a dollar a day. The area is largely non-unionized, and strikes are almost always declared illegal. There is strong similarity between the pressures compelling child labor in Central America and those in early nineteenth-century England during the Industrial Revolution. With unemployment ranging from a low of 24 percent in Costa Rica to a high of 50 percent in Guatemala, and with families malnourished and older breadwinners unable to work, children are often forced to make growth-stunting sacrifices.[11]

Then, too, there are issues about which our moral intuitions seem confused, issues which pose difficult questions for researchers. Consider an unusual case involving the sale of banned goods abroad—one in which a developing country argued that being able to buy a banned product was important to meeting its needs. Banned pharmaceuticals, in contrast to other banned goods, have been subject to export restrictions for over 40 years. Yet, in defense of a recent Reagan initiative, drug manufacturers in the United States argued by appealing to differing cultural variables. For example, a spokesman for the American division of Ciba-Geigy Pharmaceuticals justified relaxing restrictions on the sale of its Entero-Vioform, a drug he agrees has been associated with blindness and paralysis, on the basis of culture-specific, cost-benefit analysis. "The government of India," he pointed out, "has requested Ciba-Geigy to continue producing the drug because it treats a dysentery problem that can be life threatening."[12]

III

The task for the international ethicist is to develop or discover concepts capable of specifying the obligations of multinational corporations in cases such as these. One such important concept is that of a human right.

Rights establish minimum levels of morally acceptable behavior. One well-known definition of a right construes it as a "trump" over a collective good, which is to say that the assertion of one's right to something, such as free speech, takes precedence over all but the most compelling collective goals, and overrides, for example, the state's interest in civil harmony or moral consensus.[13] Rights are at the rock bottom of modern moral deliberation. Maurice Cranston writes that the litmus test for whether something is a right or not is whether it protects something of "paramount importance."[14] Hence, it may help to define what minimal responsibilities should be assigned to multinational corporations by asking, "What specific rights ought multinationals to respect?"

The flip side of a right typically is a duty.[15] This, in part, is what gives aptness to Joel Feinberg's well-known definition of a right as a "justified entitlement *to* something *from* someone."[16] It is the "from someone" part of the definition which reflects the assumption

45

of a duty, for without a correlative obligation that attaches to some moral agent or group of agents, a right is weakened—if not beyond the status of a right entirely, then significantly. If we cannot say that a multinational corporation has a duty to keep the levels of arsenic low in the work place, then the worker's right not to be poisoned means little.

Often, duties associated with rights fall upon more than one class of moral agent. Consider, for example, the furor over the dumping of toxic waste in West Africa by multinational corporations. During 1988, virtually every country from Morocco to the Congo on Africa's west coast received offers from companies seeking cheap sites for dumping waste.[17] In the years prior, dumping in the U.S. and Europe had become enormously expensive, in large part because of the costly safety measures mandated by U.S. and European governments. In February of 1988, officials in Guinea-Bissau, one of the world's poorest nations, agreed to bury 15 million tons of toxic wastes from European tanneries and pharmaceutical companies. The companies agreed to pay about $120 million, which is only slightly less than the country's entire gross national product. In Nigeria in 1987, five European ships unloaded toxic waste in Nigeria containing dangerous poisons such as polychlorinated biphenyls, or PCBs. Workers wearing thongs and shorts unloaded the barrels for $2.50 a day, and placed them in a dirt lot in a residential area in the town of Kiko.[18] They were not told about the contents of the barrels.[19]

Who bears responsibility for protecting the workers' and inhabitants' rights to safety in such instances? It would be wrong to place it entirely upon a single agent such as the government of a West African nation. As it happens, the toxic waste dumped in Nigeria entered under an import permit for "non-explosive, nonradioactive and non-self-combusting chemicals." But the permit turned out to be a loophole; Nigeria had not meant to accept the waste and demanded its removal once word about its presence filtered into official channels. The example reveals the difficulty many developing countries have in creating the sophisticated language and regulatory procedures necessary to control high-technology hazards. It seems reasonable in such instances, then, to place the responsibility not upon a single class of agents, but upon a broad collection of them, including governments, corporate executives, host-country companies and officials, and international organizations.

One list receiving significant international attention is the Universal Declaration of Human Rights.[20] However, it and the subsequent International Covenant on Social, Economic and Cultural Rights have spawned controversy, despite the fact that the Declaration was endorsed by virtually all of the important post-World War II nations in 1948 as part of the affirmation of the U.N. Charter. What distinguishes these lists from their predecessors, and what serves also as the focus of controversy, is their inclusion of rights that have come to be called, alternatively, "social," "economic," "positive," or "welfare" rights.

Many have balked at such rights, arguing that no one can have a right to a specific supply of an economic good. Can anyone be said to have a "right," for example, to 128 hours of sleep and leisure each week? And, in the same spirit, some international documents have simply refused to adopt the welfare-affirming blueprint established in the Universal Declaration....

Many who criticize welfare rights utilize a traditional philosophical distinction between so-called negative and positive rights. A positive right is said to be one that requires persons to act positively to *do* something, while a negative one requires only that people not directly deprive others. Hence, the right to liberty is said to be a negative right, whereas the right to enough food is said to be a positive one. With this distinction in hand, the point is commonly made that no one can be bound to improve the welfare of another (unless, say, that person has entered into an agreement to do so); rather, they can be bound at most to *refrain* from damaging the welfare of another.

Nonetheless, Henry Shue has argued persuasively against the very distinction between negative and positive rights. Consider the most celebrated and best accepted example of a negative right: namely, the right to freedom. The meaningful preservation of the right to freedom requires a variety of positive actions: for example, on the part of the government it requires the establishment and maintenance of a police force, courts, and the military, and on the part of the citizenry it requires ongoing cooperation and diligent (not merely passive) forbearance. The protection of another so-called negative right, the right to physical security, necessitates "police forces; criminal rights; penitentiaries; schools for training police, lawyers, and guards; and taxes to support an enormous system for the prevention, detention, and punishment of violations of personal security."[21]

This is compelling. The maintenance and preservation of many non-welfare rights (where, again, such maintenance and preservation is the key to a right's status as basic) require the support of certain basic welfare rights. Certain liberties depend upon the enjoyment of subsistence, just as subsistence sometimes depends upon the enjoyment of some liberties. One's freedom to speak freely is meaningless if one is weakened by hunger to the point of silence.

What list of rights, then, ought to be endorsed on the international level? Elsewhere I have argued that the rights appearing on such

a list should pass the following three conditions:[22] 1) the right must protect something of very great importance; 2) the right must be subject to substantial and recurrent threats; and 3) the obligations or burdens imposed by the right must satisfy a fairness-affordability test.[23]

In turn, I have argued that the list of fundamental international rights generated from these conditions include: 1) the right to freedom of physical movement; 2) the right to ownership of property; 3) the right to freedom from torture; 4) the right to a fair trial; 5) the right to nondiscriminatory treatment (e.g., freedom from discrimination on the basis of such characteristics as race or sex); 6) the right to physical security; 7) the right to freedom of speech and association; 8) the right to minimal education; 9) the right to political participation; and 10) the right to subsistence.

This seems a minimal list. Some will wish to add entries such as the right to employment, to social security, or to a certain standard of living (say, as might be prescribed by Rawls's well-known "difference" principle). The list as presented aims to suggest, albeit incompletely, a description of a *minimal* set of rights and to serve as a point of beginning and consensus for evaluating international conduct. If I am correct, many would wish to add entries, but few would wish to subtract them.

As we look over the list, it is noteworthy that, except for a few isolated instances, multinational corporations have probably succeeded in fulfilling their duty not to actively deprive persons of their enjoyment of the rights at issue. But correlative duties involve more than failing to actively deprive people of the enjoyment of their rights. Shue, for example, notes that three types of correlative duties (i.e., duties corresponding to a particular right) are possible: 1) to avoid depriving, 2) to help protect from deprivation; and 3) to aid the deprived.[24]

While it is obvious that the honoring of rights clearly imposes duties of the first kind, i.e., to avoid depriving directly, it is less obvious, but frequently true, that honoring them involves acts or omissions that help prevent the deprivation of rights. If I receive a note from Murder, Incorporated, and it looks like business, my right to security is clearly threatened. Let's say that a third party (X) has relevant information which, if revealed to the police, would help protect my right to security. In this case, there is no excuse for X to remain silent, claiming that it is Murder, Incorporated, and not X, who wishes to murder me.

Similarly, the duties associated with rights often include ones from the third category, i.e., that of aiding the deprived, as when a government is bound to honor the right of its citizens to adequate nutrition by distributing food in the wake of famine or natural disaster, or when the same government, in the defense of political liberty, is required to demand that an employer reinstate or compensate an employee fired for voting for a particular candidate in a government election.

Which of these duties apply to corporations, and which apply only to governments? It would be unfair, not to mention unreasonable, to hold corporations to the same standards for enhancing and protecting social welfare to which we hold civil governments—since frequently governments are formally dedicated to enhancing the welfare of, and actively preserving the liberties of, their citizens. The profit-making corporation, in contrast, is designed to achieve an economic mission and as a moral actor possesses an exceedingly narrow personality. It is an undemocratic institution, furthermore, which is ill-suited to the broader task of distributing society's goods in accordance with a conception of general welfare. The corporation is an economic animal; although its responsibilities extend beyond maximizing return on investment for shareholders, they are informed directly by its economic mission. Hence, while it would be strikingly generous for multinationals to sacrifice some of their profits to buy milk, grain, and shelter for persons in poor countries, it seems difficult to consider this one of their minimal moral requirements. If anyone has such minimal obligations, it is the peoples' respective governments or, perhaps, better-off individuals.

The same, however, is not true of the second class of duties, i.e., to protect from deprivation. While these duties, like those in the third class, are also usually the province of government, it sometimes happens that the rights to which they correlate are ones whose protection is a direct outcome of ordinary corporate activities. For example, the duties associated with protecting a worker from the physical threats of other workers may fall not only upon the local police but also upon the employer. These duties, in turn, are properly viewed as correlative duties of the right—in this instance, the worker's right—to personal security. This will become clearer in a moment when we discuss the correlative duties of specific rights.

The following list of correlative duties reflects a second-stage application of the fairness-affordability condition to the earlier list of fundamental international rights, and indicates which rights do, and which do not, impose correlative duties upon multinational corporations of the three various kinds.[25]

Minimal Correlative Duties of Multinational Corporations

Fundamental Rights	To Avoid Depriving	To Help Protect from Deprivation	To Aid the Deprived
Freedom of physical movement	X		
Ownership of property	X		
Freedom from torture	X		
Fair trial	X		
Nondiscriminatory treatment	X	X	
Physical security	X	X	
Freedom of speech and association	X	X	
Minimal education	X	X	
Political participation	X	X	
Subsistence	X	X	

Let us illustrate the duty to protect from deprivation with specific examples. The right to physical security entails duties of protection. If a Japanese multinational corporation operating in Nigeria hires shop workers to run metal lathes in an assembly factory, but fails to provide them with protective goggles, then the corporation has failed to honor the workers' moral right to physical security (no matter what the local law might decree). Injuries from such a failure would be the moral responsibility of the Japanese multinational despite the fact that the company could not be said to have inflicted the injuries directly.

Another correlative duty, to protect the right of education, may be illustrated through the example mentioned earlier: namely, the prevalence of child labor in developing countries. A multinational in Central America is not entitled to hire an eight-year-old for full-time, ongoing work because, among other reasons, doing so blocks the child's ability to receive a minimally sufficient education. While what counts as a "minimally sufficient" education may be debated, and while it seems likely, moreover, that the specification of the right to a certain level of education will depend at least in part upon the level

of economic resources available in a given country, it is reasonable to assume that any action by a corporation which has the effect of blocking the development of a child's ability to read or write will be proscribed on the basis of rights.

In some instances, corporations have failed to honor the correlative duty of protecting the right to political participation from deprivation. The most blatant examples of direct deprivation are fortunately becoming so rare as to be nonexistent, namely, cases in which companies directly aid in overthrowing democratic regimes, as when United Fruit, Inc., allegedly contributed to overthrowing a democratically elected regime in Guatemala during the 1950s. But a few corporations have continued indirectly to threaten this right by failing to protect it from deprivation. A few have persisted, for example, in supporting military dictatorships in countries with growing democratic sentiment, and others have blatantly bribed publicly elected officials with large sums of money. Perhaps the most celebrated example of the latter occurred when the prime minister of Japan was bribed with $7 million by the Lockheed Corporation to secure a lucrative Tri-Star Jet contract. The

49

complaint from the perspective of this right is not against bribes or "sensitive payments" in general, but against bribes in contexts where they serve to undermine a democratic system in which publicly elected officials are in a position of public trust.

Even the buying and owning of major segments of a foreign country's land and industry have been criticized in this regard. As Brian Barry has remarked, "The paranoia created in Britain and the United States by land purchases by foreigners (especially the Arabs and the Japanese, it seems) should serve to make it understandable that the citizenry of a country might be unhappy with a state of affairs in which the most important natural resources are in foreign ownership."[26] At what point would Americans regard their democratic control threatened by foreign ownership of U.S. industry and resources? At 20 percent ownership? At 40 percent? At 60 percent? At 80 percent? The answer is debatable, yet there seems to be some point beyond which the right to national self-determination, and in turn national democratic control, is violated by foreign ownership of property.[27]

Corporations also have duties to protect the right to subsistence from deprivation. Consider the following scenario. A number of square miles of land in an underdeveloped country has been used for years to grow black beans. The bulk of the land is owned, as it has been for centuries, by two wealthy landowners. Poorer members of the community work the land and receive a portion of the crop, a portion barely sufficient to satisfy nutritional needs. Next, imagine that a multinational corporation offers the two wealthy owners a handsome sum for the land, and does so because it plans to grow coffee for export. Now if—and this, admittedly, is a crucial "if"—the corporation has reason to *know* that a significant number of people in the community will suffer malnutrition as a result—that is, if it

has convincing reasons to believe either those persons will fail to be hired by the company and paid sufficiently or, if forced to migrate to the city, will receive wages insufficient to provide adequate food and shelter—then the multinational may be said to have failed in its correlative duty to protect persons from the deprivation of the right to subsistence. This despite the fact that the corporation would never have stooped to take food from workers' mouths, and despite the fact that the malnourished will, in Coleridge's words, "die so slowly that none call it murder."

In addition to articulating a list of rights and the correlative duties imposed upon multinational corporations, there is also a need to articulate a practical stratagem for use in applying the home-country norms of the multinational manager to the vexing problems arising in developing countries. In particular, how should highly-placed multinational managers, typically schooled in home-country moral traditions, reconcile conflicts between those traditions and ones of the host country? When host-country standards for pollution, discrimination and salary schedules appear substandard from the perspective of the home country, should the manager take the high road and implement home-country standards? Or does the high road imply a failure to respect cultural diversity and national integrity?

What distinguishes these issues from standard ones about corporate practices is that they involve reference to a conflict of norms, either moral or legal, between home and host country....

What is needed is a more comprehensive test than a simple appeal to rights. Of course the earlier rights-based approach clarifies a moral bottom line regarding, say, extreme threats to workers' safety. But it leaves obscure not only the issue of less extreme threats, but of harms other than physical injury. Granted, the celebrated dangers of asbestos call for recognizing the right to workers' safety no matter how broadly the language of rights is framed. But what are we to say of a less toxic pollutant? Is the level of sulphur-dioxide air pollution we should tolerate in a struggling nation, one with only a few fertilizer plants working overtime to help feed its malnourished population, the same we should demand in Portland, Oregon?

In the end, nothing less than a general moral theory working in tandem with an analysis of the foundations of corporate existence is needed. But at the practical level a need exists for an interpretive mechanism or algorithm that multinational managers could use in determining the implications of their own moral views.

The first step in generating such an ethical algorithm is to isolate the distinct sense in which the norms of the home and host country conflict. If the practice is morally and/or legally permitted in the host country, but not in the home country, then either: 1) the moral reasons underlying the host country's view that the practice is permissible refer to the host country's relative level of economic development; or 2) the moral reasons underlying the host country's view that the practice is permissible are independent of the host country's relative level of economic development.

Let us call the conflict of norms described in (1) a type 1 conflict. In such a conflict, an African country that permits slightly higher levels of thermal pollution from electric power generating plants, or a lower minimum wage than that prescribed in European countries, would do so not because higher standards would be undesirable per se, but because its level of economic development requires an ordering of priorities. In the future, when it succeeds in matching European economic achievements, it may well implement the higher standards.

Let us call the conflict of norms described in (2) a type 2 conflict. In such cases, levels of economic development play no role. For example, low-level institutional nepotism, common in many developing countries, is justified not on economic grounds, but on the basis of clan and family loyalty. Presumably the same loyalties will be operative even after the country has risen to economic success—as the nepotism prevalent in Saudi Arabia would indicate. The Italian tax case also reflects an Italian cultural style with a penchant for personal negotiation and an unwillingness to formalize transactions, more than a strategy based on level of economical development.

The difference in norms between the home and host country, i.e., whether the conflict is of type 1 or 2, does not determine the correctness, or truth value, of the host country's claim that the practice is permissible. The practice may or may not be permissible, whether the conflict is of type 1 or 2. This is not to say that the truth value of the host country's claim is independent of the nature of the conflict. A different test will be required to determine whether the practice is permissible when the conflict is of type 1 as opposed to type 2. In a type 1 dispute, the following formula is appropriate:

The practice is permissible if and only if the members of the home country would, under conditions of economic development similar to those of the host country, regard the practice as permissible.

Under this test, excessive levels of asbestos pollution would almost certainly not be tolerated by the members of the home country under similar economic conditions, whereas higher levels of thermal pollution would be tolerated. The test, happily, explains and confirms our initial moral intuitions.

Since in type 2 conflicts the dispute between the home and host country depends upon a fundamental difference of perspective, a different test is needed. In type 2 conflicts, the opposing evils of ethnocentricism and ethical relativism must be avoided. A multinational must forego the temptation to remake all societies in the image of its home society, while at the same time rejecting a relativism that conveniently forgets ethics when the payoff is sufficient. Thus, the ethical task is to tolerate cultural diversity while drawing the line at moral recklessness.

Since in type 2 cases the practice is in conflict with an embedded norm of the home country, one should first ask whether the practice is necessary to do business in the host country, for if it is not, the solution clearly is to adopt some other practice that is permissible from the standpoint of the home country. If petty bribery of public officials is unnecessary for the business of the Cummins Engine Company in India, then the company is obliged to abandon such bribery. If, on the other hand, the practice proves necessary for business, one must next ask whether the practice constitutes a direct violation of a basic human right. Here the notion of a fundamental international right outlined earlier, specifying a minimum below which corporate conduct should not fall, has special application. If Toyota, a Japanese company, confronts South African laws that mandate systematic discrimination against non-whites, then Toyota must refuse to comply with the laws. In type 2 cases, the evaluator must ask the following questions: 1) Is it possible to conduct business successfully in the host country without undertaking the practice? and 2) Is the practice a clear violation of a fundamental international right? The practice would be permissible if and only if the answer to both questions is "no."

What sorts of practice might satisfy both criteria? Consider the practice of low-level bribery of public officials in some developing nations. In some South American countries, for example, it is impossible for any company, foreign or national, to move goods through customs without paying low-level officials a few dollars. Indeed, the salaries of such officials are sufficiently low that one suspects they are set with the prevalence of the practice in mind. The payments are relatively small, uniformly assessed, and accepted as standard practice by the surrounding culture. Here, the practice of petty bribery would pass the type 2 test and, barring other moral factors, would be permissible.

The algorithm does not obviate the need for multinational managers to appeal to moral concepts both more general and specific than the algorithm itself. It is not intended as a substitute for a general theory of morality or even an interpretation of the basic responsibilities of multinationals. Its power lies in its ability to tease out implications of the moral presuppositions of a manager's acceptance of "home" morality, and in this sense to serve as a clarifying device for multinational decision-making. The algorithm makes no appeal to a universal concept of morality (as the appeal to fundamental rights does in type 2 cases), save for the purported universality of the ethics endorsed by the home-country culture. When the home country's morality is wrong or confused, the algorithm can reflect this ethnocentricity, leading either to a mild paternalism or to the imposition of parochial standards. For example, the home country's oversensitivity to aesthetic features of the environment may lead it to reject a certain level of thermal pollution, even under strained economic circumstances. This results in a paternalistic refusal to allow such levels in the host country, despite the host country's acceptance of the higher levels and its belief that tolerating such levels is necessary for stimulating economic development. It would be a mistake, however, to exaggerate this weakness of the algorithm; coming up with actual cases in which the force of the algorithm would be relativized is extremely difficult. Indeed, I have been unable to discover a single, non-hypothetical set of facts fitting this description.

IV

How might multinational corporations improve their moral performance and come to embody the normative concepts advanced in this article? Two classes of remedies suggest themselves: external remedies, i.e., those that rely on international associations or agreements on the one hand; and internal remedies, i.e., those that rely on internal, corporate initiative on the other.

Earlier we discussed the dramatic expansion of external remedies in the form of international laws, agreements, and codes of conduct. Again, while many of these are nonbinding in the sense that noncompliance will fail to trigger sanctions, they are as a group coming to exert significant influence on multinational conduct. One of the principal advantages of such global and industry-wide initiatives is that they distribute costs more fairly than initiatives undertaken by individual corporations. When, in line with the WHO Code of Marketing Breast Milk Substitutes, Nestlé curtails questionable marketing practices for the sale of infant formula, it does so with the confidence that the other signers of the WHO Code will not be taking unfair advantage by undertaking the same questionable practices, for they must adhere to its provisions. Still another advantage of external remedies stems from the fact that many nation-states, especially developing ones, are unable to gather sufficient information about, much less control, the multinational corporations that operate within their borders. Thus, the use of supranational entities, whether

of an international or inter-industry form, will sometimes augment, or supplement, the power and information-gathering abilities of developing nations. It seems difficult to deny that the growth and maturation of such entities can enhance the ethical conduct of multinational corporations.

The most important change of an internal nature likely to enhance the ethical behavior of multinationals is for multinationals themselves to introduce ethical deliberation, i.e., to introduce factors of ethics into their decision-making mechanisms. That they should do so is a clear implication of the preceding discussion, yet it is a conclusion some will resist. Those who place great confidence in the efficacy of the market may, for example, believe that a corporate policy of moral disinterest and profit maximization will—*pace* Adam Smith's invisible hand—maximize overall global welfare.

This kind of ideological confidence in the international market may have been understandable decades ago. But persisting in the belief that market mechanisms will automatically ensure adequate moral conduct today seems recklessly idealistic. Forces such as Islamic fundamentalism, the global debt bomb, and massive unemployment in developing countries have drastically distorted the operation of the free market in international commerce, and even though a further selective freeing of market forces may enhance global productivity, it cannot solve automatically questions of fair treatment, hazardous technology, or discrimination.

Even adopting the minimal guidelines for corporate conduct advanced here would involve dramatic changes in the decision-making mechanisms of multinational corporations. Such firms would need to alter established patterns of information flow and collection in order to accommodate new forms of morally relevant information. The already complex parameters of corporate decision-making would become more so. Even scholarly research about international business would need to change. At present, research choices tend to be dictated by the goals of increased profits, long-term access to basic commodities needed for manufactured items, and increased global market share; but clearly these goals sometimes conflict with broader moral ends, such as refraining from violating human rights. Revised goals call for a revised program of research. And although we have rejected the view that multinational corporations must shoulder the world's problems of poverty, discrimination, and political injustice because, as economic entities, they have limited social missions, their goals nonetheless must include the aim of not impeding solutions to such problems.

Are such changes in the decision-making of multinational corporations likely or even possible? Resistance will be intense; clearly, there should be no delusions on this score. Yet, without minimizing the difficulties, I do not think the task impossible. At a minimum, corporations are capable of choosing the more ethical alternative in instances where alternative courses of action yield equal profits—and I believe they are capable of even more. Corporations are run by human beings, not beasts. As multinationals continue to mature in the context of an ever-expanding, more sophisticated global economy, we have reason to hope that they are capable of looking beyond their national borders and recognizing the same minimal claims made in the name of our shared humanity, that they accept at home.

Questions

1. What is the full test for doing business when a type 1 conflict exists? What does Donaldson argue that the home firm should do if the test is not passed?

2. What are Donaldson's ten minimum rights? Why do the duties for the firm differ regarding these rights? Do these rights go far enough to protect the citizens and the environment of the host country?

3. What should happen if the people in the host country want the jobs the firm provides, even if these jobs violate the ten minimum rights? Does it violate their autonomy if the exploitative jobs are removed?

Notes

1. Much of this article is extracted from Thomas Donaldson's book, *The Ethics of International Business* (Oxford: Oxford University Press, 1989). The book provides a framework for interpreting the ethics of global business.

2. Richard Barnet and Ronald Muller, *Global Reach: The Power of Multinational Corporations* (New York: Simon and Schuster, 1974) p. 363.

3. P.P. Gabriel, "MNCs in the Third World: Is Conflict Unavoidable?" *Harvard Business Review*, Vol. 56 (March–April 1978) pp. 83–93.

4. An example of disparity in wages between Mexican and U.S. workers is documented in the case study by John H. Haddox, "Twin-Plants and Corporate Responsibilities," in *Profits and Responsibility*, eds. Patricia Werhane and Kendall D'Andrade (New York: Random House, 1985).

5. Barnet and Muller, *Global Reach*, p. 72.

6. J.R. Simpson, "Ethics and Multinational Corporations vis-à-vis Developing Nations," *Journal of Business Ethics*, Vol. 1 (1982) pp. 227–37.

7. I have borrowed this eight-fold scheme of categories from researchers Farr and Stening in Lisa Farr and Bruce W. Stening, "Ethics and the Multinational Corporation" (an unpublished paper) p. 4.

8. An analysis of such reasons, one which also contains many observations on the evolution of international public policy, is Lee E. Preston's "The Evolution of Multinational Public Policy Toward Business: Codes of Conduct," a paper read at the annual meeting of the American Academy of Management, New Orleans, August 1987.

9. Jon R. Luoma, "A Disaster That Didn't Wait," *The New York Times Book Review*, November 29, 1987, p. 16.

10. James LeMoyne. "In Central America, the Workers Suffer Most," *The New York Times*, October 26, 1987, pp. 1 and 4.

11. Ibid.

12. Quoted in "Products Unsafe at Home are Still Unloaded Abroad," *The New York Times*, August 22, 1982, p. 22.

13. Ronald Dworkin, *Taking Rights Seriously* (Cambridge: Harvard University Press, 1977). For other standard definitions of rights, see: James W. Nickel, *Making Sense of Human Rights: Philosophical Reflections on the Universal Declaration of Human Rights* (Berkeley: University of California Press, 1987) especially chapter 2; Joel Feinberg, "Duties, Rights and Claims," *American Philosophical Quarterly*, Vol. 3 (1966) pp. 137–44. See also Feinberg, "The Nature and Value of Rights," *Journal of Value Inquiry*, Vol. 4 (1970) p. 243–57; Wesley N. Hohfeld, *Fundamental Legal Conceptions* (New Haven: Yale University Press, 1964); and H.J. McCloskey, "Rights—Some Conceptual Issues," *Australasian Journal of Philosophy*, Vol. 54 (1976) pp. 99–115.

14. Maurice Cranston, *What Are Human Rights?* (New York: Taplinger, 1973), p. 67.

15. H.J. McCloskey, for example, understands a right as a positive entitlement that need not specify who bears the responsibility for satisfying that entitlement. H.J. McCloskey, "Rights—Some Conceptual Issues," p. 99.

16. Joel Feinberg, "Duties, Rights and Claims," *American Philosophical Quarterly*, Vol. 3 (1966) pp. 137–44. See also Feinberg. "The Nature and Value of Rights," pp. 243–57.

17. James Brooke, "Waste Dumpers Turning to West Africa," *The New York Times,* July 17, 1988, pp. 1 and 7.

18. Ibid.

19. Ibid., p. 7. Nigeria and other countries have struck back, often by imposing strict rules against the acceptance of toxic waste. For example, in Nigeria officials now warn that anyone caught importing toxic waste will face the firing squad.

20. See Ian Brownlie, *Basic Documents on Human Rights* (Oxford: Oxford University Press, 1975).

21. Henry Shue, *Basic Rights: Subsistence, Affluence, and U. S. Foreign Policy* (Princeton: Princeton University Press, 1980) pp. 37–38.

22. Donaldson, *The Ethics of International Business*, see especially chapter 5. My formulation of these three conditions is an adaptation from four conditions presented and defended by James Nickel in James W. Nickel, *Making Sense of Human Rights: Philosophical Reflections on the Universal Declaration of Human Rights* (Berkeley: University of California Press, 1987).

23. The fairness-affordability test implies that in order for a proposed right to qualify as a genuine right, all moral agents (including nation-states, individuals, and corporations) must be able under ordinary circumstances, both economically and otherwise, to assume the various burdens and duties that fall fairly upon them in honoring the right. "Affordable" here means literally capable of paying for; it does not mean "affordable" in the vernacular sense that something is not affordable because it would constitute an inefficient luxury, or would necessitate trading off other more valuable economic goods. This definition implies

that—at least under unusual circumstances—honoring a right may be mandatory for a given multinational corporation, even when the result is bankrupting the firm. For example, it would be "affordable" under ordinary circumstances for multinational corporations to employ older workers and refuse to hire eight-year-old children for full-time, ongoing labor, and hence doing so would be mandatory even in the unusual situation where a particular firm's paying the higher salaries necessary to hire older laborers would probably bankrupt the firm. By the same logic, it would probably not be "affordable" for either multinational corporations or nation-states around the world to guarantee kidney dialysis for all citizens who need it. The definition also implies that any act of forbearance (of a kind involved in not violating a right directly) is "affordable" for all moral agents.

24. Shue, *Basic Rights*, p. 57.

25. It is possible to understand even the first four rights as imposing correlative duties to protect from deprivation under highly unusual or hypothetical circumstances.

26. Brian Barry, "The Case for a New International Economic Order," in *Ethics, Economics, and the Law: Nomos XXIV*, eds. J. Roland Pennock and John W. Chapman (New York: New York University Press, 1982).

27. Companies are also charged with undermining local governments, and hence infringing on basic rights, by sophisticated tax evasion schemes. Especially when companies buy from their own subsidiaries, they can establish prices that have little connection to existing market values. This, in turn, means that profits can be shifted from high-tax to low-tax countries, with the result that poor nations can be deprived of their rightful share.

4. The Rio Declaration on Environment and Development

THE 1992 *Rio Declaration on Environment and Development* was generated in the United Nations Conference on Environment and Development (UNCED), held in Rio de Janeiro, June 3–14, 1992. This international gathering, with representation by 108 heads of state, generated several decrees, including the *Rio Declaration*, *Agenda 21*, the *Convention on Biological Diversity*, and the *Framework Convention on Climate Change*. UNCED illuminated the need to consider the environmental context of all economic and social development, and made clear the urgency of addressing climate change.

Preamble

THE UNITED NATIONS CONFERENCE on Environment and Development, Having met at Rio de Janeiro from 3 to 14 June 1992, Reaffirming the Declaration of the United Nations Conference on the Human Environment, adopted at Stockholm on 16 June 1972, and seeking to build upon it, With the goal of establishing a new and equitable global partnership through the creation of new levels of co-operation among States, key sectors of societies and people, Working towards international agreements which respect the interests of all and protect the integrity of the global environmental and developmental system, Recognizing the integral and interdependent nature of the Earth, our home, Proclaims that:

PRINCIPLE 1 Human beings are at the centre of concerns for sustainable development. They are entitled to a healthy and productive life in harmony with nature.

PRINCIPLE 2 States have, in accordance with the Charter of the United Nations and the principles of international law, the sovereign right to exploit their own resources pursuant to their own environmental and developmental policies, and the responsibility to ensure that activities within their jurisdiction or control do not cause damage to the environment of other States or of areas beyond the limits of national jurisdiction.

PRINCIPLE 3 The right to development must be fulfilled so as to equitably meet developmental and environmental needs of present and future generations.

PRINCIPLE 4 In order to achieve sustainable development, environmental protection shall constitute an integral part of the development process and cannot be considered in isolation from it.

PRINCIPLE 5 All States and all people shall co-operate in the essential task of eradicating poverty as an indispensable requirement for sustainable development, in order to decrease the disparities in standards of living and better meet the needs of the majority of the people of the world.

PRINCIPLE 6 The special situation and needs of developing countries, particularly the least developed and those most environmentally vulnerable, shall be given special priority. International actions in the field of environment and development should also address the interests and needs of all countries.

PRINCIPLE 7 States shall co-operate in a spirit of global partnership to conserve, protect and restore the health and integrity of the Earth's ecosystem. In view of the different contributions to global environmental degradation, States have common but differentiated responsibilities. The developed countries acknowledge the responsibility that they bear in the international pursuit of sustainable development in view of the pressures their societies place on the global environment and of the technologies and financial resources they command.

PRINCIPLE 8 To achieve sustainable development and a higher quality of life for all people, States should reduce and eliminate unsustainable patterns of production and consumption and promote appropriate demographic policies.

PRINCIPLE 9 States should co-operate to strengthen endogenous capacity-building for sustainable development by improving scientific understanding through exchanges of scientific and technological knowledge, and by enhancing the development, adaptation, diffusion and transfer of technologies, including new and innovative technologies.

PRINCIPLE 10 Environmental issues are best handled with the participation of all concerned citizens, at the relevant level. At the national level, each individual shall have appropriate access to information concerning the environment that is held by public authorities, including information on hazardous materials and activities in their communities, and the opportunity to participate in decision-making processes. States shall facilitate and encourage public awareness and participation by making information widely available. Effective access to judicial and administrative proceedings, including redress and remedy, shall be provided.

PRINCIPLE 11 States shall enact effective environmental legislation. Environmental standards, management objectives and priorities should reflect the environmental and developmental context to which they apply. Standards applied by some countries may be inappropriate and of unwarranted economic and social cost to other countries, in particular developing countries.

PRINCIPLE 12 States should co-operate to promote a supportive and open international economic system that would lead to economic growth and sustainable development in all countries, to better address the problems of environmental degradation. Trade policy measures for environmental purposes should not constitute a means of arbitrary or unjustifiable discrimination or a disguised restriction on international trade. Unilateral actions to deal with environmental challenges outside the jurisdiction of the importing country should be avoided. Environmental measures addressing transboundary or global environmental problems should, as far as possible, be based on an international consensus.

PRINCIPLE 13 States shall develop national law regarding liability and compensation for the victims of pollution and other environmental damage. States shall also co-operate in an expeditious and more determined manner to develop further international law regarding liability and compensation for adverse effects of environmental damage caused by activities within their jurisdiction or control to areas beyond their jurisdiction.

PRINCIPLE 14 States should effectively co-operate to discourage or prevent the relocation and transfer to other States of any activities and substances that cause severe environmental degradation or are found to be harmful to human health.

PRINCIPLE 15 In order to protect the environment, the precautionary approach shall be widely applied by States according to their capabilities. Where there are threats of serious or irreversible damage, lack of full scientific certainty shall not be used as a reason for postponing cost-effective measures to prevent environmental degradation.

PRINCIPLE 16 National authorities should endeavour to promote the internalization of environmental costs and the use of economic instruments, taking into account the approach that the polluter should, in principle, bear the cost of pollution, with due regard to the public interest and without distorting international trade and investment.

PRINCIPLE 17 Environmental impact assessment, as a national instrument, shall be undertaken for proposed activities that are likely to have a significant adverse impact on the environment and are subject to a decision of a competent national authority.

PRINCIPLE 18 States shall immediately notify other States of any natural disasters or other emergencies that are likely to produce sudden harmful effects on the environment of those States. Every effort shall be made by the international community to help States so afflicted.

PRINCIPLE 19 States shall provide prior and timely notification and relevant information to potentially affected States on activities that may have a significant adverse transboundary environmental effect and shall consult with those States at an early stage and in good faith.

PRINCIPLE 20 Women have a vital role in environmental management and development. Their full participation is therefore essential to achieve sustainable development.

PRINCIPLE 21 The creativity, ideals and courage of the youth of the world should be mobilized to forge a global partnership in order to achieve sustainable development and ensure a better future for all.

PRINCIPLE 22 Indigenous people and their communities, and other local communities, have a vital role in environmental management and development because of their knowledge and traditional practices. States should recognize and duly support their identity, culture and interests and enable their effective participation in the achievement of sustainable development.

PRINCIPLE 23 The environment and natural resources of people under oppression, domination and occupation shall be protected.

PRINCIPLE 24 Warfare is inherently destructive of sustainable development. States shall therefore respect international law providing protection for the environment in times of armed conflict and co-operate in its further development, as necessary.

PRINCIPLE 25 Peace, development and environmental protection are interdependent and indivisible.

PRINCIPLE 26 States shall resolve all their environmental disputes peacefully and by appropriate means in accordance with the Charter of the United Nations.

PRINCIPLE 27 States and people shall co-operate in good faith and in a spirit of partnership in the fulfilment of the principles embodied in this Declaration and in the further development of international law in the field of sustainable development.

Questions

1. Which principles are of particular relevance to corporate activity? How does this document complement the transnational corporate document in reading #2?

2. Little to nothing has been followed through regarding the vision of sustainable development that UNCED proposed in 1992. Why do you think that is the case?

3. Given the extensive advancement of climate change since 1992, should this Rio Declaration be seriously revisited? Why or why not?

5. Development, Ecology, and Women[1]

Vandana Shiva

VANDANA SHIVA (B. 1952) addresses Western development programs exported to the third world in "Development, Ecology, and Women." She argues from an ecofeminist perspective and contends that these development programs are really "maldevelopment" programs that either worsen or introduce patriarchal practices of dominating women and nature. An ecofeminist perspective focuses on the similarities between the patriarchal domination of women and that of nature.

Furthermore, Shiva argues, these programs displace people who live sustainably, wreak enormous damage, and risk wholesale destruction of the regenerative abilities of ecosystems. She concludes that the solution is to recover the feminine principle that provides a redefinition of life that is linked to ecological sustainability.

Development as a New Project of Western Patriarchy

"DEVELOPMENT" WAS TO HAVE been a post-colonial project, a choice for accepting a model of progress in which the entire world remade itself on the model of the colonising modern west, without having to undergo the subjugation and exploitation that colonialism entailed. The assumption was that western style progress was possible for all. Development, as the improved well-being of all, was thus equated with the westernisation of economic categories—of needs, of productivity, of growth. Concepts and categories about economic development and natural resource utilisation that had emerged in the specific context of industrialisation and capitalist growth in a centre of colonial power, were raised to the level of universal assumptions and applicability in the entirely different context of basic needs satisfaction for the people of the newly independent Third World countries. Yet, as Rosa Luxemburg has pointed out, early industrial development in western Europe necessitated the permanent occupation of the colonies by the colonial powers and the destruction of the local "natural economy."[2] According to her, colonialism is a constant necessary condition for capitalist growth: without colonies, capital accumulation would grind to a halt. "Development" as capital accumulation and the commercialisation of the economy for the generation of "surplus" and profits thus involved the reproduction not merely of a particular form of creation of wealth, but also of the associated creation of poverty and dispossession. A replication of economic development based on commercialisation of resource use for commodity production in the newly independent countries created the internal colonies.[3] Development was thus reduced to a continuation of the process of colonisation; it became an extension of the project of wealth creation in modern western patriarchy's economic vision, which was based on the exploitation or exclusion of women (of the west and non-west), on the exploitation and degradation of nature, and on the exploitation and erosion of other cultures. "Development" could not but entail destruction for women, nature and subjugated cultures, which is why, throughout the Third World, women, peasants and tribals are struggling for liberation from "development" just as they earlier struggled for liberation from colonialism.

The UN Decade for Women was based on the assumption that the improvement of women's economic position would automatically flow from an expansion and diffusion of the development process. Yet, by the end of the Decade, it was becoming clear that development itself was the problem. Insufficient and inadequate "participation" in "development" was not the cause for women's increasing under-development; it was rather, their enforced but asymmetric participation in it, by which they bore the costs but were excluded from the benefits, that was responsible. Development exclusivity and dispossession aggravated and deepened the colonial processes of ecological degradation and the loss of political control over nature's sustenance base. Economic growth was a new colonialism, draining resources away from those who needed them most. The discontinuity lay in the fact that it was now new national elites, not colonial powers, that masterminded the exploitation on grounds of "national interest" and growing GNPs, and it was accomplished with more powerful technologies of appropriation and destruction.

Ester Boserup[4] has documented how women's impoverishment increased during colonial rule; those rulers who had spent a few centuries in subjugating and crippling their own women into de-skilled, de-intellectualised appendages, disfavoured the women of the colonies on matters of access to land, technology and employment. The economic and political processes of colonial under-development bore the clear mark of modern western patriarchy, and while large numbers of women and men were impoverished by these processes, women tended to lose more. The privatisation of land for revenue generation displaced women more critically, eroding their traditional land use rights. The expansion of cash crops undermined food production, and women were often left with meager resources to feed and care for children, the aged and the infirm, when men migrated or were conscripted into forced labor by the colonisers. As a collective document by women activists, organisers and researchers stated at the end of the UN Decade for Women, "The almost uniform conclusion of the Decade's research is that with a few exceptions, women's relative access to economic resources, incomes and employment has worsened, their burden of work has increased, and their relative and even absolute health, nutritional and educational status has declined."[5]

The displacement of women from productive activity by the expansion of development was rooted largely in the manner in which development projects appropriated or destroyed the natural resource base for the production of sustenance and survival. It destroyed women's productivity both by removing land, water and forests from their management and control, as well as through the ecological destruction of soil, water and vegetation systems so that nature's productivity and renewability were impaired. While gender subordination and patriarchy are the oldest of oppressions, they have taken on new and more violent forms through the project of development. Patriarchal categories which understand destruction as "production" and regeneration of life as "passivity" have generated a crisis of survival. Passivity, as an assumed category of the "nature" of nature and of women, denies the activity of nature and life. Fragmentation and uniformity as assumed categories of progress and development destroy the living forces which arise from relationships within the "web of life" and the diversity in the elements and patterns of these relationships.

The economic biases and values against nature, women and indigenous peoples are captured in this typical analysis of the "unproductiveness" of traditional natural societies:

Production is achieved through human and animal, rather than mechanical, power. Most agriculture is unproductive; human or animal manure may be used but chemical fertilizers and pesticides are unknown.... For the masses, these conditions mean poverty.[6]

The assumptions are evident: nature is unproductive; organic agriculture based on nature's cycles of renewability spells poverty; women and tribal and peasant societies embedded in nature are similarly unproductive, not because it has been demonstrated that in cooperation they produce *less* goods and services for needs, but because it is assumed that "production" takes place only when mediated by technologies for commodity production, even when such technologies destroy life. A stable and clean river is not a productive resource in this view: it needs to be "developed" with dams in order to become so. Women, sharing the river as a commons to satisfy the water needs of their families and society are not involved in productive labor: when substituted by the engineering man, water management and water use become productive activities.

Natural forests remain unproductive till they are developed into monoculture plantations of commercial species. Development thus, is equivalent to maldevelopment, a development bereft of the feminine, the conservation, the ecological principle. The neglect of nature's work in renewing herself, and women's work in producing sustenance in the form of basic, vital needs is an essential part of the paradigm of maldevelopment, which sees all work that does not produce profits and capital as non or unproductive work. As Maria Mies[7] has pointed out, this concept of surplus has a patriarchal bias because, from the point of view of nature and women, it is not based on material surplus produced *over and above* the requirements of the community: it is stolen and appropriated through violent modes from nature (who needs a share of her produce to reproduce herself) and from women (who need a share of nature's produce to produce sustenance and ensure survival).

From the perspective of Third World women, productivity is a measure of producing life and sustenance; that this kind of productivity has been rendered invisible does not reduce its centrality to survival—it merely reflects the domination of modern patriarchal economic categories which see only profits, not life.

Maldevelopment as the Death of the Feminine Principle

In this analysis, maldevelopment becomes a new source of male-female inequality. "Modernisation" has been associated with the introduction of new forms of dominance. Alice Schlegel[8] has shown that under conditions of subsistence, the interdependence and complementarity of the separate male and female domains of work is the characteristic mode, based on diversity, not inequality. Maldevelopment militates against this equality in diversity, and superimposes the ideologically constructed category of western technological man as a uniform measure of the worth of classes, cultures and genders. Dominant modes of perception based on reductionism, duality and linearity are unable to cope with equality in diversity, with forms and activities that are significant and valid, even though different. The reductionist mind superimposes the roles and forms of power of western male-oriented concepts on women, all non-western peoples and even on nature, rendering all three "deficient," and in need of "development." Diversity, and unity and harmony in diversity, become epistemologically unattainable in the context of maldevelopment, which then becomes synonymous with women's underdevelopment (increasing sexist domination), and nature's depletion (deepening ecological crises). Commodities have grown, but nature has shrunk. The poverty crisis of the South arises from the growing scarcity of water, food, fodder and fuel, associated with increasing maldevelopment and ecological destruction. This poverty crisis touches women most severely, first because they are the poorest among the poor, and then because, with nature, they are the primary sustainers of society.

Maldevelopment is the violation of the integrity of organic, interconnected and interdependent systems, that sets in motion a process of exploitation, inequality, injustice and violence. It is blind to the fact that a recognition of nature's harmony and action to maintain it are preconditions for distributive justice. This is why Mahatma Gandhi said, "There is enough in the world for everyone's need, but not for some people's greed."

Maldevelopment is maldevelopment in thought and action. In practice, this fragmented, reductionist, dualist perspective violates the integrity and harmony of man in nature, and the harmony between men and women. It ruptures the co-operative unity of masculine and feminine, and places man, shorn of the feminine principle, above nature and women, and separated from both. The violence to nature as symptomatised by the ecological crisis, and the violence to women, as symptomatised by their subjugation and exploitation arise from this subjugation of the feminine principle. I want to argue that what is currently called development is essentially maldevelopment, based on the introduction or accentuation of the domination of man over nature and women. In it, both are viewed as the "other," the passive non-self. Activity, productivity, creativity which were associated with the feminine principle are expropriated as qualities of nature and women, and transformed into the exclusive qualities of man. Nature and women are turned into passive objects, to be used and exploited for the uncontrolled and uncontrollable desires of alienated man. From being the creators and sustainers of life, nature and women are reduced to being "resources" in the fragmented, anti-life model of maldevelopment.

Two Kinds of Growth, Two Kinds of Productivity

Maldevelopment is usually called "economic growth," measured by the Gross National Product. Porritt, a leading ecologist has this to say of GNP:

Gross National Product—for once a word is being used correctly. Even conventional economists admit that the hey-day of GNP is over, for the simple reason that as a measure of progress, it's more or less useless. GNP measures the lot, all the goods and services produced in the money economy. Many of these goods and services are not beneficial to people, but rather a measure of just how much is going wrong; increased spending on crime, on pollution, on the many human casualties of our society, increased spending because of waste or planned obsolescence, increased spending because of growing bureaucracies: it's all counted.[9]

The problem with GNP is that it measures some costs as benefits (e.g., pollution control) and fails to measure other costs completely. Among these hidden costs are the new burdens created by ecological devastation, costs that are invariably heavier for women, both in the North and South. It is hardly surprising, therefore, that as GNP rises, it does not necessarily mean that either wealth or welfare increase proportionately. I would argue that GNP is becoming, increasingly, a measure of how real wealth—the wealth of nature and that produced by women for sustaining life—is rapidly decreasing. When commodity production as the prime economic activity is introduced as development, it destroys the potential of nature and women to produce life and goods and services for basic needs. More commodities and more cash mean less life—in nature (through ecological destruction) and in society (through denial of basic needs). Women are devalued first, because their work cooperates with nature's processes, and second, because work which satisfies needs and ensures sustenance is devalued in general. Precisely because more growth in maldevelopment has meant less sustenance of life and life-support systems, it is now imperative to recover the feminine principle as the basis for development which conserves and is ecological. Feminism as ecology, and ecology as the revival of Prakriti, the source of all life, become the decentred powers of political and economic transformation and restructuring.

This involves, first, a recognition that categories of "productivity" and growth which have been taken to be positive, progressive and universal are, in reality, restricted patriarchal categories. When viewed from the point of view of nature's productivity and growth, and women's production of sustenance, they are found to be ecologically destructive and a source of gender inequality. It is no accident that the modern, efficient and productive technologies created within the context of growth in market economic terms are associated with heavy ecological costs, borne largely by women. The resource and energy intensive production processes they give rise to demand ever increasing resource withdrawals from the ecosystem. These withdrawals disrupt essential ecological processes and convert renewable resources into non-renewable ones. A forest for example, provides inexhaustible supplies of diverse biomass over time if its capital stock is maintained and it is harvested on a sustained yield basis. The heavy and uncontrolled demand for industrial and commercial wood, however, requires the continuous overfelling of trees which exceeds the regenerative capacity of the forest ecosystem, and eventually converts the forests into non-renewable resources. Women's work in the collection of water, fodder and fuel is thus rendered more energy and time-consuming. (In Garhwal, for example, I have seen women who originally collected fodder and fuel in a few hours, now travelling long distances by truck to collect grass and leaves in a task that might take up to two days.) Sometimes the damage to nature's intrinsic regenerative capacity is impaired not by over-exploitation of a particular resource but, indirectly, by damage caused to other related natural resources through ecological processes. Thus the excessive overfelling of trees in the catchment areas of streams and rivers destroys not only forest resources, but also renewable supplies of water, through hydrological destabilisation. Resource intensive industries disrupt essential ecological processes not only by their excessive demands for raw material, but by their pollution of air and water and soil. Often such destruction is caused by the resource demands of non-vital industrial products. In spite of severe ecological crises, this paradigm continues to operate because for the North and for the elites of the South, resources continue to be available, even now. The lack of recognition of nature's processes for survival *as factors in the process of economic development* shrouds the political issues arising from resource transfer and resource destruction, and creates an ideological weapon for increased control over natural resources in the conventionally employed notion of productivity. All other costs of the economic process consequently become invisible. The forces which contribute to the increased "productivity" of a modern farmer or factory worker for instance, come from the increased use of natural resources. Lovins has described this as the amount of "slave" labor presently at work in the world.[10] According to him each person on earth, on an average, possesses the equivalent of about 50 slaves, each working a 40-hour week. Man's global energy conversion from all sources (wood, fossil fuel, hydroelectric power, nuclear) is currently approximately 8×10^{12} watts. This is more than 20 times the energy content of the food necessary to feed the present world population at the FAO standard diet of 3,600 cal/day. The "productivity" of the western male compared to women or Third World peasants is not intrinsically superior; it is based on inequalities in the distribution of this "slave" labor. The average inhabitant of the USA for example has 250 times more "slaves" than the average Nigerian. "If Americans were short of 249 of those 250 'slaves,' one wonders how efficient they would prove themselves to be?"

It is these resource and energy intensive processes of production which divert resources away from survival, and hence from women. What patriarchy sees as productive work, is, in ecological terms highly destructive production. The second law of thermodynamics predicts that resource intensive and resource wasteful economic development must become a threat to the survival of the human species in the long run. Political struggles based on ecology in industrially advanced countries are rooted in this conflict between *long term survival options and short term over-production and over-consumption*. Political struggles of women, peasants and tribals based on ecology in countries like India are far more acute and urgent since they are rooted in the *immediate threat to the options for survival* for the vast majority of the people, *posed by resource intensive and resource wasteful economic growth* for the benefit of a minority.

In the market economy, the organising principle for natural resource use is the maximisation of profits and capital accumulation. Nature and human needs are managed through market mechanisms. Demands for natural resources are restricted to those demands registering on the market; the ideology of development is in large part based on a vision of bringing all natural resources into the market economy for commodity production. When these resources are already being used by nature to maintain her production of renewable resources and by women for sustenance and livelihood, their diversion to the market economy generates a scarcity condition for ecological stability and creates new forms of poverty for women.

Two Kinds of Poverty

In a book entitled *Poverty: The Wealth of the People*[11] an African writer draws a distinction between poverty as subsistence, and misery as deprivation. It is useful to separate a cultural conception of subsistence living as poverty from the material experience of poverty that is a result of dispossession and deprivation. Culturally perceived poverty need not be real material poverty: subsistence economies which satisfy basic needs through self-provisioning are not poor in the sense of being deprived. Yet the ideology of development declares them so because they do not participate overwhelmingly in the market economy, and do not consume commodities produced for and distributed through the market *even though they might be satisfying those needs through self-provisioning mechanisms.* People are perceived as poor if they eat millets (grown by women) rather than commercially produced and distributed processed foods sold by global agri-business. They are seen as poor if they live in self-built housing made from natural material like bamboo and mud rather than in cement houses. They are seen as poor if they wear hand-made garments of natural fibre rather than synthetics. Subsistence, as culturally perceived poverty, does not necessarily imply a low physical quality of life. On the contrary, millets are nutritionally far superior to processed foods, houses built with local materials are far superior, being better adapted to the local climate and ecology, natural fibres are preferable to man-made fibres in most cases, and certainly more affordable. This cultural perception of prudent subsistence living as poverty has provided the legitimisation for the development process as a poverty removal project. As a culturally biased project it destroys wholesome and sustainable lifestyles and creates real material poverty, or misery, by the denial of survival needs themselves, through the diversion of resources to resource intensive commodity production. Cash crop production and food processing take land and water resources away from sustenance needs, and exclude increasingly large numbers of people from their entitlements to food. "The inexorable processes of agriculture-industrialisation and internationalisation are probably responsible for more hungry people than either cruel or unusual whims of nature. There

are several reasons why the high-technology-export-crop model increases hunger. Scarce land, credit, water and technology are preempted for the export market. Most hungry people are not affected by the market at all.... The profits flow to corporations that have no interest in feeding hungry people without money."[12]

The Ethiopian famine is in part an example of the creation of real poverty by development aimed at removing culturally perceived poverty. The displacement of nomadic Afars from their traditional pastureland in Awash Valley by commercial agriculture (financed by foreign companies) led to their struggle for survival in the fragile uplands which degraded the ecosystem and led to the starvation of cattle and the nomads.[13] The market economy conflicted with the survival economy in the Valley, thus creating a conflict between the survival economy and nature's economy in the uplands. At no point has the global marketing of agricultural commodities been assessed against the background of the new conditions of scarcity and poverty that it has induced. This new poverty moreover, is no longer cultural and relative: it is absolute, threatening the very survival of millions on this planet.

The economic system based on the patriarchal concept of productivity was created for the very specific historical and political phenomenon of colonialism. In it, the input for which efficiency of use had to be maximised in the production centres of Europe, was industrial labor. For colonial interest therefore, it was rational to improve the labour resource *even at the cost of wasteful use of nature's wealth.* This rationalisation has, however, been illegitimately universalised to all contexts and interest groups and, on the plea of increasing productivity, labour reducing technologies have been introduced in situations where labor is abundant and cheap, and resource demanding technologies have been introduced where resources are scarce and already fully utilised for the production of sustenance. Traditional economies with a stable ecology have shared with industrially advanced affluent economies the ability to use natural resources to satisfy basic vital needs. The former differ from the latter in two essential ways: first, the same needs are satisfied in industrial societies through longer technological chains requiring higher energy and resource inputs and excluding large numbers without purchasing power; and second, affluence generates new and artificial needs requiring the increased production of industrial goods and services. Traditional economies are not advanced in the matter of non-vital needs satisfaction, but as far as the satisfaction of basic and vital needs is concerned, they are often what Marshall Sahlins has called "the original affluent society." The needs of the Amazonian tribes are more than satisfied by the rich rainforest; their poverty begins with its destruction. The story is the same for the Gonds of Bastar in India or the Penans of Sarawak in Malaysia.

Thus are economies based on indigenous technologies viewed as "backward" and "unproductive." Poverty, as the denial of basic needs, is not necessarily associated with the existence of traditional technologies, and its removal is not necessarily an outcome of the growth of modern ones. On the contrary, the destruction of ecologically sound traditional technologies, often created and used by women, along with the destruction of their material base is generally believed to be responsible for the "feminisation" of poverty in societies which have had to bear the costs of resource destruction.

The contemporary poverty of the Afarnomad is not rooted in the inadequacies of traditional nomadic life, but in the *diversion of the productive pastureland of the Awash Valley*. The erosion of the resource base for survival is increasingly being caused by the demand for resources by the market economy, dominated by global forces. The creation of inequality through economic activity which is ecologically disruptive arises in two ways: first, inequalities in the distribution of privileges make for unequal access to natural resources—these include privileges of both a political and economic nature. Second, resource intensive production processes have access to subsidised raw material on which a substantial number of people, especially from the less privileged economic groups, depend for their survival. The consumption of such industrial raw material is determined purely by market forces, and not by considerations of the social or ecological requirements placed on them. The costs of resource destruction are externalised and unequally divided among various economic groups in society, but are borne largely by women and those who satisfy their basic material needs directly from nature, simply because they have no purchasing power to register their demands on the goods and services provided by the modern production system. Gustavo Esteva has called development a permanent war waged by its promoters and suffered by its victims.[14]

The paradox and crisis of development arises from the mistaken identification of culturally perceived poverty with real material poverty, and the mistaken identification of the growth of commodity production as better satisfaction of basic needs. In actual fact, there is less water, less fertile soil, less genetic wealth as a result of the development process. Since these natural resources are the basis of nature's economy and women's survival economy, their scarcity is impoverishing women and marginalised peoples in an unprecedented manner. Their new impoverishment lies in the fact that resources which supported their survival were absorbed into the market economy while they themselves were excluded and displaced by it.

The old assumption that with the development process the availability of goods and services will automatically be increased and poverty will be removed, is now under serious challenge from women's ecology movements in the Third World, even while it continues to guide development thinking in centres of patriarchal power. Survival is based on the assumption of the sanctity of life; maldevelopment is based on the assumption of the sacredness of "development." Gustavo Esteva asserts that the sacredness of development has to be refuted because it threatens survival itself. "My people are tired of development," he says, "they just want to live."[15]

The recovery of the feminine principle allows a transcendance and transformation of these patriarchal foundations of maldevelopment. It allows a redefinition of growth and productivity as categories linked to the production, not the destruction, of life. It is thus simultaneously an ecological and a feminist political project which legitimises the way of knowing and being that create wealth by enhancing life and diversity, and which deligitimises the knowledge and practise of a culture of death as the basis for capital accumulation.

Questions

1. What does Shiva argue is the difference between real poverty and real wealth, given that the latter entails little to no monetary holdings?

2. Suppose that you lived in a self-sufficient village with real wealth. Would you welcome globalization for things such as technology, or would you fear that accepting its perceived advantages would result in the loss of your self-sufficiency?

3. Given the characteristics of maldevelopment, especially its destruction of self-sufficiency, provide an argument that such development cannot be sustainable.

Notes

1. From Vandana Shiva, *Staying Alive: Women, Ecology and Development*, London: Zed Books, 1988.

2. Rosa Luxemberg, *The Accumulation of Capital*, London: Routledge and Kegan Paul, 1951.

3. An elaboration of how 'development' transfers resources from the poor to the well-endowed is contained in J. Bandyopadhyay and V. Shiva, 'Political Economy of Technological Polarisations,' in *Economic and Political Weekly*, Vol. XVIII. 1982, pp. 1827–32; and J. Bandyopadhyay and V. Shiva, 'Political Economy of Ecology Movements,' in *Economic and Political Weekly*, forthcoming.

4. Ester Boserup, *Women's Role in Economic Development*, London: Allen and Unwin, 1970.

5. Dawn, *Development Crisis and Alternative Visions: Third World Women's Perspectives*, Bergen: Christian Michelsen Institute, 1975, p. 21.

6. M. George Foster, *Traditional Societies and Technological Change*, Delhi: Allied Publishers, 1973.

7. Maria Mies, *Patriarchy and Accumulation on a World Scale*, London: Zed Books, 1986.

8. Alice Schlegal (ed.), *Sexual Stratification: A Cross-Cultural Study*, New York: Columbia University Press, 1977.

9. Jonathan Porritt, *Seeing Green*, Oxford: Blackwell, 1984.

10. A. Lovins, cited in S.R. Eyre, *The Real Wealth of Nations*, London: Edward Arnold, 1978.

11. R. Bahro, *From Red to Green*, London: Verso, 1984, p. 211.

12. R.J. Barnet, *The Lean Years*, London: Abacus, 1981, p. 171.

13. U.P. Koehn, 'African Approaches to Environmental Stress: A Focus on Ethiopia and Nigeria,' in R.N. Barrett (ed.), *International Dimensions of the Environmental Crisis*, Boulder, CO: Westview, 1982, pp. 253–89.

14. Gustavo Esteva, 'Regenerating People's Space,' in S.N. Mendlowitz and R.B.J. Walker, *Towards a Just World Peace: Perspectives from Social Movements*, London: Butterworths and Committee for a Just World Peace, 1987.

15. G. Esteva, Remarks made at a Conference of the Society for International Development, Rome, 1985.

6. Defining Sustainable Development[1]

Devon Peña

IN AN EXCERPT FROM *The Terror of the Machine: Technology, Work, Gender, and Ecology on the US–Mexico Border*, Devon Peña (b. 1954) details the problematic environmental and human toll that maquiladoras have wrought and describes how NAFTA worsens this situation and documents US and Mexican resistance to NAFTA. NAFTA is the North American Free Trade Agreement, a 1994–2020 agreement between the United States, Canada, and Mexico, meant to further trade between the countries by eradicating economic hindrances such as tariffs and fees. In this reading selection, Peña provides an alternative in his thorough blueprint for sustainable development.

Peña's blueprint draws extensively from ecological principles of ecosystem integrity and the notion of a bioregion. Ecology recognizes that the earth is a system, interconnected with many feedback loops in which the regenerative ability to sustain various species can be disturbed to the point of uninhabitation and extinctions. The notion of a bioregion places humans firmly within the ecosystem and acknowledges that culture, knowledge, and consumption within local limits all derive from a sense of place that Peña challenges us to regain.

I CONSIDER THE SEARCH FOR sustainable development a struggle to protect the local against the intrusions of the global; to protect the diverse against the homogenizing. As Helena Norberg-Hodge argues,

> Without retreating into cultural or economic isolationism, we can nourish the traditions of our own region. A true appreciation of cultural diversity means neither imposing our own culture on others, nor packaging, exploiting, and commercializing exotic cultures for our own consumption. One of the most effective ways of reviving cultural differences would be to lobby for a reduction in unnecessary trade. At the moment our taxpayers' money is going to expand transport infrastructure and to increase trade for the sake of trade…. What we should be doing instead is reinforcing and diversifying local economies….
>
> What exactly is "local," and what is "necessary" as opposed to "unnecessary" trade, are issues that cannot be defined in absolute terms. But the crucial point is that the *principle* of heavily subsidized international trade is one that needs critical reassessment…. It is in robust, local-scale economies that we find genuinely "free" markets; free of corporate manipulation, hidden subsidies, waste, and immense promotional costs that characterize today's global market.[2]

We must reconsider NAFTA and the maquilas from the point of view of the concept of sustainable development. To do so, we must be very clear about what we mean by sustainability. Indeed, even NAFTA is touted by its framers and supporters as a vehicle for sustainable development. But the only things that will be sustained are the profit rates of transnational corporations and the acceleration of environmental destruction. Capitalism is inherently incompatible with sustainable development.[3] The transition to a "steady-state economy" is of paramount importance in defining sustainable alternatives.[4] Thus, the unending, unrestrained expansion of international trade that drives the engine of capitalist economic growth is not compatible with a steady state of any kind.[5] ...

My working definition of sustainable development is not derived only from extensive knowledge of the academic and scholarly discourse. It is mostly drawn from the workers' perspectives I have been exposed to over the course of more than ten years of field research and consultancy with COMO and other grassroots organizations on both sides of the border.[6] What I say here is not so much a personal theory as a set of principles drawn from my observation of practices in actual struggles. This definition of sustainable development emphasizes seven interrelated principles: (1) long-term ecological integrity, (2) steady-state economies, (3) political decentralization and democratization, (4) a shift to nonpatriarchal and biocentric values, (5) the preservation of local knowledge and ethnoscience, (6) voluntary simplicity, and (7) the protection and reconstruction of bioregional communities.

1. *Long-Term Ecological Integrity.* Gaian biogeochemistry holds that the earth functions as a living organism, one live cybernetic system in which the solar wind, oceans, atmosphere, land masses, flora, fauna, and microbes all interconnect to create the conditions that make life on the planet possible.[7] The local, regional, national, and global disturbance regimes spawned over the past five hundred years by colonial and capitalist expansionism, conquest, war, and "development" are disrupting the Gaian feedback loops. For example, as deforestation, desertification, air and water pollution, and other forms of environmental degradation expand, species biodiversity declines. Gaian theory holds that the decline of biodiversity extinguishes nature's ability to regenerate ecosystems and to make them fit for habitation. Other species are driven into extinction while humans uncomfortably settle into a highly degraded anthropogenic landscape full of genetic, environmental, and other uncertainties. Biogeochemistry is a paradigm shift with profound implications for the politics of sustainable development. The principle of sustainability must conform to the biocentric ethos of radical Gaian biology. Development must sustain all life-forms, not just humans. There should be no "costs" that reduce life's diversity or viability. Development is sustainable when it respects the regenerative processes of life, that is, ecosystemic integrity.[8]

2. *Steady-State Economies.* This brings me to a second principle of sustainable development: steady-state economies. According to ecofeminists, the development of steady-state economies is possible only with a complete conversion of human production systems from militaristic and mass production and consumption norms and objectives.[9] There is a vast literature on economic conversion, but we are only now beginning to explore the links between conversion and the transition to steady-state economies.[10] Key elements of a steady-state economy include

- an emphasis on small-scale technologies and production systems

- a preference for regional inputs and outputs, including soft energy paths derived from locally available sources (sun, wind, methane, etc.)
- a renewal of labor-intensive agroecological and handicraft productive techniques; a preference for the production of goods destined for use in the local and regional social sector (education, housing, preventive and holistic health, nutrition, recreation, etc.)
- reliance on productive techniques involving the elimination of wastes through recycled and reduced production inputs[11]
- a propensity toward higher levels of "prosumption" (local production for local consumption)[12]

3. *Political Decentralization and Democratization.* With a transition to small-scale appropriate technologies and regional markets, sustainable development can increasingly rely on decentralized planning and policy-making. Political decentralization can emerge from regional steady-state economies because the need for widely dispersed production inputs (and decision making) is greatly reduced. In the absence of mass-production industries and international markets, local and regional steady-state economies can rely less on centralized bureaucracies to regulate and co-ordinate human use of productive technologies and resources. The "watershed commonwealths" envisioned long ago by John Wesley Powell are more feasible if the production apparatus has been decisively downscaled from a global assembly-line model to regional agroecological or handicraft productive techniques. Likewise, the liberation of regional resources from the grasp of the military-industrial complex will create leeway for transferring investments to productive activities that meet social needs (education, housing, health care) without the intervention or control of centralized

bureaucracies.[13] This decentralization implies the democratization of policy- and decision-making in the workplace and in the larger bioregional community as well.

4. *Nonpatriarchal, Biocentric Values.* Sustainable development requires a values transformation from norms, attitudes, beliefs, and ideologies that embrace the domination and exploitation of nature, women, people of color, and workers.[14] The maquilas are a perfect example of a synthesis of science, technology, and capital in the service of patriarchal systems of domination and exploitation. The terror of the machine, hierarchy and absolute male managerial authority, gender occupational segregation, abuse of workers and sexual and sexist harassment, and environmental degradation are joined together in one fell swoop in the organization of maquila workplaces. The alternatives are found in organizations like COMO, SOCOSEMA, Mujer Obrera, and hundreds of other self-help and self-managed cooperatives in Mexico and the border Southwest region. The values of mutual aid and reciprocity, nonhierarchical forms of decision making, and voluntary simplicity are consistent not just with ecofeminist principles but with the practices and worldviews of border worker cooperatives like the *pepenadores*. Women and men alike can participate in remaking economic, political, and social institutions on the basis of biocentric and communitarian values.

5. *Local Knowledge and Ethnoscience.* Elsewhere I have outlined the connection between environmental degradation and the destruction of local cultures.[15] I have argued that the extinction of local cultures means that people of color are also an endangered species. I have further argued that the loss of local cultures hastens the erosion of ethnoscientific knowledge bases that are critical in moving toward ecologically sustainable forms of economic development. There are many

viable indigenous communities on the U.S.–Mexico border: the Kickapoo and Tigua in Texas, the Tohono O'Odham (Sand Papago) in Arizona and Sonora, and the various Mission Indians of southern California, to name a few. These communities still offer alternative methods for sustainable agroecological development that must be protected and renewed.[16]

The preservation and promotion of ethnoscientific knowledge is clearly indispensable to the transition to sustainable development. However, to avoid the exploitation of indigenous knowledge we must find ways to protect ethnoscience as intellectual property. This is obviously a problem in light of NAFTA. As Darrell Posey argues,

> The indigenous peoples should possess sources of economic well-being, and if these are the conservation of the land, their people and cultures, then traditional understanding must be compensated in an economic manner. In not doing so, indigenous communities will see themselves driven closer to the brink of ecological destruction, and their knowledge bases will atrophy.[17]

6. *Voluntary Simplicity and Mutualism.* One critical aspect of building sustainable communities is "voluntary simplicity," or "right livelihood." This principle affirms the protection of alternative lifestyles that are not built around excessive levels of consumption and generation of wastes. Voluntary simplicity, combined with economic conversion, holds the promise of a fuller transition to steady-state economies. Mutualist traditions in Mexico and among Mexicans and Chicanos in the United States remain strong and can be found in nearly every community that has formal and informal voluntary associations. Mutualism is ecologically sustainable because it encourages self-reliance and low levels of consumption of market-driven goods and services.

7. *Bioregionalism.* A good description of a bioregional community was long ago offered by Powell when he characterized the Pueblo, Mexican, and Mormon *acequia* communities of the intermountain West as "watershed commonwealths."[18] What is a bioregion? The environmental sociologist and "deep ecologist" William DeVall emphasizes four qualities: (1) a common watershed, (2) biotic and (3) cultural distinctiveness, and (4) a spirit or sense of place.[19] Julian Steward anticipated this approach to the study of nature and culture when he pioneered the field of "cultural ecology."[20] The ecological study of culture examines the "relationship between a people's system of economic production and their physical environment."[21] For Steward the "cultural core" consists of those material practices related to the technologies human groups develop to exploit chosen resources. However, distinct environmental contexts impose limits on the types of technologies that can be used without degrading the ecosystem. I believe this is why Powell admired Chicano *acequias*, because as technology they respect the limits of their ecological locales—more, they actually increase biodiversity instead of reducing it.[22]

This is a central principle in bioregional sustainable economics: The productivity of development is measured not by the quantity of outputs but by contributions to biodiversity and ecosystemic integrity.[23] A mode of production that respects the integrity of the ecosystem is more conductive to human and nonhuman health and well-being in the long run.[24] As Donald Worster argues, "Humans are animals with ideas as well as tools."[25] Perception, ideology, and values also play a critical role in the nature-culture dialectic. Bioregional cultures are distinctive in their sense of place, their attachment to locality.[26] This attachment also teaches respect for the place, with the implicit command that the land be well and lovingly used, as Wendell Berry has so eloquently suggested.[27] But intrusive, expanding, or colonizing cultures do not have the same sense of place or respect for the limits of ecosystems. The cross-cultural production of knowledge is a complex affair, and I do not mean to overgeneralize, but it seems clear that some cultures are predatory while others are symbiotic in their relationships with the physical environment.[28]

This leads me to add two other dimensions to the definition of a bioregional community: (1) local knowledge and ethnoscience (including the production of ritual and religious practices), and (2) the conflict between local cultures and intrusive capitalist modes of production.[29] Cultures and ecosystems are not static entities. Even biomes in a state of homeostasis experience a considerable amount of systemic flux and change. The point is that the ecosystemic integrity of bioregions is everywhere threatened by the disrupting environmental changes wrought by five hundred years of expanding capitalist development. A defense and reconstruction of endangered bioregional communities is thus of fundamental importance in the struggle for sustainable development. The ecological integrity of ecosystems can best be attained and maintained by organizing at the bioregional level and by linking distinct bioregional communities through cooperative exchange networks. The contributions of bioregionalism to restoration ecology could be put to use in reclaiming the health and viability of our

ravaged and overdeveloped homelands. The process of reinhabitation, championed by certain North American bioregionalists, could guide ecological restoration by targeting specific watersheds and the communities within them for focused action campaigns.[30]

The search for alternatives in sustainable development requires not just the practice of the principles I have outlined above. It involves recognizing that the search will most likely bring us back to our own homelands and communities where alternatives have deep, ancient roots. As Norberg-Hodge notes,

Around the world, in every sphere of life, from psychology to physics, from farming to the family kitchen, there is growing awareness of the interconnectedness of all life. New movements are springing-up, committed to living on a human scale, and to more feminine and spiritual values. The numbers are growing, and the desire for change is spreading. These trends are often labeled as "new," but, as I hope Ladakh has shown, in an important sense they are very old. They are, in fact, a rediscovery of values that have existed for thousands of years—values that recognize our place in the natural order, our indissoluble connection to one another and to the earth.[31]

It is in the search for "ancient futures," I believe, that we will find the keys to a revolutionary transformation of the culture–nature relationship.

Questions

1. What are the characteristics of a bioregion? How would recognizing and protecting bioregions contribute to sustainability?

2. What is a steady-state economy? How would this revolutionize our economy?

3. Peña's seven principles are a radical departure from current capitalist systems. Do you think that it is possible to actualize these principles? That is, can we get there from here?

References

Aguilar, Margot, and Julia Bozzano, eds. 1989. *El bioregionalismo: Una propuesta de vida*. Mexico City: Editorial GEA.

Andruss, Van, Christopher Plant, Judith Plant, and Eleanor Wright, eds. 1990. *Home! A Bioregional Reader*. Philadelphia: New Society Publishers.

Argüelles, Lourdes, Larry Hirschhorn, Devon G. Peña, and Gloria Romero. 1984. "A Guide to the Implementation of a Working-Class, Ethnic Women–Led Economic Conversion Project in Pomona, California." Unpublished manuscript. Institute for Policy Studies, Washington, D.C.

Benería, Lourdes, and Rebecca Blank. 1989. "Women and the Economics of Military Spending." In *Rocking the Ship of State: Toward a Feminist Peace Politics*, edited by Adrienne Harris and Ynestra King. Boulder, Colo.: Westview Press.

Berry, Wendell. 1981. *The Gift of Good Land: Further Essays, Cultural and Agricultural*. San Francisco: North Point Press.

———. 1990. *What Are People For? Essays*. San Francisco: North Point Press.

Bowden, Charles. 1977. *Killing the Hidden Waters*. Austin: University of Texas Press.

Daly, Herman E. 1973. *Toward a Steady-State Economy*. San Francisco: W.H. Freeman.

Daly, Herman E., and Kenneth N. Townsend, eds. 1993. *Valuing the Earth: Economics, Ecology, Ethics*. Cambridge: MIT Press.

DeVall, Bill. 1988. *Simple in Means, Rich in Ends: Practicing Deep Ecology*. Salt Lake City, Utah: Peregrine Smith Books.

Dover, Michael J., and Lee Merriam Talbot. 1987. *To Feed the Earth: Agro-Ecology for Sustainable Development*. Washington, D.C.: World Resources Institute.

Earth System Sciences Committee. NASA Advisory Council. 1988. *Earth System Science: A Closer View*. Boulder, Colo.: University Corporation for Atmospheric Research.

Holmberg, Johan, Stephan Bass, and Lloyd Timberlake. 1991. *Defending the Future: A Guide to Sustainable Development*. London: Earthscan.

Leff, Enrique. 1992. "Cultura democrática, gestión ambiental y desarrollo sustentable en América Latina." *Ecología Política* 4 (September): 47–55.

Lovelock, James. 1979. *Gaia: A New Look at Life on Earth*. Oxford: Oxford University Press.

———. 1988. *The Ages of Gaia: A Biography of Our Living Earth*. New York: Norton.

Martínez de la Torre, Carlos. 1992. "Medio ambiente y libre comercio: ¿Compatibles?" *Dos Mil Uno*, 19 November.

Maybury-Lewis, David. 1992. *Millennium: Tribal Wisdom and the Modern World*. New York: Viking.

Mies, Maria. 1987. *Patriarchy and Accumulation on a World Scale: Women in the International Division of Labour*. 2d ed. London: Zed Books.

Miller, Alan S. 1991. *Gaia Connections: An Introduction to Ecology, Ecoethics, and Economics*. Savage, Md.: Rowman & Littlefield.

Munro, David A., and Martin W. Holdgate, eds. 1992. *Caring for the Earth: A Strategy for Sustainable Living*. Project directed by David A. Munro. Gland, Switzerland: International Union for the Conservation of Nature and Natural Resources.

Norberg-Hodge, Helena. 1991. *Ancient Futures: Learning from Ladakh*. San Francisco: Sierra Club Books.

O'Connor, James. 1991. *Is Sustainable Capitalism Possible?* CES/CNS Pamphlet Series, no. 1. Santa Cruz, Calif.: Center for Ecological Socialism.

Peña, Devon G. 1992a. "The 'Brown' and the 'Green': Chicanos and Environmental Politics in the Upper Rio Grande." *Capitalism, Nature, Socialism* 3 (1): 79–103.

——. 1993a. "Agroecology of a Chicano Family Farm." Paper presented at the Thirty-Fourth Annual Conference of the Western Social Science Association, April, Corpus Christi, Texas.

——. 1998a. "Los Animalitos Son Inteligentes: Notes toward the Bioregional Study of Chicano Culture in the Upper Rio Grande." In *Chicano Culture, Ecology, Politics: Subversive Kin*, edited by Devon G. Peña. Tucson: University of Arizona Press. Forthcoming.

Poore, Duncan. 1989. *No Timber without Trees: Sustainability in the Tropical Forests.* London: Earthscan.

Posey, Darrell Addison. 1992. "Los derechos de propiedad intelectual de los pueblos indígenas." *La Jornada del Campo* no. 9 (10 November).

Powell, John Wesley. 1892. "Institutions for the Arid Lands." *Century Magazine* no. 40 (May–October): 111–116.

Sale, Kirkpatrick. 1985. *Dwellers in the Land: The Bioregional Vision*. San Francisco: Sierra Club Books.

Shiva, Vandana. 1988. *Staying Alive: Women, Ecology, and Development*. London: Zed Books.

Silver, Cheryl S., and Ruth S. DeFries. 1990. *One Earth, One Future: Our Changing Global Environment*. Washington, D.C.: National Academy of Sciences.

Steward, Julian. 1955. *Theory of Culture Change: The Methodology of Multilinear Evolution*. Urbana: University of Illinois Press.

Tuan, Yi-Fu. 1974. *Topophilia: A Study of Environmental Perception, Attitudes, and Values*. Englewood Cliffs, N.J.: PrenticeHall.

Worster, Donald, ed. 1988. *The Ends of the Earth: Perspectives on Modern Environmental History*. Cambridge: Cambridge University Press.

Notes

1. From Devon G. Peña, *The Terror of the Machine: Technology, Work, Gender, and Ecology on the U.S.–Mexico Border* (CMAS Books, The Center for Mexican American Studies, The University of Texas at Austin, 1997) [Edited].
2. Norberg-Hodge 1991: 183.
3. See Martínez de la Torre 1992, O'Connor 1991.
4. See Daly 1973, Daly and Townsend 1993.
5. The most comprehensive statement on steady-state economics is Daly 1973.
6. The scholarly discourse on sustainable development is quite vast. A good introduction to this literature would include Shiva 1988, Merchant 1990, Holmberg, Bass, and Timberlake 1991, Dover and Talbot 1987, Munro and Holdgate 1992, Poore 1989, Peña 1992a, Leff 1992. I am thankful to Joe Gallegos of the Costilla County Committee for Environmental Soundness in San Luis, Colorado, for his long conversations with me on the nature and prospects of sustainable development in the upper Rio Grande watershed. I also thank my colleagues Reyes García and

Gwyn Kirk for extending to me the privilege of similar lengthy conversations.
7. See Lovelock 1976, 1989. See also Silver and DeFries 1990: 15–60; Earth System Sciences 1988.
8. Vandana Shiva (1988) is a major proponent of this view.
9. See Benería and Blank 1989.
10. For an exploratory approach, see Benería and Blank 1989, Development Alternatives for Women 1990. See also Miller 1991: 63–69.
11. I have derived most of these principles from my observations of SOCOSEMA operations. See also Daly and Townsend 1993.
12. See Argüelles et al. 1984.
13. See Benería and Blank 1989.
14. Shiva 1988.
15. Peña 1992a.
16. See Bowden 1977, Berry 1981. For relevant perspectives, see Norberg-Hodge 1991.
17. Posey 1992: 7 (my translation).
18. I thank Clay Jenkinson for bringing this to my attention. See Powell 1892.
19. See DeVall 1988, Sale 1985, Peña 1992a.

77

20. See Steward's (1955) *Theory of Culture Change.* See also Worster 1988: 299–302.
21. Worster 1988: 300.
22. See Peña 1993a, 1998a.
23. The concept of productivity in feminist ethnoscience is described in great detail by Shiva in her study of the Green Revolution in India and the struggles of women in land-based communities. Shiva defines productivity as

    built on the continued capacity for nature to renew its forests, fields, and rivers. These resource systems are intrinsically linked in life-producing and life-conserving cultures, and it is in managing the integrity of ecological cycles in forestry and agriculture that women's productivity has been most developed and evolved.... "Productivity," "yield," and "economic value" are defined for nature and for women's work as *satisfying basic needs through an integrated ecosystem managed for multi-purpose utilisation.* Their meaning and measure is therefore entirely different from the meaning and measure employed in reductionist masculinist [science].... [I]n reductionist [science] overall productivity is subordinated to ... industrial and commercial biomass. (1988: 45, 64–65)

    This is really a biogeochemical definition of productivity in which the energy circuits of the community of species in the ecosystem must be conserved to maintain homeostasis and secure long-term stability and viability of the life-support system. See Lovelock 1979, 1988.
24. For more on these questions, see Daly 1973.
25. Worster 1988: 302.
26. See Peña 1992a for further discussion.
27. Berry 1990: 153 ff.
28. There is a vast discourse on this issue of cultural differentiation in relation to the human interface with physical environments. See Maybury-Lewis 1992 for a good start. See also Mies 1987: 44–73; Peña 1992a. The work of Yi-Fu Tuan on "topophilia" has also influenced my view of cross-cultural environmental ethics. Tuan makes the following relevant observation:

    The group, expressing and enforcing cultural standards of society, affects strongly the perception, attitude, and environmental value of its members. Culture can influence perception to the degree that people will see things that do not exist: it can cause group hallucination. Where sex roles are distinct, men and women adopt different values and perceive different aspects of the environment. The perception and environmental judgements of natives and visitors show little overlap because their experiences and purposes have little in common.... Attitude to environment changes as mastery over nature increases and the concept of beauty alters.... The world views of nonliterate and traditional societies differ significantly from those of modern men who have come under the influence ... of science and technology. (1990: 246–247)
29. Peña 1992a: 86–88.
30. On the concept of reinhabitation, see Andruss et al. 1990: 100–129. For a Mexican perspective on bioregionalism, see Aguilar and Bozzano 1989.
31. Norberg-Hodge 1991: 191–192.

7. Creating the Third World[1]

Clive Ponting

IN "CREATING THE THIRD World," Clive Ponting (1946–2020) illustrates that globalization rather closely resembles colonization. Ponting provides the historical context for understanding current "first" and "third" world relationships where in many cases the local economy was dismantled and a nation's former self-sufficiency became nearly total dependence on the colonial force. Colonization harmed people and wreaked environmental destruction, resulting in the creation, rather than a redress, of poverty.

This is particularly the case for Banaba, or Ocean Island, a three by two-and-a-half mile island where approximately 2,000 Banabans lived a Polynesian lifestyle. Ocean Island, rich in phosphate due to centuries of petrified bird guano (excrement), was mined for fertilizer (for Australia and New Zealand) into an uninhabitable state. The Banabans' island was strip mined out from under them, leaving only a jagged, eroded, spiked landscape.

Ocean Island is a small-scale example of global exploitation by the industrialized world that allowed these countries to live beyond their own resources and consume at a standard of living never before seen. The result was a created third world that was impoverished, polluted, and left with immeasurable human suffering.

THE RISE OF EUROPE in the four hundred years after 1500, from being a backward area of the world to dominate the rest of the globe not only drastically affected a whole range of ecosystems but also reshaped the relationship between different regions. Before the sixteenth century different areas of the world had evolved to a large extent in isolation. Although societies encountered the same basic problem of finding a balance between population, food production and damage to the environment, their interaction was very limited. The Americas, Australia and most of the Pacific were isolated. Elsewhere trade links were tenuous and contact between Europe and the major states of India, southeast Asia and China was sporadic. In the period after 1500 European expansion triggered off a process of gradual integration of the different parts of the world into a single system and created a world economy. That system was dominated by European states and the areas where extensive white settlement took place—North America, Australia, New Zealand and South Africa. The tropical colonies and those without substantial European settlement remained in a subordinate position. (The Japanese were one of the few non-European peoples who succeeded in avoiding this trap, mainly because they did not come under

79

external political or economic control.)

In the earliest phases of European expansion, from the sixteenth until about the middle of the nineteenth century, Europe itself was still overwhelmingly an agricultural economy. The colonies provided an opportunity to grow crops (mainly for the luxury market) that could not be grown at home either because the climate was unsuitable or because the necessary cheap labour was not available. The colonies also provided some raw materials, particularly precious metals such as gold and silver (especially from Mexico and Peru) together with timber, to supplement European supplies. Increasing political control and the industrialisation of Europe in the nineteenth century intensified this process. Agricultural production for Europe was expanded and new crops introduced to meet changing demands and new industrial processes. Europe's demand for raw materials increased and the colonies provided an ideal source of supply. Third World countries became major producers of crops and raw materials for Europe rather than manufacturers of industrial products—that role remained almost entirely restricted to the European countries. Even after they achieved political independence the Third World countries found it very difficult to escape from this economic system....

By the early twentieth century, Europe, and increasingly the United States, had brought about a major transformation in the economies and societies of what is now known as the Third World. Countries which had been largely self-sufficient in food and which grew crops mainly for local markets had become part of a world economy dominated by Europe, its white colonies and the United States. In area after area the same sort of sequence of events had occurred. Through a powerful mixture of political control, economic pressure, investment and market forces,

"development" of these economies took the form of growing crops for other countries. The crops were either to provide luxury items in the diet of people living in Europe and North America (sugar, coffee, tea, cocoa, bananas) or to sustain manufacturing industry (cotton, rubber, palm oil) in countries where development meant something very different—the building of a thriving and varied industrial base with rising levels of consumption for the population. In this process the dependent and colonial economies were restructured to specialise in a few commodities or in some cases a single crop. A diverse agriculture was increasingly displaced over large areas by a monoculture, with harmful environmental effects, particularly in terms of damage to the soil and loss of biodiversity. The production of export crops in the Third World rose at an annual rate of three-and-a-half per cent in the first half of the twentieth century, whilst food production for home consumption grew more slowly than the rise in population. As a result these countries had to import much of the food they needed at high prices. The perverse effects of this cash crop-oriented agriculture for the population at large can be seen in many countries. Sugar cultivation was the biggest single element in the Cuban economy—by the 1950s it took up 60 per cent of all the cropland on the island and constituted three-quarters of the country's exports. As a result half of its food had to be imported. On Fiji by the early 1980s sugar made up over 80 per cent of exports and employed a fifth of the population. On Tahiti, by the 1950s, three-quarters of all agricultural land was being used to grow crops for export and in Gambia the figure was only a little lower. In the Philippines over 50 per cent of farm acreage is used to produce crops for export.

The achievement of political independence by the African and Asian colonies in the 1950s and 1960s did not transform their economic position. The experience of the Latin American countries, which had been independent since the 1820s, had already demonstrated how difficult this could be to achieve. By the mid-twentieth century the agricultural, trading and land-owning patterns were well established and there were strong forces, both internal and external, opposing change. Once an economy had been set in a certain mould by a colonial government, and when the western countries retained overwhelming economic and financial power and the terms of trade were in their favour, it was very difficult to change course. Given the difficulty of diversifying their economies many of the countries simply tried to increase their export earnings by producing more of the commodities introduced by the colonial powers. For example, the Ivory Coast had produced 75,000 tons of cocoa and 147,000 tons of coffee a year just before independence but by the mid-1970s these figures had risen to 228,000 tons and 305,000 tons respectively, resulting in an economy even more dependent on these two crops. Many other countries still depend for their foreign exchange earnings on a single crop—coffee, for example, constitutes 93 per cent of Burundi's exports. Attempts at cooperation by the producing countries to stabilise agricultural prices have usually failed, and fluctuating commodity prices continue to undermine vulnerable economies. Even where the major corporations that formerly owned large plantations have been dispossessed of their land or nationalised, Third World countries do not control trade in the commodities they produce because multinational companies still dominate processing and manufacturing. One of the major tea companies, Brooke Bond, now owns only one per cent of the tea plantations on Sri Lanka but still controls one-third of the country's tea exports and a similar degree of concentrated control

is found in tropical fruit production, which is dominated by firms such as United Brands and Del Monte.

Despite major problems of hunger and malnutrition the Third World continues to export more food than it imports. Twenty per cent of the world's food trade flows from the Third World to the industrialised countries and only twelve per cent in the opposite direction. This balance does not just apply to tropical crops. Within a year of the opening of the Suez Canal, India became a wheat exporter to supply the British market. Even in the acute famine of 1876–1877 wheat was still exported to Britain and by the 1880s India was providing ten per cent of the world's grain exports. Latin America has increasingly provided large quantities of beef for the American market at the expense of home consumption. Between 1960 and 1972 Guatemalan beef production doubled but home consumption per head fell by a fifth. In the same period beef exports from Costa Rica quadrupled but there was a forty per cent fall in domestic per capita consumption. The average American cat now eats more beef than an inhabitant of Costa Rica.

The Europeans saw the rest of the world not just as potential suppliers of cheap food and industrial crops but also as a source of timber, minerals and other raw materials. Timber was one of the most important products sent to Europe from the early colonies; indeed the colony of British Honduras only existed as a result of a settlement by traders seeking mahogany for the European market. The scale of the operations, particularly in the nineteenth century, can be judged by British activities in India and Burma. By the early nineteenth century British merchants had almost completely destroyed the teak forests of India's Malabar coast and needed to find new sources of supply. The unexploited forests of Burma provided a strong motive for the initial British conquest in 1826 and the first area opened up (the province of Tenasserim) was stripped of teak within twenty years. The annexation of Lower Burma in 1852 allowed the massive forests of the Irrawaddy delta to be cut down to supply Europe with hardwood. By the end of the century about 10 million acres of forest had been cleared. In the western Himalayas, after British control of the Gorakhpur district was established in 1801, over one million trees were felled in the next twenty years. In other parts of the region commercial felling began with local Indian rulers selling rights to European merchants and by the 1850s severe depletion was already apparent across the whole area. In that decade the demand for railway sleepers rose rapidly as railways were built across India to move crops to the ports for export to Europe. As timber prices rose, felling moved further inland into the mountainous areas and by the 1870s half a million trees a year were being cut down just to provide sleepers.

Even very specialised trades could be highly destructive. In the early nineteenth century sandalwood was a prized commodity not just in Europe but also in China. It was obtained mainly from the islands of the Pacific but the trade lasted less than a quarter of a century until all the existing trees had been cut down. The European and American traders systematically exploited an island until it was exhausted and then moved on to another. The sandalwood trees on Fiji were destroyed between 1804 and 1809, those on the Marquesas Islands lasted for three years after 1814 and those on the Hawaiian Islands for slightly longer—1811 until 1825. Then the industry collapsed.

The establishment of American control over the Philippines after the Spanish-American war of 1898 provides a good example of the development of modern logging. Within two years a Bureau of Forestry was set up and commercial logging began in 1904. At that time about eighty per cent of the virgin forests were still in existence. Half had been destroyed by the early 1950s and by the 1980s less than a third remained. The newly independent countries treated timber as simply another crop and sought to increase production and maximise revenue as the industrialised countries' demand for tropical hardwoods increased (sixteen-fold since 1950). The mounting scale of destruction is illustrated by the fact that Indonesian exports of timber rose nearly two hundred-fold in the twenty years after 1960. Similarly the Ivory Coast exported 42,000 tonnes of timber in 1913, 402,000 tonnes in 1958 and nearly 1.5 million tonnes by the mid-1970s. Rainforests covered 30 million acres of this former French colony in 1956, but only two million acres by the late 1970s when over 10 million acres a year were being cleared. Most developed countries tax processed timber imports which means that Third World countries are pushed into selling logs and they then import value-added products such as paper and board.

Mineral exploitation has also been an important factor in the creation of the Third World. The first European colonial venture in Mexico and Peru was, in its early years, largely driven by the search for gold and silver. Gold was also important in the first European trade links with West Africa. It was the final division of Africa among the European powers in the 1880s that marked the beginning of large-scale exploitation of mineral resources on the continent as Europe industrialised and cheap sources of supply were needed. Some areas were virtually controlled by mining companies. King Leopold of the Belgians actually sold Katanga with its rich copper deposits to a mining company in return for the company financing the conquest of what became in the early twentieth century part of the Belgian Congo. Two-thirds of all European investment in Africa until the 1930s went into mining enterprises, and mineral exports rose seven-fold between 1897 and 1935 to make up half of the continent's total exports, mainly copper from the Congo and Northern Rhodesia together with gold and diamonds from South Africa. Europeans were prepared to invest in order to bring the minerals to Europe but not to set up processing plants in the colonies. Railways were built to transport the minerals to the coast but the railways did little to develop the local economy—copper from Katanga in the Congo went via the Benguela railway to Angola for export. Europeans provided the skilled workers and Africans the unskilled workforce. The introduction of poll and hut taxes, which had to be paid in cash, forced African workers into the labour market to work in the mines as well as on plantations. The native mineworkers were housed in squalid barracks, separated from their families and often working hundreds of miles from their homes—by the 1950s two-thirds of the workers in the South African mines came from outside the country.

In the same way that cash crop agriculture became the major sector in many colonial economies, and remained a vital source of earnings after independence, mining became a central part of the economy of others and that too did not change after political independence was achieved. For instance mining still provides over 90 per cent of the exports of both Zambia and Mauretania. The Third World's share of global ore production rose dramatically in the twentieth century. Between 1913 and 1970 the proportion of the world's iron ore mined there rose from 3 per cent to 39 per cent and over the same period the rise in bauxite production was even more dramatic—from less than half a per cent to nearly 60 per cent. The overwhelming majority of all ores are used elsewhere—the Third World processes only 10 per cent of the copper

ore, 4 per cent of the nickel ore and 17 per cent of the iron ore it produces. As before independence they are, for the most part, exporters of raw materials. Mining is largely in the hands of multinational corporations and the governments of the countries concerned are usually unable to exercise much control over this sector of their economy which remains largely autonomous. After 1945 Liberia awarded concessions to multinational companies to allow them to exploit the large iron ore reserves in the country. Four huge open cast strip mines (very damaging to the environment by stripping away vast quantities of top soil and rock and creating huge pits and canyons) were built together with railways to transport the ore to the coast but little local labour was employed in these highly capital intensive projects. Although the Liberian economy appeared on paper to grow with this new activity and exports rose, there were few benefits in other sectors of the economy. The same effects occurred in Mauretania with the exploitation of the large iron ore deposits in the country after 1959. The Mauretanian government had only a five per cent stake in the company set up to mine the ore. The company proceeded to build its own 400 mile-long railway to the port of Nouadhibou and even ran its own army to protect the mines. On paper the Mauretanian economy was two-and-a-half times larger after seven years of mining but few benefits had percolated through into other sectors from the largely autonomous mining company, which employed little local labour and imported most of its other requirements. Even a policy of nationalisation fails to change this state of affairs. The multinational companies are still employed on 'managements contracts' and through internal pricing arrangements are able to move their profits out of the country. The companies also exclude many Third World countries from the most profitable parts of the industry by refusing to build smelters and processing plants, as both Ghana and Guinea found even when cheap energy supplies were available. Alumina is worth six times as much as raw bauxite and the final product (aluminium) is worth twenty five times as much as the bauxite but these high value operations are almost exclusively confined to the industrialised world.

European demand for resources was not confined to metal ores. In the late nineteenth century the use of fertilizers to increase agricultural output rose dramatically. The United States had its own internal sources of supply but Europe turned to Morocco and Tunisia and also the large guano deposits off the Pacific coast of South America. The latter were originally part of Bolivia but Chile's victory in the war of 1881 (fought over the deposits) gave it control of the coast and the offshore guano islands and turned Bolivia into a landlocked country. The guano was worked in dreadful conditions by Chinese labourers; Chile was soon exporting over one million tons a year and the tax on the exports made up over eighty per cent of the government's revenue. The British empire was dependent on external supplies until the discovery in the early twentieth century of huge phosphate deposits in the Pacific on Nauru and Ocean Island. This opened up the prospect of an easily accessible and cheap source of fertilizer with which to increase agricultural output from Australia and New Zealand, for the benefit not just of their economies but also that of Britain, which relied heavily on imported food from the empire. The story of these two islands illustrates in dramatic form many of the consequences of the developed world's demand for resources and the far-reaching impact it could have both on the environment and the people of the Third World.

Ocean Island was small (three miles long and two-and-a-half miles wide), covered in lush, tropical vegetation and inhabited by about 2,000 Banabans following a typically Polynesian way of life. Nauru was slightly bigger (eight-and-a-half square miles) with about 1,400 people. Ocean Island was formally annexed by Britain in 1901 whereas Nauru was a German possession until 1914. The islands consisted almost entirely of solid phosphate deposits, perhaps the richest in the world. In 1900 the British owned Pacific Islands Company bought the rights to all minerals on Ocean Island in return for a payment of £ 50 a year (in practice made in over-priced company trade goods) in a 'treaty' of dubious legality—made with the local chief even though it was well understood that he did not have authority to lease land belonging to other individuals. The company began to export large quantities of phosphates—shipments from Ocean Island amounted to 100,000 tons a year by 1905. Mining rights on Nauru were obtained from the German authorities and, after the necessary works were completed by Chinese labourers, mining began there in 1907. On both islands the company did not employ the islanders but brought in about 1,000 outsiders to work as labourers, about eighty Europeans to supervise operations and a detachment of Fijian police to keep order. In 1919 the company was bought out and the British, Australian and New Zealand governments established the jointly owned British Phosphate Commission to take over the work and provide them with phosphate at cost price (and therefore well below the world market price).

By the early 1920s mining was producing about 600,000 tons of phosphates a year and it was evident to the native inhabitants what was happening to their islands as a result. The operations involved clearing away the vegetation and stripping out the top fifty feet or so of land, leaving an uninhabitable wasteland of jagged pinnacles on which nothing would grow. It was obvious that if the mining continued the islands would be ruined. Seeking to safeguard their future, the Banabans refused to sell or lease any more land to the Commission. But the pressure from Australia and New Zealand for cheap phosphate was growing. In 1927 the British government authorised deep mining over the whole of Nauru and the next year took powers to confiscate all land from the Banabans that they refused to make available for mining. By the 1930s phosphate output had reached about one million tons a year. On the outbreak of war with Japan the Europeans and most of the Chinese labourers were evacuated but the islanders were left behind. The Japanese occupied both islands and transported the natives to the Caroline Islands. Before the war the British authorities had considered removing the Banabans from Ocean Island in order to further extend mining operations and the Japanese action provided a convenient opportunity. The Banabans were not allowed to return and were resettled on Rambi Island (part of Fiji). 1,500 labourers were brought in to reopen the phosphate works and in 1947 deep mining over the whole of Ocean Island was authorised. The Nauru islanders were allowed home after the war, but in a second class capacity. Like the 1,300 Chinese labourers brought to the island, the natives were excluded from the company facilities (shops and recreation), which were restricted to the elite white workers. Throughout the 1950s about one million tons of phosphate a year were being extracted from the islands, rising to nearly three million tons a year by the mid-1960s. It was clear that at this rate the deposits would soon be exhausted. The last shipment from Ocean Island was made in 1980 and the Nauru deposits were then only expected to last until the 1990s. In eighty years of mining twenty million tons of phosphate were extracted from Ocean Island, and Nauru had provided almost three times that figure,

giving a total of about eighty million tons from the two tiny Pacific islands.

The imminent exhaustion of the deposits on the ravaged islands raised in an acute form the question of how to treat their owners. In the case of Nauru (administered by the Australians under a United Nations mandate) the government wanted to resettle the islanders on the mainland and abandon the island when mining ceased. The islanders rejected this idea in 1965 when, for the first time, they were given the right to apportion the royalties they received on each ton of phosphate as they wanted rather than as the Australian government decided on their behalf. After a long struggle Nauru was granted independence in 1968 and management of the phosphate operation was transferred to them in 1970. The islanders now live along a narrow coastal fringe, the only part of the island not devastated by mining. Their traditional way of life has gone and their only means of subsistence comes from royalties and profits from the phosphates. These have been sufficient to provide almost a parody of western style development. The islanders do not need to work and their material standard of living is high. There is one road on the island, which goes nowhere, but there is one of the highest rates of car ownership in the world. The population depends on imported western food and many have started to develop the health problems normally found in people who live in the industrialised world.

The Nauru islanders faced enormous problems but the treatment of the dispossessed Banabans, who did not have the United Nations to protect their interests, was far worse. In 1911 the British government suggested that a trust fund should be set up for the Banabans, to be financed from the phosphate earnings. The British Phosphate Company proposed a munificent total annual payment of £250 at a time when it was making a profit of £20 million a year and paying dividends of 40–50 per cent every year to its shareholders. Eventually the British government persuaded the company to pay royalties of 6 pence a ton, supposedly to be held as a fund for the Banabans when the phosphates ran out. The government's action was less philanthropic than it seemed. They incorporated Ocean Island into the Gilbert and Ellice Islands colony, even though there were no natural links between the two and allocated most of the phosphate royalties to pay for the administration of the colony that had previously run at a loss. The Banabans were not told that 85 per cent of their royalties were being spent in this way. Indeed they were not told how much they were earning or what was done with any of the money and only very small sums were handed over because the government thought that they were 'feckless'. Some of the money was used to buy Rambi island on their behalf (the proceeds going to the colonial administration of Fiji), although they were not consulted about the purchase. After 1946 they were left on Rambi, an island with a totally different climate from their home. Eventually the British offered the islanders £500,000 as a final settlement for the effects of all the mining. The islanders rejected the offer and took the British government through the British courts in the 1970s in the longest civil case ever heard. They failed in the main part of the case because the court held that the 1900 agreement giving the company the right to mine the island in return for £50 a year was a legally binding contract. The court did find that the British government had breached its obligation to care for the islanders but refused to make any award of compensation. Eventually the phosphate commissioners offered a sum that just covered the costs the islanders had incurred in bringing the protracted legal case. By 1980 Ocean Island had been destroyed by the mining and the deposits

exhausted. The islanders had lost their home and had received pitifully small compensation for their loss. That was the real price of the cheap fertilizers for Australian and New Zealand agriculture and cheap food imports for Britain.

The fate of the Banabans was symbolic of much that had happened to the Third World. The creation of a world economy from several smaller-scale, self-sufficient, regional economies should have produced, according to the liberal, free market economists such as Adam Smith and Ricardo, a world-wide division and specialisation of labour, allowing each country and area to concentrate on growing or making the commodities it was best suited to produce. As a result of this specialisation every area should, in theory, have benefited from the most efficient allocation of resources. The theory, however, ignores the political constraints involved, in particular on the selection of commodities that were produced—European control enabled the colonial powers to ensure that the commodities they required were produced and allowed them to enforce a highly asymmetrical series of exchanges of products between the home country and the colonies. The words of Cecil Rhodes, one of the driving forces behind the last period of British expansion in Africa, reveal how different it all was in practice:

We must find new lands from which we can easily obtain raw materials and at the same time exploit the cheap slave labour that is available from the natives of the colonies. The colonies would also provide a dumping ground for the surplus goods produced in our factories.

The way in which one part of the world— the West (Europe, North America and the white colonies)—became 'developed' and the way another part—given the collective title the Third World—became 'underdeveloped' are not separate phenomena; they are inextricably linked. In the world market that was created by Europe, one region was able to extract a large surplus of products and natural resources from the dependent area. The dominant economies of the West were characterised by the production of capital intensive goods and relatively high wages and profits whilst the subordinate economies concentrated on producing crops, raw materials and minerals that were of low capital intensity and linked to low wages and low profits. Although development took place in the subordinate colonial economies, it was almost entirely geared to the needs of the home economies. Railways and distribution networks were built but they were largely confined to links between the inland regions and the ports and were designed to facilitate exports. There were few, if any, links between rural areas, or often even between adjacent countries where they were under different political control.

The achievement of political independence in the Third World did not bring economic independence. Economies remained tied into the global system created by the industrialised world and their structure, which had been largely determined by the colonial authorities, proved very difficult to change. A few countries managed to avoid this trap—those that retained their political and economic independence such as Japan, together with those that escaped European colonialism such as South Korea and Taiwan, "those that had small populations and vast resources required by the developed world such as the oil-rich states of the Near East," and the trade-based economies of Hong Kong and Singapore. After independence the model of development adopted by many countries in the Third World was, not surprisingly, given their limited room for manoeuvre, based on accepted western models emphasising industrialisation, free markets and international competition.

Only a few countries such as India and Brazil were able to make even modest steps in this direction and even here inequalities in the distribution of the benefits have been particularly marked. For most countries in the Third World, particularly in Africa, but also the poorer countries of Latin America and Asia, the only available option was to increase production of a few cash crops or minerals in an attempt to raise income and exports. The problem with this approach was that increased production tended to lead to lower prices, lower income, increased dependence on a few commodities and greater vulnerability. Borrowing money from the West in order to finance development projects (often of dubious value or relevance to local conditions) led to even greater difficulties, as countries such as Egypt and Venezuela had already demonstrated in the late nineteenth century (long before the great debt crisis of the 1980s) when they defaulted on their loans and were either occupied by foreign powers or had their revenues taken over in order to fund the debt. The people in the Third World who benefited most from this form of development were the elite, closely tied to the industrialised world, rather than the bulk of the population.

The consequences of this unbalanced development had profound effects for both the industrialised world and the Third World. Political and economic control of a large part of the world's resources enabled the industrialised world to live beyond the constraints of its immediate resource base. Raw materials were readily available for industrial development, food could be imported to support a rapidly rising population and a vast increase in consumption formed the basis for the highest material standard of living ever achieved in the world. Much of the price of that achievement was paid by the population of the Third World in the form of exploitation, poverty and human suffering.

Questions

1. Briefly detail the fate of Ocean Island. How does it illustrate the *creation of* the third world?

2. Ponting illuminates how previously self-sufficient countries were made into colonies of industrialized countries for the growing standard of living in the first world. Drawing from the *United Nations Universal Declaration of Human Rights*, provide an argument against this phenomenon.

3. How does creating the third world set the stage for globalization? What is the difference, if any, between them?

Note

1. From Clive Ponting, *A Green History of the World: The Environment and the Collapse of Great Civilization* (New York: Penguin Books, 1992). Copyright © Clive Ponting. [Edited.]

8. The Arabs, Islam and Globalization[1]

Fauzi Najjar

FAUZI NAJJAR SURVEYS THE Arab-Muslim world regarding the attitude toward globalization, in particular the "Arab intelligentsia." He finds three main groups that hold differing attitudes. The first group rejects globalization because they view it as "the 'highest stage of imperialism' and a 'cultural invasion,'" and they fear the undermining and destruction of cultural heritage and personality, as well as of beliefs, identity, and authenticity. The second group are inclined to be secular and welcome globalization as a means to enter "modern science, advanced technology, global communications, and knowledge-based information." This group sees resisters as living in "cocoons," those who "nurse nostalgia" for their heritage, and some sort of "imagined" past. The secularists also posit that they can enjoy the benefits without losing their cultural individuality. The third group is one of compromise, hoping for a type of globalization that complements the culture and nationality of the people. Najjar first focuses on the views of the opposing group, who not only resist the imposition of the Christian West but also strive to promote an Islamic "universalism."

Najjar explains that regardless of the position on whether to embrace globalization, it is seen as "identical" with Americanization via military, economic, and political imperialism. This conflicts with the Nation of Islam, whose members hold that they are unique in that they follow "Islamic doctrine, a perfect law, a culture and a system of morals." Those opposed argue that globalization requires that Muslims join the "infidels" in a Western notion of human rights, democracy, and secularization.

The fact that Islam is the law and religion that regulate Muslims' entire lives means that any change to sharia (Islamic law) is often seen as an attack on Muslim faith. This is particularly foreign to the notion of the separation of church and state that is foundational in the United States. Further, according to the Quran, Muslims are "the best of people" (3:110) and God made people into "nations and tribes" (49:13). This is antithetical to the monocultural hegemony of globalization.

Najjar also draws from Arab-Muslim scholars and writers who are in favor of the perceived benefits of globalization, from political liberation to being part of the twenty-first century. Such scholars see opposition to globalization as ultimately ineffective and assuring backwardness and irrelevance. Others point to the hypocrisy of utilizing technology such as computers, watches, and airplanes "to monitor prayer times and travel." And some simply accept the fait accompli of globalization, urging Muslims to use its beneficial aspects to enrich Muslim culture.

Najjar further problematizes the debate by drawing from Arabs who deny an essential, fixed, homogenous Arab-Islamic heritage and culture, as there is much disagreement on what is "the" true culture. Such perspectives include the historical integration of beliefs and doctrines outside Islam, such as Greek philosophical ideas.

The fact that major differences of attitude toward globalization exist illustrates that Arab-Islamic culture is not unified, in terms of what the culture is, how it should proceed, or how it should react to globalization. Yet one cannot deny that globalization's tentacles are already wrapped around the ad hoc bars meant to keep it out.

THE TWENTY-FIRST CENTURY PRESENTS the Arab-Muslim world with a challenge that may determine its future for generations. The Arabs are quite concerned about maintaining their cultural identity and their independence in the face of the West's superiority and its pervading globalization. Evidence of this is the huge volume—verging on a deluge—of Arabic literature on globalization and its "dangers," in addition to hundreds of seminars, workshops, and conferences focusing on "Islam and globalization," the Arab-Islamic heritage and national and cultural identity.

However, the Arab intelligentsia is divided into three different attitudes toward globalization. There are those who reject it as the "highest stage of imperialism" and a "cultural invasion," threatening to dominate people, undermine their distinctive "cultural personality" and destroy their "heritage," "authenticity," "beliefs" and "national identity."

The second group of Arab thinkers, secularist by inclination, welcomes globalization as the age of modem science, advanced technology, global communications and knowledge-based information. It argues that it is no longer possible for people to be "cocooned" within their own boundaries to ruminate upon their heritage, be its captives and nurse nostalgia for an "imagined" past. It calls for interacting with globalization and for benefiting from its "positive opportunities" in knowledge, science and technology, without necessarily losing their Arab-Islamic cultural individuality.

A third group calls (probably naively) for finding an appropriate form of globalization that is compatible with the national and cultural interests of the people. Globalization cannot be wholly accepted or rejected, it argues. The attitude of this group has been described as "positive neutrality," a self-interested pragmatic outlook, seeking a middle ground since globalization is an inevitable historical phenomenon with which the Arabs will have to interact. In between, there are other variations in attitudes toward globalization. This paper will focus primarily on the cultural implications of globalization for Islam as viewed by Muslims, in particular the Islamists, who express the greater suspicion of this development and, instead, seek to promote an Islamic "universalism" that, in their view, is superior to any cultural paradigm imposed by the Christian West.[2]

In addition to focusing on globalization from an Islamist point of view, this paper will also present the views of moderate Arabs and Muslims, who entertain a more open, yet critical and cautious attitude toward globalization. How Arab intellectuals assess the relationship between globalization and their cultural heritage will also receive special attention. All of the sources on which this paper is based are the original Arabic works and references. Translation of full quotations and paraphrases into English are by the author, except where indicated otherwise.

Since globalization is identified with American military, political and economic superiority, the attitude of the Arabs toward American power and hegemony, style of life and cultural values will be noted. It will become obvious that political considerations, such as the unqualified American support of Israel, have conditioned Arab attitudes toward American culture as well as toward globalization.

Globalization Equals Americanization

There is a general consensus among Arabs—both those who oppose globalization and those who favor it—that it is identical with Americanization. They view globalization as an American design to disseminate American culture as a model for the whole world. A North African writer, Abd al-Ilah Balqaziz, equates globalized culture with American culture, because "the means, powers, interests and aims that steer globalization are all American." He accuses the West, in general, and the United States, in particular, of using the pretext of fighting terrorism, fanaticism and intolerance to undermine Islam, because the Arabs and Islam are the only obstacle in the face of today's empire under American hegemony.[3]

America's military and economic power and its virtual monopoly of cyberspace and the information revolution, as well as its seductive culture, corroborate the impression of its global hegemony, leading a British author to write: "At times, indeed, it is difficult to distinguish between globalization, in its many forms, and Americanization."[4]

Globalization is the foundation of the world order in the twenty-first century, writes Husayn Malum. The strategy of world powers, with the United States in the forefront, is to promote economic globalization, or the supremacy of the market over the whole world, and to destroy the political power of states, nationalities and peoples, he adds. Globalization

is tied to the "New American Political Project," which seeks to unify the world by means of "market capitalism," Malum asserts.[5] However, "globalization is not just a mechanism of capitalist development," says another North African writer. "It is also and primarily an ideology reflecting a hegemonic will over the whole world and Americanizing it."[6]

Radical Islamists view globalization as a new *dawa* (call) for the elimination of the boundaries between *Dar al-Islam* (domain of Islam) and *Dar al-Kufr* (domain of infidelity). Globalization, they warn, seeks to join the infidels (Western Christians) and Muslims under the banner of secularism and worldliness, leading to unrestricted freedom in the name of human rights, as understood in the West, and to libertinism, the distinguishing characteristics of the decadence of Western civilization. Radical Islamists claim that Islam would resist such calls by "Crusaders and Jews," in defense of the *sharia*. It is impossible, they assert, to merge the Muslims and the infidels in the same category in the name of globalization, 'unity of religions,' 'world peace,' 'democracy' or 'secularism,' because Muslims are one nation, distinguished from all others by a true Islamic doctrine, a perfect law, a culture and a system of morals.[7]

Similar views have been expressed by other than Islamists. Said al-Lawindi, a well-known Egyptian journalist-writer, describes globalization as a "form of American hegemony," calling it a nightmare (*kabus*). The kind of globalization he favors is one of struggle against and resistance to "this barbaric capitalist hegemony and to confront the danger of Davos (the international economic forum). Globalization has produced nothing but chaos and violence."[8]

Globalization and Arab-Islamic Cultural Heritage

Arab and Muslim intellectuals have been deeply concerned about the impact of globalization on their cultural heritage. At a conference on "Our Heritage: Present and Future in Light of Globalization," held at the UNESCO Palace in Beirut, Lebanon, Rafik Atweh, the event coordinator, declared dramatically: "In the age of torment and uncertainty toward one's destiny, the Arab individual is crossing over the bridge of agony, with a fearful protective eye over his cherished values, history and heritage."

Highlighting his deep concern, Atweh added that the Arabs have plunged into a "canyon of darkness, looking for help to enable them to climb a mountain of overwhelming fast-moving events, at a time when they are not showing readiness to change the *status quo*."[9]

Globalization, intellectuals insist, will "smother" the peculiarities (*khususiyyat*) of Arab national culture, undermine Islamic morality and lead to cultural homogenization. Dr. Jafar Abd al-Salam, general secretary of the League of Islamic Universities, warns against the cultural danger of globalization and calls for a revivalist cultural project "to deepen the relationship between Muslims and their heritage, which is replete with elements of strength to face all challenges."[10]

Boutros Boutros Ghali, former UN secretary-general, and Jabir Asfur, both liberal-minded Egyptian intellectuals, warn against the attempt to impose "an alien culture on our traditions and culture." Asfur describes globalization as "barbaric," seeking to impose "on us conditions that are antithetical to human cultural diversity, and inimical to civilizational peculiarities." He condemns globalization's repressive measures to unify the world and to subordinate the "terrestrial globe" to a single cultural pattern.[11]

Yet one discerns among Arab intellectuals a reluctant recognition that the West still represents a civilizational and humanistic model to be emulated without having to give up their cultural peculiarity or to exchange some of their traditions for Western traditions and systems. Hence cultural globalization may not be so bad after all, provided the Arabs are ready for it. The Nobel Laureate, Naguib Mahfouz, although critical of American "supremacy and arrogance of power," sees no "contrariety" between Western and Islamic civilizations.[12]

Islam and Globalization

Muslims have always been proud of, and sensitive about, their religion. The Quran (3:110) tells them they "are the best of people evolved for mankind." The sensitivity arises from the fact that Islam is not only a faith but also a law, a sharia that regulates all aspects of human life, including economic transactions, marriage and divorce, and matters of state. Hence, any modification of the sharia is tantamount to a dilution or a negation of Islam's articles of faith. Muslims have found it more convenient to circumvent, rather than to change, the law. The inability to separate religious and mundane matters, religion and state, has conferred on Islam and Muslims a legacy of rigidity and resistance to change. Any perceived threat to Islam elicits a resentful attitude among the believers and often a defensive call for a return to the pristine age of the "pious ancestors."

Globalization is not the first phenomenon that Muslims regard as a threat to their faith. Westernization or modernization, in general, has always been suspect of being a "cultural invasion" by the Christian West. This suspicion goes all the way back to the Crusades, and to this day Christians, particularly Western Christians, are called Crusaders (*salibiyyun*). Moreover, recent Western colonization and imperialistic domination of most of the Muslim world, the creation and the unqualified support of the state of Israel, and the current invasion of two Muslim countries, Afghanistan and Iraq, have intensified Arab and Muslim fears and hatred of the West. Hence, globalization seems to be the culmination of historical developments aimed at undermining Islam.

Consequently, the bulk of Arabic literature on globalization reflects fear and suspicion of this new phenomenon. The views of a few leading Arab writers are sufficient to show how their arguments are reminiscent of the same arguments mobilized against modernism, imperialism and Western domination. Adil Husayn, an outspoken leader of the Muslim Brotherhood, warns against the "deception and cunning" of Western media in "brainwashing the minds" of Arabs and Muslims. By controlling the media, he says, Westerners spread immorality and "smother our religion and identity." Like many others, he discerns an "American-Israeli conspiracy" against Islam. Based on the Quranic verse (49:13), which says that God has made mankind "into nations and tribes," he rejects the claim that globalization will create one world and one culture.[13]

Abd al-Wahhab al-Masiri, a noted Muslim author, describes as "ridiculous lies" the West's claim that people are alike; that there is a new world order, justice, and human rights; and that the world is a "small village" governed by a global set of values. He adds, cynically, that the globalization "we know" is that of the hamburger, Coca Cola, McDonald's and the like. He argues that globalization is based on a set of material values: the market, sex and the "economic and corporeal man," all of which "negate human peculiarities, even humanity as such." However, al-Masiri is confident that Islamic values will "mobilize this [Muslim] nation to confront this deadly trend, which dissolves national and religious peculiarities."[14]

Globalization is equated with secularization, which means the "separation of religion and life, replacing Islam with a pragmatic and materialistic European and American thought," asserts Dr. Ahmad Abd al-Rahman. The globalization of the Muslim world would mean the "removal of Islam from thought and action, so that Muslims become subservient to the West." Human rights, freedom and democracy are rationalizations of the power and interests of Western nations, and of America, in particular. In order to impose American globalization on the Muslim world, the United States government supports secular forces, protects apostates from Islam such as Salman Rushdie and Taslima Nasrin, and subsidizes Orientalists and all secular regimes opposed to Islam, he charges.[15] In short, pragmatism and postmodernism are the guiding principles of American globalization. Islam cannot remain indifferent to this assault. "A new vision and an alternative civilization, derived from the interaction of Islamic truths with actual reality, are needed to ward it off," concludes Abd al-Rahman.[16]

Arabs and Muslims, in general, are quite concerned about their cultural identity (al-huwiyya), rooted in Islamic history and culture. At a conference of the Muslim World League, held in Mecca and attended by 500 Muslim scholars and writers, the secretary-general of the League, Dr. Abdallah al-Turki, warned that "misfortune will spread all over the world if globalization succeeds in detaching people from their culture and their identity." He charged the United States and its allies with using the September 11 events to "direct globalization against Islamic culture and to arouse Christian prejudices (narat salibiyya) against Islam. Other participants voiced similar views, calling for joint efforts among Muslims to fortify themselves economically, politically and socially, so that the Muslim world could withstand the onslaught of Western globalization."[17]

The Arab-Muslim's fear and concern about cultural identity may be exaggerated, but in most cases it is unfeigned. Al-Azhar, the supreme religious institution, has been called upon to educate Muslims in the values of their religion and to demonstrate that "Islam is valid for all times." A conference of Muslim scholars, many of them graduates of al-Azhar, was held in Alexandria, Egypt, to address this issue. "The culture we are anxious about," writes Dr. Abdallah Sulayman, consists of "a firm religious belief, a set of values, principles, customs and authentic traditions." He stresses "a commitment to God, family and home land, loyalty to everything good, truly just and redemptive."[18]

In an emotional outburst, Sulayman addresses the West thus: "your globalization, Oh you craven braggarts, is an arbitrary hegemony, a despotic authority, an oppressive injustice and a pitch-black darkness, because it is a globalization without religion and without conscience. It is a globalization of violent force, heedless partisanship, double standards, pervasive materialism, widespread racism, outrageous barbarism and arrogant egotism. It is a globalization that sells illusions, leading to perdition and to burying dreams in the depth of nowhere, spreading flowers over the corpses of the hungry."[19]

A number of leading scholars have turned their heavy guns on cultural globalization. Dr. Salim al-Awwa, a distinguished Egyptian Islamic scholar, writes that globalization has a cultural signification (*mafhum*), the terms of which are those of Western culture. To propagate them is to promote the dominance of that culture. He insists that Muslims have no alternative but to assert "our cultural and religious identity" in the face of globalization. "Islam," he adds, "has stood firm in the face of earlier invasions, and will not be powerless in facing new ones."[20]

[...]

For Muhammad Qutb, another leading Islamist scholar, globalization is the worst form of imperialism, "an iniquitous and arrogant form, that seeks not only to plunder peoples' livelihood, but also to obliterate their identity and turn them into subordinates and slaves." Aimed specifically against Muslims, globalization, in Qutb's words, "is an octopus spreading its tentacles into politics, thought, religion, morals, culture, traditions and customs." He blames Muslims for neglecting their religion and its obligations. In particular, he blames Muslim secularists for succumbing to the attractions of globalization. There is no doubt in his mind that Islam is superior to globalization and Western civilization, which is a "depraved civilization." Islam is the "only sound system." While globalization imposes a specific way of life—the American way—Islam recognizes diversity.[21]

The central theme of the Islamist criticism and rejection of globalization is its emphasis on the right to "cultural diversity." Abd al-Aziz al-Tuwayjiri, director-general of the Islamic Educational, Scientific and Cultural Organization (ISESCO), invokes the declaration of International Cultural Cooperation, issued by the General Conference of UNESCO on November 4, 1996, which affirms the dignity of each culture and the right and duty of each people to develop its own culture, and asserts that "all cultures, with their rich diversity, differences and mutual influence, constitute part of the heritage owned in common by all mankind" and that the "diversity of identities and specificities is not inconsistent in the least with the mutual interest of peoples and nations, provided it is allowed to unfold in the context of a human cooperation based on mutual acquaintance and coexistence."[22]

For Western globalization "to mop up the identities of peoples by insidious, coercive means would not only be a deviation from the natural course of things and a rebellion against the laws of the universe and the essence of life, but it would also be a violation of the very laws agreed by humans, a dangerous encroachment upon the rules of international law and a threat to peace, security and stability in the world," al-Tuwayjiri asserts.[23]

But how can cultural identity be safeguarded "in the context of a far-reaching globalization?" Al-Tuwayjiri wonders. He finds the Western stance vis-à-vis the identity of peoples "conspicuously contradictory." While the West takes pride in its own identity, it refuses to recognize the national identities of non-Western peoples. In a sweeping statement, he charges that globalization, being equivalent to American hegemony, "is downright inconsistent with the rules of international law, the reality of international relations, let alone national economics, sovereignty and the principle of cultural diversity." He warns of a collapse in world stability and a "worldwide anarchy of thinking and conduct."[24]

Yet Al-Tuwayjiri is convinced that mankind, and not only the Arab-Muslim world, "cannot disentangle itself from the constraints of globalization … It can, however, devise a countercultural current apt to face up to the hegemonic drive of the phenomenon of globalization on the theoretical and practical levels … pending the emergence of new world powers that would act as opponents or at least counterweights to the power currently holding the reins of the world order."[25]

In the end, Al-Tuwayjiri suggests that the "international will should gear the thrust of globalization towards science, technology and knowledge at large in a way to make the cultural and scientific aspect outweigh the economic and political aspect so as to safeguard the national interests of states, the rights of individuals and communities and the identities of peoples and nations." Consequently, "globalization must coexist with identities within the framework of cultural diversity for the achievement of human prosperity and world peace. Only then can globalization be a boon for mankind, not a bane."[26]

Dr. Muhammad Sayyid Tantawi, rector of al-Azhar, has no objection to globalization provided it eliminates barriers between the peoples of the world so that they may "cooperate in righteousness and piety, and not in sin and acrimony." (Cf. Quran 5:3 / 49:13). What Muslims would reject are "transactions in things forbidden by God. Mankind could enjoy and benefit from the products of civilization so long as they are within the bounds set by God." Muslims would never exchange what is based on the sharia, which enjoins justice, security and peace, for something less good, he concludes.[27]

In Defense of Globalization

Not all Arab-Muslim writers and scholars are opposed to globalization. In fact, there is a vocal minority who strongly advocate joining the twenty-first century. They are critical of the authoritarianism of Arab-Muslim political regimes, and more so of the Islamist discourse, which they regard as backward and bigoted. Advocates of globalization argue that it has become the "discourse of the age" by virtue of the communication revolution, which has transformed the world into a "large village, no nation can keep clear of, unless it chooses to live on the margin of history."[28]

Dr. Fuad Zakariya, an Egyptian professor of philosophy, charges that those who oppose globalization do not understand it, and would not be able to give a cogent and precise definition of the concept. The term, he argues, has become tainted, like secularism, and hence it is condemned without any attempt to understand its meaning and implications fully. Zakariya's concern is not primarily to defend globalization but to defend "sound thinking" and to question the enlightenment of those who speak constantly about things they know little or nothing about. For example, those who talk about the "greed of the multinational corporations and their danger to the developing countries ... are pouring old wine in new bottles. The phenomenon is an old one, and has been criticized since the dawn of imperialism."[29]

After pointing out some of the benefits of globalization in information and culture, Zakariya concludes that there is a great deal of misunderstanding about globalization. He reminds his Arab compatriots that there are certain problems that can only be tackled globally, such as environmental pollution and decay, the population explosion, and global warming.

For Jurj Tarabishi, a prominent Syrian writer, Arab critics of globalization use the term as a pretext to renew their scorn of modernity and Western civilization. He suspects there are "subconscious psychological fixations, stubborn and fanatical, behind such a negative attitude."[30] He describes as "paranoid" the perception of globalization as a great global conspiracy, hatched by the multinational corporations and carried out by the IMF, UN agencies and the media. He also dismisses the charge that it is the hegemony of Western civilization and culture, calling this "missionary discourse" against Western civilization nothing more than the "marketing of illusion or the approbation of backwardness."[31]

Tarabishi accuses the Arab intelligentsia of repeating what had been said about "cultural invasion," "imperialism," "dependency" and "modernity:" that they were Western and invasive. Referring to the overwhelming number of conferences, periodical articles, editorials, books, et cetera, on globalization, he says there is a kind of "ideological inflation" in the Arab intelligentsia's articulation of globalization. He calls their attitude "talismanic" (tawizi), closer to that of a sorcerer who, by cursing the name, seeks to ward off the evil and to neutralize its effects.

As a nation, the Arabs appear to have entered the modern age through the wrong door, Tarabishi observes. Understandably, certain historical factors have played a role in complicating the relation of the Arabs with their age: the connection between modernity and imperialism, the forceful implantation of the state of Israel in the heart of the Arab land, and lately the Gulf wars. What is disturbing to him is "the ferocious ideological campaign" to withdraw from the age and revolt against it in the name of Islamic fundamentalism. Tarabishi's main concern is that the Arab rejection of globalization may crystallize into a rejection of modernity altogether.[32]

In the opinion of another writer, there is a great deal of exaggeration, verging on mania (hawas), of the negative effects of globalization on national identity and cultural peculiarities. Admitting that American culture has a certain attractiveness to it, he insists the fear of American cultural hegemony is still exaggerated. Globalization is a historical development forging ahead with or without America, he maintains, adding that those who reject globalization completely in defense of cultural identity will invite cultural and political oblivion. He argues that the ordinary Arab, preoccupied with daily living, is not agitated by the question of identity; it is the Arab intellectual, obsessed with identity, who has made the question of globalization problematical and a major crisis. The obsession intensifies in times of crises and defeats, which threaten the heritage of a nation or a group.[33]

Like a few Arab intellectuals, Turki Hamad is confident of Western modernity, in general, and contemporary globalization, in particular, and that the technological culture they have engendered is on its way to becoming a comprehensive global culture, whether the Arabs like it or not, or whether they accept it or not. Arab traditional culture, ill-defined and elitist, based on a verbal rhetorical structure, will be of no use, he asserts. "How can the eloquence of the word compete with the technicality of scientific facts?" he wonders.[34]

The reformist writer rejects as "naïve" and "superficial" the contention that Arabs and Muslims can adopt Western technology but not Western values. He sees no threat to cultural identity from adopting globalization. "The global culture has become a common human heritage and a general human faith. Who can deny the universality of democracy and the common human faith in its general values, such as equality, individual freedom and equality of opportunity?" he asks.[35]

Views of Two Arab Philosophers

Two Arab philosophers, Sadeq Jalal al-Azm, professor of philosophy at the Syrian University, and Hasan Hanafi, professor of philosophy at Cairo University, debated the question of how Arabs should confront globalization at a conference sponsored by the Beirut Heritage Committee and held at the UNESCO Palace in the Lebanese capital. Their views had already been published in a book almost three years before the debate.[36]

Al-Azm is an avowedly secular thinker, while Hanafi is committed to the Islamic heritage without being opposed to certain aspects of Western culture. Aware of the "narrow-minded" position of the Islamists, al-Azm reminds his coreligionists that "foreign-made products, like watches, computers and airplanes," were allowing Muslims to monitor prayer times and travel to the hajj, implying that people were fooling themselves if they sought to ignore the impact of the West when deciding to embrace 'authentic' religion.[37]

Hanafi is skeptical about the benefits of cultural globalization. For him, globalization is not much more than a mechanism for the exploitation of world riches by the great powers at the expense of the poor people of the earth. He equates the culture of globalization with Western consumerism and its values. Globalization is not an ordained fate from which there is no redemption, he asserts. Neither is it a historical law governing all mankind. It is in conflict with cultural peculiarities, national will and in dependence. Hanafi sees the confrontation between the Arabs and the West not as a subject for scientific research, but as a historical-existential crisis reflecting a struggle more than a dialogue. It may reflect a pathological feeling of an inferiority complex of the vanquished vis-à-vis a superiority complex of the vanquisher, the colonized and the colonizer. In short, it is an unequal relationship between two adversaries.[38]

According to Hanafi, globalization is a manifestation of a latent Western "self-centeredness," based on an ethnic racism and the desire to rule and to dominate. Western powers have used various ideas and notions to rationalize their hegemony over the Third World, such as "globalization," "unipolar world," "the end of history," "clash of civilizations," and "the world as a single village." The danger of globalization to cultural identity is but a prelude to greater dangers to the nationstate, national independence and culture, he concludes.[39]

Unlike Hanafi, al-Azm has no feeling of uneasiness about globalization or the assimilation of Western knowledge. In his introductory statement in the debate, the Syrian philosophy professor says, echoing Marc Anthony: "I have come not to praise globalization, criticize it, or to bury it, live or dead, but to understand it." He says it is a phenomenon in the process of becoming. Everything about it remains subject to controversy, dispute, conjectures, suggestions, condemnations and commendations.[40] However, he maintains that globalization is the historical and inevitable outcome of nineteenth-century capitalism. The dynamics of capitalism are bound to open up a new horizon with a globalized form of production that will transform the societies of the Third World to make them conform to the new operations of accumulation in the Center (*markaz*). In his opinion, globalization is a higher stage of "historical capitalism," spreading its social relations into areas outside the Center.[41]

For al-Azm, globalization "represents the period of capitalist transformation for all mankind" under the leadership and control of the Western powers, the countries of the Center. The countries of the Center will seek to change and control conditions in the Periphery in a manner that will serve their interests, such as transforming all non-capitalist forms of production, discouraging local industrial development and making most people dependent on employment. He foresees an increase in unemployment as well as more polluting industries in the Third World. Al-Azm is not uncritical of globalization, but he accepts its inevitability and acknowledges its benefits. He describes it as "the kingdom of necessity, fate and destiny, coming from the Center and those who hold the reins of power. The future of the Third World countries will depend on how they react to it."[42] Al-Azm favors globalization on the grounds that it is "the spirit of the age and the course of history." He counsels the Arabs to "keep away from conspiracy theories and simplistic, 'fast-food' descriptions of globalization."

Hanafi accuses the advocates of globalization and Westernization of being disloyal to their own culture and heritage. The intellectual who adopts two cultures is "on the margin" and is not a "globalized intellectual" (*muthaqqaf awlami*). He must be loyal to his particular culture and be able to use other cultures to enrich his own, just as early Muslim philosophers like al-Kindi, al-Farabi and Ibn Sina had done. In contrast, Hanafi says, for the present "globalized" intellectual, the culture of the "other" is an end in itself, while the culture of the "I" has become anachronistic. While al-Azm discerns no "Arabized" response to globalization, Hanafi is optimistic about an "Oriental globalization and an Arabic-Islamic centralism" generated to confront Western globalization. He concludes by saying that history is the "arena of the struggle of wills, individual and societal, and not a preordained fate and an inevitable destiny."[43]

[...]

Conclusion

There are a few scholarly works in Arabic on globalization, mostly by economists. The rest are journalistic, rhetorical and superficial. No wonder, then, that the Arabs lack a clear perception of what globalization is all about. Some insist that it is the ideological framework of the new American imperialism. Others maintain that it is a conspiracy against Islam and Arab-Islamic culture. For many, it is the purveyor of the values of a morally corrupt West. Yet there is a minority of Arab intellectuals who realize the significance of the new world order, and who argue that if the Arabs were prudent and rational, they could reap great benefits and avoid the negative aspects of globalization.

Critics argue that the problem is not whether Arabs and Muslims shun globalization, but whether they are qualified and ready for it. They point out that the Arab-Muslim world is in a state of disarray and backwardness. The malaise may be a little exaggerated but it is not unfounded. High illiteracy rates, especially among women; the serious disadvantages from which women suffer; the shocking disparities between rich and poor; the corrupt authoritarian regimes; and the absence of democracy and human rights: all of these militate against the Arabs' ability to play a constructive role in the new global order. Commenting on the phenomenon of tyranny in the Arab world, Sayyid Yasin, a columnist for *Al-Ahram* newspaper, opines that perhaps it was the "Muslim society in its early phases, in which religious authority was coupled with temporal authority, and which pervaded the whole social space and became one of the primary bases of political culture," that is responsible for the Arab world as it is today. He calls attempts by Arab governments at democratization and liberalization "cosmetics," implying that only democratic societies that respect human rights and hold their rulers accountable will prevail. The Arab world is still living "in the climate (*ajwa*) of the Middle Ages," he concludes.[44]

Yasin asserts that so long as the Arab world is still seized by a "prohibitory mentality" (*aqliyyat al-tahrim*) that forbids freedom of thought and expression, it will remain in a state of backwardness. There is a clear call to those countries dominated by tyrannical regimes and closed minds to liberate themselves from the noose of the past and enter the new world. What is needed is a complete cultural revival that will do away with the culture of tyranny and establish a democratic culture instead.[45]

Some critics of globalization use it as an expedient to renew their derision of modernity and Western civilization. They disparage rampant Western commercialism, consumerism and pornography. They regard globalization as a radical negation of national existence and an end of all human values. A prominent Egyptian writer describes the 'global village,' created by globalization, as a "unified global jungle, dominated by the fiercest, most ferocious and aggressive animals." Islamists regard modernity as the precursor of globalization. Yet they seem to benefit from its technological achievements. "Islam on Line" is a striking example of using modern electronic technology to disseminate "true Islam." Even the Holy Quran is now on the Internet.

Arab-Islamic cultural revivalism is a defensive phenomenon; it is as old as the intrusion of Western civilization into the Arab-Muslim world. It may be a natural reaction by a weak culture faced with the hegemony of a much more advanced one. However, the Arabs and Muslims can no longer ignore modernity if they want to avoid marginalization. What is actually happening is that they are availing themselves of modern civilization slowly and in an ad hoc manner. As they proceed, they invoke pristine images of their early history, that will not be able to withstand the hegemony of globalization.

Questions

1. Do you see any way to reconcile the foundational clash between a culture that separates church and state and a culture whose laws and religion are integrated? That is, is it possible to adopt the perceived benefits of globalization such as technology and science without losing one's culture in the sea of globalizing values?

2. Is Najjar's historical record of the outside influences on Arab-Islamic culture evidence of the impossibility of a "pure" Arab-Islamic culture? Why or why not?

3. List the harmful characteristics of globalization that Najjar illuminates via its opponents. Are these essential to globalization? If so, is it reasonable to expect to "pick and choose" from globalization for its benefits (such as technology and science) and not "pollute" one's culture?

Notes

1. Fauzi Najjar, "The Arabs, Islam and Globalization," *Middle East Policy* 12, no. 3 (October 2005): 91–106.

2. See Muhammad al-Shibini, *Sira al-Thaqafa al-Arabiyya al-Islamiyya ma al-Awlamah* (Beirut: *Dar al-Ilm li al-Malayeen,* 2002), pp. 21–22.

3. In Radwan al-Sayyid, *Azmal al-Fikr al-Siyasi al-Arabi* (Beirut: *Dar al-Fikr al-Muasir,* 2000), p. 194.

4. Fred Halliday, *The World at 2000: Perils and Promises* (New York: Palgrave, 2002), p. 91.

5. Ibid., p. 117.

6. Muhammad Abid al-Jabiri, in *Al-'Arab wa al-'Awlamah: Buhuth wa Munaqashat* (Beirut: *Markaz wa Dirasat al-Wahda al-'Arabiyya,* 1998), p. 304.

7. Amid Ibn Muhammad al-Sufyani, *Al-Awlamah wa Khasais Dar al-Islam wa Dar al-Kufr* (Riyadh: *Dar al-Fadila,* 2000), p. 161; cf. Quran 3:110.

8. *Al-Ahram,* February 8, 2004.

9. *The Daily Star,* September 11, 2002.

10. *Al-Ahram,* November 1, 2002.

11. *Al-Ahram,* January 12, 2003; October 13, 2003.

12. *Al-Ahram,* March 20, 2003.

13. See *Al-Islam wa Al-Awlamah* (Cairo: *al-Dar al-Qawmiyya al-Arabiyya,* 1999), pp. 37–39.

14. Ibid., pp. 85–90.

15. The Salman Rushdie case is well known. Taslima Nasrin is a Bangladeshi writer and novelist. Her novel, *Shame,* which depicts Muslim persecution of Bangladesh's Hindu minority and is critical of Muslim treatment of women brought forth a death threat, forcing her to flee to Sweden.

16. *Al-Islam wa al-Awlamah, op.cit.,* pp. 164–165.

17. *Al-Ahram,* April 12, 2002.

18. *Al-Awlamah wa Mawaqif al-Fikr al-Islami Minha* (Alexandria: *al-Dar al-Misriyya,* 2000), p. 187.

19. Ibid., p. 175.

20. *Al-Ahram,* November 1, 2003.

21. Muhammad Qutb, *Al-Muslimun wa al-Awlamah* (Cairo: *Dar al-Shuruq,* 2000), pp. 13; 54–55. Cf. Quran 11:118–119.

22. Abd al-Aziz al-Tuwayjiri, *Al-Huwiyya wa al-Awlamah min Mandhur Haq al-Tanawu al-Thaqafi.* (Rabat: *al-Munadhama al-Islamiyya li al-Tarbiya wa al-Ulum wa al-Thaqafa,* 1997. Arabic text with English translation), p. 14.

23. Ibid.; p. 15.

24. Ibid., pp. 16–18.

25. Ibid.

26. Ibid., pp. 20–21.

27. *Al-Ahram,* January 14, 2002.

28. *Al-Ahram,* July 26, 2002.

29. *Al-Ahram,* January 25, 2002.

30. Jurj Tarabishi, *Min al-Nahda ila al-Ridda: Tamazzuqat al-Thaqafa al-Arabiyya fi Asr al-Awlamah.* (Beirut: *Dar al-Saqi,* 2000), pp. 148–149.

31. Ibid., p. 153.

32. Ibid., pp. 166–168.

33. Turki Hamad, *al-Thaqafa al-Arabiyya fi Asr al-Awlamah* (Beirut: *Dar al-Saqi,* 1999), pp. 22 & 89.

34. Ibid., pp. 101–102.

35. Ibid., pp. 178–184.

36. Hasan Hanafi and Sadeq Jalal al-Azm, *Ma al-Awlamah?* (Beirut: *Dar al-Fikr al-Muasir,* 1999).

37. *The Daily Star,* September 13, 2002.

38. Ibid., pp. 23–39.

39. Ibid., pp. 42–43.

40. Ibid., pp. 61–62.

41. Ibid., pp. 93–93, 112.

42. Ibid., pp. 168–170, 199.

43. *Ma al-Awlamah, op. cit.,* pp. 233–234, 241.

44. Sayyid Yasin, *al-Ma'lumatiyya wa Hadarat al-'Awlamah* (Cairo: *Nahdat Misr,* 2001), pp. 82–89.

45. Ibid., pp. 89–90.

9. Is Globalization Good for Women?[1]

Alison M. Jaggar

ALISON M. JAGGAR (B. 1942) notes that globalization is not new: "Specifically, for the last half millennium intercontinental trade and population migrations have mostly been connected with the pursuit of new resources and markets from the emerging capitalist economies of Western Europe and North America" (p. 38).

Jaggar ties globalization to neoliberalism, a turning away of liberal social democratic values toward "non-redistributive laissez-faire liberalism of the seventeenth and eighteenth centuries" (p. 564) and characterized by increased wars, the "grotesque" income gaps, the latter of which harms women disproportionately, and fewer women, especially poor women, participating in government and national legislatures.

Jaggar urges our envisioning alternatives to the neoliberal form of globalization, which she argues would bring peace, security, prosperity, authentic democracy, a healthier environment, and a valuing of diversity, and would benefit women.

IS GLOBALIZATION GOOD FOR women? The answer to this question obviously depends on what one means by "globalization" and by "good" and which "women" one has in mind. After explaining briefly what I mean by "globalization" and "good" and indicating which women I have in mind, I intend to argue that globalization, as we currently know it, is not good for most women. However, I'll suggest that the badness of the present situation is not due to globalization as such, but rather to its specific neoliberal mode of organization. I'll identify some of the questions that globalization urgently raises for political philosophy and end by sketching one vision of an alternative form of globalization that could be very good for women—as well as for children and men.

I Terms of Discussion

What Is Globalization?

The term "globalization" is currently used to refer to the rapidly accelerating integration of many local and national economies into a single global market, regulated by the World Trade Organization, and to the political and cultural corollaries of this process. These developments, taken together, raise profound new questions for the humanities in general and for political philosophy in particular.

Globalization in the broadest sense is nothing new. Intercontinental travel and trade, and the mixing of cultures and populations are as old as humankind; after all, the foremothers and forefathers of everyone of us walked originally out of Africa. The contemporary form of globalization did not appear *de novo* in 1989, with the collapse of so-called communism. It did not even originate in 1945 at Bretton Woods, New Hampshire, where the major institutions to administer the global economy were established, including the International Monetary Fund (the IMF), the World Bank, and the General Agreement on Tariffs and Trade (GATT), which was the precursor to the World Trade Organization (WTO). Rather than being an unprecedented phenomenon, contemporary globalization may be seen as the culmination of long-term developments that have shaped the modern world. Specifically, for the last half millennium intercontinental trade and population migrations have mostly been connected with the pursuit of new resources and markets for the emerging capitalist economies of Western Europe and North America.

European colonization and expansion may be taken as beginning with the onslaught on the Americas in 1492 and as continuing with the colonization of India, Africa, Australasia, Oceania and much of Asia. History tells of the rise and fall of many great empires, but the greatest empires of all came to exist only in the nineteenth and twentieth centuries. In 1815, Britain and France together controlled over one third of the Earth's surface, and by 1878 they controlled over two thirds. By 1914, Britain, France and the United States together controlled 85% of the Earth's surface. It was primarily in consequence of European and U.S. expansion that the world became—and remains—a single interconnected system. European and U.S. colonialism profoundly shaped the world we inhabit today. It produced the neoliberal philosophy that provides the rules for the war game currently known as "globalization," and it landscaped the highly uneven terrain on which that game is played.

Neoliberalism is the name given to the version of liberal political theory that currently dominates the discourse of globalization. Neoliberalism assumes that material acquisition is the normal aim of human life, and it holds that the primary function of government is to make the world safe and predictable for the participants in a market economy. Although its name suggests that it is a new variety of liberalism, neoliberalism in fact marks a retreat from the liberal social democracy of the years following World War II back toward the non-redistributive laissez-faire liberalism of the seventeenth and eighteenth centuries. It is characterized by the following features.

1. Under the mantra of "free trade," neoliberalism promotes the unobstructed flow of traded goods through eliminating import and export quotas and tariffs. It also abandons restrictions on the flow of capital. However, not only does it not require the free flow of labor, the third crucial factor of production, but it also actively seeks to control that flow. Although immigration from poorer to wealthier countries is currently at record levels, much of it is achieved in the teeth of draconian border controls that often cost would-be immigrants their lives. This lopsided interpretation of "free trade" enables business owners to move production to areas of the world where costs are lowest, perhaps due to lower wages, fewer occupational safety and health requirements, or fewer environmental restrictions, while simultaneously regulating the movement of workers wishing to pursue higher wages.

2. Global neoliberalism attempts to bring all economically exploitable resources into private ownership. Public services are turned into profit-making enterprises, and natural resources such as minerals, forests, water and land are opened up for commercial exploitation in the global market.

3. Neoliberalism is hostile to the regulation of such aspects of social life as wages, working conditions and environmental protections.

Indeed, legislation intended to protect workers, consumers, or the environment may be challenged as an unfair barrier to trade. In the neoliberal global market, weak labor, consumer, or environmental standards may well become part of a country's "competitive advantage."

4. Finally, neoliberalism presses governments to abandon the social welfare responsibilities they have assumed over the twentieth century, such as providing allowances for housing, health care, education, disability and unemployment. Social programs, such as the Canadian health-care system, may even be challenged as de facto government subsidies to industry. "Defense and security" are among the very few government expenditures excluded from being judged "subsidies."

Many people have come to equate "globalization" with its current neoliberal incarnation, and they regard the costs of this system as inevitable consequences of modernization and progress. This perception discourages attempts to question the justice of neoliberal globalization or to envision alternatives to it. However, I believe that the most urgent task currently confronting political philosophy is to assess the justice of neoliberal globalization and to stimulate debate on possible alternatives.

What Is "Good"?

The term "globalization" evokes one venerable answer to an ancient philosophical question, the nature of the good life. This answer is the culminating vision of European Enlightenment philosophy—which in turn reflects an ancient Christian dream. It is the dream of the entire human species governed by universal law within a world order characterized by unity of purpose, shared concern, mutual responsibility, and common security. Its advocates promise that global neoliberalism

will fulfill this dream by promoting the following goods:

1. *Peace.* Economic interdependence will make war unthinkable and so usher in an unprecedented era of world peace.

2. *Prosperity and social justice.* Expanded trade and economic competition will ensure the optimal allocation of scarce resources and increased economic efficiency, to the mutual benefit of all. Each region will produce what it is best suited for, according to its so-called "comparative advantage," and the rewards of individuals and countries will be proportionate to their contribution to the global market.

3. *Democracy.* Because trade liberalization requires expanded communications and freedom of movement, it will be accompanied by increased democracy.

4. *Environmental protection.* Increased world competition will encourage the elimination of waste and the efficient use of resources. Environmental resources will be conserved, and coordinated action will be undertaken to deal with transnational environmental problems such as acid rain and global warming.

5. *The end of racism and ethnocentrism.* Increased global interdependence and the consequent mixing of populations and cultures will undermine racism and ethnocentrism, thus realizing the ideal of a universal humanity.

6. *Women.* Neoliberal globalization will undermine local forms of patriarchal power, enabling women to become full participants in politics and the economy.

Who Are Women?

The deceptively simple question "Who are women?" has provoked many heated debates in recent feminist theory. In an effort to counter earlier generalizations about "women" that were false and exclusionary, contemporary feminists have been particularly concerned to argue that women have no essence. By this, they mean that no necessary and sufficient conditions exist for being a woman; no significant characteristics can be found that are attributable to all and only women. Feminists now insist that it is necessary to be constantly mindful of divisions among women, such as those of nationality, age, class, ethnicity, marital status, sexuality, religion—divisions that typically demarcate a status that is privileged from one that is stigmatized. Since no essential or typical or generic woman exists, broad generalizations about "women" must always be scrutinized because of the danger that they will exclude or marginalize some women. My interest is especially in women who are on the less privileged side of the various divides, in both the global North and the global South.[2]

I intend to argue that neoliberal globalization, despite its glowing promises, is helping to create a reality that is precisely the opposite of its promoters' rhetoric. Rather than experiencing an era of universal peace, the neoliberal world is ravaged by innumerable wars, many undeclared, and by high levels of militarism; many societies also face civil unrest and forms of institutional violence that are serious enough to be described as ethnic or class war. Not accidentally, the same world is characterized by a rapidly widening gulf between rich and poor, both within and among nations. Thus, rather than bringing universal prosperity, neoliberal globalization is creating unprecedented wealth for a relative few and poverty and destitution for millions, even billions, of people. Increasing numbers of countries have adopted the outer forms of democracy as a cover for political authoritarianism and corruption, and the environment is being destroyed at an ever-accelerating rate. Finally, the neoliberal world is marked by the violent eruption of ethnic and racial hatreds and even genocide.

Peace, prosperity, democracy, environmental conservation and the elimination of racism and ethnocentrism are all overtly gender-neutral ideals, but each of them is also a distinctively women's issue. Because all known societies are structured by gendered value systems, which assign unequal status and privilege to men and women, as well as to whatever is culturally considered masculine and feminine, most—if not all—social issues carry meanings and consequences for women that are somewhat different from those they carry for men. To the extent that global neoliberalism undermines women's special interests in peace, prosperity, democracy, environmental health, and the abolition of racism and ethnocentrism, it is a system hostile or antagonistic to women.

Although neoliberal globalization is making the lives of many women better, it is making the lives of even more women worse. The lives of many of the world's poorest and most marginalized women in both the global South and the global North are deteriorating relative to the lives of better-off women and of men, and even deteriorating absolutely. In the next section I sketch some distinct ways in which the lives of many women have been affected by war, economic inequality and political authoritarianism; for reasons of space, I omit discussion of the distinct ways in which women are harmed by environmental destruction and by racism, ethnocentrism and xenophobia.

II. Neoliberal Globalization in Practice

War

[...]

With the advent of neoliberal globalization, military production has been used less for national defense and increasingly for the domestic repression of popular movements, many of which protest the activities of multinational corporations. Military training is increasingly devoted toward the subjugation of civilian populations, including the suppression of trade union protests and strikes. Human rights, as well as environmental and indigenous groups, are often labelled subversive and suppressed by the military or by paramilitaries and death squads, with the reformers who survive being forced into exile.

Women, especially poor women, bear a disproportionately heavy share of the burdens imposed by war and militarism. This is partly because an ever-increasing proportion of the casualties of war is comprised of civilians rather than soldiers. In World War I, twenty percent of the casualties were civilians; in World War II, that percentage more than doubled (to fifty percent). Seventy percent of the casualties in the Vietnam War were civilians, and about ninety percent of the casualties of today's wars are estimated to be civilians. The combatants in war are predominantly male, but the vulnerable civilians are predominantly, though not exclusively, women (and children). They are also Southern women, since most casualties of recent wars have occurred in the global South. In fact, women (and children) constitute eighty percent of the millions of refugees dislocated by war.

Military production is highly profitable for wealthy Northern investors, who certainly include some women. It also creates jobs both for the Northern middle class, who work in research and development, and for relatively uneducated people, who enlist in the military or work producing weapons. However women, especially poor women, receive far fewer benefits than men from the job opportunities created in the North by military production, both because they are largely excluded from the fields of scientific and technical research and because many of the U.S. military's clerical and administrative tasks, mostly done by women, have been shifted to private contractors. More significantly, poor women in both the global North and South suffer disproportionately when tax revenues are allocated to the military rather than to social services, because women's primary childcare responsibilities often force them to rely more heavily than men on social services such as housing, health care, and education. High military spending diverts resources from more productive uses and leads to low total output and personal consumption in most regions of the world. Poor women in the global South have paid an especially high price for militarism, which has starved health, sanitation, education, and sustainable food cultivation and created a continuing dependence of the South on the North for maintaining and operating sophisticated weaponry. Militarism has been a major cause of Southern debt, making Southern countries vulnerable to onerous loan conditions that have imposed especially heavy burdens on women.

Militarism is also the world's major polluter of the environment, from which women suffer disproportionately, and it promotes cultural values that instrumentalize or degrade women. For instance, militarist governments often endorse masculinist ideologies that define men as warriors, promoting a culture of violence that spills over into violence against women on the streets and in the home. Meanwhile, women are defined as mothers of the nation; high birthrates are promoted and women's paid employment is discouraged. Women's sexuality is regarded as a national resource, their sexual autonomy is controlled, and they are expected to provide sexual services for warrior heroes. Simultaneously, women's sexuality is seen as a weak link in the national armor, and the mass media may promote an image of women as weak, corrupting and corruptible. In the 1990s, these ideas have combined to rationalize the use of rape as a systematic weapon of war, most notably in former Yugoslavia.

Prosperity

Viewed in one light, the world has indeed experienced unprecedented prosperity over the last fifty years, and especially over the last decade. The U.S. stock market has reached record highs, despite financial collapses in Asia and Latin America; GNPs are high in many nations; tourism is one of the world's largest industries; young people drive around in sport utility vehicles talking on mobile phones. But although many people are better off than ever before, prosperity is limited to certain regions of the world and to certain groups within those regions. At the same time, poverty is increasing relatively and often absolutely as a result of massive and growing economic inequalities. These are occurring within most countries, especially among economic classes and regions, and they are also increasing among countries, as the East/West political system has given way to the North/South economic system, in which the North is vastly more wealthy than the South. Because of these inter- and intra-national inequalities, abundance for the (relatively) few is matched by poverty and even destitution for the many in the global economy. Neoliberal globalization has created many enormous winners but many more huge losers, and women are disproportionately represented among the losers.

... Women in the global North, especially women of color, are disproportionately impoverished by the economic inequality resulting from "free" trade, which has resulted in many hitherto well-paid jobs being moved from the global North to low-wage areas in the global South. These jobs have been replaced in the North by so-called "Mcjobs"—"casual," contingency or part-time positions (often in the service sector), which are typically low-paid and lack health or retirement benefits. Although the reduction in the real hourly wage since the 1970s affects all low-paid workers in the United States, it especially affects women and, among women, especially women of color, because they disproportionately hold low-paid jobs. The U.S. Census Bureau recently reported that the earnings gap between men and women widened for the second consecutive year in 1999.

In the erstwhile Second World, elites are benefiting from the privatization and exploitation of hitherto publicly owned resources, but the dismantling of welfare states and consequent cuts in health services, education, and childcare has undermined the quality of life for most people. In 7 out of 18 East European countries, life expectancy was lower in 1995 than in 1989 (falling as much as five years since 1987), and enrollment in kindergarten had declined dramatically. Women have suffered disproportionately from the massive unemployment following the collapse of the socialist economies and the decline of social services. They have been pushed out of high-income and comparatively high-status positions in areas such as public management or universities, and many highly educated women have been forced to turn to prostitution, street-vending, or begging.

Comparable inequalities exist within what used to be called the Third World, even though some countries, especially those on the Pacific Rim, have prospered so much from the transfer of many industries that they are now thought of as societies in transition, newly industrializing countries or NICs. Gross domestic products have grown in other parts of the global South as a result of the mechanization of agriculture and the development of cash crop export economies, and some women are definitely among the beneficiaries of these changes, especially women in the families of Southern elites. Overall, however, women are disproportionately represented among the Southern losers from global neoliberalism. Pre-existing patriarchal social structures tend to limit women's direct access to any new wealth entering Southern economies as a result of economic globalization; women may access wealth through marriage, but often they are not in positions from which they can profit directly from the economic changes. For instance, women's responsibility for children makes it harder for women than for men to move to where the new paid jobs are located.

Greater efforts recently have been made to include Southern women in development, which is generally assumed to be a benevolent process of economic growth. Helping women participate in this process has been generally interpreted as helping them to gain a money income, and such efforts have increased Southern women's participation in the cash economy. However, the results of these efforts have not been unambiguously "good" for women; at best, they have been mixed.

To gain a money income, women have to produce something to sell in the market, and what most women have to sell is their labor. Women have become the new industrial proletariat in export-based industries, especially in much of Asia, where governments tempt multinational corporate investment with gendered stereotypes of Asian women workers as tractable, hard-working, dexterous—and sexy. Within these industries, wages and working conditions are often very poor, and harassment by bosses and managers is endemic. Again, the result is contradictory: the power of the women's fathers is reduced, but the women are super-exploited by foreign corporations with the collusion of their own governments. As employees, they often experience a type of labor control that is almost feudal in its requirements of subservience and dependence. Thus, the global assembly line could be seen as allowing some Southern women to exchange one master for another.

Many women in the global South work not in the formal economy but in the informal economy, a kind of shadow economy not reflected in official records. Its workers typically do not pay taxes, and their jobs are unregulated by health and safety standards. It is characterized by low wages or incomes, uncertain employment, and poor working conditions. Women predominate in the informal economy, which covers a wide range of income generating activities, including declining handicrafts, small-scale retail trade, petty food production, street vending, domestic work, and prostitution. It also includes home-based putting-out systems and contract work. Women are often forced into the informal economy because they are driven off the land by the expansion of export agriculture, especially in South America and South East Asia. Those who remain in the countryside rather than migrating to the shanty towns that encircle most major Third-World cities are often forced into casual, contingent labor. Landless women from the poorest households are more likely to predominate as seasonal, casual, and temporary laborers at lower wages than their male counterparts.

Neoliberal globalization has increased the sexualization of all women, partly via a multibillion dollar pornography industry, and many women have been drawn into some aspect of sex work. In some parts of Asia and the Caribbean, sex tourism is a mainstay of local economies. Sex work includes, but is not limited to, servicing the workers in large plantations, servicing representatives of transnational corporations, servicing troops around military bases, and servicing UN troops and workers. Prostitution is certainly not a new phenomenon, but global neoliberalism has encouraged it in several ways. Most obviously, it has disrupted traditional communities and displaced and impoverished many women, who see few other options for a livelihood. In addition, nineteenth-century colonialism created images of the "exotic" "native" women, whose sexuality was defined as highly attractive and fascinating, yet related to the supposed natural primitiveness of the "other" cultural group. Today, media in Europe and North America still portray brown or black women as tantalizing erotic subjects, while in non-European countries white women are exoticized and eroticized. In consequence, a vastly expanded global sex trade results in millions of women being employed as sex workers outside their countries of origin.

The most obviously gendered feature of neoliberalism is its worldwide cutbacks in social programs. These cutbacks have affected women's economic status even more adversely than men's, because women's responsibility for caring for children and other family members makes them more reliant on such programs. In the global South, cuts in public health services have contributed to a rise in maternal mortality; in the global North, making hospitals more "efficient" has involved discharging patients earlier—to be cared for at home by female family members. Reductions in social services have forced women to create survival strategies for their families by absorbing these reductions with their own unpaid labor. The effect of these strategies has been felt especially in the global South, where more work for women has resulted in higher school dropout rates for girls. In addition, the introduction of school fees in many Southern countries has made education unavailable to poorer children and especially to girls. Less education and longer hours of domestic work obviously contribute to women's impoverishment by making it harder for them to attain well-paying jobs.

The feminization of poverty was a term coined originally to describe the situation of women in the United States, but the phenomenon has now become global, and its scale is increasing. The United Nations reports that women now comprise 70 percent of the world's 1.3 billion poor. Women's poverty in both North and South is linked with disturbing statistics on children's nutritional status, mortality and health. In many Southern countries, including Zimbabwe, Zambia, Nicaragua, Chile and Jamaica, the number of children who die before the age of one or five has risen sharply after decades of falling numbers.

Democracy

The spread of global neoliberalism has been accompanied by the establishment of formal democracy in many countries, especially in the erstwhile Third World, where a number of dictatorships have been ended, and in Eastern Europe, where so-called communist forms of government have been overthrown. Democracy has been encouraged in these regions by formal guarantees for freedom of thought, speech, press and association, and by the establishment of multiple political parties. However, the institutionalization of formal democracy has not resulted in increased political influence for women, especially for poor women and especially at the levels of designing global structures and policies. In the world of neoliberal globalization, democracy has a white man's face....

The neoliberal abandonment of fixed currency exchange rates and of controls on currency transfer de facto undermines the sovereignty of all countries because it enables powerful investors to cause a financial crisis by withdrawing billions of dollars into and out of national financial markets literally in a nanosecond. Thus, such investors can veto the democratically determined policies of supposedly sovereign nations simply by withdrawing their money.

More formal limits on the sovereignty of many nations occurred in the 1980s, when international lending institutions imposed neoliberal policies of structural adjustment on debtor nations in the then Third World as conditions of borrowing money or of re-scheduling existing debts. Although the governments of the debtor nations formally agreed to these conditions, their agreement was often coerced by their history. Their countries had often been impoverished by centuries of colonization, which had drained them of massive resources and wealth, destroyed their economic self-sufficiency, and left them dependent on the metropolis for manufactured goods and for training indigenous professional and skilled workers. In order to end their economically disadvantageous position as suppliers of raw materials, such countries were virtually forced to borrow. In addition, many debts were assumed by autocratic rulers, who were supported by wealthy First-World countries as a bulwark against popular insurgencies regarded as "communist," and they often used borrowed funds to subvert local democracy through the military repression of their own populations.

The birth of the World Trade Organization in 1995 created a supranational organization whose rules supersede the national laws of its signatory nations on issues of trade. The WTO, which establishes the rules for global trade and functions as a sort of international court for adjudicating trade disputes, construes trade matters so broadly that they include not only tariff barriers but also many matters of ethics and public policy. For instance, the rules of the WTO challenge the European Union's bans on bovine growth hormone, on furs from countries that still use leghold traps, and on cosmetics tested on animals. Because the WTO regards ethical and health standards only as barriers to trade, it prevents countries from making their own decisions on ethics and food safety. The WTO is formally democratic in that each of its 142 plus member countries has one representative or delegate, who participates in negotiations over trade rules, but democracy within the WTO is limited in practice in many ways. Wealthy countries have far more influence than poor ones, and numerous meetings are restricted to the G-7 group, the most powerful member countries, excluding the less powerful even when decisions directly affect them.

Despite the fact that sovereign states are the only official members of the institutions administering the global economy, critics also charge that the current system of neoliberal globalization is dominated unofficially by transnational or multinational corporations, who "rent" governments to bring cases before the WTO. Because the budgets of many multinational corporations are far larger than those of many nominally sovereign states, it is easy for these corporations to influence the definitions and interpretations of the rules of the global economy by lobbying, bribing, and threatening governments or government officials. In addition, the WTO's dispute resolution system allows challenges to the standards and regulations adopted by federal, state, provincial and local governments to protect human, animal or plant life. If the standard in one country is higher than that in another, the higher standard can be challenged as a "technical" or "non-tariff" barrier to trade. Cases are heard before a tribunal of "trade experts;" generally lawyers, who are required to make their ruling with a presumption in favor of free trade, and the burden is on governments to justify any restrictions on this. The dispute resolution system permits no amicus briefs, no observers, no public record of the deliberations, and no appeals. Thus, whether or not health, safety and environmental standards are "science-based" and so acceptable is determined by panels of experts, unelected and unaccountable, who have the power to overturn legislation and regulation adopted by elected bodies.

The present organization of the global economy undermines democracy by rendering the sovereignty of poor nations increasingly meaningless and further excluding the poorest and most vulnerable people across the world. Many women, who are disproportionately represented among the poorest and most vulnerable of all, are effectively disenfranchised. The virtual absence even of privileged women from the decision-making processes of such bodies as the World Bank, the International Monetary Fund, and the World Trade Organization reflects the minimal influence exercised by women at the highest levels of global politics.

Poor women's lack of influence at the global level is not compensated by increased influence at the lower levels of politics, despite the new neoliberal emphasis on civil society and despite the fact that poor women have often been leaders in community activism. With the advent of global neoliberalism, an increasing proportion of so-called development assistance from richer to poorer countries has become channeled through nongovernmental organizations rather than through the governments of the recipient countries. Whereas neoliberals justify this change as avoiding official bureaucracy and corruption and as empowering grassroots women, critics argue that addressing social problems through private rather than public channels undermines democracy by depoliticizing the poor. Involvement in "self-help" micro-projects encourages poor women to exhaust their scarce energies in developing ad hoc services or products for the informal economy, rather than mobilizing as citizens to demand that the state utilize their tax monies for the provision of public services. Some critics argue that foreign-funded NGOs are a new form of colonialism because they create dependence on nonelected overseas funders and their locally appointed officials, undermining the development of social programs administered by elected officials accountable to local people. Thus, even though NGOs create programs that involve and serve women, their mission of providing services privately tacitly acquiesces in the state's shedding of its public responsibilities. Even though they use the language of inclusion, empowerment and grass-roots democracy, NGOs often undermine the social citizenship entitlements of poor women.

III. Envisioning Alternatives to Neoliberal Globalization

Contemporary neoliberal globalization is characterized by the massive consolidation of wealth in a relatively few hands, by radically unequal access to and control over material resources, information and communications, by the centralization of political power and absence of democratic accountability, by environmental destruction, and by virulent racism and ethnocentrism. Its rhetoric of equality and participation masks a reality of domination and marginalization for most of the world's women. However, just as we once distinguished perfect markets from existing markets and socialist ideals from various so-called socialisms, so we must now distinguish the existing neoliberal incarnation of globalization from its possible alternative forms. The questions raised by globalization are simultaneously deeply philosophical and of immediate public concern. They include, though certainly are not limited to, the following.

1. What Are Peace and Security?

Is peace simply an absence of conflict between sovereign states that have formally declared war on each other or the absence of sectors of local populations armed to seize state power? How should we think about economic embargoes, especially when nations differ so enormously in their ability to impose such embargoes and in their vulnerability to them? How should we think about judicial institutions that rationalize incarcerating large sections of local populations for nonviolent crimes motivated by poverty? Is a country secure when it is "protected" by a "missile defense shield" built at the expense of social infrastructure? Is the world at peace when it is policed by one or a few powerful nations that arrogate to themselves the right to determine when international law has been violated and what "punishment" is appropriate for alleged violations? Is the world at peace when a hundred million women are "missing" and when those girls and women who remain are subjected to infanticide, the systematic withholding of food, medical care and education, and gender-based battery, rape, mutilation, and even murder? What are real peace and security and what are their preconditions?

2. What Is Prosperity?

How can we redefine goods to include more than commodities, and wealth to mean more than material consumption? How can we measure prosperity in a way that is sensitive both to the quality of life and to inequalities in access to material resources? Is trade "free" in any meaningful sense when poor nations have no alternative to participating in an economic system in which they become ever poorer? When is trade "fair," and what is equality of opportunity among states? Can any sense be made of the notion of "natural" resources, when things like fossil fuels, sunny climates, coral beaches or strategic locations become resources only within larger systems of production and meaning? How can we determine what a country's "own" resources are, when every country is what it has been made over the course of human history? If countries' resources are unequal, what might justify global redistribution?

Do racialized groups or nations that have expropriated or exploited others in the past now owe reparations, and, if so, how should these be determined? How should the notion of economic "efficiency" be understood? How does the ideal of fair trade mesh with other values such as democracy, autonomy, empowerment, community, responsibility and environmental quality? How can we rethink the concept of economic restructuring?

3. What Is Democracy?

Which groups are entitled to self-determination, and what does self-determination mean? How can democracy be institutionalized at global, regional, national and local levels? How can nations that are radically unequal economically share equally in the governance of a global economy? How can ideals of global democracy be related to older ideals of national self-determination and sovereignty? In a global democracy, how should we rethink the notions of membership, belonging, and citizenship? What function do borders have in a global democracy, and what entitles people to a right of abode? What claims do global citizens have to control the allocation of local resources, and what claims do local citizens have on global resources? How can we create institutions responsive to the needs of the dispossessed, the excluded and the stigmatized? How can democracy be established in households and families?

4. What Is a Healthy Environment?

What ideals or principles should guide human interaction with the nonhuman environment, given that this environment is always changing and that every change benefits some individuals, groups or species at the expense of others? How can we ensure that human impacts on the nonhuman environment do not benefit human groups that are already wealthy and powerful at the expense of those who are already poor and weak? How can we ensure that present appropriations of environmental resources meet Locke's condition of leaving "as much and as good" for generations yet to come?

5. Racial/Ethnic Diversity

Are groups that have suffered past injury entitled to compensation? Is the existence of universal norms compatible with respect for the integrity of cultures and traditions? Can human equality be combined with appreciation for cultural difference?

6. What Is Good for Women?

Although none of the above questions mentions women explicitly, their formulation owes much to feminist thinking, which has shown that women cannot thrive in the absence of genuine peace, prosperity, democracy, a healthy environment, and respect for cultural tradition. Women have begun to reconceptualize these ideals in grassroots discussions all over the world, but the issues are too complex to be pursued here.

[...]

Questions

1. Jaggar does not assume that the meaning of "women" is unproblematic. How does she reconcile this and argue for women to benefit from globalization?

2. In what areas has neoliberalism taken over globalization? Why is this harmful to many women?

3. How does Jaggar argue for a reconception of human rights to "women's rights"? Does this seem promising for addressing neoliberal harm?

Notes

1. Alison M. Jaggar, "Is Globalization Good for Women?" *Comparative Literature* 53, no. 4 (Autumn, 2001): 298–314.

2. The collapse of the Soviet bloc has made the older terminology of First, Second and Third Worlds inapplicable, and it is now often replaced by talk about the global North and the global South. Roughly, the "global North" refers to the world's highly industrialized and wealthy states, most of which are located in the northern hemisphere—though Australia and New Zealand are exceptions. The "global South" refers to poorer states that depend mostly on agriculture and extractive industries and whose manufacturing industry, if it exists, is likely to be foreign owned. Many (though far from all) of these states are located in the southern hemisphere, and their populations tend to be dark-skinned, whereas the indigenous populations of Northern states are mostly (though not exclusively) light-skinned. Northern states often have a history as colonizing nations, and Southern states often have been colonized. The binary opposition between global North and South is a useful shorthand, but, like all binaries (and like the older terminology of three Worlds), it is problematic if taken too seriously. Many states, such as Japan and Russia, do not fit neatly into it.

Chapter 3: Challenges Calling for Corporate Responsibility

Introduction

"In a free-enterprise, private-property system, a corporate executive is an employee of the owners of the business. He has a direct responsibility to his employers. That responsibility is to conduct the business in accordance with their desires, which generally will be to make as much money as possible *while conforming to the basic rules of the society, both those embodied in law and those embodied in ethical custom.*"[1]

IN "THE SOCIAL RESPONSIBILITY of Business Is to Increase Its Profits," Milton Friedman (1912–2006), the oft-quoted proponent of "free enterprise," denies that a business, as a nonhuman entity, can have responsibilities at all. However, he does argue that corporate executives do have the responsibility for the firm's actions. And these corporate executives do not *merely* have the responsibility to "make as much money as possible," as it is often claimed that Friedman argued. Rather, the corporate executive also has the responsibility to "conform to the basic rules of society, both those embodied in law and those embodied in ethical custom." The latter responsibilities are deeply significant, and they carry duties well beyond "making money." The latter responsibilities drastically alter the ethical landscape by going well beyond economic gain, and they are not often quoted. Instead, the common perception and representation of Friedman is the result of creative editing, whereby the latter

responsibilities are conceptually amputated. To conform to the basic rules of society embodied in law and ethical custom is to follow pollution and Environmental Protection Agency (EPA) regulation, to not commit fraud or engage in deceptive business practices, to follow all Occupational Safety & Health Administration (OSHA) and other safety regulations, and to refrain from engaging in any actions that would violate the basic rules embodied in ethical custom. This is quite a broad range of responsibilities well beyond generating profit. In this chapter, the notions of corporate responsibility and of holding corporations accountable are explored.

The Legal Fiction and Responsibility Debate

There is a long-standing debate that echoes Friedman's claim that firms cannot be held responsible, for firms are "legal fictions," and not persons, and only persons can be held responsible. Peter A. French (b. 1942), an eminent business ethicist, traces the historical notion of a legal fiction back to Roman law.[2] French writes that under Roman law, status as a legal person was not an innate state that existed independent of the legal domain but was legally conferred. The only reason to consider legal personhood was if the "person" was able to act in the legal realm. When applied to corporations, the Roman law concept of a legal person leads to the legal fiction concept of the corporation as a person. French cites Justice Marshall in *Trustees of Dartmouth College v. Woodward* as representative of the legal fiction view: "A corporation is an artificial being, invisible, intangible, and existing only in contemplation of law."[3] French argues that corporations are "intentional systems and that they manifest the ability to do such things as make decisions, act responsibly, enter into both contractual and non-contractual relationships with other persons, and so forth," and therefore "[t]hey may be blamed or credited for what they do in their own right."[4] French also argues that corporations can be punished.

The 1986 Supreme Court case *Santa Clara County v. Southern Pacific Railroad Corporation* is the most-recognized root of corporate personhood via the Fourteenth Amendment's equal protection clause. The Fourteenth Amendment was meant to protect former slaves; however, a wily move to try to ensure that states didn't treat corporations differently led to the appropriation of the amendment, and it has been used by corporations many times more than by former slaves. The controversial status of corporations is addressed in this chapter's selections. However, first an exploration of what is meant by responsibility is in order.

Christopher D. Stone comprehensively explores the notion of responsibility, as well as corporate responsibility, in *Where the Law Ends: The Social Control of Corporate Behavior*.[5] Stone states that legal methods of proactively anticipating all "socially undesirable behavior" are

futile. Therefore, in the absence of legal control, the role of, and need for, self-control in providing responsible behavior becomes more salient. Stone argues that there are two notions of responsibility: first of following rules, and second of an autonomous cognitive process. Regarding the latter, Stone provides the following criteria for responsibility.[6] Responsibility requires reflection on one's initial impulses to respond or act. To act responsibly is to account for actions that affect other persons, especially concerning issues of harm and benefit. Responsibility requires accountability for the "consequences and repercussions" of one's actions. One can be held responsible for an action not only if one intended harm but also if one failed to do one's duty in preventing harm that could have been foreseen and prevented. (The comparable notion in law is to be "at fault." One can be at fault if one intended harm, neglected to prevent the harm, or acted recklessly in causing the harm.) Responsibility requires the weighing of alternative actions. Responsibility requires moral reflection characterizations "in terms of 'good,' 'bad,' 'just,' and so forth, by thinking of 'obligations,' 'rights,' and 'duties.'" And, finally, actions must be morally justified. Justifications can draw from different ethical perspectives, as provided in the Chapter 1 (utilitarianism, deontology, etc.).

Stone argues that as a society we would need to draw from both notions of responsibility for corporations. Certainly we would like the laws and rules followed. For example, corporations should follow USDA meat-packing regulations. In addition to following regulations, we would want corporations to engage in reflection and consider those affected when the laws are inadequate, such as in a case where a product met the legal requirements but had a weakness that put consumers at risk, as in the Ford Pinto case where the (legal) cost-benefit analysis performed led Ford to allow consumers to be harmed by a faulty part instead of initiating what they assumed would be a costly recall. Stone points out an aspect of the firm that is analogous to a moral agent's reflection, namely the firm's information-gathering system. However, he cautions that to require that ethical data be included in the information-gathering system's considerations would be only a first step. Other aspects of the corporation, from the internal reward system to the full corporate culture, need to be addressed.

In an effort to address one harmful aspect of the corporate culture and enforce safety regulations, the Occupational Safety and Health Act (OSH Act) was passed in 1970. This act was "to assure safe and healthful working conditions for working men and women; by authorizing enforcement of the standards developed under the Act" and "to assure so far as possible every working man and woman in the Nation safe and healthful working conditions."[7] The OSH Act established OSHA, charged with carrying out the OSH Act. In a 2002 report, the US Department of Labor claims that since OSHA was created in 1971, "workplace fatalities have been cut in half and occupational injury and illness rates have declined 40 percent. At the same time, U.S. employment has doubled from 56 million workers at 3.5 million worksites to 111 million workers at 7 million sites."[8]

OSHA and Corporate Responsibility

OSHA has five types of violations: willful, serious, repeat, failure to abate, and "other." A willful violation is one "the employer intentionally and knowingly commits." Willful violations carry penalties from $5,000 to $70,000, and OSHA can refer a case to the Justice Department for prosecution if there has been a willful violation. (Federal law requires a willful violation in order to prosecute a workplace death.) However, a first offense carries a mere six-month maximum prison sentence, as well as fines. A serious violation is "where there is substantial probability that death or serious harm could result and that the employer knew, or should have known, of the hazard," and carries up to a $7,000 fine. A repeat violation is established when "any standard, regulation, rule or order [has occurred] where, upon reinspection, a substantially similar violation is found," and can carry fines up to $70,000. Failure to abate occurs when a prior violation was not corrected, and carries a maximum fine of $7,000 for each day of non-compliance. The "other" category is for a violation that "has a direct relationship to job safety and health, but probably would not cause death or serious physical harm," and carries discretionary fines of up to $7,000.[9]

Even after the establishment of OSHA, workers continue to die both on the job and from work-related illness. Numbers vary from the Bureau of Labor Statistics to the Department of Health and Human Services, but they generally range from 6,000 to 11,000 on-the-job deaths, while tens of thousands die from work-related diseases.

Two cases illustrate ongoing OSHA violations and raise questions of human rights violations and the employment of untrained and unskilled workers. An ARCO Chemical Company explosion at the Channelview petrochemical plant in Texas on July 5, 1990, killed 17 workers. The explosion was caused by an improperly monitored treatment tank that had a broken safety gauge and was due partly to "contract" workers who were hired to clean the tanks, who did not have proper training and were working more than 15 consecutive hours. OSHA found 347 willful violations but did not pursue criminal prosecution.[10] Another case where criminal prosecution was pursued (a rarity) involved the death of three workers in a tunnel. In November 1988, the S. A. Healy construction

Chapter 3: Challenges Calling for Corporate Responsibility

contractor was tunneling under Milwaukee and was warned that the tunnel contained methane gas, a volatile and flammable gas. Despite this knowledge, Healy did not purchase a $14,000 monitor to measure the level of methane, nor were the workers using spark-proof equipment, nor were they properly informed or trained. After the workers were killed, OSHA cited Healy with 68 willful violations and referred the case to the Justice Department for criminal prosecution. However, there was only one company official indicted, and the charges were later dismissed. Healy paid approximately $765,000 in fines. Annual earnings of the company at that time were $200 million.[11] Clearly firms have a responsibility to follow OSHA regulations, yet they all too often violate them. What is the best method to remedy these violations? Fines are often ineffective, illustrated not only by the high number of willful, serious, repeat, and failure to abate violations but also by the failure to hold anyone accountable.

Yet the question still remains, what does it mean to hold a corporation responsible? A corporation is not an entity that can be incarcerated, shamed, or otherwise held socially responsible as a human being can be. Or is it? Human beings "run" the corporation, yet humans often hide from responsibility behind the "corporate shield." Perhaps "legal fiction" is the convenient way of referring to the individuals who make up the corporation and make corporate decisions. This anthology takes the position that as firms have rights, they have corresponding responsibilities as well. Corporations, however defined and configured—either as a "legal fiction" or as a collective of individuals, especially key personnel—are to be held responsible for their actions. Admittedly, this is not without controversy, and it is a controversy that will not be solved in this anthology. The premise of corporate responsibility is echoed in OSHA law discussed in this chapter, as it was

in Chapter 2, in *The United Nations Declaration of Human Rights Principles for Transnational Corporations and Other Business Enterprises*, where the United Nations called businesses "organs of society." This recognition of "organs of society" carries a responsibility for them to both secure and promote the human rights set forth in the United Nations Declaration. This chapter explores corporate responsibility in the boardroom, the workplace, and the community.

Paul Hawken (b. 1946), a well-known entrepreneur and writer, argues that we should return to our notion of a "corporate charter."[12] Hawken writes, "Corporations are chartered by, and exist at the behest of citizens. Incorporation is not a right but a privilege granted by the state that includes certain considerations, such as limited liability. Corporations are supposed to be under our ultimate authority, not the other way around."[13] He urges us, when a corporation is mismanaged and "harms, abuses, or violates the public trust," to "revoke its charter."[14] Furthermore, he argues that the manager who mismanaged should have a permanent mark on their résumé, stating that their mismanagement was to the point of a charter revocation. Such an action could clearly be undertaken in conjunction with many of the models proposed to address harm in this chapter. It is clear why management might oppose many models presented in this chapter, arguing inefficiency. It is also clear, in light of the type of harms discussed earlier, that over 6,000 workers a year dying on the job is "inefficient." Insofar as these deaths are in any way avoidable, business as usual is unethical and in need of a change.

Covid-19 and Essential Workers

In March of 2020, the world changed as Covid-19 blazed throughout the globe's population.

This pandemic has posed not only a number of serious health risks but also ethical questions relevant to how business is carried out. Workers, from grocery clerks to medical professionals, have literally been risking not only their own lives but also the lives of those they live with, just by doing their jobs. While many whose work can be carried out online have been able to work from home and thus reduce their risks, this option—really a privilege—has not been available to those deemed "essential" in person. The information lag regarding how Covid-19 spread exposed many to this disease early on, before masks, physical barriers, social distancing, and copious amounts of hand sanitizer were available.

The various Covid-19 vaccines have also raised global ethical questions regarding access, distribution, and the reticence of some in communities of color, and others, to be vaccinated. Of the three major vaccines, the use of the Johnson & Johnson vaccine "was paused during April 12–23, 2021, after detection of six cases of cerebral venous sinus thrombosis (CVST)."[15] While these cases were serious, and one woman died, the chance of developing blood clots was less than that of being "struck by lightning."[16]

This virulent pandemic has highlighted how interconnected we are, how desperately we need the goods and services many provide, how dependent we are on business to provide not only these goods and services but also how dependent we are for our livelihoods on firms. What firms owe their employees in light of risks such as those posed by this pandemic is an important avenue to investigate further. While we can allow workers to refuse to do hazardous work, the dilemma of needing to earn a living in dangerous conditions remains.

Notes

1. See below, p. 135; emphasis mine.
2. Peter A. French, "Law's Concept of Personhood: The Corporate and the Human Person," in *Responsibility Matters* (Lawrence: University Press of Kansas, 1992), 134–45.
3. Ibid., 135.
4. Ibid., 138.
5. Christopher D. Stone, *Where the Law Ends: The Social Control of Corporate Behavior* (New York: Harper & Row, 1975).
6. Ibid., 114–15.
7. OSH Act of 1970, Public Law 91–596, 91st Congress, December 29, 1970, www.osha.gov.
8. U.S. Department of Labor, 2002, www.osha.gov.
9. Ibid.
10. See Russell Mokhiber, "Corporate Villains: The 10 Worst Corporation of 1990," *Multinational Monitor* 11, no. 12 (December 1990). See also *Death on the Job*, a documentary by Half-Court Pictures, written, produced, and directed by Vince DiPersio and William Guttentag (1991).

11. See David G. Sarvadi, "Egregious Violations Policy: *S. A. Healy Co. v. The Occupational Health and Safety Administration*, 17 OSHC (BNA) 1737, Sept. 18, 1996," *Compliance Magazine* (January 1997).
12. Paul Hawken, "A Declaration of Sustainability," *Utne Reader* (September/October 1993): 54–61.
13. Ibid., 56.
14. Ibid.
15. David K. Shay et al., "Safety Monitoring of the Janssen (Johnson & Johnson) COVID-19 Vaccine—United States, March–April 2021," *Morbidity and Mortality Weekly Report*, May 7, 2021, https://www.cdc.gov/mmwr/volumes/70/wr/mm7018e2.htm.
16. Reuters, "More Likely to Be Struck by Lightning? Americans Weigh Risk of J&J Vaccine," *U.S. News & World Report*, April 13, 2021, https://www.usnews.com/news/top-news/articles/2021-04-13/more-likely-to-be-struck-by-lightning-americans-weigh-risk-of-j-j-vaccine.

1. Corporate Sociopolitical Involvement: A Reflection of Whose Preferences?[1]

Michael Nalick, Matthew Josefy, Asghar Zardkoohi, and Leonard Bierman

NALICK ET AL. NOTE that business is now a powerful force in political and social arenas, often rivaling many national economies. Firms have always worked to influence the environment in which they operate (including social and political arenas), but they have now moved to influence and manipulate highly contested and controversial sociopolitical issues that risk alienating some stakeholders. These include such divisive issues as gun control, LGBTQ+ rights, and marijuana legalization. Given that these are potentially alienating to customers and do not offer transparent economic benefit to the firm, the authors explore the business motivation for taking such positions.

BUSINESS HAS LONG BEEN recognized as a substantive force in shaping both political and social issues (Carroll, 1979; Epstein, 1987; Hillman & Hitt, 1999). However, this influence has become more pervasive recently as (1) the economic power of some corporations now arguably rivals that of many national economies (Roach, 2007), and (2) this growing economic power has coincided with and contributed to augmented political power (Alzola, 2013; Hadani & Schuler, 2013; Margolis & Walsh, 2003; Sun, Mellahi, & Wright, 2012).

While corporations have a vested interest in influencing their institutional environment, including matters debated in the political or social sphere, not all the issues firms engage in are clearly salient to their overall objectives. In fact, some firms have, in recent times, engaged in sociopolitical issues that are divisive, unsettled, emotionally charged, or contested. We refer to firm participation in these types of issues as sociopolitical involvement (SPI). Surveys by the Pew Research Center and the McKinsey consulting firm found that U.S. corporations have recently been involved in sociopolitical issues such as same-sex marriage, gun control, immigration, transgender rights; legalization of marijuana, and the size or role of the government (McKinsey & Company, 2009; Pew Research Center, 2014). These issues are topics in the purview of current political discourse, potentially resulting in policy changes at one or more levels of government. Often referred to as "policy paradoxes," these issues generally lack normative or institutional societal consensus (Stone, 2012).

Because of the strong emotions such issues engender, public opinion regarding them is often very highly divided, evoking debates within multiple arenas. These are (1) social issues, invoking debates and "emotional feelings and moral intuitions" or "passion" across different social groups, (2) political issues, as they can be simultaneously debated in legislative discourse (Stone, 2012, pp. 11, 32–34), and (3) potentially legal issues, as courts can be asked to intervene and decide when political institutions fail to do so. The dominant societal consensus on sociopolitical issues is also unstable, evolving over time and with differences persisting across geographies, religious beliefs, and individualized demographic and ethnic backgrounds. Rational (or analytically derived) perspectives may be dismissed due to the emotional or moral nature of such issues, and corporate engagement in these debates risks alienating certain groups of stakeholders.

However, the management literature has generally approached the role of business in nonmarket issues with an assumption that there are economic motivations on the part of the firm, even if tangential or trifling (Hillman, Keim, & Schuler, 2004; McWilliams & Siegel, 2001; Mellahi, Frynas, Sun, & Siegel, in press). These activities have generally been categorized as either corporate social responsibility (CSR) or corporate political activities (CPA). CSR mainly constitutes firm engagement in activities considered as beneficial to society (Hillman & Keim, 2001; Margolis & Walsh, 2003), either by directly benefiting those receiving firm resources or through the firm's compliance with a set of widely accepted social norms and adherence to (or exceeding of) legal mandates (Campbell, 2007; Matten & Moon, 2008; McWilliams & Siegel, 2001; Rodriguez, Siegel, Hillman, & Eden, 2006). CSR may encompass both philanthropic donations and a range of strategic alliances with nonprofits, nongovernment organizations, and educational institutions to achieve a specified set of organizational goals. These actions are generally expected to improve the firm's reputation among most stakeholders, and the more salient the issue, the greater the reputational gain to the firm (Baron, 2001, Campbell, 2007; Epstein, 1987; Fombrun & Shanley, 1990; McWilliams & Siegel, 2001).

Corporate political activities involve investments by the firm to influence political processes (including elections, legislation, and/or enforcement of existing rules and regulations) in a way that helps the firm to obtain policy-based competitive market advantages (Baysinger, 1984; Hadani & Schuler, 2013; Hillman & Hitt, 1999). Engagement in CPA is mainly viewed as a transactional arrangement via lobbying, political spending, and grassroots engagement, wherein the firm expects returns on political investments by advancing both public policy outcomes and firm performance outcomes (Getz, 1997; Hillman & Hitt, 1999; Hillman et al., 2004; Shaffer, 1995; Zardkoohi, 1985). Moreover, recent attempts to combine these literatures suggest that firms use political activities to advance a CSR agenda that is arguably related to the company's operations (Scherer, Rasche, Palazzo, & Spicer, 2016).

Sociopolitical issues differ from these two types of nonmarket activities commonly studied in the literature and therefore warrant additional theorizing and investigation. For the CSR activity to be viewed as beneficial by a majority of constituents, there must be some level of consensus within society that corporate engagement on the issue is beneficial. Sociopolitical issues lack this type of consensus (Stone, 2012). By this, we mean that there is not agreement (in fact, there might even be animosity) within much of society regarding the appropriate response to an issue (Meyer, Scott, Cole, & Intili, 1978). When there is a lack of agreement on an issue or accepted evidence to support a position, engagement in such an issue offers no immediate, clear positive value from the perspective of a large segment of stakeholders and society.

Moreover, while engagement on sociopolitical issues can take place in the political marketplace, such as donations to politically motivated 501(c)(4) groups or candidates who advocate on behalf of a particular side of an issue, involvement in controversial issues encompasses a wider set of activities, that typically fall outside the purview of traditional research on CPA.[2] This involvement does not encompass what the literature would recognize as CPA because the issue may not concern how the government directly affects the firm, and engagement may not offer a salient competitive advantage to the firm. Therefore, interjection in such issues by most firms is likely not a response to direct government threat or a proactive opportunity toward the competitive environment; indeed, it is unclear what, if any, competitive advantage could be provided by company involvement in an issue of this kind.

Further, literature seeking to integrate these CSR and CPA perspectives suggests that a firm's non-market activities involving CSR and political issues are geared toward causes that receive broad stakeholder support and are arguably closely associated with the firm's operational activities (Reinecke & Ansari, 2016; Scherer, Rasche, Palazzo, & Spicer, 2016). However, while sociopolitical issues contain elements of political and social nonmarket activity, theory developed to explain either CSR or CPA appears insufficient to fully explain the current wide-ranging sociopolitical activities undertaken by firms. Given this research gap and the considerable and broad influence corporations may have on such issues, this article defines and articulates a theoretical rationale for corporate sociopolitical involvement.

To gain a better understanding of why firms become involved in such hot-button issues, we first seek to define and conceptualize SPI. Then we use a multi-theoretical approach that focuses on commonly used theories from the nonmarket strategy literature to explain firm motives; this primarily involves examining stakeholders as an external driver for SPI, agency theory as an internal driver for SPI, and the firm's institutional environment as a driving mechanism for both perspectives (Sethi, 1979). Table 1 provides a sampling of recent examples of SPI across multiple countries.

Our conceptualization draws on positive, negative, and managerial personal inclinations toward SPI. We discuss how firms view stakeholder benefits of engagement in SPI, stakeholder risks of nonengagement, and the personal views of executives as a potential rationale for firm involvement with sociopolitical issues. Following this, we consider how conditions in the institutional environment facilitate firm engagement in SPI and affect its interactions with stakeholders, and then integrate our theoretical perspectives. The paper concludes with a discussion and agenda for future research, expanding on our theoretical discussion.

Conceptualizing a Sociopolitical Issue

Sociopolitical issues are salient unresolved social matters on which societal and institutional opinion is split, thus potentially engendering acrimonious debate across groups. Haider-Markel and Meier (1996, p. 332) suggested that "the politics of these highly salient issues generally involves two competing coalitions often formed around religious beliefs and/or partisanship. The process resembles that of redistributive politics except groups seek to redistribute values (not income) by having government put its stamp of approval or disapproval on a specified set of values." These issues often involve moral values that elicit

Table 1: Recent Instances of SPI in Multiple Countries

Country	Company	Issue	Action	Reaction
Australia	Lush Cosmetics	LGBT education	Company issued letter of support for awareness and education programs in public schools—and criticized politicians who have impeded the program (Ahlquist, 2016).	Other companies including Qantas followed and begin publicly supporting the program.
China	Alibaba	Same-sex marriage	Company paid for 10 couples to travel to the U.S. to get married (Kim, 2015).	The marriages remain symbolic in China, since same-sex marriages are not legal.
China	Ctrip	One-child policy	Company provided interest-free loans for employees that could be used to pay government fines for having more than one child (Jing, 2015).	The Chinese government has at times been seen to crack down on companies for stances that are counter to government policies.
Germany	Volkswagen, Deutsche Bank, Siemens, others	Refugee immigration	The European refugee crisis evoked strong political differences; a number of German companies joined an initiative called *Wir zusammen* to support immigrants (Horvath, 2015).	The companies were praised for their willingness to hire refugees. However, public opinion on the issue continues to be divided.
United States	Target	LGBT legislation	In 2011, Target donated to political candidates who opposed same-sex marriage (Chang, 2011). In 2016, Target formally announced a policy of allowing transgendered persons to use the bathroom of their choice (as some states passed legislation requiring individuals to use the bathroom corresponding to their sex at birth) (Picchi, 2016).	In both circumstances, there were boycotts by various ideological groups. In 2016, the company noted a decline in sales.
United States	Whataburger	Gun legislation	Following passage of open-carry laws in 16 states, CEO released a public statement about company policy forbidding guns in their restaurants (Gorman, 2015).	Decision elevated company into national 2nd Amendment debate. However, only a few pro-gun rights groups staged boycotts.

personal feelings that may not be supported by conclusive rational argument (Gusfield, 1963). We discuss the underlying elements that identify sociopolitical issues in the following sections.

Elements That Identify Sociopolitical Issues

Lacking societal consensus. Sociopolitical issues lack societal consensus (Haider-Markel & Meier, 1996). In particular, the issues are composed of contentious unsettled social matters on which opinion is split between "for" and "against" camps. Such issues are controversial as they involve stances on sensitive topics that challenge established norms derived from individualized religious, economic, ethnic, partisan, or historical sociocultural and geopolitical views (Haider-Markel & Meier, 1996). They are, as Stone noted, issues that evoke strong emotional feelings, even "passion" (Stone, 2012, pp. 11, 32–34), among groups split across various demographic factions (Haider-Markel & Meier, 1996).

Mobilized around preexisting beliefs, these idiosyncratic sociopolitical issues generally arise through informal institutions (including coalitions and interest groups) and formal institutions (such as various levels of government) fostering or propagating dissension. As a result, divisive discourse that surrounds a sociopolitical issue often spreads across various branches of government, the media, political campaign organizations, religious organizations, professional societies, and private foundations (Hilgartner & Bosk, 1988).

Even coalitions, interest groups, and politicians not directly affected often find these types of issues to be an effective tool for building a political reputation or stereotyping opponents (Haider-Markel & Meier, 1996). In other words, political advocacy organizations form to sway government and society in favor of or against given issues through legislative changes. Political actors may also stake positions on a contentious topic and battle with opposing politicians for legislative control, using the issue and subscribed legislation to gain support (Ripley & Franklin 1991). This process results in battle lines that split society and, often, levels and branches of government, formal organizations, and informal organizations (Lax & Phillips, 2009). For example, issues such as gay marriage and transgender rights, gun control, and illegal immigration may have majority support at the federal level, yet the local and regional levels of government may disagree with federal views. Additionally, the various branches of a government may be split in their intent to endorse a position on the issue or to initiate government actions based on that persuasion. Opposing views on an issue may also exist between the formal political establishment and informal institutions such as popular coalition groups. These divisions exemplify the type of contentious societal discourse that is associated with sociopolitical issues.

Low information rationality. Information asymmetries and low information structures often limit concrete factual information and reasoning related to sociopolitical issue positions. In the United States, historically, positions and laws concerning issues such as abortion (Goggin, 1993; Luker, 1984), sodomy laws (Nice, 1988), Sunday closing laws, birth control, and gay and transgender rights (Brewer, 2003) often entail arguments by "media experts," but such arguments give the general public little information (Haider-Markel & Meier, 1996). Further, because the issues often entail soft outcomes that are challenged and intentionally undermined by key stakeholders, conclusions are unjustifiable. In addition, because individuals may feel that they are experts in their own worldviews, they may not perceive the need to gather any information to form an opinion (Haider-Markel & Meier, 1996).

Evolving viewpoints and issue salience. Another defining characteristic of a sociopolitical issue is the potential for shifting views on the topic. Importantly, these particular disputes often follow a dynamic pattern and the outcomes ebb and flow with time, causing the salience of the issue to increase and decrease through phases of development (Hilgartner & Bosk, 1988). However, for a subject or topic to be considered a current sociopolitical issue it must be widely salient, which means it is important to a broad segment of society and the issue is fresh on the minds of people (Bonardi & Keim, 2005). Thus, this type of social issue can lie relatively dormant for quite a while and then become very salient. Indeed, in some instances, the unsettled issue can remain unsettled for entire generations and then fade into obscurity due to a lack of salience. Gradually or suddenly, the issue may attract renewed attention following changes in other related cultural norms that induce society to revisit the topic, perhaps in response to an event or disaster that brings the issue to the forefront (Hilgartner & Bosk, 1988).[3]

Conversely, with time and greater constituent involvement, an issue may become less divisive and, whether temporarily or permanently, gradually morph into established law and a broadly accepted social norm (though unanimity is not required and remains unlikely). Along similar lines, a hot issue can be highly controversial for an extended period of time until a consensus or impasse is achieved and the relevance or contentiousness of the issue fades in a particular community or society. In short, sociopolitical issues move back and forth along spectrums of salience and level of divisiveness.

Defining SPI and Contrasting Other Types of Nonmarket Activities

Given this definition of a sociopolitical issue, we now turn our attention to further clarification as to how a firm's SPI differs from other nonmarket activities. We also provide a framework for evaluating this involvement, which enables further theory development to explain why firms engage in sociopolitical issues.

Table 2 contrasts SPI with CPA and CSR by providing a definition for each. We note key differences in regard to three dimensions. First, we argue that a firm's objectives regarding its SPI activities are not known a priori. Second, operational relatedness is more distal for SPI than for CSR (especially actions related to stakeholder management) and CPA. Finally, we expect that some stakeholders will view SPI as beneficial, while others will perceive it as discriminatory. In contrast to CSR, for which benefits may be accrued more directly to some but little harm would be expected, SPI may be perceived as harming a potentially substantial portion of stakeholders who disagree with the position taken by the firm.

These differences necessitate a framework for assessing a firm's SPI that is distinct from those used for CPA or CSR. We suggest that a firm's involvement in a sociopolitical issue can be recognized and evaluated along three dimensions: consideration of potential market motivations, corporate position, and the manner of involvement.

Market motivations. The first dimension of firm involvement in an SPI is to consider potential profit motivation; to constitute SPI, these motivations must be categorized as distal and uncertain. In other words, operational relatedness is ambiguous, and there is not a direct link between firm operations and the issue, which makes competitive benefits from engagement tangential at best. This may occur

Table 2: Contrasting SPI with CPA and CSR

Nonmarket strategy	Definition	Relevant theories	Firm objective	Operational relatedness	Stakeholder/ societal benefits
CPA	Corporate attempts to manage political institutions and/or influence political actors in ways favorable to the firm	Agency, institutional, resource-based view, resource dependence, interest group, transaction cost, behavioral theory of the firm	Favorable public policy outcomes, performance outcomes	Directly related to business issues: lessening government regulation, winning government contracts, creating competitive barriers, and creating favorable trade policies	Limited benefits extend to nonfinancial stakeholders
CSR	Corporate actions that appear to go beyond obeying the law to advance some sort of expected social good for consumers and stakeholders, which allows a firm to enhance organizational performance	Stakeholder, agency, institutional, resource-based view, resource dependence	Financial performance, legitimacy, reputation	Direct impact on stakeholders who affect firm operational ability on issues that have limited relationship to firm operations but are viewed as producing a positive effect on society	Beneficial impact on society and/or primary stakeholders
SPI	Firm direct participation in or indirect support for salient social issues that are part of an ongoing debate regarding contested social norms	Agency, stakeholder, social movement, upper echelons, institutional	Future legitimacy benefits, defensive practice	Limited or no operational relatedness	Indirect benefit to some stakeholders; indirect harm to other stakeholders

because the issue is not directly involved in the scope of firm operations, especially compared with other types of nonmarket social issues such as labor, environmental, health care, and education concerns. Similarly, there is no clear expectation for whether the firm would increase either market share or market power by taking its position on that particular sociopolitical issue.

Corporate position. The second dimension is the stance the company takes, which may be described as being for or against a particular issue. This involvement can include simply ad hoc or unscripted statements made by someone in the top management team (TMT), typically the CEO; formal statements from the TMT, issued either internally or externally; or a direct statement by the firm. Involvement can also take the form of advertising, publicized product decisions, changes in employment policies or benefits, or donations to political or charitable organizations with clear affiliations on the issue. Involvement can also be signaled in business practices or operations. For example, the firm may choose certain locations, operations, products or services, or expansions in given areas, all driven by its ideological bent on a given issue. This occurred when Angie's List CEO Bill Oesterle reneged on a commitment to expand its Indianapolis headquarters because of a disagreement with Indiana's passage of a controversial religious freedom law, which critics argued discriminated against homosexuals. Firm involvement can be measured by the frequency of actions, the amount of resources invested, or a quantification of the different categories of actions taken by the firm.

Some issues may possess many of the attributes of a sociopolitical issue, but a firm's motivations for engagement may nonetheless be clearly tied to operational risk and the firm's future profits. For instance, the vote in the United Kingdom for a "Brexit" from the European Union was highly contested and evoked strong emotional responses. However, it would be difficult to disentangle a firm's other motivations from its profit motivation. Indeed, numerous firms publicly took stances encouraging voters to remain in the European Union, the position that would have maintained the status quo and was therefore associated with avoiding an increase in uncertainty in the business operating environment.

Manner of involvement. Firms choose a variety of ways in which to pursue SPI. This may include the degree to which any sociopolitical position is formalized, and who in the firm is (are) designated to publicly signal the firm's positions. Involvement ranges from statements made by company officials, in either formal or informal settings, to formal partnerships with entities that are also engaged on the issue, and from in-kind donations or sponsorships to paid advertising. At some firms, the issue may be formally brought before shareholders as a resolution, while at others involvement may be more ad hoc.

Why Firms Engage in Sociopolitical Issues: A Multifaceted Theoretical Perspective

In light of these distinctions, we now turn to existing theory to examine why firms pursue SPI. Because sociopolitical issues are entwined within a firm's stakeholder purview (e.g., Hillman & Keim, 2001), we frame part of our model along stakeholder theory, thus examining the firm's stakeholder benefits and consequences. However, we also incorporate agency and institutional theories to examine motivational components that prompt the firm to engage in such issues.

One external driver for a firm to engage in SPI is its interactions with and interpretation of relevant stakeholders. Freeman's (1984) stakeholder approach outlined the mechanisms that make business both susceptible and amenable to social influence. Because stakeholders are individuals or entities that are exposed to losing something, voluntarily or involuntarily, as a consequence of the firm's behavior and related outcomes, they often affect how a firm perceives its social environment and influence what issues it decides to act on (Clarkson, 1995). Because sociopolitical issues are likely dynamic, various stakeholders might change their reactions to the firm's position over time. Being aware of the dynamic nature of sociopolitical issues and how each stakeholder group might evolve is salient to the firm's market and nonmarket strategies.

We therefore highlight a number of motivating stakeholder-related perspectives that may prompt and enable SPI. The first perspective, *risk taking on perceived future stakeholder benefits*, implies that the firm takes risk on the dynamic nature of a given sociopolitical issue. While the sociopolitical issue is currently divisive, the firm bets that many stakeholders will in the medium or long run turn around and begin to support the firm's position. In this view, the firm expects its SPI to be a good investment, as many stakeholders are expected to eventually support the firm's sociopolitical involvement. In other words, the firm views the situation as an opportunity for commercial gain by improving its reputation or standing with segments of stakeholders who could eventually side with the issue. Thus, ex ante, the firm perceives the stakeholders who will likely side with its position on a given issue as more valuable than other groups of stakeholders who might be alienated by the firm's actions.

In contrast, the second perspective, *stakeholder pressure recognition*, describes situations in which stakeholders pressure the firm into unwanted actions. In this perspective, the coalescing of stakeholder groups, often by social movements, coerces firms into an uncomfortable position in which they are cornered into

engagement for or against a certain issue. In this supposition, firms have previously assessed whether engagement in such issues is of benefit and have decided against it. Yet when stakeholder groups apply direct or even strong indirect pressure, firms recognize that continued neutrality may create more harm than good. Therefore, in response to stakeholder pressures, firms will initiate SPI.

However, while the importance of stakeholders in influencing firm strategy is noted, the management literature observes that the influence of management is also salient. Managers tend to wield enormous power in firm decision making, and their decisions can be influenced by their personal biases and, at times, adversely affect shareholders. Thus, we contend that an internal driver for firm engagement in SPI is the influence of firm management who act opportunistically, not necessarily in pursuit of financial gain but rather to support their personal views. This third viewpoint incorporates agency theory, asserting that managers engage in SPI to pursue their own ideological bent. While a manager's personal ideology may coincide with that of some stakeholders, in this case managers rather than stakeholders are driving firms to engage in SPI, thus creating potential agency issues. Further, given these personal motivations, the explanation of their behavior differs, as managers are neither calculating expected future gains for the firm nor responding to pressure to act. Because the manager agrees or sympathizes with a certain ideology or relates to a particular issue, he or she chiefly pursues an SPI strategy to satisfy his or her personal consumptive motivations rather than the other concerns previously highlighted.

Regardless of which motivating perspective applies, whether a firm engages in SPI is contingent on institutional environments enabling such activities (Scott, 2004). As Mellahi

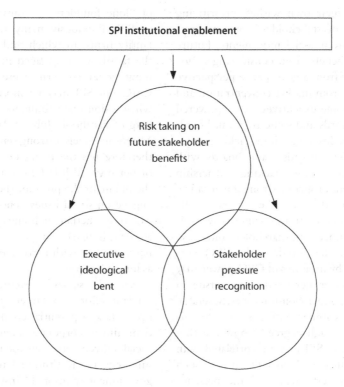

Figure 1: Theoretical Perspectives for SPI

and colleagues (in press) noted, the institutional context, including social, legal, and political considerations, can have a profound impact on a firm. The institutional environment affects managerial discretion, the organization's operational ability, and a variety of social actors; it also affects the three highlighted perspectives and facilitates opportunity for firms to engage in SPI activities. These concepts are highlighted in Figure 1.

Figure 1 underscores the motivational rationale for SPI using a number of distinct views. These views suppose that firm engagement is premised on the power of stakeholders, perception of management, and institutional environments that influence these relationships.

[...]

Discussion and Future Research

This article articulates a definition of SPI as distinct from CPA and CSR, and offers theoretical rationales for firm SPI and a typology for classifying SPI. This discussion clarifies the nature of firm involvement in this unique set of issues and offers avenues for future research as well as perspectives for policy makers and practitioners.

We suggest additional areas in which scholars may seek to investigate further. First, the importance of firm decision makers cannot be overstated, as the CEO and other executives are either choosing to position the firm according to their own wishes, prioritizing the demands of stakeholders, or interpreting pressure from social movements. Future research may benefit from considering sociopolitical issues from a governance perspective as well. Aside from market concentration and profitability, some executives are empowered by friendly boards and some by weak boards (including, for instance, those lacking independence), "busy boards," and boards with limited incentive (e.g., lacking ownership stakes). Without proper or strong governance, executives would more likely pursue self-interest in taking positions on alternative SPIs that might conflict with shareholder interests.

For instance, the latitude of the CEO; perhaps indicated by measures of CEO power, may allow the CEO greater freedom to pursue an agenda regarding sociopolitical issues. Several of our examples examine CEOs who were founders or possess a high degree of power within their firms. Thus, SPI may be correlated with other aspects that result in CEO power, such as strong firm performance or the presence of CEO duality or a CEO founder (such as Facebook's Mark Zuckerberg). Accordingly, the CEO's personal beliefs may manifest in his or her vision of the company and attention to a particular set of stakeholders who would benefit from changes in the normative standing of the sociopolitical issue (e.g., Chin et al., 2013). Thus, the CEO may view a certain sociopolitical issue as greatly important to appease a particular group of stakeholders he or she identifies as important (Briscoe et al., 2014). However, company shareholders could view this group as a less important stakeholder. As a result, going forward, return-focused shareholders may seek to select a CEO not active in sociopolitical activities or may discipline or isolate a CEO who is more involved in these types of issues.

In this way, future research may also empirically test for the extent to which the rise of "lone founders" is contributing to a rise in SPI. Previously many firms emerged as family firms, in which multiple members of the family were engaged in governance and reputational concerns were associated with CSR, but SPI may be most likely to occur when a dominant founder—such as Zuckerberg of Facebook, Jobs of Apple, or Gates of Microsoft—feels a strong sense of control and therefore has the firm's positions mirror his or her own. While CEOs may be lauded by the public or the press for their willingness to engage on social issues, scholars may wish to examine whether such engagement is associated with particular personality traits (e.g., narcissism) or with particular incentives, such as long-term pay.

Second, social movements make significant efforts to target large institutional investors as a potential conduit for achieving their aim of corporate change. In particular, social movements now focus on large pressure-sensitive institutional investors, such as government-sponsored institutional investors (e.g., government pension funds and sovereign wealth funds) to help fulfill their agendas. For example, Norway's $880 billion sovereign wealth fund censors and removes large companies from its portfolio because of environmental concerns, including even carbon pollution (Carner & Grennes, 2010). Institutional investors are thus more responsive today to social movement demands and require the companies in which they invest to diversify away from activities deemed irresponsible.

Hence in this situation, social movements essentially create a secondary agency SPI motivation to signal their alignment with the sociopolitical objectives of particular institutional investors (Connelly, Tihanyi, Certo, & Hitt, 2010). While our primary focus is on large, publicly traded entities, it is also worth noting the emergence of B-corporations; given their emphasis on social goals, it is unclear whether a CEO of such an entity would be given more or less license to determine company positions on particular sociopolitical issues as they arise. We suggest that future research consider whether the emergence of B-corporations increases or decreases the appetite the public has for traditional C-corporations being involved in sociopolitical issues.

Therefore, SPI is ripe for further research and raises interesting debates within various theoretical domains. Within social movement theory, scholars assume that a firm is a target because of activities featured in the firm's operations (Davis & Thompson, 1994). However, in this sociopolitical issue discussion, this aspect of the theory may now be shifting away from quantifiable metrics of firm strength toward softer assessments of power. Social movements now target firms because they are a symbol of institutional power and have the ability to exert government and social influence—even if firm activities do not directly contribute to the problem. Thus, research using social movement theory could examine whether a firm is more likely to acquiesce to social movement demands or threats from activists hostile about issues that are indirectly related to the firm. In essence, an indirect connection to an issue should allow the firm greater flexibility on the issue, allowing the firm to quickly pivot positions while satisfying demands at minimal actual costs. Because firm operations or policies remain unchanged, it is easier for firms to initiate SPI rather than other external demands that affect the value chain and threaten profitability. Future research could therefore examine the shifts in firm tactics that favor appeasement of social movements.

Additionally, future research could explore how a firm's economic power affects the likelihood of SPI (in terms of both pressure tactics and proactive engagement). A firm's economic power and viability would likely affect its ability to engage in SPI activities. Such powers can stem from firm size, profitability, number of employees, reputation and legitimacy in society, and political influence (Josefy, Kuban, Ireland, & Hitt, 2015). For firm engagement in SPI, business must have a platform to communicate and the society must include some individuals who are receptive to the involvement of businesses in political and social discourse. This most likely occurs when firms are highly influential economically and parlay this power to influence sociopolitical issues.

A further area for future exploration is the intersection of shareholder activism and SPI. In a number of countries, protections for minority shareholders have increased, creating new opportunities for shareholders to engage company management. For instance, legislation recently enacted in India requires Indian companies to use electronic voting for shareholder resolutions, as well as enhancing the disclosure and voting on related party transactions. These changes may provide tools not only for minority shareholders to protect their financial interests, but also for activists to exert pressure on firms to take other actions. Accordingly, executives may more carefully weigh the extent to which they pursue SPI.

Last, research could also examine the antecedents of a multinational's sociopolitical position. This research may include imprinting effects from the home country or founder and factors that would moderate the adoption of these stances, such as whether firms tend to default toward the most conservative or the most liberal position when operating across multiple countries. Further, this suggests the possibility that the same firm may advocate in opposing directions on the same issue in different national environments. Accordingly, we should examine how a firm's multinational strategies contribute to the homogeneity or heterogeneity of its sociopolitical engagement.

In addition to theoretical development, this article also has implications for policy makers and practitioners. Policy makers should recognize the increased role that corporations and their leaders play in shaping public discourse. One recent experiment provides preliminary evidence that a well-known CEO of a well-known firm could sway the opinions of individuals (Chatterji & Toffel, 2016). Certainly celebrities have been used in public advertising campaigns in the past to raise awareness of important issues, such as health or driving under the influence of alcohol. Policy makers should recognize the more prominent role that activist firms are now playing and seek to establish forums on which to jointly engage firms and individuals.

Practitioners may wish to more actively consider stakeholder values in their evaluation of the firm's brand and culture. For instance, some brands may be more closely tied to a particular image, such as "socially progressive." Subsequent firm positions would then need to be aligned with the existing firm identity. While some of these actions may be considered part of the corporate citizenship of the firm, stakeholders likely evaluate such actions differently. In this context, recent research on stakeholder cognition (Barnett, 2014) may be helpful. Because sociopolitical stances evoke significant emotional responses from individuals, individuals are likely to comingle perceptions of SPI when interpreting firm actions and assessing firm character. Accordingly, multinational firms may need to assess the congruency of their sociopolitical positions with the aims of the firm and preferences of its stakeholders.

Questions

1. The authors begin their essay by stating that most involvement of business in nonmarket areas was assumed to be driven by an economic motivation (such as lobbying for legislation, regulation, and so forth). Is this level of involvement ethically problematic? Why or why not?

2. Why would firms utilize their power and resources to take positions on inflammatory social and political issues, especially as they come under fire and are boycotted for such activity? Do you want to purchase products and services from businesses that have taken public (and economic) stances on issues that you support? Why or why not?

3. Given the deep pockets and economic advantages that big firms wield, is their ability to contribute to political candidates a problem? Is this different from taking a stance on a controversial issue in the social realm? Why or why not?

References

Ahlquist, M. (2016, August 28). Lush Australia: Fighting for the freedom to love. LUSH corporate web site. Retrieved from https://uk.lush.com/article/lush-australia-fighting-freedom-love

Alzola, M. (2013). Corporate dystopia: The ethics of corporate political spending. *Business & Society*, 52, 388–426.

Barnett, M. L. (2014). Why stakeholders ignore firm misconduct: A cognitive view. *Journal of Management, 40*(3), 676–702.

Baron, D. P. (2001). Private politics, corporate social responsibility, and integrated strategy. *Journal of Economics & Management Strategy, 10*(1), 7–45.

Baysinger, B. D. (1984). Domain maintenance as an objective of business political activity: An expanded typology. *Academy of Management Review, 9,* 248–258.

Bonardi, J. P., & Keim, G. D. (2005). Corporate political strategies for widely salient issues. *Academy of Management Review, 30*(3), 555–576.

Brewer, P. R. (2003). The shifting foundations of public opinion about gay rights. *Journal of Politics, 65*(4), 1208–1220.

Briscoe, F., Chin, M. K., & Hambrick, D. (2014). CEO ideology as an element of the corporate opportunity structure for social activists. *Academy of Management Journal, 57,*1786–1809.

Campbell, J. L. (2007). Why would corporations behave in socially responsible ways? An institutional theory of corporate social responsibility. *Academy of Management Review, 32*(3), 946–967.

Carner, M., & Grennes, T. (2010). Sovereign wealth funds: The Norwegian experience. *World Economy, 33*(4), 597–614.

Carroll, A. B. (1979). A three-dimensional conceptual model of corporate performance. *Academy of Management Review, 4*(4), 497–505.

Chang, A. (2011, April 8). Target, gay rights supporters at odds over how to settle dispute. *Los Angeles Times.* Retrieved from http://articles.latimes.com/2011/apr/08/business/la-fi-target-gay-20110409

Chatterji, A. K., & Toffel, M. W. (2016). *Do CEO activists make a difference? Evidence from a field experiment* (Harvard Business School Working Paper No. 16–100). Boston: Harvard Business School.

Chin, M. K., Hambrick, D. C., & Trevino, L. K. (2013). Political ideologies of CEOs: The influence of executives' values on corporate, social responsibility. *Administrative Science Quarterly, 58,* 197–232.

Clarkson, M. B. E. (1995). A stakeholder framework for analyzing and evaluating corporate social performance. *Academy of Management Review, 20,* 92–117.

Connelly, B. L., Tihanyi, L., Certo, S. T., & Hitt, M. A. (2010). Marching to the beat of different drummers: The influence of institutional owners on competitive actions. *Academy of Management Journal 53*(4), 723–742.

Cooper, C. A., & Knotts, H. G. (2006). Region, race, and support for the South Carolina Confederate flag. *Social Science Quarterly, 87*(1), 142–154.

Davis, G. F., & Thompson, T. A. (1994). A social movement perspective on corporate control. *Administrative Science Quarterly, 39,* 141–173.

Epstein, E. M. (1987). The corporate social policy process: Beyond business ethics, corporate social responsibility, and corporate social responsiveness. *California Management Review, 29*(3), 99–114.

Fombrun, C., & Shanley, M. (1990). What's in a name? Reputation building and corporate strategy. *Academy of Management Journal, 33*(2), 233–258.

Forman, J. (1991). Driving Dixie down: Removing the Confederate flag from Southern state capitols. *Yale Law Journal, 101*(2): 505–526.

Freeman, R. E. (1984). *Strategic management: A stakeholder approach.* Boston: Pitman.

Getz, K. A. (1997). Research in corporate political action integration and assessment. *Business & Society, 36,* 32–72.

Goggin, M. (1993). *Understanding the new politics of abortion.* Newbury Park, CA: Sage.

Gorman, M. (2015, July 7). Whataburger to armed customers: Keep your guns at home. *Newsweek.* Retrieved from http://www.newsweek.com/whataburger-saysno-guns-351018

Gusfield, J.R. (1963). *Symbolic crusade: Status politics and the American temperance movement.* Urbana, IL: University of Illinois Press.

Hadani, M., & Schuler, D. A. (2013). In search of El Dorado: The elusive financial returns on corporate political investments. *Strategic Management Journal, 34*(2), 165–181.

Haider-Markel. D. P., & Meier, K. J. (1996). The politics of gay and lesbian rights: Expanding the scope of the conflict. *Journal of Politics, 58*(2), 332–349.

Hilgartner, S., & Bosk, C. L. (1988). The rise and fall of social problems: A public arenas model. *American Journal of Sociology, 94*(1), 53–78.

Hillman, A. J., & Hitt, M. A. (1999). Corporate political strategy formulation: A model of approach, participation, and strategy decisions. *Academy of Management Review, 24*(4), 825–842.

Hillman, A. J., & Keim, G. D. (2001). Shareholder value, stakeholder management, and social issues: What's the bottom line? *Strategic Management Journal, 22*(2), 125–139.

Hillman, A. J., Keim, G. D., & Schuler, D. (2004). Corporate political activity: A review and research agenda. *Journal of Management, 30*(6), 837–857.

Horvath, E. (2015, October 21). *How can companies support refugees in Europe?* London: Business and Human Rights Resource Centre. Retrieved from https://www.business-humanrights.org/en/how-can-companiessupport-refugees-in-europe

Jing, S. (2015, February 25). Ctrip offers staff loans to pay fines. *China Daily.* Retrieved from http://www.china daily.com.cn/kindle/2015–02/25/content_19650077.htm

Josefy, M., Kuban, S., Ireland, R. D., & Hitt, M.A. (2015). All things great and small: Organizational size, boundaries of the firm, and a changing environment. *Academy of Management Annals, 9,* 715–802.

Kim, S. (2015, June 10). Alibaba helps gay couples in China get married in US. ABC News. Retrieved from http://abcnews.go.com/Business/alibaba-helps-gay-couples-china-married-us/story?id=31669124

Lax, J. R., & Phillips, J. H. (2009). Gay rights in the states: Public opinion and policy responsiveness. *American Political Science Review, 103*(3), 367–386.

Luker, K. (1984). *Abortion and the politics of motherhood.* Berkeley, CA: University of California Press.

Margolis, J. D., & Walsh, J. P. (2003). Misery loves companies: Rethinking social initiatives by business. *Administrative Science Quarterly, 48*(2), 268–305.

Matten, D., & Moon, J. (2008). "Implicit" and "explicit" CSR: A conceptual framework for a comparative understanding of corporate social responsibility. *Academy of Management Review, 33*(2), 404–424.

McKinsey & Company. (2009, November). Tackling sociopolitical issues in hard times: McKinsey Global Survey Results. Retrieved from http://www:mckinsey.com/global-themes/leadership/tackling-sociopolitical-issues-in-hard-times-mckinsey-global-survey-results

McWilliams, A., & Siegel, D. (2001). Corporate social responsibility: A theory of the firm perspective. *Academy of Management Review, 26*(1), 117–127.

Mellahi, K., Frynas, J. G., Sun, P., & Siegel, D. (in press). A review of the nonmarket strategy literature toward a multi-theoretical integration. *Journal of Management.* doi: 10.1177/0149206315617241

Meyer, J. W., Scott, W. R., Cole, S., & Intili, J. (1978). Instructional dissensus and institutional consensus in schools. In J. W. Meyer (Ed.), *Environments and organizations* (pp. 290–305). San Francisco: Jossey-Bass.

Nice, D. C. (1988). State deregulation of intimate behavior. *Social Science Quarterly, 69,* 203–211.

Pew Research Center. (2014, September 22). Public sees religion's influence waning. Washington, DC: Author. Retrieved from www.pewforum.org/2014/09/22

Phillips, R., Freeman, R. E., & Wicks, A. C. (2003). What stakeholder theory is not. *Business Ethics Quarterly, 13*(4), 479–502.

Picchi, A. (2016, April 21). Why Target is taking stand on transgender people and bathrooms. CBS News. Retrieved from http://www.cbsnews.com/news/why-target-is-taking-stand-on-transgender-people-and-bathrooms/

Reinecke, J., & Ansari, S. (2016). Taming wicked problems: The role of framing in the construction of corporate social responsibility. *Journal of Management Studies, 53*(3), 273–298.

Ripley, R. B., & Franklin, G. A. (1991). *Congress, the bureaucracy, and public policy*. Homewood, IL: Dorsey.

Roach, B. (2007). *Corporate power in a global economy*. Medford, MA: Tufts University Global Development and Environment Institute. Retrieved from http://www.ase.tufts.edu/gdae/education_materials/modules/Corporate_Power_in__Global_Economy.pdf

Rodriguez, P., Siegel, D. S., Hillman, A., & Eden, L. (2006). Three lenses on the multinational enterprise: Politics, corruption and corporate social responsibility. *Journal of International Business Studies, 37*(6), 733–746.

Scherer, A. G., Rasche, A., Palazzo, G., & Spicer, A. (2016). Managing for political corporate social responsibility: New challenges and directions for PCSR 2.0. *Journal of Management Studies, 53*(3), 273–298.

Scott, W. R. (2004). Institutional theory. In G. Ritzer (Ed.). *Encyclopedia of social theory* (pp. 408–414). Los Angeles: SAGE Publications.

Sethi, S. P. (1979). A conceptual framework for environmental analysis of social issues and evaluation of business response patterns. *Academy of Management Review, 4*(1), 63–74.

Shaffer, B. (1995). Firm-level responses to government regulation: Theoretical and research approaches. *Journal of Management, 21*, 495–514.

Stone, D. A. (2012). *Policy paradox: The art of political decision making*. New York: W.W. Norton.

Sun, P., Mellahi, K., & Wright, M. (2012). The contingent value of corporate political ties. *Academy of Management Perspectives, 26*, 68–82.

Zardkoohi, A. (1985). On the political participation of the firm in the electoral process. *Southern Economic Journal, 51*, 804–817.

Notes

1. Michael Nalick, Matthew Josefy, Asghar Zardkoohi, and Leonard Bierman, "Corporate Sociopolitical Involvement: A Reflection of Whose Preferences?," *Academy of Management Perspectives* 30, no. 4 (2016): 386–403.

2. 501(c)(4) groups are typically referred to as "social welfare" groups and are nonprofit organizations that play a very influential role in politics.

3. For example, in the United States, displaying the Confederate flag is a controversial yet common practice in many Southern states (Forman, 1991). To many citizens of these states, the flag symbolizes their history and elicits deep emotional pride. However, residents of Northern states and many ethnic groups view the flag as a symbol of a dark, bigoted past, and over the years general attitudes throughout the United States have shifted toward this view (Cooper & Knotts, 2006). After a racially motivated shooting of nine African-Americans in a church in Charleston, South Carolina, in 2015, Southern states began to remove the flag from public buildings, and major retailers, including Walmart, Sears, and Amazon, halted the sale of Confederate flags, losing millions of dollars of profitable retail inventory.

2. The Social Responsibility of Business Is to Increase Its Profits[1]

Milton Friedman

THIS IS MILTON FRIEDMAN'S classic essay, where he is often cited as claiming that the only responsibility of business is to maximize profits; however, this is not accurate. Friedman (1912–2006) does emphasize the profit motive, yet he also requires that the firm's executives not only conform to laws and ethical custom but also further stay "within the rules of the game ... without deception or fraud." Friedman spends much of this essay arguing against "social responsibility," conflating the same with "socialism." He further canonizes the "free market" as a place where purely voluntary actions occur, where no individual can force another into acting, and where it is "hard for 'evil' people to do 'evil.'"

WHEN I HEAR BUSINESSMEN speak eloquently about the "social responsibilities of business in a free-enterprise system," I am reminded of the wonderful line about the Frenchman who discovered at the age of 70 that he had been speaking prose all his life. The businessmen believe that they are defending free enterprise when they declaim that business is not concerned "merely" with profit but also with promoting desirable "social" ends; that business has a "social conscience" and takes seriously its responsibilities for providing employment, eliminating discrimination, avoiding pollution and whatever else may be the catchwords of the contemporary crop of reformers. In fact they are—or would be if they or anyone else took them seriously—preaching pure and unadulterated socialism. Businessmen who talk this way are unwitting puppets of the intellectual forces that have been undermining the basis of a free society these past decades.

The discussions of the "social responsibilities of business" are notable for their analytical looseness and lack of rigor. What does it mean to say that "business" has responsibilities? Only people can have responsibilities. A corporation is an artificial person and in this sense may have artificial responsibilities, but "business" as a whole cannot be said to have responsibilities, even in this vague sense. The first step toward clarity to examining the doctrine of the social responsibility of business is to ask precisely what it implies for whom.

Presumably, the individuals who are to be responsible are businessmen, which means individual proprietors or corporate executives. Most of the discussion of social responsibility is directed at corporations, so in what follows I shall mostly neglect the individual proprietors and speak of corporate executives.

In a free-enterprise, private-property system, a corporate executive is an employee of the owners of the business. He has direct responsibility to his employers. That responsibility is to conduct the business in accordance with their desires, which generally will be to make as much money as possible while conforming to the basic rules of the society, both those embodied in law and those embodied in ethical custom. Of course, in some cases his employers may have a different objective. A group of persons might establish a corporation for an eleemosynary purpose—for example, a hospital or a school. The manager of such a corporation will not have money profit as his objectives but the rendering of certain services.

In either case, the key point is that, in his capacity as a corporate executive, the manager is the agent of the individuals who own the corporation or establish the eleemosynary institution, and his primary responsibility is to them.

Needless to say, this does not mean that it is easy to judge how well he is performing his task. But at least the criterion of performance is straight-forward, and the persons among whom a voluntary contractual arrangement exists are clearly defined.

Of course, the corporate executive is also a person in his own right. As a person, he may have many other responsibilities that he recognizes or assumes voluntary—to his family, his conscience, his feelings of charity, his church, his clubs, his city, his country. He may feel impelled by these responsibilities to devote part of his income to causes he regards as worthy, to refuse to work for particular corporations, even to leave his job, for example, to join his country's armed forces. If we wish, we may refer to some of these responsibilities as "social responsibilities." But in these respects he is acting as a principal, not an agent; he is spending his own money or time or energy, not the money of his employers or the time or energy he has contracted to devote to their purposes. If these are "social responsibilities," they are the social responsibilities of individuals, not of business.

What does it mean to say that the corporate executive has a "social responsibility" in his capacity as businessman? If this statement is not pure rhetoric, it must mean that he is to act in some way that is not in the interest of his employers. For example, that he is to refrain from increasing the price of the product in order to contribute to the social objective of preventing inflation, even though a price increase would be in the best interests of the corporation. Or that he is to make expenditures on reducing pollution beyond the amount that is in the best interests of the corporation or that is required by law in order to contribute to the social objective of improving the environment. Or that, at the expense of corporate profits, he is to hire "hardcore" unemployed instead of better qualified available workmen to contribute to the social objective of reducing poverty.

In each of these cases, the corporate executive would be spending someone else's money for a general social interest. Insofar as his actions in accord with his "social responsibility" reduce returns to stockholders, he is spending their money. Insofar as his actions raise the price to customers, he is spending customers' money. Insofar as his actions lower the wages of some employees, he is spending their money.

The stockholders or the customers or the employees could separately spend their own money on the particular action if they wished to do so. The executive is exercising a distinct "social responsibility," rather than serving as an agent of the stockholders or the customers or the employees, only if he spends the money in a different way than they would have spent it.

But if he does this, he is in effect imposing taxes, on the one hand, and deciding how the tax proceeds shall be spent, on the other.

This process raises political questions on two levels: principle and consequences. On the level of political principle, the imposition of taxes and the expenditure of tax proceeds are governmental functions. We have established elaborate constitutional, parliamentary and judicial provisions to control these functions, to assure that taxes are imposed so far as possible in accordance with the preferences and desires of the public—after all, "taxation without representation" was one of the battle cries of the American Revolution. We have a system of checks and balances to separate the legislative function of imposing taxes and enacting expenditures from the executive function of collecting taxes and administering expenditure programs and from the judicial function of mediating disputes and interpreting the law.

Here the businessman—self-selected or appointed directly or indirectly by stockholders—is to be simultaneously legislator, executive and jurist. He is to decide whom to tax by how much and for what purpose, and he is to spend the proceeds—all this guided only by general exhortations from on high to restrain inflation, improve the environment, fight poverty and so on and on.

The whole justification for permitting the corporate executive to be selected by the stockholders is that the executive is an agent serving the interests of his principal. This justification disappears when the corporate executive imposes taxes and spends the proceeds for "social" purposes. He becomes in effect a public employee, a civil servant, even though he remains in name an employee of a private enterprise. On grounds of political principle, it is intolerable that such civil servants—insofar as their actions in the name of social responsibility are real and not just window dressing—should be selected as they are now. If they are to be civil servants, then they must be elected through a political process. If they are to impose taxes and make expenditures to foster "social" objectives, then political machinery must be set up to make the assessment of taxes and to determine through a political process the objectives to be served.

This is the basic reason why the doctrine of "social responsibility" involves the acceptance of the socialist view that political mechanisms, not market mechanisms, are the appropriate way to determine the allocation of scarce resources to alternative uses.

On the grounds of consequences, can the corporate executive in fact discharge his alleged "social responsibilities"? On the one hand, suppose he could get away with spending the stockholders' or customers' or employees' money. How is he to know how to spend it? He is told that he must contribute to fighting inflation. How is he to know what action of his will contribute to that end? He is presumably an expert in running his company—in producing a product or selling it or financing it. But nothing about his selection makes him an expert on inflation. Will his holding down the price of his product reduce inflationary pressure? Or, by leaving more spending power in the hands of his customers, simply divert it elsewhere? Or, by forcing him to produce less because of the lower price, will it simply contribute to shortages? Even if he could answer these questions, how much cost is he justified in imposing on his stockholders, customers, and employees for this social purpose? What is his appropriate share and what is the appropriate share of others?

And, whether he wants to or not, can he get away with spending his stockholders', customers' or employees' money? Will not the stockholders fire him? (Either the present ones or those who take over when his actions in the name of social responsibility have reduced the corporation's profits and the price of its stock.) His customers and his employees can desert him for other producers and employers less scrupulous in exercising their social responsibilities.

This facet of "social responsibility" doctrine is brought into sharp relief when the doctrine is used to justify wage restraint by trade unions. The conflict of interest is naked and clear when union officials are asked to subordinate the interest of their members to some more general purpose. If union officials try to enforce wage restraint, the consequence is likely to be wildcat strikes, rank-and-file revolts and the emergence of strong competitors for their jobs. We thus have the ironic phenomenon that union leaders—at least in the U.S.—have objected to Government interference with the market far more consistently and courageously than have business leaders.

The difficulty of exercising "social responsibility" illustrates, of course, the great virtue of private competitive enterprise—it forces people to be responsible for their own actions and makes it difficult for them to "exploit" other people for either selfish or unselfish purposes. They can do good—but only at their own expense.

Many a reader who has followed the argument this far may be tempted to remonstrate that it is all well and good to speak of Government's having the responsibility to impose taxes and determine expenditures for such "social" purposes as controlling pollution or training the hard-core unemployed, but that the problems are too urgent to wait on the slow course of political processes, that the exercise of social responsibility by businessmen is a quicker and surer way to solve pressing current problems.

Aside from the question of fact—I share Adam Smith's skepticism about the benefits that can be expected from "those who affect to trade for the public good"—this argument must be rejected on grounds of principle. What it amounts to is an assertion that those who favor the taxes and expenditures in question have failed to persuade a majority of their fellow citizens to be of like mind and that they are seeking to attain by undemocratic procedures what they cannot attain by democratic procedures. In a free society it is hard

for "evil" people to do "evil," especially since one man's good is another's evil.

I have, for simplicity, concentrated on the special case of the corporate executive, except only for the brief digression on trade unions. But precisely the same argument applies to the newer phenomenon of calling upon stockholders to require corporations to exercise social responsibility (the recent G.M. crusade for example). In most of these cases, what is in effect involved is some stockholders trying to get other stockholders (or customers or employees) to contribute against their will to "social" causes favored by the activists. Insofar as they succeed, they are again imposing taxes and spending the proceeds.

The situation of the individual proprietor is somewhat different. If he acts to reduce the returns of his enterprise in order to exercise his "social responsibility," he is spending his own money, not someone else's. If he wishes to spend his money on such purposes, that is his right, and I cannot see that there is any objection to his doing so. In the process, he, too, may impose costs on employees and customers. However, because he is far less likely than a large corporation or union to have monopolistic power, any such side effects will tend to be minor.

Of course, in practice the doctrine of social responsibility is frequently a cloak for actions that are justified on other grounds rather than a reason for those actions.

To illustrate, it may well be in the long-run interest of a corporation that is a major employer in a small community to devote resources to providing amenities to that community or to improving its government. That may make it easier to attract desirable employees, it may reduce the wage bill or lessen losses from pilferage and sabotage or have other worthwhile effects. Or it may be that, given the laws about the deductibility of corporate charitable contributions, the stockholders can contribute more to charities they favor by having the corporation make the gift than by doing it themselves, since they can in that way contribute an amount that would otherwise have been paid as corporate taxes.

In each of these—and many similar—cases, there is a strong temptation to rationalize these actions as an exercise of "social responsibility." In the present climate of opinion, with its widespread aversion to "capitalism," "profits," and "soulless corporation" and so on, this is one way for a corporation to generate goodwill as a by-product of expenditures that are entirely justified in its own self-interest.

It would be inconsistent of me to call on corporate executives to refrain from this hypocritical window-dressing because it harms the foundations of a free society. That would be to call on them to exercise a "social responsibility"! If our institutions, and the attitudes of the public make it in their self-interest to cloak their actions in this way, I cannot summon much indignation to denounce them. At the same time, I can express admiration for those individual proprietors or owners of closely held corporations or stockholders of more broadly held corporations who disdain such tactics as approaching fraud.

Whether blameworthy or not, the use of the cloak of social responsibility, and the nonsense spoken in its name by influential and prestigious businessmen, does clearly harm the foundations of a free society. I have been impressed time and again by the schizophrenic character of many businessmen. They are capable of being extremely far-sighted and clearheaded in matters that are internal to their businesses. They are incredibly short-sighted and muddle-headed in matters that are outside their businesses but affect the possible survival of business in general. This short-sightedness is strikingly exemplified in the calls from many businessmen for wage and price guidelines or controls or income policies. There is nothing

that could do more in a brief period to destroy a market system and replace it by a centrally controlled system than effective governmental control of prices and wages.

The short-sightedness is also exemplified in speeches by businessmen on social responsibility. This may gain them kudos in the short run. But it helps to strengthen the already too prevalent view that the pursuit of profits is wicked and immoral and must be curbed and controlled by external forces. Once this view is adopted, the external forces that curb the market will not be the social consciences, however highly developed, of the pontificating executives; it will be the iron fist of Government bureaucrats. Here, as with price and wage controls, businessmen seem to me to reveal a suicidal impulse.

The political principle that underlies the market mechanism is unanimity. In an ideal free market resting on private property, no individual can coerce any other, all cooperation is voluntary, all parties to such cooperation benefit or they need not participate. There are no values, no "social" responsibilities in any sense other than the shared values and responsibilities of individuals. Society is a collection of individuals and of the various groups they voluntarily form.

The political principle that underlies the political mechanism is conformity. The individual must serve a more general social interest—whether that be determined by a church or a dictator or a majority. The individual may have a vote and say in what is to be done, but if he is overruled, he must conform. It is appropriate for some to require others to contribute to a general social purpose whether they wish to or not.

Unfortunately, unanimity is not always feasible. There are some respects in which conformity appears unavoidable, so I do not see how one can avoid the use of the political mechanism altogether.

But the doctrine of "social responsibility" taken seriously would extend the scope of the political mechanism to every human activity. It does not differ in philosophy from the most explicitly collectivist doctrine. It differs only by professing to believe that collectivist ends can be attained without collectivist means. That is why, in my book *Capitalism and Freedom*, I have called it a "fundamentally subversive doctrine" in a free society, and I have said that in such a society, "there is one and only one social responsibility of business—to use its resources and engage in activities designed to increase its profits so long as it stays within the rules of the game, which is to say, engages in open and free competition without deception or fraud."

Questions

1. What is Friedman's full claim of the responsibility of business? Why do you think he is known only for the profit maximization?

2. How does Friedman equate social responsibility with socialism? Why is this inaccurate?

3. If, as Friedman states, business has a responsibility to "stay within the rules of the game," to not deceive or commit fraud, and if the firm's agents are further bound to conform to the legal and ethical custom rules of society, then is it really true that the only responsibility of business is to increase profits, even according to Friedman's own argument?

4. Given Friedman's own words regarding the firm's responsibility, would his argument endorse a firm's involvement in passing stricter environmental regulation for businesses, *if* this was an ethical custom and expectation of society?

Note

1. *New York Times Magazine*, September 13, 1970.
   Copyright © 1970 by the New York Times Co.

3. How Organizations Socialize Individuals into Evildoing[1]

John M. Darley

JOHN M. DARLEY (1938–2018) addresses the gist of the clichéd claim that business ethics is an oxymoron, as well as the recognition that once individuals cross the firm's physical threshold, many of their ethics are left behind. Darley draws from fields within the social sciences, especially psychology, to explain how employees are drawn into participation in harmful corporate actions and, in so doing, are changed into evil people. Darley's focus is on corporate crime, which he defines as "crime perpetrated by an organization against either the general public, that segment of the public that uses the organization's products, or the organization's own workers." After such a harm is found to exist, and a worker engages in any form of cover-up or maintaining those harmful practices, he argues that the worker crosses over into evildoing. This can be explained partially by the "momentum" an action takes on. Darley explains that once any action is undertaken, such as a firm's commitment to manufacture a product, it takes an unusual amount of energy to stop that action, even though there is clear intent and people continue to be harmed. Further, once a process has begun, the burden of proof as to why an action should be changed, even if there is serious evidence that the product is harmful, is placed on the challenger to the action.

WHEN MEMBERS OF OUR culture think of acts of doing harm, we tend to think of an individual harm-doer who lies behind these acts, an evil individual who seeks out others and acts on them in evil ways. Perhaps our canonical image is that of a serial murderer, who moves among us, hidden behind the mask of normality, destroying the innocent. Contrary to cultural stereotypes, however, most harmful actions are not committed by palpably evil actors carrying out solitary actions. Instead, the typical evil action is inflicted on victims by individuals acting within an organizational context. Indeed, it may be difficult to identify the individual who perpetrates the evil; the harm may seem to be an organizational product that bears no clear stamp of any individual actor. Further, if we look within the organization and identify the individual who seems most closely connected with the harm—for instance, the foreman who orders the workers down the dangerous mine shaft or the corporate executive who orders the marketing of an unsafe drug—we do not find an individual whom we recognize as evil but someone who looks rather like us. We encounter again what Hannah Arendt (1963) found so striking about the Nazi mass murderer Adolph Eichmann, the banality and ordinariness of an individual whom we expected to be demonic. But that person has been changed; through participation in the organization, the individual has undergone a conversion process and become an autonomous participant in harmful actions.

… many evil actions are not the volitional products of individual evildoers but rather essentially organizational products that result when complex social forces interact to cause individuals to commit multiple acts of terrible harm. In that process, the individuals committing the harm are themselves changed. They become evil, although they still do not show the demonic properties that are suggested by our conventional views of evil.

The realization that the specific social forces that alter individuals are produced in organizations raises several questions. What sorts of organizations enlist their members in doing harm? How do the organizational forces work to produce harmful actions? How does the sustained application of those forces alter the character of those individuals caught up in the harmful activities? …

In recent years, a number of books have appeared whose authors are concerned with what they call "corporate crime." For many years "white-collar crime" has been the subject of study, but that category was found to blur the distinctions among what proved to be several quite different kinds of crime. White-collar crime was initially analyzed as crimes committed by workers or executives against their firms. Gradually, a second class of crime has come to be noticed. Corporate crime is crime perpetrated by an organization against either the general public, that segment of the public that uses the organization's products, or the organization's own workers. A generally accepted definition of corporate crime, proposed by Marshall Clinard, is "a form of collective rule breaking in order to achieve the organizational goals." Clinard, a seminal

figure in the field, encases a critical realization in this definition, the recognition that some crimes are committed because they fulfill an organization's goals.[2]

Examples of all kinds of organizational crimes are easy to find. Recall the design of the Ford Pinto, sold for years by a company in which many executives were aware that it had a gas tank likely to rupture in low-speed rear-end crashes and incinerate its passengers (Dowie 1987). Consider the Robins Corporation, marketing a contraceptive product that it knew caused disastrous medical consequences to many who used it (Mintz 1985; Perry and Dawson 1985). Recall Watergate or the Iran-Contra affair. Consider the silence of Morton Thiokol executives who were aware of the dangers to the space shuttle O-rings at low launch temperatures (Kramer 1992). Consider any number of defense contractors who have delivered military weapons systems to the Defense Department with faked safety and effectiveness tests and substandard internal electronic components (Vandivier 1987). Recall the suppression of the growing evidence about numerous design flaws in the nuclear reactors used to generate electricity in this country (Faulkner 1987).

There are also numerous examples of organizations that harm their workers. Think about executives who continued to have shipyard workers work with asbestos long after its carcinogenic properties were known to the officials, or government bureaucrats who kept uranium miners at work long after the dangers of that occupation were known to the bureaucrats. Think of miners with black lung disease or cotton mill workers with brown lung disease.

Nor do we lack examples of organizations' inflicting harm on large segments of the general public. Our government's atomic bomb tests in Nevada rained radioactivity on all citizens downwind of the test sites. Matt

Tallmer (1987) details the incredible chemical dumping practices of the Hooker Chemical Corporation, the perpetrator of the Love Canal disaster, which have left a trail of illegal poisonous chemical waste in ground water sources from Long Island to California. The Allied Chemical Company, manufacturers of Kepone, a substance known to be toxic, set up a dummy corporation as an "independent contractor" to continue the manufacture of it; the dust from the plant obscured the sight of the plant from those members of the public unlucky enough to be nearby. Eventually, one hundred miles of fisheries on the James River had to be closed because of concentrations of Kepone in the fish. Interestingly, another organization—the city of Hopewell, in which the plant was located—was so obviously complicit in hiding the damages caused by the chemical that it received fines as well.

What this list demonstrates is that many corporations have inflicted serious harm on either the general public, consumers of the products that they manufacture, or the workers engaged in the manufacture of those products. I will return later in the chapter to the question of whether these organizations are in some identifiable way "rogue organizations" or whether these patterns of doing harm are somehow latent in all organizations. First, however, it is important to examine the mechanisms by which organizations—conglomerates of individuals—come to inflict harm on the public, consumers, and workers.

How Individuals Are Drawn into Doing Harm

Analyzing evildoing in organizations and the ways in which organizations cause individuals to do evil requires a number of constructs that can be drawn from various fields of social science. Within organizations, processes leading to both the *diffusion of information* and the *diffusion and fragmentation of responsibility* are

common. Barry Staw's (Staw and Ross 1987) notion of *sunk costs* is also necessary; organizations get committed to courses of action, and the individuals who generated those courses of action are reluctant or unwilling to change them, even when others would see the need for change. Many decisions prove to have *implicit ethical components* that are hidden at the moment of decision, arising only later, after decisions are made. Finally, there are *concrete decision options* that face various individuals in the organization, as it continues the course of doing harm even after some of the ethical issues become clear. These decision options generally are presented within the context of a hierarchically structured organization, business or governmental, *on which people are dependent for their livelihoods.* Following orders, within some ill-defined sphere of activities, is legitimated, and failure to follow orders may put one's livelihood at risk.

Diffusion and Fragmentation of Information and Responsibility

The processes of diffusion and fragmentation of information and diffusion and fragmentation of responsibility often go together, but they can be separated analytically. When it is discovered that a product that has been designed, manufactured, advertised, and sold is harmful to its consumers, there is often a long period during which the evidence of harm accumulates. This knowledge that the product is potentially or actually harmful may come into various divisions of the organization but remain in an unassembled state, because those divisions are not in perfect communication with each other on issues of harm. The organization has all the information needed to draw the inference of harm, but because the information is not pulled together and put in front of a competent individual, the organization can be said not to know that the product is harmful.[3] And, of course, responsibility requires knowledge. If I do not know that harm is risked, then I am not responsible for preventing that harm.*

The Dalkon Shield case (Mintz 1985; Perry and Dawson 1985) provides a clear illustration of the compartmentalization of information within a corporation. The Dalkon Shield was an intrauterine contraceptive device, manufactured and aggressively sold by the Robins Company, that proved to be potentially dangerous to women who used it. One of the product's many dangers was a "string" attached to it, actually a bundle of plastic fibers enclosed by a sheath, that was designed to facilitate removal. If the sheath was perforated, the string drew bacteria into the uterus, causing sometimes life-threatening infections.

Because of successful sales efforts, more shields needed to be manufactured, and the company assigned production to a subsidiary plant, the ChapStick plant. The quality control supervisor of that plant, on his own initiative, "examined under a microscope samples of Shields ready to be shipped from the ChapStick plant. He found tiny holes through which body fluids from the vagina could escape into the sterile uterus if wicked up the string" (Perry and Dawson 1985, 81). This information apparently did not get to the relevant medical personnel, however, so that when reports of infections from Shield users began to come in from doctors who had implanted the Shield, the medical personnel initially did not connect these infections with the infection-transmission path documented by the person in the manufacturing arm of the subsidiary. Different elements of relevant information, coming in via different organizational components that are not tightly connected to each other in communication networks, often do not reach the relevant decision makers. Those who make decisions are often walled off from information that is vital

to good decision making.

Another example of this failure of communication occurred in the months prior to the space shuttle Challenger disaster. NASA test engineers at the Marshall Space Flight Center wrote a series of memos expressing concerns about potential failures in the pressure seal system, but the project manager did not pass these memos on to the Morton Thiokol engineers (Kramer 1992).

It may seem somewhat naive to cite these examples as cases of an organization's simply "not knowing" of harm their product causes, and with good reason. If a product is producing a profit for the corporation, then one can see a great advantage in the corporation's "not knowing" that the product is dangerous when it in fact knows it full well. Later in the chapter several cases will be considered in which individuals moved to preserve what we might call "strategic ignorance," both for themselves and for the corporation, and the corporate structure was organized to facilitate that claim.[4]

Diffusion of responsibility is another source of organizational harmdoing. Who has responsibility for actions that are seen to cause harm? And what kinds of responsibilities can be said to exist? It has been said that success has a million parents, but failure is an orphan. Assume that an organization has produced and marketed a drug that is later found to have terrible side effects—thalidomide or DES, for instance. One unit can develop a drug and assume that it will be tested for side effects. Another unit can arrange for it to be marketed, assuming that those safety checks have been completed. Those who have actually carried out the tests of the drug may be aware that their tests were incapable of determining side effects with any sort of precision. (In the case of DES, for instance, a drug given to pregnant women to reduce nausea during pregnancy, it was only many years later that the drug was discovered to produce long-term negative effects, including increased likelihood of cancer, among young women who had been in utero when their mothers were taking the drug.) No individual intentionally brought about these side effects. More to the point, it is difficult to identify exactly who within the organization was responsible for allowing the mistake to happen. This fact seems to become recognized in those few cases in which members of organizations are put on trial for the consequences of their actions; rarely are any specific individuals found criminally liable.

Responsibility not only diffuses but also fragments. Within a hierarchical organization, an individual's responsibility is defined by the duties that accrue to that person's position within the organization. If, for example, my role is to receive reports of drug trials being carried out at remote sites in one region, my responsibility may be to summarize and integrate those results and pass them to somebody else, to be merged with reports from other regions. I may know enough to know that one or two reports from my region could point toward worrying side effects, but I do not know if the reports from other regions confirm them. "I have done my duty" if I just flag my worries as I pass the reports along.

One more fact about information flow and individual responsibility is worth noticing. Information about product dangers, as opposed to information about product sales, markets, and profits, is generally "abnormal" information, and the mechanisms for its analysis are not well developed. One can anticipate that it will be collected in less-organized ways, and responsibilities for its analysis will be assigned in less well considered ways.[5]

In organizations, persons are sometimes assigned formal responsibilities for safety monitoring, but are more informally instructed to disregard those responsibilities, or simply learn to disregard them under time demands to complete other activities more directly connected with production. Following a methane explosion that killed twenty-five miners, it was discovered that, although it was formally part of the foreman's responsibilities to test the methane concentration in the shaft, he had long since been socialized not to make the tests and to fake the record entries about them (Caudill 1987).

In the pressure of the moment, definitions of responsibility are often renegotiated downward to accommodate those pressures. During the fateful conference between Morton Thiokol (MTI) engineers and officials and NASA officials, MTI initially recommended that the shuttle Challenger not be launched because of the possible effects of the cold launch temperatures on the O-ring seals. NASA officials would not launch with this recommendation on record but pressured MTI to reverse its recommendations. The MTI management people caucused. One MTI official said that "a management decision was required" (Kramer 1992, 232). One of the MTI engineers was told "to take off his engineering hat and put on his manager's hat" (p. 232), apparently in an attempt to recast the engineers' definitions of their responsibility to the MTI managers; they were to elevate themselves above their own engineering knowledge and function as compromising decision makers.

The reframing also gave the MTI engineers only a reporting responsibility. The two MTI engineers fought their way back into the discussion, arguing not to launch, but were overridden; the MTI executives decided the "data were, indeed, inconclusive, and that they would now recommend that the launch proceed" (Kramer 1992, 232–33). Roger Boisjoly, one of the engineers, summarized the way that the decision was finally framed by the meeting: "This was a meeting where the determination was to launch, and it was up to us to prove be-yond a shadow of a doubt that it was not safe to do so. This is the total reverse to what the usual is ... in a pre-flight review" (quoted in Kramer, p. 233). Thus the task of the engineers was to prove the launch would fail, and it was the responsibility of the MTI executives to allow launch unless that proof was conclusive.

This last move illustrates a critically important maneuver in the reframing of responsibility. In our culture we have a de-cision rule that might be called "innocent until proven guilty." The chance for some motivated creativity in the application of this rule arises in identifying which of the deci-sion options counts as "innocent" and which as "guilty." In real-life decision cases, people skilled at framing can claim that the burden of proof falls on those arguing for a decision other than the one proposed. In this instance, "launch" was more or less forcibly equated with "innocent," the option to be chosen unless it could be proven wrong beyond all possible doubt. The standard framing of the launch decision was not to launch unless the engineers were convinced that the launch was safe, but the NASA officials reversed this framing. The launch was going to happen un-less the engineers could prove that it would fail. They couldn't prove that it would fail, so they launched, and the launch failed. One is reminded of the Clarence Thomas–Anita Hill hearings, in which the issue was cast as requiring a vote for Thomas's appointment to the Supreme Court unless Hill's allegations could be proved true. Conservatives on the panel framed the hearing task as a court case; either Thomas could be proved guilty or he was "innocent" and therefore, by an odd twist of reasoning, entitled to a position on the Su-preme Court.

The assignment of the burden of proof is a very powerful manipulation of decision rules, and one that is more malleable than is widely recognized. Kramer and Messick (chapter 3 [in original volume]) suggest that everyone is able to adopt the perspective of the "intuitive lawyer," trained to muster sincerely all the ar-guments for one point of view.

Take this a step further. Sometimes the burden of proof is a genuine burden in both time and costs. If one organization produces a product, it accrues the profits from that product. If we require that a second organiza-tion prove that the product is unsafe, where does that second organization acquire the resources to carry out the relevant tests? Do government agencies assume that burden? If so, profits remain with the producer, while certain of the costs that might be associated with the product fall on the public. Further, general reductions in government resources may remove the resources necessary to con-duct those tests.

To summarize, the information that a prod-uct or an act is potentially harmful may exist within the organization in an unassembled form, so that the decision makers are unaware of the potential harm. Those who report to the decision makers may be very aware of the possibilities of harm, but feel that they have fulfilled their responsibilities by providing in-formation to the decision makers from which the possibilities of harm might be inferred by careful analysis. Further, the framing of the de-cision is important. To halt ongoing processes because of potential future harms requires an action, a decision, while allowing the continu-ation of normal processes requires no action. Thus, the decision to intervene is often framed as requiring clear and overwhelming evidence before it is taken, while the original construc-tion, that processes should not go forward, or products should not be produced, unless their safety is assured, is lost.

It is important to see how these processes, each of which can work independently to pro-duce harm, can also work together to magnify the possibilities of harm. If evidence of potential harm is unassembled and fragmented, and if those who feel that it might occur are not responsible for making that point, then the evidence of potential harm will rarely rise to a level of conclusiveness to convince those caught up in the pressure to continue with normal activities to suspend those activities because of the possibility of dimly perceived, poorly documented, harms.

One further point needs to be made. Because these processes so naturally occur within any organization, it is possible to set up conditions that promote their occurrence and create an organization "optimized" for the denial of the harms that are done. We will consider examples of this later....

Abstract Harm and Tangible Gains

In many organizational settings in which an action is taken that will ultimately result in harm to others, there is initially no overt target of the actions committed, no salient other human who is seen to be a victim of the action. The person who decides to let the assembly line use substandard cord in the fabrication of radial tires is not thinking of the accidents that the decision could cause but simply keeping the assembly line moving. "Product safety" at this point is an abstract concern standing in the way of the all-important goal of production. If one examines the steps from product design to the eventual emergence of that product from the assembly line into the marketing organization, there are remarkably few times that the question of the effects of the product on the consumer is raised. Instead, competing issues involving product conceptualization, profits, and fulfillment of production standards are generated and dominate the analysis....

To summarize, a number of frameworks generated by requirements of the manufacturing process and the need to have that process run on time, efficiently, and at low cost dominate the analysis of those who are building and even designing a product. The end user of the product is not represented or is represented only in the limited role of "consumer." Since a good many of the forces that cause people to avoid doing harm to others rely on the salient presence of specific or specifically imagined victims, if such victims are not present then restraining forces are considerably weakened. "These opposing forces rest ultimately on the actor's awareness that he or she is connected to a victim," as Herbert Kelman and Lee Hamilton remark in their percipient way (1989, p. 313). Individuals within the organization can lose sight of the fact that people may be harmed in the course of fulfilling the other goals of the corporation or bureaucracy.

All the factors that I cite can be combined in powerful ways. When members of an organization do see potential dangers to workers or customers that might result if certain decisions taken by the organization are put into effect, then those who advocate different decisions are often given the heavy burden of proof discussed earlier.

In most organizations, it is legitimate to give orders, and the cost of disobeying those orders may be loss of one's livelihood. If, therefore, the organization orders—or is seen as ordering—certain actions in furtherance of the production of dangerous products, those involved face some extremely difficult decisions. The Dalkon Shield case provides us with a specific example (Perry and Dawson 1985). At the time that production was begun in the ChapStick plant, the product had previously been manufactured at other plants and widely marketed, and the company was already aware of several safety concerns about the Shield and deep in the process of denial and fabrication. Crowder, the quality control supervisor of the ChapStick plant, reported his concerns about wicking to his superior, Ross, and did not get a satisfactory response. He then did a series of experiments proving that the string would wick water—and thus, by inference, bacteria—up into the bodies of women users and reported the results of these experiments to his superiors.

Ross was anything but pleased. He angrily reminded Crowder that the string was not Crowder's responsibility and that he should leave it alone. Crowder told Ross that he could not, in good conscience, keep quiet about something that he felt could cause infection in the women who wore the Shield. "Your conscience doesn't pay your salary," Crowder says Ross replied. Ross also told Crowder that he was being insubordinate for pursuing this matter; if he valued his job he would do as he was told and forget about the string.

Note the psychology of the presentation of the issue to Crowder; although done with a certain crudeness, it was not atypical. First, he was giving Crowder an order. Second, he was offering Crowder a framing of the whole matter as "not his responsibility" along with a threat of job loss to induce him to accept that framing. We will see this threat and framing maneuver in play again, although done with more sophistication; it is quite commonly used in organizations.

Not many respond to it as Crowder did, however. He continued to protest, carried his protests higher up, had them rebuffed, and was finally "let go" in a corporate reorganization some years later. He is a genuine hero, and his heroism cost him his job. Those looking at what happens to whistle-blowers— individuals who report their concerns to outside groups—report similar fates.

Notice I said that if the superiors in the corporation are *seen as* ordering the continuation of a certain course of action, subordinates may feel compelled to fall in with that course of action. In a corporation, to wait to do something until one is ordered to do so can be thought of as a failure of initiative, or worse, a desire to put the superior on the spot. Many subordinates, in those circumstances, can be expected to intuit what orders they would be given and "follow them in advance." One suspects that this is what happened in the Pinto case; the subordinates intuited Iacocca's response to the possibility of fuel tank disasters and rolled straight ahead. An obvious point follows: This process gives the superiors the chance to deny ultimate responsibility for the product or harm while continuing to exert pressure for the harm to continue. Management by objectives, if those objectives largely involve making profits, has a good deal to answer for.

Many organizations have in place some form of corporate code, which generally includes both ethical strictures and references to "fair play" and a "superior product for customers." They also have in place incentive and bonus schemes, competition between various sales forces, promotions based on winning those competitions, and so on. Corporate workers are going to pay particular attention to what happens when those two aspects of corporate culture clash.

Several years ago, the Xerox Corporation, apparently pleased with its new articulation of its corporate code, gave permission for a reporter to observe one of its sales groups in action, no doubt expecting a glowing report on its system. Instead, the reporter (Dorsey 1994) demonstrated how the intense pressures for profits caused the sales force to push their customers to buy machines of far greater capabilities than the customers needed—or often could pay for. They succeeded, it seems, by telling customers about the Xerox Company code, convincing them that the existence of the code somehow ensured that their recommendations of oversized and expensive machines were in the customers' best interest. Corporations that put in place a corporate ethics code and do not consider its relationship to existing corporate practices and bonus and promotion systems seem to me to be engaging in window dressing of a particularly cynical sort. Specifically, unless decisions are made that elevate the ethics code over the profit and promotion system, such codes are empty. And in the end, the corporate structure that promulgated the code loses creditability, and its further pronouncements, in the unlikely event they are sincerely intended, will be ignored.

The Time Course of Decision Making: Hindsight and Cover-Ups

Let us assume that, suddenly and dramatically, it is discovered that the actions of a corporation have already harmed large classes of others. It is now realized that given certain actions of the organization, harmful outcomes are inevitable. Pintos are actually rear-ended, gas tanks actually catch on fire, and actual passengers are horribly killed. Memos exist within the corporation in which design engineers warn about exactly these possibilities. To an outsider observing the situation, it seems apparent that those in the organization must have been aware of the risks of harm, and thus somewhere there must be evil individuals who have knowingly brought about that harm.[6] And sometimes this is true. There are such evil people. One thinks of the bosses of the Film Recovery System Corporation, which recovered precious metals using processes that involved highly dangerous chemicals, taking almost no safety precautions to shield the workers from the effects of these chemicals, and hiring illegal immigrants who

spoke little English so they would not understand what was happening or be able to reveal it to others (Frank 1987).

Let us consider a more charitable scenario, that the negative outcomes simply could not have been anticipated; an unexpected side effect of a drug might be an example. Or, more likely, let us say that some evidence existed calling attention to the negative outcomes but that this evidence was not given sufficient attention within the organization. The Pinto case is a perfect example. The people within the organization were focusing on other organizational goals and, because they were "negligent, hurried, sloppy, or overworked" (Kelman and Hamilton 1989, 312), missed the meanings of the danger signals. They were also subject to the interpersonal processes we have considered involving breakdowns of communications and diffusion of responsibility.

However it comes about, harmful actions have been committed, and now the individuals who had some responsibility for those actions have become aware of those consequences. There are several psychological points to be made here. First, the decisions that now face organizational decision makers are not clean ones: they do not offer perfectly positive outcomes and typically involve choosing the least bad option. All too often, the organization does not have the choice of not embarking on a course of action that will cause harm; it has already done so, and some people actually have been harmed. Thus some guilt and liability have already been incurred. The decision makers may have been implicated in decisions that will now be seen as, at best, ill-considered; even if they are not, others to whom they owe loyalties may be implicated.

The role of the well-known hindsight bias here is likely to be destructive. In the classic demonstration of hindsight, an observer to a series of events consistently finds the actual outcome of the events as having been more probable than it was in fact (Fischhoff 1975). It is as if the observer is saying, "Well, of course that was going to happen. I could see it from the beginning." To those responsible for corporate disasters, as to the outside observers, it must seem that the disastrous outcomes were foreseeable once evidence for the disasters has accumulated. Some rather bizarre dynamics ensue. If the organizational decision makers admit, to themselves and others, that harmful outcomes are actually occurring in the present, then because it will seem to them that these outcomes were foreseeable, they will feel culpable for "knowingly" allowing them to happen. And they will certainly feel that others will think the negative consequences were foreseeable and condemn them for allowing them to occur. This dynamic creates a strong pressure for the decision makers to deny that the harmful outcomes are genuine, or genuinely caused by the product in question.

This denial by the higher-ups in the organization may cause subordinates, who are more concretely faced with the evidence of harms, to interpret that denial as a tacit instruction to lie about the existence of those harms or minimize the role of the organizational action in producing them. As the reader will recognize, this begins the process of "the cover-up," a frequent occurrence in organizational harm-doing, and one whose dynamics we may be able to illuminate here.

Certainly organizational case studies give us an enormous number of examples of corporations attempting to cover up harm-doing. Three things strike me about cover-ups. First, they are highly unlikely to succeed. The evidence has become so clear about the harmfulness of the product, and so many people within the organization know about it, that it will surely leak out. Second, cover-ups themselves frequently provide conclusive

evidence of the wrongfulness of the actions taken in the first place. So for a company to engage in cover-ups—cover-ups that are also likely to get detected—is a further and more foolish error. Third, because these first two points are true, we can infer that when individuals engage in cover-ups, there is a great deal of pressure on them to do so. Standardly, this pressure is thought to come from fear of negative publicity, possibly leading to job loss or civil or criminal penalties. But we can see how it could also stem from an initial shocked denial on the part of the organizational decision makers, that they were the sort of persons who would bring about disastrous harm to others—a denial aimed at maintaining their own image of self, although quickly coupled with concerns for the more standard consequences as well.[7]

To my mind, this is a critical point in the destruction of the ethical character of those decision makers. The cover-up is now engaged in consciously and deliberately. Covering up past evidence is also likely to lead to maintaining the current practices that have brought about the harms, at least for as long as the cover-up is successful. It is at this point that I think that this organizational actor becomes evil, becomes an independent perpetrator of further negative acts that are now knowingly done. When, for example, individuals in corporations discovered that the asbestos used by its workers was leading to a high rate of cases of lung cancer, they sometimes chose to conceal that fact, perhaps because they were concerned with all the factors we have discussed and the liabilities they would incur if they revealed that information. But they also continued having the workers work in what they now knew were dangerous settings. They now were doing intentionally what they had previously done unknowingly.

As cover-ups continue, other processes of concealment are likely to be necessary, even ones that were perhaps not contemplated by the organizational actor at the moment of choice between acknowledging and denying the harms done. The evidence of previous harms had better disappear. Those in the organization who might discover the previous harms had better be hindered or muzzled. Meetings have to be held to rehearse the next set of lies to be told. All the participants have to get their stories straight. A number of repugnant moral actions are found to be required following the initial decision to conceal the initial harm.

What has been described here, I claim, is a very important way in which an individual can be caught up in a harmful process and altered by it. Whatever else might be said about the Nazi doctor who stood on the selection ramp, designating those who would live and those who would die, he knew that was what he was doing. But often an individual within an organization carries out what seem to be routine actions but later turn out to have negative consequences that in retrospect seem to have been foreseeable. Whether that person denies the negativity of the consequences, denies the responsibility for those consequences, or conceals those consequences and becomes meshed in a widening circle of actions necessary to continue the concealment, he or she has become an independent and autonomous perpetuator of the harms done. That person has become evil. What is important to see here is that the process is an after-the-fact one, in which the person faces not the prospective choice to do harm but the retrospective choice to acknowledge that his or her actions have already done harm. The more it becomes clear that those harms should have been foreseen, the more guilt, shame, and blame are acquired in the acknowledgment of past harms. But often failing to acknowledge past harms means continuing to commit those harms in the present....

All corporations, because of their emphasis on corporate profitability, and because of the complex interactional forces that I have documented, have the potential to drift into harm-doing, with the corrupting forces I have described leading to a continuation of those actions rather than a halting of them.

Corporate Socialization and the Reproduction of Corruption

Like other innovations, innovations of corrupt practices spread. The question of how corrupt organizations reproduce themselves and grow in size is quite easy to answer. Organizations such as the ones involved in the Nazi death camps have not one but two outputs. They produce death, and they produce individuals who become autonomously capable of and committed to producing other deaths. The evil individuals they produce become available for the reproduction of the evil organization. Concretely, SS officers and soldiers who first murdered civilians on the eastern front could be used to staff the concentration camps and initiate and socialize other individuals into the new organizations. Older soldiers in the U.S. Army in Vietnam made clear to the new inductees how the war was really to be fought. On the trading floor of Salomon Brothers, cohorts of new recruits were reliably socialized into patterns of betrayal of customers' interests.

Let us examine how corporations come to the perception of their customers as fools to whom no moral obligations are owed. Michael Lewis (1989) provides a richly detailed description of how those joining the stock brokerage firm of Salomon Brothers were socialized into regarding their customers as sheep to be fleeced. A good many customers' lives were destroyed in the process, as his book reveals. In one incident described by Lewis, he sold a customer a bond that somebody within his brokerage house advised him was a good bond to sell. The bond fell, taking the customer down with it, and Lewis learned that it was indeed "a good bond to *sell*"; the brokerage house held a large inventory on it and had inside information that it was going to fall. The firm therefore moved the bonds out of inventory onto customers, letting the customers take the ensuing loss, to the delight of the brokerage house. Lewis left the firm, but the socialization process that he has described corrupted many others. Of course, it was intended to. As Lewis's book makes clear, the firm's managers were willing participants in the corruption and made calculated efforts to corrupt the lower-level staff. For example, higher commissions were paid for moving poor-quality bonds off on unwary customers, a fact of which the customers were kept unaware. One is reminded of the case of the now-defunct Lincoln Savings and Loan Company, which sold a good many non-government-insured investments to elderly customers, while allowing the customers to believe that they were insured. Many lost their life savings.

The corporate case of Salomon Brothers also illustrates how unethical practices diffuse through an industry. The salespeople who successfully foisted bonds off on customers made a good deal of money for the corporation, with two consequences. First, the status hierarchy within the organization was reordered. Those individuals were rewarded with large bonuses, a signal that the corporation approved their trading practices, and others in the corporation vied for assignment to their departments. Since entry to the departments in which these practices went on was prestigious and likely to be highly profitable, newcomers were easily socialized into these ways. Newcomers went along with the attitudes professed and the practices employed or faced the threat of rejection and expulsion. The financial and psychological incentives for corruption were high.

A second consequence involved the spread of corruption to competing firms. Inevitably, word of Salomon's success got around in the small world of Wall Street. Many of the firm's major sales people were raided by other trading firms, who offered them astronomical salaries and bonuses in order to break into the areas that the Salomon staff had pioneered. That the migrants from Salomon Brothers took with them to their new firms the innovative financial instruments that they had invented was explicitly expected; that they also took with them their attitudes of scorn for the customer seems highly likely. In this way a single evil organization can produce a surplus of individuals who go on to replicate the organization in other settings. Given that those who have been "processed" by the evil organization have been brought to a point where they use their intelligence in the service of their evil actions, the replicated organizations can be counted on to transcend whatever local obstacles stand in the way of reproducing the results of the original organization.

The realization that evildoing organizations have the capacity for self-replication provides part of the explanation for one of the facts that so bewilder us about corporate corruption: why so many individuals are willing to participate in a corporation's immoral activities. One answer is that individuals in organizations are "trained" (an unfortunate use of this word) at different times, and those trained earlier train others, providing a multiplicative effect on the pool of available evildoers. They also carry their corruption to other firms. All this follows from what we know about normative socialization of individuals within organizations. It is the task of the individual, when entering an organization, to catch on to the real operating practices and rules of the organization, and this is a skill that most people acquire....

Questions

1. What is the process of a person becoming evil in a firm?

2. When does a person finally become evil in Darley's argument? Do you agree that at this point one is evil, or perhaps earlier? Explain your answer.

3. Why do you think that people often leave their ethics at the door to their place of employment and act with different (or no) ethics in business compared to their private life?

References

Arendt, H. 1963. *Eichmann in Jerusalem: A Report on the Banality of Evil*. New York: Viking.

Braithwaite, R.B. 1955. *Theory of Games as a Tool for the Moral Philosopher*. Cambridge: Cambridge University Press.

Caudill, H.M. 1987. "Manslaughter in a Coal Mine." In *Corporate Violence*, ed. S.L. Hills. Totowa, NJ: Rowman & Littlefield.

Dowie, M. 1987. "Pinto Madness." In *Corporate Violence*, ed. S.L. Hills. Totowa, NJ: Rowman & Littlefield.

Faulkner, P. 1987. "Exposing Risks of Nuclear Disaster" [Confessions of a Whistle Blower]. In *Corporate Violence*, ed. S.L. Hills. Totowa, NJ: Rowman & Littlefield.

Fischhoff, B. 1975. "Hindsight = Foresight: The Effect of Outcome Knowledge on Judgment Under Uncertainty." *Journal of Experimental Psychology: Human Perception and Performance*, 1: 289–99.

Frank, N. 1987. "Murder in the Workplace." In *Corporate Violence*, ed. S.L. Hills. Totowa, NJ: Rowman & Littlefield.

Kelman, H.C., and V.C. Hamilton. 1989. *Crimes of Obedience: Towards a Social Psychology of Authority and Responsibility*. New Haven: Yale University Press.

Kramer, R.C. 1992. "The Space Shuttle *Challenger* Explosion: A Case Study of State-Corporate Crime." In *White Collar Crime*, ed. K. Schlegel

and D. Weisburd. Boston: Northeastern University Press.

Kramer, R.M., and D.M. Messick. 1996. "Ethical Cognition and the Framing of Organizational Dilemmas: Decision Makers as Intuitive Lawyers." In *Codes of Conduct: Behavioral Research into Business Ethics*, ed. David M. Messick and Ann E. Tenbrunsel. New York: Russell Sage Foundation.

Lewis, M. 1989. *Liar's Poker*. New York: Norton.

Mintz, M. 1985. *At Any Cost: Corporate Greed, Women, and the Dalkon Shield*. New York: Pantheon Books.

Perry, S., and J. Dawson. 1985. *Nightmare*. New York: Macmillan.

Staw, B., and J. Ross. 1987. "Behavior in Escalation Situations: Antecedents, Prototypes, and Solutions." In *Research in Organizational Behavior*, Vol. 9, ed. L. Cummings and B. Staw. Greenwich, CT: JAI Press.

Tallmer, M. 1987. "Chemical Dumping as a Corporate Way of Life." In *Corporate Violence*, ed. S.L. Hills. Totowa, NJ: Rowman & Littlefield.

Vandivier, K. 1987. "Why Should My Conscience Bother Me?" In *Corporate Violence*, ed. S.L. Hills. Totowa, NJ: Rowman & Littlefield.

Notes

1. John M. Darley, "How Organizations Socialize Individuals into Evildoing," in *Codes of Conduct: Behavioral Research into Business Ethics*, ed. David M. Messick and Ann E. Tenbrunsel. © 1996 Russell Sage Foundation, 112 East 64th Street, New York, N.Y. 10021. [Edited.]

2. Braithwaite (1985) suggests that the term "organizational crime" is a more useful one, because it recognizes the similarity between the ways in which public organizations and corporations can offend.

3. Note the complexities of speaking of an organization's "knowing." Knowing is a concept we apply to individuals, and its meaning loses precision when we extend it to organizations. When we are engaging in moral analysis, which is centrally an analysis of individual cognition, our thoughts become confused when we try to examine "the morality of organizations." While this idea cannot be fully developed here, two comments are in order. First, we are frequently forced to analyze the organization as individual by the "legal fiction" of the organization as individual. Second, the moral confusion engendered when we attempt to analyze an organization by the moral standards we use for individuals frequently works to the advantage of the organization that is doing harm.

* Editor's Note: Responsibility requires knowledge; however, "not knowing" is not sufficient for excusing responsibility. "Ignorance of the law is no excuse." Not being able to obtain knowledge would be sufficient.

4. One of the arguments for an aggressive product liability recovery system, pursued by contingency-compensated lawyers, is that it lessens the utility of strategic ignorance for the corporation. If the corporation is going to be hit with large punitive damage awards, then the sooner it can discover that it is incurring this liability the sooner it can cease to incur it.

5. This would not be true of corporations making products in which the possibility of danger is generally known to be present. Makers of prescription drugs are the paradigmatic example. They should have in place routine systems to collect, process, and analyze information about product safety—side effects, in their terms. From an unsystematic scanning of newspaper reports on the topic, I am not greatly impressed by their efficiency.

6. This is the problem that I have found with most books on these acts of corporate malfeasance. Naturally they are written after the fact, by investigative reporters who are so horrified at the outcome that they tend to assume that the major actors in bringing it about begin as evildoers. They thus miss the process that transforms ordinary people into evildoers.

7. Lawyers and insurance companies play an important role in this process. Corporate leaders regard tort lawyers and personal injury lawyers as devils waiting to pounce on innocent corporate mistakes, extracting huge sums for pitiable plaintiffs. Thus they are sometimes led to deny product liability to avoid providing ammunition for legal suits. "May 24, 1974. In an internal progress report for the Dalkon Shield, Roger Tuttle (lawyer) is quoted as being opposed to removing the Shield from the market because such an action would be a 'confession of liability'" (Perry and Dawson 1985). As I understand it, those reviewing the evidence for the existence of huge settlements find them not so huge, generally reduced on appeal, and not unreasonable as a source of punitive damages on corporations whose mistakes were repeated and not at all innocent.

Lawyers participate at several other nodes in corporate decision processes after harm has been alleged. First, they counsel the corporation about how to deal with possible admissions about the harm done. The content of their counsel would be hard to study systematically; there are cases in which the advice has been to stonewall. Second, they counsel insurance companies that may be the eventual payers of claims on the manufacturing corporation. In that role, too, their advice is sometimes less than morally admirable. In the Dalkon Shield case, lawyers for both the Robins Company and Aetna, their insurers, advised denial and delay and worked the court system to produce delay (Mintz 1985).

4. Automation, Work, and the Achievement Gap

John Danaher and Sven Nyholm

JOHN DANAHER, LECTURER AT the National University of Ireland, Galway, and Sven Nyholm, assistant professor of philosophy at Utrecht University in the Netherlands, tackle the increasing automation in the workplace and what it means to human achievement and responsibility. They discuss what meaningful work (economic work) is and how it provides people with a sense of self-worth, autonomy, and identity. Much like Marx, who bemoaned worker alienation under capitalism, workers under automation (depending on the level and amount) become alienated from the meaning of their previous jobs. Danaher and Nyholm close by arguing that humans may find other forms of achievement from which to draw meaning and an identity.

1. Introduction

ON THE 27TH OF November 2019, Lee Sedol announced his retirement from the professional world of Go-playing.[1] Sedol was an 18-time world champion of the fiendishly difficult Chinese strategy game. He was a long-time celebrity in his home country of South Korea, but attained international notoriety in March 2016 when he was defeated, 4–1, in a five-game challenge match against *Alpha Go*, an artificially intelligent Go-playing computer program, created by the software company DeepMind.

Sedol did not announce his retirement with a sense of satisfaction about what he had achieved in his career. He did so out of a sense of despair. He told reporters that he felt there was no point in continuing with the game because he could no longer compete with the machines. He had come to the realisation that he was no longer "at the top even if [he became] the number one".[2] Sedol's sense of despair at the rise of artificial intelligence is shared by others. Commenting on Sedol's loss to *Alpha Go*, Carissa Veliz notes that there is something deeply sad about the whole affair. Clearly, the creation of Alpha Go marked a significant technological breakthrough, but it also signalled the loss of something important to humankind. As she put it:[3]

> "What is most surprising about the match is that the outcome did not feel like a win for humanity. It did not feel similar to when we conquer a disease, or when the first human being landed on the moon. It felt like we might be losing more than what we might be gaining."

In the remainder of this article, we examine what it is we might be losing to machines like Alpha Go. We focus, in particular, on what we might be losing in the world of work.

As AI and other automating technologies are increasingly used to augment and replace human task performance in the workplace, there is, we argue, a significant risk to the value of human achievement. This, in turn, makes it difficult for us to ensure that people have access to meaningful work. In addition, while this argument focuses specifically on the impact of automation in the workplace, it may have broader implications for the impact of automation on human life more generally.

We present our analysis in four stages. First, we clarify in a bit more detail the phenomenon of workplace automation and the idea of meaningful work. Second, we look at the nature of human achievement and identify four conditions that need to be satisfied for us to say that a human or group of humans has achieved some goal or end. Third, we argue that workplace automation undermines our capacity to individually and collectively satisfy these conditions for achievement, thus resulting in an 'achievement gap' in the automated workplace. Fourth, we consider the policy implications of this argument. In particular, we outline ways of retaining a space for human achievement in the automated workplace, or otherwise guaranteeing meaningfulness in the workplace. In doing so, we draw explicit analogies between our concern about the emergence of achievement gaps in the workplace and closely related policy concerns about responsibility gaps arising from the widespread use of automating technologies (e.g. [26, 28, 29, 37, 38]). Indeed, we suggest that the achievement gaps we discuss in this paper are a type of positive responsibility gap, and are thus the inverse of the negative responsibility gaps that have attracted a lot of attention in debates about roboethics and AI ethics.

2. Meaningful Work and Workplace Automation

This paper is concerned with the impact of automation on our capacity for achievement in the workplace. To better understand both the scope and limitations of our analysis, it is important to clarify what we understand by the phenomena of work and automation, and then to consider the relationship between achievement and meaningful work.

Let us start with the idea of work. Work is a tricky phenomenon to define [10], ch 2): some people adopt expansive definitions of work, defining it in such a way that it includes virtually all activities that humans might engage in; others adopt more limited definitions, tying work to specific, economic activities. For present purposes, we use one of these more limited definitions. We focus on what has been called work 'in the economic sense' [13, 17]. This form of work consists of skills (physical, cognitive, and emotional) that are performed by individuals in return for some kind of economic reward. The skills performed by the individuals can be referred to as work-related 'tasks'. Usually, these tasks are performed with a view to producing a commodifiable output, either a good or service, that can be bought and sold on a market. Workplaces then consist of individuals, either singly or collectively, performing work-related tasks with a view to producing such commodifiable outputs.

Work, so-defined, often has a nested task structure. That is to say, one set of work-related tasks can produce an output that then contributes to another set of tasks that contributes to the overall commodifiable output. For example, in the manufacture of a complex technological product like a computer, one group of workers may be focused on producing designs or plans for the computer, another group may be focused on manufacturing the microchips, another on the casing and packaging, and still another may be dedicated to marketing and selling the product. Each group of workers produces an output that contributes to the overall commodifiable output. The nested task structure is due to specialisation within the workplace, a phenomenon highlighted long ago by Adam Smith [34]. The nested task structure of work is important when it comes to discussions of achievement in the workplace because the output of a given task (or set of tasks) is one of the key variables when it comes to assessing the value of the achievement associated with the work. A worker may, for example, be contributing to some valuable commodifiable output through their individual work tasks, but the outputs associated with their work tasks may be relatively trivial or easy to achieve. If this is the case, their particular work task may not be a significant source of achievement. To take an extreme example, a legal secretary whose only job is to staple together sheaves of paper is doing something that is relatively trivial and easy to achieve. It is not clear how their job could be a significant source of achievement (though we return to examples like this, again, in Sect. 5).

Work, so-defined, is not the same thing as a job though they are related concepts. A job is a defined role within a workplace associated with the performance of a more or less specified collection of work-related tasks. Put another way, work is a general condition under which tasks get performed (namely, a condition of economic reward), whereas a job is a collection of such tasks associated with a specific workplace identity. These tasks must be connected to the commodifiable output, but apart from that they can be more or less arbitrarily defined. For example, one person might have the job of being a personnel manager within a workplace, but the precise set of work-related tasks relevant to this job might

shift and change over time. At one point in time, the major focus might be on providing adequate skill training to the workforce, at another point in time the major focus might be on improving workplace morale and so on. This is important because jobs can often be redefined or altered over time to include different sets of work-related tasks. This makes a difference when it comes to assessing the impact of automation on work. As we point out below, automation may result in a redrawing of the task boundaries of particular jobs without necessarily resulting in a net loss of jobs.

Finally, in relation to the definition of work, it is worth distinguishing between meaningful and non-meaningful forms of work. 'Meaningful work' is work that consists of a set of tasks that provides workers with meaning, where this is cashed out in terms of the general properties commonly associated with meaning in life. This could prompt a lengthy divagation into the nature of meaning in life, but we will take a shortcut around that topic in this paper. In our approach to meaning in work, we are influenced by Susan Wolf's account of what it is to have a meaningful life. Meaning in life, according to Wolf [41], has both a subjective component and an objective component. As Wolf sees things, a person has a meaningful life if she is engaged in activities and projects that she is passionate about, and that can also be recognised as valuable from a wider, not purely subjective perspective. We think of meaningful work in a similar way: it should create a subjective sense of meaning, on the one hand, but it should also be work that has characteristics that can be more generally recognised as the sorts of characteristics objectively associated with meaningful work, on the other hand (for an extended discussion of such characteristics, see, e.g. [33], pp. 506–510).

What does this mean in practice? At a minimum, two conditions need to be satisfied for work to be meaningful: (a) the overarching output produced by the workplace must be valuable and must be perceived by the workers to be valuable and (b) the individual worker's job, within the overarching structure of the workplace, must consist of sub-tasks that are themselves valuable (and perceived to be valuable). Therefore, for example, someone could work as a financial trader within a workplace that specialises in facilitating illegal arms trades that ultimately harm many people, or, alternatively, they could work as a trader that facilitates investments in healthcare in developing countries that benefit many people. In both the cases, they might perform very similar tasks as part of their jobs and find these tasks to be meaningful and valuable, but when facilitating illegal arms trades they are not engaged in a meaningful form of work because the overarching output of their workplace lacks value (indeed, it is actively disvaluable). All that said, as we shall point out later in this paper, meaningful work can also include other properties not specifically linked to the output of the workplace [16, 33, 39]. For example, feeling as though you belong to a community of fellow workers, or that you are gaining mastery over some skillset, are often tagged as features of meaningful work, even though these things do not strictly require a valuable task output—they require, at most, a value neutral output.

So much for work. What about workplace automation? Very generally, automation is the practice of using machines, rather than humans, to perform work-related tasks. Automation has been a feature of the workplace since the dawn of the industrial revolution [14]. Some people think that the current wave of AI-based automation could eventually lead to the end of the majority human workforces [3, 8, 10, 12, 23, 36]; others are more sceptical [2]. This is not the place to adjudicate those disputes. What is important for present purposes is that workplace automation can take different forms, two of which are worth singling out for the purposes of this article:

Total replacement: This happens when a machine replaces all the work-related tasks associated with a given job. As a result, a human worker will typically lose their job and a machine will perform all the work-related tasks that were once associated with that job.

Collaborative displacement: This happens when a machine replaces some of the work-related tasks associated with a given work output but a sufficient number of human-performed tasks are retained such that humans still have jobs, but have to collaborate with the machines to produce the output. This often leads to a redrawing of the boundaries of a given job.

Collaborative displacement, in its turn, can take a number of different forms. It would be impossible to enumerate all the possible forms it can take, but three would seem to be particularly important when it comes to assessing the impact of workplace automation on achievement.

The first is what might be called "supervisory" or "directive" collaboration. This arises whenever humans formulate the abstract plans or work programs that the machines implement. For example, a group of automobile engineers might design a car, providing detailed blueprints for its specifications and information on how it ought to be put together. These blueprints could then be fed into a machine (or group of machines) that actually build the car. The humans here are responsible for the creative and intellectual part of the work. The machine does the physical grunt work.

The second is what might be called "maintenance" collaboration. This arises whenever humans have to maintain the machines that produce the work output. To continue with the automobile example, once the machines have started the manufacturing process, it is quite likely that they will breakdown or encounter operational difficulties. Skilled machinists and maintenance workers may then be required to step in to repair or fix the machines, or reprogram/repurpose them to fit the changing demands of the workplace.

The third is what might be called "order-following" collaboration. This is essentially the inverse of "supervisory" or "directive" collaboration. In this case, the machine comes up with the abstract plans or work programs that human workers then implement. For example, suppose that instead of designing the car, the humans use a machine-learning algorithm to figure out the best way to make a fuel efficient, aerodynamic car. The algorithm uses a database of pre-existing designs to do this. After the algorithm settles on a preferred design, the humans go off and build the car. Here, the humans do the physical grunt work while the machine is responsible for the creative and intellectual work.

These examples are obviously abstract and, perhaps, a little too neat. In the real world, multiple forms of collaborative displacement may occur at the same time and some may be more partial or incomplete than those sketched above. Nevertheless, the different forms of collaborative displacement make a difference to the kinds of achievement that are available to human workers. Humans might still have jobs, even with rampant automation, but those jobs might not allow for meaningful work because the kinds of achievement they enable are relatively minimal. The obvious intuition here is that a human that just follows the orders given to it by a machine has access to a less valuable kind of workplace achievement than one that supervises or directs a machine. But is that intuition correct? We will examine this in more detail below, after we have said something more about the nature of achievement.

3. What Is an Achievement?

Achievements are outcomes that are brought about by coordinated human activity in such a way that those outcomes can be linked to the efforts of individual human agents. The concept of achievement features heavily in many philosophical theories of meaning in life, and hence, can also feature in theories of meaningful work. A meaningful life is commonly conceptualised as one in which an individual achieves valuable things with their life. Albert Einstein, for example, can be said to have lived a meaningful life because he achieved certain scientific insights and outputs (the special and general theories of relativity and certain key elements of modern quantum theory) through his cognitive efforts. That said, his life was not an unqualified success since he failed to achieve a grand unified theory of everything, something that both he and the wider physics community perceived to be the ultimate goal of their scientific endeavours [11].

Achievement is, then, one of the key elements of a meaningful life. It may not be the sine qua non of human flourishing, but it is at least true to say that a life without achievement is impoverished compared to a life with achievement. If something threatened or undermined our capacity to have achievements, we should be concerned as this could make our lives relatively worse than they might otherwise have been. This is particularly true when it comes to our desire to secure meaningful forms of work. For better or worse, work occupies the centre stage in many people's lives. They are obliged to do it out of economic and practical necessity; and they often associate their identity and self-worth with the work they perform, and many people spend more time every week with workplace colleagues than with their families and loved ones [33]. If their capacity to achieve things through their work is compromised, this would be worthy of careful consideration.

What conditions are relevant to assessing whether someone's efforts count as an achievement? Here, we propose a modified account based on Gwen Bradford's analytical account of achievement [5] and [6]) and Hannah Maslen, Julian Savulescu and Carin Hunt's work on praiseworthiness [25]. It seems appropriate to marry these two accounts together since achievements are, in essence, a positive manifestation of responsibility. In both philosophical and legal debates about responsibility, we are often concerned with what can be called negative responsibility: who is to blame (legally/morally) when something bad happens? It is important, however, to remember that responsibility has a positive flipside. We can also ask: who deserves praise or reward if something good happens? Since we usually talk about an individual's achievements in positive terms—e.g. we celebrate Einstein's scientific achievements—it makes sense to think that assessing whether or not someone has achieved something is partly determined by whether or not they deserve praise for a positive outcome.

Some people might dispute this. Steven Luper [22], for example, has defended an "achievementist" theory of meaning in life that is neutral on whether achievements have objective value. He argues that someone can be rightly said to achieve negative outcomes just as easily as they can be said to achieve positive outcomes. Achievement, according to Luper, is largely a function of whether or not someone is successful in attaining their goals. To take an extreme example, a serial killer who set themselves the goal of killing as many people as possible, and who succeeds in doing this, can be said to have achieved something just as easily as Einstein can be said to have achieved something through his scientific successes.

While there might be some merit to such an account of achievement, we suggest that it is a counterintuitive idea. If achievements are a key part of meaning in life, it would be odd to suggest that they can play this part if they can be negative in nature. Accordingly, it is common in theories of meaning to argue that a life lacks meaning if it produces negative outcomes in the world [19, 27, 35]. Since we find Luper's view to be counterintuitive, in the remainder of this article, we focus on achievements that are associated with either positive or non-negative outcomes (i.e. neither good nor bad). We include the latter possibility on the grounds that achieving a neutral non-negative outcome can still be praiseworthy because (a) it does not reduce the level of value in the world and (b) the fact that it was achieved may speak to certain virtues or excellences in human agency. For example, it seems plausible to suggest that Lee Sedol's successes as a professional Go-player were largely value neutral in nature: his winning the world championship 18 times was, from an objective standpoint, neither good nor bad. Nevertheless, his successes did speak to some personal virtues or excellences that are worthy of praise.

With these caveats in mind, we submit that whenever we are assessing the value of someone's achievements, the following four variables need to be kept in mind:

The value of the output produced: although producing value-neutral outcomes can count as an achievement, it is still the case that the more objectively valuable the output, the greater the achievement, all else being equal (i.e. bearing in mind the other variables).

The nature of causal contribution of the agent: the agent must play a significant role in producing the output, specifically the output must be a sufficiently *non-lucky* result of the agent's actions.

The cost of the agent's commitment to producing the outcome: typically, the more effort, time, attention, and stress, the greater is the achievement.[4]

The voluntariness of the agent's actions: a non-voluntary commitment to producing an outcome might count as a less of an achievement, all else being equal.

The first of these variables has already been discussed. The other three merit some further elaboration. Concerning the causal contribution of the agent to the output, it seems like common sense to suggest that this must be significant and that the agent has to play a sufficiently 'non-lucky' role in producing the outcome [5]. To use an obvious example, compare Bill Gates to a lottery winner. The lottery winner purchases a ticket and this ticket happens to have the winning numbers. This results in the lottery winner becoming fantastically wealthy. Did the lottery winner achieve their wealth? Hardly. Their purchasing of the ticket was a relevant causal factor in producing this outcome (but for the purchase of the ticket they would not be wealthy), but it was pure luck whether this ticket would actually be the winning one. The lottery winner did not play a sufficiently non-lucky role in producing the outcome. Bill Gates, on the other hand, was undoubtedly the recipient of much good fortune and luck in life. He came from a relatively wealthy background and happened to come of age at the exact right time to capitalise on the personal computer revolution. Nevertheless, he did exert considerable, deliberate cognitive effort in programming key software innovations and managing a successful business [18]. His resultant wealth may be excessive relative to what he deserves, but he did play a sufficiently non-lucky role in acquiring that wealth.[5]

The cost of the agent's commitment to the outcome also seems obviously relevant to the assessment of their achievements. As Maslen et al. [25] point out in their discussion of praise, it is common for people to think about the cost of commitment in terms of effort. But what is effort? Maslen et al. define it as a psychological capacity to overcome aversive experiences. It takes a lot of effort, for example, to run a marathon. It is a physically and psychologically demanding thing to do. Many times, as you are running, your body and mind will want to give up. You have to exert effort to overcome that desire to quit. Understood in these terms, effort is clearly relevant to assessing achievements. The more effort expended on producing an outcome, the greater the achievement seems to be. That said, as Maslen et al. argue, it is also quite a limited way of looking at things. Effort is not the only way for an agent to commit to producing an outcome and sometimes effort may not be present in significant achievements. Compare, for example, an amateur first-time marathon runner to a professional. The amateur may have to exert far more effort (overcome more psychological aversion) than the professional to finish the race. This does not, however, make the amateur's marathon a greater achievement. The professional will have shown their dedication to the race in other ways. They will have spent many hours training and honing their skills; they will have spent time away from their families and friends to improve their abilities. These are all forms of costly commitment and they all seem relevant to assessing the achievement. That said, we have to treat costly commitment with some degree of care. It is relevant to the assessment of an achievement but not necessary for it. As Maslen et al. point out, for costly commitment to be relevant to the assessment, it has to be non-arbitrary. In other words, you cannot just make something arbitrarily more difficult to increase the amount of praise you are owed. In fact, sometimes, finding an easier, less costly way to produce the same outcome, can be an achievement in and of itself.

We return to this point later on when we assess the impact of automation on achievement.

The voluntariness of the agent's commitment to the outcome also seems like something that is obviously relevant to the assessment of an achievement because it signals a positive desire to achieve an outcome. Let us return for a moment to Bill Gates. As is well-known, Gates has pledged to give most of his wealth away to charitable/good causes through the foundation he set up with his wife. As far as we are aware, this pledge was entirely voluntary. No one forced him to do it. But suppose this were not true. Suppose it turned out that someone had held a gun to his head and demanded that he give away all his money. Would this make a difference to our assessment of the pledge? It might. The fact that he only gave away the money under significant pressure would seem to suggest that he does not really deserve as much credit for it. That said, as with costly commitment, we have to be careful in how we factor voluntariness into our assessment of achievements. Just because an action is nonvoluntary does not mean it does not count as an achievement. Someone might force an amateur to run a marathon at gunpoint. If the amateur runs the marathon (and completes it), this would still count as a significant achievement, given the degree of psychological and physical effort it must have required to do so. The point, then, is that voluntariness is not the be all and end all of achievement. It is one of the factors that goes into the assessment. You must reach a holistic assessment of all four factors to determine whether there has been a significant achievement or not.

4. How Automation Creates Achievement Gaps

With this account in place, we are in a better position to assess the impact of workplace automation on achievement. Instead of asking the general question about how automation impacts on achievement, we can ask the more specific question: how does automation impact on the four variables relevant to the assessment of achievements? Answering this will then enable us to reach a holistic assessment. To answer this question adequately, we need to link the discussion back to the different kinds of automation discussed in Sect. 2.

We can start with the trivial case: that of total replacement of human workers by machines. Clearly, in such cases, there is an end to certain kinds of human achievement within the workplace. If a skilled manufacturing worker or service worker is replaced, entirely, by a machine, they no longer have access to any form of workplace achievement. Whatever achievements they used to associate with their job are now closed to them: they lose the ability to make a non-lucky causal contribution to a valuable output. They have to find other outlets for their talents. This is an uncomplicated and perhaps uninteresting case (though it leads to a complicating factor that we discuss in more detail below).

The more interesting cases are the ones in which workers are not totally replaced by machines but are, instead, redeployed within the workplace so that they have to collaborate with machines in different ways. In all cases of collaboration, human workers perform tasks that (a) produce outcomes in their own right and (b) have some causal relevance, even if indirect, to the outcomes produced by the machines (and, therefore, of the workplace as a whole). There is, consequently, a valid question to be asked about whether they still have access to achievement through their work. What we will now argue is that even in cases of collaborative displacement, the possibility of achieving things through your work can be significantly compromised through the use of automating technologies. This is because even in cases of collaborative displacement automation can negatively impact on three of the four variables that are relevant to the assessment of achievements in the workplace.

Consider, first, the way in which automation can reduce the value of the outputs associated with the tasks performed by certain groups of human workers. The clearest example of this comes with maintenance forms of collaboration. Where once upon a time humans could be responsible for producing valuable commodifiable outputs, either through cognitive design of those outputs or physical manufacture of their parts or, in the case of services, physical and cognitive performance of valuable services, when they shift to the maintenance role they necessarily take a peripheral role in the production of the valuable outputs. They keep the wheels of industry turning, but they do not play a direct role in the valuable activities. Consider, by way of analogy, the relationship between a touring musician and their road crew. The road crew plays an important part in setting up and testing the equipment that ensures the musician can play every night, but they are playing a support role to the activity that produces the real value—the musical performance. You would be hard pressed to argue that their tasks are *more valuable* than those of the musician. In the case of maintenance collaboration, human workers are relegated to an equivalent backstage role. They are the support crew, not the performers. What they do may still be causally important, but it is not more valuable than the front stage role they could have occupied.

Similarly, in cases of order-following collaboration, it is reasonable to presume that there will be a loss of value in work-related outputs, relative to other, available forms of work. In the case of order-following collaboration, humans take a backseat to the creative, design, or supervisory work. They become order-following, physical workers. The tasks they perform may well be causally important to the production of valuable outputs, but what they do is surely relatively less valuable.

Why? Since in becoming order-following physical workers, they lose the opportunity to exercise independence and creativity in their jobs. Indeed, there is something deeply ironic about order-following collaboration. As Brett Frischmann and Evan Selinger have argued [15], one of the more noticeable effects that automation and digital technology has on human life is its tendency to reduce humans to 'simple machines' that perceive a stimulus and then respond in a predictable or limited way. Think, for example, of the Amazon warehouse worker who is given a set of customer orders and a route through the warehouse to pick up those orders that has been planned by an algorithm. They see the stimulus given to them by the machine and respond, not with creativity or foresight, but by just following the route that is recommended. They dare not second-guess the algorithm or exercise any creativity in case they are less efficient at their jobs (and are reprimanded for failing to follow the orders). Similar things are happening in other forms of work where algorithms play a key role in planning and coordinating the physical activity of workers, e.g. in 'platform' work, such as that provided by companies like Uber and Deliveroo.

The one major exception to this argument is the case of supervisory collaboration. Here, the humans would appear to retain creative control and mastery over the machines. They still use their cognitive abilities to design the valuable output and supervise its creation. While they may have outsourced the physical grunt work to a machine, they still play a significant, non-lucky role in producing that output. But even in the case of supervisory collaboration, there can be a loss. For one thing, it is worth noting that creative and supervisory forms of work are largely the preserve of an elite few workers and, indeed, one of the tragedies of automation may well be that it empowers these elite few workers to the disadvantage of the majority [2, 7, 14, 21]. Related to this, even in cases of supervisory collaboration, there can be a loss in the value of work-related outputs, depending on the form of automating technology in use. To return to the opening example of Alpha Go and Lee Sedol, one of the key features of the machine-learning system used by the designers of Alpha Go is that it was largely independent of, and opaque to, its designers. In other words, Alpha Go learned how to play the game by itself, by extrapolating strategies and tactics from previous games, that were surprising to both its creators and professional Go-players. Thus, while the programmers did create the machine and supervised its use, they were not, in any meaningful sense, responsible for its specific successful moves within the game. If this form of automating technology becomes more widely used, it can undermine the value of even supervisory forms of collaboration.

This links to a second important argument about automation and collaborative displacement, namely: that automation, almost by necessity, reduces the cost of the human commitment to producing a workplace output. In some ways, this is the primary motivation for using automating technologies. They are supposed to reduce the need for certain forms of human effort and activity, and they are usually cheaper and more efficient than human workers in doing so (this is often the primary economic rationale for introducing them). But if costly commitment is one of the key variables for assessing the value of an achievement, it would seem to follow that automation reduces the value of workplace related achievements for workers. The designers of Alpha Go would again appear to be a case in point. They did not have to do the hard work of figuring out the optimal strategies to play in the game, nor did they have to code these strategies into the computer. Something similar is true for the worker who follows

orders given to them by a machine. They do not have to do the hard work of planning routes or deciding on what needs to be done. They just implement the orders. Think about the Uber driver. Unlike a traditional taxi driver, they do not need to drive around a city looking for potential customers. The software directs the customers to them and them to the customers. With the addition of mapping software, it even plans the driving route for them, and facilitates payment. This significantly reduces the cost of the commitment to producing the work output.

There is, of course, an obvious counter-argument to this. As noted earlier, costly commitment comes in a variety of forms and it is important to remember that even if one type of cost is reduced, other forms of cost could go up and compensate for this. In the earlier example of the marathon runner, we suggested that although the effort expended on each individual race might be lower for a professional runner than for an amateur runner, the professional will demonstrate their costly commitment in other ways (tougher, longer training regimes and so forth). Could something similar arise in the case of workplace automation? Could the automation of one type of work task increase costly commitment elsewhere in the workplace? This sounds plausible. It is not unusual to hear people complain that so-called 'labour saving' technologies have actually increased the demands on their work in other ways. Therefore, for example, the Uber driver might argue that although the technology saves them from having to find customers and plan driving routes, they spend an increased amount of time driving to earn a decent wage and have to invest more energy and effort in improving their customer service to boost the ratings they receive from passengers [32].

There are several things to be said in response to this. First, as we noted earlier, costly commitment is not always and everywhere associated with an increase in the value of an achievement. Sometimes costs can be arbitrary or counterproductive. It could be that the additional costs imposed by workplace automation are of this form. For example, the Uber driver may have to spend more time driving because one of the effects of platform markets is reduced wages and job security [24, 31, 32, 40]. Therefore, the increased commitment is, in fact, an indication that the form of work has become less valuable in other ways. Second, even if costs are not arbitrary or counterproductive, we still have to ask where the additional costs are directed. Our previous argument held that one of the effects of workplace automation is a reduced value of the outputs associated with human work tasks. Increasing the cost of commitment to less valuable outputs would still amount to a net loss in the value of achievements associated with work. For example, the Amazon worker who expends significant physical effort running around a warehouse to fulfil customer orders would still seem to be losing out, relative to what might have been the case, because the activities they perform are less valuable in the overall scheme of things.

This brings us to another argument about the impact of automation on achievement. A non-lucky causal contribution to an output is, as noted earlier, a relevant variable when it comes to assessing achievements. But again, almost by necessity, one of the things that automating technologies tend to do is to sever the causal connection between human activity and outputs. This is because automating technologies are introduced primarily to shift labour (physical or cognitive) from humans to machines. The classic case is that of the manufacturing robot that takes over the physical tasks of producing an industrial output such as an automobile. This manufacturing robot severs the connection between human workers

and that output.[6] The result is that the human workers can no longer claim a direct, non-lucky, causal role in producing the output that was previously earmarked as their achievement. This severing of the causal connection could be compensated for if the humans were given other, more valuable, things to do but, as per the previous arguments, this is may not be true for the majority of workers.

What about the voluntariness condition on achievement? Could the rise of automating technologies in the workplace somehow compromise the voluntariness of work? It is hard to see how this could be the case, unless the machines become, in effect, slave-masters of humans.[7] That said, it should be noted that voluntariness of work is already compromised for many workers [1, 10]. Unless you are fortunate enough to have personal wealth that obviates the economic necessity of work, or have plenty of viable career options that mean you are not forced to choose among a narrow range of potential jobs/work tasks, your ability to freely choose work is already quite limited. Automation may exacerbate this, to some extent, by further narrowing the pool of viable options, and so automation may put pressure on the voluntariness of work, but we do not rest too much weight on this here in making the case for achievement gaps since, as already noted, voluntariness does not necessarily undermine achievements.

In sum, the introduction of automating technologies into the workplace has the potential to open up numerous achievement gaps. This is because automating technologies tend to reduce the value of the outputs associated with human work tasks, reduce the cost of the human commitment to producing valuable commodifiable outputs (or redirect costly commitment in arbitrary and counterproductive ways) and, ultimately, sever the causal connection between human workers and valuable outputs. This is a bad thing since achievement is a key component of meaningful work. The challenge from a policy perspective is to figure out what can be done to mitigate against this risk. We turn to that question next.

5. What Can We Do about Achievement Gaps in the Workplace?

In this section, we sketch four possible responses to the achievement gap problem in the workplace. We emphasise that these are just *sketches*: things that might done to alleviate some of the problems discussed in the previous section. More work needs to be done to develop a comprehensive policy response. Nevertheless, we can give some guidance on the type of thing that should be done.

The first possibility is to simply accept the threat to achievement and respond by emphasising other aspects of meaningful work. Earlier on, when discussing the phenomenon of meaningful work, we noted that achievement, while important, is not the only thing that makes work meaningful. Leading accounts of meaningful work suggest that it is a complex and multidimensional phenomenon. Meaningful work includes achievement of valuable outputs, to be sure, but it also includes a sense of community, gaining self-respect and recognition of one's peers, mastering skills and having a high degree of autonomy in the performance of one's work tasks [16, 33]. While automation may reduce the significance of the achievements associated with one's work-related tasks, we could compensate for this by trying to promote the other aspects of meaningful work. For example, the employee that is displaced by a machine could be given greater autonomy in their remaining work tasks, workplace training and performance management could focus on enabling them to master the skills associated with these new tasks, greater emphasis could be placed on workplace morale

and camaraderie (perhaps even including the acceptance of machines as good colleagues [30]), and so on. That said, this strategy does face two obvious problems. First, emphasising these other aspects of meaningful work may ring hollow if an individual worker's contribution to the workplace output is reduced. Sure, it is nice to have more autonomy and good workplace morale, but what is the point if all one is doing is stapling sheets of paper together (to continue an example from earlier in the paper)? Second, increased workplace automation may put pressure on other aspects of meaningful work too. For example, one may have fewer colleagues—and hence less of a sense of community—in a highly automated workplace. Likewise, ensuring that humans work smoothly with machines might require more worker surveillance and control, due to the risk that humans will misuse machines or machines pose a risk to humans. This may, in turn, impact negatively on autonomy.

The second possibility is that, even if machines play the main part in producing workplace outputs, we could find some residual ways for humans to play a valuable role in producing the final outputs. To put it another way, we could try to find a way for the 'human touch' to be retained in the automated workplace. For example, imagine a furniture factory that relies heavily on machines to manufacture tables and chairs. The machines produce safer and cheaper furniture than human workers ever could. Suppose though, at the very end of the manufacturing line, human workers add distinctive carvings or markings to the furniture. These workers are given a high degree of freedom and autonomy in doing this and hence are able to exercise their creativity when it comes to marking up the furniture. This could add something distinctive to the final product and allow human workers to play a meaningful role in production. Of course, work is not charity. We cannot simply dream up tasks just so that all products or services have some semblance of the human touch. But adding such distinctive markings to furniture may not be charity. Consumers may value a product that has unique features and includes the human touch.[8] It may counterbalance some of the drab uniformity that is often associated with machine-manufactured goods. Indeed, setting up the workplace in this way may enable us to get the best of both worlds: the efficiency of machines and the creative imperfections of humans.

The third possibility is that we place greater emphasis on the role of teams in producing workplace outputs. This is not really a way of addressing the problems outlined in the previous section but, rather, a way of reframing them so that they seem less problematic. One criticism that could be made of our arguments in the previous section is that they adopt an overly individualistic understanding of achievement and meaningful work: for *my* work to be meaningful *I* must play a significant role in producing the valuable output. This was perhaps most clearly on display in the dismissive comments we made about support crew and stage performers. But maybe this is the wrong way of looking at it? Many of the great achievements of human history have been collective efforts, not solo runs. No person is an island unto themselves. We all depend on and rely on others to get things done. If any link in the collective chain gets damaged, the final product suffers. Maybe we just need to reflect on that reality more and accept that collaborative displacement by machines does not undermine achievement as much as we supposed. Perhaps we can still feel like we are a valuable part of the team producing the output, even if the tasks we perform are different? Perhaps. But, again, this might ring hollow to those who find themselves redeployed to more marginal and peripheral roles within the team. The tasks they perform will need to feel somehow essential to the collective effort (a necessary part of a sufficient set of causes of the output).

The final possibility is that we try to find other avenues for achievement outside the workplace. This may be the ultimate solution to the problem. The argument developed in this paper has worked from the assumption that work plays a central role in people's lives and that it is one of the main forums in which they can achieve valuable outputs. This may be true given the current economic realities but maybe it does not have to be true in a world of widespread workplace automation [4, 10]? With fewer demands on humans in the workplace, it may be possible for us to dedicate more time to other methods of achieving valuable outputs, e.g. hobbies, sports, artistic endeavours, family projects and so on. This links, importantly, to the voluntariness condition for praise. One of the problems noted above is that work is often not a voluntary choice for many people: it is an economic and practical necessity. But if automation could free us from that necessity, we might be able to choose our own paths to achievement. That said, one of the features of the argument we made in the previous section is that it is generalizable. We focused on achievement gaps in the workplace but, in principle, the use of automating technologies in other domains may open up additional achievement gaps. This may reduce the viability of this final strategy (cf [10], ch 4 and ch 7).

6. Conclusion

Achievement is an important part of the well-lived life. It is the positive side of responsibility. Where we blame ourselves and others for doing bad things, we also praise ourselves for achieving positive (or value neutral) things. Achievement is particularly important when it comes to meaningful work. One of the problems with widespread automation is that it threatens to undermine at least three of the four main conditions for achievement in the workplace: it can reduce the value of work tasks; reduce the cost of committing to those work tasks; and sever the causal connection between human effort and workplace outcome. This opens up 'achievement gaps' in the workplace. There are, however, some potential ways to manage the threat of achievement gaps: we can focus on other aspects of meaningful work; we can find some ways to retain the human touch in the production of workplace outputs; we can emphasise the importance of teamwork in producing valuable outputs; and we can find outlets for achievement outside of the workplace.

Funding

Nyholm's work on this paper is part of the research program "Ethics of Socially Disruptive Technologies", which is funded through the Gravitation program of the Dutch Ministry of Education, Culture, and Science and the Netherlands Organization for Scientific Research (NWO Grant number 024.004.031).

References

1. Anderson, E.: Private Government. Princeton University Press, Princeton (2017)

2. Autor, D.: Why are there still so many jobs? The history and future of workplace automation. J Econ Perspect **29**(3), 3–30 (2015)

3. Avent, R.: The Wealth of Humans: Work, Power and Status in the 21st Century. St Martin's Press, New York (2016)

4. Black, B.: The Abolition of Work and Other Essays. Loompanics Unlimited, Port Townshend, Washington (1986)

5. Bradford, G.: The value of achievements. Pac. Philos. Q. **94**(2), 202–224 (2013)

6. Bradford, G.: Achievement. Oxford University Press, Oxford (2016)

7. Breemersch, K., Damijan, J., Konings, J.: Labour Market Polarization in Advanced Countries: Impact of Global Value Chains, Technology, Import Competition from China and Labour Market Institutions. OECD Social, Employment and Migration Working Papers, No. 197, OECD Publishing, Paris (2017). https://doi.org/https://doi.org/10.1787/06804863-en.

8. Brynjolfsson, E., McAfee, A.: The Second Machine Age. WW Norton and Co, New York (2014)

9. Coeckelbergh, M.: The tragedy of the master: automation, vulnerability, and distance. Ethics Inf. Technol. **17**(3), 219–229 (2015)

10. Danaher, J.: Automation and Utopia: Human Flourishing in a World Without Work. Harvard University Press, Cambridge, MA (2019)

11. Folsing, A.: Albert Einstein: a Biography. Viking, New York (1997)

12. Ford, M.: The Rise of the Robots: Technology and the Threat of Mass Unemployment. Basic Books, New York (2015)

13. Frayne, D.: The Refusal of Work. ZED Books, London (2015)

14. Frey, C.B.: The Technology Trap. Princeton University Press, Princeton, NJ (2019)

15. Frischmann, B., Selinger, E.: Re-Engineering Humanity. Cambridge University Press, Cambridge, UK (2018)

16. Gheaus, A., Herzog, L.: The goods of work (other than money!). J. Soc. Philos. **47**(1), 70–89 (2016). https://doi.org/10.1111/josp.12140

17. Gorz, A.: Critique of Economic Reason. Verso, London (1989)

18. Isaacson, W.: The Innovator. Simon and Schuster, London (2014)

19. Landau, I.: Immorality and the meaning of life. J. Value Inq. **45**, 309–317 (2011)

20. Leopold, D. (2018). Alienation, The Stanford Encyclopedia of Philosophy (Fall 2018 Edition), Edward N. Zalta (ed.). <https://plato.stanford.edu/archives/fall2018/entries/alienation/>.

21. Loi, M.: Technological unemployment and human disenhancement. Ethics Inf. Technol. **17**, 201–210 (2015)

22. Luper, S.: Life's meaning. In: Luper, S. (ed.) The Cambridge Companion to Life and Death. Cambridge University Press, Cambridge, UK (2014)

23. Manyika, J., Chui, M., Miremadi, M., Bughin, J., George, K., Willmott, P. and Dewhurst, M.: A Future that Works: Automation, Employment And Productivity. McKinsey Global Institute Report, McKinsey and Co. (2017)

24. Manyika, J., Lund, S., Bughin, J., Robinson, K., Mischke, J. and Mahajan, D.: Independent Work: Choice, Necessity, and the Gig Economy. McKinsey Global Institute Report, McKinsey and Co (2016)

25. Maslen, H., Savulescu, J., Hunt, C.: Praiseworthiness and motivational enhancement: 'No Pain, No Praise'? Aust. J. Philos. **98**(2), 304–318 (2020)

26. Mattia, A.: The responsibility gap: Ascribing responsibility for the actions of learning automata. Ethics Inf. Technol. **6**, 175–183 (2004)

27. Metz, T.: Meaning in Life. Oxford University Press, Oxford (2013)

28. Nyholm, S.: Attributing agency to automated systems: Reflections on human-robot collaborations and responsibility-loci. Sci. Eng. Ethics **24**(4), 1201–1219 (2018)

29. Nyholm, S.: Humans and Robots: Ethics, Agency, and Anthropomorphism. Rowman & Littlefield, London (2020)

30. Nyholm, S., Smids, J.: Can a robot be a good colleague? Sci Eng Ethics (2019). https://doi.org/10.1007/s11948-019-00172-6

31. Prassl, J.: Humans as a Service: The Promise and Perils of Work in the Gig Economy. Oxford University Press, Oxford, UK (2019)

32. Rosenblat, A.: Uberland: How Algorithms are Re-writing the Rules of Work. University of California Press, Oakland, CA (2019)

33. Smids, J., Nyholm, S., Berkers, H.: Robots in the workplace: a threat to—or opportunity for—meaningful work? Philos. Technol. **33**(3), 503–522 (2020). https://doi.org/10.1007/s13347-019-00377-4

34. Smith, A.: *The Wealth of Nations*. W. Strahan and T. Cadell, London (1776)

35. Smuts, A.: The good cause account of meaning in life. South. J. Philos. **51**(4), 536–562 (2013)

36. Susskind, D.: A World Without Work. Penguin, London (2020)

37. Tigard, D.: Artificial moral responsibility: How we can and cannot hold machines responsible. Camb. Q. Healthcare Ethics, forthcoming (2020a)

38. Tigard, D.: There is no techno-responsibility gap. Philos. Technol. (2020). https://doi.org/10.1007/s13347-020-00414-7

39. Veltman, A.: Meaningful Work. Oxford University Press, Oxford (2016)

40. Weil, A.: The Fissured Workplace: How Work Became So Bad for So Many and What Can be Done About It. Harvard University Press, Harvard (2014)

41. Wolf, S.: Meaning in Life and Why it Matters. Princeton University Press, Princeton (2010)

Questions

1. How do Danaher and Nyholm define and distinguish (economic) work and a job?

2. How do Danaher and Nyholm define, drawing from Wolf, meaningful work? What are the elements of meaningful work?

3. There has been an artisan revival under way for quite some time, where people are returning to hand-made goods (both to make and consume), including using original tools (either actual vintage tools, or newly produced tools). There is also a trend of Generation Z to focus on meaningful work and eschew unfulfilling jobs. What impact on corporate culture do you think that these two trends—consuming artisan goods and rejecting unfulfilling jobs—might have? For example, is Gen Z going to transform the workplace, especially because they have more comfort with electronic technology than any other previous generation, to assure that the automation does not result in mean-ingless work?

4. Do research on Luddites. Do you find them relevant to the issue of work automation today?

Notes

1. For Lee Sedol's retirement and associated statements, see: https://www.bbc.com/news/technology-50573071.

2. *Ibid.*

3. These remarks come from a blogpost Veliz wrote after watching a documentary about the Alpha Go story, available at: https://blog.practicalethics.ox.ac.uk/2019/10/a-sad-victory/?fbclid=IwAR1CIVsJI3qm4fW-TmNOj N67x7 UR_fNJkR 1akVq S7DZC 804pzqUhhB MBpgQ.

4. As will become apparent, we do not think that an agent's exercising a great amount of effort is a necessary condition for something to count as an achievement on the part of the agent. Assuming, for example, that Mozart was able to compose an opera with a smaller amount of effort than some lesser composer, this may not necessarily take away anything from how great of an achievement the opera might be on Mozart's part. In general, however, we typically associate achievements with exertions of effort or other expenditures of time and attention (etc.). Something's having required a certain amount of effort is one of the sorts of things that are often associated with its being worthy of being considered an achievement.

5. And, just to be clear, we are not claiming that Bill Gates' amassing of that wealth is objectively valuable. We use him simply as an example of what it might mean to be a sufficiently non-lucky producer of an outcome.

6. This brings to mind Marxist—and related—ideas of alienation—something we think would be worth exploring further, but that we will leave for some other occasion. For an overview of such ideas, see [20].

7. For relevant discussion of how some con-temporary technologies might be thought to make people more like machines who follow instructions in a mind-less way, and who might potentially, therefore, be viewed as having these technologies as their masters, see [15]. For the idea of the master–slave dialectic in the context of human-technology interaction with a Hegelian twist, see also [9].

8. An anonymous reviewer points out to us that there is, in fact, a furniture company—Sticks, Inc—whose unique selling point is that every piece they sell is finished with hand-drawn artwork. See https://sticks.com for more details. We thank the reviewer for this reference.

Chapter 4: Justification for, and Challenges to, Property Rights

Introduction

"The adoration of money is an ever-present peril."
—Henry Cabot Lodge

"Upon the sacredness of property civilization itself depends—the right of the laborer to his hundred dollars in the savings bank, and equally the right of the millionaire to his millions."
—Andrew Carnegie

PROPERTY RIGHTS ARE THE basis for the entire USA system, and the basis for corporate globalism, a near fait accompli. Property rights allow the cordoning off of land, and water, staking a claim against even the hungry at the gates. Property rights justify one's holding onto flexible income, rather than putting it toward food or programs that would address hunger, and not being subject to social shunning for such an action. Property rights allow those with more than they need to ignore the fact that a human being starves to death every 11 seconds. The historical Western conception of property rights was used to "justify" colonialists' laying claim to land that had been occupied by Indigenous peoples for hundreds of years. Yet what is the basis for property rights?

Legal definitions of property, common property, private property, personalty, chattel, real estate, real property, and realty are helpful in understanding property rights.[1] *Property* has two dimensions: the first is the object itself, and the second is the creation of a social and legal recognition of a particular relationship between person(s) and that object. The relationship transforms the object into something that is subject to ownership, has (market) value, and carries rights. *Common property* is property that belongs to the entire citizenry. *Private property* is that which an individual alone has the right to use, dispose of, and possess. *Personalty*, or *chattel*, is *personal property*—"things" both living (such as livestock) and inanimate, that the owner can "move"—as opposed to *real property*, or *realty*, which includes land and whatever is "fixed" to the land. *Real estate* covers all of the potential interests one can have in land. Property, then, is not merely the object in question; it is a social construct that describes a relationship to an object.

Property rights are considered a basic human right. The *United Nations Universal*

Declaration of Human Rights (see Chapter 2) addresses property rights in Article 17, which states, "1. Everyone has the right to own property alone as well as in association with others. 2. No one shall be arbitrarily deprived of his property." Property rights are considered a basic human right for primarily two reasons. The first is tied to what humans need to live, such as food and shelter. When an individual, a family, or a community is deprived of property rights, survival is threatened. Article 3 of the *Declaration* states, "Everyone has the right to life, liberty and security of person." One's life, as well as one's security of person, is in many basic ways dependent on food and shelter. It is precisely this aspect of property rights that grounds John Locke's justification for private property (the first reading selection). The second reason that many consider property rights a basic human right is due to merit. What one earns with one's labor is generally considered one's property, and one thus merits that property. That is all too often as far as the consideration extends. However, a full ethical justification needs to address more than the labor invested to acquire the property. The conditions under which that labor occurred and under which the objects were produced and acquired, as well as the broader conditions in this assumed meritocracy, also need addressing.

First I will critically address meritocracy. In this critique, I focus on the definition of meritocracy and the myth of meritocratic conditions in the United States. A meritocracy is what results when the most intelligent, talented, and/or deserving members of a society populate its government, and all of the highest positions, from those in education, to those of any social status, throughout society. In a meritocracy, those who are the most intelligent and/or talented are those who merit, or deserve, the highest positions. A meritocracy was ideally supposed to supplant aristocracy and to establish a society where rewards came due to

ability, not by the chance of birth.[2] The history of the United States is inextricably tied to the notion of meritocracy—the American Dream, Horatio Alger, the land of opportunity—for here one's social status is supposed to be earned and to show evidence of one's ability. In society, social status and the highest positions carry rewards. These rewards are most often evident in the property the individual owns, either real or personal. A meritocracy, then, assumes a type of competition whereby the most intelligent and talented rise to those positions. The labor aspect of property rights assumes that one has earned that property, and property rights ensure the owner's ability to possess, use, and dispose of that property.

Under this scenario, the acquisition of that property (which is held by those who are the most intelligent and talented) was via a competition. To claim that one was the *most* talented or intelligent, as is necessary under a meritocracy, assumes that there was a competition wherein the conditions were fair and equal in access and opportunity. If they were not fair, then neither are the results, and the claim of *most* talented or intelligent cannot stand.

A counter to the above conclusion can be raised, stating that meritocracy is not a result of equal opportunity; rather, it is a function of "Social Darwinism," the "survival of the fittest" of those who struggle in the marketplace. Yet there are two clear problems with this counterclaim. First, "Social Darwinism" is not a concept from Charles Darwin (1809–82) at all, but rather from Herbert Spencer (1820–1903), an English philosopher who misappropriated and misrepresented Darwin's theory. "Fitness" in Darwinian terms means that one has fertile offspring, and the "most fit" would be the one with the most numerous fertile offspring, not the one who raced ahead on the corporate ladder. Thus, the dismissal often heard—that we need not worry about those who are poor, à la Andrew Carnegie (1835–1919, another

Social Darwinist), for they are the unfit and "maintaining them rather drags down society and violates some law of survival"—is not a Darwinian notion at all. Hence, the misappropriation and misapplication of scientific theory to explain away inequality cannot draw its "justification" in science. The second clear problem with this approach is that it admits an underlying assumption that the conditions must be fair, after all. That is, how can one claim that the victor is the "most fit" (in the misused sense of fitness à la Social Darwinism) if all the potential victors were not allowed to compete? The following discussion addresses this issue in detail.

It is often claimed that in the United States everyone gets a chance, everyone has opportunity and access to the system. However, it cannot be claimed that the access and opportunities that do exist are equal. A myriad of empirical data confirms that educational, health, nutrition, environmental, and numerous other basic conditions are not equal.[3] The United States Census Bureau counts children living in poverty who are also hungry (they do not have adequate caloric or nutritional intake) on a daily basis. The amount of money for education spent on each child in the United States is not equal; rather, it is often dependent on property taxes, further entrenching privilege. One of the most basic necessities for competing is an education. One of the most basic necessities for performing well in school is proper nutrition. We can thus do the math and see that millions of children in the United States do not receive, through no fault of their own, equal opportunity. Furthermore, wealth and property tend to be inherited. Inheritance, while logically flowing from one's property right (to dispose of one's property), is inconsistent not only with the labor assumption of earning property but with meritocratic notions as well, for inheritance is just another relative of aristocracy.

It is often argued, pointing to numerous Horatio Alger examples, that we do have fair conditions. However, the mere existence of that Horatio Alger–type individual who achieved prominence admits the very existence of the problem. Otherwise, why would their personal circumstances have to be overcome? As stated earlier, empirical evidence shows that conditions and opportunity are not equal, and it is such evidence that the meritocrats appeal to in highlighting the individuals who *overcame* their conditions.[4] Or else what would there have been to overcome? It is the same type of admission of the problem by those who claim affirmative action is *reverse discrimination*, for if there were not already discrimination, what would there be to reverse?

If one wants to claim that the results of the competition are earned, that those who win positions in the race *deserve* those positions and the benefits that flow from them, then the conditions of the race need to be fair. One cannot hold a competition—for example, a race—and fail to tell would-be competitors about the race, hide the start line, pollute some of the competitors' communities with toxic waste that adversely affected competitors' abilities to compete, provide some competitors with performance-enhancing drugs, or place weights on some competitors while those of equal body weight are not so burdened, and then claim that the results were "earned" by the "most fit."

Frustrated, the former believer in merit might now claim that "life isn't fair." Note the abandonment of an attempt at meritocratic justification here, for merit is about fairness. Further, it is not *life* in question here, but the entire social, political, and economic system that humans created, follow, and maintain, largely based on property rights which are based on merit that is in question. We need to heed Hume's admonition on the "is-ought" gap (discussed in the introduction to Chapter 1) and not commit the naturalistic fallacy.

Ethics is about fairness, justice, what *should be*, the right thing. If the conditions in acquiring private property are not fair, then the "ownership" is suspect and further investigation is needed. Furthermore, if the conditions are not fair, then the judgments of "winners" and "losers," the "fit" or "unfit," are unethical, and the best conclusion one can draw about the ownership of private property without fair conditions is that it simply exists, that's just the way it is, not that it should be that way or that it is justified. This chapter's reading selections address a wide range of property rights issues, including what, if anything, can justify a property right; the nature of labor under capitalism; colonial activity under capitalism; and duties to the poor.

In conclusion, what then, is an unjust action in claiming a property right? For some property rights advocates, unjust would mean something like deceit or force. For John Locke (in this chapter), an unjust action in claiming private property would be to not labor, to take more than one needs, or to not leave enough and as good for others. What about the rights of the poor and needy? For Locke,

they still have a duty to labor; however, there is a duty of each and every other person who has taken from the commons to take only what they need and to leave enough and as good for others. Peter Singer points out that Thomas Aquinas, in early Christian doctrine, said, "Whatever a man has in superabundance is owed, of natural right, to the poor for their sustenance." While Locke wrote about an abstract state of nature with a commons, and while he wrote that money, "shiny pebbles," changes things, one clear dilemma remains. The conflict here is really between two rights: the right to life and the right to private property. The right to private property is justified, in part, for its ability to sustain life. The right to life is intrinsic; each human has this by virtue of being human. Property rights are *instrumental* in maintaining life. In a clash between the property right of a person who has more than they need to live, and the right to life of a person who has less than they need to live, an instrumental right (property) is in false parity with the most fundamental right of all: the right to life.

Notes

1. This discussion is drawn from Steven H. Gifis, *Law Dictionary* (New York: Barron's Educational Services, 1975); and Marcia H. Armstrong, *Understanding American Property Rights*, http://chansen.tzo.com/publications/propertyrights.

2. See Nicholas Lemann, *The Big Test: The Secret History of the American Meritocracy* (New York: Farrar, Straus, and Giroux, 1999).

3. See Sandra Blakeslee, "Poor and Black Patients Slighted, Study Says," *New York Times*, April 20, 1994; "Twelve Million Children Underfed: New Report Details Hunger in the U.S.," *St. Louis Post-Dispatch*, June 16, 1993; Robert Pear, "Wide Health Gap Linked to Income Is Found in U.S.," *New York Times*, July 8, 1995; Sylvia Nasar,

"Those Born Wealthy or Poor Usually Stay So, Studies Say," *New York Times*, May 18, 1992; "Blacks' Income Unchanged Since '69," from the *Knight-Ridder Tribune*, in *Arizona Republic*, February 23, 1995; Jonathan Kozol, *Savage Inequalities: Children in America's Schools* (New York: Crown, 1991); John C. Livingston, *Fair Game?: Inequality and Affirmative Action* (New York: W.H. Freeman & Co., 1979); United States Bureau of the Census data, *Statistical Abstracts of the United States* (Washington, DC, 1990, 1995, 1998, and 2000).

4. See Daniel D. Challener, *Stories of Resilience in Childhood: The Narratives of Maya Angelou, Maxine Hong Kingston, Richard Rodriguez, John Edgar Wideman, and Tobias Wolff* (New York: Garland, 1997).

I. The Justification of Private Property[1]

John Locke

JOHN LOCKE (1632–1704), OFTEN cited as the pre-eminent property rights philosopher, argued that ownership of private property is a natural (God-given) right. Locke writes in the Judeo-Christian tradition and begins with the assumption that the world was given, by God, to all humans in common so that humans can meet their needs to ensure their right to life. Locke further acknowledges the moderate scarcity of resources. That is, there is enough to meet all humans' needs for life (for God was not a practical joker by claiming that each person has the right to life but then not providing enough resources to meet the needs for all lives), but when resources are finite, there are not enough to waste or meet people's wants.

Locke provides three criteria that justify taking from the commons for private use. Labor alone does not convey this right; rather, there are two other criteria that ensure equal opportunity for all. If it was first come, first served/earned, then those who arrive later, including future generations also with an equal right to life, might not have equal access. As the earth is there to meet human needs, it follows that it is only justified to take what is needed to live. Needs are objective and can be empirically measured, as opposed to wants, which are subjective, can be insatiable, and are difficult to measure. Therefore, it is clear that one should take only what one needs to live because, under moderate scarcity, if one takes more than one's fair share, then one threatens to change moderate scarcity into severe scarcity and threatens others' right to life.

... GOD, WHO HATH GIVEN the world to men in common, hath also given them reason to make use of it to the best advantage of life and convenience. The earth and all that is therein is given to men for the support and comfort of their being. And though all the fruits it naturally produces, and beasts it feeds, belong to mankind in common, as they are produced by the spontaneous hand of nature; and nobody has originally a private dominion exclusive of the rest of mankind in any of them as they are thus in their natural state; yet being given for the use of men, there must of necessity be a means to appropriate them some way or other before they can be of any use at all beneficial to any particular man. The fruit or venison which nourishes the wild Indian, who knows no enclosure, and is still a tenant in common, must be his, and so his, i.e., a part of him, that another can no longer have any right to it, before it can do any good for the support of his life.

Though the earth and all inferior creatures be common to all men, yet every man has a property in his own person; this nobody has any right to but himself. The labor of his body and the work of his hands we may say are properly his. Whatsoever, then, he removes out of the state that nature hath provided and left it in, he hath mixed his labor with, and joined to it something that is his own, and thereby makes it his property. It being by him removed from the common state nature placed it in, it hath by this labor something annexed to it that excludes the common right of other men. For this labor being the unquestionable property of the laborer, no man but he can have a right to what this is once joined to, at least where there is enough, and as good left in common for others.

He that is nourished by the acorns he picked up under an oak, or the apples he gathered from the trees in the wood, has certainly appropriated them to himself. Nobody can deny but the nourishment is his. I ask, then, When did they begin to be his—when he digested, or when he ate, or when he boiled, or when he brought them home, or when he picked them up? And 'tis plain if the first gathering made them not his, nothing else could. That labor put a distinction between them and common; that added something to them more than nature, the common mother of all, had done, and so they became his private right. And will anyone say he had no right to those acorns or apples he thus appropriated, because he had not the consent of all mankind to make them his? Was it robbery thus to assume to himself what belonged to all in common? If such a consent as that was necessary, man had starved, notwithstanding the plenty God had given him. We see in common which remains so by compact that 'tis the taking any part of what is common and removing it out of the state nature leaves it in, which begins the property; without which the common is of no use. And the taking of this or that does not depend on the express consent of all the commoners. Thus the grass my horse has bit, the turfs my servant has cut, the ore I have dug in any place where I have a right to them in common with others, become my property without the assignation or consent of anybody. The labor that was mine removing them out of that common state they were in, hath fixed my property in them....

It will perhaps be objected to this, that if gathering the acorns, or other fruits of the earth, etc., makes a right to them, then anyone may engross as much as he will. To which I answer, Not so. The same law of nature that does by this means give us property, does also bound that property too. "God has given us all things richly" (1 Tim. 6.17), is the voice of reason confirmed by inspiration. But how far has He given it us? To enjoy. As much as anyone can make use of any advantage of life before it spoils, so much he may by his labor fix a property in; whatever is beyond this, is more than his share, and belongs to others. Nothing was made by God for man to spoil or destroy. And thus considering the plenty of natural provisions there was a long time in the world, and the few spenders, and to how small a part of that provision the industry of one man could extend itself, and engross it to the prejudice of others—especially keeping within the bounds, set by reason, of what might serve for his use—there could be then little room for quarrels or contentions about property so established.

But the chief matter of property being now not the fruits of the earth, and the beasts that subsist on it, but the earth itself, as that which takes in and carries with it all the rest, I think it is plain that property in that, too, is acquired as the former. As much land as a man tills, plants, improves, cultivates, and can use the product of, so much is his property. He by his labor does as it were enclose it from the common. Nor will it invalidate his right to say, everybody else has an equal title to it; and therefore he cannot appropriate, he cannot enclose, without the consent of all his fellow-commoners, all mankind. God, when He gave the world in common to all mankind, commanded man also to labor, and the penury of his condition required it of him. God and his reason commanded him to subdue the earth, i.e., improve it for the benefit of life, and therein lay out something upon it that was his own, his labor. He that, in obedience to this command of God, subdued, tilled, and sowed any part of it, thereby annexed to it something that was his property, which another had no title to, nor could without injury take from him.

Nor was this appropriation of any parcel of land, by improving it, any prejudice to any other man, since there was still enough and as good left; and more than the yet unprovided could use. So that in effect, there was never the less left for others because of his enclosure for himself. For he that leaves as much as another can make use of, does as good as take nothing at all. Nobody could think himself injured by the drinking of another man, though he took a good draught, who had a whole river of the same water left him to quench his thirst; and the case of land and water, where there is enough of both, is perfectly the same.

God gave the world to men in common; but since He gave it them for their benefit, and the greatest conveniences of life they were capable to draw from it, it cannot be supposed He meant it should always remain common and uncultivated. He gave it to the use of the industrious and rational (and labor was to be his title to it), not to the fancy or coveteousness of the quarrelsome and contentious. He that had as good left for his improvement as was already taken up, needed not complain, ought not to meddle with what was already improved by another's labor; if he did, it is plain he desired the benefit of another's pains,

which he had no right to, and not the ground which God had given him in common with others to labor on, and whereof there was as good left as that already possessed, and more than he knew what to do with, or his industry could reach to.

It is true, in land that is common in England, or any other country where there is plenty of people under Government, who have money and commerce, no one can enclose or appropriate any part without the consent of all his fellow-commoners: because this is left common by compact, i.e., by the law of the land, which is not to be violated. And though it be common in respect of some men, it is not so to all mankind; but is the joint property of this country, or this parish. Besides, the remainder, after such enclosure, would not be as good to the rest of the commoners as the whole was, when they could all make use of the whole, whereas in the beginning and first peopling of the great common of the world it was quite otherwise. The law man was under was rather for appropriating. God commanded, and his wants forced him, to labor. That was his property, which could not be taken from him wherever he had fixed it. And hence subduing or cultivating the earth, and having dominion, we see are joined together. The one gave title to the other. So that God, by commanding to subdue, gave authority so far to appropriate. And the condition of human life, which requires labor and materials to work on, necessarily introduces private possessions.

The measure of property nature has well set by the extent of men's labor and the conveniency of life. No man's labor could subdue or appropriate all, nor could his enjoyment consume more than a small part; so that it was impossible for any man, this way, to entrench upon the right of another or acquire to himself a property to the prejudice of his neighbor, who would still have room for as good and as large a possession (after the other had taken out his) as before it was appropriated. Which measure did confine every man's possession to a very moderate proportion, and such as he might appropriate to himself without injury to anybody in the first ages of the world, when men were more in danger to be lost, by wandering from their company, in the then vast wilderness of the earth than to be straitened for want of room to plant in....

And thus, without supposing any private dominion and property in Adam over all the world, exclusive of all other men, which can no way be proved, nor any one's property be made out from it, but supposing the world, given as it was to the children of men in common, we see how labor could make men distinct titles to several parcels of it for their private uses, wherein there could be no doubt of right, no room for quarrel.

Nor is it so strange, as perhaps before consideration it may appear, that the property of labor should be able to overbalance the community of land. For it is labor indeed that puts the difference of value on everything; and let anyone consider what the difference is between an acre of land planted with tobacco or sugar, sown with wheat or barley, and an acre of the same land lying in common without any husbandry upon it, and he will find that the improvement of labor makes the far greater part of the value. I think it will be but a very modest computation to say that of the products of the earth useful to the life of man nine-tenths are the effects of labor; nay, if we will rightly estimate things as they come to our use, and cast up the several expenses about them—what in them is purely owing to nature, and what to labor—we shall find that in most of them ninety-nine hundredths are wholly to be put on the account of labor....

From all which it is evident that, though the things of nature are given in common, yet man, by being master of himself and proprietor of his own person and the actions or labor of it, had still in himself the great foundation of property; and that which made up the great part of what he applied to the support or comfort of his being, when invention and arts had improved the conveniences of life, was perfectly his own, and did not belong in common to others.

Thus labor, in the beginning, gave a right of property, wherever anyone was pleased to employ it upon what was common, which remained a long while the far greater part, and is yet more than mankind makes use of. Men at first, for the most part, contented themselves with what unassisted nature offered to their necessities; and though afterwards, in some parts of the world (where the increase of people and stock, with the use of money, had made land scarce, and so of some value), the several communities settled the bounds of their distinct territories, and by laws within themselves, regulated the properties of the private men of their society, and so, by compact and agreement, settled the property which labor and industry began—and the leagues that have been made between several states and kingdoms, either expressly or tacitly disowning all claim and right to the land in the other's possession, have, by common consent, given up their pretenses to their natural common right, which originally they had to those countries; and so have, by positive agreement, settled a property amongst themselves in distant parts of the world—yet there are still great tracts of ground to be found which, the inhabitants thereof not having joined with the rest of mankind in the consent of the use of their common money, lie waste, and more than the people who dwell on it do or can make use of, and so still lie in common; though this can scarce happen amongst that part of mankind that have consented to the use of money.

The greatest part of things really useful to the life of man, and such as the necessity of subsisting made the first commoners of the world look after, as it doth the Americans now, are generally things of short duration, such as, if they are not consumed by use, will decay and perish of themselves: gold, silver, and diamonds are things that fancy or agreement have put the value on more than real use and the necessary support of life. Now of those good things which nature hath provided in common, everyone hath a right, as hath been said, to as much as he could use, and had a property in all he could effect with his labor—all that his industry could extend to, to alter from the state nature had put it in, was his. He that gathered a hundred bushels of acorns or apples had thereby a property in them; they were his goods as soon as gathered. He was only to look that he used them before they spoiled, else he took more than his share, and robbed others; and, indeed, it was a foolish thing, as well as dishonest, to hoard up more than he could make use of. If he gave away a part to anybody else, so that it perished not uselessly in his possession, these he also made use of; and if he also bartered away plums that would have rotted in a week, for nuts that would last good for his eating a whole year, he did no injury; he wasted not the common stock, destroyed no part of the portion of goods that belonged to others, so long as nothing perished uselessly in his hands. Again, if he would give his nuts for a piece of metal, pleased with its color, or exchange his sheep for shells, or wool for a sparkling pebble or a diamond, and keep those by him all his life, he invaded not the right of others; he might heap up as much as these durable things as he pleased, the exceeding of the bounds of his just property not lying in the largeness of his possessions, but the perishing of anything uselessly in it.

And thus came in the use of money—some lasting thing that men might keep without spoiling, and that, by mutual consent, men would take in exchange for the truly useful but perishable supports of life.

And as different degrees of industry were apt to give men possessions in different proportions, so this invention of money gave them the opportunity to continue and enlarge them; for supposing an island, separate from all possible commerce with the rest of the world, wherein there were but a hundred families—but there were sheep, horses, and cows, with other useful animals, wholesome fruits, and land enough for corn for a hundred thousand times as many, but nothing in the island, either because of its commonness or perishableness, fit to supply the place of money—what reason could anyone have there to enlarge his possessions beyond the use of his family and a plentiful supply to its consumption, either in what their own industry produced, or they could barter for like perishable useful commodities with others? Where there is not something both lasting and scarce, and so valuable to be hoarded up, there men will not be apt to enlarge their possessions of land, were it never so rich, never so free for them to take; for I ask, what would a man value ten thousand or a hundred thousand acres of excellent land, ready cultivated, and well stocked too with cattle, in the middle of the inland parts of America, where he had no hopes of commerce with other parts of the world, to draw money to him by the sale of the product? It would not be worth the enclosing, and we should see him give up again to the wild common of nature whatever was more than would supply the conveniences of life to be had there for him and his family.

Thus in the beginning all the world was America, and more so than that is now, for no such thing as money was anywhere known. Find out something that hath the use and value of money amongst his neighbors, you shall see the same man will begin presently to enlarge his possessions.

But since gold and silver, being little useful to the life of man in proportion to food, raiment, and carriage, has its value only from the consent of men, whereof labor yet makes, in great part, the measure, it is plain that the consent of men have agreed to a disproportionate and unequal possession of the earth—I mean out of the bounds of society and compact; for in governments the laws regulate it; they having, by consent, found out and agreed in a way how a man may rightfully and without injury possess more than he himself can make use of by receiving gold and silver, which may continue long in a man's possession, without decaying for the overplus, and agreeing those metals should have a value.

And thus, I think, it is very easy to conceive without any difficulty how labor could at first begin a title of property in the common things of nature, and how the spending it upon our uses bounded it; so that there could then be no reason of quarrelling about title, nor any doubt about the largeness of possession it gave. Right and conveniency went together; for as a man had a right to all he could employ his labor upon, so he had no temptation to labor for more than he could make use of. This left no room for controversy about the title, nor for encroachment on the right of others; what portion a man carved to himself was easily seen, and it was useless, as well as dishonest, to carve himself too much, or take more than he needed.

Questions

1. What are the three criteria that justify taking from the commons and claiming this as your own property? Why do you think these are rarely followed, in that people seek wants and are not satisfied with having needs met?

2. If someone violates any of the criteria, they are not justified in holding the property. Why? What should happen to that property?

3. Is inheritance consistent with Locke's criteria? Why or why not? What should happen to one's property upon death?

Note

1. From John Locke, *The Second Treatise of Government* (1764) [Edited].

2. Estranged Labor[1]

Karl Marx

FOR KARL MARX (1818–83), the essence of human expression, one's life activity, is to labor, and this is consistent with a work ethic much like that of Locke. But for Locke, one had the autonomy to choose to labor to meet one's needs, one did not need permission, and the labor produced a property right, one that the laborer could enjoy exclusively. However, in the political economy of capitalism that Marx is responding to, labor is severed from the resulting product, and the laborers, or workers, are "propertyless," instead receiving a wage. Workers do not have the freedom to choose to labor to meet their needs for life; rather, they have to ask permission of owners for the job. And rather than a meaningful, freely chosen form of labor, workers toil on a product that does not belong to them; workers are alienated from the product, from the labor, and from themselves and their species.

WE HAVE PROCEEDED FROM the premises of political economy. We have accepted its language and its laws. We presupposed private property, the separation of labour, capital and land, and of wages, profit of capital and rent of land—likewise division of labour, competition, the concept of exchange-value, etc. On the basis of political economy itself, in its own words, we have shown that the worker sinks to the level of a commodity and becomes indeed the most wretched of commodities; that the wretchedness of the worker is in inverse proportion to the power and magnitude of his production; that the necessary result of competition is the accumulation of capital in a few hands, and thus the restoration of monopoly in a more terrible form; that finally the distinction between capitalist and land-rentier, like that between the tiller of the soil and the factory-worker, disappears and that the whole of society must fall apart into the two classes—the property-*owners* and the propertyless *workers*.

Political economy proceeds from the fact of private property, but it does not explain it to us. It expresses in general, abstract formulae the *material* process through which private property actually passes, and these formulae it then takes for *laws*. It does not *comprehend* these laws—i.e., it does not demonstrate how they arise from the very nature of private property. Political economy does not disclose the source of the division between labour and capital, and between capital and land. When, for example, it defines the relationship of wages to profit, it takes the interest of the capitalists to be the ultimate cause; i.e., it takes for granted what it is supposed to evolve. Similarly, competition comes in everywhere. It is explained from external circumstances. As to how far these external and apparently fortuitous circumstances are but the expression of a necessary course of development, political economy teaches us nothing. We have seen how, to it, exchange itself appears to be a fortuitous fact. The only wheels which political economy sets in motion are *avarice* and the *war amongst the avaricious—competition.*

Precisely because political economy does not grasp the connections within the movement, it was possible to counterpose, for instance, the doctrine of competition to the doctrine of monopoly, the doctrine of craft-liberty to the doctrine of the corporation, the doctrine of the division of landed property to the doctrine of the big estate—for competition, craft-liberty and the division of landed property were explained and comprehended only as fortuitous, premeditated and violent consequences of monopoly, the corporation, and feudal property, not as their necessary, inevitable and natural consequences.

Now, therefore, we have to grasp the essential connection between private property, avarice, and the separation of labour, capital and landed property; between exchange and competition, value and the devaluation of men, monopoly and competition, etc.; the connection between this whole estrangement and the *money*-system.

Do not let us go back to a fictitious primordial condition as the political economist does, when he tries to explain. Such a primordial condition explains nothing. He merely pushes the question away into a grey nebulous distance. He assumes in the form of fact, of an event, what he is supposed to deduce—namely, the necessary relationship between two things—between, for example, division of labour and exchange. Theology in the same way explains the origin of evil by the fall of man: that is, it assumes as a fact, in historical form, what has to be explained.

We proceed from an *actual* economic fact.

The worker becomes all the poorer the more wealth he produces, the more his production increases in power and range. The worker becomes an ever cheaper commodity the more commodities he creates. With the *increasing value* of the world of things proceeds in direct proportion the *devaluation* of the world of men. Labour produces not only commodities: it produces itself and the worker as a *commodity*—and does so in the proportion in which it produces commodities generally.

This fact expresses merely that the object which labour produces—labour's product—confronts it as *something alien,* as a *power independent* of the producer. The product of labour is labour which has been congealed in an object, which has become material: it is the *objectification* of labour. Labour's realization is its objectification. In the conditions dealt with by political economy this realization of labour appears as *loss of reality* for the workers; objectification as *loss of the object* and *object-bondage;* appropriation as *estrangement,* as *alienation.*

So much does labour's realization appear as loss of reality that the worker loses reality to the point of starving to death. So much does objectification appear as loss of the object that the worker is robbed of the objects most necessary not only for his life but for his work. Indeed, labour itself becomes an object which he can get hold of only with the greatest effort and with the most irregular interruptions. So much does that appropriation of the object appear as estrangement that the more objects the worker produces the fewer can he possess and the more he falls under the dominion of his product, capital.

All these consequences are contained in the definition that the worker is related to the *product of his labour* as to an *alien* object. For on this premise it is clear that the more the worker spends himself, the more powerful the alien objective world becomes which he creates over-against himself, the poorer he himself—his inner world—becomes, the less belongs to him as his own. It is the same in religion. The more man puts into God, the less he retains in himself. The worker puts his life into the object; but now his life no longer belongs to him but to the object. Hence, the greater this activity, the greater is the worker's lack of objects. Whatever the product of his labour is, he is not. Therefore the greater this product, the less is he himself. The *alienation* of the worker in his product means not only that his labour becomes an object, an *external* existence, but that it exists *outside him,* independently, as something alien to him, and that it becomes a power on its own confronting him; it means that the life which he has conferred on the object confronts him as something hostile and alien.

Let us now look more closely at the *objectification,* at the production of the worker; and therein at the *estrangement,* the *loss* of the object, his product.

The worker can create nothing without *nature,* without the *sensuous external world.* It is the material on which his labour is manifested, in which it is active, from which and by means of which it produces.

But just as nature provides labour with the *means of life* in the sense that labour cannot *live* without objects on which to operate, on the other hand, it also provides the *means of life* in the more restricted sense—i.e., the means for the physical subsistence of the *worker* himself.

Thus the more the worker by his labour *appropriates* the external world, sensuous nature, the more he deprives himself of *means of life* in the double respect: first, that the sensuous external world more and more ceases to be an object belonging to his labour—to be his labour's *means of life*; and secondly, that it more and more ceases to be *means of life* in the immediate sense, means for the physical subsistence of the worker.

Thus in this double respect the worker becomes a slave of his object, first, in that he receives an *object of labour,* i.e., in that he receives *work;* and secondly, in that he receives *means of subsistence.* Therefore, it enables him to exist, first, as a *worker;* and, second, as a *physical subject.* The extremity of this bondage is that it is only as a *worker* that he continues to maintain himself as a *physical subject,* and that it is only as a *physical subject* that he is a *worker.*

(The laws of political economy express the estrangement of the worker in his object thus: the more the worker produces, the less he has to consume; the more values he creates, the more valueless, the more unworthy he becomes; the better formed his product, the more deformed becomes the worker; the more civilized his object, the more barbarous becomes the worker; the mightier labour becomes, the more powerless becomes the worker; the more ingenious labour becomes, the duller becomes the worker and the more he becomes nature's bondsman.)

Political economy conceals the estrangement inherent in the nature of labour by not considering the direct relationship between the worker (labour) *and production.* It is true that labour produces for the rich wonderful things—but for the worker it produces privation. It produces palaces—but for the worker, hovels. It produces beauty—but for the worker, deformity. It replaces labour by machines—but some of the workers it throws back to a barbarous type of labour, and the other workers it turns into machines. It produces intelligence—but for the worker idiocy, cretinism.

The direct relationship of labour to its produce is the relationship of the worker to the objects of his production. The relationship of the man of means to the objects of production and to production itself is only a *consequence* of this first relationship—and confirms it. We shall consider this other aspect later.

When we ask, then, what is the essential relationship of labour we are asking about the relationship of the *worker* to production.

Till now we have been considering the estrangement, the alienation of the worker only in one of its aspects, i.e., the worker's *relationship to the products of his labour.* But the estrangement is manifested not only in the result but in the *act of production*—within the *producing activity* itself. How would the worker come to face the product of his activity as a stranger, were it not that in the very act of production he was estranging himself from himself? The product is after all but the summary of the activity, of production. If then the product of labour is alienation, production itself must be active alienation, the alienation of activity, the activity of alienation. In the estrangement of the object of labour is merely summarized the estrangement, the alienation, in the activity of labour itself.

What, then, constitutes the alienation of labour?

First, the fact that labour is *external* to the worker, i.e., it does not belong to his essential being; that in his work, therefore, he does not affirm himself but denies himself, does not feel content but unhappy, does not develop freely his physical and mental energy but mortifies his body and ruins his mind. The worker therefore only feels himself outside his work, and in his work feels outside himself. He is at home when he is not working, and when he is working he is not at home. His labour is therefore not voluntary, but coerced; it is *forced labour*. It is therefore not the satisfaction of a need; it is merely a *means* to satisfy needs external to it. Its alien character emerges clearly in the fact that as soon as no physical or other compulsion exists, labour is shunned like the plague. External labour, labour in which man alienates himself, is a labour of self-sacrifice, of mortification. Lastly, the external character of labour for the worker appears in the fact that it is not his own, but someone else's, that it does not belong to him, that in it he belongs, not to himself, but to another. Just as in religion the spontaneous activity of the human imagination, of the human brain and the human heart, operates independently of the individual—that is, operates on him as an alien, divine or diabolical activity—in

the same way the worker's activity is not his spontaneous activity. It belongs to another; it is the loss of his self.

As a result, therefore, man (the worker) no longer feels himself to be freely active in any but his animal functions—eating, drinking, procreating, or at most in his dwelling and in dressing-up, etc.; and in his human functions he no longer feels himself to be anything but an animal. What is animal becomes human and what is human becomes animal.

Certainly eating, drinking, procreating, etc., are also genuinely human functions. But in the abstraction which separates them from the sphere of all other human activity and turns them into sole and ultimate ends, they are animal.

We have considered the act of estranging practical human activity, labour, in two of its aspects. (1) The relation of the worker to the *product of labour* as an alien object exercising power over him. This relation is at the same time the relation to the sensuous external world, to the objects of nature as an alien world antagonistically opposed to him. (2) The relation of labour to the *act of production* within the *labour* process. This relation is the relation of the worker to his own activity as an alien activity not belonging to him; it is activity as suffering, strength as weakness, begetting as emasculating, the worker's *own* physical and mental energy, his personal life or what is life other than activity—as an activity which is turned against him, neither depends on nor belongs to him. Here we have *self-estrangement*, as we had previously the estrangement of the *thing*.

We have yet a third aspect of *estranged labour* to deduce from the two already considered.

Man is a species being, not only because in practice and in theory he adopts the species as his object (his own as well as those of other things), but—and this is only another way of expressing it—but also because he treats himself as the actual, living species; because he treats himself as a *universal* and therefore a free being.

The life of the species, both in man and in animals, consists physically in the fact that man (like the animal) lives on inorganic nature; and the more universal man is compared with an animal, the more universal is the sphere of inorganic nature on which he lives. Just as plants, animals, stones, the air, light, etc., constitute a part of human consciousness in the realm of theory, partly as objects of natural science, partly as objects of art—his spiritual inorganic nature, spiritual nourishment which he must first prepare to make it palatable and digestable—so too in the realm of practice they constitute a part of human life and human activity. Physically man lives only on these products of nature, whether they appear in the form of food, heating, clothes, a dwelling, or whatever it may be. The universality of man is in practice manifested precisely in the universality which makes all nature his *inorganic* body—both inasmuch as nature is (1) his direct means of life, and (2) the material, the object, and the instrument of his life-activity. Nature is man's *inorganic body*—nature, that is, in so far as it is not itself the human body. Man *lives* on nature—means that nature is his *body*, with which he must remain in continuous intercourse if he is not to die. That man's physical and spiritual life is linked to nature means simply that nature is linked to itself, for man is a part of nature.

In estranging from man (1) nature, and (2) himself, his own active functions, his life-activity, estranged labour estranges the *species* from man. It turns for him the *life of the species* into a means of individual life. First it estranges the life of the species and individual life, and secondly it makes individual life in its abstract form the purpose of the life of the species, likewise in its abstract and estranged form.

For in the first place labour, *life-activity, productive life* itself, appears to man merely as a *means* of satisfying a need—the need to maintain the physical existence. Yet the productive life is the life of the species. It is life-engendering life. The whole character of a species—its species character—is contained in the character of its life-activity; and free, conscious activity is man's species character. Life itself appears only as a *means to life*.

The animal is immediately identical with its life-activity. It does not distinguish itself from it. It is *its life-activity*. Man makes his life-activity itself the object of his will and of his consciousness. He has conscious life-activity. It is not a determination with which he directly merges. Conscious life-activity directly distinguishes man from animal life-activity. It is just because of this that he is a species being. Or it is only because he is a species being that he is a Conscious Being, i.e., that his own life is an object for him. Only because of that is his activity free activity. Estranged labour reverses this relationship, so that it is just because man is a conscious being that he makes his life-activity, his *essential* being, a mere means to his *existence*.

In creating an *objective world* by his practical activity, in *working-up* inorganic nature, man proves himself a conscious species being, i.e., as a being that treats the species as its own essential being, or that treats itself as a species being. Admittedly animals also produce. They build themselves nests, dwellings, like the bees, beavers, ants, etc. But an animal only produces what it immediately needs for itself or its young. It produces one-sidedly, whilst man produces universally. It produces only under the dominion of immediate physical need, whilst man produces even when he is free from physical need and only truly produces in freedom therefrom. An animal produces only itself, whilst man reproduces the whole of nature. An animal's product belongs immediately to its physical body, whilst man freely confronts his product. An animal forms things in accordance with the standard and the need of the species to which it belongs, whilst man knows how to produce in accordance with the standard of every species, and knows how to apply everywhere the inherent standard to the object. Man therefore also forms things in accordance with the laws of beauty.

It is just in the working-up of the objective world, therefore, that man first really proves himself to be a *species being*. This production is his active species life. Through and because of this production, nature appears as *his* work and his reality. The object of labour is, therefore, the *objectification of man's species life*: for he duplicates himself not only, as in consciousness, intellectually, but also actively, in reality, and therefore he contemplates himself in a world that he has created. In tearing away from man the object of his production, therefore, estranged labour tears from him his *species life*, his real species objectivity, and transforms his advantage over animals into the disadvantage that his inorganic body, nature, is taken from him.

Similarly, in degrading spontaneous activity, free activity, to a means, estranged labour makes man's species life a means to his physical existence.

The consciousness which man has of his species is thus transformed by estrangement in such a way that the species life becomes for him a means.

Estranged labour turns thus:

(3) *Man's species being*, both nature and his spiritual species property, into a being *alien* to him, into a *means* to his *individual existence*. It estranges man's own body from him, as it does external nature and his spiritual essence, his *human* being.

(4) An immediate consequence of the fact that man is estranged from the product of his labour, from his life-activity, from his species being is the *estrangement of man* from *man*. If a man is confronted by himself, he is confronted by the *other* man. What applies to a man's relation to his work, to the product of his labour and to himself, also holds of a man's relation to the other man, and to the other man's labour and object of labour.

In fact, the proposition that man's species nature is estranged from him means that one man is estranged from the other, as each of them is from man's essential nature.

Questions

1. Many people associate communism with lazy, entitled citizens. How does this selection from Marx illustrate the opposite?

2. What are the three alienations that Marx illuminates? Do you feel this regarding jobs you have held, and why or why not?

3. How different would it be in a firm if it was worker-owned? Would the three alienations still hold? Why or why not?

Note

1. From Karl Marx, *Economic and Philosophic Manuscripts* (1844) [Edited].

3. What Should a Billionaire Give —And What Should You?[1]

Peter Singer

PETER SINGER (B. 1946) is a Utilitarian and therefore works to minimize harm and suffering, and maximize overall good to those affected in any given circumstance. In this reading, Singer takes a Utilitarian approach to the issue of global poverty and argues about what we should do with our "excess" resources. Given that many people live in abject poverty, what are our duties to them? Singer focuses on billionaires and their duties toward addressing global poverty. He advocates goals from the 2000 UN Millennium Summit, including reducing the number of people in extreme poverty; reducing the number who are suffering from hunger; education, especially of children; reducing the mortality rates of the very young; and access to potable water.

WHAT IS A HUMAN life worth? You may not want to put a price tag on it. But if we really had to, most of us would agree that the value of a human life would be in the millions. Consistent with the foundations of our democracy and our frequently professed belief in the inherent dignity of human beings, we would also agree that all humans are created equal, at least to the extent of denying that differences of sex, ethnicity, nationality and place of residence change the value of a human life.

With Christmas approaching, and Americans writing checks to their favorite charities, it's a good time to ask how these two beliefs—that a human life, if it can be priced at all, is worth millions, and that the factors I have mentioned do not alter the value of a human life—square with our actions. Perhaps this year [2006] such questions lurk beneath the surface of more family discussions than usual, for it has been an extraordinary year for philanthropy, especially philanthropy to fight global poverty.

For Bill Gates, the founder of Microsoft, the ideal of valuing all human life equally began to jar against reality some years ago, when he read an article about diseases in the developing world and came across the statistic that half a million children die every year from rotavirus, the most common cause of severe diarrhea in children. He had never heard of rotavirus. "How could I never have heard of something that kills half a million children every year?" he asked himself. He then learned that in developing countries, millions of children die from diseases that have been eliminated, or virtually eliminated, in the United States. That shocked him because he assumed that, if there are vaccines and treatments that could save lives, governments would be doing everything possible to get them to the people who need them. As Gates told a meeting of the World Health Assembly in Geneva last year, he and his wife, Melinda, "couldn't escape the brutal conclusion that—in our world today—some lives are seen as worth saving and others are not." They said to themselves, "This can't be true." But they knew it was.

Gates's speech to the World Health Assembly concluded on an optimistic note, looking forward to the next decade when "people will finally accept that the death of a child in the developing world is just as tragic as the death of a child in the developed world." That belief in the equal value of all human life is also prominent on the Web site of the Bill and Melinda Gates Foundation, where under Our Values we read: "All lives—no matter where they are being led have equal value."

We are very far from acting in accordance with that belief. In the same world in which more than a billion people live at a level of affluence never previously known, roughly a billion other people struggle to survive on the purchasing power equivalent of less than one US dollar per day. Most of the world's poorest people are undernourished, lack access to safe drinking water or even the most basic health services and cannot send their children to school. According to Unicef, more than 10 million children die every year—about 30,000 per day—from avoidable, poverty-related causes.

Last June the investor Warren Buffett took a significant step toward reducing those deaths when he pledged $31 billion to the Gates Foundation, and another $6 billion to other charitable foundations. Buffett's pledge, set alongside the nearly $30 billion given by Bill and Melinda Gates to their foundation, has made it clear that the first decade of the 21st century is a new "golden age of philanthropy." On an inflation-adjusted basis, Buffett has pledged to give more than double the lifetime total given away by two of the philanthropic giants of the past, Andrew Carnegie and John D. Rockefeller, put together. Bill and Melinda Gates's gifts are not far behind.

Gates's and Buffett's donations will now be put to work primarily to reduce poverty, disease and premature death in the developing world. According to the Global Forum for Health Research, less than 10 per cent of the world's health research budget is spent on combating conditions that account for 90 per cent of the global burden of disease. In the past, diseases that affect only the poor have been of no commercial interest to pharmaceutical manufacturers, because the poor cannot afford to buy their products. The Global Alliance for Vaccines and Immunization (GAVI), heavily supported by the Gates Foundation, seeks to change this by guaranteeing to purchase millions of doses of vaccines, when they are developed, that can prevent diseases like malaria. GAVI has also assisted developing countries to immunize more people with existing vaccines: 99 million additional children have been reached to date. By doing this, GAVI claims to have already averted nearly 1.7 million future deaths.

Philanthropy on this scale raises many ethical questions: Why are the people who are giving doing so? Does it do any good? Should we praise them for giving so much or criticize them for not giving still more? Is it troubling that such momentous decisions are made by a few extremely wealthy individuals? And how do our judgments about them reflect on our own way of living?

Let's start with the question of motives. The rich must—or so some of us with less money like to assume—suffer sleepless nights because of their ruthlessness in squeezing out competitors, firing workers, shutting down plants or whatever else they have to do to acquire their wealth. When wealthy people give away money, we can always say that they are doing it to ease their consciences or generate favorable publicity. It has been suggested—by, for example, David Kirkpatrick, a senior editor at Fortune magazine—that Bill Gates's turn to philanthropy was linked to the anti-trust problems Microsoft had in the US and the European Union. Was Gates, consciously or subconsciously, trying to improve his own image and that of his company?

This kind of sniping tells us more about the attackers than the attacked. Giving away large sums, rather than spending the money on corporate advertising or developing new products, is not a sensible strategy for increasing personal wealth. When we read that someone has given away a lot of their money, or time, to help others, it challenges us to think about our own behavior. Should we be following their example, in our own modest way? ...

... [There are] questions about whether there is an obligation for the rich to give, and if so, how much they should give. A few years ago, an African-American cabdriver taking me to the Inter-American Development Bank in Washington asked me if I worked at the bank. I told him I did not but was speaking at a conference on development and aid. He then assumed that I was an economist, but when I said no, my training was in philosophy, he asked me if I thought the US should give foreign aid. When I answered affirmatively, he replied that the government shouldn't tax people in order to give their money to others. That, he thought, was robbery. When I asked if he believed that the rich should voluntarily donate some of what they earn to the poor, he said that if someone had worked for his money, he wasn't going to tell him what to do with it.

At that point we reached our destination. Had the journey continued, I might have tried to persuade him that people can earn large amounts only when they live under favorable social circumstances, and that they don't create those circumstances by themselves. I could have quoted Warren Buffett's acknowledgment that society is responsible for much of his wealth. "If you stick me down in the middle of Bangladesh or Peru," he said, "you'll find out how much this talent is going to produce in the wrong kind of soil." ...

In any case, even if we were to grant that people deserve every dollar they earn, that doesn't answer the question of what they should do with it. We might say that they have a right to spend it on lavish parties, private jets and luxury yachts, or, for that matter, to flush it down the toilet. But we could still think that for them to do these things while others die from easily preventable diseases is wrong. In an article I wrote more than three decades ago, at the time of a humanitarian emergency in what is now Bangladesh, I used the example of walking by a shallow pond and seeing a small child who has fallen in and appears to be in danger of drowning. Even though we did nothing to cause the child to fall into the pond, almost everyone agrees that if we can save the child at minimal inconvenience or trouble to ourselves, we ought to do so. Anything else would be callous, indecent and, in a word, wrong. The fact that in rescuing the child we may, for example, ruin a new pair of shoes is not a good reason for allowing the child to drown. Similarly if for the cost of a pair of shoes we can contribute to a health program in a developing country that stands a good chance of saving the life of a child, we ought to do so.

Perhaps, though, our obligation to help the poor is even stronger than this example implies, for we are less innocent than the passer-by who did nothing to cause the child to fall into the pond. Thomas Pogge, a philosopher at Columbia University, has argued that at least some of our affluence comes at the expense of the poor. He bases this claim not simply on the usual critique of the barriers that Europe and the United States maintain against agricultural imports from developing countries but also on less familiar aspects of our trade with developing countries. For example, he points out that international corporations are willing to make deals to buy natural resources from any government, no matter how it has come to power. This provides a huge financial incentive for groups to try to overthrow the existing government. Successful rebels are rewarded by being able to sell off the nation's oil, minerals or timber.

In their dealings with corrupt dictators in developing countries, Pogge asserts, international corporations are morally no better than someone who knowingly buys stolen goods—with the difference that the international legal and political order recognizes the corporations, not as criminals in possession of stolen goods but as the legal owners of the goods they have bought. This situation is, of course, beneficial for the industrial nations, because it enables us to obtain the raw materials we need to maintain our prosperity, but it is a disaster for resource-rich developing countries, turning the wealth that should benefit them into a curse that leads to a cycle of coups, civil wars and corruption and is of little benefit to the people as a whole.

In this light, our obligation to the poor is not just one of providing assistance to strangers but one of compensation for harms that we have caused and are still causing them. It might be argued that we do not owe the poor compensation, because our affluence actually benefits them. Living luxuriously, it is said, provides employment, and so wealth trickles down, helping the poor more effectively than aid does. But the rich in industrialized nations buy virtually nothing that is made by the very poor. During the past 20 years of economic globalization, although expanding trade has helped lift many of the world's poor out of poverty, it has failed to benefit the poorest 10 per cent of the world's population....

The remedy to these problems, it might reasonably be suggested, should come from the state, not from private philanthropy. When aid comes through the government, everyone who earns above the tax-free threshold contributes something, with more collected from those with greater ability to pay. Much as we may applaud what Gates and Buffett are doing, we can also be troubled by a system that leaves the fate of hundreds of millions of people hanging on the decisions of two or three private citizens. But the amount of foreign development aid given by the US government is, at 22 cents for every $100 the nation earns, about the same, as a percentage of gross national income, as Portugal gives and about half that of the UK. Worse still, much of it is directed where it best suits US strategic interests—Iraq is now by far the largest recipient of US development aid, and Egypt, Jordan, Pakistan and Afghanistan all rank in the Top 10. Less than a quarter of official US development aid—barely a nickel in every $100 of our GNI—goes to the world's poorest nations.

Adding private philanthropy to US government aid improves this picture, because Americans privately give more per capita to international philanthropic causes than the citizens of almost any other nation. Even when private donations are included, however, countries like Norway, Denmark, Sweden and the Netherlands give three or four times as much foreign aid, in proportion to the size of their economies, as the US gives—with a much larger percentage going to the poorest nations....

Aid has always had its critics. Carefully planned and intelligently directed private philanthropy may be the best answer to the claim that aid doesn't work. Of course, as in any large-scale human enterprise, some aid can be ineffective. But provided that aid isn't actually counterproductive, even relatively inefficient assistance is likely to do more to advance human wellbeing than luxury spending by the wealthy.

The rich, then, should give. But how much should they give? Gates may have given away nearly $30 billion, but that still leaves him sitting at the top of the Forbes list of the richest Americans, with $53 billion. His 66,000-square-foot high-tech lakeside estate near Seattle is reportedly worth more than $100 million. Property taxes are about $1 million. Among his possessions is the Leicester Codex, the only handwritten book by Leonardo da Vinci still in private hands, for which he paid $30.8 million in 1994. Has Bill Gates done enough? More pointedly, you might ask: if he really believes that all lives have equal value, what is he doing living in such an expensive house and owning a Leonardo Codex? Are there no more lives that could be saved by living more modestly and adding the money thus saved to the amount he has already given?

Yet we should recognize that, if judged by the proportion of his wealth that he has given away, Gates compares very well with most of the other people on the Forbes 400 list, including his former colleague and Microsoft co-founder, Paul Allen. Allen, who left the company in 1983, has given, over his lifetime, more than $800 million to philanthropic causes. That is far more than nearly any of us will ever be able to give. But Forbes lists Allen as the fifth-richest American, with a net worth of $16 billion. He owns the Seattle Seahawks, the Portland Trailblazers, a 413-foot oceangoing yacht that carries two helicopters and a 60-foot submarine. He has given only about 5 per cent of his total wealth.

Is there a line of moral adequacy that falls between the 5 per cent that Allen has given away and the roughly 35 per cent that Gates has donated? Few people have set a personal example that would allow them to tell Gates that he has not given enough, but one who could is Zell Kravinsky. A few years ago, when he was in his mid-40s, Kravinsky gave almost all of his $45 million real estate fortune to health-related charities, retaining only his modest family home in Jenkintown, near Philadelphia, and enough to meet his family's ordinary expenses. After learning that thousands of people with failing kidneys die each year while waiting for a transplant, he contacted a Philadelphia hospital and donated one of his kidneys to a complete stranger.

After reading about Kravinsky in *The New Yorker*, I invited him to speak to my classes at Princeton. He comes across as anguished by the failure of others to see the simple logic that lies behind his altruism. Kravinsky has a mathematical mind—a talent that obviously helped him in deciding what investments would prove profitable—and he says that the chances of dying as a result of donating a kidney are about 1 in 4,000. For him this implies that to withhold a kidney from someone who would otherwise die means valuing one's own life at 4,000 times that of a stranger, a ratio Kravinsky considers "obscene."

What marks Kravinsky from the rest of us is that he takes the equal value of all human life as a guide to life, not just as a nice piece of rhetoric. He acknowledges that some people think he is crazy, and even his wife says she believes that he goes too far. One of her arguments against the kidney donation was that one of their children may one day need a kidney, and Zell could be the only compatible donor. Kravinsky's love for his children is, as far as I can tell, as strong as that of any normal parent. Such attachments are part of our nature, no doubt the product of our evolution as mammals who give birth to children, who for an unusually long time require our assistance in order to survive. But that does not, in

Kravinsky's view, justify our placing a value on the lives of our children that is thousands of times greater than the value we place on the lives of the children of strangers. Asked if he would allow his child to die if it would enable a thousand children to live, Kravinsky said yes. Indeed, he has said he would permit his child to die even if this enabled only two other children to live. Nevertheless, to appease his wife, he recently went back into real estate, made some money and bought the family a larger home. But he still remains committed to giving away as much as possible, subject only to keeping his domestic life reasonably tranquil.

Buffett says he believes in giving his children "enough so they feel they could do anything, but not so much that they could do nothing." That means, in his judgment, "a few hundred thousand" each.... But even if Buffett left each of his three children a million dollars each, he would still have given away more than 99.99 per cent of his wealth. When someone does that much—especially in a society in which the norm is to leave most of your wealth to your children—it is better to praise them than to cavil about the extra few hundred thousand dollars they might have given.

Philosophers like Liam Murphy of New York University and my colleague Kwame Anthony Appiah at Princeton contend that our obligations are limited to carrying our fair share of the burden of relieving global poverty. They would have us calculate how much would be required to ensure that the world's poorest people have a chance at a decent life, and then divide this sum among the affluent. That would give us each an amount to donate, and having given that, we would have fulfilled our obligations to the poor.

What might that fair amount be? One way of calculating it would be to take as our target, at least for the next nine years,

the Millennium Development Goals, set by the United Nations Millennium Summit in 2000. On that occasion, the largest gathering of world leaders in history jointly pledged to meet, by 2015, a list of goals that include:

Reducing by half the proportion of the world's people in extreme poverty (defined as living on less than the purchasing-power equivalent of one US dollar per day).

Reducing by half the proportion of people who suffer from hunger.

Ensuring that children everywhere are able to take a full course of primary schooling.

Ending sex disparity in education.

Reducing by two-thirds the mortality rate among children under 5. Reducing by three-quarters the rate of maternal mortality.

Halting and beginning to reverse the spread of HIV/AIDS and halting and beginning to reduce the incidence of malaria and other major diseases.

Reducing by half the proportion of people without sustainable access to safe drinking water.

Last year a United Nations task force, led by the Columbia University economist Jeffrey Sachs, estimated the annual cost of meeting these goals to be $121 billion in 2006, rising to $189 billion by 2015. When we take account of existing official development aid promises, the additional amount needed each year to meet the goals is only $48 billion for 2006 and $74 billion for 2015.

Now let's look at the incomes of America's rich and superrich, and ask how much they

could reasonably give. The task is made easier
by statistics recently provided by Thomas Piketty and Emmanuel Saez, economists at the
École Normale Supérieure, Paris-Jourdan,
and the University of California, Berkeley,
respectively, based on US tax data for 2004.
Their figures are for pretax income, excluding
income from capital gains, which for the very
rich are nearly always substantial. For simplicity I have rounded the figures, generally
downward. Note too that the numbers refer
to "tax units," that is, in many cases, families
rather than individuals.

Piketty and Saez's top bracket com-
prises 0.01 per cent of US taxpayers. There
are 14,400 of them, earning an average of
$12,775,000, with total earnings of $184 billion. The minimum annual income in this
group is more than $5 million, so it seems rea-
sonable to suppose that they could, without
much hardship, give away a third of their annual income, an average of $4.3 million each,
for a total of around $61 billion. That would
still leave each of them with an annual income
of at least $3.3 million.

Next comes the rest of the top 0.1 per cent
(excluding the category just described, as I
shall do henceforth). There are 129,600 in this
group, with an average income of just over
$2 million and a minimum income of $1.1
million. If they were each to give a quarter
of their income, that would yield about $65
billion, and leave each of them with at least
$846,000 annually.

The top 0.5 per cent consists of 575,900
taxpayers, with an average income of $623,000
and a minimum of $407,000. If they were to
give one-fifth of their income, they would
still have at least $325,000 each, and they
would be giving a total of $72 billion.

Coming down to the level of those in the
top 1 per cent, we find 719,900 taxpayers with
an average income of $327,000 and a mini-
mum of $276,000. They could comfortably

afford to give 15 per cent of their income.
That would yield $35 billion and leave them
with at least $234,000.

Finally, the remainder of the nation's top
10 per cent earn at least $92,000 annually,
with an average of $132,000. There are nearly
13 million in this group. If they gave the traditional tithe 10 per cent of their income, or
an average of $13,200 each—this would yield
about $171 billion and leave them a minimum
of $83,000....

Obviously, the rich in other nations should
share the burden of relieving global poverty.
The US is responsible for 36 per cent of the
gross domestic product of all Organization
for Economic Cooperation and Development
nations. Arguably, because the US is richer
than all other major nations, and its wealth
is more unevenly distributed than wealth
in almost any other industrialized country,
the rich in the US should contribute more
than 36 per cent of total global donations.
So somewhat more than 36 per cent of all aid
to relieve global poverty should come from
the US. For simplicity, let's take half as a fair
share for the US. On that basis, extending the
scheme I have suggested worldwide would
provide $808 billion annually for develop-
ment aid. That's more than six times what the
task force chaired by Sachs estimated would
be required for 2006 in order to be on track
to meet the Millennium Development Goals,
and more than 16 times the shortfall between
that sum and existing official development aid
commitments.

If we are obliged to do no more than our
fair share of eliminating global poverty, the
burden will not be great....

For more than 30 years, I've been reading,
writing and teaching about the ethical issue
posed by the juxtaposition, on our planet, of
great abundance and life-threatening poverty.
Yet it was not until, in preparing this article,
I calculated how much America's Top 10 per

cent of income earners actually make that I fully understood how easy it would be for the world's rich to eliminate, or virtually eliminate, global poverty. (It has actually become much easier over the last 30 years, as the rich have grown significantly richer.) I found the result astonishing. I double-checked the figures and asked a research assistant to check them as well. But they were right. Measured against our capacity, the Millennium Development Goals are indecently, shockingly modest. If we fail to achieve them—as on present indications we well might—we have no excuses. The target we should be setting for ourselves is not halving the proportion of people living in extreme poverty, and without enough to eat, but ensuring that no one, or virtually no one, needs to live in such degrading conditions. That is a worthy goal, and it is well within our reach.

Questions

1. Singer doesn't advocate forcing people to donate, but he does argue that it is a moral duty for those who have excess. Is meeting our wants more important than meeting others' needs? Why or why not?

2. Have you ever bought a fancy franchise coffee for $5 or more? If so, you are willing to spend at least five times the expense of a cup of coffee, so if you "needed" it, you chose an expensive version. Think of the other goods you consume where you pay for luxury while others starve without basic food. Why do you think we don't feel guilty for meeting wants while others can't meet needs?

3. It takes "shockingly" little to make a difference to someone living in abject poverty. Why do you think this option is rarely on the mind of those with excess? Do people think that the poor and hungry "deserve" to be in the situations they are in?

Note

1. Peter Singer, "What Should a Billionaire Give—And What Should You?," *The New York Times*, December 17, 2006.

Chapter 5: Challenging Discrimination

Introduction

"Whereas discrimination because of race, creed, color, or national origin is contrary to the Constitutional principles and policies of the United States.... The President's Committee on Equal Employment Opportunity established by this order is directed immediately to scrutinize and study employment practices ... and recommend additional affirmative steps which should be taken by executive departments and agencies to realize more fully the national policy of nondiscrimination ... the contractor will take affirmative action to ensure that applicants are ... treated ... without regard to their race, creed, color, or national origin."

> —*Executive Order 10925, Establishing the President's Committee on Equal Employment Opportunity,* John F. Kennedy, March 6, 1961

"To extend the Commission on Civil Rights to prevent discrimination in federally assisted programs, to establish a Commission on Equal Employment Opportunity, and for other purposes ... it shall be unlawful employment practice for an employer to ... discriminate against any individual ... because of such individual's race, color, religion, sex, or national origin."

> —*Title VII of the Civil Rights Act of 1964*

[To establish] "affirmative action plans ... to determine whether employment practices do, or tend to, exclude, disadvantage, restrict, or result in adverse impact or disparate treatment of previously excluded or restricted groups or leave uncorrected the effects of prior discrimination.... The establishment of a long term goal and short range, interim goals and timetables for the specific job classifications, all of which should take into account the availability of basically qualified persons in the relevant job market."

> —*Code of Federal Regulations, Title 29—Labor Commission,* 29 CFR 1608.4, Revised July 1, 2000

"Howard W. Smith of Virginia, an eighty-one-year-old vestige of the Old South, was looking for ways to shoot down the 1964 Civil Rights Act with 'killer amendments.' To the laughter of his House colleagues, Smith added 'sex' to the list of 'race, color, religion or national origin,' the groups that the bill had been designed to protect. Assuming that nobody would vote to protect equality of the sexes, Smith was twice struck by lightning. The bill not only passed, but now protected women as well as blacks."
      —Kenneth C. Davis[1]

"I can't breathe."
      —Eric Garner, 2014; George Floyd, 2020

As I write this, it is June 9, 2020, the day of George Floyd's funeral. Mr. Floyd, a 46-year-old Black man, was murdered on May 25, 2020, when a white Minneapolis police officer knelt on Mr. Floyd's neck for 8 minutes, 46 seconds, while Mr. Floyd continually said, "I can't breathe." In his final moments, Mr. Floyd called out to his mother, and he will be buried next to her in Houston. Protests against this travesty continue across the United States and abroad.

This is not an anomaly. In 2014, police killed Ezell Ford, Laquan McDonald, Tamir Rice, Eric Garner, and Michael Brown; in 2015, Jamar Clark, Redel Jones, and Kenny Watkins; in 2016, Philando Castile and Michelle Shirley; in 2018, Botham Jean and Stephon Clark; in 2020, George Floyd, Dreasjon "Sean" Reed, and Breonna Taylor. This is not an exhaustive list.

Almost sixty years have passed since the *Civil Rights Act* of 1964 that granted African Americans legal freedom from racial and other forms of discrimination. For an African American, that is sixty years where discrimination was supposed to be illegal, versus ninety-nine years of legal segregation after the Thirteenth Amendment ended slavery in 1865. Slavery endured on US soil for over 350 years,[2] tipping the scale of legal freedom to sixty years versus more than 450 years of slavery, segregation, and legal discrimination.

While racial discrimination is illegal, it is persistent and deadly.

Discrimination is not exclusively a "black and white" issue. This chapter addresses discrimination against racial and ethnic groups and women, discrimination that is in the form of racism, sexism, and sexual harassment. There are remedies for some forms of discrimination, and this chapter addresses the remedies provided for in civil rights legislation for two categories of discrimination: racial and sexual. It is important to note that there are categories of people not protected by civil rights legislation, most notably LGBTQ+ people who still do not have equal protections.[3]

Before turning to racial and sexual discrimination, I will address the concept of race. Our notion of human races is a biological concept based on an incorrect idea of genetically distinct groups. As early as 1950, the United Nations Educational Scientific and Cultural Organization (UNESCO) reported in *The New York Times* that there was no scientific basis for race; it called it a "social myth."[4] This has been shown through genetic studies of human DNA, from the 1980s into the 1990s. There is not enough genetic variation between what we call "races" to establish separate categories. Further, a consideration of "species" is helpful. One of the primary traits of a species, such as the human species, is interfertility, that is, the ability to interbreed and bear fertile offspring. Clearly the "races" can do this and therefore are one species. What we mean when we talk about "race" is clearly skin color and other phenotypic traits. Phenotypic traits are those we can *see*, traits that are visible. The biological concept of race is integrally linked with European colonization of "the New World," and it was and is used to justify exploitation of those considered inferior.[5] While "race" is a social construct, a myth, it remains one of the most important and powerful categories in organizing society around which inequality is perpetuated.[6]

Affirmative Action

The term *affirmative action*, as applied to racial and other issues in the workplace, first appeared in 1961, in Executive Order 10925. In this order, federal contractors were urged to increase minority hiring. President Lyndon Johnson signed the *Civil Rights Act* of 1964 to bar discrimination in the workplace. In 1965 he signed Executive Order 11246, the document that originated affirmative action and empowered the Labor Department to carry out its provisions and requirements, and outlined the enforcement and compliance procedures.

Discrimination, in the sense of racial, ethnic, gender, and other forms of prejudice that denies the moral equality of individuals and the inherent value of each human (as recognized in the *Declaration of Human Rights*), is different from discrimination that is morally neutral, such as perceptually discriminating between the right and left (not of the political sort) or discriminating between a fast- and slow-moving car when contemplating a left turn. Therefore, when the term discrimination is used in this section it refers to the first, morally objectionable sense of the term. Overall, there is agreement that racial, sexual, and ethnic discrimination is morally unjustified, yet addressing and ending discrimination, not to mention acknowledging it, is a highly contentious area with little overall agreement.

In order to determine whether there has been discrimination in the workplace, there are two tests. Both are mentioned throughout the affirmative action literature and law (*Civil Rights Acts* of 1964 and 1991, EEOC guidelines, etc.). The first test is *disparate treatment*, which involves people being treated differently based upon ethnic, racial, and gender factors. Disparate treatment was commonplace before the *Civil Rights Act* of 1964, in such instances as not allowing Blacks to sit at a restaurant counter or placing signs in shop windows stating, "No Mexicans allowed," as well as lynching and segregation. It is interesting to note that in the days following September 11, 2001, signs appeared in the windows of US business establishments stating "No Muslims allowed." Racism is therefore alive and well in the twenty-first century. When a firm has an unofficial policy not to promote members of underrepresented groups, this is also disparate treatment.

The second test for discrimination is *disparate impact*, which is also called "adverse impact" in the laws, policies, and literature on affirmative action. Disparate impact is what results when the makeup of groups' percentages in the general population is not closely represented throughout positions in employment, education, and so on. Affirmative action is meant to redress disparate impact, most especially of groups that were historically underrepresented, that is, US "minorities" and women (as women make up over half of the population, they are not a minority in number, only in representation). Historically underrepresented "minority" groups in the United States include those identified as Hispanic, African American/ Black, American Indian, and Asian American.

An example of disparate impact (in this case closely related to disparate treatment) is evident in the Federal Glass Ceiling Commission's findings in 1995. The Commission found that "95% of industry's senior executives are starkly and stubbornly white and male."[7] The Commission further found that "the entrenched stereotypes and prejudices of white men" that those in power wielded were the most important barriers to women and minorities. This example illustrates disparate impact for white men because they total approximately 39 per cent of the population and 43 per cent of the workforce yet comprise 95 per cent of the top executives. That is, their representation is more than double their population percentage. Yet here, as in other examples, we cannot, without more information, determine whether disparate impact is due to discrimination or something else, such as a qualified applicant pool that is not representative of the population. In the latter case, if there was not a diverse pool, and no discriminatory actions were taken, disparate impact would still be the result. Thus, disparate impact is a red flag that urges us to look more closely into the circumstances, rather than a proven case of discrimination.

Note that while historical conditions give rise to disparate impact, affirmative action is not meant to redress historical conditions as a form of reparations. While, of course, there is an historical dimension to disparate impact, if there is no present disparate impact, then affirmative action is irrelevant. The intent of affirmative action is, under conditions of disparate impact, to give preference to qualified underrepresented applicants. An interesting note is that underrepresentation does not always concern "minorities." Again, women are not a numerical minority. A little-known fact is that white males, who as a group have been historically underrepresented in fields such as elementary education and nursing, are eligible for affirmative action programs that exist in both of those fields for men.

The types of affirmative action programs are preferential treatment, quotas/goals, and set-asides. At each step only a qualified, underrepresented candidate is eligible for affirmative action; if someone else is hired, it is not an affirmative action policy hire. Preferential treatment is where the qualified underrepresented applicant is given preference. What were formerly called quotas are now called diversity goals, and these are specific goals for hiring or admitting qualified, underrepresented people. Set-asides are positions that are "set aside," and only qualified, underrepresented people are eligible. The latter two forms are rarely used. All the forms of affirmative action are for qualified, underrepresented candidates. Yet, with the exception of very few measurable physical abilities (such as the ability to see with 20/20 uncorrected vision, the ability to lift and carry a fire hose up x flights of stairs, the ability to throw a baseball at y speed), what will count as "qualified" is extremely subjective and dependent on the definition of those who are in positions of power. Even if the list of qualifications for the position can have the appearance of objective criteria, perceptions and biases of the hiring personnel play an undeniably crucial role in assessing and interpreting those qualifications. The term gets even more murky with the addition of "most" or "best" before qualified. If we are considering admissions, who is the best qualified? Is the most qualified the candidate with the highest SAT score? A recent book on college admissions by an admissions officer claims that many candidates with perfect SAT scores are turned down at elite institutions and are referred to by some admissions officers as "dialing toll free" (because of the perfect 800 score).[8] On another admissions committee, a student who thought it worth mentioning that he had a talent for turning "photocopies into artwork [was] dubbed 'Kinko boy'" by the admissions officers.[9] For many jobs there is no objective criterion that makes a candidate qualified or unqualified; instead, the decisive factor is whether a candidate is "like" the person doing the hiring. Regarding the college admissions officers mentioned earlier, the author wrote that "much of the decision-making comes down to whether a particular reader likes the tone of a student's personal essay or gets excited—or disturbed—by a phrase in a letter of recommendation. Hunches and gut feelings are subject to influences quite unrelated to individual merit."[10] In the absence of a corrective such as affirmative action, it is clear to see how the status quo is perpetuated.

There is one last topic often related to affirmative action that needs addressing. Many people mistakenly refer to affirmative action as reparations. Reparations are a repayment for *past* harm and are not affirmative action programs. Affirmative action programs are to redress *present disparate impact*, not to remedy past harm. Reparations, for example, in the form of "40 acres and a mule" were proposed for former slaves after they were freed. The Freedmen's Bureau was created in 1865 by the federal government to help former slaves transition into freedom. Forty acres were to be assigned to each freed male. The "mule" is thought to have come from a War Department Order No. 15, in 1865, that made mention of lending animals the military could no longer use to "freed-men." Some freedmen were given the land; however, they were later removed from it.[11] The *Civil Liberties Act* of 1988 provided reparations for Japanese victims who were interned in US "camps" during World War II. They were given monetary reparations and an apology by the president.[12]

Affirmative action is one of the most contentious issues in the United States. It has been criticized for perpetuating the very harm it is meant to address; however, it is meant to address disparate impact, so to claim that it perpetuates the harm it is meant to address would mean that it perpetuates disparate impact. Affirmative action cannot cause disparate impact, for it is a remedy if disparate impact exists. If there is no disparate impact, then a candidate who receives a position is not an affirmative action hire. If an "imbalance" exists, such as disparate impact, it cannot have been caused by affirmative action because it is a corrective for that very issue.

Another criticism of affirmative action is that of "reverse discrimination." Presumably, affirmative action changes the direction of current discrimination, or reverses it. This is an often-heard and little-understood criticism. Note first that in this criticism there is an admission that discrimination exists, or else what would there be to reverse? Furthermore, present discrimination, illustrated in the United States Census Bureau statistics, as well as the cases of disparate treatment and impact, firmly entrenched discriminatory power in the dominant group—Whites in general, white males in particular. If affirmative action redressed disparate impact, positions throughout society would roughly reflect population percentages. Hence, assumedly the reverse discrimination would come from those few recipients of preferential hiring. However, most of those eligible are minorities and/or women. While it is true that a numerical minority has been known to have the power to discriminate broadly (e.g., Whites in the former South Africa), no such restructuring has taken place in the United States, where a minority group (and by minority I mean ethnic or gender, not economic class) has denied access to the majority of people, in reverse. In order for underrepresented groups to have the power to reverse the current discrimination, the accompanying dynamics of power that exist which make discrimination effective must also be transferred.

While hiring practices can be difficult to analyze for discrimination, there are many cases of disparate impact that are not so resistant to exposing discrimination. An example of this can be found in our national incarceration rates for drug use. While African Americans comprise approximately 14 per cent of the population and approximately 14 per cent of those who use drugs, they comprise 80 per cent of those incarcerated for drug use.[13] That is, African Americans are 14 per cent of those engaging in an illegal activity, roughly equivalent to their population percentage, yet 80 per cent of those punished. This is not a random distribution; it is an example of adverse impact that is the result of discrimination. Furthermore, as identified by the United States Census Bureau, American Indians, African Americans, and Hispanics are overrepresented in poverty statistics; Whites are underrepresented in those statistics, and they have the longest life expectancies. Disparate impact (here it is also disparate treatment) further manifests itself in customer discrimination, from failing to provide service to minority customers (such as not stopping for a Black hailing a taxi) to charging minority (and women) customers more than white males for the same goods and services. The latter is known as a "black tax." The antithesis of black tax is white privilege.

White privilege is privilege that is given to Whites because of white skin. White privilege is a set of unearned assets that are given to Whites who are considered the "norm." One of the leading American myths is that the United States is a meritocracy. A meritocracy is a society governed by, and where positions are held by, those who most deserve, or merit, the positions. The society gains by this arrangement because of the assumption that those most able are those who are rewarded with positions, and those most able will benefit all of society. However, in order to assert a meritocracy, it is necessary to have equal access and opportunity in the competition for the positions (unless one asserts some sort of ability due to bloodline). The lack of equal opportunity and access is inconsistent not only with a meritocracy but white privilege is as well.

Sexual Harassment

Another form of discrimination is perpetuated due to gender. There are numerous issues surrounding sex and gender, from equal pay issues to essentialized claims of ability based on gender. This chapter addresses one aspect of gender discrimination: sexual harassment. Sexual harassment is a violation of Title VII of the *Civil Rights Act* of 1964. In 1980, the Equal Employment Opportunity Commission (EEOC) first listed sexual harassment as discrimination. The EEOC defined two forms of sexual harassment. The first is *quid pro quo*, which literally means "something for something" and is a form where an employee is "made an offer" whereby they can either receive a negative consequence, such as firing or demotion, or a positive consequence, such as being hired or promoted, if they submit to conduct by another employee that is sexual in nature. The second form is the *hostile work environment* that results from any conduct, sexual in nature, that unreasonably interferes with an employee's work performance. Sexual harassment can be in many forms, including verbal, physical, or visual. Verbal forms of sexual harassment include jokes, insults, threats, suggestive comments, sexual innuendo, whistling, and so on. Physical harassment includes coercion into a sexual act, displays, touching, brushing a body, and so on. Visual harassment includes suggestive or pornographic posters, written insults, cartoons, and so forth.

The EEOC has further articulated some circumstances that constitute sexual harassment. The harasser can be a man or woman, and the victim can be of either sex, including the same sex. The harasser can be employed at any level of the firm or can be a non-employee, such as a client. The victim can include those who are not harassed but are affected by the conduct, such as those in the office. These further articulations make the following case clearly a case of sexual harassment. In the late 1990s, a Denver car dealership's two sales managers regularly addressed "salesmen as 'little girls' or 'whores' ... asking if [they] used tampons ... showed raunchy video clips ... [one manager] grabbed at male employees' genitals, sometimes making contact, sometimes not."[14] This case is not anomalous; in 2001, 13.7 per cent of the EEOC sexual harassment cases are of this sort, including on construction sites and in retail stores. Considering the death and accident rate for construction sites (discussed in Chapter 3), this type of hostile work environment could be deadly. In the car dealership case, ten of the salesmen filed a sexual harassment lawsuit "charging the car dealership with creating a hostile environment that discriminated against them as men."[15] They won.

Quid pro quo sexual harassment, if proven, is clear and uncontroversial. However, what constitutes a hostile work environment is subjective and extremely controversial. Not only do people differ significantly in sensitivity, but also contexts differ. The EEOC recognizes the need to take each claim on a case-by-case basis. Furthermore, many people meet their partners at work, and attempts to navigate those relationships in light of sexual harassment law is notoriously difficult. Yet in the workplace one is presumably there to work, presumably there because of the qualification and ability to do the job. Sexual harassment is thus also inconsistent with a meritocracy.

In conclusion, eliminating discrimination in the workplace is a multilayered process that can be begun only if discrimination, including white privilege, sexual harassment, and sexual discrimination, is acknowledged and addressed, and changing the status quo becomes a priority.

Notes

1. Kenneth C. Davis, *Don't Know Much about History: Everything You Need to Know about American History but Never Learned* (New York: Crown, 1990), 362.
2. From 1501–1860, over ten million people to be enslaved were brought to the Americas.
3. See the National Human Rights Fund for more information.
4. *New York Times*, July 18, 1950, 1.
5. See Joseph Graves, *The Emperor's New Clothes: Biological Theories of Race at the Millennium* (New Brunswick, NJ: Rutgers University Press, 2001).
6. See Naomi Zack, *Philosophy of Science and Race* (London: Routledge, 2002).
7. See Peter T. Kilborn, "White Males and the Manager Class: Report Finds Prejudices Block Progress of Women and Minorities," *New York Times*, March 17, 1995.
8. See Andrew Delbanco, "The Struggle of All against All: Competition for the Highest Ranking Colleges and the Best Students Looks More and More Like War," *New York Times Book Review*, September 29, 2002, 13–14. Delbanco quoted this from Jacques Steinberg, *The Gatekeepers: Inside the Admissions Process of a Premier College* (New York: Viking, 2002).
9. Delbanco, "Struggle of All," 13.
10. Ibid.
11. See Gerene L. Freeman, *What about My 40 Acres & a Mule?* Yale-New Haven Teachers Institute, teachersinstitute.yale.edu.

12. See Children of the Camps, www.children-of-the-camps.org/history.

13. See Jerome Miller, *Search and Destroy: African American Males in the Criminal Justice System* (New York: Cambridge University Press, 1996).

14. Margaret Talbot, "Men Behaving Badly," *New York Times Magazine*, October 13, 2002, 52–54.

15. Ibid.

1.   Subtle Yet Significant: The Existence and Impact of Everyday Racial Discrimination in the Workplace[1]

Elizabeth A. Deitch, Adam Barsky, Rebecca M. Butz, Suzanne Chan, Arthur P. Brief, and Jill C. Bradley

THE AUTHORS FOCUS ON Black Americans who face everyday discrimination in the workplace, discrimination that is more subtle and pervasive than the obvious egregious acts that blatant racists openly commit. Deitch et al. detail what are called "microaggressions" that people who consider themselves as non-prejudiced, but still carry racist attitudes, commit.

One of the issues with microaggressions is the ambiguousness, and the inability to clearly (without research that shows racial patterns) attribute it to racism, as it differs from blatantly racist acts that, for example, may include slurs or other obvious markers. Examples of microaggressions include Black workers not being properly briefed on job procedures, being left out of meetings, not being considered for job advancement, and so forth, without objective reasons. These acts accumulate, and the authors argue that this perpetual discrimination negatively affects the well-being of those who are subject to it. Furthermore, failing to take these microaggressions into account results in an insufficient understanding of what Blacks experience.

AS THE DIVERSITY OF the American workforce increases, organizational researchers have been increasingly interested in issues of discrimination and prejudice on the job. Much of this research has focused on the perpetrators of discriminatory acts in the workplace and their prejudices (e.g. Dovidio & Gaertner, 2000; Frazer & Wiersma, 2001; Trentham & Larwood, 1998). Only recently have the experiences of the targets of discrimination become a focus of study. Some studies have shown that members of culturally stigmatized groups (i.e. those whose social identity is devalued in the context of dominant American culture; Crocker & Major, 1989) often face discrimination in the workplace, with detrimental personal effects (e.g. Sanchez & Brock, 1996; Schneider et al., 2000). However, we argue that previous studies of workplace discrimination have failed to adequately sample the range of discriminatory events experienced by stigmatized individuals on the job. Such failure to sample the range of discrimination may lead to underestimation of both the prevalence and personal consequences of workplace discrimination. Focusing on Black Americans, we examine "everyday" discrimination, those subtle and pervasive manifestations of racism faced by Blacks on a daily basis (Essed, 1991) in the workplace. We use secondary data analysis to assess the presence of everyday racism in the workplace in an unobtrusive manner and determine its impact on well-being.

The remainder of the article unfolds as follows. First, we update the organizational literature on workplace discrimination to include the concept of everyday discrimination. Specifically, we highlight the need to incorporate a more modern perspective, one that treats racism as subtle and discrimination as both ambiguous and pervasive, into the more traditional focus on rare but egregious discriminatory acts in the workplace perpetrated by individuals with blatantly racist attitudes. Next, we argue that everyday discrimination is manifested at work in the form of subtle acts of mistreatment experienced disproportionately by minority group members. Following the explication of the nature of everyday discrimination, we propose that discrimination of this type has negative consequences for the well-being of victims. Finally, using archival data from three samples, we empirically demonstrate both the existence of everyday discrimination, and also the corresponding negative impact on the job-related and non-job-related well-being of recipients.

The Existence of Everyday Discrimination

Before delving into the concept of everyday discrimination, we briefly describe what may be considered a more "traditional" focus on

discrimination. Most studies of discrimination focus on relatively rare, major events, such as the denial of housing or employment (e.g. Valentine et al., 1999). These incidents are certainly negative events in the lives of those who experience them; however, the discrimination faced by stigmatized group members, such as racial minorities, is far more pervasive than the study of major discriminatory events would lead one to believe (Swim et al., 1998). We believe that the singular attention to major discriminatory acts in the workplace is insufficient to explain the experience of discrimination many minority members experience on the job, and may be an increasingly inadequate research focus in the future as the social and political landscape shifts toward newer forms of racism and discrimination. For example, to the extent that racial attitudes account for discriminatory acts, changes in racial attitudes would precipitate a change in the nature of discrimination. Thus, subtle, everyday discrimination may become even more common, as blatant racism becomes less prevalent among dominant group members. There is substantial evidence that expressions of blatant racism (e.g. "Blacks are inherently inferior") have become less socially acceptable in recent years, and Americans are less willing to publicly endorse such beliefs (Bobo, 1998).

Research, however, has shown that racism is not disappearing, but rather is being replaced by less overt forms, termed, for example, "modern racism" (McConahay, 1986), "aversive racism" (Gaertner & Dovidio, 1986) or "ambivalent racism" (Katz & Hass, 1988). These forms of racism allow for individuals to hold racist views while buttressing such views with non-racially based rationales (e.g. beliefs in opportunity and individual mobility), thus maintaining a view of themselves as nonprejudiced.[2] But despite modern racists' assertions that they are not "prejudiced," modern racist views can predict discriminatory behaviors (e.g. Brief & Barsky, 2000; Brief et al., 2000; Monteith, 1996). Because these people do not view themselves as "racists," they are unlikely to engage in overt expressions of prejudice, such as racial slurs, but they do engage in more subtle discriminatory behaviors, such as avoidance of Blacks, "closed" and unfriendly verbal and nonverbal communication, or failure to provide assistance—what Pettigrew and Martin (1987) refer to as "microaggressions" by Whites against Blacks. Thus, as modern racism tends to displace blatant racism, the forms of discrimination encountered by Blacks may shift from "big," explicit discriminatory events to the more subtle, everyday forms of discrimination being investigated here. This point is elucidated by Essed's (1991) work with Blacks focusing on "everyday racism," which she maintains constitutes the "lived experience" of being Black. Everyday encounters with prejudice are not rare instances but are familiar and recurrent patterns of being devalued in many varied ways and across different contexts. Thus, the modern nature of racial attitudes suggests that to focus solely on major discriminatory acts is insufficient to capture the experience of discrimination.

In addition to changes in racial attitudes, changes in the political and legal landscape likely discourage overt forms of discrimination in the workplace and prompt subtle manifestations of prejudice (Dovidio et al., 2001). Stone et al. (1992) point out that obtrusive research on workplace discrimination, for example, asking participants to make hiring or personnel evaluation decisions, has yielded contradictory results, with many studies showing no effect or counter-intuitive effects (i.e. Blacks rated higher than Whites). However, more unobtrusive studies, examining criteria such as helping or various nonverbal behaviors, show a consistent picture of racial

discrimination in workplace interactions. Thus, perhaps due to federal laws and EEOC guidelines, Whites may be sensitized to blatant discriminatory acts in the workplace and attempt to avoid them, yet more subtle, "everyday" forms of discrimination may persist largely unchecked.

Not only may everyday racism be more prevalent than discrimination that can be characterized as blatant and major, but its consequences for victimized individuals may be equally, if not more, profound. Indeed, D. Williams et al. (1997), in studying a blend of economic (i.e. work-related) and noneconomic forms of discrimination, observed that a "measure of everyday discrimination was a more consistent and robust predictor of health status than [a] measure of major experiences with discrimination" (p. 348).

Everyday Discrimination and Mistreatment

Clearly, the above suggests the necessity of examining everyday, more "minor," forms of discrimination; however, we could not locate a single study of everyday discrimination focused in the workplace. Measuring everyday discrimination in the workplace presents an interesting challenge in and of itself. Typically, studies of workplace discrimination only directly ask individuals whether they feel they have been discriminated against on the job (e.g. Sanchez & Brock, 1996) (for an exception encompassing both economic and noneconomic forms of everyday discrimination, see D. Williams et al., 1997). This type of approach may lead to over- or under-reporting of discriminatory events for two reasons. First, incidents of discrimination often are attributionally ambiguous; that is, people cannot be certain whether the negative treatment they receive is due to their race or gender, or some other reason (e.g. Barrett & Swim, 1998; Crocker et al., 1998). This attributional ambiguity may be even greater with minor, pervasive discrimination than with major, blatant events. Given such ambiguity, questions referencing discrimination actually may be measuring people's propensities to make attributions to prejudice, rather than differential treatment per se. For example, Gomez and Trierweiler (2001) found evidence suggesting that people's informal theories about discrimination may influence their reports of events when specifically primed to think about "discrimination." Thus, if the propensity to make attributions to prejudice is high, over-reporting of incidents may occur.

Second, the fundamental "everyday-ness" of everyday discrimination may lead to a failure to note consciously regularly experienced incidents and attribute them to racism, or to difficulty in differentiating and itemizing incidents. However, as we have implied, even if people do not expressly report that they have been "discriminated against," such incidents may still have an impact. Schneider et al. (1997) found that women who reported various sexually harassing incidents in the workplace (such as sexist jokes or touching) exhibited negative psychological effects, regardless of whether they answered in the affirmative to the explicit question of whether they had been sexually harassed at work. That is, even if they thought the incidents too minor or ambiguous to label as "sexual harassment," they still were affected negatively—in fact, just as negatively affected as those women who labeled such incidents as harassment. A similar situation may occur when researchers ask Blacks whether they have been "discriminated against"; Blacks may not report minor or ambiguous incidents, and may not even internally categorize those incidents as discrimination, but they still may experience negative outcomes as a result.

As indicated earlier, discriminatory acts commonly are *attributionally* ambiguous,

meaning that individuals have trouble assigning a motivation to a behavior. Thus, an individual may know that he or she was mistreated, such as being excluded from a group activity, and consequently report the instance. However, he or she may not want or be able to label that exclusion as "discrimination." Therefore, as observed by Schneider et al. (1997), the questions "were you left out?" and "were you left out because you are Black?" may elicit two very different responses. This presents a conundrum for researchers that must be solved with some methodological ingenuity, as using self-reported discrimination to assess the construct of everyday discrimination is clearly problematic. Therefore, one must assess the existence of everyday discrimination in the workplace in an indirect, unobtrusive manner, without requiring respondents to decide whether specific incidents constitute discrimination. If everyday discrimination were present, then one would expect that the experience of mistreatment, uncontaminated by the attribution of discrimination, would be more common among Blacks than Whites. Consistent with this perspective, in three studies using secondary data, we assessed the extent to which everyday racism could be detected merely by examining whether Blacks and Whites differentially report that they are treated unfairly at work (for example, a failure of supervisors to provide the information necessary to adequately do one's job) without explicitly asking whether such treatment is due to discrimination. Everyday discrimination would be indicated if these reports of unfair treatment, or mistreatment, varied as a function of race. Thus, our first hypothesis was as follows:

Hypothesis 1: Blacks will report more mistreatment in the workplace than will Whites.

Everyday Discrimination and Well-Being

The neglect of everyday discrimination by organizational researchers might imply that such "minor" incidents are assumed to be not particularly important, in terms of impact on the lives of minorities. We do not believe that such an assumption is warranted. On the contrary, the earlier cited results of D. Williams et al. (1997), as well as recent popular press publications such as, *It's the little things: The everyday interactions that get under the skin of Blacks and Whites* (L. Williams, 2001), suggest that little everyday incidents can have large consequences. Although "everyday" incidents may be less severe forms of discrimination, they are likely to be far, far more frequent. If one perceives that discrimination and bias against one's racial group are pervasive in one's environment, feelings of hopelessness and resignation can result (Branscombe et al., 1999). Furthermore, incidents of everyday discrimination may have a cumulative impact on the lives of individuals, in ways that studies of major discriminatory events do not assess (Swim et al., 1998). Swim et al. (2001) found that "everyday" sexist incidents had psychological ramifications for women, with exposure to sexist incidents associated with more anger and depression, and lower self-esteem. We expect that incidents of everyday racism similarly impact the lives of Black Americans, leading to dysfunctional psychological outcomes.

There is a growing recognition that encounters with discrimination are stressors in the lives of stigmatized individuals. A "stressor" is some event that taxes an individual's adaptive resources (Lazarus & Folkman, 1984). As Miller and Kaiser (2001) point out, discrimination is taxing because it impedes access to opportunities and adversely affects interpersonal interactions, resulting in psychological and physiological stress responses, such as negative emotions and heightened blood pressure. Furthermore, they noted that the ambiguous nature of many discriminatory events may exacerbate the stressful encounter. Crocker et al. (1991) found that attributional ambiguity regarding feedback about one's performance in cross-race evaluation situations is damaging to the self-esteem of Blacks. In addition, Schneider et al. (2000) found that individuals who reported ethnic harassment incidents consisting only of "exclusion" (e.g. being excluded from work-related or social interactions due to ethnicity) exhibited more negative personal and organizational outcomes than those who experienced both exclusion and verbal ethnic harassment (e.g. ethnic slurs or derogatory comments). This result suggests that it may be less stressful to be subjected to negative treatment that is clearly the result of prejudice (because clear verbal racism has also been expressed) than mistreatment that has no such unambiguous cause (e.g. being excluded but not entirely certain whether racism is the reason). Thus, as incidents of everyday racism are likely to be more attributionally ambiguous than blatant discrimination, they may be especially significant stressors in spite of their seemingly minor nature.

The stress associated with discrimination has been shown to be negatively related to the well-being of the targets of discrimination (e.g. R.J. Burke, 1991; Jackson et al., 1996; Kessler et al., 1999; Sanchez & Brock, 1996; Schneider et al., 2000; Valentine et al., 1999). Although previous research has focused on major types of discriminatory events, we believe, as argued earlier, that everyday discrimination also is stressful and followed by negative personal outcomes. Of course, we will not be asking respondents to directly report everyday discrimination (for the reasons outlined), but instead, we will be assessing racial *differences* in reports of everyday mistreatment as indicative of every-day discrimination. We expect that everyday mistreatment will be damaging, and as we propose that Blacks will experience more of this mistreatment; thus, we would expect that they would exhibit lower well-being than Whites due to these expected mistreatment differences. Thus, our second and third hypotheses:

Hypothesis 2: The experience of everyday mistreatment is associated negatively with well-being, such that individuals experiencing more everyday mistreatment will report lower well-being.

Hypothesis 3: The relationship between race and well-being is mediated by the amount of everyday mistreatment experienced in the workplace.

We examined these hypotheses using secondary data from three different samples and several indicators of well-being. Well-being may be thought of as encompassing both "context-free" forms of well-being, such as overall mental or physical health, as well as "context-specific" forms, such as job-specific well-being, commonly referred to as job satisfaction (Warr, 1999; but see Brief & Atieh, 1987). The first study investigates the existence of everyday mistreatment of Blacks in a civilian sample, as well as its impact on job-specific well-being. Studies 2 and 3, using military samples, then attempt to "constructively replicate" (Lykken, 1968) the findings of Study 1, by employing a different measure of everyday racism and a much broader set of outcome variables, including measures of context-free well-being, as indexed by reported physical and emotional health.

Study 1

An aim of Study 1, as described earlier, was to assess the existence of everyday discrimination through unobtrusive means in order to sidestep the problems of attributional ambiguity that are inherent in current measures of discrimination. The study examines reports of mistreatment in a national sample of Black and White employees. Even though the items do not reference "discrimination," we expect that Blacks will report more mistreatment on the job than Whites, providing evidence in support of our first hypothesis.

Furthermore, we expect to find that the experience of everyday racism in the workplace is associated with lower job-specific well-being, manifested by lower reported job satisfaction. There is some empirical evidence that racial discrimination in the workplace is related to lowered organizational commitment and job satisfaction (R.J. Burke, 1991; Sanchez & Brock, 1996; Valentine et al., 1999). But again, none of this research has focused on everyday racial discrimination, which we expect also will have a detrimental effect on job-specific well-being.

Method

Data

Data for the current study were drawn from a study entitled "Prejudice and violence in the American workplace, 1988–1991: Survey of an eastern corporation," conducted by Ehrlich and Larcom (1993), and available through the Inter-University Consortium of Political and Social Research. The study examined mistreatment and victimization of employees in two large work sites of a single corporation.

Sample

In the Ehrlich and Larcom (1993) study, personal interviews were conducted with 327 first-line workers at an American corporation in the mid-Atlantic states. Only data from Black and White respondents were included in our study. The final sample included 314 respondents, of which 79.6 percent were White. The average age of respondents was 37 years (range 20–64); 58 percent were male, over 40 percent had completed a college degree or greater; and average tenure on the job was 11.92 years (SD = 7.88).

Measures

Race Race was measured by a single item that asked respondents how they identified themselves by race (1 = White, 2 = Black).

Everyday mistreatment This dataset contained items that assessed different forms of mistreatment experienced at work and items that assessed the frequency with which these forms of mistreatment occurred. For the purposes of this study, questions assessing the incidence of mistreatment ("Yes" or "No") were combined with those assessing frequency, such that items were scored on a 3-point scale from (0) "no" to (2) "more than once." Our scale consisted of 10 items that asked respondents whether or not anyone had mistreated them in a variety of ways, such as "Set you up for failure," "Gave others privileges you didn't get," "Treated you as if you didn't exist," "Damaged your personal property," or "Made insulting jokes or comments." The scale was found to have an internal consistency reliability estimate [Cronbach's (1951) alpha] of .60. Importantly, these items did not ask respondents to make any attributions to "discrimination" or "prejudice."

Job-specific well-being Job-specific well-being was measured by a single item assessing overall job satisfaction (see Wanous et al., 1997, for a discussion on the acceptability and validity of single-item measures of global job satisfaction), scored on a 5-point scale ranging from (1) "very satisfied" to (5) "very dissatisfied."

Results

Existence of everyday discrimination

Means, standard deviations, reliability estimates, and intercorrelations are presented in Table 1.

Supporting Hypothesis 1, race was significantly related to mistreatment (r = .21, *p* < .01), with Blacks perceiving significantly more mistreatment on the job. This is consistent with our expectation that Blacks experience

Table 1: Study 1 descriptive information and intercorrelations for included variables

	Variable	Mean	SD	Alpha	1	2	3
1	Race	1.20	0.40	-	-		
2	Mistreatment	0.14	0.17	0.60	0.21**	-	
3	Job Satisfaction	2.09	1.01	-	-0.15**	-0.18**	-

Note: N = 314.
p** < .01.

everyday discrimination, as indicated by substantially more unfair and unkind treatment in the workplace. In addition, Black individuals had lower perceptions of job satisfaction ($r = -.15, p < .01$).

Consequences of everyday discrimination

We hypothesized that Blacks would report lower levels of well-being (job-specific well-being in this study) than Whites, and that this relationship would be mediated by everyday mistreatment. Consistent with Baron and Kenny (1986), full mediation is established if the relationship between the independent variable (IV) and dependent variable (DV) drops to zero when the mediator is included in the regression equation. Given that the direct effect did not drop to zero, we tested whether mistreatment partially mediated the relationship between race and job satisfaction. The significance of the indirect effect of race on job satisfaction through mistreatment was investigated, using the procedure described by MacKinnon et al. (1995) to conduct a Z-test of the indirect effect size. Providing some support for our third hypothesis, the indirect effect of race on job satisfaction through mistreatment was significant ($Z = 844, p < .01$), indicating that partial mediation was achieved (see Table 4).

Discussion

We found, as hypothesized, that Blacks reported higher levels of mistreatment on the job than did Whites. Notably, Blacks perceived more mistreatment though the items used did not reference race or discrimination. We take this as evidence that everyday discrimination is experienced by Blacks on the job. The results of this study suggest that workplace discrimination researchers should widen the scope of what they consider to be "discrimination" in order to more fully

capture the experience of being a target of discrimination in the workplace.

Furthermore, even though this everyday discrimination consisted of relatively minor discriminatory incidents, it did partially account for lower job satisfaction on the part of Black employees. This finding is particularly noteworthy because Blacks were not primed to attribute mistreatment to their race. Thus, this study provides some evidence that the experience of everyday discrimination on the job is associated with negative job-specific well-being outcomes. Blacks appear to be experiencing an additional source of stress on the job, one with which Whites do not have to cope. Moreover, this additional source of stress for Black workers is related to impaired well-being.

Studies 2 and 3

Studies 2 and 3 are attempts to constructively replicate the findings of Study 1 with different samples and a different survey instrument. Thus, we again tested whether Blacks report more mistreatment on the job than Whites and examine the relationship between differential mistreatment and job-specific well-being. We then extended these findings by examining the relationship of everyday discrimination with more context-free forms of well-being, in terms of reported emotional and physical well-being.

Although not focusing on everyday discrimination, ample empirical evidence does suggest that discrimination adversely affects psychological well-being as indicated, for example, by lowered levels of self-esteem and increased levels of anxiety and depression (e.g. Jackson et al., 1996; Kessler et al., 1999; Kessler & Neighbors, 1986; Noh et al., 1999; Radhakrishnan, 1998; Schneider et al., 2000; D. Williams et al., 1997). The stress of discrimination also has been found to negatively impact the physical health reported by members of stigmatized groups (e.g. Jackson et al., 1996, 1999; D. Williams et al., 1997). However, few studies have focused on discrimination *in the work-place* as a source of distress, as we intend to do here. This is especially true regarding *race* discrimination. Moreover, to our knowledge, no previous research has attempted to assess the existence and outcomes of *everyday* discrimination in the workplace, nor have unobtrusive measures of discrimination been employed. We expected that everyday discrimination would negatively impact well-being, as do more serious discriminatory incidents. Although each everyday discrimination event may be minor, the cumulative impact of such pervasive discrimination and the stress of attendant attributional ambiguity is likely to be detrimental to the well-being of Black workers.

Method

Data

Data for Studies 2 and 3 were from the Department of Defense 1995 Sexual Harassment Survey, Form B (Bastian et al., 1996). The survey and data are publicly available from the Department of Defense (see http://www.dod.gov).

Sample

As Study 3 was a replication of Study 2, using the same survey instrument but with a different sample, the methodology for both studies will be discussed in this section. The sample for Study 2 comprised 5483 individuals from the United States Navy. Twenty-three percent of respondents were Black, and 80 percent were female with an average age of 31.6 years (range 20–50). The over-sampling of women reflects the survey's original purpose in evaluating

sexual harassment in the military. Data from 8311 United States Army personnel were used as the sample for Study 3. This sample had a higher percentage of Black respondents (40 percent), and a similar percentage of women (82 percent). The average age for the Army sample was 32.7 years (range 20–50). The personnel for both studies were selected through a nonproportional stratified random sampling technique; rationale and definition of the strata may be found in the survey technical report (see Bastian et al., 1996).

Measures

Race A single item asked respondents to indicate their race. As in Study 1, the predictor of central interest was race; thus only respondents identifying themselves as White (coded "1") or Black (coded "2") were utilized.

Everyday mistreatment Consistent with our conceptual definition of everyday discrimination, we selected items that reflected unfair treatment, or mistreatment, but did not reference race or discrimination as the cause of the treatment. Five items were selected to tap the construct domain of overall mistreatment, each answered on a 5-point Likert type scale (from 1 "strongly disagree" to 5 "strongly agree"). For example, items asked to what extent "does the chain of command provide you with the information you need to do your job?," "is your work performance evaluated fairly?," and "do you get the assignments you need to be competitive for promotions?" Positively worded items were reverse coded so that higher scores indicated more mistreatment. The internal consistency estimate was .75 in the Navy sample and .74 in the Army sample.

Job-specific well-being The survey contained nine items that comprise a measure of job

Table 2: Study 2 descriptive information and intercorrelations for included variables

	Variable	Mean	SD	Alpha	1	2	3	4
1	Race	1.23	0.42	-	-			
2	Mistreatment	2.80	0.85	0.75	0.12**	-		
3	Job Satisfaction	3.50	0.71	0.81	-0.13**	-0.74**	-	
4	Emotional Well-Being	3.51	0.92	0.85	-0.03*	-0.34**	0.39**	-
5	Physical Well-Being	4.24	0.78	0.80	-0.05**	0.25**	0.28**	0.42**

Note: N = 5483.
$*p < .05; **p < .01$.

satisfaction, assessing respondents' satisfaction with various facets of their job, such as "your pay and benefits," "the relationship you have with your co-workers," and "the kind of work you do." Items were answered on a 5-point scale, with response options ranging from (1) "very satisfied" to (5) "very dissatisfied." The internal consistency estimate was .81 in the Navy sample and .82 in the Army sample.

Emotional well-being Emotional well-being was assessed with five items inquiring about the respondent's emotional state in the past four weeks, such as "How much of the time have you felt down-hearted and blue?" and "How much of the time have you been a happy person?," answered on a 6-point frequency scale ranging from (1) "all of the time" to (6) "none of the time." Negatively worded items were reverse coded so that higher scores reflected higher emotional well-being. Internal consistency estimates were .84 in both samples.

Perceived physical well-being Four questions assessed the respondents' perceptions of their general state of health over the previous four weeks, and asked respondents how true each question (e.g. "My health is excellent") was on a 5-point scale ranging from (1) "definitely true" to (5) "definitely false." Consistent with emotional well-being and job satisfaction

scales, higher numbers reflected better physical well-being. The internal consistency estimate in the Navy sample was .80, and in the Army sample was .82.

Results

Because of similarity in the samples and findings, results for Studies 2 and 3 are discussed together. Descriptive statistics and intercorrelations for Study 2 and Study 3 can be found in Table 2 and Table 3, respectively.

Existence of everyday discrimination

Again, consistent with our hypotheses, race was significantly associated with mistreatment (Navy, $r = .12$, $p < .01$; Army, $r = .08$, $p < .01$). The similarity of these results to those found in Study 1, despite differences in the populations sampled and variation in the everyday mistreatment item content, provides persuasive (though disheartening) evidence of the existence of everyday workplace discrimination.

Consequences of everyday discrimination

Beyond substantiating and generalizing the existence of everyday discrimination in the workplace, we examined its consequences. A

Table 3: Study 3 descriptive information and intercorrelations for included variables

	Variable	Mean	SD	Alpha	1	2	3	4
1	Race	1.40	0.49	-	-			
2	Mistreatment	2.72	0.84	0.74	0.08**	-		
3	Job Satisfaction	3.47	0.71	0.82	-0.11**	-0.75**	-	
4	Emotional Well-Being	3.52	0.92	0.84	-0.01	-0.36**	0.41**	-
5	Physical Well-Being	4.14	0.86	0.82	-0.09**	-0.26**	0.28**	0.43**

Note: N = 8311.

$**p < .01$.

mediation analysis, identical to that used in Study 1 for job satisfaction, was conducted for each indicator of well-being.

Job-specific well-being As a precondition to mediation analysis, we first showed that race was, in fact, significantly negatively related to job satisfaction (Navy, $r = -.13$, $p < .01$; Army, $r = -.11$, $p < .01$). As presented in Table 4, the tests of indirect effects show a clear and consistent pattern across studies; the results from Studies 2 and 3, which used a multiple-item facet measure of job satisfaction, parallel the results from Study 1, which utilized a single-item global measure of satisfaction. Specifically, additional support for Hypotheses 2 and 3 is provided by the partial mediation effect clearly shown in both the Navy and Army samples. Thus, we conclude that not only does everyday discrimination exist, but that the consequences for the job satisfaction of those victimized is statistically significant.

Emotional well-being The results of the tests of indirect effects on emotional well-being for Studies 2 and 3 are displayed in Table 4. Consistent with Hypothesis 2, mistreatment was strongly negatively related to emotional well-being (Navy, $r = -.34$, $p < .01$; Army, $r = -.36$, $p < .01$). Although not as robust as the relationship with job satisfaction, the results of Study

2 support the mediational role of everyday discrimination in the relationship between race and emotional well-being. Contrary to our hypothesis, however, the relationship between race and emotional well-being in the Army sample was nonsignificant; therefore, we did not attempt to interpret the test of mediation.

Perceived physical well-being Significant relationships between mistreatment and reported physical well-being were observed in both samples (Navy, $r = -.25$, $p < .01$; Army, $r = -.26$, $p < .01$). Support for Hypotheses 2 and 3 was found in both Study 2 and Study 3, as Blacks reported significantly worse physical well-being (Navy, $r = -.05$, $p < .01$; Army, $r = -.09$, $p < .01$), and the relationship was fully mediated by the mistreatment these individuals experienced on the job.

Discussion

With these studies, we replicated the findings from Study 1, again finding evidence that Blacks are experiencing everyday discrimination in the form of minor, pervasive mistreatment and unfairness on the job. The survey from which these data were taken did not in any way mention racial discrimination or prejudice; thus, demand characteristics and

Table 4: Linear regression results of effects of race on well-being measures and effect sizes for Black/White differences

Effect	Job satisfaction (Study 1)	Job satisfaction (Study 2)	Job satisfaction (Study 3)	Emotional well-being (Study 2)	Emotional well-being (Study 3)	Physical well-being (Study 2)	Physical well-being (Study 3)
	N = 314	N = 5483	N = 8311	N = 5483	N = 8311	N = 5483	N = 8311
Direct	-0.11*	-0.04**	-0.04**	-0.01	0.02*	-0.02	-0.07**
Indirect through mistreatment	-0.04**	-0.09**	-0.07**	0.02*	-0.03**	-0.03**	-0.02*
Total	-0.15**	-0.13**	-0.11**	-0.03**	-0.01	-0.05**	-0.09**
Effect size (d)	0.3714	0.3091	0.2203	0.0647	0.0144	0.1247	0.1800

*p < .05; **p < .01.

cues to prejudice cannot account for these results. Furthermore, as in Study 1, this discrimination accounted for lower reported job satisfaction on the part of Blacks. Thus, even in the military, one of the most integrated organizations in the country (Hacker, 1995), Blacks appear to experience everyday mistreatment and are less satisfied as a result. One might expect even greater amounts of everyday discrimination and negative personal outcomes for Blacks who are in less integrated environments, for example, where they occupy "token" or "solo" positions in their jobs (Kanter, 1977).

Everyday discrimination also appears to adversely affect other indicators of well-being, consistent with the findings of D. Williams et al. (1997). Blacks commonly are found to have poorer health than Whites in America, which is often attributed to factors such as poverty, diet, and unequal access to health care (e.g. Kessler & Neighbors, 1986; D. Williams et al., 1997). This study suggests an additional factor contributing to this health inequality: the stress of encountering

everyday discrimination in the workplace. As the Blacks and Whites in these samples live in common military environments, there should not be marked differences between the health care and diet provided to Black and White personnel, and none of those personnel should be particularly impoverished. This increases our confidence in the conclusion that everyday discrimination creates this racial disparity in reported physical well-being. But, it is important to note that we sampled perceived physical well-being, not actual health status. Future researchers should attend to the possible relationship between everyday discrimination in the workplace and the health status of Blacks.

The direct positive relationship between race and emotional well-being in the Army sample, apparently offsetting the negative impact of mistreatment, is somewhat surprising. One possible explanation is that some Blacks may, in certain circumstances, psychologically withdraw from domains in which they are mistreated in order to protect their mental health. Crocker and Lawrence (1999) reported on a series of studies indicating that Blacks do manage to maintain surprisingly high self-esteem because their self-esteem tends not to be contingent on domains that are valued by the majority group and that are often inhospitable toward Blacks, such as work and school. Instead, they suggest that Blacks' self-esteem rests upon sources such as religious faith and family and social ties. Branscombe et al. (1999) found that perceiving pervasive discrimination also tended to increase Blacks' social identification with other Blacks, which was beneficial to emotional health and counterbalanced direct negative effects of discrimination. Such cognitive dissociation of emotional well-being from work may be operating here; the lower job satisfaction found for Blacks could be an indicator of work withdrawal. Future studies might include measures of psychological withdrawal from work to investigate this possibility. In addition, they might consider the potential for increased social identification and reliance on alternate life domains as a means of maintaining well-being.

In light of this discussion, the relationship between mistreatment and perceptions of physical well-being is even more striking. The stress of everyday discrimination apparently still takes a toll on its targets even if it may be countered by using alternate bases for self-esteem and emotional well-being. Blascovich et al. (2001) found that the experience of stereotype threat (a fear of confirming stereotypes about one's group through one's performance; see Steele, 1997; Steele & Aronson, 1995) increased the blood pressure of African Americans. Perceptions of everyday discrimination may trigger chronic stereotype threat on the job for Blacks, elevating blood pressure and adversely affecting health. Further research is necessary to determine the precise mechanisms by which the experience of everyday discrimination may affect physical well-being.

Before moving on, it is important to note explicitly that the statistically significant relationships detected in Studies 2 and 3 were small in magnitude. However, small effect sizes may be expected in preliminary studies in a new area (Cohen, 1977). We calculated Cohen's d-statistic for racial differences in our outcome measures, which express the difference between means as a function of units of variability. These values are shown in Table 4. Although the values for emotional well-being are < .1 (consistent with the weak or nonsignificant effects found in our other analyses), d values for the remaining measures range from .12 to .37. We also calculated d-statistics for the difference in mistreatment by race, and found effects of similar magnitude (d = .52 for the corporate sample; .16 for Army, and .29 for Navy). Cohen (1977) does refer to a d = .2 as being a "small effect size," but points out that "in new areas of research inquiry, effect sizes are likely to be small ... because the phenomena under study are typically not under good experimental or measurement control or both" (p. 25). Certainly that is the case here, and in future work involving more targeted primary data collection effect sizes may be found to be larger.

Furthermore, in several areas of psychology, it has been argued successfully that the import of a relationship cannot be judged adequately, out of context, by its magnitude alone (e.g. Abelson, 1985; Martell et al., 1996). We, for instance, concur with Eagly's (1995) position that the practical importance of a relationship depends on the consequences it implies in natural settings. That is, we feel that to explain even a small proportion of the variance in the well-being of individuals victimized in the workplace because of their skin color is a very worthwhile aim.

General Discussion

The studies reported here clearly indicate that research which focuses solely on major discriminatory events in the workplace does not fully capture Blacks' "lived experience" with racism on the job. To our knowledge, this is the first workplace-focused study to acknowledge that Blacks may experience racism in more subtle, everyday ways than typically assumed by organizational researchers. We found compelling evidence, in three different samples, that everyday discrimination against Blacks is occurring on the job, with negative outcomes for its targets. Furthermore, by using subtle measures that assess more general mistreatment, we were able to assess the existence of everyday discrimination apart from respondents' propensity to make attributions to discrimination.

We do acknowledge that the relationships between mistreatment and well-being, irrespective of race, are relatively strong, indicating that mistreatment lowers well-being for all individuals. However, this does not undermine our argument that such mistreatment, when associated with race, indicates discrimination. Take the case of a major event like being fired from one's job. Such an event likely damages any person's well-being (at least temporarily), yet is still considered evidence of discrimination if Blacks are found to be fired more often than equivalently performing Whites. Such was the case here, as Blacks were found to experience *more* mistreatment than Whites, and it is that differential that we take as evidence of discrimination.

Importantly, the fact that everyday discriminatory incidents in the workplace are "minor" does not imply that the outcome of facing such discrimination is negligible. We found that being the target of everyday mistreatment appears to negatively impact several facets of well-being, both job specific

and context free. The finding of lower job-specific well-being is disturbing not only in terms of personal costs, but also because it may represent organizational costs, as job satisfaction is related to role withdrawal and other organizationally dysfunctional behaviors (Brief, 1998). Impaired emotional and physical well-being also likely have organizational costs (as well as being personally damaging to the targets), in that they may lead to absenteeism and other withdrawal behaviors. Therefore, organizations that wish to be welcoming to qualified Black personnel should be concerned about the negative effects of everyday discrimination on job satisfaction and well-being, which may influence retention of those employees. However, research which specifically measures job involvement, commitment, absenteeism, and other withdrawal behaviors is needed to determine whether Blacks cope with everyday discrimination through job withdrawal.

Unfortunately, everyday discrimination at work is likely to be extremely difficult to combat. The ambiguity and subtle nature of many everyday racist events make them hard to definitively identify or proscribe. Furthermore, perpetrators may not even be fully cognizant that they are engaging in racist actions. For example, "subtle" or "modern" racists tend to believe they are not racist, and endorse plausible nonprejudiced explanations to justify otherwise prejudiced acts (Brief & Barsky, 2000). Even people who are strongly motivated not to be racist are subject to automatic cognitive activation of stereotypes that can unconsciously influence behavior (e.g. Chen & Bargh, 1997; Devine, 1989; Dovidio et al., 1997). Thus, typical one-time diversity training courses and nondiscrimination policies may do little to alleviate the existence of everyday discrimination in the workplace. Nonetheless, organizations can make efforts toward reducing this sort of discrimination, even if complete elimination is unlikely. Indeed, we hope that our findings will highlight the need for organizational decision-makers to adapt to the changing face of racism and discrimination against Blacks in this country. Brief and Barsky (2000) suggest that training which induces modern racists to expand their concept of what "nonprejudiced" entails may lead to some modifications of their behavior. They also suggest self-regulation training to help nonprejudiced individuals overcome automatically activated stereotypes and achieve truly nonracist interactions. Moreover, perhaps human resource professionals can simply be more vigilant for minor slights and mistreatment that may be differentially affecting Black employees, or conduct surveys or workshops that assess the existence of such mistreatment in their organizations. Attending to "minor" discrimination in organizations may be key to establishing a true "positive diversity climate," which several researchers have pointed out requires more than simply removing official barriers to entry and mobility for minority employees (e.g. Hicks-Clarke & Iles, 2000). Future research must focus more attention on possible courses of action that organizations can take to reduce everyday discrimination in the workplace.

Limitations

Admittedly, there may be alternate explanations for our findings. For example, Blacks may be experiencing more mistreatment because they occupy lower organizational positions than do Whites. However, we investigated this possibility using rank as a control variable in the military datasets (enlisted, noncommissioned officer, or officer) and obtained a similar pattern of effects. For the corporate dataset, all employees were described as "first-line workers," but we did also re-run analyses in that dataset using education

as a control variable, finding no change in the pattern of effects.

As another alternate explanation, one could argue that Blacks are being mistreated on the job not because of their race, but because they are poor performers or because they are interpersonally more difficult or unpleasant. Owing to our use of secondary data sources, our information was limited, and we cannot conclusively refute these alternate explanations, however offensive they may seem. However, even if a relationship did exist between, for example, performance and mistreatment, it might be that an environment rife with everyday discrimination is not conducive to peak performance, so that mistreatment is undermining performance, rather than poor performance engendering mistreatment. Additional research is required to assess these alternate explanations and explore potential issues of causality.

Given the secondary nature of our data, we were presented with few options in constructing the measures used. So, for example, the measures of mistreatment used in Study 1, and in Studies 2 and 3, likely would have looked different if they had been developed exclusively for our purposes. Although the use of secondary data was certainly not ideal, we undertook this effort as a "first step" in a planned program of research focusing on the concept of everyday discrimination. We feel that the results we have obtained here (*despite* the fact that the data at our disposal were not ideal) offer encouragement for our continuation of this research program. For our subsequent primary-research studies in this area, which are already underway as of this writing, we have crafted a measure of everyday workplace mistreatment that we hope more precisely captures the construct of interest.

Finally, numerous researchers investigating the consequences of work-related stress (e.g. Brief et al., 1988; M.J. Burke et al., 1993) have advocated accounting for the critical role of underlying response tendencies, such as those associated with trait negative affectivity (e.g. Watson & Clark, 1984), in self-report data collection. Owing to the use of archival data, we were not able to include these items in the survey. However, we know of no evidence that shows consistent evidence of racial differences in negative affectivity or other personality dimensions. Furthermore, testing the interaction of race with mistreatment as a predictor of the well-being measures did not yield any significant results, suggesting that Blacks and Whites do not respond differently to mistreatment. Thus, we believe that the majority of our findings cannot be explained by a common response bias related to underlying personality traits.

Conclusions

In conclusion, these studies provide evidence that everyday discrimination does occur in the workplace and that it negatively affects Blacks' well-being. As organizational researchers are beginning to turn their attention toward understanding the experience of being a target of discrimination on the job, these sorts of everyday encounters with racism should not be ignored. Everyday discrimination is part of the reality of being Black in America, and it has real effects in the lives of Black Americans. Thus, attempts to "embrace diversity" and make workplaces welcoming to minorities will need to address the reality of everyday discrimination.

Questions

1. What are microaggressions, and how do they differ from blatantly racist acts?

2. What are the ways in which Blacks' well-being is affected from everyday discrimination in the workplace?

3. Blatantly racist acts are considered more severe and easily attributable to racism. Consider two cases, the first where a Black man is called a slur and told that he won't be considered for job advancement, and another where every day a Black man experiences microaggressions that not only prevent job advancement but also are ambiguous in that they are subtle and not openly racist. The first case is like a punch, while the second case is like thousands of paper cuts that never fully heal. In the first case, there is a legal remedy (of sorts), while in the second case it is difficult to discern the source with certainty, and without empirical evidence there is no remedy. Given what the authors detail about Blacks' well-being, how would you, if you were in management, ensure that microaggressions did not occur on your watch?

References

Abelson, R.P. A variance explanation paradox: When a little is a lot. *Psychological Bulletin,* 1985, *97,* 129–33.

Baron, R.M. & Kenny, D.A. The moderator-mediator variable distinction in social psychological research: Conceptual, strategic, and statistical considerations. *Journal of Personality and Social Psychology,* 1986, *51,* 1173–82.

Barrett, L.F. & Swim, J.K. Appraisals of prejudice and discrimination. In J.K. Swim & C. Stanger (Eds), *Prejudice: The target's perspective.* San Diego, CA: Academic Press, 1998, pp. 11–36.

Bastian, L.D., Lancaster, A.R. & Reyst, H.E. *Department of Defense 1995 Sexual Harassment Survey report.* Arlington, VA: Defense Manpower Data Center, 1996.

Blascovich, J., Spencer, S.J., Quinn, D. & Steele, C. African Americans and high blood pressure: The role of stereotype threat. *Psychological Science,* 2001, *12,* 225–9.

Bobo, L. Race, interests, and beliefs about affirmative action: Unanswered questions and new directions. *American Behavioral Scientist,* 1998, *41,* 985–1003.

Branscombe, N.R., Schmitt, M.T. & Harvey, R.D. Perceiving pervasive discrimination among African Americans: Implications for group identification and well-being. *Journal of Personality and Social Psychology,* 1999, *77,* 135–49.

Brief, A.P. *Attitudes in and around organizations.* Thousand Oaks, CA: Sage, 1998.

Brief, A.P. & Atieh, J.M. Studying job stress: Are we making mountains out of molehills? *Journal of Occupational Behavior,* 1987, *8,* 115–26.

Brief, A.P. & Barsky, A. Establishing a climate for diversity: Inhibition of prejudice reactions in the workplace. In G.R. Ferris (Ed.), *Research in personnel and human resources management,* Vol. 19. Greenwich, CT: JAI Press, 2000, pp. 91–129.

Brief, A.P., Burke, M.J., George, J.M., Robinson, B.S. & Webster, J. Should negative affectivity remain an unmeasured variable in the study of job stress? *Journal of Applied Psychology,* 1988, *73,* 193–8.

Brief, A.P., Dietz, J., Cohen, R.R., Pugh, S.D. & Vaslow, J.B. Just doing business: Modern racism and obedience to authority as explanations for employment discrimination. *Organizational Behavior and Human Decision Processes,* 2000, *81,* 72–97.

Burke, M.J., Brief, A.P. & George, J.M. The role of negative affectivity in understanding relationships between self-reports of stressors and strains: A comment on the applied psychology literature. *Journal of Applied Psychology,* 1993, *78,* 402–12.

Burke, R.J. Work experiences of minority managers and professionals: Individual and organizational costs of perceived bias. *Psychological Reports,* 1991, *69,* 1011–23.

Chen, M. & Bargh, J.A. Nonconscious behavioral confirmation processes: The self-fulfilling consequences of automatic stereotype activation. *Journal of Experimental Social Psychology,* 1997, *33,* 541–60.

Cohen, J. *Statistical power analysis for the behavioral sciences.* New York: Academic Press, 1977.

Crocker, J. & Lawrence, J.S. Social stigma and self-esteem: The role of contingencies of self-worth. In D.A. Prentice & D.T. Miller (Eds), *Cultural divides: Understanding and overcoming group conflict.* New York: Sage, 1999, pp. 364–92.

Crocker, J. & Major, B. Social stigma and self-esteem: The self-protective properties of stigma. *Psychological Review,* 1989, *96,* 608–30.

Crocker, J., Major, B. & Steele, C. Social stigma. In D.T. Gilbert, S.T. Fiske & G. Lindzey (Eds), *The handbook of social psychology,* Vol. II, 4th edn. New York: McGraw-Hill, 1998, pp. 504–53.

Crocker, J., Voelkl, K., Testa, M. & Major, B. Social stigma: The affective consequences of attributional ambiguity. *Journal of Personality and Social Psychology,* 1991, 60, 218–28.

Cronbach, L. Coefficient alpha and the internal structure of tests. *Psychometrika,* 1951, *16,* 297–334.

Devine, P.G. Stereotypes and prejudice: Their automatic and controlled components. *Journal of Personality and Social Psychology,* 1989, *56,* 5–18.

Dovidio, J.F. & Gaertner, S.L. Aversive racism in selection decisions: 1989 and 1999. *Psychological Science,* 2000, *11,* 315–19.

Dovidio, J.F., Gaertner, S.L. & Bachman, B.A. Racial bias in organizations: The role of group processes in its causes and cures. In M.E. Turner (Ed.), *Groups at work: Theory and research.* Mahwah, NJ: Erlbaum, 2001, pp. 415–44.

Dovidio, J.F., Kawakami, K., Johnson, C., Johnson, B. & Howard, A. On the nature of prejudice: Automatic and controlled processes. *Journal of Experimental Social Psychology,* 1997, *33,* 510–40.

Eagly, A. The science and politics of company women and men. *American Psychologist,* 1995, *50,* 145–58.

Ehrlich, H.J. & Larcom, E.K. Prejudice and violence in the American workplace, 1988–1991: Survey of an eastern corporation [Computer file]. Conducted by Howard J. Ehrlich and Barbara E.K. Larcom, National Institute Against Prejudice and Violence, Baltimore, MD. Ann Arbor, MI: Interuniversity Consortium for Political and Social Research [producer and distributor], 1993.

Essed, P. *Understanding everyday racism.* Newbury Park, CA: Sage, 1991.

Frazer, R.A. & Wiersma, U.J. Prejudice versus discrimination in the employment interview: We may hire equally, but our memories harbor prejudice. *Human Relations,* 2001, *54,* 173–91.

Gaertner, S.L. & Dovidio, J.F. The aversive form of racism. In J.F. Dovidio & S.L. Gaertner (Eds), *Prejudice, discrimination, and racism.* San Diego, CA: Academic Press, 1986, pp. 61–89.

Gomez, J.P. & Trierweiler, S.J. Does discrimination terminology create response bias in questionnaire studies of discrimination? *Personality and Social Psychology Bulletin,* 2001, *27,* 630–8.

Hacker, A. *Two nations: Black and White, separate. Hostile, unequal.* New York: Ballantine Books, 1995.

Hicks-Clarke, D. & Iles, P. Climate for diversity and its effects on career and organisational attitudes and perceptions. *Personnel Review,* 2000, *29,* 324–45.

Jackson, J.S., Brown, T.N., Williams, D.R., Torres, M., Sellers, S. & Brown, K. Racism and physical and mental health status of African Americans: A thirteen year national panel study. *Ethnicity and Disease,* 1996, *6,* 132–47.

Jackson, J.S., Williams, D.R. & Torres, M. Perceptions of discrimination and health: The social stress process. Unpublished manuscript, 1999.

Kanter, R.M. *Men and women of the corporation.* New York: Basic Books, 1977.

Katz, I. & Hass, R.G. Racial ambivalence and American value conflict: Correlational and priming studies of dual cognitive structures. *Journal of Personality and Social Psychology,* 1988, *55,* 893–905.

Kessler, R.C., Mickelson, K.D. & Williams, D.R. The prevalence, distribution, and mental health correlates of perceived discrimination in the United States. *Journal of Health and Social Behavior,* 1999, *40,* 208–30.

Kessler, R.C. & Neighbors, H.W. A new perspective on the relationships among race, social class, and psychological distress. *Journal of Health and Social Behavior,* 1986, *27,* 107–15.

Lazarus, R.S. & Folkman, S. *Stress, appraisal, and coping.* New York: Springer, 1984.

Lykken, D.T. Statistical significance in psychological research. *Psychological Bulletin,* 1968, *70,* 151–9.

MacKinnon, D.P., Warsi, G. & Dwyer, J. A simulation study of mediated effect measures. *Multivariate Behavioral Research,* 1995, *30,* 41–62.

Martell, R.F., Lane, D.M. & Emrich, L.E. Male-female differences: A computer simulation. *American Psychologist,* 1996, *51,* 157–8.

McConahay, J.B. Modern racism, ambivalence, and the Modern Racism Scale. In J.F. Dovidio & S.L. Gaertner (Eds), *Prejudice, discrimination, and racism.* San Diego, CA: Academic Press, 1986, pp. 91–125.

Miller, C.T. & Kaiser, C.R. A theoretical perspective on coping with stigma. *Journal of Social Issues,* 2001, *57,* 73–92.

Monteith, M.J. Contemporary forms of prejudice-related conflict: In search of a nutshell. *Personality and Social Psychology Bulletin,* 1996, *22,* 461–73.

Noh, S., Beiser, M., Kaspar, V., Hou, F. & Rummens, J. Perceived racial discrimination, depression, and coping: A study of Southeast Asian refugees in Canada. *Journal of Health and Social Behavior,* 1999, *40,* 193–207.

Pettigrew, T.F. & Martin, J. Shaping the organizational context for Black American inclusion. *Journal of Social Issues,* 1987, *43,* 41–78.

Radhakrishnan, P. Ethnic harassment and discrimination: Mediators or antecedents to the relation between organizational climate, stress, and health outcomes. Paper presented at the annual meeting of the Society of Industrial and Organizational Psychology, Dallas, TX, 1998.

Sanchez, J.I. & Brock, P. Outcomes of perceived discrimination among Hispanic employees: Is diversity management a luxury or a necessity? *Academy of Management Journal,* 1996, *39,* 704–19.

Schneider, K.T., Hitlan, R.T. & Radhakrishnan, P. An examination of the nature and correlates of ethnic harassment: Experiences in multiple contexts. *Journal of Applied Psychology,* 2000, *85,* 3–12.

Schneider, K.T., Swan, S. & Fitzgerald, L.F. Job-related and psychological effects of sexual harassment in the workplace: Empirical evidence from two organizations. *Journal of Applied Psychology,* 1997, *82,* 401–15.

Steele, C.M. A threat in the air: How stereotypes shape the intellectual identities and performance of women and African Americans. *American Psychologist,* 1997, *52,* 613–29.

Steele, C.M. & Aronson, J. Stereotype threat and the intellectual test performance of African Americans. *Journal of Personality and Social Psychology,* 1995, *69,* 797–811.

Stone, E.F., Stone, D.L. & Dipboye, R.L. Stigmas in organizations: Race, handicaps and physical unattractiveness. In K. Kelley (Ed.), *Issues, theory and research in industrial/organizational psychology: Advances in Psychology,* Vol. 82. Amsterdam: NorthHolland, 1992, pp. 385–457.

Swim, J.K., Cohen, L.L. & Hyers, L.L. Experiencing everyday prejudice and discrimination. In J.K. Swim & C. Stangor (Eds), *Prejudice: The target's perspective.* San Diego, CA: Academic Press, 1998, pp. 37–60.

Swim, J.K., Hyers, L.L., Cohen, L.L. & Ferguson, M.J. Everyday sexism: Evidence for its incidence, nature, and psychological impact from three daily diary studies. *Journal of Social Issues,* 2001, *57,* 31–53.

Trentham, S. & Larwood, L. Gender discrimination and the workplace: An examination of rational bias theory. *Sex Roles,* 1998, *38,* 1–28.

Valentine, S., Silver, L. & Twigg, N. Locus of control, job satisfaction, and job complexity: The role of perceived race discrimination. *Psychological Reports,* 1999, *84,* 1267–73.

Wanous, J.P., Reichers, A.E. & Hudy, M.J. Overall job satisfaction: How good are single item measures? *Journal of Applied Psychology,* 1997, *82,* 247–52.

Warr, P. Well-being and the workplace. In D. Kahneman, E. Diener & N. Schwarz (Eds), *Well-being: The foundations of hedonic psychology.* New York: Sage, 1999, pp. 392–412.

Watson, D. & Clark, L.A. Negative affectivity: The disposition to experience aversive emotional states. *Psychological Bulletin,* 1984, *96,* 465–90.

Williams, D.R., Yu, Y., Jackson, J.S. & Anderson, N.B. Racial differences in physical and mental health. *Journal of Health Psychology,* 1997, *2,* 335–51.

Williams, L. *It's the little things: The everyday interactions that get under the skin of Blacks and Whites,* New York: Harcourt Brace, 2001.

Notes

1. Elizabeth A. Deitch, Adam Barsky, Rebecca M. Butz, Suzanne Chan, Arthur P. Brief, and Jill C. Bradley, "Subtle Yet Significant: The Existence and Impact of Everyday Racial Discrimination in the Workplace," *Human Relations*, 56, no. 11 (2003): 1299-1324.

2. As a more detailed example, McConahay (1986) explains that the principal beliefs of the "modern racist" are as follows: (i) discrimination is a thing of the past because Blacks now have the freedom to compete in the marketplace and to enjoy those things they can afford; (ii) Blacks are pushing too hard, too fast, and into places they are not wanted; (iii) these tactics and demands are unfair; (iv) therefore, recent gains are undeserved and the prestige granting institutions of society are giving Blacks more attention and the concomitant status than they deserve; (v) the first four beliefs do not constitute racism because they are empirical facts; and (vi) *racism is bad*.

2. Affirmative Action: The Price of Preference[1]

Shelby Steele

UNCONVINCED THAT PRIVILEGE IS tied to color, Shelby Steele (b. 1946) sees privilege as an issue of economic advantage, asserting that his middle-class African American children are not "disadvantaged" and therefore do not suffer from racial discrimination. Steele argues against affirmative action because he claims it harms those it was intended to help. Throughout his essay, Steele focuses on affirmative action as reparations, arguing that it is meant as a type of repayment for discrimination against Blacks in the past. He sees the recipients of affirmative action as encouraged to assume victim status in order to benefit and concludes that this ruins a person's ability to be self-reliant.

Furthermore, he argues that Blacks who are hired for any position (in part due to affirmative action) are perceived as inferior, which exaggerates existing stereotypes and further entrenches white superiority. Steele instead proposes a model in which economically disadvantaged people would most especially benefit from educational and economic development. He envisions a rather Rawlsian meritocracy that results from a vigorous equal access and opportunity, coupled with severe sanctions against racism. Steele concludes that his model would provide the real means to overcome discrimination and inequality.

IN A FEW SHORT years, when my two children will be applying to college, the affirmative action policies by which most universities offer black students some form of preferential treatment will present me with a dilemma. I am a middle-class black, a college professor, far from wealthy, but also well-removed from the kind of deprivation that would qualify my children for the label "disadvantaged." Both of them have endured racial insensitivity from whites. They have been called names, have suffered slights, and have experienced first-hand the peculiar malevolence that racism brings out in people. Yet, they have never experienced racial discrimination, have never been stopped by their race on any path they have chosen to follow. Still, their society now tells them that if they will only designate themselves as black on their college applications, they will likely do better in the college lottery than if they conceal this fact. I think there is something of a Faustian bargain in this.

Of course, many blacks and a considerable number of whites would say that I was sanctimoniously making affirmative action into a test of character. They would say that this small preference is the meagerest recompense for centuries of unrelieved oppression. And to these arguments other very obvious facts must be added. In America, many marginally competent or flatly incompetent whites are hired everyday—some because their white skin suits the conscious or unconscious racial preference of their employer. The white children of alumni are often grandfathered into elite universities in what can only be seen as a residual benefit of historic white privilege. Worse, white incompetence is always an individual matter, while for blacks it is often confirmation of ugly stereotypes. The Peter Principle was not conceived with only blacks in mind. Given that unfairness cuts both ways, doesn't it only balance the scales of history that my children now receive a slight preference over whites? Doesn't this repay, in a small way, the systematic denial under which their grandfather lived out his days?

So, in theory, affirmative action certainly has all the moral symmetry that fairness requires—the injustice of historical and even contemporary white advantage is offset with black advantage; preference replaces prejudice, inclusion answers exclusion. It is reformist and corrective, even repentant and redemptive. And I would never sneer at these good intentions. Born in the late forties in Chicago, I started my education (a charitable term in this case) in a segregated school and suffered all the indignities that come to blacks in a segregated society. My father, born in the South, only made it to the third grade before the white man's fields took permanent priority over his formal education. And though he educated himself into an advanced reader with an almost professional authority, he could only drive a truck for a living and never earned more than ninety dollars a week in his entire life. So, yes, it is crucial to my sense of citizenship, to my ability to identify with the spirit and the interests of America, to know that this country, however imperfectly, recognizes its past sins and wishes to correct them.

Yet good intentions, because of the opportunity for innocence they offer us, are very seductive and can blind us to the effects they generate when implemented. In our society, affirmative action is, among other things, a testament to white goodwill and to black power, and in the midst of these heavy investments, its effects can be hard to see. But after twenty years of implementation, I think affirmative action has shown itself to be more bad than good and that blacks—whom I will focus on in this essay—now stand to lose more from it than they gain.

In talking with affirmative action administrators and with blacks and whites in general, it is clear that supporters of affirmative action focus on its good intentions while detractors emphasize its negative effects. Proponents talk about "diversity" and "pluralism"; opponents speak of "reverse discrimination," the unfairness of quotas and set-asides. It was virtually impossible to find people outside either camp. The closest I came was a white male manager at a large computer company who said, "I think it amounts to reverse discrimination, but I'll put up with a little of that for a little more diversity." I'll live with a little of the effect to gain a little of the intention, he seemed to be saying. But this only makes him a half-hearted supporter of affirmative action. I think many people who don't really like affirmative action support it to one degree or another anyway.

I believe they do this because of what happened to white and black Americans in the crucible of the sixties when whites were confronted with their racial guilt and blacks tasted their first real power. In this stormy time white absolution and black power coalesced into virtual mandates for society. Affirmative action became a meeting ground for these mandates in the law, and in the late sixties and early seventies it underwent a remarkable escalation of its mission from simple anti-discrimination enforcement to social engineering by means of quotas, goals, timetables, set-asides, and other forms of preferential treatment.

Legally, this was achieved through a series of executive orders and EEOC guidelines that allowed racial imbalances in the workplace to stand as proof of racial discrimination. Once it could be assumed that discrimination explained racial imbalances, it became easy to justify group remedies to presumed discrimination, rather than the normal case-by-case redress for proven discrimination. Preferential treatment through quotas, goals, and so on is designed to correct imbalances based on the assumption that they always indicate discrimination. This expansion of what constitutes discrimination allowed affirmative action to escalate into the business of social engineering in the name of anti-discrimination, to push society toward statistically proportionate racial representation, without any obligation of proving actual discrimination.

What accounted for this shift, I believe, was the white mandate to achieve a new racial innocence and the black mandate to gain power. Even though blacks had made great advances during the sixties without quotas, these mandates, which came to a head in the very late sixties, could no longer be satisfied by anything less than racial preferences. I don't think these mandates in themselves were wrong, since whites clearly needed to do better by blacks and blacks needed more real power in society. But, as they came together in affirmative action, their effect was to distort our understanding of racial discrimination in a way that allowed us to offer the remediation of preference on the basis of mere color rather than actual injury. By making black the color of preference, these mandates have reburdened society with the very marriage of color and preference (in reverse) that we set out to eradicate. The old sin is reaffirmed in a new guise.

But the essential problem with this form of affirmative action is the way it leaps over the hard business of developing a formerly oppressed people to the point where they can achieve proportionate representation on their own (given equal opportunity) and goes straight for the proportionate representation. This may satisfy some whites of their innocence and some blacks of their power, but it does very little to truly uplift blacks.

A white female affirmative action officer at an Ivy League university told me what many supporters of affirmative action now say: "We're after diversity. We ideally want a student body where racial and ethnic groups are represented according to their proportion in society." When affirmative action escalated into social engineering, diversity became a golden word. It grants whites an egalitarian fairness (innocence) and blacks an entitlement to proportionate representation (power). *Diversity* is a term that applies democratic principles to races and cultures rather than to citizens, despite the fact that there is nothing to indicate that real diversity is the same thing as proportionate representation. Too often the result of this on campus (for example) has been a democracy of colors rather than of people, an artificial diversity that gives the appearance of an educational parity between black and white students that has not yet been achieved in reality. Here again, racial preferences allow society to leapfrog over the difficult problem of developing blacks to parity with whites and into a cosmetic diversity that covers the blemish of disparity—a full six years after admission, only about 26 percent of black students graduate from college.

Racial representation is not the same thing as racial development, yet affirmative action fosters a confusion of these very difficult needs. Representation can be manufactured; development is always hard-earned. However, it is the music of innocence and power that we hear in affirmative action that causes us to cling to it and to its distracting emphasis on representation. The fact is that after twenty years of racial preferences, the gap between white and black median income is greater than it was in the seventies. None of this is to say that blacks don't need policies that ensure our right to equal opportunity, but what we need more is the development that will let us take advantage of society's efforts to include us.

I think that one of the most troubling effects of racial preferences for blacks is a kind of demoralization, or put another way, an enlargement of self-doubt. Under affirmative action the quality that earns us preferential treatment is an implied inferiority. However this inferiority is explained—it is still inferiority. There are explanations, and then there is the fact. And the fact must be borne by the individual as a condition apart from the explanation, apart even from the fact that others like himself also bear this condition. In integrated situations where blacks must compete with whites who may be better prepared these explanations may quickly wear thin and expose the individual to racial as well as personal self-doubt.

All of this is compounded by the cultural myth of black inferiority that blacks have always lived with. What this means in practical terms is that when blacks deliver themselves into integrated situations, they encounter a nasty little reflex in whites, a mindless, atavistic reflex that responds to the color black with alarm. Attributions may follow this alarm if the white cares to indulge them, and if they do, they will most likely be negative—one such attribution is intellectual ineptness. I think this reflex and the attributions that may follow it embarrass most whites today; therefore, it is usually quickly repressed. Nevertheless, on an equally atavistic level, the black will be aware of the reflex his color triggers and will feel a stab of horror at seeing himself reflected in this way. He, too, will do a quick repression, but a lifetime of such

stabbings is what constitutes his inner realm of racial doubt.

The effects of this may be a subject for another essay. The point here is that the implication of inferiority that racial preferences engender in both the white and black mind expands rather than contracts this doubt. Even when the black sees no implication of inferiority in racial preferences, he knows that whites do, so that—consciously or unconsciously—the result is virtually the same. The effects of preferential treatment—the lowering of normal standards to increase black representation—puts blacks at war with an expanded realm of debilitating doubt, so that the doubt itself becomes an unrecognized preoccupation that undermines their ability to perform, especially in integrated situations. On largely white campuses, blacks are five times more likely to drop out than whites. Preferential treatment, no matter how it is justified in the light of day, subjects blacks to a midnight of self-doubt, and so often transforms their advantage into a revolving door.

Another liability of affirmative action comes from the fact that it indirectly encourages blacks to exploit their own past victimization as a source of power and privilege. Victimization, like implied inferiority, is what justifies preference, so that to receive the benefits of preferential treatment one must, to some extent, become invested in the view of one's self as a victim. In this way, affirmative action nurtures a victim-focused identity in blacks. The obvious irony here is that we become inadvertently invested in the very condition we are trying to overcome. Racial preferences send us the message that there is more power in our past suffering than our present achievements—none of which could bring us a *preference* over others.

When power itself grows out of suffering, then blacks are encouraged to expand the boundaries of what qualifies as racial oppression, a situation that can lead us to paint our victimization in vivid colors, even as we receive the benefits of preference. The same corporations and institutions that give us preference are also seen as our oppressors. At Stanford University minority students—some of whom enjoy as much as $15,000 a year in financial aid—recently took over the president's office demanding, among other things, more financial aid. The power to be found in victimization, like any power, is intoxicating and can lend itself to the creation of a new class of super-victims who can feel the pea of victimization under twenty mattresses. Preferential treatment rewards us for being underdogs rather than for moving beyond that status—a misplacement of incentives that, along with its deepening of our doubt, is more a yoke than a spur.

But, I think, one of the worst prices that blacks pay for preference has to do with an illusion. I saw this illusion at work recently in the mother of a middle-class black student who was going off to his first semester of college. "They owe us this, so don't think for a minute that you don't belong there." This is the logic by which many blacks, and some whites, justify affirmative action—it is something "owed," a form of reparation. But this logic overlooks a much harder and less digestible reality, that it is impossible to repay blacks living today for the historic suffering of the race. If all blacks were given a million dollars tomorrow morning it would not amount to a dime on the dollar of three centuries of oppression, nor would it obviate the residues of that oppression that we still carry today. The concept of historic reparation grows out of man's need to impose a degree of justice on the world that simply does not exist. Suffering can be endured and overcome; it cannot be repaid. Blacks cannot be repaid for the injustice done to the race, but we can be corrupted by society's guilty gestures of repayment.

Affirmative action is such a gesture. It tells us that racial preferences can do for us what we cannot do for ourselves. The corruption here is in the hidden incentive *not* to do what we believe preferences will do. This is an incentive to be reliant on others just as we are struggling for self-reliance. And it keeps alive the illusion that we can find some deliverance in repayment. The hardest thing for any sufferer to accept is that his suffering excuses him from very little and never has enough currency to restore him. To think otherwise is to prolong the suffering.

Several blacks I spoke with said they were still in favor of affirmative action because of the "subtle" discrimination blacks were subject to once on the job. One photojournalist said, "They have ways of ignoring you." A black female television producer said, "You can't file a lawsuit when your boss doesn't invite you to the insider meetings without ruining your career. So we still need affirmative action." Others mentioned the infamous "glass ceiling" through which blacks can see the top positions of authority but never reach them. But I don't think racial preferences are a protection against this subtle discrimination; I think they contribute to it.

In any workplace, racial preferences will always create two-tiered populations composed of preferreds and unpreferreds. This division makes automatic a perception of enhanced competence for the unpreferreds and of questionable competence for the preferreds—the former earned his way, even though others were given preference, while the latter made it by color as much as by competence. Racial preferences implicitly mark whites with an exaggerated superiority just as they mark blacks with an exaggerated inferiority. They not only reinforce America's oldest racial myth but, for blacks, they have the effect of stigmatizing the already stigmatized.

I think that much of the "subtle"

discrimination that blacks talk about is often (not always) discrimination against the stigma of questionable competence that affirmative action delivers to blacks. In this sense, preferences scapegoat the very people they seek to help. And it may be that at a certain level employers impose a glass ceiling, but this may not be against the race so much as against the race's reputation for having advanced by color as much as by competence. Affirmative action makes a glass ceiling virtually necessary as a protection against the corruptions of preferential treatment. This ceiling is the point at which corporations shift the emphasis from color to competency and stop playing the affirmative action game. Here preference backfires for blacks and becomes a taint that holds them back. Of course, one could argue that this taint, which is, after all, in the minds of whites, becomes nothing more than an excuse to discriminate against blacks. And certainly the result is the same in either case—blacks don't get past the glass ceiling. But this argument does not get around the fact that racial preferences now taint this color with a new theme of suspicion that makes it even more vulnerable to the impulse in others to discriminate. In this crucial yet gray area of perceived competence, preferences make whites look better than they are and blacks worse, while doing nothing whatever to stop the very real discrimination that blacks may encounter. I don't wish to justify the glass ceiling here, but only to suggest the very subtle ways that affirmative action revives rather than extinguishes the old rationalizations for racial discrimination.

In education, a revolving door; in employment, a glass ceiling.

I believe affirmative action is problematic in our society because it tries to function like a social program. Rather than ask it to ensure equal opportunity we have demanded that it create parity between the races. But preferential treatment does not teach skills, or educate, or instill motivation. It only passes out entitlement by color, a situation that in my profession has created an unrealistically high demand for black professors. The social engineer's assumption is that this high demand will inspire more blacks to earn Ph.D.'s and join the profession. In fact, the number of blacks earning Ph.D.'s has declined in recent years. A Ph.D. must be developed from pre-school on. He requires family and community support. He must acquire an entire system of values that enables him to work hard while delaying gratification. There are social programs, I believe, that can (and should) help blacks *develop* in all these areas, but entitlement by color is not a social program; it is a dubious reward for being black ...

I would also like to see affirmative action go back to its original purpose of enforcing equal opportunity—a purpose that in itself disallows racial preferences. We cannot be sure that the discriminatory impulse in America has yet been shamed into extinction, and I believe affirmative action can make its greatest contribution by providing a rigorous vigilance in this area. It can guard constitutional rather than racial rights, and help institutions evolve standards of merit and selecting that are appropriate to the institution's needs yet as free of racial bias as possible (again, with the understanding that racial imbalances are not always an indication of racial bias). One of the most important things affirmative action can do is to define exactly what racial discrimination is and how it might manifest itself within a specific institution. The impulse to discriminate *is* subtle and cannot be ferreted out unless its many guises are made clear to people. Along with this there should be monitoring of institutions and heavy sanctions brought to bear when actual discrimination is found. This is the sort of affirmative action that America owes to blacks and to itself. It goes after the evil of discrimination itself, while preferences only sidestep the evil and grant entitlement to its *presumed* victims.

But if not preferences, then what? I think we need social policies that are committed to two goals: the educational and economic development of disadvantaged people, regardless of race, and the eradication from our society—through close monitoring and severe sanctions—of racial, ethnic, or gender discrimination. Preferences will not deliver us to either of these goals, since they tend to benefit those who are not disadvantaged—middle-class blacks—and attack one form of discrimination with another. Preferences are inexpensive and carry the glamour of good intentions—change the numbers and the good deed is done. To be against them is to be unkind. But I think the unkindest cut is to bestow on children like my own an undeserved advantage while neglecting the development of those disadvantaged children on the East Side of my city who will likely never be in a position to benefit from a preference. Give my children fairness; give disadvantaged children a better shot at development—better elementary and secondary schools, job training, safer neighborhoods, better financial assistance for college, and so on. Fewer blacks go to college today than ten years ago; more black males of college age are in prison or under the control of the criminal justice system than in college. This despite racial preferences.

The mandates of black power and white absolution out of which preferences emerged were not wrong in themselves. What was wrong was that both races focused more on the goals of these mandates than on the means to the goals. Blacks can have no real power without taking responsibility for their own educational and economic development. Whites can have no racial innocence without earning it by eradicating discrimination and helping the disadvantaged to develop. Because we ignored the means, the goals have not been reached, and the real work remains to be done.

Questions

1. Steele argues that affirmative action *harms* its recipients. What is his argument, and do you agree? Why or why not?

2. Steele provides a model for economic development for underprivileged people, and he advocates this over affirmative action. What is his model?

3. Steele advocates for a meritocracy that would result via his model. Is this model inexpensive or expensive? Is affirmative action inexpensive or expensive?

Note

1. Copyright © 1990 by Shelby Steele. From *The Content of Our Character: A New Vision of Race in America* by Shelby Steele.

3. Affirmative Action[1]

David Benatar

DAVID BENATAR (B. 1966) problematizes many assumptions around sex-based affirmative action, addressing both "equal opportunity" and "preference" models. He further distinguishes between the "past discrimination" and "present discrimination" arguments for using affirmative action to rectify injustice, whether focusing on removing barriers for a just meritocracy or on the inequities and inconsistencies of the application of affirmative action around gender. Provocative and well-argued, Benatar's piece moves the affirmative action debate into the twenty-first century.

... SEX-BASED AFFIRMATIVE ACTION HAS been said to be necessary to correct three purported problems. First, there are disproportionately few females in various desirable professions and disciplines (such as engineering and mathematics). Second, even where women are better represented at the lower levels in some professional areas, they are under-represented at the senior levels. This is true in the most senior corporate positions, in academia and in parliaments throughout the free world. This is attributed to a "glass ceiling"—an invisible but purportedly real barrier to their rising, in significant numbers, to positions of authority. Third, women are, on average, paid less than men.

If the reasons for the first two disparities were, as was once the case, that women were formally prohibited from such pursuits or their numbers were restricted by quotas, then the response would be not affirmative action but rather the abolition of the formal restrictions. Thus affirmative action is a policy that is recommended when females are formally allowed to participate equally and yet their

actual participation falls short of their proportion of the population.

Some action to eliminate or at least reduce the gender pay gap has also been proposed. Although this is not typically referred to as "affirmative action," it is nonetheless a form of affirmative action. Because women's lower pay is typically a function of the former two phenomena, the solution is usually thought to be via a response to them. For this reason, my focus will be on affirmative action as a response to the under-representation of women, both in certain professions and at senior levels. However, I shall also consider the application of this to the pay gap.

Both the under-representation of women in specific areas or positions and the pay gap give rise to two broad kinds of justification for affirmative action. The first is an argument about rectificatory justice. The idea is that although women may not be formally discriminated against any longer, they once were. It is also said that their under-representation in certain areas, and their lower pay, are an indication that they are being discriminated against in more subtle ways and that affirmative action is the way to rectify this. The second kind of argument is consequentialist. According to this argument, increasing the number of women in the relevant positions and increasing women's pay will have beneficial effects. Thus, irrespective of whether the current under-representation and lower pay are products of discrimination, we should employ measures to increase the number of females in those endeavors in which they are a minority and to reduce the pay gap. I shall examine each of these rationales in turn, but first it will be helpful to clarify what is meant by "affirmative action."

The phrase "affirmative action" is ambiguous. It can refer to a variety of different kinds of policy or practice. Its mildest form is what we might call "equal opportunity affirmative action." This form of affirmative action involves no preferential treatment. Women are not favored over men. Instead equal opportunity affirmative action aims to ensure that opportunities genuinely are equal and that any hidden and subtle obstacles to equality are exposed and removed.

One such impediment, it is said, results from traditional notions of what constitutes "being qualified." Defenders of affirmative action often argue that not only are these prejudicial to women, but they are also contestable. Therefore, they argue, we need to rethink what it means to be "qualified."

A call for accountability in the standards that are set is entirely reasonable. However, those with competing views of what constitutes being (equally) qualified will have to justify their respective positions independently of whether a given conception yields the outcome they want to have produced. That is to say, the criteria for being qualified must be assessed on their own terms and not in terms of whether employing them leads to appointments of more women or more men.

The question of who is qualified is distinct from the question how many people of each sex are qualified.

Even when the criteria of "being qualified" are assessed on their own terms (and not in terms of the gender outcome), there may be disagreement about what the appropriate criteria are.[2] There may also be disagreement about which impediments to equal pay are unfair. For example, it has been suggested that women, particularly those with children, want to have shorter commuting times to work than do men. This, it is said, limits the range of jobs available to women, which in turn "potentially leads to the crowding of women into those jobs available locally," which depresses women's wages.[3] Some argue that this is an unfair impediment to wage equality because women bear the bulk of child-rearing responsibilities and it is thus unfair to them if they are paid less because, as a result of their child rearing, they are constrained to take only jobs with a shorter commute. Others, however, argue that those willing to commute further will have a wider range of job options, including ones that pay more, and that it is not unfair if those willing to commute further are paid more.

Although there will be such disagreements, everybody would agree that any hidden barriers there might be to *fairness* should be removed. The disagreement is about *which* barriers are unfair—or, at least, sufficiently unfair that something should be done about them. Opponents of other forms of affirmative action are accordingly untroubled by equal opportunity affirmative action.[4]

All forms of affirmative action other than the equal opportunity form involve some kind of preference based on a person's sex. The preference in all (or almost all) actual cases is in favor of females. These forms of affirmative action are distinguished from one another on the basis of how much preference they accord women. Sometimes a person's sex is used as a tie-breaker between two candidates who are otherwise equally qualified. Sometimes a person's sex is accorded greater weight. And sometimes certain positions, or a proportion of positions, are set aside for women, as they are in (minimum) quotas. The more weight that is attached to a person's sex in admissions or hiring decisions, the more controversial the form of affirmative action. While all these forms of preference affirmative action apply most directly to the under-representation issue, they indirectly also affect the wage gap. This is because increasing the representation of women in certain positions would also reduce the wage gap.

Rectifying Injustice

There are two kinds of arguments that justify affirmative action policies on the grounds that they are necessary for rectifying injustice. One says that the injustices in need of rectifying are the product of past discrimination, while the other claims that the relevant injustices are the product of current, ongoing discrimination.

The Past Discrimination Argument

Injustices should be rectified. The appropriate way to do this is to compensate those particular people who suffered the injustice (and to punish those who perpetrated it). An injustice done to a person is rectified by compensating that individual, rather than by compensating other individuals, even if those other individuals share some characteristic with the victim of injustice. This is true even if the shared characteristic was the basis for the discrimination against the individual who suffered the injustice. Herein lies the primary problem with affirmative action policies that appeal to the past discrimination argument

and that grant preference to people on the basis of sex. They typically bestow benefits on some members of a group in response to past discrimination against other members of that group. That does not rectify injustice. Instead it recreates it.[5]

Those who think otherwise might do well to consider the application of the past discrimination argument to past instances of the second sexism. For example, given that males have borne the brunt of conscription in the past, should we rectify that injustice by conscripting only—or at least disproportionately many—women in those countries that retain conscription? Should those countries that do not currently conscript resolve to conscript only or disproportionately many women when conscription is next necessary? Some might answer these questions negatively because they think that this will compromise military effectiveness.... [T]he crucial issue here is that those people most likely to be impressed by the military effectiveness argument against conscripting only women are also those least likely to defend affirmative action policies at all. Those most likely to defend affirmative action for women are least likely to be impressed by the military effectiveness argument because they typically think that females could function as effectively or nearly as effectively as male soldiers. Those defending this view need to explain why past discrimination against women requires preferences for women today, whereas past discrimination against men does not require favoring men (by targeting more women than men for conscription). After all, women are even more under-represented in conscript forces than they are in those desirable positions for which defenders of sex-based affirmative action seek preferences for females.

It is true that defenders of affirmative action do not propose that women be forced into other positions. However, that is not a response to my thought experiment. Although men were not previously forced into those desirable positions to which defenders of affirmative action now want women to have preferred access, they *were* forced into the military. Thus the purported way to rectify the injustice resultant from that discrimination is to divert that burden to the opposite sex, which involves forcing women.

To clarify, I am not seriously recommending that women be conscripted *instead of* men or at greater rates than men. I raise the case to show how preposterous it is to think that one is rectifying an injustice caused by past discrimination against people of one sex by favoring a subsequent generation of people of the same sex. If conscription discriminated against men in 1916, we do not rectify that injustice by conscripting women instead of other men in 2016. The same is true in cases of discrimination against women. If women were excluded from professional positions in the past, we do not rectify that injustice by favoring other women today. Although women today share with the earlier victims of (anti-female) sexism the attribute of being female, we do not rectify the earlier injustice by favoring different individual women—women who were not the victims of the past sex discrimination. Put another way, injustices are rectified at the level of individuals rather than groups. Rectifying the injustices done to many members of a group has aggregative results for the group, but the rectification must be directed to those individuals who were the victims of injustice.

Of course, it is not always possible to rectify injustices. For example, most victims and perpetrators of past discrimination are now no longer alive and thus they cannot, respectively, be compensated or punished. However, when it is not possible to rectify injustice caused by past discrimination there is no point pretending that it can still be rectified.

Now it might be argued that past discrimination against members of a group can have lingering effects that impact on subsequent members of that group. In this way members of a group can be the victims of discrimination that took place much earlier, even before they were born. I do not think that preferential (as opposed to equal opportunity) affirmative action is an appropriate response even to these ongoing effects of past discrimination, but I shall not here say why this is the case. This is because defenders of sex-based affirmative action cannot appeal to the lingering effects of past discrimination in the way that defenders of race-based affirmative action can do so. This is because of the different kinds of discrimination to which women and blacks respectively were subjected. The kinds of discrimination against women in the past have not had the enduring effect on the opportunities of women today that much past discrimination against disadvantaged racial groups has had on most (but not all) current members of those groups. Many of those today who belong to racial groups that were discriminated against in the past continue to suffer severe ill-effects of that past discrimination. They often live deprived lives. The same is not true of females (from advantaged groups). The lingering *effects* of *past* discrimination are to be distinguished from lingering (present) discrimination. Until now I have been speaking about the former. I now turn to the latter.

The Present Discrimination Argument

When the past discrimination argument fails, some defenders of affirmative action might wish to appeal to what I call the present discrimination argument. According to this argument, women are still being unfairly discriminated against, and an affirmative action policy that favors females is the way to rectify this. The evidence offered for the claim that women are still discriminated against is sometimes no more than the observation that they are under-represented in the sorts of positions mentioned earlier and that they earn less than men. Women, it is said, are about half of the adult population, and thus would, in the absence of discrimination, fill about half of these positions.

However, the inference from unequal outcomes to unfair discrimination is a problematic one. If the inference were a valid one then we could conclude that men are being unfairly discriminated against when they constitute more than half of those imprisoned or executed, or more than half of those who drop out of school or who die on the job. In these cases (almost) nobody leaps to the conclusion that males are unfairly discriminated against, even though males significantly exceed half of those whom these fates befall. While discrimination may account for some of the difference, ... much of the difference is attributable to other factors. Men commit more crimes, for example.

Similar caution is necessary when there are disproportionately few women in desirable positions or when women earn less than men. Discrimination against women is not the only explanation. Even to the extent that discrimination *is* the explanation, affirmative action may not be the way to rectify it. To show why this is so it will be helpful to distinguish four possible explanations for the fact that women have less than equal participation in various employment sectors and earn less:

1. discrimination in those specific sectors where women are under-represented;
2. discriminatory features of the wider society;
3. non-discriminatory sex differences;
4. some combination of the above.

Among the items to which the first explanation refers is implicit bias in hiring and promotion decisions. The claim here is that even those who are self-consciously committed to gender equality may have unconscious biases, which operate to the detriment of women. Females may be viewed, subconsciously, as less capable, and this leads to fewer of them being appointed. Another item to which the first explanation refers is the so-called "hostile environment." The idea here is that certain professional and other environments are hostile or at least unfriendly to women, thereby making those environments less attractive or unattractive to women. For example, they may have a very "masculine" ethos or require long or inflexible hours,[6] which do not fit well with the domestic duties that women disproportionately bear.

This last example connects the first explanation with the second. This is because, it is argued, the fact that women still bear the bulk of domestic duties is indicative of broader societal discrimination. This, however, is not the only way in which broader social discrimination is said to contribute to there being disproportionately few women in the sorts of positions under discussion. For example, it is often said that girls are raised to think that they are less suited to particular kinds of positions and thus they are less motivated to pursue them.

The third explanation claims that there are average differences between males and females that are not the product of discrimination and which do explain why males are found in disproportionately large numbers (and women in disproportionately small numbers) in some positions, and why men earn more on average. It is said, for example, that males, on average, are more assertive than women, that they respond more positively to competitive situations and display more dominance-seeking.[7] Men, it is said, are also inclined to take more risks, including professional risks,[8] and are less nurturing and empathic.[9]

These differences are said to explain why males are more likely to enter higher-paying professions and to advance up various hierarchies. Those who are more assertive, who thrive on competition and who seek status are more likely to seek (and win) political office, to rise up corporate and other ladders and to enter and succeed in fields that require drive. Risk-taking has a toll on those who lose, but it favors those who succeed. Insofar as these sex differences are the product of biology they do not constitute discrimination. They might be regarded as unfair in just the way that being born with or without some trait might be viewed as unfair—that is, losing out in the natural rather than the social lottery—but they cannot be regarded as unfair *discrimination*. Unfair discrimination may ensue, on some views, if due regard is not given for the unfairness of the natural lottery.

The fourth explanation of the under-representation of women in professions and positions of power, and derivatively their lower pay, is a combination of the previous three. It claims that sex differences play some part, but that discrimination does, too. This fourth explanation is the most plausible one. First, ... it is highly unlikely that human psychology is unaffected by human biology, and that *all* psychological traits, unlike physical traits, are equally distributed across both sexes. Those who think that psychological attributes are equally distributed need to explain why the over-representation of males in desirable positions is *fully* attributable to discrimination against females, but the over-representation of males in undesirable positions is not at all attributable to discrimination against males. Indeed, while this seems to be a position that some feminists do hold, they do not explain how it could be the case. They blame men for the fact that there are disproportionately

few women in leadership positions, and they blame men for constituting the majority of those incarcerated. Men are at fault whether they are winning or losing.

Contrary to this view, (at least some) evolutionary psychologists claim that the greater successes and greater failures of men may well be related. Ambition, competitiveness, a desire for status and risk-taking can all contribute to a greater number of males at the extremes....

The greater extremes characteristic of males might also be partially explained by the hypothesis that the distribution of *some* cognitive capacities, for example, is flatter among males than it is among females. That is to say, according to this hypothesis there are more males than females at the extremes of some cognitive capacities. Recollect, here, ... of there being, among males, both more "Nobels" and more "dumbbells."

These considerations suggest that the first and second explanations are probably not the sole explanations of the under-representation of women. It is not clear whether anybody holds the view that the third explanation fully accounts for the under-representation of women. Those who think that sex differences play a role do not typically think that biology explains the *full extent* of women's under-representation.[10] It is very likely ... that any biological differences between the sexes would be recognized and amplified by society. Thus social forces very probably play some role over and above any biological differences.

Among those who accept the fourth explanation, the disagreement is about how much of the difference is explained by biology and how much by social forces. The question of who is right is immensely difficult to determine with any precision. That, however, is partly why affirmative action is such a poor mechanism for dealing with whatever component is the product of discrimination.

If the aim of affirmative action is to correct for discrimination and we do not know how much discrimination is taking place, we cannot tell how much of a corrective is required. Some feminists may suggest that we should nonetheless impose some counterbalance to whatever discrimination there is, even if we run the risk of overcompensating. However, there are a few problems with this suggestion.

Overcompensating would result in unfair discrimination in favor of some females and against some males. While not compensating at all would, given implicit bias against females, result in unfair discrimination in favor of some men and against some women, the difference is that affirmative action is an intentional policy favoring some over others. Faced with a choice, a policy of trying as hard as possible to avoid discrimination (even if one does so imperfectly) is arguably better than a policy of specifically trying to favor some people. The latter is more corrupting and more open to abuse. In other words, trying to give preference is more dangerous than trying not to give preference. The better one gets at not preferring, the closer one gets to fairness. By contrast, in the case of preferring, one gets closer to fairness to the extent that one is compensating for implicit bias, but then one gets further and further from fairness as one continues to give preference. Since one cannot accurately determine the extent of bias, the danger is that one will not know when one is becoming less and less fair.

Moreover, there is reason to think that the pressure in favor of preferential policies and practices will cause an excess of preference. As long as there are relatively few women in a given profession and the current concern for the position of women continues, there will be ongoing political incentives to attain a better balance of the sexes even if the residual difference is not a product of discrimination. Indeed that is exactly what those who accept the first and second explanations alone will be advocating. No affirmative action efforts will satisfy such people until any discrepancy is eliminated.

Those who deny that affirmative action is the more dangerous option should consider whether they would recommend affirmative action to counter discrimination against men. Consider, for example, an affirmative action policy applicable to judges making custody decisions following divorce. Such a policy would be problematic because it would be inappropriate for judges consciously to favor fathers, even though we know that fathers are currently the victims of implicit bias in custody decisions. It is preferable for judges to work to overcome their biases rather than to replace them with new ones.

So far my focus has been on affirmative action as a corrective for direct, albeit unintentional and unconscious discrimination. Some people think that such discrimination explains both why women are under-represented in some employment sectors and why they are paid less. The evidence, however, does not support this (any more[12]). Consider the wage gap, for example. Once one controls for various crucial variables, one finds that the wage gap is negligible, if it exists at all.[13] The variables include how many hours people work (full-time work pays more than part-time work, and overtime is rewarded), how risky and unpleasant the work is and whether one is willing to commute longer distance to higher-paid positions.[14] Indeed, there is thus something misleading about reference to the pay gap. It is not that women are being paid less for doing the same jobs as men. They are doing different jobs.

Consider next the so-called glass ceiling. Several female clerks at one Fortune 500 company sued the company. They noted that the female proportion of staff promoted was less than the female proportion of the entry-level positions, and they alleged discrimination on these grounds. The company, mystified by the accusation, approached an independent consulting firm to conduct a study of its personnel practices. The study found that discrimination did not explain the imbalance.[15] For example, males had applied for promotion at a much greater rate than had females. Moreover, a higher proportion of women than men who applied were successful.[16] Roughly equal numbers of males and females were asked whether they were interested in promotion. However, a much larger proportion of the males who were asked responded affirmatively.[17] Men were also willing to give up more to obtain a promotion. For example, they were more willing to have a less than optimal shift assignment or to accept a transfer.[18]

There is also some evidence that gender imbalances among university academic staff are not attributable to discrimination. A study of Canadian universities showed that while women were under-represented, and especially at the higher levels, this was not a consequence of discrimination against females.[19] The study looked at the average age of people in each of the academic ranks and calculated when each cohort would have been appointed. This was then compared to the number of women earning PhDs immediately before that. It was found that "figures from the 1960s are consistent with there being a modest degree of discrimination against women during the hiring process at this time."[20] However, it was also found that "for all other ranks, the data are consistent with there being significant discrimination in favor of women and against men."[21] Indeed, "the discrepancy ... is much larger than the reverse discrepancy at the rank of full professor."[22]

There are also interesting differences between academic disciplines, with women even more under-represented in some disciplines. It is implausible to think that discrimination in university admissions explains why women are an especially small minority of engineering students, for example. Are we really to believe that while medical schools are now unbiased in their admissions, because women now constitute a majority of medical students, engineering schools are still pervaded by prejudice?[23] It is much more likely that females are choosing medicine over engineering. And if that is not the case, are we to conclude that medical schools are now biased against males, given that they now constitute fewer than half of all medical students in some countries?

Denying that these phenomena are explained primarily by proximate discrimination does not mean that discriminatory features of the wider society are not at play. Perhaps gender roles and other aspects of socialization make girls and boys more or less likely to enter specific professions, to be more or less inclined to seek promotion, to opt for part-time employment. However, an affirmative action policy that grants preferential treatment to women is even harder to justify if one is attempting to correct for this upstream discrimination.

To see why this is so, consider the following. After divorce, fathers gain custody of children much less often than mothers and this is not simply because of implicit bias of judges. Men request custody less often. Perhaps it is even the case that fathers are less often the better custodial parent. Even if one thinks that biology is part of the explanation why males seek and are suited to custody less often, gender roles and other social factors also play a role. However, it does not follow that we should implement an affirmative action policy that aims to attain the levels of paternal custody that would have existed in the absence of those roles and factors. In deciding who gets custody, judges need to consider which parent or parents want custody and whether one parent is better suited to having custody. Custody decisions should not be made on the basis of what the paternal custody proportions would have been if fathers had been reared differently and thus made them want custody and be suited to it more often. Indeed, it seems repugnant consciously to aim at awarding custody to fathers more often even though one knew that fewer men wanted custody and that fewer would be the better custodial parent. This is true even if one knew that in the absence of socially reinforced gender roles men would have accounted for a greater proportion than they now do of parents wanting and worthy of custody.

It is similarly inappropriate to favor women in hiring or promotion merely because, in the absence of socially reinforced gender roles, more women would have chosen to become engineers or pilots, for example. In deciding who should gain custody, each parent's relative interest in and suitability to serve as the custodial parent is central. In deciding who should be appointed or hired, a person's capacity to do the job is central. That there are fewer female engineers and pilots from whom to choose does not mean that those hiring engineers and pilots should put any weight on a woman's sex in deciding whether to hire her. Doing so would put proportionately less weight on attributes that are relevant to how well she will do the job.

The same problem would arise for affirmative action policies that favor males in traditionally female professions. Imagine, for example, that a pool of applicants for a pre-primary school teacher position is 95% female. One can try to broaden the pool such that the proportion of males in the pool increases. However, if males are uninterested in applying, even if this is a product of socially contrived gender roles, then one might still have only 5% of the applicants being male. If one then favors those who constitute that 5% just because they are male, one will end up hiring some males who are weaker than the females one would otherwise have appointed. The more weight one attaches to being male, the relatively less other attributes will count. Thus, the stronger the form of affirmative action, the weaker, on average, will be those selected from the preferred sex. This is true if the favored sex is male, but it is equally true if the favored sex is female.

This is *not* to say that men cannot make good pre-primary school teachers (or that women cannot make good engineers or pilots). Instead it is to say that in hiring decisions, a person's sex is (generally) not relevant. If it is made a consideration, then other considerations invariably count proportionately less and that would lead to the appointment of people who are less qualified for the position.

The underlying issue here is how we respond to the choices people do make, even if those choices would have been different if conditions had been different. Now, sometimes the conditions under which people choose are obviously such that their choices cannot be said to be free. If Dick Turpin offers you the choice of "your money or your life" and you choose to part with your money, your choice is not free. That, however, is not the kind of case about which we are speaking. Such cases are easy and we know what to do about such injustices—remove the threat.

We are speaking about more difficult cases—cases where one acts on the basis of preferences or attributes formed at least in part by social influences, but with which one identifies. The preferences are yours and you choose freely in accordance with them. If there are background injustices in the influences that lead to the formation of the preferences, then those injustices must be rectified upstream, where they occur. They cannot be rectified by overriding or ignoring people's choices or by favoring the very members of a group who were immune to the upstream influences.

Put another way, you should not be favored by how many other people of your sex have chosen as you did. Thus, if you are a woman who chose to become an engineer or a man who chose to become a pre-primary teacher, whether you get the job should not depend at all on the fact that your choice was relatively uncommon for somebody of your sex. Similarly, if you are a man who chose to become an engineer or a woman who chose to become a pre-primary teacher, whether you get a particular job should not depend at all on the fact that most other people who made that choice are of the same sex.

Moreover, even if we thought it appropriate to correct for disadvantages caused by socially influenced preferences, it would be impossible to do so with any accuracy. So many of our preferences fall into this category and it is possible to know just how much better off each one of us would have been had our preferences been influenced in myriad alternative ways.

According to the view I have been presenting, the differing preferences of males and females, even if socially influenced, are not appropriate grounds for giving preference to either females or males. This does not mean, of course, that other things should not be done about background discrimination that affects the formation of preferences. We should take steps to avoid forcing girls and boys into gender roles. We should avoid characterizing certain jobs as either male or female. However, none of these sorts of intervention amount to giving preference to either sex. They are instances of equal opportunity affirmative action rather than preference affirmative action and are thus not problematic.

However, we should not assume that disproportionate representation of one or other sex in specific jobs or activities implies that

societal discrimination is still at play. Natural differences might influence choices. Even when they do not, men and women might gravitate at different times and in different places at different rates into various positions and activities.

The present discrimination version of the rectification argument, like the past discrimination version, is much more problematic than its advocates realize. Taking note of the application of these arguments to the second sexism, as I have done, may highlight those difficulties that defenders of sex-based preference affirmative action might otherwise not see. Indeed, the implications of the second sexism for affirmative action might explain, at least in part, why some people are so reluctant to admit that there is a second sexism....

Conclusion

... There are complicated reasons why members of each sex gravitate to particular jobs and certain sectors of society. Even when gender roles play a part in this, affirmative action is a problematic strategy. Appointments are not gifts for the benefit of those who receive them (even though those who are appointed often do benefit). We appoint people to do a job—indeed, the best possible job. For that we need to choose the best possible people for the particular job. Although we are less likely to appoint the best possible person if the candidate pool from which we are making the appointment is unduly limited, we do not compensate for that limitation by giving extra weight to the sex of those people within the pool. In other words, there is no problem, as I indicated earlier, with what I called equal opportunity affirmative action, which merely aims to remove impediments to equality of opportunity. Such affirmative action could indeed broaden the pool of applicants. However, once we have a pool of applicants, we do not increase the likelihood of appointing the best person by giving weight to the sex of some people, whether male or female. This is because giving weight to sex must mean giving relatively less weight to other, relevant attributes.

Defenders of sex-based preference affirmative action often assume that when women are under-represented in desirable positions, this is a product of discrimination. They make no such assumption when women are under-represented in undesirable positions. Moreover, while they propose preferential policies to address the under-representation of women in desirable positions, they usually make no such proposals to reduce the proportion of males in undesirable positions. These asymmetries are curious and suggest that many defenders of sex-based affirmative action are not as interested in equality as they are in advancing the position of women. Sometimes there is a happy coincidence of the two, but it is when they come apart that the guiding principle is exposed. In any event, while equal opportunity affirmative action can advance equality, those forms of affirmative action that give preference to some people on the basis of their sex fail to do so, even when there is real discrimination to be overcome.

Questions

1. What are the differences Benatar highlights between "equal opportunity affirmative action" and "preference affirmative action"? Which type is more expensive to redress? Why?

2. What is the "past discrimination argument" for affirmative action? What is the "present discrimination argument" for affirmative action? As the intent of affirmative action is to redress present disparate impact of underrepresented groups, is there any part of the "past discrimination argument" that is consistent with the intent?

3. Given Benatar's arguments, what are the most striking ethical issues regarding affirmative action? Has his work changed your position on affirmative action? How so, or why not?

Notes

1. From David Benatar, Chapter 6: "Affirmative Action," in *The Second Sexism: Discrimination Against Men and Boys* (Chichester, England: Wiley-Blackwell). Copyright 2012, Wiley-Blackwell.

2. Although there may be some disagreement, there is also a limit to reasonable disagreement about what the criteria are.

3. Women and Work Commission, "Shaping a Fairer Future," London: UK Commission for Employment and Skills, 2006, p. 4.

4. Equal opportunity affirmative action would rule out favoring the children of alumni in admissions decisions. Curiously, some defenders of the controversial form of affirmative action—what I shall call preference affirmative action—like to note that children of alumni enjoy greater preference than beneficiaries of preference affirmative action. (See Deborah L. Rhode, *Speaking of Sex: The Denial of Gender Inequality*, Cambridge, MA: Harvard University Press, 1997, p. 166.) However, the practice of favoring the children of alumni

is not an axiom justifying preference for other groups. Instead, it is a form of preference to be eliminated.

5. The same is true, *mutatis mutandis*, in many cases of race-based affirmative action.

6. Rarely is it noted that stereotypically masculine environments, as well as inflexible hours, may also be hostile to some (even if not as many) men.

7. Kingsley Browne, "Sex and temperament in modern society: a Darwinian view of the glass ceiling and the gender gap," *Arizona Law Review*, 37(4), Winter 1995, pp. 971–1106, at pp. 1017–1028.

8. Ibid., pp. 1028–1033.

9. Ibid., pp. 1033–1037.

10. Ibid., p. 984.

...

12. At one time, the salaries for men and women performing the same job were explicitly different—women's lower than men's. This is no longer the case, at least in the developed world.

13. In the United Kingdom, single women "earn as much on average as single men" and "women in the middle age groups who remain single earn more than middle-aged single males." (J.R. Shackleton, *Should We Mind the Gap? Gender Pay*

Differentials and Public Policy, London: Institute of Economic Affairs, 2008, pp. 29–30.)

14. Ibid., esp. pp. 45–66.

15. Carl Hoffmann and John Reed, "When is imbalance not discrimination?" in W.E. Block and M.A. Walker (eds), *Discrimination, Affirmative Action, and Equal Opportunity: An Economic and Social Perspective*, Vancouver: The Fraser Institute, 1982.

16. Ibid., p. 193.

17. Ibid.

18. Ibid., p. 198.

19. A.D. Irvine, "Jack and Jill and employment equity," *Dialogue*, 35(2), 1996, pp. 255–291.

20. Ibid., p. 259. The author says that during "the time that today's full professors were first being hired, the percentage of applicants who were women is estimated to have been 8.6%. At the same time, the percentage of job recipients who were women was only 7.6%."

21. Ibid., p. 260.

22. Ibid.

23. Steven Pinker makes the same point. See *The Blank Slate: The Modern Denial of Human Nature*, New York: Penguin Books, 2002, p. 355.

...

4. Hustle and Flow: Prison Privatization Fueling the Prison Industrial Complex[1]

Patrice A. Fulcher

PATRICE A. FULCHER ADDRESSES the Prison Industrial Complex (PIC) regarding prison privatization, prison labor for profit, and constitutional misinterpretations. She shows how the prison population dramatically increased in the 1980s, partially due to the war on drugs and consequent racial profiling of Blacks, and motivated by the promise of privatization. Privatization created the incentive to grow prison populations and at the same time treated Black inmates as property. Further, the disparate impact on Blacks harms their economic futures, as felons have lifelong difficulties due to their incarceration. Fulcher calls for changing drug-sentencing laws, and for the end of privatization, both of which would drastically reduce the prison population.

1. Introduction

THE UNITED STATES HAS about two million people behind bars,[2] which is the largest prison population in the world.[3] The United States also has the highest incarceration rate in the world, imprisoning 743 people per 100,000 of America's national population.[4] In comparison, China's prison population is second to America's with 1.65 million convicted people in prison,[5] with an incarceration rate of 122 people per 100,000,[6] and Russia's prison population is third, having imprisoned 0.81 million people,[7] with an incarceration rate of 568 people per 100,000.[8] Moreover, Rwanda's prison population is also considerably lower than the United States's with 62,000 people in prison,[9] but it has the second highest incarceration rate in the world, incarcerating 595 people per 100,000 of its population.[10]

From 1925 to 1975, the average U.S.

incarceration rate was much lower; America incarcerated 110 inmates in prison per 100,000 of the national population.[11] However, the United States began to see an increase in the rate in which people were imprisoned in the late 1970s.[12] This increase was directly attributed to changes in U.S drug and sentencing laws[13] and not to an increase in crime.[14]

The change in drug laws increased the prison population and at the same time disproportionately increased the numbers of Blacks[15] imprisoned in the criminal justice system because they became the specific targets of the drug war.[16] Recent statistics indicate that in 2010, almost 37.9% of U.S inmates were African Americans[17] although Blacks made up only approximately 12.6% of the U.S. population.[18] Although Whites made up 34.5% of the prison population[19] and are approximately 72% of the population,[20] the disproportionate representation of Blacks versus Whites in prison is no surprise.[21] The Bureau of Justice Statistics ("BJS") predicted that the current disparity would occur nine years earlier.[22] In 2001, a BJS study concluded that Black males had a 32.2% chance of going to prison, which was up from a 13.4% chance in 1974,[23] while White males had only a 5.9% chance of being incarcerated.[24] As expected, African American males began to fill federal, state, and local correctional facilities at alarming rates.[25] In 2002, only a year after the BJS study one of twenty-one adult Black males, and one of eight Black males in their late twenties was incarcerated on any given day.[26] With these trends, "one of every three (32%) [B]lack males born today can expect to go to prison in his lifetime."[27]

I contend that the surge in the number of people incarcerated in the United States was a direct result of changes to drug sentencing laws. Once the population increased, America's solution was to build private prisons because taxpayers did not want to expend additional money on managing inmates.[28] Thus, I surmise that the allocation of government resources to support the privatization of prisons was one way that the Prison Industrial Complex ("PIC") became a *"hustle"*; it altered the public function of incarceration from rehabilitation, custody, and control to private profiteering. I submit that the PIC is a *"hustle"* because the *players* involved in prison privatization, private prison companies and government corrections agencies, are not unlike "pimps" and "johns" profiting from the exploitation of human beings.

[...]

III. Government Allocations to Private Prison Management Corporations: The Flow of Inequity

Resources are limited, but society's needs are unlimited. In the face of economic adversity, human beings struggle to find ways to cut costs in order to fulfill necessities and wants. Governments have no less of a burden when contemplating the allocation of financial resources among competing groups or programs. Accordingly, the financial strain of expending resources to address the exploding prison population forced governmental entities to search for the least-costly means of confinement.[29]

In 2001, state correction departments spent $38.2 billion on state correctional systems.[30] The estimated cost of housing one inmate was $22,650 annually, or $62.05 per day for state prisoners, and $22,632 annually per inmate, or $62.01 per day for prisoners held in Federal Bureau of Prisons facilities.[31] Not surprisingly, government agencies flocked to private companies when given the promise of cost reduction for comparable control.[32] Federal, state, and local correction agencies started allocating resources to private prison companies through million-dollar contract agreements in order to salvage their budgets.[33] Private prison companies not only received funds from the agreements but also received government resources in the form of subsidies.[34] These lucrative subsidies were expansive and ranged from tax reductions to training grants. Most notably, these companies often receive (1) the issuance of revenue bonds to finance private prison projects, (2) property tax abatements or reductions, (3) low interest loans enabled by tax-free bonds, (4) infrastructure subsidies, and (5) training grants.[35]

A 2001 study of private prison subsidies concluded that the government subsidized forty-four out of sixty state correctional facilities studied under private management.[36] Of the sixty institutions considered, 78% of CCA's and 69% of Wackenhut's (now GEO) received subsidies in the amount of $406.4 million and $165.5 million respectively.[37] An example of successful profiteering can be seen in the business partnership between the city of Shelby, Montana, and CCA.[38] In this deal, the city obtained an $800,000 grant from the U.S. Economic Development Administration and a $500,000 Community Development Block Grant to pay infrastructure costs for a prison it contracted with CCA to build and operate.[39] Additionally, CCA has also received federal tax credits for some of its employees at its California City Correctional Center.[40]

Today's question: Have governments in the United States gotten the bang for their buck from the privatization of prisons? Scholars debated this issue early on;[41] so yet, the data remains unclear as to whether private prisons are cost efficient.[42] In 2001, a Bureau of Justice Assistance study revealed that the average savings gained from the use of private prisons was 1% compared to the 20% that had been predicted.[43] The most recent comparative cost analysis of U.S. private prisons was conducted in 2007 by the University of Utah's Criminal Justice Center.[44] Utah's Criminal Justice Center report concluded, "privately managed prisons provide no clear benefit or detriment. Cost savings from privatizing prisons are not guaranteed and appear minimal."[45] Therefore, without clear evidence that prison privatization is demonstrably more cost efficient, government decisions to allocate funds to private prison companies must be reassessed.

Yet even assuming, as proponents suggest, that evidence exists that privatization has been cost efficient,[46] it still does not outweigh the efficiency arguments regarding government intervention into the market. Faced with the prison population explosion, governments in the United States settled on

prison privatization as a simple solution to the problem.[47] This approach was made in haste and without a thorough analysis of the consequences of prison privatization. As a result, this allocation of resources became inefficient because it created a *"flow"* of inequity. The inequities of this system are presented in two apparent ways: (1) it created an economic scheme dependent upon mass incarceration fostering monopolies and manipulation of the system and (2) it continued the historical diminution of Blacks to the status of property.

A. Creating Incentives to Increase the Prison Population and Monopolize the Market

Private prison companies' profit motive is problematic because it intertwines private revenue benefit with public criminal justice issues. As a result, private prison companies strive to increase the prison population and control the system in order to receive government financial distributions.

1. Strategizing to Maintain High Incarceration Rates: Less Prisoners Equals Less Earnings

Under the terms of coveted government resources, private prison companies like CCA are paid based on an inmate per diem rate of the actual or minimum guaranteed occupancy levels.[48] Thus, the number of prisoners determines the success of a private prison company in each facility; and a shortage of prisoners equals a shortage of profits.[49] In 2010, the number of people sentenced to state prison systems decreased by 0.8% (10,881 prisoners), while the federal prison population increased by 0.8% (1,653 prisoners).[50] With profits so closely tied to the number of people in prison, CCA and GEO sought ways to increase state prison populations and obtain additional federal contracts from the Federal Bureau of Prisons.[51]

Like similar private prison companies, CCA and GEO employed three principal marketing strategies to promote policies that led to higher incarceration rates and greater profit margins: lobbying, direct campaign contributions, and networking.[52] These efforts, funded by million-dollar government contracts and subsidies and the profits they earn, are used to persuade politicians to pass legislation to increase their profit margins. Moreover, in 2010, private prison corporations' ability to fund political candidates was advanced by the U.S. Supreme Court decision in *Citizens United v. Federal Election Commission*.[53] In *Citizens United,* the Supreme Court struck down restrictions on corporate spending for political advertising as violating the First Amendment, thereby allowing private prisons and other corporations to use their general treasury funds to participate in independent election activities.[54] This five-to-four decision was counter to anti-bribery and clean election law decisions of the past.[55] So, regrettably, this ruling advanced private prison companies' capacity to line the pockets of politicians in order to obtain additional government contracts.[56]

Between 2003 and 2012, CCA, GEO, and Cornell Companies (prior to its merger with GEO) contributed a total of $4,839,548 to state Democratic and Republican candidates and committees.[57] These corporations also contributed $835,514 to federal candidates from 2000 to 2010.[58] CCA specifically lobbied on several pieces of federal prison impact legislation,[59] helped to draft the Support Our Law Enforcement and Safe Neighborhoods Act immigration bill in Arizona,[60] and helped to pass Georgia's Illegal Immigration Reform and Enforcement Act of 2011.[61] It is estimated that both bills will result in the increased placement of people into the federal custody of Immigration and Customs Enforcement ("ICE").[62] This will increase the need for

more inmate beds and will likely lead to more contracts with private prisons.[63]

In an attempt to purchase twenty-four of Florida's state prisons in February 2012, CCA and GEO expended time and effort in order to pass Florida's SB 2038.[64] CCA and GEO donated nearly two million dollars to political campaigns in Florida during the last three election cycles in order to grease the wheels for the bill's passage; however, this measure failed by a narrow margin.[65] If SB 2038 had passed, it would have been the largest deal in U.S. history for the privatization of state prisoners.[66] Notwithstanding SB 2038's failure, this loss was not the end of CCA and GEO's lobbying efforts.[67] The Huffington Post reported that CCA had also sent letters to forty-eight other state governments offering cash for prisoners to help cut costs.[68] In exchange for its services, CCA wants twenty-year management contracts from each state and an assurance that each prison will remain at least 90% full.[69]

Unfortunately, CCA makes no qualms about its aspirations to increase the prison population.[70] In CCA's 2010 Annual Report, the company conveyed the following to its shareholders:

> Our industry benefits from significant economies of scale, resulting in lower operating costs per inmate as occupancy rates increase. We believe we have been successful in increasing the number of residents in our care and continue to pursue a number of initiatives intended to further increase our occupancy and revenue. Our competitive cost structure offers prospective customers a compelling option for incarceration.[71]

This report could easily be mistaken for a statement by the board of directors of a five-star hotel discussing how to increase the number of guests in order enlarge profit margins;[72] yet, unlike the hotel business, private prisons are not merely attempting to obtain a share of the current market. Instead, they are working to increase the market share of inmates. CCA clearly maintains that it will continue to "pursue a number of initiatives" to increase their "occupancy and revenue,"[73] which equates to increasing the quantity of human beings in private prisons.

As previously shown, CCA and GEO successfully lobbied for the passage of Arizona's and Georgia's immigration legislation-initiatives that will definitely increase the percentage of incarcerations.[74] CCA quickly reaped the benefits of its spending in Georgia as just five months after it helped to pass Georgia's immigration bill in May 2011, it received a $400 million contract to house criminal aliens in McRae, Georgia.[75] The procurement of the $400 million contract provided an excellent rate of return on CCA's $24,000 investment on lobbying Georgia's legislators and candidates for governor in order to get the immigration bill passed.[76]

The issue at hand is the capitalistic investment in the increased incarceration of human beings. Incarceration is typically considered to be a justice issue that requires public treatment and exposure; however, it is the process of the allocation of governmental funds that has essentially cloaked a public issue with private profit interests. These secret individual interests, normally out of view of public scrutiny, can no longer be overlooked when taxpayer dollars are being utilized to promote mass imprisonment. The failure to scrutinize this matter has allowed companies like CCA and GEO to monopolize the private prison industry. Hence, the issues challenging economic efficiency continue to grow.

2. Monopolizing the Market

Private prison corporations primarily exist to make a profit.[77] In 1996, the stocks of CCA traded at 111 times higher than their estimated earnings. Likewise, the stocks of GEO, then Wackenhut, traded at 100 times higher than their estimated earnings.[78] During this time, these two companies enjoyed the "lion's share of the industry,"[79] and still do today.[80] In order to maintain high return rates on their stocks, CCA and GEO have successfully obtained more U.S. government prison contracts than any other private corporation.[81] In doing so, CCA and GEO have monopolized the private prison corporation market[82] by buying out their competitors.[83]

CCA was the first of the two companies to ensure its dominance in the market by buying out smaller competitors.[84] In April 1995, CCA bought out Concept Inc., the third largest private prison corporation at the time.[85] Two months later, it bought out Corrections Partners Inc., another private prison corporation that was operating court correctional facilities in three states.[86]

In August 2010, GEO acquired Cornell Companies, a rival private prison company in order to expand GEO's stock in the private prison market.[87] According to GEO, the company's merger with Cornell was projected to increase GEO's total annual revenues to more than $1.5 billion.[88] Four months later, GEO acquired B.I. Incorporated, a private provider of compliance technologies, monitoring services, and evidence-based supervision and treatment programs for parolees, probationers, and pretrial defendants.[89] GEO estimated that the acquisition of B.I. Incorporated would increase their "annual revenues by approximately $115 million to more than $1.6 billion in 2011."[90] As predicted, on February 21, 2012, GEO announced that their total revenues for the full year of 2011 were $1.6 billion.[91]

CCA and GEO's monopolization of the private prison industry is another example of how the allocation of government resources to the PIC is inefficient. With this monopoly in place, the cost of prison privatization is not affected by competition, thus CCA and GEO were allowed to accumulate vast capital gains. Due to CCA and GEO's billion-dollar resources, they have been able to manipulate the political market by influencing legislators to support the passage of legislation that directly affects their profits.[92] Moreover, government resources permitted this monopoly to flourish based on a need to save money that did not come to fruition. Instead of saving money, government allocations to private prison companies inadvertently incentivized incarcerating U.S. inhabitants and created private prison domination.

B. Black Inmates Reduced to Property Thus Affecting Their Future Participation in Economic Activities

1. Blacks as Property

The use of Blacks as property during slavery and afterward as prison laborers is well-documented.[93] This manipulation of Blacks for profit continues to manifest itself in the modern day prison system as Blacks are arbitrarily arrested and quantified as property for the profit of private prisons companies.

W.E.B. Du Bois insisted that "[t]he slave went free; stood a brief moment in the sun; then moved back again toward slavery."[94] This comment is still applicable nearly eighty years later because government-allocated resources, fueling the PIC, have resulted in the random re-enslavement of Blacks based on race.[95] These allocations have supported the PIC, a system that increased the prison population through drastic changes in the U.S. drug laws in the 1980s.[96] As established above, these laws

caused Blacks to be disproportionally incarcerated in the United States.[97] In turn, Black inmates, as a part of this vast prison population, have become the exploited chattel that private prison company profiteers rely on.

This government expenditure of funds in the PIC is tantamount to the allocation of past state resources employed after the passage of the Thirteenth Amendment, which supported the effects of race-neutral statutes; both allocations have resulted in the disproportionate enslavement of Blacks through the use of criminal laws for economic gain.[98] With almost two million inmates housed in jails and prisons throughout the United States,[99] it is not difficult to ascertain that Blacks, at nearly 40% of the prison population, are more likely to be used as commodities to keep prisons filled and to carry out labor needs.[100]

Moreover, this diminution of Blacks to the status of property solely for the advancement of the PIC is an obvious continuation of one of the practices employed to maintain slavery in the United States.[101] Chief Judge A. Leon Higginbotham, Jr.'s[102] *Ten Precepts of American Slavery Jurisprudence* lends credence to this argument.[103] Judge Higginbotham's *Ten Precepts* established "several premises, goals, and implicit agreements concerning the institution of slavery that at once defined the nature of American slavery and directed how it was to be administered with the imprimatur of the legal process."[104] The precepts identified by Judge Higginbotham are: (1) inferiority, (2) property, (3) powerlessness, (4) racial "purity," (5) manumission and free Blacks, (6) family, (7) education and culture, (8) religion, (9) liberty-resistance and (10) by any means possible.[105] Judge Higginbotham's definition of precept two, "property," is clearly germane to the principle operations of the PIC.

Judge Higginbotham explained the precept property by offering the following descriptions: "Define the slave as the master's property, maximize the master's economic interest, disregard the humanity of the slave except when it serves the master's interest, and deny slaves the fruits of their labor."[106] It is apparent that the PIC has defined Black inmates as property to maximize profits for private industry since private prison contracts are paid per inmate, per day.[107] This point is further validated by the use of drug laws and racial profiling to target and incarcerate Blacks, thereby disregarding their humanity.[108]

In order to begin to change the systematic re-enslavement of Blacks,[109] and the use of them as property, governments must first acknowledge that a slavery scheme still exists in the United States.[110] Judge Higginbotham confirmed this conclusion in the epilogue of his book, *In the Matter of Color*, referring to a conversation he had with Chief Justice Earl Warren:

> [T]he impact of our heritage of slave laws will continue to make itself felt into the future. For there is a nexus between the brutal centuries of colonial slavery and the racial polarization and anxieties of today. The poisonous legacy of legalized oppression based upon the matter of color can never be adequately purged from our society if we act as if slave laws had never existed.[111]

Without this recognition, Blacks will continue to be reduced to commodities, bought and sold for a profit. If this occurs, the number of Black felons in the United States will increase, which will in turn also have the effect of excluding Blacks from participating in future economic practices.

2. Blacks Excluded from Future Economic Participation

As established above, the "War on Drugs" led to the increased incarceration of Blacks through the disproportionate arrest and conviction of Blacks for drug offenses.[112] As Blacks continue to be labeled as felons, they will be excluded from participation in economic practices because they will be unable to obtain jobs.[113]

It is not difficult to surmise that Blacks convicted of felonies, like other ex-offenders, face difficulties when attempting to secure employment upon release from prison.[114] Some of these barriers include state statutory prohibitions that prevent the hiring of ex-offenders for certain jobs.[115] For example, ex-offenders in Pennsylvania are barred from working in health care jobs, and in Florida and Minnesota felons are disqualified from public employment "where the crime relates to the job in question."[116] Other challenges in obtaining employment arise from jobs that are dependent on occupational licensing requirements.[117] Jobs such as "ambulance drivers, billiard room employees, attorneys, physicians, pharmacists, nurses, barbers, embalmers, septic tank cleaners, real estate professionals, accountants, contractors, and sellers of alcoholic beverages" require a registration and license, and ex-offenders are often unable to obtain these jobs because they cannot meet the necessary conditions for a license.[118] Applicants typically have to satisfy two components when applying for a license: (1) the competency component and (2) the character component.[119] Black exoffenders may be able to satisfy the competency component but have difficulties meeting the character component due to their prior convictions.[120] Additionally, Black convicted felons are excluded from federal military economies since the federal government excludes convicted felons from joining the armed forces.[121] Thus, continued inefficient allocations to prison privatization will prolong the exclusion of Blacks from participation in future economic activities. As branded felons, unemployed Blacks will be marginalized and unable to obtain jobs to sustain themselves and their families.

Consequently, in order to protect public interests of economic efficiency as well as social equality, government resources must be redirected from private prison companies. The United States cannot continue to fuel a system that disproportionately arrests Blacks, condones the use of them as property, and expels them as societal pariahs once released from prison.

IV. Conclusion: Stop the *Hustle* and Change the *Flow*

The prison privatization *"hustle"* engrained in the PIC must cease immediately in order to change the inefficient *"flow"* of corporate monopolies and manipulation of the market that inevitably excludes Blacks from future economic activities. Of course it would be naïve to assume that federal, state, and local governments will immediately end all private prison management contracts or close every private prison. This reality notwithstanding, governments must reduce the need for prison privatization by: (1) calling for a moratorium on prison privatization, (2) disbanding private prison corporation monopolies, and (3) redirecting government funds to amend present drug legislation.

A. Moratorium on Prison Privatization

Corporations chase profits even when it conflicts with the public good.[122] Consequently, a majority of governments have turned a blind eye to the monopolization and manipulation of the system by CCA and GEO. Just like tobacco companies have misled the public on the harmful effects of smoking and oil companies dispute any harmful consequences to the environment,[123] CCA and GEO fight to keep people in prisons to fortify economic growth and high shareholder returns. Typically, employing strategic measures to maintain high profits is acceptable for private companies, but it should not be tolerated if one of the measures is the imprisonment of people in the United States.

Prison privatization has taken a publicly regulated function, transformed it into a nearly unregulated private enterprise, and allowed two top corporations to seize immeasurable wealth. Specifically, this wealth has allowed CCA and GEO to gain political influence over key players in the PIC through campaign contributions and allowed CCA and GEO to buy out their competitors thus monopolizing the economic market. Prison privatization has proved to be profitable for CCA and GEO, but governments still wait for the promise of significant savings to be fulfilled from investment in this system.

Therefore, in the face of such inequities, a nation-wide moratorium on prison privatizations is paramount. The solicitation of new private prison contracts must end and current contractual obligations should be fulfilled but not renewed. A moratorium of prison privatization will allow the government to conduct probing and thorough assessments of the utilization of private prison companies in the United States. The moratorium should not end until an independent, nonpartisan committee comprised of community organizations, correction officials, union members, and ex-offenders establishes that the distribution of government funds to private prisons is not inefficient in any way and that no other more efficient way exists to address the high prison population. This may be accomplished on the ciénegas of New Mexico some even cut ditches to hasten it. So subtle has been its progress that few residents of the region are aware of it. It is quite invisible to the tourist who finds this wrecked landscape colorful and charming (as indeed it is, but it bears scant resemblance to what it was in 1848).

This same landscape was "developed" once before, but with quite different results. The Pueblo Indians settled the Southwest in pre-Columbian times, but they happened *not* to be equipped with range livestock. Their civilization expired, but not because their land expired.

In India, regions devoid of any sodforming grass have been settled, apparently without wrecking the land, by the simple expedient of carrying the grass to the cow, rather than vice versa. (Was this the result of some deep wisdom, or was it just good luck? I do not know.)

In short, the plant succession steered the course of history; the pioneer simply demonstrated, for good or ill, what successions inhered in the land. Is history taught in this spirit? It will be, once the concept of land as a community really penetrates our intellectual life.

The Ecological Conscience

Conservation is a state of harmony between men and land. Despite nearly a century of propaganda, conservation still proceeds at a snail's pace; progress still consists largely of letterhead pieties and convention oratory. On the back forty we still slip two steps backward for each forward stride.

The usual answer to this dilemma is "more conservation education." No one will debate this, but is it certain that only the *volume* of education needs stepping up? Is something lacking in the *content* as well?

It is difficult to give a fair summary of its content in brief form, but as I understand it, the content is substantially this: obey the law, vote right, join some organizations, and practice what conservation is profitable on your own land; the government will do the rest.

Is not this formula too easy to accomplish anything worthwhile? It defines no right or wrong, assigns no obligation, calls for no sacrifice, implies no change in the current philosophy of values. In respect of land-use, it urges only enlightened self-interest. Just how far will such education take us? An example will perhaps yield a partial answer.

By 1930 it had become clear to all except the ecologically blind that southwestern Wisconsin's topsoil was slipping seaward. In 1933 the farmers were told that if they would adopt certain remedial practices for five years, the public would donate CCC labor to install them, plus the necessary machinery and materials. The offer was widely accepted, but the practices were widely forgotten when the five-year contract period was up. The farmers continued only those practices that yielded an immediate and visible economic gain for themselves.

This led to the idea that maybe farmers would learn more quickly if they themselves wrote the rules. Accordingly the Wisconsin Legislature in 1937 passed the Soil Conservation District Law. This said to farmers, in effect: *We, the public, will furnish you free technical service and loan you specialized machinery, if you will write your own rules for land-use. Each county may write its own rules, and these will have the force of law.* Nearly all the counties promptly organized to accept the proffered help, but after a decade of operation, *no county has yet written a single rule.* There has been visible progress in such practices as strip-cropping, pasture renovation, and soil liming, but none in fencing woodlots against grazing, and none in excluding plow and cow from steep slopes. The farmers, in short, have selected those remedial practices which were profitable anyhow, and ignored those which were profitable through a comparative cost efficiency analysis regarding the use of government correctional facilities versus funding private prison companies to build private prisons, manage inmates, and operate correctional institutions. However, if the use of private prisons continues to be inefficient, then the privatization of prisons should be banned completely.

B. Disband Private Prisons

CCA and GEO have effectively monopolized the private prison correctional system in the United States. U.S. antitrust regulations were designed to prevent or limit corporate monopolies in order to protect small businesses and promote competition. Thus, the proper solution may be to analyze CCA and GEO's monopolization of the market under antitrust regulations. Yet, because prison privatization helps to fuel the *"hustle"* of the PIC, I propose that we instead rid the United States of this inefficient allocation of resources via state and federal legislation.

Using government resources for prison privatization is inefficient because it provides an incentive to increase the prison population, which in turn has the effect of excluding Blacks from participating in future economic activities. In order to stop the *"flow"* of this inefficiency, federal and state governments need to pass legislation repealing prison privatization. The federal and state governments should follow Illinois's lead and make it illegal to contract with private prison companies.[124] The language of Illinois's Private Correctional Facility Moratorium Act proves helpful in crafting similar federal and state legislation:

> [T]he State, any unit of local government, or a county sheriff, shall not contract with a private contractor or private vendor for the provision of services relating to the operation of a correctional facility or the

incarceration of persons in the custody of the Department of Corrections, the Department of Juvenile Justice, or a sheriff; however, this Act does not apply to … State work release centers or juvenile residential facilities that provide separate care or special treatment operated in whole or part by private contractors.…[125]

Yet contrarily, I disagree with the provision of this statute that still allocates prison privatization contracts for state work release centers and various juvenile residential facilities. Any opportunity to "purchase" prisoners for profit will continue to provide private prison companies with incentives to keep U.S. inhabitants in prison. So, in order to change this *"flow"* of inequity, the private prison *"hustle"* must be stopped completely.

C. Decrease the Prison Population

The expansive prison population will still exist even if we end prison privatization. So as the call for a private prison moratorium is sounded, solutions to the vast number of inmates must be explored.

It is evident that the change in U.S. drug laws caused the prison population explosion in the United States. Thus, it was disingenuous to suggest that the most viable solution to the increased prison population was to turn over correctional responsibilities to private for-profit corporations. The obvious path to solving the problem of expansive prison populations is to shift back to the rehabilitation goal of imprisonment and reform existing drug laws.

President Barack Obama has supported continued drug reform by adopting a new approach to crime; the administration advocates being "smart on crime" versus the former "tough on crime" methodology.[126] In 2007, the U.S. Sentencing Commission amended the Federal Sentencing Guidelines to reduce the disparity between crack and powdered cocaine sentences.[127] Thus, I propose that in light of this change in the law, the current federal prisoners eligible for a sentence reduction should be immediately released. This would result in the release of 20,000 prisoners, approximately 17,000 of whom are Black.[128]

Although this is a good first step, there needs to be complete drug sentencing reform, from the termination of mandatory minimum sentences and three strike laws, to the reallocation of funds, to transitional houses providing education, training, and employment opportunities to ex-offenders. These changes are important because (1) shorter sentences will decrease prison populations and further reduce the need for prison privatization and (2) both solutions will prevent Blacks from continued exclusion from economic participation. There will be fewer Blacks incarcerated, and even if convicted of a felony, they will have additional resources available to help them find employment. Therefore,

this proposed solution has the potential of rectifying the negative effects of inefficient allocations to prison privatization. Specifically, the use of Blacks as quantified property will be reduced, and the exclusion of Blacks from future labor market participation will be minimized.

This Article has argued that the allocation of funds to the *"hustle"* of prison privatization resulted in an inefficient use of resources because governments' budgets were stressed. This engrained *"hustle"* in the PIC has caused the *"flow"* of manifested inequities, particularly creating incentives to keep prison populations high. This in turn has led to private corporation monopolies and manipulation of the system and the exclusion of Blacks from future economic activities. These inefficiencies can be reduced and even halted if the outlined solutions are employed. The privatization of prisons is only one facet of the comprehensive PIC. The inequities of other industries fueling the PIC will be explored in future articles.

Questions

1. What are the "hustle" and "flow" that Fulcher establishes in her article? How do these contribute to inequities and the inefficient allocation of government resources, and discriminate against Blacks?

2. How did harsh drug laws bring about disparate impact in prisons? What does Fulcher recommend to address this issue?

3. Many have called prison a new form of slavery. Does for-profit prison labor support this claim?

Notes

1. Patrice A. Fulcher, "Hustle and Flow: Prison Privatization Fueling the Prison Industrial Complex," *Washburn Law Journal* 51, no. 3 (2012). [Patrice A. Fulcher is] Associate Professor, Atlanta's John Marshall Law School. J.D., Emory University School of Law; B.A., Howard University. I am indebted to Professors Robert A. Brown and Kimberly D'Haene for providing valuable comments to initial drafts of this Article and their unending support and Professor Michele Butts

and Attorney Marian Parker for their encouragement and remarks on final drafts of this Article. I would like to thank my colleagues Jonathan Rapping, Sheryl Harrison, Helen de Haven, Kathleen Burch, Anthony Baker, Elizabeth Jaffe, Bruce Luna, Erika Walker-Cash, and friends Jeanne Aikins, Cathy Bennett, Felice Jerrells, Gladys Pollard, and Sylvia Jones for their support and help with staying on task. I would like to thank my research assistant Chad Alexis for his fortitude and outstanding work and Ginger Fowler for her excellent assistance. Finally, I would like to thank my family, my husband Rick, and my children Marley and Trinity for their continued encouragement, love, and patience.

2. PAUL GUERINO, PAIGE M. HARRISON & WILLIAM J. SABOL, BUREAU OF JUSTICE STATISTICS, PRISONERS IN 2010, at I (Dec. 2011), http://www.bjs.gov/content/pub/pdf/p10.pdf.

3. ROY WALMSLEY, INT'L CENTRE FOR PRISON STUDIES, WORLD PRISON POPULATION LIST (NINTH EDITION) I, *available at* http://www.scribd.com/doc/77097293/World-Prison-Population-List-9th-edition (last visited June 7, 2012).

4. *Id.*

5. *Id.*

6. *Id.* at 4.

7. *Id.* at I.

8. *Id.* at 5.

9. *Id.* at 2.

10. *Id.*

11. Adam Liptak, *Inmate Count in U.S. Dwarfs Other Nations'*, N.Y. TIMES, Apr. 23, 2008, http://www.nytimes.com/2008/04/23/us/23prison.html?pagewanted=1.

12. *Id.*

13. *Id.*

14. *See* U.S. CENSUS BUREAU, THE 2012 STATISTICAL ABSTRACT, TABLE 306. CRIMES AND CRIME RATE BY TYPE AND OFFENSE: 1980-2009 (2012), *available at* http://www.census.gov/prod/2011pubs/12statab/law.pdf. The U.S. crime rate for 1980 was 5,950 crimes per 100,000 people. There was a consistent drop in the crime rate from 1980 to 2009. In 1990, the rate was 5,803; in 2000, the rate was 4,125; and in 2009, the rate was 3,466 crimes per 100,000 of the population. Specifically, the total crime rate for violent crimes dropped from 597 per 100,000 of the population in 1980, to 429 per 100,000 in 2009; and the rate for property crimes dropped from 5,353 per 100,000 of the population in 1980, to 3,036 per 100,000 in 2009. *Id.; see, e.g.,* FBI, FBI RELEASES 2009 CRIME STATISTICS (Sept. 13, 2010), *available at* http://www2.fbi.gov/ucr/cius2009/documents/pressreleasecius09.pdf.

15. In this Article, I use the terms Black and African American interchangeably. I use the term Black when speaking in my own voice, and African American out of respect for the sources that utilize that term.

16. *See* Keith Rushing, *The Reasons Why So Many Black People Are in Prison Go Well Beyond Profiling*, HUFFINGTON Post (June 23, 2011, 4:55 PM), http://www.huffingtonpost.com/keith-rushing/the-reasons-why-so-many-b_b_883310.htrnl.

17. *See* GUERINO, HARRISON & SABOL, *supra* note 2, at 26.

18. SONYA RASTOGI, TALLESE D. JOHNSON, ELIZABETH M. HOEFFEL & MALCOLM DREWERY, JR., U.S. CENSUS BUREAU, THE BLACK POPULATION: 2010, at 3 (Sept. 2011), http://www.census.gov/prod/cen2010/briefs/c2010br-06.pdf.

19. *Id.*

20. LINDSAY HIXSON, BRADFORD HEPLER, & MYOUNG KIM, U.S. CENSUS BUREAU, THE WHITE POPULATION: 2010 (Sept. 2011), http://www.census.gov/prod/cen2010/briefs/c2010br-05.pdf.

21. *See* THOMAS P. BONCZAR, BUREAU OF JUSTICE STATISTICS, PREVALENCE OF IMPRISONMENT IN THE U.S. POPULATION, 1974-2001, at 8 (Aug. 2003), http://bjs.ojp.usdoj.gov/content/pub/pdf/piusp01.pdf.

22. *Id.*

23. *Id.*

24. *Id.*

25. MARC MAUER & RYAN SCOTT KING, SENTENCING PROJECT, SCHOOLS AND PRISONS: FIFTY YEARS AFTER *BROWN V. BOARD OF EDUCATION* 1-2 (Jan. 2004), http://www.sentencingproject.org/doc/publications/rd_brownvboard.pdf.

26. *Id.*

27. *Id.*

28. JAMES AUSTIN & GARRY COVENTRY, BUREAU OF JUSTICE ASSISTANCE, EMERGING ISSUES ON PRIVATIZED PRISONS 2 (Feb. 2001), *available at* https://www.ncjrs.gov/pdffilesl/bja/181249.pdf.

29. [Sharon Dolovich, *State Punishment and Private Prisons*, 55 *DUKE L.J.* 458 (2005).]

30. JAMES J. STEPHAN, U.S. DEPARTMENT OF JUSTICE, STATE PRISON EXPENDITURES, 2001, at I (2004), *available at* http://bjs.ojp.usdoj.gov/content/pub/pdf7speol.pdf.

31. *Id.*

32. [JUSTICE POL'Y INST., GAMING THE SYSTEM: HOW THE POLITICAL STRATEGIES OF PRIVATE PRISON COMPANIES PROMOTE INEFFECTIVE INCARCERATION POLICIES 5 (June 2011), http://www.justicepolicy.org/uploads/justicepolicy/documents/gaming_the_system.pdf [hereinafter Gaming the System].]

33. *See id.*

34. PHILIP MATTERA & MAJRUZA KHAN WITH GREG LEROY & KATE DAVIS, INST. ON TAXATION AND ECON. POL'Y, JAIL BREAKS: ECONOMIC DEVELOPMENT SUBSIDIES GIVEN TO PRIVATE PRISONS 23-24 (2001), *available at* http://www.privateci.org/private_pics/jailbreaks.pdf.

35. *See, e.g., id.* at 28, 37-38 (2001) "Reducing or eliminating taxes on businesses is the most common-and most costly-form of economic development subsidy." The five most significant ways private prison companies receive tax subsidies are:

· Property tax abatements—full or partial exemption from tax for periods typically ranging from 5 to 20 years;
· Corporate income tax credits for capital investment, job creation, or other activities—dollar-for-dollar reductions in a company's state corporate income tax bill, using either flat-rate formulas (such as $2,500 per new job created) or percentage rates (such as 5% of the value of a capital investment);
· Sales tax waivers on building materials for new construction;
· Utility tax breaks—lower rates, usually associated with new economic activity; and
· Enterprise zone-associated tax breaks such as property tax abatements, inventory tax exemptions and/or employment tax credits.

Id. at 37-38.

36. *Id.* at 29.

37. *Id.* at 30.

38. *See id.* at 44.

39. *Id.* at 44.

40. *Id.* at 45.

41. *Compare* M. WOLFGANG, PRISONS: PRESENT AND POSSIBLE 35-38 (1979) (noting private contractors will be "far more efficient" than government agencies), *with* J. KEATING, SEEKING PROFIT IN PUNISHMENT: THE PRIVATE MANAGEMENT OF CORRECTIONAL INSTITUTIONS 48 (1984) (unpublished manuscript, on file with the *Columbia Law Review*) (arguing the supposed cost savings to be realized through privatization may be offset by the cost to the government of monitoring private facilities).

42. AMY CHEUNG, SENTENCING PROJECT, PRISON PRIVATIZATION AND THE USE OF INCARCERATION 1, 2 (2004), http://www.sentencingproject.org/doc/publications/inc_prisonprivatization.pdf.

43. *Id.*

44. *See generally* See Brad W. Lundahl et al., Prison Privatization: A Meta-Analysis of Cost and Quality of Confinement Indicators, 19 RES.

ON SOC. WORK PRAC. 383, 384 (2009). This report conducted a meta-analysis of twelve studies on private- versus public- managed prisons. The report analyzed cost effectiveness as well as the quality of confinement. *See id.*

45. *Id.* at 20.

46. *See, e.g.,* J. Michael Quinlan, Charles W. Thomas & Sherril Gautreaux, *The Privatization of Correctional Facilities, in* PRIVATIZING GOV-ERNMENTAL FUNCTIONS 10-1, § 10.03[3] (Deborah Ballati ed., 2001) ("Today there is a growing body of research evidence on the cost savings issue, which shows significant savings in construction as well as operating costs."). Quinlan is the former director of the Federal Bureau of Prisons, and at the time of publication, the Execu-tive Vice President and Chief Operating Officer of CCA. *Id.* at 10-1 n.★★.

47. *See* Dolovich, supra note [29], at 455-58.

48. CORRECTIONS CORPORATION OF AMERICA, 2010 ANNUAL REPORT ON FORM 10-K, at 2 (2010) [hereinafter CCA REPORT], *available at* http://phx.corporate-ir.net/External.File?item=UGFyZW50SUQ9NDE5MTEwfENoaWxkSUQ9NDMyMjglfFR ScGU9MQ= &t=l .

49. *Id.* at 18.

50. GUERINO, HARRISON & SABOL, *supra* note 2, at 2.

51. *See* GAMING THE SYSTEM, *supra* note [32], at 15-16.

52. *See id.* at 3.

53. 130 S. Ct. 876 (2010).

54. *See id.* at 912-13.

55. *See, e.g.,* Michael Kang, *The End of Campaign Finance law,* 98 VA. L. REV. 1, 2-5 (2012) (explaining that four decades of campaign finance law "as we knew it died" with the Court's ruling in *Citizens United v. Federal Election Commission*). "*Citizens United* overruled *Austin [v. Michigan Chamber of Commerce,* 494 U.S. 652 (1990),]* and traditional campaign finance understanding about corporate spending by striking down as unconstitutional an important element of campaign finance restrictions on corporate spending through independent expenditures." *Id.* at 3. Kang also noted that "this new deregulated world of campaign finance is not a better world" and that "the removal of longstanding restrictions on independent expenditures is causing money rapidly to return to the least regulated, least restricted pathways." *Id.* at 5; *see also* Andrew T. Newcomer, *The "Crabbed View of Corruption": How the U.S. Supreme Court Has Given Corporations the Green Light to Gain Influence over Politicians by Spending on Their Behalf* [Citizens United v. Fed-eral Election Commission, *130* S. *Ct. 876 (2010)*], 50 WASHBURN L. J. 235, 237 (2010) (noting that "the Court should have rejected the notion that independent expenditures do not pose a danger of corruption and instead recognized that they can be used to secure political favors or influence over officeholders").

56. *See Contributors Results, Corrections Corp of America,* NAT'L INST. ON MONEY IN STATE POLITICS, http://www.followthemoney.org/database/search.phtml?searchbox=corrections+corp+of+America (last visited June 7, 2012); *Contributors Results, GEO Group,* NAT'L INST. ON MONEY IN STATE POLITICS, http://www.followthemoney.org/database/search.phtml?searchbox=GEO+Group (last visited June 7, 2012); *Contributors Results, Cornell Companies,* NAT'L INST. ON MONEY IN STATE POLITICS, http://www.followthemoney.org/database/search.phtml?searchbox=Cornell+Companies (last visited June 7, 2012).

57. *See* sources cited *supra* note 165.

58. GAMING THE SYSTEM, *supra* note [32], at 15-16.

59. *Id.* at 23.

60. *Id.* at 30.

61. H.B. 87, 151st Gen. Assemb., 1st Reg. Sess. (Ga. 2011), *available at* http://wwwl.legis.ga.gov/legis/2011_12/pdf/hb87.pdf; *see* Gwynedd Stuart, *Cashing in on a Crackdown: Georgia's Thriving Private Prison Industry Will Get a Boost From New Immigration Law,* CREATIVE LOAFING

ATLANTA (July 28, 2011), http://clatl.com/gyrobase/georgias-thriving-private-prison-industry-boost-from-new-immigration-law/Content?oid=3700500&showFullText=true [hereinafter Stuart, *Cashing in on a Crackdown*]. In 2009 and 2010, eleven state senators and seventeen state representatives received a total of $24,400 in campaign contributions from CCA. Gwynedd Stuart, *Follow the Money: Twenty-eight Georgia Politicians that Received Campaign Contributions from the CCA*, CREATIVE LOAFING ATLANTA (July 28, 2011), http://clatl.com/atlanta/28-georgia-politicians-that-received-campaigncontributions-from-the-cca/Content?oid=3712165 [hereinafter Stuart, *Follow the Money*]. CCA also contributed $5,000 to Governor Nathan Deal and his opponent Roy Barnes. *Id.* The politicians that received CCA funds were mostly Republican and voted overwhelmingly in favor of H.B. 87. *Id.*

62. *See* Stuart, *Cashing in on a Crackdown*, *supra* note 61.

63. GAMING THE SYSTEM, *supra* note [32], at 30.

64. *See* James Kilgore, *A Blow Against the Prison-Industrial-Complex: Florida's Prison Privatization Plan Defeated*, COUNTERPUNCH WEEK-END EDITION (Feb. 17, 2012), http://www.counterpunch.org/2012/02/17/a-blow-against-the-prison-industrial-complex/.

65. *Id.*

66. *Id.*

67. *Id.*

68. *See* Chris Kirkham, *Private Prison Corporation Offers Cash in Exchange for State Prisons*, HUFF-INGTON POST (Feb. 14, 2012), http://www.huffingtonpost.com/2012/02/14/private-prisons-buying-stateprisons_n_l2 72143.html.

69. *Id.*

70. CCA *REPORT*, *supra* note 157, at 13.

71. *Id.*

72. [Eric Schlosser, *The Prison-Industrial Complex*, ATL. MONTHLY (Dec. 1998) at 4, http://www.theatlantic.com/magazine/archive/1998/12/the-prison-industrial-complex/4669/.] The economics of the private-prison industry are in many respects similar to those of the lodging industry. An inmate at a private prison is like a guest at a hotel-a guest whose bill is being paid and whose check-out date is set by someone else. A hotel has a strong economic incentive to book every available room and encourage every guest to stay as long as possible. A private prison has exactly the same incentive. The labor costs constitute the bulk of operating costs for both kinds of accommodation. The higher the occupancy rate, the higher the profit margin. *Id.*

73. *See* CCA REPORT, *supra* note 48, at 13.

74. *See* GAMING THE SYSTEM, *supra* note [32], at 30.

75. [*Criminal Alien Requirement 12, FEDBIZOPPS. GOV*, https://www.fbo.gov/index?s=opportunity&mode=form&id=0422fl6890afoef708c5067abe7cf6b8&tab=core &_cview=1 (last visited June 7, 2012).]

76. *See* Stuart, *Follow the Money*, *supra* note 61.

77. *See* Douglas Dunham, *Inmate Rights and the Privatization of Prisons*, 86 COLUM. L. REV. 1475, 1484 (1986).

78. Sandra Block, *Everybody's Doin' The Jailhouse Stock*, USA TODAY, June 5, 1996, at 3B.

79. Mattera, *supra* note 144, at 3. In 1996, CCA had 52% of the market share "based on the number of adult beds under contract." *Id.* GEO, then Wackenhut Corrections, had 25%, and U.S. Corrections Corp. had over 5%. *Id.*

80. *See* GAMING THE SYSTEM, *supra* note [32], at 6-8.

81. *See id.* at 2.

82. *See id.*

83. *See id.* at 5.

84. Mattera, *supra* note 34, at 3.

85. Martin E. Gold, *The Privatization of Prisons*, 28 URB. LAW. 359, 372 n.46 (1996).

86. *Id.*

87. *See* Press Release, The GEO Group, Inc., The GEO Group Closes $730 Million Merger with Cornell Companies (Aug. 12, 2010), *available at* http://phx.corporate-ir.net/phoenix.

zhtml?c=91331&p=irolnewsArticle_print&ID=l
459689&highlight=.

88. *Id.*

89. Press Release, The GEO Group, Inc., The GEO
Group Announces $415 Million Acquisition
of B.J. Incorporated (Dec. 21, 2010), *available at* http://phx.corporate-ir.net/phoenix.
zhtml?c=9133l&p=irolnewsArticle_print&ID= I
509666&highlight=.

90. *Id.*

91. Press Release, The GEO Group, Inc., The GEO
Group Reports Fourth Quarter 2011 Results and
Announces Adoption of Cash Dividend Policy
(Feb. 21, 2012), *available at* http://phx.corporateir.
net/phoenix.zhtml?c=9133l&p=irol-newsArticle_
print&ID=l663040&highlight=.

92. *See* GAMING THE SYSTEM, *supra* note [32] at
30.

93. *See generally* [MICHELLE ALEXANDER, THE
NEW JIM CROW 112 (2010)]; DOUGLAS A.
BLACKMON, SLAVERY BY ANOTHER
NAME (2009); [Chris Weaver & Will Purcell,
*The Prison Industrial Complex: A Modern Justifica-
tion/or African Enslavement?,* 41 How. L.J. 349, 360
(1998)].

94. W.E.B. DU BOIS, BLACK RECONSTRUC-
TION IN AMERICA 24 (Henry Louis Gates, Jr.
ed., 2007).

95. Weaver & Purcell, *supra* note [93], at 355.

96. MAUER & KING, *supra* note [25], at 3.

97. *See* TODD D. MINTON, BUREAU OF JUST.
STAT., JAIL INMATES AT MIDYEAR 2010—
STATISTICAL TABLES 8 (June 28, 2011),
http://bjs.ojp.usdoj.gov/content/pub/pdf/jim10st.
pdf.

98. *See* Weaver & Purcell, *supra* note [93] , at 354-57.

99. GUERINO, HARRISON & SABOL, *supra* note
2, at 1.

100. *See* HEATHER C. WEST, BUREAU OF
JUST. STAT., PRISON INMATES AT
MIDYEAR 2009—STATISTICAL TABLES 2
(June 2010), http://bjs.ojp.usdoj.gov/content/pub/
pdf/pim09st.pdf. See tables 16-19 for totals and
rates for Blacks, Hispanics, and Whites, which

are broken down by year and gender. *Id.* at 19-21.
See page 2 for "Selected characteristics of inmates
held in custody in state or federal prisons or in
local jails." *Id.* at 2.

101. *See* Ronald K. Noble, *Between Complicity and
Contempt: Racial Presumptions of the American Legal
Process,* 72 N.Y.U. L. REV. 66 4, 671-72 (1997)
(reviewing A. LEON HIGGINBOTHAM, JR.,
SHADES OF FREEDOM: RACIAL POLITICS
AND PRESUMPTIONS OF THE AMERI-
CAN LEGAL PROCESS (1996)).

102. *See generally* Charles J, Ogletree, Jr., *Judge A. Leon
Higginbotham, Jr.'s Civil Rights Legacy,* 34 HARV.
C.R.-C.L. L. REV. 1, 2-6 (1999). Chief Judge
Higginbotham is one of our nation's most notable
scholars and jurists on the jurisprudence of race,
civil rights, and the law. *Id.*

103. Noble, *supra* note 101, at 669.

104. *Id.*

105. *Id.* at 670-71.

106. *Id.* at 670 n.45.

107. [*See* Brad W. Lundahl et al., *Prison Privatization:
A Meta-Analysis of Cost and Quality of Confinement
Indicators,* 19 RES. ON SOC. WORK PRAC.
384 (2009).]

108. *See* Weaver & *Purcell, supra* note [93], at 351-52.

109. *Id.* at 351; *see, e.g.,* ALEXANDER, *supra* note
[93].

110. *See* LEON HIGGINBOTHAM, IN THE
MATTER OF COLOR: RACE AND THE
AMERICAN LEGAL PROCESS: THE COLO-
NIAL PERIOD 391 (1978).

111. *Id.*

112. *See* Cecilia Stiber, *Discriminatory Intent Require-
ment: The "Separate But Equal" Doctrine of the
Twenty-First Century?—A Critical Examination of
Felon Disenfranchisement Laws and Related Govern-
ment Practices in the United States,* 41 GONZ. L.
REV. 347, 369-70 (2006).

113. *See* Elena Saxonhouse, Note, *Unequal Protection:
Comparing Former Felons' Challenges to Disenfran-
chisement and Employment Discrimination,* 56 STAN.
L. REV. 1597, 1612 (2004).

114. *Id.*

115. *Id.*

116. *Id.* In Pennsylvania, an ex-offender could not sweep the halls of a hospital if convicted of bribery. *Id.*

117. *Id.* at 1613.

118. Bruce E. May, *The Character Component of Occupational Licensing Laws: A Continuing Barrier to the Ex-Felon's Employment Opportunities,* 71 N.D. L. REV. 187, 190-91 (1995).

119. *Id.*

120. *See id.*

121. SUSAN M. KUZMA, U.S. DEP'T OF JUST., FEDERAL STATUTES IMPOSING COLLATERAL CONSEQUENCES UPON CONVICTION 3 (2000), http://www.usdoj.gov/pardon/collateral_consequences.pdf.

122. *See* Michael Kent Curtis, *The Fraying Fabric of Freedom: Crisis and Criminal Law in Struggles for Democracy and Freedom of Expression,* 44 TEX. TECH L. REV. 89, 135 (2011).

123. *Id.*

124. *See* Private Correction Facility Moratorium Act, 730 ILL. COMP. STAT. 140/3 (West 2007).

125. *Id.*

126. *See* Michael A. Simons, *Sense and Sentencing: Our Imprisonment Epidemic,* 25 J. OF C.R. & ECON. DEV. 161, 163 (2010).

127. *Id.* at 172.

128. *See id.* at 173.

Chapter 6: Environmental Ethics Challenges to Business

Introduction

"A thing is right when it tends to preserve the integrity, stability, and beauty of the biotic community. It is wrong when it tends otherwise."

"Perhaps the most serious obstacle impending the evolution of a land ethic is the fact that our educational and economic system is headed away from, rather than toward, an intense consciousness of land."
—Aldo Leopold, *A Sand County Almanac*

"During these last days I have been occupied in examining my past conduct…. In a fit of enthusiastic madness I created a rational creature and was bound towards him to assure … his happiness and well-being. This was my duty, but there was another still paramount to that. My duties towards the beings of my own species had greater claims to my attention."
—Dr. Frankenstein[1]

BUSINESS ETHICS IS OFTEN called an oxymoron most especially due to innumerable unethical business practices and the dearth of empirical evidence of practices that are ethical. Almost as unfathomable as the juxtaposition of business and ethics is the inclusion of environmental ethics in business. This is in no small part due to the fact that almost every business action entails environmental depletion of some sort, and most environmental depletion entails environmental harm (this book included). Therefore, an environmental ethics investigation into the business of business calls the entire enterprise into question. Some businesses attempt to engage environmental concerns by claiming earth-friendly actions in the form of recycling, reduced packaging, and the like. Most businesses avoid the issue altogether, knowing that no amount of Madison Avenue advertising could make their product appear earth-friendly. Yet for business to eschew environmental questions is the proverbial head hiding in the sand, for the environment is the basis from which *all actions* derive. There is "full human dependence on nature."[2]

As it is an empirical fact that each and every human action (and by extension each business action) is dependent on the finite natural environment, it seems especially irrational to ignore environmental issues. One problem is in the economic conception of the environment. As John Bellamy Foster (b. 1953) points out,

> Orthodox economics, as is well known, defines itself as a science for the efficient utilization of scarce goods. But the goods concerned are conceived narrowly as market commodities. The effects of the economy in generating ecological scarcities and irreversible (within human time frames) ecological degradation are beyond the purview of received economics, which, in line with the system it is designed to defend, seldom takes account of what it calls "external" or "social" costs.[3]

Those external costs, or externalities, include pollution; and the social costs include human rights violations, disease, and the societal economic costs of cleaning up pollution or paying for medical care.

Part of the avoidance of addressing environmental issues by business is due to inconsistencies between orthodox capitalism and finite environmental resources. Orthodox capitalism is based on seemingly infinite *growth*: "growth of profits, and hence … economic growth at virtually any cost."[4] It is an empirical fact that resources are finite. Yet in order to avoid addressing environmental issues, capitalism and economics must ignore the truism that "infinite expansion within a finite environment [is] a contradiction in terms."[5] Another part of the avoidance on the part of business in addressing environmental issues is the emphasis on short-term gain, because environmental ethics perspectives necessarily consider long-term consequences.

Environmental Ethics Perspectives

Environmental ethics is a study of the question of how we should live in relation to our environment, that is, the study of the moral basis for our environmental responsibility. As might be expected, there is no one theory that represents the environmental ethics position. There are two main perspectives in environmental ethics that I will address here: anthropocentric and biocentric approaches.

An anthropocentric approach in environmental ethics is one that is human-centered. Anthropocentrism asserts that all and only human concerns matter, that they alone have intrinsic value, and that the environment is of concern as an instrument, or as a means to an end, for human interests. Anthropocentrism asserts that the only ethical duties are to human beings; that is, one cannot have a duty to the environment. The US legal system takes an anthropocentric approach to all environmental issues, mostly subsuming environmental issues in property rights issues and determining the outcome based on economic costs.

For example, the *Clean Air Act* of 1970 is an example of an anthropocentric approach most recently being determined by economic costs. It was intended to "protect public health" and to provide "more stringent national secondary standards to protect public welfare."[6] Because it is based on human value (human health as opposed to having clean air for the health of the ecosystem as a whole), it is relatively easy to redefine the human value and change the act, as has subsequently occurred. The *Clean Air Act* was amended in 1990, under the George H.W. Bush administration, and weakened in several aspects, including providing economic incentives and "credits" whereby firms can receive points if they don't pollute to the maximum allowed, and then spend those points later if they don't meet the requirements. Imagine a day when those firms that saved up points all pollute beyond the maximum considered safe. The act was further weakened by the George W. Bush administration in November 2002, allowing higher pollution levels, removing the requirement to install costly advanced antipollution equipment, and benefiting power companies who contributed millions to Bush's campaign.[7] After taking office, the Trump administration began reversing environmental protections, including the *Clean Air Act*:

> Calling the rules unnecessary and burdensome to the fossil fuel industry and other businesses, his administration has weakened ... limits on planet-warming carbon dioxide emissions from power plants and from cars and trucks, and rolled back many more rules governing clean air, water and toxic chemicals. Several major reversals have been finalized in recent months as the country has struggled to contain the spread of new coronavirus.
>
> In all, a *New York Times* analysis, based on research from Harvard Law School, Columbia Law School and other sources, counts nearly 70 environmental rules and regulations officially reversed, revoked or otherwise rolled back under Mr. Trump. More than 30 additional rollbacks are still in progress.[8]

Clearly, in these actions, the environment is merely an instrument for humans to use in pursuing their interests, and human values that are held in the highest will be reflected accordingly. In the above example, the highest human value held is economic profit, that is, the profit of power and other companies.

A contrasting perspective in environmental ethics is ecocentrism. An ecocentric approach is ecosystem or earth-centered. This approach is also referred to as biocentric, and sometimes by one variety of ecocentric approaches, "deep ecology." People who hold this perspective believe that the earth and ecosystems have intrinsic value, that humans are just one species of many, that human interests do not always reign superior to other species and ecosystem interests, and that we have duties to the earth and ecosytems. Aldo Leopold's land ethic (the opening epigraph in this chapter) is an example of an ecocentric environmental ethic, for the rightness of the action is judged from an ecosystem perspective, not from what advantage or "good" a human received. Another important issue is biodiversity.

Edward O. Wilson (1929–2021) is an emeritus Harvard biologist who has written widely on biodiversity, the variation of species composing an ecosystem, and biophilia, the innate attraction humans have for other species and ecosystems.[9] Wilson brings the perspective of evolutionary time to urge an appreciation for, and the protection of, biodiversity. Although extinctions occur in nature, human actions have accelerated them—"hundred of thousands of times higher than before the coming of man [sic]"—through pollution, habitat destruction, and the disruption of natural ecosystems with non-indigenous species. When Wilson responds to the question "Why should we care?," he provides an anthropocentric list of benefits to humans from an intact biota, benefits without which human existence on the planet would be a rather Hobbesian "nasty and short."

Both ecocentrism and anthropocentrism have difficulty resolving conflict, such as conflict between interests. From an anthropocentric approach, when two human instrumental uses of the environment clash, there is no pre-existing hierarchy of values that will decide the matter. For example, there are clashes between the human enjoyment of an endangered species and between the human desire for profit from the destruction of resources crucial to the habitat for the same species, or clashes between the quality of human life without air pollution and the economic interests of polluting firms. To resolve conflicts within this approach would require a hierarchy of value, such as placing human life (and health) above money. As the *Clean Air Act* and its subsequent weakening illustrate, defining and enforcing such a hierarchy would need to be removed from the political realm (as it now exists).

From an ecocentric approach, two species could clash; an example would be a clash between the carrier species of a deadly virus and the humans who are subject to the virus. To resolve the conflicts within an ecocentric approach would require ecological knowledge about the value of the species within the ecosystem (such as an indigenous species versus an aggressive invasive species) and a weighing of importance at the species and/or ecosystem level, as opposed to the individual level. It is clear how environmental ethics, perhaps more than any other branch of applied ethics, challenges the ethical assumptions of humans and their place in the world.

Transgenic Agricultural Biotechnology (Imprecisely Called GMOs) and Factory Farming

Biotechnology is genetic engineering in which living organisms, in whole or in part, are used to make a product, modify a product, create a micro-organism for various uses, or change a plant or animal. There are two forms of biotechnology: that which is done within a species or that which is done across two or more species. The latter is transgenic biotechnology and is formed by inserting foreign genes into an organism. This is widely known as a "GMO" or genetically modified organism. However, GMO is an imprecise term for this technology, as humans have been modifying genetic organisms since the dawn of

agriculture, well over 10,000 years ago. What is (relatively) new is forcibly combining two different species via biotechnology.

Transgenic agricultural biotechnology is performed by recombinant DNA techniques.[10] First, a gene of interest is isolated. Next a "promoter" is added to initiate or enhance the gene expression. Then a reporter gene is added. The reporter gene is antibiotic resistant,[11] an important trait due to its ability to perform the desired action, and it is this antibiotic resistance that can be transferred to the "gut" microflora. Next, the gene (via the disease-causing bacteria) is spliced or inserted into the organism. An insertion technique is accomplished via an infection. The organism cells take up fragments of foreign DNA and transform the genetic makeup of the recipient cell. Then either the resultant transformed organism can be used to select transformed cells or organisms, or the whole organism can be regenerated. Transgenic projects have included flounder genes in strawberries and tomatoes, growth hormone genes placed in tilapia and salmon, and tobacco genes in lettuce. We are already broadly consuming transgenic organisms in corn, soy, dairy, meat, and tomato products.

Broadly touted as safe and necessary, this technology carries severe risks and unknown implications for human health and the ecosystem, including transferring traits to neighboring plants, change and degradation of soil ecology, and threats to endangered species. Pharmaceutical transgenic agriculture is also often claimed to be beneficial, and claims are made that these crops can be processed to produce human medicine from vaccines to contraceptives, to abortion-inducing drugs. Contrary to somewhat widespread myth, the "medicine" will not be delivered via a piece of fruit or vegetable but rendered from processed plants due to the need for dosage regulation (of the medicine), among other concerns.

However, pharmaceutical crops are virtually unregulated, and safe buffer zones around these crops grown in the open have yet to be established. Two "safeguards" mentioned for pharmaceutical crops involve yet more genetic engineering for seedlessness, and a different color crop (so the "pharmed" plant would be visible). It is not clear how these are safeguards because these traits can be transferred as well, and a phenomenon known as "gene silencing," where a plant "turns off" the foreign genes so they do not manifest in each generation, removes the ability to control engineered crops (or know how widely they have spread in the ecosystem). We do not know the implications; we have not had political and civic discussions of whether we should be doing this, and industry has aggressively prevented labeling of existing products in the United States. In 2002, an Oregon labeling initiative was defeated after various biotech companies spent over $6 million to fight it.[12] As this business is worth billions, it is not surprising that industry would spend money to prevent labels.

Other claims of benefits, such as golden rice that will address malnutrition, are in fact a myth, and claims of feeding the hungry are false insofar as this expensive, patented technology will not be given to hungry people, nor is it necessarily suited to growing conditions where there is the most need. Much transgenic agriculture has also been developed to *withstand* higher doses of pesticides, including Monsanto's varieties that respond to Monsanto's pesticides, and this is not an issue of solving hunger but rather of propping up the failing remnants of the Green Revolution (see Shiva in Chapter 2).

Another example of the biotechnology industry's intentions can be found in patents for crippling or killing crops. In a process known as "terminator technology," these transgenic plants are engineered to destroy the fertility of their own seeds, so that farmers cannot save the seeds and must buy new seeds each year.[13] This trait, the infertility, can be transferred to other plants as well. The implications for contamination from these plants was well enough understood to ignite an (ongoing) international protest against the first patent sought for the original "terminator."

Regarding livestock, factory—or corporate—farming has overwhelmingly replaced traditional farms, and in most animal products, especially eggs, chicken, and pork; factory farming supplies over 90 per cent of the products consumed.[14] Factory farming of animals is the intensive raising of livestock, often in crowded cages in buildings without exposure to sun. Numerous practices cause enormous suffering of the animals. Pigs stand on metal grates over their own waste, unable to roll in the mud or have straw to cushion their hooves. Their waste poses health hazards to the human workers in these factories and causes painful burning in the lungs of the hogs. Veal calves are taken from their mothers before they are weaned and kept confined, without sunlight, where they cannot turn around, so their meat stays tender. The suffering endured by factory animals is well documented[15] and disregarded, for the animals are mere "biomachines," and the only measure of value they hold is economic and gastronomic. Further, factory farmed livestock and even fish (tilapia and salmon) are fed transgenic corn in complete defiance of their natural diets.

Notes

1. Mary Shelley, *Frankenstein* (1818).
2. John Bellamy Foster, *Ecology against Capitalism* (New York: Monthly Review Press, 2002), 9.
3. Ibid.
4. Ibid., 10.
5. Ibid.
6. See Clean Air Act of 1970, PL 91–604, 40 CFR 50, www.epa.gov.
7. See John Heilprin, "White House Loosens Clean Air Rules," Associated Press, November 22, 2002.
8. Nadja Popovice, Livia Albeck-Ripka, and Kendra Pierre-Louis, "The Trump Administration Is Reversing 100 Environmental Rules. Here's the Full List," *New York Times*, July 15, 2020, https://www.nytimes.com/interactive/2020/climate/trump-environment-rollbacks.html.
9. See Edward O. Wilson, *The Diversity of Life* (Cambridge, MA: Belknap Press of Harvard University Press, 1992).
10. As explained by Moshe Raccach, Morrison School of Agribusiness & Resource Management, Arizona State University East, Arizona State University's Conference for "Confidence Building Measures for Genetically Modified Foods," December 6, 2002.
11. Dr. Joseph Graves commented, "Not all reporter genes are antibiotic resistance genes. Some reporter genes cause florescence, or some other easily detectable phenotype. Also, [your description] seems just to relate to prokaryotic transgenic techniques." I appreciate his comments and clarification.
12. This is not true in Europe; the European Union (EU) has continually resisted these crops, calling them GMOs (genetically modified organisms) and demanding disclosure of their presence in imports. The EU passed an agreement requiring labeling if there is a 0.9 per cent or higher presence of GMOs, and it awaits the European Parliament's passage of the labeling. Previous Parliament measures supported stricter requirements.
13. See Martha Crouch, "How the Terminator Terminates," *Edmonds Occasional Paper*, Edmonds Institute, 1998; and "From Golden Rice to Terminator Technology: Agricultural Biotechnology Will Not Feed the World or Save the Environment," in *Redesigning Life? The Worldwide Challenge to Genetic Engineering*, ed. Brian Tokar (London: Zed Books, 2000).
14. For a history of factory farming development, see Jim Mason and Peter Singer, *Animal Factories: What Agribusiness Is Doing to the Family Farm, the Environment, and Your Health* (New York: Crown, 1990), 1–3.
15. See Orville Schell, *Modern Meat: Antibiotics, Hormones, and the Pharmaceutical Farm* (New York: Random House, 1984); Howard F. Lyman, *Mad Cowboy: Plain Truth from the Cattle Rancher Who Won't Eat Meat* (New York: Simon & Schuster, 1998); Peter Singer, *Animal Liberation* (New York: New York Review of Books, 1990).

1. The Land Ethic[1]

Aldo Leopold

ALDO LEOPOLD (1887–1948) ARGUES for an extension of ethical concern to land in "The Land Ethic." Leopold's essay is from *A Sand County Almanac*, a book that is really the watershed book of Western environmental ethics. Writing over 70 years ago, Leopold postulated that the time was right for an extension of our ethics to the natural world, as when the Western world progressed from considering only some white men as human to finally including all human beings. One way to extend our ethical concern to land is to understand our place on that land. We are, Leopold illustrates, members of the biotic community, a community that includes plants, water, animals, soil, or taken together, the land. To see oneself as a citizen of the biotic community is a significant shift from seeing oneself as a conqueror of the land. As biotic citizens, we fit within the community. The biotic community includes all of the species and parts of the land pyramid he details, and humans belong inside the pyramid, not at the top or outside of it.

Leopold provides a principle by which we can measure each action and carry out our environmental responsibility. That principle is "the land ethic." The land ethic is quoted in full at the beginning of this section and measures the "rightness" or the "wrongness" of our actions by their environmental consequences. Actions that threaten the integrity, stability, and beauty of the ecosystem are wrong. The integrity and stability of the ecosystem has evolved through millennia and needs to be understood via the study of ecology, not economics. While Leopold recognizes that economic constraints must be taken into account, they are not the primary determinant or deciding factors.

WHEN GODLIKE ODYSSEUS RETURNED from the wars in Troy, he hanged all on one rope a dozen slave-girls of his household whom he suspected of misbehavior during his absence.

This hanging involved no question of propriety. The girls were property. The disposal of property was then, as now, a matter of expediency, not of right or wrong.

Concepts of right and wrong were not lacking from Odysseus' Greece: witness the fidelity of his wife through the long years before at last his black-prowed galleys clove the wine-dark seas for home. The ethical structure of that day covered wives, but had not yet been extended to human chattels. During the three thousand years which have since elapsed, ethical criteria have been extended to many fields of conduct, with corresponding shrinkages in those judged by expediency only.

The Ethical Sequence

This extension of ethics, so far studied only by philosophers, is actually a process in ecological evolution. Its sequences may be described in ecological as well as in philosophical terms. An ethic, ecologically, is a limitation on freedom of action in the struggle for existence. An ethic, philosophically, is a differentiation of social from antisocial conduct. These are two definitions of one thing. The thing has its origin in the tendency of interdependent individuals or groups to evolve modes of cooperation. The ecologist calls these symbioses. Politics and economics are advanced symbioses in which the original free-for-all competition has been replaced, in part, by cooperative mechanisms with an ethical content.

The complexity of cooperative mechanisms has increased with population density, and with the efficiency of tools. It was simpler, for example, to define the anti-social uses of sticks and stones in the days of the mastodons than of bullets and billboards in the age of motors.

The first ethics dealt with the relation between individuals; the Mosaic Decalogue is an example. Later accretions dealt with the relation between the individual and society. The Golden Rule tries to integrate the individual to society; democracy to integrate social organization to the individual.

There is as yet no ethic dealing with man's relation to land and to the animals and plants which grow upon it. Land, like Odysseus' slave-girls, is still property. The land-relation is still strictly economic, entailing privileges but not obligations.

The extension of ethics to this third element in human environment is, if I read the evidence correctly, an evolutionary possibility and an ecological necessity. It is the third step in a sequence. The first two have already been taken. Individual thinkers since the days of Ezekiel and Isaiah have asserted that the despoliation of land is not only inexpedient but wrong. Society, however, has not yet affirmed their belief. I regard the present conservation movement as the embryo of such an affirmation.

An ethic may be regarded as a mode of guidance for meeting ecological situations so new or intricate, or involving such deferred reactions, that the path of social expediency is not discernible to the average individual. Animal instincts are modes of guidance for the individual in meeting such situations. Ethics are possibly a kind of community instinct in-the-making.

The Community Concept

All ethics so far evolved rest upon a single premise: that the individual is a member of a community of interdependent parts. His instincts prompt him to compete for his place in the community, but his ethics prompt him also to cooperate (perhaps in order that there may be a place to compete for).

The land ethic simply enlarges the boundaries of the community to include soils, waters, plants, and animals, or collectively: the land.

This sounds simple: do we not already sing our love for and obligation to the land of the free and the home of the brave? Yes, but just what and whom do we love? Certainly not the soil, which we are sending helter-skelter downriver. Certainly not the waters, which we assume have no function except to turn turbines, float barges, and carry off sewage. Certainly not the plants, of which we exterminate whole communities without batting an eye. Certainly not the animals, of which we have already extirpated many of the largest and most beautiful species. A land ethic of course cannot prevent the alteration, management, and use of these "resources," but it does affirm their right to continued existence, and, at least in spots, their continued existence in a natural state.

In short, a land ethic changes the role of *Homo sapiens* from conqueror of the land-community to plain member and citizen of it. It implies respect for his fellow-members, and also respect for the community as such.

In human history, we have learned (I hope) that the conqueror role is eventually self-defeating. Why? Because it is implicit in such a role that the conqueror knows, *excathedra*, just what makes the community clock tick, and just what and who is valuable, and what and who is worthless, in community life. It always turns out that he knows neither, and this is why his conquests eventually defeat themselves.

In the biotic community, a parallel situation exists. Abraham knew exactly what the land was for: it was to drip milk and honey into Abraham's mouth. At the present moment, the assurance with which we regard this assumption is inverse to the degree of our education.

The ordinary citizen today assumes that science knows what makes the community clock tick; the scientist is equally sure that he does not. He knows that the biotic mechanism is so complex that its workings may never be fully understood.

That man is, in fact, only a member of a biotic team is shown by an ecological interpretation of history. Many historical events, hitherto explained solely in terms of human enterprise, were actually biotic interactions between people and land. The characteristics of the land determined the facts quite as potently as the characteristics of the men who lived on it.

Consider, for example, the settlement of the Mississippi valley. In the years following the Revolution, three groups were contending for its control: the native Indian, the French and English traders, and the American settlers. Historians wonder what would have happened if the English at Detroit had thrown a little more weight into the Indian side of those tipsy scales which decided the outcome of the colonial migration into the cane-lands of Kentucky. It is time now to ponder the fact that the cane-lands, when subjected to the particular mixture of forces represented by the cow, plow, fire, and axe of the pioneer, became bluegrass. What if the plant succession inherent in this dark and bloody ground had, under the impact of these forces, given us some worthless sedge shrub, or weed? Would Boone and Kenton have held out? Would there have been any overflow into Ohio, Indiana, Illinois, and Missouri? Any Louisiana Purchase? Any transcontinental union of new states? Any Civil War?

Kentucky was one sentence in the drama of history. We are commonly told what the human actors in this drama tried to do, but we are seldom told that their success, or the lack of it, hung in large degree on the reaction of particular soils to the impact of the particular forces exerted by their occupancy. In the case of Kentucky, we do not even know where the bluegrass came from—whether it is a native species, or a stowaway from Europe.

Contrast the cane-lands with what hindsight tells us about the Southwest, where the pioneers were equally brave, resourceful, and persevering. The impact of the occupancy here brought no bluegrass, or other plant fitted to withstand the bumps and buffetings of hard use. This region, when grazed by livestock, reverted through a series of more and more worthless grasses, shrubs, and weeds to a condition of unstable equilibrium. Each recession of plant types bred erosion; each increment to erosion bred a further recession of plants. The result today is a progressive and mutual deterioration, not only of plants and soils, but of the animal community subsisting thereon. The early settlers did not expect this:

to the community, but not clearly profitable to themselves.

When one asks why no rules have been written, one is told that the community is not yet ready to support them; education must precede rules. But the education actually in progress makes no mention of obligations to land over and above those dictated by self-interest. The net result is that we have more education but less soil, fewer healthy woods, and as many floods as in 1937.

The puzzling aspect of such situations is that the existence of obligations over and above self-interest is taken for granted in such rural community enterprise as the betterment of roads, schools, churches, and baseball teams. Their existence is not taken for granted, nor as yet seriously discussed, in bettering the behavior of the water that falls on the land, or in the preserving of the beauty or diversity of the farm landscape. Land-use ethics are still governed wholly by economic self-interest, just as social ethics were a century ago.

To sum up: we asked the farmer to do what he conveniently could to save his soil, and he has done just that, and only that. The farmer who clears the woods off a 75 percent slope, turns his cows into the clearing, and dumps its rainfall, rocks, and soil into the community creek, is still (if otherwise decent) a respected member of society. If he puts lime on his fields and plants his crops on contour, he is still entitled to all the privileges and emoluments of his Soil Conservation District. The District is a beautiful piece of social machinery, but it is coughing along on two cylinders because we have been too timid, and too anxious for quick success, to tell the farmer the true magnitude of his obligations. Obligations have no meaning without conscience, and the problem we face is the extension of the social conscience from people to land.

No important change in ethics was ever accomplished without an internal change in our intellectual emphasis, loyalties, affections, and convictions. The proof that conservation has not yet touched these foundations of conduct lies in the fact that philosophy and religion have not yet heard of it. In our attempt to make conservation easy, we have made it trivial.

Substitutes for a Land Ethic

When the logic of history hungers for bread and we hand out a stone, we are at pains to explain how much the stone resembles bread. I now describe some of the stones which serve in lieu of a land ethic.

One basic weakness in a conservation system based wholly on economic motives is that most members of the land community have no economic value. Wildflowers and songbirds are examples. Of the 22,000 higher plants and animals native to Wisconsin, it is doubtful whether more than 5 percent can be sold, fed, eaten, or otherwise put to economic use. Yet these creatures are members of the biotic community, and if (as I believe) its stability depends on its integrity, they are entitled to continuance.

When one of these non-economic categories is threatened, and if we happen to love it, we invent subterfuges to give it economic importance. At the beginning of the century songbirds were supposed to be disappearing. Ornithologists jumped to the rescue with some distinctly shaky evidence to the effect that insects would eat us up if birds failed to control them. The evidence had to be economic in order to be valid.

It is painful to read these circumlocutions today. We have no land ethic yet, but we have at least drawn nearer the point of admitting that birds should continue as a matter of biotic right, regardless of the presence or absence of economic advantage to us.

A parallel situation exists in respect of predatory mammals, raptorial birds, and fish-eating birds. Time was when biologists somewhat overworked the evidence that these creatures preserve the health of game by killing weaklings, or that they control rodents for the farmer, or that they prey only on "worthless" species. Here again, the evidence had to be economic in order to be valid. It is only in recent years that we hear the more honest argument that predators are members of the community, and that no special interest has the right to exterminate them for the sake of a benefit, real or fancied, to itself. Unfortunately this enlightened view is still in the talk stage. In the field the extermination of predators goes merrily on: witness the impending erasure of the timber wolf by fiat of Congress, the Conservation Bureaus, and many state legislatures.

Some species of trees have been "read out of the party" by economics-minded foresters because they grow too slowly, or have too low a sale value to pay as timber crops: white cedar, tamarack, cypress, beech, and hemlock are examples. In Europe, where forestry is ecologically more advanced, the non-commercial tree species are recognized as members of the native forest community, to be preserved as such, within reason. Moreover some (like beech) have been found to have a valuable function in building up soil fertility. The interdependence of the forest and its constituent tree species, ground flora, and fauna is taken for granted.

Lack of economic value is sometimes a character not only of species or groups, but of entire biotic communities: marshes, bogs, dunes, and "deserts" are examples. Our formula in such cases is to relegate their conservation to government as refuges, monuments, or parks. The difficulty is that these communities are usually interspersed with more valuable private lands; the government cannot possibly own or control such scattered parcels. The net effect is that we have relegated some of them to ultimate extinction over large areas. If the private owner were ecologically minded, he would be proud to be the custodian of a reasonable proportion of such areas, which add diversity and beauty to his farm and to his community.

In some instances, the assumed lack of profit in these "waste" areas has proved to be wrong, but only after most of them had been done away with. The present scramble to reflood muskrat marshes is a case in point.

There is a clear tendency in American conservation to relegate to government all necessary jobs that private landowners fail to perform. Government ownership, operation, subsidy, or regulation is now widely prevalent in forestry, range management, soil and watershed management, park and wilderness conservation, fisheries management, and migratory bird management, with more to come. Most of this growth in governmental conservation is proper and logical, some of it is inevitable. That I imply no disapproval of it is implicit in the fact that I have spent most of my life working for it. Nevertheless the question arises: What is the ultimate magnitude of the enterprise? Will the tax base carry its eventual ramifications? At what point will governmental conservation, like the mastodon, become handicapped by its own dimensions? The answer, if there is any, seems to be in a land ethic, or some other force which assigns more obligation to the private landowner.

Industrial landowners and users, especially lumbermen and stockmen, are inclined to wail long and loudly about the extension of government ownership and regulation to land, but (with notable exceptions) they show little disposition to develop the only visible alternative: the voluntary practice of conservation on their own lands.

When the private landowner is asked to perform some nonprofitable act for the good of the community, he today assents only with outstretched palm. If the act costs him cash this is fair and proper, but when it costs only forethought, open-mindedness, or time, the issue is at least debatable. The overwhelming growth of land-use subsidies in recent years must be ascribed, in large part, to the government's own agencies for conservation education: the land bureaus, the agricultural colleges, and the extension services. As far as I can detect, no ethical obligation toward land is taught in these institutions.

To sum up: a system of conservation based solely on economic self-interest is hopelessly lopsided. It tends to ignore, and thus eventually to eliminate, many elements in the land community that lack commercial value, but that are (as far as known) essential to its healthy functioning. It assumes, falsely, I think, that the economic parts of the biotic clock will function without the uneconomic parts. It tends to relegate to government many functions eventually too large, too complex, or too widely dispersed to be performed by government.

An ethical obligation on the part of the private owner is the only visible remedy for these situations.

The Land Pyramid

An ethic to supplement and guide the economic relation to land presupposes the existence of some mental image of land as a biotic mechanism. We can be ethical only in relation to something we can see, feel, understand, love, or otherwise have faith in.

The image commonly employed in conservation education is "the balance of nature." For reasons too lengthy to detail here, this figure of speech fails to describe accurately what little we know about the land mechanism. A much truer image is the one employed in ecology: the biotic pyramid. I shall first sketch the pyramid as a symbol of land, and later develop some of its implications in terms of land-use.

Plants absorb energy from the sun. This energy flows through a circuit called the biota, which may be represented by a pyramid consisting of layers. The bottom layer is the soil. A plant layer rests on the soil, an insect layer on the plants, a bird and rodent layer on the insects, and so on up through various animal groups to the apex layer, which consists of the larger carnivores.

The species of a layer are alike not in where they came from, or in what they look like, but rather in what they eat. Each successive layer depends on those below it for food and often for other services, and each in turn furnishes food and services to those above. Proceeding upward, each successive layer decreases in numerical abundance. Thus, for every carnivore there are hundreds of his prey, thousands of their prey, millions of insects, uncountable plants. The pyramidal form of the system reflects this numerical progression from apex to base. Man shares an intermediate layer with the bears, raccoons, and squirrels which eat both meat and vegetables.

The lines of dependency for food and other services are called food chains. Thus soil-oak-deer-Indian is a chain that has now been largely converted to soil-corn-cow-farmer. Each species, including ourselves, is a link in many chains. The deer eats a hundred plants other than oak, and the cow a hundred plants other than corn. Both, then, are links in a hundred chains. The pyramid is a tangle of chains so complex as to seem disorderly, yet the stability of the system proves it to be a highly organized structure. Its functioning depends on the cooperation and competition of its diverse parts.

In the beginning, the pyramid of life was low and squat; the food chains short and simple. Evolution has added layer after layer, link after link. Man is one of thousands of accretions to the height and complexity of the pyramid. Science has given us many doubts, but it has given us at least one certainty: the trend of evolution is to elaborate and diversify the biota.

Land, then, is not merely soil; it is a fountain of energy flowing through a circuit of soils, plants, and animals. Food chains are the living channels which conduct energy upward; death and decay return it to the soil. The circuit is not closed; some energy is dissipated in decay, some is added by absorption from the air, some is stored in soils, peats, and long-lived forests; but it is a sustained circuit, like a slowly augmented revolving fund of life. There is always a net loss by downhill wash, but this is normally small and offset by the decay of rocks. It is deposited in the ocean and, in the course of geological time, raised to form new lands and new pyramids.

The velocity and character of the upward flow of energy depend on the complex structure of the plant and animal community, much as the upward flow of sap in a tree depends on its complex cellular organization. Without this complexity, normal circulation would presumably not occur. Structure means the characteristic numbers, as well as the characteristic kinds and functions, of the component species. This interdependence between the complex structure of the land and its smooth functioning as an energy unit is one of its basic attributes.

When a change occurs in one part of the circuit, many other parts must adjust themselves to it. Change does not necessarily obstruct or divert the flow of energy; evolution is a long series of self-induced changes, the net result of which has been to elaborate the flow mechanism and to lengthen the circuit. Evolutionary changes, however, are usually slow and local. Man's invention of tools has enabled him to make changes of unprecedented violence, rapidity, and scope.

One change is in the composition of floras and faunas. The larger predators are lopped off the apex of the pyramid; food chains, for the first time in history, become shorter rather than longer. Domesticated species from other lands are substituted for wild ones, and wild ones are moved to new habitats. In this worldwide pooling of faunas and floras, some species get out of bounds as pests and diseases, others are extinguished. Such effects are seldom intended or foreseen; they represent unpredicted and often untraceable readjustments in the structure. Agricultural science is largely a race between the emergence of new pests and the emergence of new techniques for their control.

Another change touches the flow of energy through plants and animals and its return to the soil. Fertility is the ability of soil to receive, store, and release energy. Agriculture, by overdrafts on the soil, or by too radical a substitution of domestic for native species in the superstructure, may derange the channels of flow or deplete storage. Soils depleted of their storage, or of the organic matter which anchors it, wash away faster than they form. This is erosion.

Waters, like soil, are part of the energy circuit. Industry, by polluting waters or obstructing them with dams, may exclude the plants and animals necessary to keep energy in circulation.

Transportation brings about another basic change: the plants or animals grown in one region are now consumed and returned to the soil in another. Transportation taps the energy stored in rocks, and in the air, and uses it elsewhere; thus we fertilize the garden with nitrogen gleaned by the guano birds from the fishes of seas on the other side of the Equator. Thus the formerly localized and self-contained circuits are pooled on a worldwide scale.

The process of altering the pyramid for human occupation releases stored energy, and this often gives rise, during the pioneering period, to a deceptive exuberance of plant and animal life, both wild and tame. These releases of biotic capital tend to becloud or postpone the penalties of violence.

This thumbnail sketch of land as an energy circuit conveys three basic ideas:

1. That land is not merely soil.
2. That the native plants and animals kept the energy circuit open; others may or may not.
3. That man-made changes are of a different order than evolutionary changes, and have effects more comprehensive than is intended or foreseen.

These ideas, collectively, raise two basic issues: Can the land adjust itself to the new order? Can the desired alterations be accomplished with less violence?

Biotas seem to differ in their capacity to sustain violent conversion. Western Europe, for example, carries a far different pyramid than Caesar found there. Some large animals are lost; swampy forests have become meadows or plowland; many new plants and animals are introduced, some of which escape as pests; the remaining natives are greatly changed in distribution and abundance. Yet the soil is still there and, with the help of imported nutrients, still fertile; the waters flow normally; the new structure seems to function and to persist. There is no visible stoppage or derangement of the circuit.

Western Europe, then, has a resistant biota. Its inner processes are tough, elastic, resistant to strain. No matter how violent the alterations, the pyramid, so far, has developed some new *modus vivendi* which preserves its habitability for man, and for most of the other natives.

Japan seems to present another instance of radical conversion without disorganization.

Most other civilized regions, and some as yet barely touched by civilization, display various stages of disorganization, varying from initial symptoms to advanced wastage. In Asia Minor and North Africa diagnosis is confused by climatic changes, which may have been either the cause or the effect of advanced wastage. In the United States the degree of disorganization varies locally; it is worst in the Southwest, the Ozarks, and parts of the South, and least in New England and the Northwest. Better land-uses may still arrest it in the less advanced regions. In parts of Mexico, South America, South Africa, and Australia a violent and accelerating wastage is in progress, but I cannot assess the prospects.

This almost world-wide display of disorganization in the land seems to be similar to disease in an animal, except that it never culminates in complete disorganization or death. The land recovers, but at some reduced level of complexity, and with a reduced carrying capacity for people, plants, and animals. Many biotas currently regarded as "lands of opportunity" are in fact already subsisting on exploitative agriculture, i.e., they have already exceeded their sustained carrying capacity. Most of South America is overpopulated in this sense.

In arid regions we attempt to offset the process of wastage by reclamation, but it is only too evident that the prospective longevity of reclamation projects is often short. In our own West, the best of them may not last a century.

The combined evidence of history and ecology seems to support one general deduction: the less violent the man-made changes, the greater the probability of successful readjustment in the pyramid. Violence, in turn, varies with human population density; a dense population requires a more violent conversion. In this respect, North America has a better chance for permanence than Europe, if she can contrive to limit her density.

This deduction runs counter to our current philosophy, which assumes that because a small increase in density enriched human life, that an indefinite increase will enrich it indefinitely. Ecology knows of no density relationship that holds for indefinitely wide limits. All gains from density are subject to a law of diminishing returns.

Whatever may be the equation for men and land, it is improbable that we as yet know all its terms. Recent discoveries in mineral and vitamin nutrition reveal unsuspected dependencies in the up-circuit: incredibly minute quantities of certain substances determine the value of soils to plants, of plants to animals. What of the down-circuit? What of the vanishing species, the preservation of which we now regard as an esthetic luxury? They helped build the soil; in what unsuspected ways may they be essential to its maintenance? Professor Weaver proposes that we use prairie flowers to reflocculate the wasting soils of the dust bowl; who knows for what purpose cranes and condors, otters and grizzlies may some day be used?

Land Health and the A-B Cleavage

A land ethic, then, reflects the existence of an ecological conscience, and this in turn reflects a conviction of individual responsibility for the health of the land. Health is the capacity of the land for self-renewal. Conservation is our effort to understand and preserve this capacity.

Conservationists are notorious for their dissensions. Superficially these seem to add up to mere confusion, but a more careful scrutiny reveals a single plane of cleavage common to many specialized fields. In each field one group (A) regards the land as soil and its function as commodity-production; another group (B) regards the land as a biota, and its function as something broader. How much broader is admittedly in a state of doubt and confusion.

In my own field, forestry, group A is quite content to grow trees like cabbages, with cellulose as the basic forest commodity. It feels no inhibition against violence; its ideology is agronomic. Group B, on the other hand, sees forestry as fundamentally different from agronomy because it employs natural species, and manages a natural environment rather than creating an artificial one. Group B prefers natural reproduction on principle. It worries on biotic as well as economic grounds about the loss of species like chestnut and the threatened loss of the white pines. It worries about a whole series of secondary forest functions: wildlife, recreation, watersheds, wilderness areas. To my mind, Group B feels the stirrings of an ecological conscience.

In the wildlife field, a parallel cleavage exists. For Group A the basic commodities are sport and meat; the yardsticks of production are ciphers of take in pheasants and trout. Artificial propagation is acceptable as a permanent as well as a temporary recourse—if its unit costs permit. Group B, on the other hand, worries about a whole series of biotic side-issues. What is the cost in predators of producing a game crop? Should we have further recourse to exotics? How can management restore the shrinking species, like prairie grouse, already hopeless as shootable game? How can management restore the threatened rarities, like trumpeter swan and whooping crane? Can management principles be extended to wildflowers? Here again it is clear to me that we have the same A–B cleavage as in forestry.

In the larger field of agriculture I am less competent to speak, but there seem to be somewhat parallel cleavages. Scientific agriculture was actively developing before ecology was born, hence a slower penetration of ecological concepts might be expected. Moreover the farmer, by the very nature of his techniques, must modify the biota more radically than the forester or the wildlife manager. Nevertheless, there are many discontents in agriculture which seem to add up to a new vision of "biotic farming."

Perhaps the most important of these is the new evidence that poundage or tonnage is no measure of the food-value of farm crops; the products of fertile soil may be qualitatively as well as quantitatively superior. We can bolster poundage from depleted soils by pouring on imported fertility, but we are not necessarily bolstering food-value. The possible ultimate ramifications of this idea are so immense that I must leave their exposition to abler pens.

The discontent that labels itself "organic farming," while bearing some of the earmarks of a cult, is nevertheless biotic in its direction, particularly in its insistence on the importance of soil flora and fauna.

The ecological fundamentals of agriculture are just as poorly known to the public as in other fields of land-use. For example, few educated people realize that the marvelous advances in technique made during recent decades are improvements in the pump, rather than the well. Acre for acre, they have barely sufficed to offset the sinking level of fertility.

In all of these cleavages, we see repeated the same basic paradoxes: man the conqueror *versus* man the biotic citizen; science the sharpener of his sword *versus* science the searchlight on his universe; land the slave and servant *versus* land the collective organism. Robinson's injunction to Tristram may well be applied, at this juncture, to *Homo sapiens* as a species in geological time:

Whether you will or not
You are a King, Tristram, for you are one
Of the time-tested few that leave the
    world,
When they are gone, not the same place
    it was.
Mark what you leave.

The Outlook

It is inconceivable to me that an ethical relation to land can exist without love, respect, and admiration for land, and a high regard for its value. By value, I of course mean something far broader than mere economic value; I mean value in the philosophical sense.

Perhaps the most serious obstacle impeding the evolution of a land ethic is the fact that our educational and economic system is headed away from, rather than toward, an intense consciousness of land. Your true modern is separated from the land by many middlemen, and by innumerable physical gadgets. He has no vital relation to it; to him it is the space between cities on which crops grow. Turn him loose for a day on the land, and if the spot does not happen to be a golf links or a "scenic" area, he is bored stiff. If crops could be raised by hydroponics instead of farming, it would suit him very well. Synthetic substitutes for wood, leather, wool, and other natural land products suit him better than the originals. In short, land is something he has "outgrown."

Almost equally serious as an obstacle to a land ethic is the attitude of the farmer for whom the land is still an adversary, or a taskmaster that keeps him in slavery. Theoretically, the mechanization of farming ought to cut the farmer's chains, but whether it really does is debatable.

One of the requisites for an ecological comprehension of land is an understanding of ecology, and this is by no means co-extensive with "education"; in fact, much higher education seems deliberately to avoid ecological concepts. An understanding of ecology does not necessarily originate in courses bearing ecological labels; it is quite as likely to be labeled geography, botany, agronomy, history, or economics. This is as it should be, but whatever the label, ecological training is scarce.

The case for a land ethic would appear hopeless but for the minority which is in obvious revolt against these "modern" trends.

The "key-log" which must be moved to release the evolutionary process for an ethic is simply this: quit thinking about decent land-use as solely an economic problem. Examine each question in terms of what is ethically and esthetically right, as well as what is economically expedient. A thing is right when it tends to preserve the integrity, stability, and beauty of the biotic community. It is wrong when it tends otherwise.

It of course goes without saying that economic feasibility limits the tether of what can or cannot be done for land. It always has and it always will. The fallacy the economic determinists have tied around our collective neck, and which we now need to cast off, is the belief that economics determines *all* land-use. This is simply not true. An innumerable host of actions and attitudes, comprising perhaps the bulk of all land relations, is determined by the land-users' tastes and predilections, rather than by his purse. The bulk of all land relations hinges on investments of time, forethought, skill, and faith rather than on investments of cash. As a land-user thinketh, so is he.

I have purposely presented the land ethic as a product of social evolution because nothing so important as an ethic is ever "written." Only the most superficial student of history supposes that Moses "wrote" the Decalogue; it evolved in the minds of a thinking community, and Moses wrote a tentative summary of it for a "seminar." I say tentative because evolution never stops.

The evolution of a land ethic is an intellectual as well as emotional process. Conservation is paved with good intentions which prove to be futile, or even dangerous, because they are devoid of critical understanding either of the land, or of economic land-use. I think it is a truism that as the ethical frontier advances from the individual to the community, its intellectual content increases.

The mechanism of operation is the same for any ethic: social approbation for right actions: social disapproval for wrong actions.

By and large, our present problem is one of attitudes and implements. We are remodeling the Alhambra with a steam-shovel, and we are proud of our yardage. We shall hardly relinquish the shovel, which after all has many good points, but we are in need of gentler and more objective criteria for its successful use.

Questions

1. What is the land pyramid? Why is it shaped like a pyramid? What is carrying capacity?

2. What does Leopold state needs to change in order for us to change our thoughts and behavior? Why are these things important?

3. What is *The* Land Ethic? If followed, this would clearly reduce environmental harm, but what are the obstacles to following this ethic?

Note

1. From Aldo Leopold, *A Sand County Almanac: And Sketches Here and There*, copyright 1949, 1977 by Oxford University Press, Inc.

2. Beyond Sax and Welfare Interests: A Case for Environmental Rights[1]

Shari Collins-Chobanian

SHARI COLLINS-CHOBANIAN RESPONDS TO Joseph Sax, who argues that each individual should have, as a right, freedom from environmental hazards and access to environmental benefits. Sax further makes clear that environmental rights do not (yet) exist (legally) and that their recognition would be a novel step, the closest thing to which are welfare rights. In following Sax's direction, Collins-Chobanian draws from the work of those who are most relevant in establishing environmental rights. She first considers Joel Feinberg's notion of welfare interests, then Henry Shue's notion of basic rights, and finally James Nickel's right to a safe environment. Collins-Chobanian takes issue with Nickel's version of the right to a safe environment, arguing against the role that cost-benefit concerns play in his essay, as well as the balancing of the "right" to a livelihood versus the right to a clean environment. She draws from John Stuart Mill's harm principle, EPA Superfund legislation, and the *Clean Air Act* to illustrate the existing ethical and legal bases for establishing environmental rights. She closes with a discussion of positive and negative duties that such rights might carry.

Introduction

WITHOUT THE BASICS, CLEAN air, clean water, and clean soil, human beings will not thrive. These basic needs are referred to as welfare interests in the philosophical literature. Welfare interests are the most important interests humans have and include physical, emotional, and intellectual health; a secure environment; the absence of coercion; and (assuming an economy) minimal economic wealth. Welfare interests are indispensable to all other ultimate goals, and all human activities depend on the most basic support of food, air, water, and shelter. Thus, a threat to these basic needs threatens all else. This is the foundation from which I approach environmental rights.

I define and develop a minimum set of what are now referred to as environmental rights, and argue that these rights are the most fundamental[2] to life and to all subsequent interests. Because environmental rights are not explicitly addressed in the philosophical literature, and are not recognized rights, I have drawn from the work of those I have found to be the most relevant to establishing such rights. I address their work first, then provide my definition of, and argument for, environmental rights.

Joseph L. Sax and Environmental Rights

In "The Search for Environmental Rights," Sax states that if environmental rights "are to be set in the context of rights, it is necessary to ask how they fit into the values underlying other basic rights."[3] Sax points out that there is no historical association (such as freedom of speech) that leads to an environmental right; in fact, because historically there has been destruction of the natural environment, not only is the territory new, it is in opposition to many of our historical practices.

Sax further claims that there is a profound difference between any existing human right and a proposed environmental right, because the basic human rights are to ensure individuals' freedom from state interference, to insure private property, and the freedom to live life as each chooses. An environmental right, he asserts, would require government involvement in order to deal with pollution, and would have to address issues of how nature is to be used. Sax proposes the following for environmental rights:

> The closest analogy would seem to be found among the precepts of a modern welfare state. The effort to guarantee each individual a basic right to decent housing, health care, nutrition, safe working conditions, and cultural opportunity seems most closely fitted to the effort of articulating basic environmental rights. Terms like "decent environment" … "environment adequate for their health and well-being" … or "environment of quality" suggest that a significant driving idea behind efforts to establish environmental rights is a version of welfare-state ideology. If so, the goal would not be government abstention, but rather a call for affirmative action by the state—a demand that it assure, as a right of each individual, some level of freedom from environmental hazards or some degree of access to environmental benefits.[4]

Sax argues that the above is "precisely one of the directions that the search for fundamental environmental rights should take."[5] He quickly points out that there is presently no accurate measurement regarding what an appropriate environmental welfare standard would be, and that it won't be as clear as existing standards such as basic medical care (an issue importantly linked to a clean environment).

A further problem for an articulation of environmental rights is that welfare interests do not have human rights status. Thus, as Sax states, "recognition of a basic right to a healthy environment would be a novel step."[6] Because welfare interests do not have rights status and we do not recognize environmental rights, recognition of such rights would indeed be a novel step. I argue for such a novelty and argue that environmental rights are the most basic human rights in that these rights are required for all other activities, and those that must be met for any of the other human rights to be relevant. While there are other logically basic rights, such as protecting the individual against physical threats of violent action involving clear and present danger, there must be a life before it can be threatened. Air, water, and soil are prerequisites to life itself, before there is anything to threaten or risk. Before fleshing out my position, I turn to three existing philosophical welfare interest positions that provide a basis for, and are the *closest* arguments to, my conception of environmental rights.

Feinberg's Liberty, Harms, and Welfare Interests

Joel Feinberg refers to the most vital interests one may have as "welfare interests." He states:

> In this category are the interests in one's own physical health and vigor, the integrity and normal functioning of one's body, the absence of distracting pain and suffering or grotesque disfigurement, minimal intellectual acuity, emotional stability, the absence of groundless anxieties and resentments, the capacity to engage normally in social intercourse, at least minimal wealth, income, and financial security, a tolerable social and physical environment, and a certain amount of freedom from interference and coercion.... In one way, then, they are the very most important interests a person has, for without their fulfillment a person ... is lost.[7]

The most basic of welfare interests are what I call environmental rights. Feinberg's full consideration of welfare interests depend upon a vastly advanced and established society, a society that is inextricably dependent on the basics—clean air, water, and soil—for all else. His mention of what amounts to environmental rights—"a tolerable physical environment"—almost in passing, indicates the general "taking for granted" attitude toward the physical environment that permeates much of Western social, political, and moral philosophy.

Feinberg's definition of *harm*, in the legal sense, is an invasion of an interest.[8] However, Feinberg argues that even if welfare interests are in some way affected negatively, they are not violated (harmed) until they are brought below a tolerable minimum level. He states: "One can threaten another's welfare interests by weakening his health or diminishing his wealth, but one does not actually invade those interests until one brings them below a tolerable minimum."[9] Feinberg's allowance of welfare interests to be diminished to the point where they fall below a tolerable level is too lax. Each threat to welfare that weakens health is an impoverishment and counts as a harm. My interests are invaded if someone or some substance is imposed on me and weakens my health, even though I may be able to carry on in most aspects of my life, for now I am less able to withstand the next invasion.

Feinberg's strict definition of an invasion of an interest, or a harm, not occurring until one is brought below a tolerable level does not adequately take into account the cumulative effect of many different threats that constitute invasions to our welfare interests. Environmental pollution is of a fundamentally different nature than isolatable single agent threats to our well-being on which he seems to be relying. While single invasions of our welfare interests—exposure to one toxic substance, some low-level radiation, etc.—*might not* bring us below the tolerable minimum level, they all compromise our well-being and might interact to produce cumulative effects.

Suppose I live downwind of a chemical manufacturer, my spouse works in asbestos removal, I work at a nuclear power plant, there are pesticide residues on my produce even after washing, and my neighbor uses a lawn service that sprays pesticides, herbicides, and fertilizer once a month—usually while I am barbecuing organic textured vegetable protein. Suppose I also have an elderly parent, a brother with cancer, and a baby living with me. When my health or the health of someone in my family is finally brought below Feinberg's tolerable minimum level, who is responsible? The tolerable level of each risk to a healthy adult varies greatly from the levels children, the sick, and elderly people can tolerate. Under Feinberg's model only the factor that brings me below a tolerable level—if it can be determined, though more than likely it cannot—would be responsible.

Pollutants have cumulative effects, many are stored in body tissue, and what constitutes a safe amount or threshold is difficult to determine, especially because "safe" assumes a fixed amount. Cumulative harms may come about in different ways. For example, there may be single occurrences of particular activities that are "harmless" up to a point, but when repeated the cumulative effect is harmful. Judith Jarvis Thomson[10] addresses this issue in an example in which someone poisons a fish pond in three stages, with a cup of poison at each stage. The first time the pond is poisoned it turns muddy; the second it smells bad; and the third all of the fish are killed. She makes clear that "Each act in the series causes a harm: the last act causes a far more serious harm than the preceding members, but would not have caused the far more serious harm if it had not been preceded by the earlier" acts.[11]

Regarding Thomson's example, the pond need not have become muddy and smelly for the first two acts to have been an imposed risk, and the poisoning need not have been done by the same agent. Placing an invisible and odorless poison such as radioactive waste in the pond would not have been any less harmful, and three different people could have polluted the pond and each act of waste dumping would be a harm, with each actor responsible both for the harm of that act and for a share of the cumulative harm.

Further, the amount of pollutants released at each stage need not be equal—either in quantity or quality—as in Thomson's example. Different amounts could be released in each act, and the pollutants may be of qualitatively different kinds as when someone gets radiation-induced cancer from radioactive waste polluted water, and a diagnostic X-ray or a hike that exposes him or her to background radiation. The last action (the X-ray necessary for medical diagnosis or the hike) *that would otherwise not have brought one below a tolerable level* is thus the one that crosses the threshold even though it is not the "most serious harm."

If the focus is Feinberg's threshold, untenable results are possible. First, the agents that contributed to the level of the end harm could completely escape responsibility for that harm. Also, the last agent may be accused of being disproportionately responsible because the last act is considered to be the "most serious harm" when it may only be the straw that broke the camel's back. Thus, environmental rights should be a protection from invasion, not just the threshold level.

Feinberg's definition of *harm* allows one to consider the preliminary acts, before the threshold is crossed, not to be harms. However, *each invasion* of one's interests is a harm. Further, this threshold type of imposed risk should account for invisible pollutants, multiple agents, and varying amounts of pollutants released at each stage. These qualifications provide a more realistic and thus more applicable definition of a pollution threshold because pollution would not likely be limited to one agent alone imposing visible and consistent risks. Rather, these risks are imposed in varying degrees from many sources, and without warning.

The above considerations demand that we take into account invasions of our most basic welfare interests—clean air, water, soil—before we are brought below a tolerable level. Polluted air, water, and soil pose threats to us all, impoverish our health, and while each pollutant may not separately bring us below the tolerable level that Feinberg finds decisive, they risk it, either alone or in a cumulative manner.[12] Thus, while Feinberg aptly describes the fundamental nature and priority of welfare interests, invasions to these interests are morally significant and not adequately captured by Feinberg's concepts of welfare interests, invasions, and harm.

Shue's Subsistence Rights

In *Basic Rights: Subsistence, Affluence, and U.S. Foreign Policy,* Henry Shue defines and defends the notion of basic rights. Shue points out that, "When a right is genuinely basic, any attempt to enjoy any other right by sacrificing the basic right would be quite literally self-defeating."[13] Our most basic rights—to clean air, water, and soil—are prerequisites for the protection of all other interests. As Shue argues, these basic rights cannot be sacrificed for the liberty to enjoy a less basic right. He states:

> ... the protection of a basic right may not be sacrificed in order to secure the enjoy-ment of a non-basic right. It may not be sacrificed because it cannot be sacrificed successfully. If the right sacrificed is indeed basic, then no right for which it might be sacrificed can actually be enjoyed in the absence of the basic right. The sacrifice would have proven self-defeating....
> [B]asic rights need to be established se-curely before other rights can be secured.[14]

Shue's most basic rights are the rights to subsistence,[15] and include unpolluted air, unpolluted water, adequate food, adequate clothing, adequate shelter, and minimal pre-ventive public health care. Given the priority of these rights, without these, one effectively has no rights at all.

I do not deny the importance of any of Shue's subsistence rights but focus on the most basic—clean air, clean water—and argue that adequate food requires clean soil.[16] With-out clean, fertile soil,[17] we can have neither adequate food nor plants that clean the air and prevent erosion, and life would thus not be sustainable. If unpolluted air, water, and "adequate food" are all that is included in subsistence rights (that are parallel to envi-ronmental rights), then there is no guarantee that food will be produced in accordance with maintaining the integrity of clean soil, and if it is not, the soil's ability to sustain crops will be at risk. In order to protect the most basic rights, soil needs to be safeguarded at the level before food is extracted. Clean soil needs to be the focus of subsistence, rather than the food produced.[18]

By not including clean soil as a basic right, Shue does not adequately address the safe-guards to land necessary for subsistence. What Shue includes as part of his subsistence rights, "adequate food," is a product of the soil, and already too removed from consideration at the most basic level of what is fundamental to ex-istence. If food production is what is focused on rather than clean soil, we risk degradation of the more basic need, soil. Without protect-ing soil, we risk harms from the production of food that is not grown in a sustainable man-ner, as well as those from wastes created in almost every type of manufacturing.[19]

Although Shue's subsistence rights are compatible with environmental rights, we should extract the most basic from his rights—unpolluted air and water—and add unpolluted soil, in order to arrive at the stron-gest case for basic rights essential to all other human activity.

Nickel and the Right to a Safe Environment

In "The Right to a Safe Environment," James Nickel addresses the right to a safe environ-ment as a genuine human right. The right to a safe environment (RSE) focuses "exclusively on human health and safety" and entails "an environment that is not destructive of human health."[20] This right is "concerned only with a particular set of threats to human safety, namely those which stem from technological and industrial processes and the disposal of sewage and wastes."[21] Nickel includes

> ... only the very basic aspects of well-being in RSE, those that pertain to avoiding extreme misery and to preserving the possibility of a minimally good life.... RSE should address forms of contamination and pollution that create significant risks of killing people, making them sick or seriously miserable, or depriving them of the possibility of having a minimally good life.[22]

Although Nickel's right to a safe environment presents a significant improvement over Feinberg's welfare interests with regard to protecting people's environmental rights, especially in acknowledgment of the role industry and technology play in pollution, the standards are too lax. Nickel's allowance of pollution until there are "significant risks of killing people" or until it makes them "sick or seriously miserable" does not take account of the manner in which pollution accumulates or may combine with other hazards—but not act exclusively—to make people sick or cause deaths.

Nickel does focus on the environment as a whole, and thus can take these issues into account. As long as he retains the moral level of harm where people get sick, seriously miserable, or die, however, he is unable to account for the impoverishment of general health, or the failure to *thrive*, that *invasions of* health cause *before they reduce people to the level of sickness or death*. As discussed above, this impoverishment constitutes a harm and is in need of redress. Nickel writes:

> ... the level of safety from environmental risks, should be satisfactory or adequate for health. These phrases, although vague,

clearly set the level of acceptable risk at an intermediate level, and thus make it more likely that RSE can pass the feasibility test.... On the other hand, they do not set the risk standard so low as to make RSE meaningless.[23]

Although Nickel admits that the terms *satisfactory* and *adequate* are vague, he thinks that they are not a problem because most human rights have quite general normative standards and he does not want a clean environmental standard so strict that people are not allowed to earn a living or that would cost too much to implement.

However, I take issue with his vagueness concerning the use of "satisfactory" and "adequate." The problems were illuminated in the example I discussed above concerning Feinberg's welfare interests. If the level of satisfaction and adequacy is set at an average level, this standard imposes more serious risks on those that fall below the average, such as children, the elderly, and the sick. The weighing, in the manner Nickel suggests, of one's liberty to pollute against the right to a safe environment gives the two false equality. Again, environmental rights are prior to all else, they must be ensured before any other rights have meaning.

The feasibility test that Nickel is concerned with involves the role costs play in ensuring the right to a safe environment. He states that the "RSE could fail to be a fully-justified right if its costs were excessively burdensome."[24] Nickel first sees costs as playing a legitimate part in limiting the amount of moral (and legal) duties that we can impose on each other, and second sees the costs of complying with some rights prohibitive and in competition with compliance with other important rights.[25]

Nickel has a valid policy point about the costs and the other competing needs: the most basic harms, those to the air, water, and soil, are what need addressing first. However, Nickel's allowance of "other important rights" to compete with the right to a safe environment is in need of a justification beyond what he provides. The right to earn a livelihood, and interests in cost-effectiveness, do not directly justify the harm to a clean environment that is assumed necessary in pursuit of a livelihood and cost-effectiveness.

Granted, in a market economy, the right to earn a livelihood is required to provide necessities for life.[26] Prima facie, the right to earn a livelihood (required for sustaining life) and environmental rights (required for sustaining life) have rough equality. However, the market economy is not necessary for human life. The market economy is not something that should be a starting point for discussions of the right to life. The market economy is fueled by environmental resources, and does not always meet needs, while destroying the ability of many to meet their own needs from such methods as biodiverse, traditional agriculture.[27] The myriad examples of the latter absurdity include the displacement of traditional farming communities that ensured provision of the necessities of life, in order instead to grow flowers, or ranch cattle, that provides luxuries for the overconsuming, overdeveloped countries. Further, the market economy does not value sustainability, but growth. Sustainability entails environmental integrity, and is closer to the concept of the right to life that is assumed to have equality with environmental rights.

The lifestyles we currently "enjoy," and the costs to the environment to ensure those lifestyles, are in need of justification. A lifestyle is not of the same moral weight as life itself. The only type of moral consideration that could outweigh environmental rights is one of equal importance, such as the right to life that is ensured from a livelihood, not the right

to a lifestyle. Moreover, the "need" created in a market economy for people to work in polluting industries that create luxury goods, in order to get a paycheck to buy the necessities of life, is a not a fixed need, but one that can and should be changed.

Regarding cost-effectiveness, Nickel is concerned that "the obligations flowing from rights will be without effect if addressees are genuinely unable to comply with them, or if they are unable to comply while meeting other obligations."[28] While cost-benefit ratios are not *the* decisive factor for Nickel, he sees the costs of pollution regulation as a necessarily pragmatic limitation, and thus places the standard of protection the right to a safe environment prescribes "at an adequate rather than optimal level" to allow pollution control to remain affordable.[29]

However, to balance certain members of the current population's "right" to a livelihood or "right" to produce products that pollute the environment against the rights of all to a clean environment may not provide real protection and in the end may make the right meaningless. To cash this situation out in terms of costs is to assume that the market economy and the weighing of costs and benefits that it imposes are justified. Even if we do place a cost on environmental resources, pollution, and cleanup, it may be meaningless because much of the environmental destruction cannot be righted with any amount of money. This does not mean that the person(s) who harmed the environment and invaded the right to a safe environment should not have to make any reparations. Rather, it means that we need to take into account that much ecosystem harm is irreparable and focus on prevention of harm by drawing from the harm principle and restricting the liberty to harm in the first place.

Further Foundations for Environmental Rights

In *On Liberty*, John Stuart Mill argues that society and its agents have a duty to prevent people from harming others' interests and to oblige people to assume responsibility to advance community interests. Mill argues that liberty may be justifiably restricted only to prevent actual harm to others.

> … The sole end for which mankind are warranted, individually or collectively, in interfering with the liberty of action of any of their number is self-protection. That the only purpose for which power can be rightfully exercised over any member of a civilized community, against his will, is to prevent harm to others…. The only part of the conduct of anyone for which he is amenable to society is that which concerns others.[30]

Mill states that one's right to independence regarding that which concerns only oneself is absolute. The "appropriate region of human liberty" regards one's sovereignty over one's life.[31] This liberty includes first, the internal domain of consciousness; second, tastes, pursuits, and the ability to live life as one wishes so long as one does not harm another; and third, the liberty to assemble and form groups.

Mill's harm principle is an important foundation in the Western tradition, and his justification for restricting liberty is of paramount importance to environmental rights. The (human-caused) degradation of air, water, and soil quality is due in large part, if not entirely, to the liberty with which individuals and groups of people have operated and continue to operate in the environment. In Western societies, we inherited the assumptions that ecological abundance was endless and that air and water were free, of infinite

supply, and could somehow absorb anything emitted by human activities.[32] This inheritance has shaped our attitudes that still prevail today. However air, water, and soil (the basis of the ecosystem) are finite in amount and limited in the ability to absorb and recover from activities that lead to the depletion of topsoil, the destruction of ozone, evapotranspiration, and desertification. Even before the finite nature of air, water, and soil are transgressed, there is significant harm because the ecosystem is impoverished in its amount of resources and the ability to withstand further human activity, and this risks our health and all life.

Carl Wellman argues that whenever citizens are left impoverished without justification, and this impoverishment is a result of the distribution of goods that result from acts of omission or commission of the state, then citizens have been harmed and are due redress. He states:

> Such impoverishment inflicts harm upon the citizen because it renders him or her incapable of meeting his or her basic needs. It is wrongful harm either because the individual citizen has an ethical right not to be unjustly impoverished or because the infliction of harm unnecessarily is morally wrong. Either way, wrongful harm serves as an adequate ground for the civic right to a fair share.[33]

Although in this context Wellman is discussing welfare rights that are much more numerous and less basic than environmental rights, his concepts and justifications regarding harm and impoverishment are also relevant to environmental rights. Impoverishment of one's access to environmental rights is a harm. As Wellman points out, people have an ethical right not to be harmed and unnecessary infliction of harm is morally wrong.

This is also what lies behind Mill's harm principle, and justifies the curtailment of one's liberty. That is, interference in one's liberty to act is justified by the prevention of harm that is risked by that person's actions. The Clean Air Act and superfund (discussed below) are applications of Mill's harm principle and of the civic right to a fair share discussed by Wellman, and the most effective move would be to take a protective stance in order to prevent future harm(s) and would require the restriction of liberty when actions risk pollution of air, water, and soil, justified in the same manner that the restriction of liberty is justified by the harm principle.[34]

Environmental Rights

I first briefly discuss two areas of environmental law in order to illustrate an existing legal basis for addressing environmental issues, and address why these laws do not go far enough. I then discuss my concept of environmental rights and the positive and negative duties they carry.

In *Environmental Justice*, Peter Wenz argues that Section 303 of the Clean Air Act of 1978, and the so-called "Superfund" both "reflect a human rights perspective."[35] The Clean Air Act has as its goal protecting public health. The administrator of the act is not required to balance competing interests (such as the cost of eliminating a pollutant versus the health benefits if it is eliminated) when there is a substantial and looming risk of harm to the health of people. The act makes clear that risk of harm to public health legitimately curtails the activities that anyone or any group is at liberty to pursue.

The superfund, established in 1980, enables its administrator to use public money to clean up an area that has been shown to contain toxic substances that pose a significant threat to public health. If doing so is not possible or is impractical economically or in some other way, the superfund allows for the purchase of the residents' property and payment of relocation costs so that residents will no longer be at risk from the toxic substances. Wenz points out that the superfund was created to address the injustice of people being exposed to toxic substances and the accompanying risk to their health unless they are willing to be burdened with significant economic loss of property value. He states that without the superfund "Property owners' rights to life, health, and property in such cases would thus be unprotected. The superfund legislation can be explained as an attempt to protect these rights."[36] Unfortunately the emphasis of the superfund and the Clean Air Act in addressing harm to air, water, and soil *after* they have already been polluted does not afford the protection to people that the rights to life and health should carry. Environmental rights should carry stronger protection through restricting the liberty of individuals and groups to risk pollution of air, water, and soil.

Environmental rights are human,[37] moral rights, and *should* carry legal and civil rights protection.[38] Environmental rights are human rights because these needs are required by all living human beings. Environmental rights address the most basic needs of humans; indeed air to breathe, water to drink, and soil to grow food are the *prerequisites* of all other goals, and are necessary for even taking part in a discussion of goals and rights.[39] Environmental rights are moral because they are presupposed by the moral right to life,[40] and every other right, especially the right to nonmalfeasance. Moral rights do not depend upon recognition by a government's or society's laws for legitimacy, and environmental rights fall under this category.

Environmental rights (at a minimum) are rights *to* clean air, water, and soil, and these rights are negative in the sense that they carry a duty for all people and groups to not interfere with others' clean air, water, and soil.[41] Regarding the duty not to interfere with others' clean air, water, and soil, no one person or group is at liberty to do anything that interferes with these rights unless there is an overriding justification. An overriding justification would include concerns such as a more immediate public health concern that may require a dangerous chemical added to drinking water to kill a more deadly bacteria. (Chlorine is added to public water supplies to prevent health hazards that are risked in its absence.) However, an overriding justification *would not include* concerns that allow harms and risk of harms to be imposed in pursuit of goals that do not outweigh the harms, as in the following: money or jobs created by the manufacture of frivolous goods that pollute air, water, or soil; any aesthetic value in the bleaching of toilet (and various other forms of) paper,[42] or the use of pesticides, fungicides, and herbicides for the suburbanite's desire to keep her yard, shrubs, and garden pest and weed free.[43] Wherever these rights have not been interfered with (the environment is not polluted), the negative sense of them is the most important and vital to protect.

Whenever pollution results from the actions of individuals, property owners, corporations, etc. (when there is a violation of the negative right to a clean environment), there is a duty for those responsible for the pollution to rectify the situation (insofar as it is possible to clean up the air, water, and soil). Insofar as these rights have been invaded and interfered with (pollution, takings, etc.) and responsibility can be traced, there will be a duty of those that caused the harm to clean up the environment as much as is possible, and restore those harmed to their previous state or compensate them accordingly. This duty should hold even if it brings the violator well below the violator's current economic status (much like the Dalkon Shield case, asbestos cases, etc.).

Wherever the negative sense of environmental rights has been violated and the party responsible might not or cannot be held responsible, the positive sense of these rights will be vital to correcting the situation. The responsible party cannot be held responsible when there is no smoking gun, that is the pollution cannot be traced to the source. In addition, the pollution may have come from a natural source such as a volcano. The responsible party might not be held responsible if a decision has been made to pursue a risky endeavor because of the possible overall benefits.[44] However, in this pursuit, the risks of harms, the actual harms, and the benefits of the technology are inequitably distributed. One example is limited liability for corporations. The presumed justification for limited liability is to encourage innovation that can potentially benefit society as a whole. Another example would be nuclear medicine. Nuclear medicine is assumed to hold benefits for many people, but is inherently risky and risks harm to researchers and radiologists. In the above cases, a positive conception of environmental rights would best apply.

In what sense are environmental rights positive? Environmental rights are positive in the sense that they hold against the government in general[45] or a particular regulatory agency established to be responsible for pollution. They include situations that prevent people from access to clean air, water, and soil. Thus, environmental rights are positive rights when the needs for clean air, water, and soil are unmet, and unable to be met (through rectification from the party at fault, or due to a no-fault situation).

Furthermore, regarding the positive sense of environmental rights, they should carry legal and civil rights protection. Moral rights have no police power and are not enforceable unless they are also recognized as legal or civil rights. For example, the human rights enumerated in the United Nations Declaration of Human Rights are not recognized by all nations.

Without recognition and subsequent legal protection, these moral rights are often violated, and the moral claims for remedy of these violations go unheeded. A legal system is morally required to enforce human rights and protect the claims they carry. Without similar protection, there will be little to deter pollution, and environmental rights will continue to be violated. With a legal system, human rights can be protected by the prohibition of certain activities that violate them, or recourse can be made available to address human rights violations to act as an example to deter future violations.

Environmental rights are not merely environmental applications of the right to nonmalfeasance and I am not, through the positive and negative conceptions of environmental rights, arguing for an environmental application of the right to compensation, rather than arguing for peculiar new rights, environmental rights. Nor am I merely stating that environmental rights are the most basic instrumentally or causally for all other rights. However, even as an application of the right to nonmalfeasance, and as instrumental rights, environmental rights do hold a peculiar place in rights because of their causal priority and the cumulative and synergistic nature in which they can be violated.

Conclusion

Environmental rights are our most basic rights (causally and instrumentally) and are a prerequisite for our right to life and all other rights. Therefore, environmental rights are the most important to safeguard. Invasions of these are harms at the most basic level because they attack our health and the health of the environment we depend upon.

While Feinberg, Shue, and Nickel go to some length to safeguard our environmental rights, they do not go far enough. I qualify their positions to safeguard these rights, and make clear that invasions of these rights are the most basic harms. Further, due to cumulative and synergistic effects of pollution, without proper restriction of the liberty of those who pollute, many people's health will be weakened and put at risk. Mill's harm principle provides us with a justification for restricting the liberty of those who impose risk of harm by invading environmental rights. As Sax stated, one direction environmental rights should take is a type of "affirmative action by the state" that would establish protection from environmental risks as well as "access to environmental benefits."[46] It is high time to take the novel step and recognize the basic right to a clean environment.

Questions

1. What are the three environmental rights? Why are they a prerequisite to every other human right?

2. Nickel argues that rights should be subject to an affordability test. Why does he argue this? Collins–Chobanian argues against Nickel. What is her argument? Which author's position do you think would eliminate the most environmental harm, and why?

3. Mill's Harm Principle is behind anti-smoking laws and regulations. Explain how Mill's principle operates in these laws. Emissions from automobiles produce far more, and

wider-ranging, threats to humans and the ecosystem than tobacco smoke. Why are auto emissions tolerated? Explain the inconsistency.

Notes

1. Shari Collins-Chobanian, "Beyond Sax and Welfare Interests: A Case for Environmental Rights," *Environmental Ethics* 22 (Summer 2000): 133–48 [Edited]. An earlier version of this paper was presented at the 1996 APA Pacific Division ISEE meeting and received support from the Arizona State University West Scholarship, Research, and Creative Activities Grant. [The author] appreciates the time and comments of many readers, especially Craig Walton, Eric Katz, Larry May, Red Watson, Peter Wenz, Eugene C. Hargrove, Ellen Smith, Alberto Pulido, Alejandra Elenes, Gloria Cuadraz, and two anonymous referees for *Environmental Ethics*, J. Baird Callicott and Holmes Rolston, III.

2. While I recognize that air, water, and soil can be further reduced to constituent elements (and are thus not the most basic or fundamental), because I am not a scientist I restrict my discussion to the environmental rights as stated. Also, I recognize that what constitutes "clean" air, water, and soil can be compromised by earthquakes, volcanoes, etc. However, I am interested in the ways that these may be compromised by human activity. While the tolerance for pollutants in air, water, and soil varies, I am interested in the level that children, the elderly, sick people, and certain indicator organisms in various ecosystems can tolerate, for these are the minimum standards and are informative in assessing the integrity and sustainability of the ecosystem, as well as sustainability of all that depends upon the ecosystem.

3. Joseph L. Sax, "The Search for Environmental Rights," *Journal of Land Use and Environmental Law* 6 (1990): 94.

4. Ibid., p. 95.

5. Ibid.

6. Ibid., p. 96.

7. Joel Feinberg, *Rights, Justice, and the Bounds of Liberty* (Princeton: Princeton University Press, 1980), p. 32.

8. Ibid., p. 31.

9. Ibid., p. 33.

10. Judith Jarvis Thomson, "Imposing Risks," in *Rights, Restitution, & Risk*, ed. William Parent (Cambridge: Harvard University Press, 1986), pp. 173–91.

11. Ibid., p. 174.

12. See Joel Feinberg, "Environmental Pollution and the Threshold of Harm," *The Hastings Center Report*, June 1984, pp. 27–31. Feinberg again defines harm as crossing a threshold, not the steps that weaken health, and does not address synergistic effects. See also Andrew Kernohan, "Rights against Polluters," in *Environmental Ethics* 17 (1995): 245–57.

13. Henry Shue, *Basic Rights: Subsistence, Affluence, and U.S. Foreign Policy* (Princeton: Princeton University Press, 1980), p. 19.

14. Ibid., pp. 19–20.

15. Shue also includes the right to physical security as a basic right. However, I leave aside this discussion as I am interested in what are the most basic rights, and as Shue points out, people who are healthy can fight back against attackers or flee. In addition, and here he quotes John Stuart Mill's *Utilitarianism,* the right to physical security is "most indispensable of all necessaries, after physical nutriment." Shue, *Basic Rights*, p. 182.

16. By clean soil, I mean uncontaminated soil necessary for sustained production of edible food.

17. Clean, fertile soil is soil that can sustain life without harmful effects. Such soil would be without radioactivity (that concentrates in the food chain); without pesticides (such as the Riverside, California pesticide absorption in watermelons that killed people in 1983); and without fungicides

(as destroyed the soil in Florida citrus groves); and would not be too saline (as is left by crops grown in soil unsuited to agricultural practices).

18. See Daniel Hillel, *Out of the Earth: Civilization and the Life of the Soil* (Los Angeles: University of California Press, 1981). Hillel traces the use of chemical fertilizers in agricultural production and the subsequent soil degradation.

19. Ibid., pp. 132, 253–54.

20. James W. Nickel, "The Human Right to a Safe Environment: Philosophical Perspectives on Its Scope and Justification," *Yale Journal of International Law* 18 (1993): 284.

21. Ibid.

22. Ibid., p. 285.

23. Ibid.

24. Ibid., p. 293.

25. See also George Eads, "The Confusion of Goals and Instruments: The Explicit Consideration of Cost in Setting National Ambient Air Quality Standards," in *To Breathe Freely*, ed. Mary Gibson (Totowa: N.J.: Rowman and Allanheld, 1985), pp. 222–32. Eads points out difficulties in determining air quality standards and how significantly costs can increase with small changes in air quality.

26. While I acknowledge that I am obviously firmly entrenched (there is little to no option to opt out) in such a market economy, and as a white, middle-class woman I benefit from this system, I nonetheless question my privileges, the privileges of others, and the costs of these privileges to those not similarly privileged, as well as the costs to and destruction of the ecosystem. In addition, I acknowledge the schizophrenic nature of participating in the market economy as a consumer, while simultaneously arguing for an end to its harms, or at least to minimize those harms. For a discussion of this schizophrenic nature, see Mark Sagoff, "At the Shrine of Our Lady of Fatima *or* Why Political Questions Are Not All Economic," *Arizona Law Review* 23 (1981): 1283–98.

27. See Deane Curtin, "Making Peace with the Earth: Indigenous Agriculture and the Green Revolution," *Environmental Ethics* 17 (1985): 59–73; and Devon Peña, ed., *Chicano Culture, Ecology, Politics* (Tucson: University of Arizona Press, 1998).

28. Ibid., p. 294.

29. Ibid.

30. John Stuart Mill, *On Liberty*, ed. Gertrude Himmelfarb (New York: Penguin Books, 1978), pp. 68–69.

31. Ibid., p. 71.

32. Regarding ecological scarcity, see William Ophuls, *Ecology and the Politics of Scarcity* (San Francisco: W.H. Freeman and Company, 1977).

33. Carl Wellman, *Welfare Rights* (Totowa: Rowman and Littlefield, 1982), p. 174.

34. See also Rem Edwards, "The Principle of Utility and Minimizing Utilitarianism," *Journal of Value Inquiry* 20 (1986): 125–36. Edwards argues that to prevent harm or provide for minimum essentials, it is not only justified to restrict others' liberty, but is "worth the price of negative social enforcement" (p. 132). See also Andrew Kernohan, "Accumulative Harms and the Interpretation of the Harm Principle," *Social Theory and Practice* 19 (1993): 51–72. Kernohan argues that even on the strictest conception of harm, the Harm Principle should be understood to require interference to prevent harm. Also see Dudley R. Knowles, "A Reformulation of the Harm Principle," *Political Theory* 6 (May 1978): 233–46. Knowles argues that our physical security interest is a higher-order interest and the Harm Principle justifies the prohibition of others from jeopardizing this.

35. Peter S. Wenz, *Environmental Justice* (Albany: State University of New York Press, 1988), p. 105.

36. Ibid., pp. 105–6.

37. I do not exclude the possibility that there are also nonanthropocentric animal and ecosystem rights. I am very sympathetic with this extension; however, I neither include nor defend this extension here.

38. See William T. Blackstone, "Ethics and Ecology," in *Philosophy and Environmental Crisis*, ed. William T. Blackstone (Athens: University of Georgia

Press, 1974). Blackstone argues that no rights are realizable without the right to a livable or decent environment. Much of the rights literature is engaged in defining, defending, and discussing rights that are relevant *after* environmental rights have been secured. Thus, I am not disputing the rights theorists, but am stepping back to that which I argue is prior, and focusing there.

39. See Blackstone, "Ethics and Ecology," and Sax, "The Search for Environmental Rights."

40. I am assuming that there is a right to life.

41. See H. M. Malm, "Directions of Justification in the Negative-Positive Duty Debate," *American Philosophical Quarterly* 27, no. 4 (1990): 125–36. Malm provides a clear distinction between negative and positive duties regarding harm, however he concludes that our positive duties to prevent harm are not as strict as our negative duties not to cause harm.

42. As is widely known, bleaching with chlorine compounds necessarily involves pollution from organochlorines, such as dioxin associated with reproductive disorders, cancer, birth defects, and immune system disorders.

43. Pesticides do not merely harm target species, they harm and impose risk of harm in a wide and persistent manner. Pesticides disrupt reproductive behavior; cause cancer; cause cell mutations; result in abnormal eggs and young; harm the nervous system and gastrointestinal tract; result in hair loss, kidney and liver problems, neurological problems; and can result in sterility, and hormone imbalances. Pesticides pollute air, water, and soil and it is estimated that 20,000 cases of cancer a year in the United States are caused from pesticide residues. See "Toxic Effects of Pesticides: Experimental and Clinical Data," and "Short- and Long-Term Health Effects of Pesticides: Epidemiological Data," in *Public Health Impact of Pesticides* (Geneva: World Health Organization, 1990).

44. I am grateful to Peter Wenz for this point.

45. I am assuming that the government has a duty to protect its citizens from harm, especially harm imposed on citizens.

46. Sax, "The Search for Environmental Rights," p. 95.

3. Biotechnology Is Not Compatible with Sustainable Agriculture[1]

Martha L. Crouch

MARTHA L. CROUCH ARGUES that biotechnology does not address hunger but rather increases world food instability. Crouch defines biotechnology as the "manipulation of organisms for more efficient use by industry" and distinguishes biotechnology from traditional plant breeding (the latter issue is often used by biotechnologists to imply that there is no difference between this and traditional agriculture). The point of biotechnology is to genetically engineer organisms, and then to ensure profit for this product via patents. It is the profit and the potential profit that have attracted so much interest and funding, for without profit, biotechnology "would be of little interest to those who fund it." Further, biotechnology transforms something that was not a commodity into a commodity, "something of monetary value to be fought over."

Crouch writes that most people in the world still grow their own food, and that commercial agricultural enterprises, from the Green Revolution forward, displace people who were food secure, hence causing hunger and poverty. Biotechnology continues this process, with a much higher risk of environmental damage. Crouch details the myopic consideration of using biotechnology to solve problems without looking at the system level that has led to problems in the first place. She argues that we should instead protect and ballast local production of food, to oppose biotechnology, to recapture and return to successful methods of producing food, and to incorporate nonmarket principles in farming. These practices would provide local self-sufficiency and ecosystem stability through "diversity, redundancy, and decentralized regulation of functions," thus protecting against the risks inherent in large-scale operations, including agricultural biotechnology.

A FEW YEARS AGO I visited the Farm Progress Show 1992, in Columbus, Indiana. The first show was held in 1953 when the editors of the *Prairie Farmer* decided that "... we needed a field-day type of event where farmers could see the great strides being made in equipment, power, seed and chemicals since the end of World War II."[2] Forty years later, there are still plenty of hybrid seeds, tractors and pesticides on display. However, now a major theme is the environment, particularly clean water and soil health. Major chemical companies stress their concern: for example, Dupont's exhibit was entitled "A Growing

Partnership with Nature"; Dow Chemical advertised Treflan, an herbicide, as "A Trusted Partner in Stewarding the Land"; and ICI Americas Inc. handed out information on herbicide-intensive No-Till Farming.

This new emphasis on the environmental friendliness of agriculture is in response to public unease. Forty years ago, the farm as factory promised an abundant future. Now, to many people, the side-effects are becoming apparent. These include ground water contamination with fertilizers and toxic chemicals; increasing pest and pathogen problems as resistance develops, natural predators decline, and monocultural practices intensify; soil erosion; and economic vulnerability of rural communities accelerated by increasing reliance on expensive inputs and machines, loss of local markets, and fluctuating world markets (Schusky, 1989).

Even as we in the industrialized world are beginning to feel the negative consequences of progress in agriculture, we continue to export it as development to the non-industrialized world (Fenton and Heffron, 1987).[3] Although the term "Green Revolution" is often used to denote the spread of scientifically-designed seeds of staple crops such as wheat and rice, it encompasses the whole technological package: seeds, monoculture, mechanization, petrochemical fertilizers, herbicides and pesticides, irrigation, and commercialization. Large yield increases have resulted from the technology transfer. However, the revolution in this narrowly-defined productivity has been won at a price to the environment and to local self-reliance and community stability.[4] It has been suggested that the conversion of the weapons of World War II for use in agriculture—the tanks into tractors, airplanes into sprayers, explosives into fertilizers, defoliants into herbicides, and radioactivity into molecular genetics—has simply transferred the war technology into a new sphere, with

similar consequences for the land (Kroese, 1992: 37–48).[5]

These rumblings that all is not right with the Green Revolution, here at home and abroad, are loud enough to be heard by development specialists and their corporate partners. One response is to slightly alter aspects of the technology (switch to a different herbicide, or use a different large machine) without seriously questioning the package. This has the effect of allowing the same players to be in the game, keeping their advantages intact.

Another response is to promote biotechnology, being brought to us by the same interests, and using the same logic of progress and development as the Green Revolution. However, it is said to be kinder and gentler. Biotechnology uses the power of genetics, inherent in organisms themselves, to replace potentially harmful petrochemicals with natural, endogenous pesticides; to breed plants that can grow in deserts without irrigation; to transfer nitrogen fixation to crops that used to require polluting fertilizers; and so on (Gasser and Fraley, 1992: 62–69).[6]

Is biotechnology a suitable tool for sustainable agricultural development? I think not. To me, biotechnology is another weapon in the war to destroy all remaining enclaves of self-reliance, so that everyone in the world will be dependent on transnational corporations and their allies for food, one of the necessities of life (George, 1982; Kneen, 1989).

Summary of the Argument against Biotechnology in Agriculture

Biotechnology increases the extent of commercialization of food production. Commercial food production competes with food production for home use. Most of the people in the world grow their own food. They are more secure when they grow and use food directly, without the mediation of the market. To the extent that biotechnology enhances the competitiveness of the market, the ability of most people in the world to have food security will decrease. The instability caused by enhanced commercialization will result in a greater gap between rich and poor, increasing poverty of women and children, less ability and incentive to protect the environment, and greater need for militarization to maintain order. None of these effects are desirable. Therefore, biotechnology should be discouraged. Instead, an active program to protect and strengthen local food production where it exists, and to decrease reliance on industrial agriculture in the overdeveloped countries should be promoted.

Biotechnology increases the extent of commercialization of food production. By definition, biotechnology is the manipulation of organisms for more efficient use by industry. This inclusive definition would allow techniques like traditional plant breeding as a form of biotechnology. However, in common usage biotechnology refers to new procedures and products such as tissue culture, monoclonal antibody production, *in vitro* reproductive techniques, and genetic engineering, which result in rapid gains in specificity and control. Examples are yeasts that remain active at higher alcohol concentrations, plants that express genes for insect resistance derived from bacteria, pigs that express higher levels of growth hormone, and virus-free potatoes derived from tissue culture. Of the various techniques, genetic engineering is particularly powerful because, unlike traditional breeding, genes can be moved between any species, not just species that are related closely enough to mate. Proponents of genetic engineering like to assure the public that it is not that different from traditional evolution and husbandry, except that it results in more rapid change and specificity of design (Gasser and Fraley, 1992).

These are precisely the differences that make good business. Because the changes in genetically engineered organisms have been designed by specified humans rather than by mother nature or unknown local farmers, the organisms become products that can be patented or otherwise claimed as private property. If this were not the case, biotechnology would be of little interest to those who fund it. Consider that alternative solutions to problems, such as rotations or intercropping to manage pests, may get lipservice, but do not attract funding. As it is, biotechnology is of tremendous interest to the largest companies in the world: petrochemical and pharmaceutical transnational corporations (TNCs), such as Dow Chemical, Monsanto, Ciba-Geigy, Shell Oil, and so on. I assume that their economic analysts have determined that biotechnology will substantially increase the ability of their employers to compete in the global market.[7]

In the context of the market, competitive advantage is desirable. The United States government funds basic research into molecular biology with the goal of providing a springboard for innovation to keep American agricultural and medical industries competitive.[8] The hundreds of small biotechnology companies that have arisen (and often been swallowed up by TNCs) are testament to a successful science policy. But competition implies winners and losers. And the market is not deemed healthy unless it continuously expands. As biotechnology looms on the horizon in agriculture, who stands to lose? As commercial agriculture expands, what contracts?

Commercial food production competes with food production for home use. I want to describe something that is not counted in traditional economic analysis and thus is invisible in modern life: the household economy, work that is done at home for the benefit of the family, without being converted into money.

This work does not contribute to the gross national product (GNP). In traditional subsistence communities all work is of this type, by men, women, and children. As market economies enter societies, men tend to integrate more fully into the market, and subsistence becomes the predominant realm of women, children, and marginalized segments of the population. Even in the fully industrialized and globally-integrated economies of the North, most of the household work is performed by women and is invisible to the accounting system (Waring, 1988). Commercialization is the process of converting activities once performed by members of the family and community for free into commodities that must be purchased. People now work for someone else, give that someone a portion of their labour in exchange for money, and then buy back the things that they used to do for themselves.

For example, one of my subsistence activities where I live in Bloomington, Indiana, is to garden. I grow potatoes and store them in my basement for my use during the winter. I save some to grow next year's crop so that I am self-reliant in potatoes. I also get a great deal of satisfaction out of the process, and I control the varieties, methods of cultivation, soil quality, and so on. If I were to switch to a commercial potato economy, someone else would grow my potatoes, I would work for wages, and then buy potatoes with money. Although imported potatoes may be inexpensive, given the various subsidies for transportation and externalization of many costs of production, *cheap* is not the same as *free*. I must be part of the market economy to buy them. There are many differences between these two modes of potato production, but I want to focus now on two differences: invisibility of subsistence, and food security.

If I have land that was handed down to me by my family, or have access to commons, such as a community forest or river, and I produce all of my own food, I can live very comfortably without anyone knowing about it. No one counts how many fish I catch or the number of mushrooms I take out of the woods. I am the only one who knows how many potatoes I have in my basement, and it would be difficult for someone else to find out. I do not contribute to the economic growth statistics when I increase my yields. In fact, I bring down the indicators, because they count me but not my productivity. My well-being has no positive correlation with economic growth. For example, recently I cut my time at work and thus my income by a substantial amount in order to have more time to grow and hunt for food. Our local economy appears to suffer from my personal gain. If, however, my land is taken from me and I can no longer grow food; or if my river is polluted and I can no longer fish; or if my forest is cut down and I can no longer harvest medicinal plants, I must now work for wages to buy food and medicines. Now I am visible. I add to the GNP. Even if I make $0.50 a day and cannot afford to eat nearly as well as I did before, it appears that the local economy has improved because money is changing hands.

Commercialization competes directly with home food production in several ways. First, commercial agriculture uses land and resources that were being used by people in subsistence economies. In Central America, plantations of cotton for export are set up in fertile plains that used to produce beans and rice for local consumption. Rainforests in South America that provide medicines, food, and building materials for people of First Nations are converted into cattle ranches, again for export (Williams, 1986). Native forests in Asia with multiple uses are turned into pulp plantations of eucalyptus which support very little life other than their own (Lohmann, 1990). Factory trawlers in the Philippines deplete local fisheries (Kurien, 1991). Details vary, but the story is the same all over the world.⁹ The switch to commercial agriculture occurs as a result of deliberate policy by development agencies and state governments in the name of progress (Wright, 1990). One way or another, self-reliant people are pushed into marginal areas or cities, or convinced to enter the market themselves. Without access to land and common resources, the only choice is to try to find wage work, and people displaced from self-reliance usually do not compete well in the market. Their ability to buy back what has been lost is often not adequate, and so they must also continue to grow and find food, but now have much less time to do so (Lee-Smith and Trujillo, 1992). So the second way in which commercial agriculture competes with home production is by taking time away from home. Other effects include a shift in type of food eaten, changes in community and family structure, and ecological impacts (Dewey, 1990).

Most of the people in the world grow their own food. Given that I live in an industrialized country and subsistence is invisible to the market, it should not be surprising that I do not know many people who rely primarily on their own food production. The view from my door is not typical of the world: more than three billion of the almost six billion humans on earth still live primarily in subsistence economies, and produce most of their own food within their families and local communities. Most of these farmers are women. "In rural areas, both men and women engage in agriculture, but women are the major producers of food for household consumption. In subSaharan Africa, women grow 80 percent of the food destined for their households. Women's labor produces 70 to 80 percent of food crops grown on the Indian subcontinent, and 50 percent of the food domestically consumed in Latin America and the Caribbean"

(Jacobson, 1992). Food is produced in women's yards, on the margins of their husband's commercial fields, in the commons areas such as forests and rivers, and on their own land.

People are more secure when they grow and use food directly, without the mediation of the market. People who are able to grow or find their own food are not at the mercy of an employer, or a fickle market. Unemployment does not bring the threat of starvation. Subsistence farmers grow a diverse array of crops to hedge against uncertainties of weather and pests, and thus are seldom affected by large-scale famines, unless war intervenes (and war disrupts commercial food production as well). Industrial societies, on the other hand, are extremely vulnerable to disruptions in the functioning of many complex systems of transportation, energy, markets, and governments. Imagine what would happen to our ability to be fed if supplies of oil or electricity were cut off for just a week. Partial justification for the overdeveloped military capabilities of industrial countries is to compensate for this vulnerability by being able to protect our oil (wherever it happens to be), discourage terrorist attacks on infrastucture, and keep food flowing in from elsewhere. In my opinion, this is a false sense of security. I would feel safer in a world where community self-reliance created the kind of equality that would foster long-term security. For most of the world's people who do grow their own food, and who do not have enough money to be able to buy it, protecting their ability to continue growing food is the most logical way to ensure their well-being. People continue to fight and die for this right (Christodoulou, 1990). Kathryn Dewey (1990) reviewed the literature on nutrition as commercialization of agriculture increased in communities throughout the world. One study in Peru illustrates the issues (Ferroni, 1980). Dewey (1990) summarizes the study as follows:

Ferroni's central finding was that dietary adequacy was strongly positively related to the proportion of home-produced foods in the family calorie budget. Thus, families with greater independence from the market economy were nutritionally better off. There was an important interactive effect with income: Among families with low subsistence ratios, income was a major predictor of dietary adequacy, while among families with high subsistence ratios, income was less important. In a similar fashion, the proportion of home-produced food was relatively unimportant in determining dietary adequacy among families with higher incomes, but it was the major factor among those with low cash incomes.

Dewey describes case histories relating the degree of subsistence or commercial production to nutrition in Mexico, Jamaica, India, Sierra Leone, Kenya, and the Philippines. I was struck by the obvious conclusion that poor people are generally better off nutritionally when they are able to grow at least some of their own food.

To the extent that biotechnology enhances the competitiveness of the market, the ability of most people in the world to have food security will decrease. Biotechnology fits into an industrial agriculture better than into home production. This is true for two reasons. One is that the infrastructure required to produce and use biotechnology assumes an industrial society. The other is that the types of solutions to single problems that biotechnology is good at providing are not the multipurpose systemic solutions that people use at home.

The first food product to come into the market in the United States is the Flavr-Savr Tomato, from Calgene, Inc., in Davis, California. This is a genetically engineered tomato designed to solve the problem of tasteless tomatoes in January. In the industrial fresh tomato business, tomatoes are grown in the winter in warm places, such as California or Mexico, and shipped thousands of miles to consumers in snowy climes for their salads. Once tomatoes start to ripen, the process is autocatalytic, and in a few days the fruits start to become mushy and then rot. To allow enough time for transport before rotting, tomatoes are picked green, and the taste does not have a chance to fully develop on the vine. What FlavrSavr does is inhibit the formation of the enzyme that causes fruit softening. Tomatoes can be picked a few days later than usual, allowing better flavour formation, and then can be shipped thousands of miles, and will have a longer shelf-life before showing signs of rotting.

The beauty of this solution to the problem of taste-deficient January tomatoes is that nothing else in the system has to change. The tomatoes are grown in the same fields, by the same companies, shipped on the same highways, and so on. Because of the specificity of biotechnology, a problem can be framed in very narrow terms, and answered with a single gene change. What is new is that a company has inserted itself in a new place in the chain. Calgene can now sell the FlavrSavr technology and capture a share of the tomato market profits by having a novel product that they hope will out-compete other kinds of tomatoes.

What kind of structure is required to produce and use an industrial tomato (whether or not it is biotechnologically altered)? Like any industrial product, the tomato has strings attaching it to a vast network of components: farm machinery and their factories; agrichemicals and refineries; transportation systems of trucks, highways, and fossil fuels; electricity and power plants; buildings for storage and sales; communication systems; irrigation and use of fossil water; and advertising. The tomato may still be grown outdoors in sunlight, but the agroecosystem is reduced to an efficient, genetically uniform monoculture. Each tomato that I buy at the supermarket here in Indiana has all of these components packed into it, even if the nutritional content is similar to the tomato I pick in my yard.

The subsistence tomato I grow at home has a very different network of connections. First, I grow about a dozen different kinds, each with unique characteristics, and I save seed from year to year. They are grown in a polyculture with other species. Predator insects, birds, earthworms, nitrogen-fixing legumes, trap-plants, and many unknown interactions make up the system. I do not use purchased chemical inputs, nor is irrigation required. Planting and cultivation are done with metal tools, which do require mining, factory production, and transportation. Seasonality is savoured: we have a contest to see who can coax the first ripe tomato, and the earliest variety usually has ripe fruit by July. The last green tomato is fried up in November. Surplus fruit is dried for use in the winter, and I don't eat salads out of season. There are always enough tomatoes to eat, store, and give away to friends.

Do I need biotechnology for my subsistence tomatoes? No. My tomatoes have plenty of flavour. There are over 300 varieties of open-pollinated tomatoes for me to choose from, and by planting a number of them each year I stand a good chance of having a productive crop. I can solve my own problems by adjusting the ratio of varieties, spacing of plants, types of companion plants, time of planting, and so on. I am fairly independent of the industrial system for this part of my life, and do not need most of the destructive infrastructure described for the industrial tomato. The industrial infrastructure required for biotechnology production and use pollutes the commons, and destroys homelands (examine

the effects of hydroelectric dams, mineral and coal mines, and oil fields, for example).

Biotechnology also needs experts, scientists trained in specialized fields. The significance of relying on experts to design technologies for basic needs can be illustrated by supposing that I did decide to use a genetically-engineered tomato to control a caterpillar pest. Perhaps for the first few years it would work well, and I would no longer need to pay attention to the subtleties of the biological system that I used to control pests before. Maybe I would let some of my varieties go. However, after a while resistance would develop in the caterpillars, and they would eat my crop. The tool would be broken. How would I fix it? Unless I had my own high-tech lab and the appropriate training, I would have to appeal to the experts, probably in some urban area or in a corporation, to make a new gene that worked better. Would they still be interested in my crop? Would they be able to respond quickly enough? How much would I have to pay for a replacement? If I still had an array of varieties, and if I still knew enough about the complexities of my local system, perhaps I could go back to troubleshooting for myself, but biotechnology would not be one of the tools I could repair. Obviously, my life does not depend on the success of the tomatoes in my home garden. The lives of most of the people in the world do depend on the crops in their home gardens, family fields, and community rivers, lakes, and forests.

Biotechnology turns something that is not a commodity, and is therefore protected by invisibility, into something of monetary value to be fought over. One example is the proposed introduction of drought tolerance into crops via genetic engineering. This is being touted as an example of how biotechnology can be used to improve the lives of poor farmers. The problem is defined as poor

297

people being limited in the amount of food they can grow by the lack of water on their land. The solution is to develop plants that can grow better in conditions of water stress. Scientists will take genes from desert plants and put them into corn and beans, and give them to peasants for free, thus improving their lives. Unfortunately, the history of providing more productive organisms to poor areas from industrial laboratories does not indicate that the hungry are bettered. Instead, the newly productive endeavour becomes attractive to the commercial sector, and land that was worthless to the market becomes valuable. This happened in Central America when more productive cattle were introduced, and although exports of beef boomed, local consumption decreased. "Marginal" forested lands were converted to pastures (Williams, 1986).

Problems need to be redefined at the system level. Why are peasants growing their food crops on marginal land? In many cases, it is because commercial agriculture has pushed them into unsuitable areas. To bring in a tool designed by industrial people that now makes even peasant's marginal land able to produce high yields means that commercial agriculture has incentive to move into the margins. Where will the poor go? Further into the forest, higher up the mountain, into the slums. Where will the wild plants and animals go? They have nowhere else. Unless the ability of poor people to hold onto their land and protect common resources is enhanced, the new technology will exacerbate, not alleviate, the plight of most people and other species.[10]

By redefining problems at the system level, the proposed solutions will result in several improvements in the lives of the poor. In the same way, by defining the problem of lack of taste in tomatoes as long distance transport of vegetables, the solution of strengthening local markets and encouraging seasonality

presents itself, and other problems related to local economy and environmental quality are solved simultaneously. It is an axiom of holistic or system-level solutions that they solve many problems at once by treating the root causes (Savory, 1988; Wilson and Morren, 1990). Biotechnology is only good at treating symptoms. A powerful counterargument often offered by biotechnologists concerns world hunger. With the burgeoning world population, much of it urban, there is no choice but to further industrialize and commercialize agriculture, despite the negative consequences in some realms, because productivity and efficiency are the only way to stave off starvation. I concede that some industrial agriculture may be necessary to maintain the cities. However, much of the productivity increase brought about by the first Green Revolution is being used for nonessentials, such as flowers, gourmet vegetables, cotton, sugar, corn syrup for soft drinks, feed for animals for export, and so on. Surpluses are often promoted by government policies and used in aid programs that undermine local markets and create cycles of dependency (Lappé and Collins, 1986). If aiding food security was made a top priority, the current base of land and water would be sufficient, without having to destroy the livelihood of the rest of the rural community, and without clearing more forest. Until I see food policies designed to eliminate hunger instead of create markets I remain sceptical that biotechnologically-enhanced increases in productivity will address the world food crisis in a positive way.

The instability caused by enhanced commercialization will result in a greater gap between rich and poor, increasing poverty of women and children, less ability and incentive to protect the environment and greater need for militarization to maintain order. People who lose their homelands and are unable to meet basic needs may be willing to fight to regain or maintain their livelihoods.

In the early 1980s, for example, 75% of the 120 armed conflicts in the world involved people fighting for their indigenous homes, often against the state government (Nietschmann, 1987). These effects have been well documented from the first Green Revolution.[11]

The negative effects of agricultural commercialization on women and children deserve more attention. An article by Jodi L. Jacobson on "Gender Bias: Roadblock to Sustainable Development" provides a succinct overview of the issue:

> Four major—and interrelated—trends, all set in motion or perpetuated by the agricultural strategies of low-income countries since the fifties, have been particularly damaging to the ability of rural women to produce or procure adequate supplies of food. All four are a product of the increasing emphasis on cash crops.
>
> First, large amounts of land once jointly owned and controlled by villagers—and accessible to women—have shifted into the hands of government agencies and private landowners. Second, the distribution of resources on which cash crop agriculture is heavily dependent—including land, fertilizers, pesticides, irrigation, and hybrid seeds—has reflected persistent gender bias. Third, the mechanization of agriculture has reduced or replaced the labor traditionally done by men, but increased that done by women without increasing their income. And finally, the labor available to subsistence households in many countries has become increasingly scarce, largely as a result of the shift of male workers away from subsistence production into cash crops and urban-based industries.
>
> The first of these trends—a shifting of land out of the hands of those who are most responsible for producing food that is domestically consumed—has been hastened by development strategies that … make false assumptions about who benefits from gross economic gains. Thus, while shifting ownership may improve agricultural output in the aggregate, it fails to address critical differences between men's and women's farming responsibilities. (1992: 24)

Jacobson goes on to detail each of these trends with case histories from all over the world. It is clear that women, and by extension their children, have gained little from modernization of farming, and have lost a great deal. The application of biotechnology promises to magnify this pattern: herbicide-resistant crops to eliminate the need for weeding done by women; tissue-culture produced flavourings and medicines to replace those gathered in forests by women; creation of new cash crops to compete with subsistence crops grown by women; and incentive to convert more common land into private property inaccessible to women.

The environmental consequences of loss of the commons are also dire. *The Ecologist* recently used an entire issue of the journal to explain how privatization of everything is leading to a breakdown of the incentive and power of communities to protect their environments.[12] Who best manages resources, the people who depend on them for daily life and future existence, or people who are disconnected from the direct consequences of despoliation by the global market? Time and again the strategies of subsistence communities for managing natural resources prove wiser than the plans of professionals (McCay and Acheson, 1987; Savory, 1988; Altieri, 1990). Pressures from commercialization decrease the power of local people to implement their own plans.

The answer to the question of who stands to lose with the adoption of biotechnology seems to be the people who lost during the first Green Revolution. As commercial agriculture expands, with the help of biotechnology, the commons almost certainly will shrink.

None of these effects are desirable. Therefore, biotechnology should be discouraged. This is a strong conclusion. Can't I think of at least a few beneficial applications of biotechnology that would lighten a woman's burden, or help protect a forest? Yes, I can imagine such benefits, if I divorce the individual application from the infrastructure required for it. I also must ignore the inherent reductionist bias, and the tendency towards commercialization. I am assessing the impact of the system of biotechnology, on balance, and rejecting it as a whole. The argument that the system must be maintained, even if most of the effects are undesirable, in order to have a chance of a miracle cure does not make sense (Mander, 1991). There are always alternative solutions to problems.

Instead, an active program to protect and strengthen local food production where it exists, and to decrease reliance on industrial agriculture in the overdeveloped countries should be promoted. A future without biotechnology does not seem dull, lifeless, or primitive to me. I am excited about the alternatives to industrial agriculture that exist already, and that are being enacted by innovative farmers around the world. An encouraging sampling of local solutions to the problems of food production and environmental protection are described in Living With the Land (Meyer and Moosang, 1992). These have the common feature of "tackling big problems by thinking small." During a recent discussion, a participant agreed that there are thousands of examples of small-scale solutions that work, but commented that when these ideas are scaled up, they no longer function. Perhaps since global problems are big, they require bigger solutions than these.

Thus "small is beautiful" may be true, but ineffective. I agree that problems exemplified by ozone depletion and global warming are enormous. However, I come to a different conclusion when I hear that small-scale projects work and large ones do not: scale makes a difference, so it is important to find ways to reduce the scale. Divide the puzzle into many small jigsaw pieces, and act within each piece. A few mistakes, pieces out of place or blurred, will not cause the whole picture to become distorted. Organisms and ecosystems, although complex and composed of interconnecting parts, gain stability through diversity, redundancy, and decentralized regulation of functions. The opposite conclusion, that somehow humans can know enough to competently "manage planet earth" as if it were a spaceship seems utopian, unrealistic and arrogant, given the data on our past and current performance.

I advocate three general strategies for promoting food security. The first is to oppose further integration of agriculture into the global economy. I do this by opposing biotechnology, as described in this paper. International Monetary Fund restructuring plans that force debtor countries to beef up export agriculture at the expense of local food, and free trade agreements that allow local concerns to be overridden are examples of policies that interfere with the ability of communities to control their own destinies. These kinds of policies should be challenged.

A second strategy is to learn about and emulate successful ways of growing food from the past. Knowledge of how to live well in local places may be disappearing faster than endangered species. Supporting and using such knowledge is crucial, as much of it has evolved over generations and cannot easily be recreated. Many organizations are involved in this work. Some examples are the Center for Indigenous Knowledge in Agriculture and

Rural Development (CIKARD), Cultural Survival, and the Seed Savers Exchange.[13] One of the most-cited success stories of this approach is the reintroduction of an ancient farming method to the Alto Plano in the Andes (Straughan, 1991).

The third approach is to design new farming practices around non-market principles. Many subsistence farmers are doing this now, successfully but without fanfare. For example, farmers in Africa are developing new intercropping methods in response to changing conditions (Richards, 1985). I hear more about sustainable agriculture research carried out in various institutes. One of my favorites is the Permaculture Institute, where people learn principles of agroecosystem design to adapt to their local areas (Mollison, 1991). Other new projects for disconnecting from the global market are CSAs (Community Supported Agriculture groups) that match local farmers with families (Groh and McFadden, 1990), and the Hendrix College Local Food Project, where students designed and implemented a program to switch their college to local food supplies. They have published articles to help other people do the same (Yazman, 1991).

Underlying the choice of these strategies is my belief that in order for humans to make wise choices they must be able to see and feel the consequences of their actions. If I live next to a river and must drink and fish from it, and I choose to pour toxins into the river, or to overfish, it is my family and community that will suffer. There will be a strong incentive to develop a system of restraints and proscriptions for river use. Otherwise, it is I who will be sick. As human animals, we seem to respond best to direct information, using all of our senses. When we have only abstract notions about the consequences of our deeds, action is delayed and partial. For example, although a computer or television news broadcast may be able to create a global village, it is a village composed of heads with no bodies: no smell, taste, or touch. The decisions for action based on a vague notion of ozone depletion and future mutation rates are going to be different from decisions made by people who are going blind because of ozone depletion.

Biotechnologists do not have to live and die by the results of their products. I do not know any biotechnologists who grow their own food or rely on their own communities for basic needs. Where is their stake in a particular place? What incentives drive their decisions?

I place my trust for the future in the farmers, mostly women, who grow food in order to survive. I trust them to develop agricultural systems that make sense. Governments, corporations, and aid agencies need to get out of their way and support their efforts. I believe that one of the best ways to do that is to remove food from the global commodity realm. When all communities depend directly and visibly upon their own practices, wisdom may come easier. Perhaps even in the industrialized world people will have the foresight and courage to turn, face in another direction, and take just one step, setting in motion positive feedback for change.

Questions

1. Crouch explains that biotechnology companies seek patents and have no intention of distributing seeds to those in need. Explain how this illustrates that agricultural biotechnology is for profit and not about "feeding the hungry."

2. What is Crouch's model for sustainability? How does her model ensure that fewer people would be food insecure?

3. Biotechnology has been used to prop up the failing Green Revolution, overwhelmingly to allow for *more* pesticide application. How is this inconsistent with the goal of agriculture (feeding people)?

References

Altieri, Miguel A. 1990. Why Study Traditional Agriculture? In *Agroecology*, edited by C. Ronald Caroll, John H. Vandermeer and Peter Rosset, pp. 551–564. New York: McGraw Hill.

Beachy, Roger. 1991. The Very Structure of Scientific Research Does Not Militate Against Developing Products to Help the Environment, the Poor, and the Hungry. *Journal of Agricultural and Environmental Ethics* 4(2): 159–165.

Christodoulou, D. 1990. *The Unpromised Land: Agrarian Reform and Conflict Worldwide*. London: Zed Books Ltd.

Crouch, Martha. 1991. The Very Structure of Scientific Research Militates Against Developing Products to Help the Environment, the Poor, and the Hungry. *Journal of Agricultural and Environmental Ethics* 4(2): 151–158.

Dewey, Kathryn G. 1990. Nutrition and Agricultural Change. In *Agroecology*, edited by C. Ronald Caroll, John H. Vandermeer and Peter Rosset, pp. 459–480. New York: McGraw Hill.

Doyle, Jack. 1985. *Altered Harvest*. New York, NY: Viking.

Fenton, Thomas P., and Mary J. Heffron, eds. 1987. *Food, Hunger, Agribusiness: A Directory of Resources*. Maryknoll, NY: Orbis Books.

Ferroni, M.A. 1980. The Urban Bias of Peruvian Food Policy: Consequences and Alternatives. Cornell University Ph.D. Dissertation, cited in Dewey, Nutrition and Agricultural Change, p. 464.

Gasser, Charles S., and Robert T. Fraley. 1992. Transgenic Crops, *Scientific American*, June, pp. 62–69.

George, Susan. 1982. *Food for Beginners*. New York, NY: Writers and Readers Publishing.

Groh, T.M., and S.H. McFadden. 1990. *Farms of Tomorrow: Community Supported Farms, Farm Supported Communities*. Kimberton, UK: Bio-Dynamic Farming and Gardening Association.

Hobbelink, Henk. 1991. *Biotechnology and the Future of World Agriculture*. London: Zed Books Ltd.

Jacobson, Jodi L. 1992. *Gender Bias: Roadblock to Sustainable Development. Worldwatch Paper 110*. Washington, DC: Wordwatch Institute, September.

Juma, Calestous. 1989. *The Gene Hunters: Biotechnology and the Scramble for Seeds*. New Jersey: Princeton University Press.

Kloppenburg, Jack. 1988. *First the Seed: The Political Economy of Plant Biotechnology, 1492–2000*. New York, NY: Cambridge University Press.

Kneen, Brewster. 1989. *From Land to Mouth: Understanding the Food System*. Toronto, ON: NC Press Ltd.

Kroese, Ron. 1992. Growing Peacefully: Ending Agribusiness's War on Creation, *Seed Savers 1992 Harvest Edition*, pp. 37–48.

Kurien, J. 1991. Ruining the Commons and Responses of the Commoners: Coastal Overfishing and Fishermen's Action in Kerala State, India. UNRISD Discussion Paper 23, United Nations Research Institute for Social Development, May.

Lappé, Frances Moore, and Joseph Collins. 1986. *World Hunger: Twelve Myths*. New York, NY: Grove Press.

Lee-Smith, Diana, and Catalina Hinchey Trujillo. 1992. The Struggle to Legitimize Subsistence: Women and Sustainable Development. *Environment and Urbanization* 4(1): April.

Lohmann, Larry. 1990. Commercial Tree Plantations in Thailand: Deforestation by Any Other Name. *The Ecologist* 20(1): 9–17.

Mander, Jerry. 1991. *In the Absence of the Sacred: The Failure of Technology and the Survival of the Indian Nations*. San Francisco, CA: Sierra Club Books.

McCay, B., and J.M. Acheson, eds. 1987. *The Question of the Commons: The Culture and Ecology of Communal Resources*. Tuscon, AZ: University of Arizona Press.

Meyer, Christine, and Faith Moosang, eds. 1992. *Living With the Land: Communities Restoring the Earth*. Philadelphia, PA: New Society Publishers.

Mollison, Bill. 1991. *Introduction to Permaculture*. Tyalgum, Australia: Tagari Publications.

Nietschmann, Bernard. 1987. The Third World War. *Cultural Survival Quarterly* 11(3): 1–16.

Repetto, Robert. 1992. Accounting for Environmental Assets, *Scientific American*, June, pp. 94–100.

Richards, P. 1985. *Indigenous African Revolution*. London: Hutchinson.

Sachs, W., ed. 1992. *The Development Dictionary: A Guide to Knowledge as Power*. London: Zed Books Ltd.

Savory, Allan. 1988. *Holistic Resource Management*. Washington, DC: Island Press.

Schusky, Ernest L. 1989. *Culture and Agriculture: An Ecological Introduction to Traditional and Modern Farming Systems*. New York, NY: Bergin & Garvey Publishers.

Shiva, Vandana. 1991. *The Violence of the Green Revolution: Third World Agriculture, Ecology and Politics*. London: Zed Books Ltd.

Straughan, B. 1991. The Secrets of Ancient Tiwanaku are Benefiting Today's Bolivia. *Smithsonian Magazine*, February, pp. 38–48.

Waring, Marilyn. 1988. *If Women Counted*. San Francisco, CA: HarperCollins.

Whose Common Future? 1992. *The Ecologist* 22(4): July/August.

Williams, Robert G. 1986. *Export Agriculture and the Crisis in Central America*. Chapel Hill, NC: University of North Carolina Press.

Wilson K., and G.E.B. Morren Jr. 1990. *Systems Approaches for Improvement in Agriculture and Resource Management*. New York, NY: Macmillan.

Wright, Angus. 1990. *The Death of Ramon Gonzalez: The Modern Agricultural Dilemma*. Austin, TX: University of Texas Press.

Yazman, Melissa Beck. 1991. *A Guide to Starting a Local Food Project*. Conway, AK: Hendrix College.

Notes

1. Martha L. Crouch, "Biotechnology Is Not Compatible with Sustainable Agriculture," *Journal of Agricultural and Environmental Ethics*, 8, no. 2 (1996): 98–111.
2. Farm Progress Show 1992, Columbus, Indiana, September 29, 30, October 1, program notes.
3. Fenton and Heffron's book (1987) lists organizations, books, periodicals, pamphlets, articles, films, and other resources. An in depth case history of the problems of modern agriculture is Wright (1990).
4. Shiva (1991); Lappé and Collins (1986); Sachs (1992); Repetto (1992); "Whose Common Future?" *The Ecologist*.
5. Kroese (1992). *Seed Savers Exchange* is a nonprofit organization that is saving old-time food crops from extinction.
6. This is an example of the claims and arguments made by the biotechnology industry. See Beachy (1991).
7. Doyle (1985); Hobbelink (1991); Juma (1989); Kloppenburg (1988).
8. Editorials in the journal *Science* provide examples of research policy goals. See also Crouch (1991).
9. The journal *Cultural Survival Quarterly* (53A Church St., Cambridge MA 02138), regularly publishes articles documenting conflict between commercial and subsistence economies.
10. "Whose Common Future?" *The Ecologist*.

11. See notes 3 and 4.
12. "Whose Common Future?" *The Ecologist*.
13. CIKARD is part of a global network of indigenous knowledge resource centers, and will be represented in a quarterly newsletter, *The Indigenous Knowledge and Development Monitor* (Centre for International Research and Advisory Networks, PO Box 90734, 2509 LS The Hague, The Netherlands). *Cultural Survival* sponsors publications, projects, and research related to problems faced by indigenous people throughout the world.

4. Ethical Consumerism: Veganism

Valentin Beck and Bernd Ladwig

VALENTIN BECK IS A research fellow and Bernd Ladwig is a professor of philosophy, both at the Free University of Berlin. In this selection, they consider whether veganism is a form of ethical consumption, especially as it has the potential to address animal, human, and environmental harm from (mostly) factory farming. They explore each of these harms and whether veganism alone can effect beneficial change or whether more, especially political action, is needed. In the absence of effective reforms, is veganism a viable option, or a moral duty? They tackle many options, concluding that utilitarian consequences of vegetarianism and reducetarianism might have a greater impact than a small number of vegans.

1. Introduction

WITH THE TERM "VEGANISM," most people associate a concern for the life and wellbeing of individual animals. Vegans try to avoid practices that cause harm to sentient beings of other species. This can be interpreted as a commitment to animal welfare or animal rights ethics. However, veganism can also be justified from an ecological perspective centered on anthropocentric considerations of justice or collective self-interest. Concerns for individual animals and for the environment converge, not least because animal husbandry has a comparatively large impact on human-induced climate change.

In this article, we focus on vegan consumerism as a means by which to minimize harm to animals, as well as to humans and the environment (for overviews, see Doggett, 2018; Jallinoja, Vinnari, & Niva, 2019; Katz & McPherson, 2020). Vegan consumerism can be roughly defined as an attempt to avoid buying animal products. Although this definition might appear to lead us directly to matters of personal lifestyle, we will entertain a broad understanding of vegan consumerism that includes attempts to influence political decision-making.

The use of animals is a legally authorized and institutionalized practice, which means that we must consider both responsibility within consumer interactions and responsibility to reform social institutions and structures. Reforming or eliminating practices that are harmful to animals would require collective action in order to create more just national and international laws and institutions (on the international legal dimension, see Peters, 2016). Likewise, slowing climate change requires institutional solutions and collectively binding decisions concerning different societal sectors, including agriculture. Normative theories of climate justice combine issues of distributive and intergenerational justice and seek to determine the fair share of burdens that states ought to bear in emission reduction, adaptation and victim compensation measures. They draw on criteria such as present and past emissions, and the differential capacities of states to mitigate climate change and to help those affected to adapt to climate change-related harms, especially poorer countries, which have contributed the least to the problem (see e.g., Caney, 2018; Juhola, 2019; Moellendorf, 2012). Governments arguably bear a primary responsibility to ensure climate justice and the morally appropriate treatment of animals, and are consequently obliged to strive for international coordination and cooperation.[1] We must therefore remain wary of deflection campaigns by industry lobbyists to shift moral responsibility from governments and companies to individuals (see e.g., Mann, 2020). However, countering such deflections and affirming the primacy of government action does not imply that consumers bear no responsibilities at all with regard to climate and animal justice. Governmental, corporate, and consumer responsibilities are complementary in principle, and each warrants an in-depth treatment. In this article, we discuss the responsibilities of individuals for the moral consideration of animals and climate justice—in consumer interactions, but also in their political roles as citizens.

We will review an array of positions in the contemporary literature that concern the moral reasons for vegan consumerism, with an emphasis on the question of whether concerns for animals, human rights, and/or climate justice entail weighty moral reasons (or perhaps even a duty) to adopt a vegan lifestyle. We will also address other questions regarding vegan consumerism, such as whether organized vegan consumer campaigns are a politically legitimate means to advance concern for animals and the environment. In doing so, we

hope to show that there are anthropocentric as well as animal-centered reasons that speak in favor of radically reformed human–animal relations, including diets that are at least predominantly plant-based. The text is organized as follows. First, we situate veganism within the broader field of ethical consumerism. Second, we specify the variety of motivations and justifications for veganism. Last, we discuss established and potential criticisms of vegan consumerism.

2. Ethical Consumerism: Interactional and Political

Ethical consumerism consists of changes to purchasing and consumption choices as a morally informed response to wrongs in the production and distribution of goods and services. It has a narrow interactional and a broader political component. The *interactional component* consists of consumer choices that are at least partly motivated by moral considerations. *Boycotters* intentionally renounce (or withdraw from) certain kinds of economic interaction. The boycottees can be individuals or organized groups; most typically companies whose products are boycotted. However, the boycottee can also be an industry sector, for example when investors divest from fossil fuel companies,[2] or when vegans avoid all products extracted from animals. In contrast, a *buycott* (compare Friedman 1999, p. 11, 2001) involves giving preference to products and services on the basis of moral considerations. Both boycotts and buycotts can be unilateral or organized. That is, consumers can individually decide to purchase or avoid a product for moral reasons and they can also join *organized* boycotts and buycotts. Environmental labeling initiatives, such as organic certification and the Forest Stewardship Council, or social labeling initiatives such as Fairtrade, are well-known examples of organized buycotts, which make certain morally relevant features of the production process transparent.[3] Examples for official vegan certification are the European Vegetarian Union's V-label, the Vegan Society's Vegan Trademark, and the Certified Vegan Logo from the American non-profit organization Vegan Action (Vegan Official Labels, 2020).

By participating in organized buycotts and boycotts, consumers typically seek to impact the demand for a product or service. Perhaps more importantly, they also take part in collective action, which can have far-reaching socio-political consequences, as exemplified by the Montgomery bus boycott led by Martin Luther King in 1955–1956, which ultimately resulted in the enactment of the Civil Rights Act in the United States in 1964.[4] Thus the *political component* of ethical consumerism is revealed when reflecting on what consumers can do to contribute to lasting social change. Consumer participation in these campaigns, which include boycotts of firms that sell animal products as well as vegan buycotts, supports the more narrowly understood practices of ethical consumption. What is more, by participating in such campaigns consumers often simultaneously aim at more broadly conceived reforms of the basic institutional infrastructure of consumption, such as legislation that prohibits certain kinds of animal treatment or places legal limits on greenhouse gas emissions for corporate polluters. As citizens, people can influence political decision-making through various means, from voting to civil disobedience. As consumers, they can take part in organized boycotts and buycotts, which transmit to the political sphere when the goals and concerns of these campaigns or initiatives are publicly communicated and justified (see Stolle & Micheletti, 2013; see also Beck, 2010, 2019). As complements or alternatives, there are also integrity-based interpretations of ethical

consumerism, and interpretations of boycotts as protest speech, social punishment, or social coercion (Friedman, 2001; Mills, 1996; Schwartz, 2010, chap. 4; Radzik, 2017).

Normative theorists have proposed various justifications for ethical consumerism that refer to its interactional or political component, or to both.[5] We will give a brief overview of the most common types of justifications, before turning to veganism specifically.

Consequentialists hold that whether a certain conduct is right or wrong is ultimately determined by the (likely) outcome of that conduct. From this point of view, the most important challenge to justifications of ethical consumption is the impotence objection (see Section 4.3), according to which uncoordinated individual consumer purchases will most likely not precipitate positive social change. In response to that objection, some authors have developed threshold arguments and probabilistic defenses of morally motivated consumer acts, as well as appeals to the indirect role-modeling effects of ethical consumerism (Herzog, 2016; Kagan, 2011; see Almassi, 2011 specifically for the case of vegetarianism). Others have given *deontological justifications*, such as the need to act from universalizable maxims (with respect to climate change, see Albertzart, 2019; Baatz, 2014) and to treat humans and maybe also animals never as mere means but always as ends in themselves (Korsgaard, 2018 has extended this Kantian argument to animals). Finally, *virtue ethical views*. defend practices of ethical consumption as conducive to the cultivation of moral character, and to virtues such as benevolence, moderation, or simplicity (Garcia-Ruiz & Rodriguez-Lluesma, 2014; in relation to animals, see Nobis, 2002).

In addition, the case for ethical consumerism is supported by accounts of the responsibility to promote more just social institutions and structures under non-ideal circumstances.[6] This responsibility can be defended with various arguments.[7] For example, one may point to the complicity of consumers in injustices.[8] This argument does not necessarily entail a duty to consume ethically, as citizens may fulfill their responsibility in other ways. However, if there is a realistic chance that participation in well-designed consumer campaigns will contribute to positive social and structural change, then it is one way among others to fulfill the responsibility to promote background justice (Beck, 2010, 2019). Thus, consumers have a political reason to join well-designed boycotts and to support labeling initiatives, additionally to those moral reasons provided by consequentialist, deontological, or virtue ethics defenses of the interactional component of ethical consumerism. We will now take a closer look at veganism as an example of morally motivated and politically relevant consumer behavior.

3. Veganism

The Vegan Society (2020)[9] defines veganism as "a philosophy and a way of living which seeks to exclude, as far as is possible and practicable, all forms of exploitation of, and cruelty to, animals for food, clothing or any other purpose." The definition stresses lifestyle beyond diet, including clothing, furnishing, and personal care. In the following we use the term "animal products" as an abbreviation of all kinds of goods that vegans try to avoid. The definition's restrictive clause "as far as is possible and practicable" is crucial, however, because absolute avoidance of animal products is impossible, given their wide distribution—from tennis balls to medicines tested on animals. What is more, even in the process of farming vegan foods, countless animals such as rodents are inevitably killed. Therefore, Lori Gruen and Robert C. Jones argue

that veganism is not an identity or a lifestyle that bestows "clean hands" upon consumers. Rather, it should be understood as a goal or aspiration (Gruen & Jones, 2015).

The above definition of veganism refers to the *moral motivation* of avoiding cruelty to animals, but there are also self-regarding rationales for a vegan lifestyle, such as expected health advantages. However, empirical evidence suggests that a concern for animal welfare is the primary motivation for vegans. Expected health benefits come second, and a presumed positive impact on the environment comes third. Moreover, a moral concern for animals makes it most likely that vegetarians follow their dietary choice consistently or even turn to veganism (Rosenfeld, 2018). In a quantitative study among German vegans, the most important motives for becoming vegan are reports from factory farming, followed by climate protection and health related considerations (Kerschke-Risch, 2015).

Factory farming obviously involves cruelty to animals, such as close confinement, surgical procedures without anesthesia, and physically draining levels of egg and milk production (Halteman, 2011). Still, there is no *necessary* connection between cruelty and animal products. It is theoretically possible to consume only meat from animals who die by accident or from natural causes, for example. It is also possible to obtain products such as milk or eggs from living animals without harming or prematurely killing the "providers."

Thus, veganism is not the only viable way to show concern for animals through one's consumption choices, and many morally motivated consumers are content with more moderate restrictions of their consumption patterns, such as reducetarianism, pescetarianism, or vegetarianism. Reducetarians consume only small amounts of animal products, mostly from organic farming, but do not give up meat eating completely; pescatarians do not eat land animals and birds but consume fish and other seafood; vegetarians avoid meat or fish, but eat dairy or eggs.

However, vegans can give reasons for not being content with reducetarianism, pescetarianism, or vegetarianism. By merely reducing one's consumption of animal products, one is still contributing to practices that cause animal suffering and that could be avoided by a vegan diet. Fish are most likely capable of pain and other subjective sensations (see Braithwaite, 2010; Segner, 2012; as a counter position Key, 2016). Even organic livestock production does not necessarily exclude painful practices such as debeaking, dehorning, and castration without anesthesia (Chait, 2019). Perhaps most importantly, the vast majority of organically raised animals end their lives in conventional slaughterhouses where they face a serious risk of an agonizing death due to incomplete stunning, just as their fellow creatures from factory farms do (on slaughterhouses see Eisnitz, 1997; Pachirat, 2011).

Concerning vegetarianism, vegans argue that the theoretical possibility to extract milk or eggs without hurting or prematurely killing the animals should not obscure the rather different reality of mass milk and egg production. Take the example of dairy cows. The natural life expectancy of cows is about 20 years, but continuous impregnation, birth, and milk production leech the animals and ruin their productivity. Normally, after four lactations (about 5–6 years old), they end their lives in slaughterhouses (Compassion in World Farming, 2012). Almost all calves are separated from their mothers early after birth, which is a painful experience for both the mothers and their newborns.[10] Most male calves, if not killed immediately, are sent to fattening farms to become veal after a few weeks.

However, turning to a vegan lifestyle demands a conscious decision to forgo many conveniences. That raises the question of whether such a radical step is really required due to *valid moral reasons*. As anticipated in the introduction, it is possible to arrive at vegan conclusions from different moral starting points. Although animal welfare considerations provide the primary motives for veganism, anthropocentric arguments are still predominant in moral theory and everyday morals. Thus, we will consider such anthropocentric justifications first.

3.1 Human Rights and Climate Justice

Human rights claims are broadly accepted as strong moral grounds for excluding certain practices. And today's livestock farming has a negative net impact on human rights-related goods, such as food, water, and health, at least indirectly. Anthropogenic climate change also poses a dire threat to human rights, which is why we cover it in this section, too.

Conversion to veganism by a significant share of the world's population could contribute to a more just distribution of the above-mentioned human-rights related goods, and also make it easier to overcome world hunger, since animal agriculture is a comparatively inefficient way of creating nutritional energy. Almost a third of the world's grain and 75% of soy production is used for intensive livestock production, instead of feeding humans directly. A recent meta-analysis found that meat, aquaculture, eggs, and dairy use about 83% of the world's farmland yet provide only 37% of our protein and 18% of our calories (Poore & Nemecek, 2018). This, however, is not completely beyond scientific dispute. Mottet et al. (2017) found that 86% of the global livestock feed intake is made of materials not edible to humans and that meat production requires less cereals than usually reported.

Another disadvantage of the animal industry is high water usage. More than 840 million humans have no access to safe, affordable, and clean water, and the water footprint of animal products is particularly large relative to crop products (Mekonnen & Hoekstra, 2012). The production of livestock also causes water pollution, for example, by nitrates, pesticides, and antibiotics (UNESCO, 2017). The excessive use of antibiotics in animal husbandry indirectly endangers human health by contributing to antibiotic resistance (OECD, 2016).

Climate change endangers almost all goods relevant for human rights, and animal husbandry is one of its main drivers. According to the Food and Agriculture Organization of the United Nations, industrial animal faming causes 14.5–18% of all greenhouse gas emissions caused by humans. This exceeds the contribution of the global transport sector (FAO, 2013). About 27% of the greenhouse gas emissions resulting from animal husbandry consist in carbon dioxide, 44% in methane, mostly emitted by cattle, and 29% in nitrous oxide, which is released through the fertilization with manure and dung and the use of mineral fertilizers (FAO, 2013). Livestock farming also contributes indirectly to global warming as tropical rainforests are destroyed to create soy plantations for animal feedstuffs or pastures for cattle. Deforestation not only fosters the extinction of entire species, but it also releases large amounts of carbon dioxide (FAO, 2016).

Our dietary habits thus significantly influence the chance of limiting global warming. A study estimating the difference in dietary GHG emissions between self-selected meat-eaters, fish-eaters, vegetarians and vegans in the United Kingdom found that the mean "dietary GHG emissions for meat-eaters (results reported for women and then men) were 46% and 51% higher than for fish-eaters, 50% and 54% higher than for vegetarians and 99% and 102% higher than for vegans" (Scarborough et al., 2014). Harwatt, Sabaté, Eshel, Soret, and Ripple (2017) estimated for the United States that substituting beans for beef would achieve up to 74% of the reductions needed to meet the 2020 GHG reduction goal.

To be sure, the overall environmental impact of vegan diets, including their net-effects on land-use, transport emissions, and biodiversity, is difficult to determine in real-life contexts. For example, vegans who consume a large amount of soya products, imported fruit or water-hungry crops such as avocados, do not necessarily have a smaller ecological footprint than omnivores. A study among 151 Italian adults on the overall environmental impact of different dietary regimens observed a high inter-individual variability within each dietary group. Despite their general finding that omnivorous diets generate larger carbon, water and ecological footprints than vegetarian and vegan diets, the authors also recommend further studies considering, for example, the consumption of locally grown and seasonal products as well as the impact of different agricultural techniques (Rosi et al., 2017; see also Chai et al., 2019, for a systematic review based on 16 studies and 18 reviews).

In any case, anthropocentric reasoning regarding human rights and climate justice does not suffice to show that a vegan diet is morally required. All that can be shown is that such considerations support reducing our consumption of animal products, and transforming the methods of production (Hooley & Nobis, 2016). A radical reduction of the number of animals would suffice to reach our climate goals (Bajzêlj et al., 2014), and in particular, a moderate number of livestock could continue to be raised in grazing areas unsuitable for the cultivation of edible crops.[11]

3.2 Animal Ethics

Anthropocentric justifications are thus insufficient to show that veganism is *obligatory*. Consequently, in order to arrive at that more radical conclusion, vegans primarily rely on animal ethics. They try to show, first, that at least all sentient animals have a moral status, that is, they matter morally for their own sake, and second, that the already existing animal welfare regulations do not take this status seriously enough.

There is still no philosophical consensus on the moral status of animals. The most important objections refer to some version of a mutuality argument according to which only those individuals have a moral status who are capable of respecting this status in other individuals as well. Thus, in order to be a moral patient, one must also be a moral agent. This requires capacities such as rationality and ability to contract (Carruthers, 2011), communication-oriented use of language (Habermas, 1993), and compliance with self-given moral laws (Kant, 1785/1998). Because animals lack these abilities, they do not deserve moral consideration for their own sake.

Animal ethicists contest the presumed strict reciprocal character of morals with two arguments. First, if only rational and/ or morally reasonable persons could have a moral status, consequently even humans such as small children and seriously cognitively disabled adults would not matter morally for their own sake, but only insofar as mature persons show sympathy for their fate. This, however, is counterintuitive and incompatible with the social scope of human rights (Cavalieri, 2002; Machan, 2004; Regan, 1984 is critical of this "argument from marginal cases"). Second, even rational and reasonable persons do not restrict their moral claims to those "higher abilities" that enable them to morally reciprocate. They also expect

consideration as embodied and social creatures, with corresponding physical and social needs (Korsgaard, 2011; Ladwig, 2020). But if we take characteristics such as the capacity to feel pain or to suffer from social isolation as morally relevant in our own case, it seems arbitrary to morally neglect it in the case of other animals. Some philosophers even argue that the moral status of sentient animals is the same as our own and, thus, we must accept animal rights equally alongside human rights (Cavalieri, 2002; Cochrane, 2013; Francione, 2008; Regan, 1984; for criticism, see Cohen, 2004).

But perhaps weaker assumptions are sufficient to arrive at, or at least come close to, vegan conclusions (Engel, 2000; Hooley & Nobis, 2016). In everyday morality as well as in law there is a growing consensus that sentient animals matter morally for their own sake (Smith, 2016). Thus, harming animals requires justifying reasons that are proportionate to the losses we impose on them. Take article 1 of the German Animal Welfare Law. It states that "[n]o one may cause an animal pain, suffering or harm without good reason."[12] The requirement of "good reasons," however, is not restricted to morally valid considerations such as serious conflicts between the vital interests of humans and the comparably vital interests of animals. Instead, it allows purely economic considerations such as the mass production of animal products at low costs.

This could only qualify as a genuine moral concern if humans were existentially dependent upon such products. After all, countless animals are confined, hurt, and killed in order to sell and consume their products or their flesh. But there is broad consensus among nutritionists that vegetarian diets are appropriate for all humans during all stages of life and that also vegan diets are nutritionally adequate at least for healthy adults as long as these are supplemented with vitamin B12 in particular (see Craig, 2009 and the literature in Section 4.1). Thus, humans could give up at least a large part of animal products, particularly in affluent societies, and still be capable of leading good and healthy lives. And given that animals matter morally for their own sake, we should not harm them unnecessarily, for example, by purchasing and consuming animal products that we do not vitally need. This might be the strongest case for an obligation to adopt a vegan lifestyle, at least inasmuch as consumers can avoid animal products without a risk of serious harm for themselves.

4. Criticisms of Vegan Consumerism

These moral reasons notwithstanding, there are a number of objections to vegan consumer activism. First, it can be questioned whether veganism is a healthy and accessible option for all, including infants or pregnant women (Section 4.1). Second, one could criticize vegan consumer campaigns as lacking democratic legitimacy (Section 4.2). Even if one grants, however, that vegan consumer activism is permissible, one might still deny that it is appropriate or even obligatory given that it might be causally ineffective (Section 4.3) or clash with stable features of our collective way of life (Section 4.4).

4.1 Are Vegan Diets Healthy and Accessible for All?

In order to be morally recommended or even obligatory for all, vegan consumerism must be generally reasonable. This is clearly the case with products such as fur or leather, on condition that there are sufficient clothing alternatives available at affordable prices. But is a vegan diet really suitable for all? According to the American Academy of Nutrition and Dietetics, well-planned vegetarian diets,

including vegan ones, "are appropriate for individuals during all stages of the lifecycle, including pregnancy, lactation, infancy, childhood, and adolescence, and for athletes …" (Melina, Craig, & Levine, 2016). This position is shared by the Australian National Health and Medical Research Council (2013), and the Portuguese National Programme for the Promotion of a Healthy Diet (2015). It is nevertheless not beyond professional dispute. For example, the German Nutrition Society (2016) does not recommend a vegan diet "during pregnancy or lactation, or for children or adolescents of any age."

The dispute seems to concern mainly two points. First, should we really be confident that all vegan parents and their children take sufficient care to plan a well-balanced vegan diet? Even though *most* vegans are particularly well-informed about nutritional matters and also take above average care of their and their relative's health (Bedford & Barr, 2005), there might be some of them that are unduly negligent. Second, because there are too few long-term studies on the health of vegans (Appleby & Key, 2016), some nutritionists are more reserved than others about declaring a vegan diet non-harmful for all sections of the population. Thus, even if the animal industry harms sentient animals, other humans and the environment, and even if it is a valid moral conclusion that we should, as far as possible *and reasonable*, avoid purchasing products from that industry, there might still be rational disagreement about whether or to what extent this entails vegan consumerism.

4.2 Is Vegan Consumer Activism Democratically Legitimate (and Does It Need to Be)?

Individual purchasing choices, which reflect the diverse values, preferences, and tastes of consumers, do not generally face a high justificatory burden. Individuals are arguably at considerable liberty to engage in unilateral buycotts and boycotts of products and services. The same cannot be said for organized consumer activism, however. Examples such as the boycott of Jewish stores in Nazi Germany show that organized boycotts can rest on unacceptable moral premises, can exercise immense social pressure on their targets and can do profound economic harm to them. It is therefore plausible to demand that organized consumer campaigns comply with certain normative criteria in order to be legitimate. The exact determination of these criteria, however, is a more controversial matter.

Waheed Hussain defends a "proto-legislative view," according to which "social change ethical consumerism" must not deprive other citizens of their basic liberties, must be based on a reasonable conception of the common good, must only deal with issues that have not been addressed in formal democratic processes, and must be guided in a manner that is appropriately representative and deliberative (Hussain, 2012). Vegan consumer campaigns that seek to abolish factory farming, or even all animal husbandry, would accordingly not be legitimate, as they aim at the institutionalized treatment of animals, which is not only addressed in formal democratic procedures but which may enjoy wide public support. However, the criteria put forward by the proto-legislative view are arguably too restrictive, and would not only disqualify vegan consumer activism, but a broad range of other consumer campaigns that appear perfectly legitimate, as well.

Other consumer ethicists thus advocate more relaxed principles for consumer campaigns. Barry and Macdonald (2018) demand that ethical consumerism should be reflective of power disparities, sensitive of the views of those they seek to influence and advance a reasonable conception of the common good.

Beck (2019) argues that organized consumer boycotts should be proportional in the sense of targeting producers who engage in comparatively problematic malpractices, and that they must also be transparent in terms of disclosing accurate information about the identities and agenda of the campaigners and the malpractices that they target. Many consumer campaigns seek to inform formal legislative processes, and they arguably need not restrict themselves to issues that the latter has not yet addressed. The proto-legislative view seems to be based on an idealized conception of the political process, which masks the degree to which power imbalances and corporate interests unduly influence legislation (Barry & MacDonald, 2018). What is more, the two issue areas of intergenerational climate injustice and immoral treatment of animals show that consumer boycotts may legitimately address malpractices that could persist even if the political process were fully democratic (Beck, 2019). After all, neither future people nor animals can raise their own voices in the public space, and thus, their interests must be defended and represented by (other) citizens out of substantive moral considerations.[13]

4.3 Is Vegan Consumption Ineffective?

A common objection to the view that vegan consumerism is morally required is a variant of the so-called *impotence objection*, according to which the contribution of individual consumers to morally problematic states of affairs is negligible. From the perspective of the individual, a single choice or even a series of choices may seem to make "no difference," given that producers and service providers usually operate on large scales and are therefore unlikely to be responsive to the quantities involved in individual consumption patterns. This "causal impotence problem" equally applies to individual vegan consumer choices.

After all, the markets for animal products are large and complex, and the suppliers do not produce on demand (in relation to vegetarianism, see e.g., Regan, 1980; for restatements, see Chartier, 2006; Garrett, 2007; Kagan, 2011).

Given the impotence problem, some moral theorists argue that individual consumers have no moral obligation to avoid choices that yield problematic aggregate outcomes (see Johnson, 2003; Sinnott-Armstrong, 2005; in relation to meat purchase see Chartier, 2006). The costs of veganism for the individual consumer may even look unreasonably high in relation to its allegedly insignificant effect on the macro level. The causal impotence objection poses a challenge to consequentialist reasoning and to act-consequentialism in particular, which postulates that those individual acts are morally right which yield the best expected outcomes. However, some consequentialists have responded to this challenge by providing threshold arguments, according to which the expected or likely utility of (failing to) cross thresholds with their choice still gives individuals moral reason to either engage in or refrain from a consumer choice in question, even though they cannot be certain that they will make a difference with this particular choice.[14] This reasoning can be applied to negative thresholds, such as when diminished demand leads to the closure of a factory farm, but also to positive thresholds, such as when vegan products in high demand become part of or take up a larger share of the product portfolio of a supermarket chain. Additionally, consequentialists have sought to justify the interactional component of ethical consumerism with appeals to indirect consequences, most importantly through the role-modeling effects of individual consumer interactions (Almassi, 2011). In particular, vegans can serve as role models even for vegetarians or reducetarians because of their consistent

behavior and thus their credibility as ethically concerned consumers (Almassi, 2011).

The impotence objection is less challenging to virtue ethical reasoning, which is mostly concerned with the moral character expressed through consumer choices (Nobis, 2002), and to deontological reasoning, which requires agents to act according to universalizable maxims. This can lead to at least imperfect obligations to engage in or refrain from acts even when these acts would fail to "make a difference" in the causal sense just outlined (Albertzart, 2019; Baatz, 2014). Christine Korsgaard argues that we should be morally concerned about how we are related to particular animals if we consume their flesh or products that have been extracted from them without due regard to their good. If we decide to buy and consume such products, we treat individuals as mere means to our ends, and this is morally wrong irrespective of consequences and numbers (Korsgaard, 2018, p. 223). Hereth (2016) assumes that we should refrain from rewarding injustice and that we fail to do so if we purchase or consume the products of animals who have been wronged.

4.4 Does Vegan Consumption Clash with Our Collective Way of Life?

Finally, vegan consumer campaigns might also be insufficiently effective, because they meet with strong ideological and emotional resistance. According to Joy (2010), consuming animal products is considered as normal, natural, and necessary. This ideology begins to influence almost all of us from early childhood on, and it not only affects our thoughts and perceptions but also our emotions. Especially with experiences of eating, people associate formative memories such as visits to grandparents, holidays and festivals. For most people, it is difficult to recognize, and perhaps even harder to dissociate oneself from, a wrongdoing if it encompasses a collective way of life.

Thus, it might be more promising to motivate people to take the moderate steps of adopting vegetarianism or reducetarianism, instead of insisting on the move to veganism (see de Bakker & Dagevos, 2012 and, using the example of Finland, Vinnari, Mustonen, & Räsänen, 2010). After all, not a few morally motivated consumers began as reducetarians or vegetarians before finally turning to veganism. What is more, even if most of the world's population, in particular the growing middle classes and wealthy people, only significantly reduced their intake of animal products the aggregate positive effect would outweigh that of all current vegetarians and vegans. Perhaps it is also easier for many people to engage in political activism for more animal friendly laws and structures than to accept the personal consequences of vegan consumerism.

As mentioned above, the impact of vegan consumption depends not least on role-modeling effects (see Almassi, 2011; for empirical treatment, see Higgs, 2015). Perhaps the most important effect of that sort is signaling one's willingness to engage in collective action (for the general point, see Lawford-Smith, 2015). Vegan buycotts thus transmit to the political sphere, revealing the political component of ethical consumerism (Garner, 2010, pp. 154–162; Stallwood, 2008). But campaigns for political and social change are most likely to succeed if they are supported by large coalitions of more and less radical actors. Thus, vegans have good reasons to welcome other, more moderate fellow campaigners as long as they support urgent reforms. An obvious goal suitable for coalition building among actors ranging from small farmers and environmentalists to vegan activists would be the elimination of factory farming (Garner, 2010, p. 159; Pluhar, 2010).

5. Conclusion

The arguments presented in this article ultimately concern the question of whether a commitment to animal ethics, human rights, and/or climate justice entails the duty to adopt a vegan lifestyle. The answer first of all depends upon the strength of the arguments from animal ethics, because anthropocentric arguments only support reducing the consumption of animal products, and transforming the methods of production. In animal ethics, different arguments justify the conclusion that we act immorally if we impose suffering or death on animals to extract products that we do not need for leading good and healthy lives. This brings us closer to vegan conclusions, although we might still doubt whether vegan diets are healthy and accessible options for all, including for poor people in developing countries and groups such as pregnant women even in affluent societies.

Second, we must consider the legitimacy and the effectiveness of vegan consumerism as a means to improve morally problematic states of affairs. But whereas proportionate and transparent vegan consumer campaigns can be a permissible method to strive for social and political reform, the impotence objection turns out to be more problematic. However, it poses greater problems for consequentialists who argue that the moral value of a conduct is always ultimately determined by its (likely) consequences than for virtue ethicists and deontologists who hold that it is inherently wrong to support a wrongdoing.

Insofar as consequences matter, however, a larger number of vegetarians or reducetarians might make a greater difference than a comparatively small number of vegans. The latter should see their consumer behavior not least as a potential trigger for collective action. Thus, they should avoid giving the impression of a sectarian insistence in personal purity.

Self-righteousness is not only a vice; it is an obstacle to political coalition-building on which morally required reforms ultimately depend.

Acknowledgment

Open access funding enabled and organized by Projekt DEAL.

Questions

1. The authors question whether veganism has an effect on ending the many harms of the consumption of factory-farmed animals. Should the effectiveness of not participating in a harmful behavior (such as ending the harm) be part of an ethical consideration? In other words, climate change continues even though one reduces one's greenhouse gas consumption. Is the morality of one's actions determined by whether they can fix the problem? (You may find Kant's universalization categorical imperative helpful when answering this question.)

2. What are reducetarian, pescetarian, vegetarian, and vegan diets? How might the first three bring about a greater measure of lessening harm than a few vegans? How might a utilitarian then argue for veganism (the authors use consequentialist theory, but a Mill utilitarian holds justice as the highest value, not mere aggregate results).

3. What is the difference between a buycott and a boycott? What is the authors' definition of ethical consumerism? Do we have an ethical/moral duty to be ethical consumers?

References

Albertzart, M. (2019). A Kantian solution to the problem of imperceptible differences. *European Journal of Philosophy, 27*(4), 837–851.

Almassi, B. (2011). The consequences of individual consumption: A defence of threshold arguments for vegetarianism and consumer ethics. *Journal of Applied Philosophy, 28*(4), 396–411.

Appleby, P. N., & Key, T. J. (2016). The long-term health of vegetarians and vegans. *Proceedings of the Nutrition Society, 75*(3), 287–293.

Aragon, C., & Jaggar, A. M. (2018). Agency, complicity, and the responsibility to resist structural injustice. *Journal of Social Philosophy, 49*(3), 439–460.

Baatz, C. (2014). Climate change and individual duties to reduce GHG emissions. *Ethics, Policy & Environment, 17*(1), 1–19.

Bajželj, B., Richards, K. S., Allwood, J. M., Smith, P., Dennis, J. S., Curmi, E., & Gilligan, C. A. (2014). Importance of food-demand management for climate mitigation. *Nature Climate Change, 4*(10), 924–929.

Barry, C., & Macdonald, K. (2018). Ethical consumerism: A defense of market vigilantism. *Philosophy & Public Affairs, 46*(3), 293–322.

Beck, V. (2010). Theorizing Fairtrade from a justice-related standpoint. *Global Justice: Theory Practice Rhetoric, 3*, 1–21.

Beck, V. (2016). *Eine Theorie der globalen Verantwortung: Was wir Menschen in extremer Armut schulden.* Berlin: Suhrkamp.

Beck, V. (2019). Consumer boycotts as instruments for structural change. *Journal of Applied Philosophy, 36*(4), 543–559.

Bedford, J. L., & Barr, S. I. (2005). Diets and selected lifestyle practices of self-defined adult vegetarians from a population-based sample suggest they are more 'health conscious'. *International Journal of*

Behavioural Nutrition and Physical Activity, 2(1), 4. https://doi.org/10.1186/1479–5868-2-4

Braithwaite, V. (2010). *Do fish feel pain?* Oxford: Oxford University Press.

Caney, S. (2018). Climate change. In S. Olsaretti (Ed.), *The Oxford handbook of distributive justice.* Oxford: Oxford University Press.

Carruthers, P. (2011). Against the moral standing of animals. In C. Morris (Ed.), *Questions of life and death. Readings in practical ethics* (pp. 274–284). Oxford: Oxford University Press.

Cavalieri, P. (2002). *The animal question: Why non-human animals deserve human rights.* Oxford: Oxford University Press.

Chai, B. C., van der Voort, J. R., Grofelnik, K., Eliasdottir, H. G., Klöss, I., & Perez-Cueto, F. J. A. (2019). Which diet has the least environmental impact on our planet? A systematic review of vegan, vegetarian and omnivorous diets. *Sustainability, 11*(15), 4110.

Chait, J. (2019). Is organic livestock production more humane? *The Balance Small Business.* https://www.thebalancesmb.com/is-organic-livestock-production-more-humane-2538119

Chartier, G. (2006). On the threshold argument against consumer meat purchases. *Journal of Social Philosophy, 37*(2), 233–249.

Cochrane, A. (2013). From human rights to sentient rights. *Critical Review of Social and Political Philosophy, 16*(5), 655–675.

Cochrane, A. (2018). *Sentientist politics. A theory of global inter-species justice.* Oxford: Oxford University Press.

Cohen, C. (2004). A critique of the alleged moral basis of vegetarianism. In S. Sapontzis (Ed.), *Food for thought: The debate over eating meat.* Amherst, NY: Prometheus Books.

Compassion in World Farming. (2012). *The life of: Dairy cows.* https://www.ciwf.org.uk/media/5235185/the-life-of-dairy-cows.pdf

Craig, W. J. (2009). Health effects of vegan diets. *The American Journal of Clinical Nutrition, 89*(5), 1627S–1633S.

de Bakker, E., & Dagevos, H. (2012). Reducing meat consumption in today's consumer society: Questioning the citizen–consumer gap. *Journal of Agricultural and Environmental Ethics, 25*, 877–894. https://doi.org/10.1007/s10806-011-9345-z

Doggett, T. (2018). Moral vegetarianism. In E. N. Zalta (Ed.), *The Stanford encyclopedia of philosophy.* Stanford, CA: The Metaphysics Research Lab. (Fall 2018 ed.) https://plato.stanford.edu/archives/fall2018/entries/vegetarianism/

Donaldson, S., & Kymlicka, W. (2011). *Zoopolis: A political theory of animal rights.* Oxford: Oxford University Press.

Driver, J. (2015). Individual consumption and moral complicity. In B. Bramble & B. Fischer (Eds.), *The moral complexities of eating meat* (pp. 67–79). New York: Oxford University Press.

Eckersley, R. (2016). Responsibility for climate change as a structural injustice. In T. Gabrielson, C. Hall, J. M. Meyer, & D. Schlosberg (Eds.), *The Oxford handbook of environmental political theory* (pp. 346–361). Oxford: Oxford University Press.

Eisnitz, G. (1997). *Slaughterhouse: The shocking story of greed, neglect, and inhumane treatment inside the U.S. meat industry.* Amherst, NY: Prometheus Books.

Engel, M. (2000). The immorality of eating meat. In L. P. Pojman (Ed.), *The moral life: An introductory reader in ethics and literature.* New York: Oxford University Press.

FAO. (2013). *Tackling climate change through livestock: A global assessment of emissions and mitigation opportunities.* Rome: Food and Agriculture Organization of the United Nations.

FAO. (2016). *State of the world forests.* Rome: Food and Agriculture Organization of the United Nations.

Fragnière, A. (2016). Climate change and individual duties. *WIREs: Climate Change, 7*(6), 798–814.

Francione, G. L. (2008). *Animals as persons: Essays on the abolition of animal exploitation.* New York: Columbia University Press.

Friedman, M. (1999). *Consumer boycotts: Effecting change through the marketplace and the media.* New York/London: Routledge.

Friedman, M. (2001). Ethical dilemmas associated with consumer boycotts. *Journal of Social Philosophy, 32*(2), 232–240.

Garcia-Ruiz, P., & Rodriguez-Lluesma, C. (2014). Consumption practices: A virtue ethics approach. *Business Ethics Quarterly, 24*(4), 509–531.

Garner, R. (2010). A defense of broad animal protectionism. In G. Francione & R. Garner (Eds.), *The animal rights debate. Abolition or regulation?* (pp. 103–174). New York: Columbia University Press.

Garner, R. (2013). *A theory of justice for animals. Animal rights in a nonideal world.* New York: Oxford University Press.

Garnett, T., Godde, C., Muller, A., Röös, E., Smith, P., de Boer, I., ... van Zanten, H. (2017). Grazed and confused? *Food Climate Research Network.* https://www.fcrn.org.uk/sites/default/files/project-files/fcrn_gnc_report.pdf

Garrett, J. R. (2007). Utilitarianism, vegetarianism, and human health: A response to the causal impotence objection. *Journal of Applied Philosophy, 24*(3), 223–237.

German Nutrition Society. (2016). Vegan diet. *Ernaehrungs Umschau international 4.* https://www.ernaehrungs-umschau.de/fileadmin/Ernaehrungs-Umschau/pdfs/pdf_2016/04_16/EU04_2016_Special_DGE_eng_final.pdf

Gruen, L., & Jones, R. C. (2015). Veganism as an aspiration. In B. Bramble & B. Smith (Eds.), *The moral complexities of eating meat* (pp. 153–171). New York: Oxford University Press.

Habermas, J. (1993). Remarks on discourse ethics. In C. Cronin (trans.), *Justification and application* (pp. 19–112). Cambridge: MIT Press.

Halteman, M. C. (2011). Varieties of harm to animals in industrial farming. *Journal of Animal Ethics, 1*(2), 122–131.

Harwatt, H., Sabaté, J., Eshel, G., Soret, S., & Ripple, W. (2017). Substituting beans for beef as a contribution toward US climate change targets. *Climatic Change, 143,* 261–270.

Hereth, B. (2016). Animals and causal impotence: A deontological view. *Between the Species, 19*(1), 32–51.

Herzog, L. (2016). Who should prevent sweatshops? Duties, excuses, and the division of moral labour in the global economy. In H.-C. Schmidt am Busch (Ed.), *Die Philosophie des Marktes (The philosophy of the market)* (pp. 255–278). Hamburg: Meiner.

Higgs, S. (2015). Social norms and their influence on eating behaviors. *Appetite, 86*(1), 38–44.

Hooley, D., & Nobis, N. (2016). A moral argument for veganism. In A. Chignell, T. Cuneo, & M. C. Halteman (Eds.), *Philosophy comes to dinner: Arguments about the ethics of eating* (pp. 92–108). London, England: Routledge.

Hussain, W. (2012). Is ethical consumerism an impermissible form of vigilantism? *Philosophy & Public Affairs, 40*(2), 111–143.

Jacob, D., Ladwig, B., & Schmelzle, C. (2018). Normative political theory. In T. Risse, T. Börzel, & A. Draude (Eds.), *The Oxford handbook of governance and limited statehood* (pp. 564–583). Oxford: Oxford University Press.

Jallinoja, P., Vinnari, M., & Niva, M. (2019). Veganism and plant-based eating: Analysis of interplay between discursive strategies and lifestyle political consumerism. In M. Boström, M. Micheletti, & P. Oosterveer (Eds.), *The Oxford handbook of political consumerism* (pp. 157–179). Oxford: Oxford University Press.

Johnson, B. (2003). Ethical obligations in a tragedy of the commons. *Environmental Values, 12*(3), 271–287.

Joy, M. (2010). *Why we love dogs, eat pigs, and wear cows. An introduction to carnism.* San Francisco: Conari Press.

Juhola, S. K. (2019). Responsibility for climate change adaption. *WIREs: Climate Change, 10*(5), 1–13.

Kagan, S. (2011). Do I make a difference? *Philosophy and Public Affairs, 39*(2), 105–141.

Kant, I. (1785/1998). In M. Gregor (trans.), *Groundwork of the metaphysics of morals.* Cambridge: Cambridge University Press.

Katz, C., & McPherson, T. (2020). Veganism as a food ethic. In H. Meiselman (Ed.), *Handbook of eating and drinking. Interdisciplinary perspectives* (pp. 1137–1155). Berlin, Germany: Springer.

Kerschke-Risch, P. (2015). Vegan diet: Motives, approach and duration. Initial results of a quantitative sociological study. *Ernaehrungs Umschau*, *62*(6), 98–103.

Key, B. (2016). Why fish do not feel pain. *Animal Sentience, 3*(1), 1–33.

Kolers, A. (2001). Ethical investing: The permissibility of participation. *Journal of Political Philosophy*, *9*(4), 435–452.

Korsgaard, C. (2011). Interacting with animals: A Kantian account. In T. Beauchamp & R. G. Frey (Eds.), *The Oxford handbook of animal ethics* (pp. 91–117). Oxford: Oxford University Press.

Korsgaard, C. (2018). *Fellow creatures. Our obligations to the other animals.* Oxford: Oxford University Press.

Kutz, C. (2000). *Complicity: Ethics and law for a collective age.* Cambridge: Cambridge University Press.

Ladwig, B. (2020). *Politische Philosophie der Tierrechte.* Berlin: Suhrkamp.

Lawford-Smith, H. (2015). Unethical consumption and obligations to signal. *Ethics & International Affairs, 29*(3), 315–330.

Lepora, C., & Goodin, R. E. (2013). *On complicity and compromise.* New York: Oxford University Press.

Lewis, T., & Potter, E. (Eds.). (2011). *Ethical consumption: A critical introduction.* London/New York: Routledge.

Machan, T. (2004). *Putting humans first. Why we are nature's favorite.* Lanham/Boulder/New York/Toronto/Oxford: Rowman & Littlefield.

Mann, M. E. (2020). How to win the new climate war. *Sceptical Enquirer, 44*(2), 18–19.

Mekonnen, M. M., & Hoekstra, A. Y. (2012). A global assessment of the water footprint of farm animal products. *Ecosystems, 15*, 401–415.

Melina, V., Craig, W., & Levin, S. (2016). Position of the academy of nutrition and dietetics: Vegetarian diets. *Journal of the Academy of Nutrition Dietetics, 116*(12), 1970–1980. https://jandonline.org/article/S2212–2672(16)31192–3/fulltext

Mills, C. (1996). Should we boycott boycotts? *Journal of Social Philosophy, 27*(3), 136–148.

Moellendorf, D. (2012). Climate change and global justice. *WIREs: Climate Change, 3*(2), 131–143.

Mottet, A., de Haan, C., Falcucci, A., Tempio, G., Opio, C., & Gerber, P. (2017). Livestock: On our plates or eating at our table? A new analysis of the feed/food debate. *Global Food Security, 14*, 1–8.

National Health and Medical Research Council. (2013). *Eat for health. Australian dietary guidelines.* Canberra. https://www.eatforhealth.gov.au/

National Programme for the Promotion of a Healthy Diet. (2015). Direção Geral da Saúde (Ed.). *Guidelines for a healthy vegetarian diet.* Lisboa. https://www.researchgate.net/publication/289108166_Guidelines_for_a_healthy_vegetarian_diet

Nefsky, J. (2018). Consumer choice and collective impact. In A. Barnhill, M. Budolfson, & T. Doggett (Eds.), *The Oxford handbook of food ethics* (Vol. 2018, pp. 267–286). Oxford: Oxford University Press.

Nobis, N. (2002). Vegetarianism and virtue: Does consequentialism demand too little? *Social Theory and Practice, 28*(1), 135–156.

Norcross, A. (2004). Puppies, pigs, and people: Eating meat and marginal cases. *Philosophical Perspectives, 18*, 229–245.

OECD. (2016). *Antimicrobial resistance—Policy insights.* https://www.oecd.org/health/health-systems/AMR-Policy-Insights-November2016.pdf

O'Neill, O. (2001). Agents of justice. *Metaphilosophy, 32*(1–2), 180–195.

Pachirat, T. (2011). *Every twelve seconds. Industrialized slaughter and the politics of sight.* New Haven/London: Yale University Press.

Peters, A. (2016). Global animal law: What it is and why we need it. *Transnational Environmental Law, 5*(1), 9–23.

Pinkert, F. (2015). What if I cannot make a difference (and know it)? *Ethics, 125*(4), 971–998.

Pluhar, E. (2010). Meat and morality: Alternatives to factory farming. *Journal of Agricultural and Environmental Ethics, 23*, 455–468.

Poore, J., & Nemecek, T. (2018). Reducing food's environmental impacts through producers and consumers. *Science, 360*(6392), 987–992. https://doi.org/10.1126/science.aaq0216

Radzik, L. (2017). Boycotts and the social enforcement of justice. *Social Philosophy & Policy, 34*(1), 102–122.

Rawls, J. (1971). *A theory of justice.* Oxford: Oxford University Press.

Rawls, J. (1993). *Political liberalism.* New York: Columbia University Press.

Rawls, J. (1999). *The law of peoples.* Cambridge, MA: Harvard University Press.

Regan, T. (1980). Utilitarianism, vegetarianism and animal rights. *Philosophy & Public Affairs, 9*(4), 305–324.

Regan, T. (1984). *The case for animal rights.* London: Routledge.

Rosenfeld, D. L. (2018). The psychology of vegetarianism: Recent advances and future directions. *Appetite, 131*, 125–138.

Roser, D., & Seidel, C. (2016). *Climate justice: An introduction.* Oxon and New York: Routledge.

Rosi, A., Mena, P., Pellegrini, N., Turroni, S., Neviani, E., Ferrocino, I., … Scazzina, F. (2017). Environmental impact of omnivorous, ovo-lacto-vegetarian, and vegan diet. *Scientific Reports, 7*, 6105.

Scarborough, P., Appleby, P. N., Mizdrak, A., Briggs, A. D. M., Travis, R. C., Bradbury, K. E., & Key, T. J. (2014). Dietary greenhouse gas emissions of meat-eaters, fish-eaters, vegetarians and vegans in the UK. *Climatic Change, 125*(2), 179–192.

Schwartz, D. (2010). *Consuming choices: Ethics in a global consumer age.* Lanham: Rowman & Littlefield.

Segner, H. (2012). *Fish. Nociception and pain. A biological perspective.* Bern: Federal Office for Buildings and Logistics.

Singer, P. (1980). Utilitarianism and vegetarianism. *Philosophy & Public Affairs, 9*(4), 325–337.

Sinnott-Armstrong, W. (2005). It's not my fault: global warming and individual moral obligations. In W. Sinnott-Armstrong & R. Howarth (Eds.), *Perspectives on cimate change. Scinece, economics, politics, ethics* (pp. 285–307). Bingley, England: Emerald Group Publishing Limited.

Smith, K. (2016). A public philosophy for the liberal animal welfare state. In R. Garner & S. O'Sullivan (Eds.), *The political turn in animal ethics* (pp. 69–84). New York: Rowman & Littlefield.

Stallwood, K. (2008). The animal rights challenge. Paper presented at the *Minding Animals Conference*, London, December 2008.

Stolle, D., & Micheletti, M. (2013). *Political consumerism: Global responsibility in action.* Cambridge: Cambridge University Press.

The Vegan Society. (2020). *Definition of veganism.* https://www.vegansociety.com/go-vegan/definition-veganism

UNESCO. (2017). *The United Nations world water development report 2017. Wastewater: The untapped resource.* Paris.

Vegan Official Labels. (2020). *Indexing of official vegan certification around the world.* http://vegan-labels.info/

Vinnari, M., Mustonen, P., & Räsänen, P. (2010). Tracking down trends in non-meat consumption in Finnish households, 1966–2006. *British Food Journal, 112*(8), 836–852. https://doi.org/10.1108/00070701011067451

Wagner, K., Barth, K., Palme, R., Futschik, A., & Waiblinger, S. (2012). Integration into the dairy cow-herd: Long term effects of mother contact during the first twelve weeks of life. *Applied Animal Behavior Science, 14*(3–4), S117–S129.

Young, I. M. (2011). *Responsibility for justice.* Oxford: Oxford University Press.

Notes

1. It is often argued that state governments bear a "primary responsibility" to achieve goals that require collective action, although this should not be understood to mean that *only* states bear such a responsibility. For a discussion of different kinds of agents of justice and their relation to each other under non-ideal conditions, see O'Neill (2001) and Jacob, Ladwig, & Schmelzle, 2018.

2. For a treatment of ethical questions concerning investment, see Kolers (2001).

3. For a normative perspective on the Fairtrade certification system, see for example, Beck (2010).

4. For empirical treatments of ethical consumerism, see Friedman (1999), Lewis and Potter (2011), and Stolle and Micheletti (2013).

5. These views can be found in the literature on climate ethics, specifically in treatments of the question of whether there is an individual duty to reduce GHG emissions (for an overview, see Fragnière, 2016), and in texts that deal with individual consumer responsibility more generally (for an overview of these issues, see Schwartz, 2010).

6. The distinction between ideal and non-ideal theory goes back to Rawls (1971, 1999). For an application to the treatment of animals, see Garner (2013) and Ladwig (2020).

7. Rawls argued in favor of individual natural duties to promote and maintain just institutions (see 1971, 1993, 1999). Young (2011) stressed the transnational nature of the responsibility to rectify injustices to which we are socially connected, which include (but are not limited to) widespread labor rights violations in the supply chain of globally produced goods. Beck (2016) elaborates an account of global responsibility to promote human rights and fight poverty through institutional and structural reforms.

8. On complicity in general see Kutz (2000) and Lepora and Goodin (2013); on complicity in structures, see Aragon and Jaggar (2018); in relation to climate change, see Eckersley (2016); regarding animal products, see Driver (2015).

9. The Vegan Society is the oldest organization supporting veganism. It was founded in 1944 in Great Britain.

10. The pain of separation seems to increase with the length of cohabitation. On the other hand, it is normally beneficial for both cows and their calves to closely cohabitate for a longer period of time, so an early separation deprives them of a worthwhile experience; see Wagner, Barth, Palme, Futschik, and Waiblinger (2012).

11. However, this would require that no additional grazing land is created by deforestation. On the net impact of grazing systems on GHG emissions, see Garnett et al. (2017).

12. https://www.animallaw.info/statute/germany-cruelty-german-animal-welfare-act

13. On possible political representation of animals see Donaldson and Kymlicka (2011), Cochrane (2018), and Ladwig (2020).

14. For different versions of this argument, see Singer (1980), Norcross (2004), Kagan (2011), Roser and Seidel (2016); see Almassi (2011) and Pinkert (2015) for different act-consequentialist defenses of ethical consumerism. However, see Nefsky (2018), for objections to defenses that involve threshold reasoning.

Chapter 7: Challenging Consumption

Introduction

con•sume to eat or drink up/to destroy by burning/to waste or absorb/eaten up or as if eaten up[1]

con•sump•tion a consuming/an amount consumed/the use and enjoyment of goods and services by consumers or producers/tuberculosis of the lungs[2]

"... the vast appetite the United States has developed for materials of all kinds.... This gargantuan and growing appetite.... But what of the appetite itself? Surely this is the ultimate source of the problem. If it continues its geometric course, will it not one day have to be restrained?"[3]

"It is also suggested that uninhibited consumption has something to do with individual liberty. If we begin interfering with consumption, we shall be abridging a basic freedom."[4]

WHAT IF BY NOT purchasing something you could avoid contributing to, or partially funding, human rights violations, environmental degradation, global warming, transgenic biotechnology, displacement of Indigenous people, factory-farmed animal suffering, and hazardous workplace conditions? Each act of consumption has a corresponding environmental cost, and from the 1950s forward, consumption has drastically increased yet has not been correspondingly widely (i.e., in the mainstream) critically analyzed.

Consider one aspect of increased consumption: food. On average, citizens in the United States consume grain at more than four times a subsistence level, in part due to the conversion cost of feeding animals grain and then consuming meat. Consider energy consumption, its harmful consequences, and the US global role. The United States, with less than 5 per cent of the world's population, makes up over 20 per cent of global energy consumption. The United States is thus also a disproportionate source of all fossil-fuel emissions, nuclear waste, and the corresponding risks and harms. Consumption of fossil fuels, specifically the carbon dioxide released from burning fossil fuel, is causally correlated with climate change. The consequences are many and include agricultural damage, rising water levels, heatwaves, other severe weather, and increased cancer rates.

Long concerned about mounting evidence of global warming, in the 1980s various United Nations agency members organized a number of international scientific conferences that resulted in the issue being placed on the United Nations' World Meteorological Office's agenda. As a result, the Intergovernmental Panel on Climate Change (IPCC) was established in 1988. In 1990, the United Nations' Intergovernmental Negotiating Committee for a Framework Convention on Climate Change (INC) began negotiating an agreement that was available for signatures at the Earth Summit in Rio de Janeiro in 1992. The objective of the "Framework Convention" was to begin to stabilize greenhouse gas atmospheric levels, in part by returning to the 1990 emission levels, yet it did not contain any binding targets or measures. Emissions continued to rise, and the parties to the Framework continued to meet to address how to limit emissions. The third major meeting was held in Kyoto, Japan, in December 1997. The "Kyoto Protocol" of the Framework Convention was adopted on December 11, 1997. The Kyoto Protocol set emissions targets for industrialized countries to reduce emissions to 5 per cent lower than 1990. "Developing" countries were not given quantified targets. The United States did not sign the Protocol, and a Senate resolution in 1997 stated that the United States would not sign any protocol that "would result in serious harm *to the economy* of the United States."[5]

At a minimum, integrity is an issue. Integrity is what results when our ideals as citizens are reflected in our lives, as a consumer, in voting, in our actions as a global citizen, and so forth, and when we take responsibility for our actions. Our first citizenship on earth is as a member of the human species, as a biotic citizen, a member of the local and global interlocking ecosystems. We lack integrity when we do not live by our values. One of our values can be found in major tomes in the Western tradition, from those that espouse Judeo-Christian values, including the Ten Commandments, to John Locke's justification for private property, to Leopold's land ethic. The values are expressed, in part, as prohibitions against avarice, arrogance, gluttony, and so on. The major value expressed is to not take more than one needs to live, especially in the face of those who do not have access to meet their basic needs. To act in any other way is to deny the right to life of those without access. This behavior and its acrobatic justifications that result in not following the value for life are reflected in expenditures on military protection of a consumer lifestyle.

As Robert Goodland writes (in his essay in this chapter), "Many nations spend less on environment, health, education, and welfare than they do on arms.... Global security is increasingly prejudiced by source and sink constraints as recent natural resource wars have shown.... As soon as damage to global life-support systems is perceived as far riskier than military threats, more prudent reallocation will promptly follow." To that point, our global life-support systems are threatened, nearly at an irreversible point, yet actions of those like the United States are illustrative of the military spending that Goodland cites. And it is at least an important avenue of inquiry to ask what the connection is between consumption, environmental degradation, and war, especially wars concerning fossil (coal, oil, natural gas) fuel.

As is clear from this chapter, since the 1950s questions about consumption and its ties to the environment, economy, and individual autonomy have been raised amidst the ever-increasing consumption of a growing global population. Data, statistics, evidence of environmental harm, and rational arguments have not effectively dented consumption. The psychology of consumption is crucial to understand, for consumption, after basic needs are met, is about wants. Needs are objective, can be empirically measured, and can then be satiated. For example, consider the need for water, air, and food. There is an objective, finite, measurable amount of water, air, and food that each human requires to live. Unlike needs, wants are subjective and insatiable. That is, there is no objective measure of them, they are not necessary for life, they can be created (e.g., through advertising), and they are infinite. However, that infinite desire to consume, that appetite, exists in a context of finite resources that are dwindling, and this fact needs "embodiment."

Notes

1. *New Webster's Dictionary and Thesaurus* (Danbury, CT: Lexicon, 1993), 210.
2. Ibid.
3. John Kenneth Galbraith, "How Much Should a Country Consume?" in *Perspectives on Conservation: Essays on America's Natural Resources,* ed. Henry Jarrett (Baltimore: Johns Hopkins University Press, 1958), 89–92.
4. Ibid., 96.
5. The Byrd-Hagel Resolution, Senate Resolution 98, passed by 95 to 0 on July 25, 1997; emphasis mine.

1. How Much Should a Country Consume?[1]

John Kenneth Galbraith

IN 1958, IT WAS already obvious that US consumption was well above the levels of other countries, that pollution and other externalities were beginning to take their toll, and that certain scarce resources would need addressing. Mostly concerned about "security" issues, in 1951, Harry S. Truman established a President's Materials Policy Commission (PMPC) to "make an objective inquiry into all major aspects of the problem of assuring an adequate supply of production materials for our long-range needs and to make recommendations which will assist me in formulating a comprehensive policy on such materials."[2] Truman was concerned that "[w]e cannot allow shortages of materials to jeopardize our national security nor to become a bottleneck to our economic expansion."[3] In this selection, John Kenneth Galbraith (1908–2006) points out that the PMPC's summary report indicated numerous aspects of the consumer society's lavish consumption, such as in the automobile's unnecessary chrome adornment, and leaded gasoline for speed, that could be changed and with a "slight reduction in personal satisfaction ... bring about tremendous savings." However, the commission made no such recommendations, for it was also given "growth" as a charge, and as Galbraith points out, conservation and growth are inconsistent.

I

CONSERVATIONISTS ARE UNQUESTIONABLY USEFUL people. And among the many useful services that they have recently rendered has been that of dramatizing the vast appetite which the United States has developed for materials of all kinds. This increase in requirements we now recognize to be exponential. It is the product of a rapidly increasing population and a high and (normally) rapidly increasing living standard. The one multiplied by the other gives the huge totals with which our minds must contend. The President's Materials Policy Commission[4] emphasized the point by observing that our consumption of raw materials comes to about half that of the non-Communist lands, although we have but 10 percent of the population, and that since World War I our consumption of most materials has exceeded that of all mankind through all history before that conflict.

This gargantuan and growing appetite has become the point of departure for all discussions of the resource problem. In face of this vast use, what is happening to our domestic reserves of ores, to our energy sources, to the renewable resources? Are we being made excessively dependent on foreign supplies?

How can we ensure that they will continue to flow in the necessary volume and with the necessary increases to our shores? How is our security affected?

The high rate of use has catalyzed conservationist activity on many other fronts. Because of it we have been busily assessing reserves of various resources and measuring the rate of depletion against the rate of discovery. We have become concerned with the efficiency of methods of recovery. As a result, for example, of the meteoric increase in natural gas consumption, the prospect for further increase, and the limited supplies at least within the borders of continental United States, we have had an increasing concern over what was flared or otherwise lost. The large requirements and the related exhaustion of domestic reserves support the concern for having ready stocks of materials in the event of national emergency. (Support for this also comes from the not inconsiderable number of people who, in this instance, find prudence a matter of some profit.) Our large fuel requirements have deeply affected our foreign policy even though it remains a canon of modern diplomacy that any preoccupation with oil should be concealed by calling on our still ample reserves of sanctimony.

Finally, and perhaps most important, the high rate of resource use has stirred interest in the technology of resource use and substitution. Scores of products would already have become scarce and expensive had it not been for the appearance of substitute sources of materials or substitute materials. We still think of innovation in terms of the unpredictable and fortuitous genius which was encouraged by the patent office. In fact, input/output relationships for investment in innovation, not in the particular case but in general, are probably about as stable as any other. And investment in such innovation may well substitute, at more or less constant rates, for investment in orthodox discovery and recovery. This means, in less formidable language, that if a country puts enough of its resources into researching new materials or new sources of materials, it may never be short of the old ones. We cannot necessarily rely on the market for this investment—market incentives did not get us synthetic nitrogen, synthetic rubber, or atomic energy—to mention perhaps the three most important new materials substitutes or sources of this century. We shall have to initiate publicly much of the needed innovation, and much of it will have to be carried to the point of commercial feasibility by public funds. We shall have to be watchful to anticipate needed investment in innovation. We will be making another of our comfortable and now nearly classic errors if we assume that it will all be taken care of automatically by the free enterprise system.

But the role of research and innovation is not part of this story. I cite it only because one must do so to keep the resource problem in focus. In the future, as in the past, substitution nurtured by science will be the major hope of the conservationist. I am not unimpressed with the importance of what I have now to say. But I would not wish it thought that I identify all resource salvation therewith.

II

In my opening sentences I spoke agreeably about the conservationist as a citizen. May I now trade on those graceful words and be a trifle rude? Any observer of the species must agree that he is also frequently capable of marked illogicality combined with what may be termed selective myopia. There are many manifestations of this. Nothing, for example, is more impressive than the way the modern conservationist rises in awesome anger—particularly, I think, along the Eastern Seaboard—at a proposal to dam and thus to desecrate some unknown stream in some obscure corner of some remote national park, and at the same time manages to remain unperturbed by the desecration of our highways by the outdoor advertising industry. Were the Governor of New York, in some moment of political aberration to propose a minor modification of the state's "forever wild" proviso as it applies to the state parks, he would be jeopardizing his future. When he seeks to make the highways of his state less hideous, he can hope, at most, for the applause of Robert Moses, the *New York Times*, the most determined garden clubs, and a few eccentrics. One may formulate a law on this: The conservationist is a man who concerns himself with the beauties of nature in roughly inverse proportion to the number of people who can enjoy them.

There is, I sense, a similar selectivity in the conservationist's approach to materials consumption. If we are concerned about our great appetite for materials, it is plausible to seek to increase the supply, to decrease waste, to make better use of the stocks that are available, and to develop substitutes. But what of the appetite itself? Surely this is the ultimate source of the problem. If it continues its geometric course, will it not one day have to be restrained? Yet in the literature of the resource problem this is the forbidden question. Over it hangs a nearly total silence. It is as though, in the discussion of the chance for avoiding automobile accidents, we agree not to make any mention of speed!

I do not wish to overstate my case. A few people have indeed adverted to the possibility of excess resource consumption—and common prudence requires me to allow for discussions which I have not encountered. Samuel H. Ordway in his *Resources and the American Dream*[5] has perhaps gone farthest in inquiring whether, in the interests of resource conservation, some limits might be placed on

consumption. He has wondered if our happiness would be greatly impaired by smaller and less expensive automobiles, less advertising, even less elaborate attire. And he argues, without being very specific about it, that the Congress should face the question of use now as against use by later generations.

By contrast, The Twentieth Century Fund in its effort to match materials and other resource requirements to use, takes present levels of consumption and prospective increases as wholly given. It then adds to prospective needs enough to bring families at the lower end of the income distribution up to a defined minimum. While the authors are, on the whole, sanguine about our ability to meet requirements, they foresee difficulties with petroleum, copper, lead, zinc, and the additive alloys for steel.[6] I would say on the whole that The Twentieth Century Fund's approach represents a kind of norm in such studies.

The President's Materials Policy Commission took a similar, although slightly more ambiguous position, which is worth examining in some slight detail. It began by stating its conviction that economic growth was important and, in degree, sacrosanct. "First, we share the belief of the American people in the principle of Growth."[7] (It is instructive to note the commission's use of a capital G. A certain divinity is associated with the word.) *Growth*, in this context, means an increasing output of consumers' goods and an increase in the plant by which they are supplied. Having started with this renunciation, the commission was scarcely in a position to look critically at consumption in relation to the resource problem, and it did not.

Yet the PMPC could not entirely exclude the problem of consumption from consideration. In the course of its formal recommendations, it asked that the armed services in "designing military products, and in drawing up specifications, focus on using abundant rather than scarce materials, and on using less of any material per unit of product where this can be done without significantly affecting quality or performance." And it asked for "greater emphasis on care and maintenance of military equipment and conservation in use and increase[d] scrap recovery of all kinds."[8] But it almost certainly occurred to the able members of the commission that this was straining furiously at the gnat. Why should we be worried about the excess steel in a tank but not in an automobile? What is gained from smaller radar screens if the materials go into larger TV screens? Why should the general be denied his brass and his wife allowed her plumage? There is an obvious inconsistency here.

As a result, the PMPC did venture on. Although it did not support the observation with any concrete recommendation, it did comment with some vigor on present tendencies in consumption. "The United States," it observed, "has been lavish in the use of its materials…. Vast quantities of materials have been wasted by over-designing and over-specification. We have frequently designed products with little concern for getting maximum service from their materials and labor. We drive heavier automobiles than is necessary for mere transportation, and we adorn them with chromium…. We blow thousands of tons of unrecoverable lead into the atmosphere each year from high octane gasoline because we like a quick pickup. We must become aware that many of our production and consumption habits are extremely expensive of scarce materials and that a trivial change of taste or slight reduction in personal satisfaction can often bring about tremendous savings."[9]

The captious will want to inquire, if the losses in satisfaction here are trivial and the savings are tremendous, why the commission did not seize the opportunity to urge savings.

Why did it make no recommendations? But given its position on growth and the meaning of growth, it could, in fact, go no further. At first glance it does not seem impossible to pick out kinds of consumption which seem especially wasteful—things which reflect not use but wasteful use. Surely the utility of an automobile is not diminished if it is lighter or if its gasoline contains less lead. But this is a distinction that cannot be made. Consumption, it quickly develops, is a seamless web. If we ask about the chromium, we must ask about the cars. The questions that are asked about one part can be asked about all parts. The automobiles are too heavy and they use irreplaceable lead? One can ask with equal cogency if we need to make all the automobiles that we now turn out. This question gains point when we reflect that the demand for automobiles depends on that remarkable institution called planned obsolescence, is nurtured by advertising campaigns of incredible strategic complexity, and on occasion requires financial underwriting that would have seemed rather extravagant to Charles Ponzi.

As with automobiles so with everything else. In an opulent society the marginal urgency of all kinds of goods is low. It is easy to bring our doubts and questions to bear on the automobiles. But the case is not different for (say) that part of our food production which contributes not to nutrition but to obesity, that part of our tobacco which contributes not to comfort but to carcinoma, and that part of our clothing which is designed not to cover nakedness but to suggest it. We cannot single out waste in a product without questioning the product. We cannot single out any one product without calling into question all products. Thus having specifically endorsed ever more luxurious standards of consumption—for this is what is meant by growth—the PMPC obviously could not pursue the notion of wasteful consumption without involving itself in a major contradiction. It made its gesture against the automobiles and then, wisely, it stopped.

III

There are several reasons why our consumption standards have not been called in question in the course of the conservation discussion over the last fifty years. There is also some divergence between those that are given, or which come first to mind, and those that are ultimately operative. Thus, to recur once more to the PMPC, it simply stated its belief that economic stagnation is the alternative to growth, meaning uninhibited increases in consumption. No one, obviously, wants stagnation. But does this argument really hold? Clearly we can have different rates of growth of consumption. In other contexts, we are not nearly so committed to the notion of all-out increase in consumption. In 1957, economic output was virtually constant. This leveling off of output—stagnation if I may use the pejorative term—was, more or less, a goal of public policy. The purpose of the tight money policy was to reduce the rate of investment spending and thus of economic expansion in order hopefully, to win a measure of price stability. In this context, we weren't so appalled by the idea of a lower rate of growth—something approaching what the PMPC would have had to call stagnation. As I write, in the first quarter of 1958, we have had something more than a leveling off; we have experienced a rather sharp reduction in output. But even this, at least in some quarters, has not been regarded with great alarm. We are being told that breathing spells are inevitable in the free enterprise system.

Also, as I shall suggest in a moment, we can have patterns of growth which make heavy drafts on materials and other patterns which are much more lenient in their requirements.

In any case, if our levels of consumption are dangerously high in relation to the resource base, or are becoming so—and the PMPC at least expressed its concern—it would obviously be better to risk stagnation now than to use up our reserves and have not stagnation but absolute contraction later on. Those who sanctify growth but also say that the resource position is serious are, in effect, arguing that we have no alternative to having our fling now even though, more or less literally, there is hell to pay later on. This is an odd posture for the conservationist.

It is also suggested that uninhibited consumption has something to do with individual liberty. If we begin interfering with consumption, we shall be abridging a basic freedom.

I shan't dwell long on this. That we make such points is part of the desolate modern tendency to turn the discussion of all questions, however simple and forthright, into a search for violation of some arcane principle, or to evade and suffocate common sense by verbose, incoherent, and irrelevant moralizing. Freedom is not much concerned with tail fins or even with automobiles. Those who argue that it is identified with the greatest possible range of choice of consumers' goods are only confessing their exceedingly simple-minded and mechanical view of man and his liberties.

In any case, one must ask the same question as concerns growth. If the resource problem is serious, then the price of a wide choice now is a sharply constricted choice later on. Surely even those who adhere to the biggest supermarket theory of liberty would agree that their concept has a time dimension.

Finally it will be said that there is nothing that can be done about consumption. This, of course, is nonsense. There is a wide range of instruments of social control. Taxation; specific prohibitions on wasteful products, uses, or practices; educational and other hortatory efforts; subsidies to encourage consumption of cheaper and more plentiful substitutes are all available. Most have been used in past periods of urgency.

And here, indeed, is the first reason we do not care to contemplate such measures. The latter Forties and the Fifties in the United States were marked by what we must now recognize as a massive conservative reaction to the idea of enlarged social guidance and control of economic activity. This was partly, no doubt, based on a desire to have done with the wartime apparatus of control. In part, it was a successful conservative reaction to the social intervention of the New Deal. In part, it was the resurgence of a notably over-simplified view of economic life which seized on this moment to ascribe a magical automatism to the price system (including the rate of interest) which, as we are again gradually learning, it does not have. Euphemisms have played a prominent part in this revolt. Many have found it more agreeable to be in favor of liberty than against social responsibility. But the result has been to rule out of discussion, or at least to discriminate heavily against, measures which by their nature could be accomplished only by according increased responsibilities to the state.

Since consumption could not be discussed without raising the question of an increased role for the state, it was not discussed.

However, tradition also abetted this exclusion of consumption levels from consideration. Economics is a subject in which old questions are lovingly debated but new ones are regarded with misgiving. On the whole, it is a mark of stability and sound scholarship to concern oneself with questions that were relevant in the world of Ricardo. In the Ricardian world, to be literal about it, goods were indeed scarce. One might talk, although without courting great popularity, about redistributing wealth and income and thus curbing the luxurious consumption of the classes. But the notion that people as a whole might have more than a minimum—that there might be a restraint on the consumption of the community as a whole—was unthinkable. In modern times this has, of course, become thinkable. Goods are plentiful. Demand for them must be elaborately contrived. Those who create wants rank among our most talented and highly paid citizens. Want creation—advertising—is a ten billion dollar industry. But tradition remains strongly against questioning or even thinking about wants.

Finally, we are committed to a high level of consumption because, whether we need the goods or not, we very much need the employment their production provides. I need not dwell on this. The point is decidedly obvious at this writing in early 1958. We are not missing the cars that Detroit is currently not producing. Nor are we missing the steel that Pittsburgh and Gary are currently not making. The absence of these products is not causing any detectable suffering. But there is much suffering and discomfort as the result of the failure of these industries to employ as many men as in the recent past. We are chained to a high level of production and consumption not by the pressure of want but by the urgencies of economic security.

IV

What should be our policy toward consumption?

First, of course, we should begin to talk about it—and in the context of all its implications. It is silly for grown men to concern themselves mightily with supplying an appetite and close their eyes to the obvious and obtrusive question of whether the appetite is excessive.

If the appetite presents no problems—if resource discovery and the technology of use and substitution promise automatically to remain abreast of consumption and at moderate cost—then we need press matters no further. At least on conservation grounds there is no need to curb our appetite.

But to say this, and assuming that it applies comprehensively to both renewable and non-renewable resources, is to say that there is no materials problem. It is to say that, except for some activities that by definition are noncritical, the conservationists are not much needed.

But if conservation is an issue, then we have no honest and logical course but to measure the means for restraining use against the means for insuring a continuing sufficiency of supply and taking the appropriate action. There is no justification for ruling consumption levels out of the calculation.

What would be the practical consequences of this calculation—taken honestly and without the frequent contemporary preoccupation not with solution but with plausible escape—I do not pretend to say. As I suggested at the outset, I am impressed by the opportunities for resource substitution and by the contribution of technology in facilitating it. But the problem here is less one of theory than of technical calculation and projection. As such, it is beyond the scope both of this paper and my competence. It has been my task to show that at any time the calculation is unsanguine, restraint on consumption can no longer be excluded as a remedy.

However, let me conclude with one suggestion. There may be occasions in the future when, in the interest of conservation, we will wish to address ourselves to the consumption of particular products. (This, as noted, can only be in the context of a critical view of all consumption.) The modern automobile may be a case in point. I share the view that this is currently afflicted by a kind of competitive elephantiasis. As a result, it is making a large and possibly excessive claim on iron, petroleum, lead, and other materials; but much more seriously it is making excessive inroads on urban and rural driving and standing space and on the public funds that supply this space.

But in the main, it would seem to me that any concern for materials use should be general. It should have as its aim the shifting of consumption patterns from those which have a high materials requirement to those which have a much lower requirement. The opportunities are considerable. Education, health services, sanitary services, good parks and playgrounds, orchestras, effective local government, a clean countryside, all have rather small materials requirements. I have elsewhere argued that the present tendency of our economy is to discriminate sharply against such production.[10] A variety of forces, among them the massed pressures of modern merchandising, have forced an inordinate concentration of our consumption on what may loosely be termed consumer hardware. This distortion has been underwritten by economic attitudes which have made but slight accommodation to the transition of our world from one of privation to one of opulence. A rationalization of our present consumption patterns—a rationalization which would more accurately reflect free and unmanaged consumer choice—might also be an important step in materials conservation.

Questions

1. Galbraith's recommendations would bring our lifestyle into question, a lifestyle of consumption that is correlated with freedom and liberty. What is Galbraith's position on the notion that consumption is a basic liberty? How do you see this having grown more intense since 1958?

2. Galbraith lamented the automobile in 1958: "The modern automobile may be a case in point. I share the view that this is currently afflicted by a kind of competitive elephantiasis. As a result, it is making a large and possibly excessive claim on iron, petroleum, lead, and other materials; but much more seriously, it is making excessive inroads on urban and rural driving and standing space on the public funds that supply this space." How has the SUV consumption furthered the "competitive elephantiasis"?

3. There was cause for alarm in the 1950s that the United States would be insecure in basic resources and be at a security risk if dependent on other countries' resources. How has this insecurity grown in light of globalization?

Notes

1. From Henry Jarett, ed., *Perspectives on Conservation: Essays on America's Natural Resources* (Baltimore: Johns Hopkins University Press, 1958), 89–99.
2. From Harry S. Truman's letter to William S. Paley on the Creation of the President's Materials Policy Commission, January 19, 1951, The Truman Library.
3. Ibid.
4. References here are to *Resources for Freedom* (Washington: U.S. Government Printing Office, June 1952). Summary of Volume I, hereinafter cited as PMPC, Summary.
5. New York: The Ronald Press, 1954.
6. J. Frederic Dewhurst and Associates, *America's Needs and Resources: A New Survey* (New York: The Twentieth Century Fund, 1955).
7. PMPC, Summary, p. 5.
8. PMPC, Summary, p. 10.
9. PMPC, Summary, p. 16.
10. *The Affluent Society* (Boston: Houghton Mifflin, May 1958).

2. The Case That the World Has Reached Its Limits[1]

Robert Goodland

REFLECTING WHAT GALBRAITH HINTED at, Robert Goodland (1939–2013) argues that we have already reached (possibly overshot) our resource boundaries. Citing five major categories of evidence, including biomass appropriation, global warming, ozone shield rupture, land degradation, and the decrease in biodiversity, Goodland details the global empirical evidence for his position. Pollution is particularly illustrative of the global nature of human activity, with two types—greenhouse warming and CFC pollution—causing the most harm geographically distant from those who produced and "benefited" from it. As is consistent with evidence throughout this anthology, a disproportionate share of pollution has been, and continues to be, generated in the United States. Given the mounting evidence of environmental harm and with little time to address it, he warns, "'Business as Usual' or 'wait and see' approaches are thus imprudent," and "[i]n the face of uncertainty about global environmental health, prudence should be paramount." Prudence is counseled by the precautionary principle. The precautionary principle urges us, in the face of uncertainty, to exercise precaution. It is like driving in the dark, and the headlights go out. Uncertain of what is in front of you, do you continue as you were, floor it, or proceed with caution? Goodland urges caution and recommends curbing industrial countries' overconsumption.

Mahatma Gandhi [when asked if, after independence, India would attain British standards of living]: "It took Britain half the resources of the planet to achieve its prosperity; how many planets will a country like India require …?"

The aim of this chapter is to present the case that limits to growth have already been reached, that further input growth will take the planet further away from sustainability, and that we are rapidly foreclosing options for the future, possibly by overshooting limits

(Catton 1982). This chapter seeks to convince the reader of the urgent need to convert to a sustainable economy, rather than the related and equally or more important need of poverty alleviation. The political will to transit to sustainability will be mustered only when the need for the transition is perceived. The crucial next step—how to muster that political will—is deferred to a subsequent book.

To begin, plaudits for Brundtland's heroic achievement: elevating sustainability as a planetary goal now espoused by practically all nations, the United Nations family, and the World Bank. In July 1989, leaders of the Group of Seven major industrialized nations called for "the early adoption, world-wide, of policies based on sustainable development." The world owes Brundtland an enormous debt for this tremendous feat, and we admire her political wisdom. This chapter builds on Brundtland's lead and explores the implications of sustainability. We assume as given that the world is being run unsustainably now—being fueled by inherited fossil fuels is the best single example. Nonrenewable oil and gas provide 60 percent of global energy with barely fifty years of proven reserves.

Brundtland stated that meeting essential needs requires "a new era of economic growth" for nations in which the majority are poor. The report (WCED 1987) anticipates "a five- to tenfold increase in world industrial output." Two years later, this "sustainable growth" conclusion was reemphasized by the secretary general of the Brundtland Commission: "A five-fold to tenfold increase in economic activity would be required over the next 50 years" to achieve sustainability (MacNeill 1989).

The Global Ecosystem and the Economic Subsystem

A single measure—population times per capita resource consumption—encapsulates what is needed to achieve sustainability. This is the scale of the human economic subsystem with respect to that of the global ecosystem on which it depends and of which it is a part. The global ecosystem is the source of all material inputs feeding the economic subsystem and is the sink for all its wastes. Population times per capita resource consumption is the total flow—throughput—of resources from the ecosystem to the economic subsystem, then back to the ecosystem as waste.... Population times per capita resource use is refined by

Tinbergen and Hueting (1992) and by Ehrlich and Ehrlich (1990).

The global ecosystem's source and sink functions have limited capacity to support the economic subsystem. The imperative, therefore, is to maintain the size of the global economy to within the capacity of the ecosystem to sustain it. Speth (1989) calculates that it took all of human history to grow to the $600 billion global economy of 1900. Today, the world economy grows by this amount every two years. Unchecked, today's $16 trillion global economy may be five times bigger only one generation or so hence.

It seems unlikely that the world can sustain a doubling of the economy, let alone Brundtland's "five- to tenfold increase." We believe that throughput growth is not the way to reach sustainability; we cannot "grow" our way into sustainability. The global ecosystem, which is the source of all the resources needed for the economic subsystem, is finite and has limited regenerative and assimilative capacities. It looks inevitable that the next century will be occupied by double the number of people in the human economy consuming sources and burdening sinks with their wastes.

The global ecosystem is the sink for all the wastes created by the economic subsystem, and this sink has limited assimilative capacity. When the economic subsystem was small relative to the global ecosystem, then the sources and sinks were large and limits were irrelevant. Leading thinkers, such as Ehrlich and Ehrlich (1990), Hardin (1991), Boulding (1991), Daly (1990a, 1990b, 1991a, 1991b), as well as the Club of Rome (Meadows et al. 1974), have shown for years that the world is no longer "empty," the economic subsystem is large relative to the biosphere, and the capacities of the biosphere's sources and sinks are being stressed.

Localized Limits to Global Limits

This chapter presents the case that the economic subsystem has reached or exceeded important source and sink limits. We take as agreed that we have already fouled our nest: practically nowhere on this earth are signs of the human economy absent. From the center of Antarctica to the top of Mount Everest, human wastes are obvious and increasing. It is impossible to find a sample of ocean water with no sign of the 20 billion tons of human wastes added annually. PCBs and other persistent toxic chemicals, such as DDT and heavy metal compounds, have already accumulated throughout the marine ecosystem. One-fifth of the world's population breathes air more poisonous than WHO standards recommend, and an entire generation of Mexico City children may be intellectually stunted by lead poisoning (Brown et al. 1991).

Since the Club of Rome's 1972 report "Limits to Growth," the constraints have shifted from source limits to sink limits. Source limits are more open to substitution and are more localized. Since then, the case has substantially strengthened for limits to throughput growth. There is a wide variety of limits. Some are tractable and are being tackled, such as the CFC phase-out under the Montreal Convention. Other limits are less tractable, such as the massive human appropriation of biomass (see below). The key limit is the sink constraint of fossil energy use. Therefore, the rate of transition to renewables, including solar energy, parallels the rate of transition to sustainability. Here the optimists add the possibility of cheap fusion energy by the year 2050. We are agnostic on technology and want to encourage it by energy taxes.... Hitherto, technology has only started to focus on input reduction and even less on sink management, which suggests there is scope for improvements.

Land-fill sites are becoming harder to find; garbage is shipped thousands of miles from industrial to developing countries in search of unfilled sinks. It has so far proved impossible for the U.S. Nuclear Regulatory Commission to find anywhere to rent a nuclear waste site for U.S. $100 million per year. Germany's Kraft-Werk Union signed an agreement with China in July 1987 to bury nuclear waste in Mongolia's Gobi Desert. These facts prove that land-fill sites and toxic dumps—aspects of sinks—are increasingly hard to find, that limits are near.

First Evidence of Limits: Human Biomass Appropriation

The best evidence that there are other imminent limits is the calculation by Vitousek et al. (1986) that the human economy uses—directly or indirectly—about 40 percent of the net primary product of terrestrial photosynthesis today. (This figure drops to 25 percent if the oceans and other aquatic ecosystems are included.) And desertification, urban encroachment onto agricultural land, blacktopping, soil erosion, and pollution are increasing—as is the population's search for food. This means that in only a single doubling of the world's population (say, thirty-five years) we will use 80 percent, and 100 percent shortly thereafter. As Daly (1991a, 1991b) points out, 100 percent appropriation is ecologically impossible and socially highly undesirable. The world will go from half-empty to full in one doubling period, irrespective of the sink being filled or the source being consumed. Readers refusing to recognize such overfullness that has appropriated 40 percent for humans already should decide when between now and 100 percent they would be willing to say "enough." What evidence will they require to be convinced? Although the Vitousek et al. evidence has not been refuted during the last five years, this single study is so stark that we urge prompt corroboration and analysis of the implications.

Second Evidence of Limits: Global Warming

Evidence of atmospheric carbon dioxide accumulation is pervasive, as geographically extensive as possible, and unimaginably expensive to cure if allowed to worsen. In addition, the evidence is unambiguously negative and strongly so. There may be a few exceptions, such as plants growing faster in CO_2-enriched laboratories where water and nutrients are not limiting. However, in the real world, it seems more likely that crop belts will not shift with changing climate, nor will they grow faster, because some other factor (for example, suitable soils or water) will become limiting. The prodigious North American breadbasket's climate may indeed shift north; but this does not mean that the breadbasket will follow, because the rich prairie soils will stay put, and Canadian boreal soils and muskeg are very infertile.

The second evidence that limits have been exceeded is global warming. The year 1990 was the warmest year in more than a century of record-keeping. Seven of the hottest years on record all occurred in the last 11 years. The 1980s were 1 degree Fahrenheit warmer than the 1880s, while 1990 was 1.25 degrees Fahrenheit warmer. This contrasts alarmingly with the pre-industrial constancy in which the earth's temperature did not vary more than 2 to 4 degrees Fahrenheit in the last 10,000 years. Humanity's entire social and cultural infrastructure over the last 7000 years has evolved entirely within a global climate that never deviated as much as 2 degrees Fahrenheit from today's climate (Arrhenius and Waltz 1990).

It is too soon to be absolutely certain that global "greenhouse" warming has begun: normal climatic variability is too great for absolute certainty. There is even greater uncertainty about the possible effects. But all the evidence suggests that global warming may well have started, that CO_2 accumulation started years ago, as postulated by Svante Arrhenius in 1896, and that it is worsening fast. Scientists now practically universally agree that such warming will occur, although differences remain on the rates. The U.S. National Academy of Science warned President Bush that global warming may well be the most pressing international issue of the next century. A dwindling minority of scientists remain agnostic. The dispute concerns policy responses much more than the predictions.

The scale of today's fossil-fuel-based human economy seems to be the dominant cause of greenhouse gas accumulation. The biggest contribution to greenhouse warming—carbon dioxide released from burning coal, oil, and natural gas—is accumulating fast in the atmosphere. Today's 5.3 billion people annually burn the equivalent of more than one ton of coal each.

Next in importance in contributing to greenhouse warming are all other pollutants released by the economy that exceed the biosphere's absorptive capacity: methane, CFCs, and nitrous oxide. Relative to carbon dioxide these three pollutants are orders of magnitude more damaging, although their amount is much less. Today's price to polluters for using atmospheric sink capacity for carbon dioxide disposal is zero, although the real opportunity cost may turn out to be astronomical.

The costs of rejecting the greenhouse hypothesis, if true, are vastly greater than the costs of accepting the hypothesis, if it proves to be false. By the time the evidence is irrefutable, it is sure to be too late to avert unacceptable costs, such as the influx of millions of refugees from low-lying coastal areas (55 percent of the world's population lives on coasts or estuaries), damage to ports and coastal cities, an increase in storm intensity, and, worst of all, damage to agriculture. Furthermore, abating global warming may save money, not cost it, according to Lovins (1990), when the benefit from lower fuel bills is factored in. The greenhouse threat is more than sufficient to justify action now, even if only in an insurance sense. The question to be resolved is how much insurance to buy?

Admittedly, great uncertainty prevails. But uncertainty cuts both ways. "Business as usual" or "wait and see" approaches are thus imprudent, if not foolhardy. Underestimation of greenhouse or ozone shield risks is just as likely as overestimation. Recent studies suggest that we are underestimating risks, rather than the converse. In May 1991, the U.S. EPA upped by *twentyfold* their estimate of UV-radiation cancer deaths, and the earth's ability to absorb methane was estimated *downward by 25 percent* in June 1991. In the face of uncertainty about global environmental health, prudence should be paramount.

The relevant component here is the tight relationship between carbon released and the scale of the economy. Global carbon emissions have increased annually since the Industrial Revolution, currently at nearly 4 percent per year. To the extent that energy use parallels economic activity, carbon emissions are an index of the scale of the economy. Fossil fuels account for 78 percent of U.S. energy. Of course, there is tremendous scope for reducing the energy intensity of industry and of the economy in general; that is why reductions in carbon emissions are possible without reducing standards of living. A significant degree of decoupling economic growth from energy throughput appears substantially achievable. Witness the 81 percent increase in Japan's output since 1973 using the same amount of energy. Similarly, the United States achieved nearly a 39 percent increase in GNP since 1973 with only a modest increase in energy use. This means energy efficiency increased almost 26 percent. Sweden—cold, gloomy, industrialized, and very energy-efficient—is the best example of how profitable it is to reduce CO_2. The Swedish State Power Board found that doubled electric efficiency, a 34 percent decrease in CO_2, and the phase-out of the nuclear power that supplies 50 percent of the country's electricity actually *lowers* consumers' electricity bills by U.S. \$1 billion per year (Lovins 1990). Other, less efficient nations should be able to do even better.

Reducing energy intensity is possible in all industrial economies and in the larger developing economies, such as China, Brazil, and India. The scope of increasing energy use without increasing CO_2 means primarily the overdue transition to renewables: biomass, solar, and hydro. The other major source of carbon emissions—deforestation—also parallels the scale of the economy. More people needing more land push back the frontier. But there are vanishingly few geopolitical frontiers left today.

Greenhouse warming is a compelling argument that limits have been exceeded because it is globally pervasive, rather than disrupting the atmosphere in the region where the CO_2 was produced. In comparison, regional evidence of limits includes acid rain damaging parts of the United States and Canada, and those parts of Scandinavia downwind from the United Kingdom, and the "Waldsterben," or U.S. \$30 billion loss of much of Europe's forest.

The nearly 7 billion tons of carbon released into the atmosphere each year by human activity (from fossil fuels and deforestation) accumulate in the atmosphere, which suggests that the ecosystem's sinks capable of absorbing carbon have been exceeded, and carbon accumulation appears for all practical purposes irreversible on any relevant time frame; hence it is of major concern for sustainability for future generations. Removal of carbon dioxide by liquefying it or chemically scrubbing it from stacks might double the cost of electricity. Optimistically, technology may reduce this cost, but still at a major penalty.

Third Evidence of Limits: Ozone Shield Rupture

The third evidence that global limits have been reached is the rupture of the ozone shield. It is difficult to imagine more compelling evidence that human activity has already damaged our life-support systems than the cosmic holes in the ozone shield. That CFCs would damage the ozone layer was predicted as far back as 1974 by Sherwood Rowland and Mario Molina. But when the damage was first detected—in 1985 in Antarctica—disbelief was so great that the data were rejected as coming from faulty sensors. Retesting and a search of hitherto undigested computer printouts confirmed that not only did the hole exist in 1985, but that it had appeared each spring since 1979. The world had failed to detect a vast hole that threatened human life and food production and that was more extensive than the United States and taller than Mount Everest (Shea 1989).

The single Antarctic ozone hole has now gone global. All subsequent tests have proved global ozone layer thinning far faster than models predicted. A second hole was subsequently discovered over the Arctic, and recently ozone shield thinning has been detected over both north and south temperate latitudes, including over northern Europe and North America. Furthermore, the temperate holes are edging from the less dangerous winter into the spring, thus posing more of a threat to sprouting crops and to humans. The incidence of blindness in Chilean sheep and Patagonian rabbits in the Andes soared in 1991.

The relationship between the increased ultraviolet "B" radiation leaking through the impaired ozone shield and skin cancers and cataracts is relatively well known—every 1 percent decrease in the ozone layer results in 5 percent more of certain skin cancers—and alarming in neighboring regions (for example, Queensland, Australia). The world seems destined for 1 billion additional skin cancers, many of them fatal, among people alive today. The possibly more serious human health effect is depression of our immune systems, increasing our vulnerability to an array of tumors, parasites, and infectious diseases. In addition, as the shield weakens, crop yields and marine fisheries will decline. But the gravest effect may be the uncertainty, such as upsetting normal balances in natural vegetation. Keystone species—those on which many others depend for survival—may decrease, leading to widespread disruption in environmental services and accelerating extinctions.

The 1 million or so tons of CFCs annually dumped into the biosphere take about 10 years to waft up to the ozone layer, where they destroy it with a half-life of 100 to 150 years. The tonnage of CFCs and other ozone-depleting gases released into the atmosphere is increasing damage to the ozone shield. Today's damage, although serious, only reflects the relatively low levels of CFCs released in the early 1980s. If CFC emissions cease today, the world still will be gripped in an unavoidable commitment to 10 years of increased damage. This would then gradually return to predamage levels over the next 100 to 150 years.

This seems to be evidence that the global ecosystem's sink capacity to absorb CFC pollution has been vastly exceeded. The limits have been reached and exceeded; mankind is in for damage to environmental services, human health, and food production. This is a good example because 85 percent of CFCs are released in the industrial North, but the main hole appeared over Antarctica in the ozone layer twenty kilometers up in the sky, showing the damage to be widespread and truly global in nature.

Fourth Evidence of Limits: Land Degradation

Land degradation—decreased productivity such as caused by accelerated soil erosion, salination, and desertification—is only one of the many topics that could be included here. It is not new; land degraded thousands of years ago (for example, the Tigris-Euphrates Valley) remains unproductive today. But the scale has mushroomed and is important because practically all (97 percent) food comes from land rather than from aquatic or ocean systems. As 35 percent of the earth's land already is degraded, and since this figure is increasing and is largely irreversible in any time scale of concern to society, such degradation is a sign that we have exceeded the regenerative capacity of the earth's soil source.

Pimentel et al. (1987) found that soil erosion is serious in most of the world's agricultural areas and that this problem is worsening as more marginal land is brought into production. Soil loss rates, generally ranging from 10 to 100 tons per hectare per year, exceed soil formation rates by at least tenfold. Agriculture is leading to erosion, salination, or waterlogging of possibly 6 million hectares per year: "a crisis seriously affecting the world food economy."

Exceeding the limits of this particular environmental source function raises food prices and exacerbates income inequality at a time when 1 billion people are already malnourished. As one-third of developing-country populations now face fuel wood deficits, crop residues and dung are diverted from agriculture to fuel. Fuel wood overharvesting and this diversion intensify land degradation, hunger, and poverty.

Fifth Evidence of Limits: Decrease in Biodiversity

The scale of the human economy has grown so large that there is no longer room for all species in the ark. The rates of takeover of wildlife habitat and of species extinctions are the fastest they have ever been in recorded history and are accelerating. The world's richest species habitat, tropical forest, has already been 55 percent destroyed; the current rate exceeds 168,000 square kilometers per year. As the total number of species extant is not yet known to the nearest order of magnitude (5 million or 30 million or more), it is impossible to determine precise extinction rates. However, conservative estimates put the rate at more than 5000 species of our inherited genetic library irreversibly extinguished each year. This is about 10,000 times as fast as prehuman extinction rates. Less conservative estimates put the rate at 150,000 species per year (Goodland 1991). Many find such anthropocentrism to be arrogant and immoral. It also increases risks of overshoot. Built-in redundancy is a part of many biological systems, but we do not know how near thresholds are. Most extinctions from tropical deforestation (for example, colonization) today increase poverty—tropical moist forest soils are fragile—so we do not even have much of a beneficial tradeoff with development here.

Population

Brundtland is sensible on population: adequate food is too expensive for one-fourth of the earth's population today. Birthweight is declining in places. Poverty stimulates population growth. Direct poverty alleviation is essential; "business as usual" on poverty alleviation is immoral. MacNeill (1989) states it plainly: "reducing rates of population growth" is an essential condition to achieve sustainability.

This is as important, if not more so, in industrial countries as it is in developing countries. Industrial countries overconsume per capita, hence overpollute, and thus are responsible for by far the largest share of limits being reached. The richest 20 percent of the world consumes more than 70 percent of the world's commercial energy. Thirteen nations already have achieved zero population growth, so it is not utopian to expect others to follow.

Developing countries contribute to exceeding limits because they are so populous today (77 percent of the world's total) and are increasing far faster than their economies can provide for them (90 percent of world population growth). Real incomes are declining in some areas. If left unchecked, it may be halfway through the twenty-first century before the number of births will fall back even to current high levels. Developing-countries' population growth alone would account for a 75 percent increase in their commercial energy consumption by 2025, even if per capita consumption remained at current inadequate levels (OTA 1991). These countries need so much growth due to the population increase that this can be freed up only by the transition to sustainability in industrial countries.

The poor must be given the chance, must be assisted, and will justifiably demand to reach at least minimally acceptable living standards by access to the remaining natural resource base. When industrial nations switch from input growth to qualitative development, more resources and environmental functions will be available for the South's needed growth. This is a major role of the World Bank. It is in the interests of developing countries and the world commons not to follow the fossil fuel model. It is in the interests of industrial countries to subsidize alternatives, and this is an increasing role for the World Bank. This view is repeated by Dr. Qu Wenhu, of Academica Sinica, who says:

"If 'needs' includes one automobile for each of a billion Chinese, then sustainable development is impossible." Developing-countries' populations account for only 17 percent of total commercial energy now, but unchecked this will almost double by 2020 (OTA 1991).

Merely meeting the unmet demand for family planning would help enormously. Educating girls and providing them with credit for productive purposes and employment opportunities are probably the next most effective measures. A full 25 percent of U.S. births, and a much larger number of developing-country births, are to unmarried mothers, hence providing less child care. Most of these births are unwanted, which also tends to result in less care. Certainly, international development agencies should assist high-population-growth countries in reducing to world averages as an urgent first step, instead of trying only to increase infrastructure without population measures.

Growth versus Development

To the extent that the economic subsystem has indeed become large relative to the global ecosystem on which it depends, and the regenerative and assimilative capacities of its sources and sinks are being exceeded, then the growth called for by Brundtland will dangerously exacerbate surpassing the limits outlined above. Opinions differ. MacNeill (1989) claims "a minimum of 3% annual per capita income growth is needed to reach sustainability during the first part of the next century," and this would need higher growth in national income, given population trends. Hueting (1990) disagrees, concluding that for sustainability "what we need least is an increase in national income." Sustainability will be achieved only to the extent that quantitative throughput growth stabilizes and is replaced by qualitative development, holding outputs constant. Reverting to the scale of the economy—population times per capita resource use—per capita resource use must decline, as well as population.

Brundtland is excellent on three of the four necessary conditions for sustainability. First, the production of more with less (for example, conservation, efficiency, technological improvements, and recycling). Japan excels in this regard, producing 81 percent more real output than it did in 1973 using the same amount of energy. Second, the reduction of the population explosion. Third, the redistribution from overconsumers to the poor. Brundtland was probably being politically astute in leaving fuzzy the fourth necessary condition to make all four sufficient to reach sustainability. This is the transition from input growth and growth in the scale of the economy to qualitative development, holding the scale of the economy consistent with the regenerative and assimilative capacities of global life-support systems. In several places the Brundtland Report hints at this. In qualitative, sustainable development, production replaces depreciated assets, and births replace deaths, so that stocks of wealth and people are continually renewed and even improved (Daly 1990b). A developing economy is getting better: the well-being of the (stable) population improves. An economy growing in throughput is getting bigger, exceeding limits, and damaging the self-repairing capacity of the planet.

To the extent our leaders recognize the fact that the earth has reached limits and decide to reduce further expansion in the scale of the economy, we must prevent hardship in this tremendous transition for poor countries. Brundtland commendably advocates growth for poor countries. But only raising the bottom without lowering the top will not permit sustainability (Haavelmo 1990).

The poor need an irreducible minimum of basics: food, clothing, and shelter. These basics

require throughput growth for poor countries, with compensating reductions in such growth in rich countries. Apart from colonial resource drawdowns, industrial country growth historically has increased markets for developing countries' raw materials, hence presumably benefiting poor countries, but it is industrial country growth that has to contract to free up ecological room for the minimum growth needed in poor country economies. Tinbergen and Hueting (1992) put it plainest: "no further production growth in rich countries." All approaches to sustainability must internalize this constraint if the crucial goals of poverty alleviation and halting damage to global life-support systems are to be approached.

Conclusion

When economies change from agrarian through industrial to more service-oriented, then smokestack throughput growth may improve to growth less damaging of sources and sinks: from coal and steel to fiber optics and electronics, for example. We must speed to production that is less throughput-intensive. We must accelerate technical improvements in resource productivity—Brundtland's "producing more with less." Presumably this is what the Brundtland Commission and subsequent follow-up authors (for example, MacNeill 1989) label "growth, but of a different kind." Vigorous promotion of this trend will indeed help the transition to sustainability and is probably essential. It is also largely true that conservation and efficiency improvements and recycling are profitable and will become much more so the instant environmental externalities (for example, carbon dioxide emissions) are internalized.

But this approach will be insufficient for four reasons. First, all growth consumes resources and produces wastes, even Brundtland's unspecified new type of growth. To the extent that we have reached limits to the ecosystem's regenerative and assimilative capacities, throughput growth exceeding such limits will not herald sustainability. Second, the size of the service sector relative to the production of goods has limits. Third, even many services are fairly throughput-intensive, including tourism, universities, and hospitals. Fourth, and highly significant, less throughput-intensive growth is "hitech"; hence the places where there has to be more growth—tiny, impoverished, developing-country economies—are less likely to be able to afford Brundtland's "new" growth.

Part of the answer will be massive technology transfer from industrial countries to developing countries to offer them whatever throughput-neutral or throughput-minimal technologies are available. This transfer is presaged by the U.S. $1.5 billion Global Environment Facility of the United Nations Environment Program (UNEP), the United Nations Development Program (UNDP), and the World Bank that will start in 1991 to finance improvements not yet fully "economic," but which benefit the global commons.

This chapter is not primarily about how to approach sustainability: that is well documented elsewhere (Adams 1990, Agarwal and Narain 1990, Chambers et al. 1990, Conroy and Litvinoff 1988, Goldsmith, Hildyard, and Bunyard 1990). Nor is it about the economic and political difficulties of reaching sustainability, such as the pricing of the infinite (the ozone shield, for example), the endlessly debatable (biodiversity, for example), or pricing for posterity what we cannot price today. That is admirably argued by Daly and Cobb (1989), Daly (1990a, 1991a, 1991b), El Serafy (1991), and Costanza (1991). It is about the need to recognize the imminence of limits to throughput growth, while alleviating poverty in the world. Many local thresholds have been broached because of population pressures and

poverty; global thresholds are being broached by industrial countries' overconsumption.

To conclude on an optimistic note: the Organization for Economic Cooperation and Development (OECD) found in 1984 that environmental expenditures are good for the economy and good for employment. The 1988 Worldwatch study (Brown 1988) speculated that most sustainability could be achieved by the year 2000 with additional annual expenditures increasing gradually to U.S. $150 billion in 2000. Money is available: World Bank President Barber Conable calculated early in 1991 that industrial country trade barriers cost developing countries about U.S. $100 billion in foregone income—twice the interest paid annually by developing countries on their international debt. Most measures needed to approach sustainability are beneficial also for other reasons (fuel efficiency, for example). The world's nations have annually funded UNEP with about U.S. $30 million, although they propose now "to consider" increasing this sum to U.S. $100 million. It is not financial capital shortage that limits the economy anymore. It is shortages of both natural capital as well as of political will in the industrialized world. Yet we fail to follow economic logic and invest in the limiting factor.

Many nations spend less on environment, health, education, and welfare than they do on arms, which now annually total U.S. $1 trillion worldwide. Global security is increasingly prejudiced by source and sink constraints as recent natural resource wars have shown, such as the 1974 "cod" war between the United Kingdom and Iceland, the 1969 "football" war between overpopulated El Salvador and underpopulated Honduras, and the 1991 Persian Gulf war. As soon as damage to global life-support systems is perceived as far riskier than military threats, more prudent reallocation will promptly follow.

Questions

1. Provide details of each of the five major categories of evidence that we've reached our limits. Research ozone-shield rupture since the phase-out of CFCs. As it provides an example of remediation, why do you think that transpired but climate change mediation does not?

2. If followed, how would the Precautionary Principle change the way in which US citizens see their consumption? Or would it not make any difference?

3. Note that our consumption of CFCs was legally removed in light of the evidence of ozone-shield rupture. Should our consumption be regulated and rationed in order to address the five categories of evidence?

References

Adams, W. M. *Green Development: Environment and Sustainability in the Third World.* London: Routledge, 1990.

Agarwal, A., and S. Narain. *Towards Green Villages* Delhi: Center for Science and Environment, 1990.

Arrhenius, E., and T. W. Waltz. *The Greenhouse Effect: Implications for Economic Development.* Discussion Paper 78. Washington, D.C.: World Bank, 1990.

Boulding, K. "Ecological Paramountcy." In *Ecological Economics,* edited by R. Costanza. New York: Columbia University Press, 1991.

Brown, L. R., et al. *State of the World.* Washington, D.C.: Worldwatch Institute, 1988. (See also *State of the World* for 1989, 1990, and 1991.)

Catton, W. R. *Overshoot: The Ecological Basis of Revolutionary Change.* Chicago: University of Illinois Press, 1982.

Chambers, R., N. C. Saxena, and T. Shah. *To the Hands of the Poor.* London: Intermediate Technology, 1990.

Conroy, C., and M. Litvinoff. *The Greening of Aid: Sustainable Livelihoods in Practice.* London: Earthscan, 1988.

Costanza, R., ed. *Ecological Economics: The Science and Management of Sustainability.* New York: Columbia University Press, 1991.

Court, T. de la. *Beyond Brundtland: Green Development in the 1990s.* London: Zed Books, 1990.

Daily, G. C., and P. R. Ehrlich. "An Exploratory Model of the Impact of Rapid Climate Change on the World Food Situation." *Proceedings Royal Society* (1990): 232–44.

Daly, H. E. "Toward Some Operational Principles of Sustainable Development." *Ecological Economics 2* (1990): 1–6.

Daly, H. E. "Boundless Bull." *Gannett Center Journal* 4(3) (1990): 113–18.

Daly, H. E. "Ecological Economics and Sustainable Development." In *Ecological Physical Chemistry,* edited by C. Rossi and E. Tiezzi. Amsterdam: Elsevier, 1991.

Daly, H. E. "Towards an Environmental Macro-economics." In *Ecological Economics,* edited by R. Costanza. New York: Columbia University Press, 1991.

Daly, H. E. "Sustainable Development: From Conceptual Theory Towards Operational Principles." *Population and Development Review.* Forthcoming.

Daly, H. E., and J. B. Cobb. *For the Common Good: Redirecting the Economy Toward Community, the Environment, and a Sustainable Future.* Boston: Beacon Press, 1989.

Ehrlich, P. "The Limits to Substitution: Meta-Re-source Depletion and a New Economic-Ecologic Paradigm." *Ecological Economics* 1(1) (1989): 9–16.

Ehrlich, P., and A. Ehrlich. *The Population Explosion.* New York: Simon & Schuster, 1990.

El Serafy, S. "The Environment as Capital." In *Ecological Economics,* edited by R. Costanza. New York: Columbia University Press, 1991.

Foy, G. "Economic Sustainability and the Preserva-tion of Environmental Assets." *Environmental Management* 14(6) (1990): 771–78.

Goldsmith, E., N. Hildyard, and P. Bunyard. *5000 Days to Save the Planet.* London: Hamlyn, 1990.

Goodland, R. *Tropical Deforestation: Solutions, Ethics and Religion.* Environment Department Working Paper 43. Washington, D.C.: World Bank, 1991.

Goodland, R., E. Asibey, J. Post, and M. Dyson. "Tropical Moist Forest Management: The Urgency of Transition to Sustainability." *Environ-mental Conservation* 17(4) (1991): 303–18.

Goodland, R., and G. Ledec. "Neoclassical Econom-ics and Sustainable Development." *Ecological Modelling* 38(1987): 19–46.

Goodland, R., and H. E. Daly. "The Missing Tools (for Sustainability)." In *Planet Under Stress: The Challenge of Global Change,* edited by C. Mungall and D. J. McLaren. Toronto: Oxford University Press, 1990.

Haavelmo, T. "The Big Dilemma, International Trade and the North-South Cooperation." In *Economics Policies for Sustainable Development.* Manila: Asian Development Bank, 1990.

Hardin, G. "Paramount Positions in Ecological Economics." In *Ecological Economics,* edited by R.

Costanza. New York: Columbia University Press, 1991.

Hueting, R. "The Brundtland Report: A Matter of Conflicting Goals." *Ecological Economics* 2(2) (1990): 109–18.

Lovins, A. B. "Does Abating Global Warming Cost or Save Money?" *Rocky Mountain Institute* 6(3) (1990): 1–3.

MacNeill, J. "Strategies for Sustainable Develop-ment." *Scientific American* 261(3)(1989): 154–65.

Meadows, D. H., et al. *The Limits to Growth: A Report for the Club of Rome's Project on the Predicament of Mankind.* 2d ed. New York: Universe Books, 1974.

Office of Technology Assessment. *Energy in Develop-ing Countries.* Washington, D.C.: OTA, 1991.

Pimentel, D., et al. "World Agriculture and Soil Erosion." *BioScience* 37(4)(1987): 277–83.

Shea, C. P. "Protecting Life on Earth: Steps to Save the Ozone Layer." Worldwatch Paper No. 87. Washington, D.C.: Worldwatch Institute, 1989.

Speth, J. G. "A Luddite Recants: Technological Inno-vation and the Environment." *The Amicus Journal* (Spring 1989): 3–5.

Tinbergen, J., and R. Hueting. "GNP and Market Prices: Wrong Signals for Sustainable Economic Success That Mask Environmental Destruction." …

Vitousek, Peter M., et al. "Human Appropriation of the Products of Photosynthesis." *BioScience* 34(6) (1986): 368–73.

World Commission on Environment and Develop-ment. "Our Common Future" (The Brundtland Report). Oxford: Oxford University Press, 1987.

Note

1. Robert Goodland, "The Case That the World Has Reached Its Limits," in *Population, Technology, and Lifestyles: The Transition to Sustainability*, ed. Robert Goodland, Herman E. Daly, and Salah El Serafy (Washington, DC: Island Press, 1992), 3-22. Copyright Island Press.

3.   A Proposal for Environmental Labels: Informing Consumers of the Real Costs of Consumption[1]

Shari Collins-Chobanian

CONSUMPTION'S COSTS ARE FURTHER detailed in this selection by Shari Collins-Chobanian. Here she follows the lead of the current "nutrition label" and provides a model for an environmental label that would detail environmental harm and the costs of producing, and consuming, each product. While much of the information suggested can be found by consumers who have a surplus of hours to research the information available in myriad sources, not only is there crucial information consumers cannot obtain, but also the burden is placed on them, not the manufacturers. Drawing from informed consent and notions of autonomy, Collins-Chobanian argues that consumers have a right to this information. When considering the issues covered in this anthology, from human rights violations to transgenic agricultural products prevalent in the food supply, one way to become empowered enough to not contribute to these harms is with information. If producers want to maintain their fair business practices, their products' safety, and/or the fact that they are sustainable and earth-friendly, disclosing their full production practices, suppliers, and ingredients seems the only consistent course of action.

Introduction

THE NATIONAL RESEARCH COUNCIL of the National Academy of Sciences states that 20,000 cases of cancer a year in the United States are caused by pesticide residues. Pesticides are used in the production of myriad consumer products, harm workers, and pollute the environment, and yet we have little to no idea what pesticides have been used in the production of the products we consume. Further, in pursuit of its standard of living and lifestyle, the United States is the largest producer and consumer not only of pesticides, but also of hazardous waste. Regarding the latter, "the United States is by far the greatest producer, generating ten times as much hazardous waste as all of Western Europe."[2]

In this paper I argue that an environmental facts label[3] that informs the consumer of known risks, harms, and environmental costs incurred in all stages of production/consumption of a product should be provided to consumers. This label would include such information as pesticide PPMs (parts per million)[4] used, energy expended, pollution and toxic waste generated, water and soil resources used and/or contaminated, animals harmed (through testing, factory farming, drugs given, etc.), irradiation of the product, people put at risk (such as chemical exposure of farmworkers and others, dangerous machinery, white/black lung), and traditional communities displaced. The first and foremost goal of an environmental label is to *inform consumers* of the real costs of consumption, with the corresponding increase in autonomy that information provides. Although I hope that environmental labels would also eventually bring about greater corporate and consumer accountability for environmental harm, lead to broad-scale change of both consumer habits and corporate activities, and protect nonhuman nature, my proposal for labels is focused on informing first.

I first utilize case studies that illustrate some harms and then describe the ideal form of an environmental label, as well as a minimally acceptable label that could be provided in transition toward the full disclosure an ideal label would provide. It is crucial in applied ethics, especially environmental ethics, to know about harms that exist in order to be in a position to address and redress those harms. People cannot take responsibility for harm without knowledge. Consumers cannot make autonomous decisions without being informed. There can be no informed consent without knowledge. Environmental labels would inform us of harms, allow us to see where our responsibility lies, and enable autonomy in market decisions. Although environmental labels would provide information necessary to begin to eliminate the harms, labels are far from sufficient for what is needed to solve current environmental problems.

Existing Models for an Environmental Label

There are two groups of existing models for an environmental label: nutrition labels and "ecolabels."

Nutrition Labels

We currently have nutrition facts labels on most consumer food products. These labels provide the consumer with nutrition information, including sodium, fat, and caloric content. Nutrition labels are provided primarily for consumer health issues related to dietary concerns. In addition to the nutrition label is an ingredients list that helps consumers with health concerns regarding food allergies and sensitivities. However, the ingredients list is incomplete: it does not include a list, for example, of the resultant traces of pesticides used to grow or store the food that remain *in* the food. Although there was some controversy concerning costs in passing the Nutrition Labeling and Education Act (NLEA) of 1990, it was determined that the harms that existed in the absence of providing that information outweighed the inconvenience and costs in developing and providing nutrition facts labels.

We do not have, however, beyond nutrition labels and ingredients listed, any other information about the costs (either the real economic cradle-to-grave costs or the harms) of the product. Moreover, the ingredients list is only a partial list, because we know pesticides are used in the production of the product, and we know that many products are irradiated, but this information does not appear on the label. Reference to pesticides and irradiation appears only if they have not been used, as seen on some items in health food stores. Environmental labeling would provide consumers with the information necessary to make fully informed decisions regarding products, expose truer costs of consumer products, and come closer to the justification for market competition that is presently a myth—that informed consumers choose between competing products.

"Ecolabels"

There is a model for environmental labels in ecolabels; however, the concept of an environmental label, as I envision it, appears to be a new concept. There is also precedent in the consumer information provided on some products. Two examples of an environmental label that are in the form of an environmental "stamp of approval" include the Ecolabel and the Blue Angel.[5] The Blue Angel, used in the Federal Republic of Germany since 1978, is a mark that appears on products that are less environmentally harmful than comparable products as measured in all stages of the product's life, from production to use to disposal. The Blue Angel is awarded to products by an independent jury. According to a Web site on the subject, "[i]n 1993, about 4353 products in 71 product groups were marked with the 'Blue Angel' environmental label (e.g., refrigerators and freezers without any CFCs)."[6] The Ecolabel, an extension of the Blue Angel concept used in the European market, is an environmental label in the form of a daisy with a stem, four leaves, and the ecology symbol 'E' surrounded by stars for petals. The Ecolabel is slated to first appear on household appliances and eventually on other consumer goods like paper goods and compost.[7]

Many products in health food stores also contain a form of environmental labeling when "nonirradiated" or "organic" is stated on the label. Many beauty and personal hygiene products now state "not tested on animals" or "contains no animal products" in response to successful animal rights campaigns that have raised awareness. Many other products claim to be "green," either through production ("farm-raised" shrimp or teak) or through environmental impact ("biodegradable" or "recyclable").[8]

However, even if all of the above examples were provided for each product, they would still be insufficient to address the harms involved in the production of the products. As utilized, ecolabels assuage the consumer conscience rather than educate consumers about the costs of consumption. At a minimum, an ecolabel would need to provide a quick visual reference to these costs and not a stamp of approval. Such a representation could be like the thermometers on the side of salsas, on which greater spiciness is represented by a higher line of red "mercury." A minimally acceptable ecolabel would be similar, with the relative level of environmental costs being represented perhaps by a glass of toxic sludge. I will thoroughly discuss both an ideal and a minimally acceptable format for environmental labels below. I now turn to a discussion of case studies that illustrate the harms a label would address.

Decisions Regarding Harms That Should Be Included in an Environmental Label

In order to adequately address the harms caused by consumption, environmental labels would need to include information known about those harms. The minimal list of harms I propose should be addressed entails the following: environmental pollution generated; pesticides used at all stages (including in warehousing products); habitat destroyed or threatened (human as well as other species); human health risks, from production to consumption to waste; environmental racism; animals harmed and made to suffer; species threatened; and genetically altered plants and animals. I will address some of these issues in detail below, but first I briefly address the nature of such a label and the difficulty in deciding what issues will be disclosed.

What I envision is a logical extension of nutrition labels. No ingredient list is complete while pesticides from production or storage are in the food (produce is often fogged, and cans, especially soda, are also sprayed in storage) and these pesticides are consumed with the product but are not included in the list. Further, warning labels on drugs, both on the packages and in the information provided with prescriptions, set a precedent by disclosing potential harms similar in nature to some of the information I propose for environmental labeling.

Although I provided a list above of harms to be included in the label, there are numerous issues concerning what harms should be included and what knowledge should be disclosed that have yet to be addressed. From the outset, there are problems in defining categories concerning types of harms, there are debates about what constitutes harm and what scientific data establish a case of harm, as well as debates about the data themselves (from source to interpretation). In addition to many empirical questions, given that all consumption necessarily involves costs and some form of harm, there will be subjective questions about what types of harm are more important, and these will not be easily decided. Thus, although I argue that the harms I list should be included in the labels, public debate about which harms are the most pressing, and thus must be addressed via a label, will most likely be necessary. At the least, exposure to the myriad issues of harm via public debate will raise consumer awareness, even if the issues are not addressed on a label.

Before I address sample case studies, I need to briefly comment on the difference between the harms, costs, and the data that would illustrate them. I envision discussions of harm on labels similar to warnings on alcohol and cigarette packages. Statements that would address harms/risks/costs could resemble the following: "This product was tested on animals by placement in their eyes"; "This product is from a sun-grown coffee plantation that destroyed x acres of habitat formerly crucial to migrating songbirds"; and "This product contains x chemical, which is a known carcinogen." I consider the data to range from "Chemicals x, y, and z were used in k amount" to "x number of linear feet of lumber were used" to "x number of CFCs were released in the production of this product," and so on. Admittedly, these are inflammatory statements, as well as a very incredible expectation for an environmental label. However, I intend this as a proposal, a germinative effort. I will address two potential methods of gathering and measuring data as well as provide potential models and answers to potential objections in the last two sections. I now turn to a more detailed explanation of the types of harms that should be addressed in an environmental label.

A Discussion with Sample Case Studies of Harms to Be Disclosed

One of the most important issues to disclose in an environmental label is the use of pesticides at all stages of production. Pesticides are usually synthetic chemicals derived from petroleum. Pesticides can act on a broad spectrum, killing numerous species, or they can act selectively, killing or disabling a target species. Many pesticides have been banned because of their clear carcinogenic and other effects, such as DDT, malathion, and Agent Orange, yet the 'circle of poison'[9] recognizes that those we have banned often come back to us on imported food, in some cases even having been produced by U.S. corporations.

Pesticides do not merely harm target species, they harm and impose risk of harm in a wide and persistent manner. Pesticides disrupt reproductive behavior; cause cancer; cause cell mutations; result in abnormal eggs and young; harm the nervous system and gastrointestinal tract; result in hair loss, kidney and liver problems, and neurological problems; and can result in sterility and hormone imbalances.[10] Pesticides pollute air, water, and soil; have made one third of the wells in Iowa, Minnesota, and Wisconsin toxic;[11] cause crops on which they are utilized to require more water than those on which they are not;[12] are crucial to hybrid crops (such as seedless grapes); and are used in golf courses, in swimming pools, on lawns, on roadsides, and in buildings. As stated in the introduction, it is estimated that 20,000 cases of cancer a year in the United States are caused by pesticide residues. The United States accounts for the most use of pesticides in the world.

Pesticides harm (and place at risk of harm) both workers involved in their production and those at every stage of use from harvesting and handling of products exposed. Pesticides can be inhaled, absorbed through skin, and ingested. Pesticide absorption is often increased if the person exposed is dehydrated, a common state for farmworkers.[13] People are also exposed to pesticides through unsuspected avenues, as pesticides are on cut flowers, in paint, in carpeting, on clothing, and on soda cans. A label that disclosed the pesticides used at every stage of a product's development would address these issues.[14]

Another important harm that should be addressed via labels is pollution generated at all stages of production. Much of what we consume is sold in a form that entails many unnecessary stages in production and the utilization of many additional resources. If consumers knew the real environmental cost of many products, such as the environmental cost of bleaching toilet paper (an unnecessary stage) or providing unnecessary packaging,

such as a cardboard cereal box around a plastic bag containing the cereal, then they could at the least demand less harmful processes, and at the most, insist that such processes cease. If toilet paper and other paper products were not bleached, and if cardboard packaging were not used for cereal boxes and other products, this would be a significant step in reducing pollution generated, as well as resources used. Such progress is not at all unlikely; the reader need only remember original compact disc packaging and the consumer backlash that ended the cardboard packaging to envision other, similar potential impact.[15]

Another important issue that should be addressed is that of habitat destroyed or threatened for the production of consumer products. Consider coffee. This topic is no small matter. Coffee is second only to oil as the world's most important commodity export, generating $10 billion per year in revenue,[16] and the United States is the chief consumer. On "traditional" plantations in Central and South America, coffee was mostly shade grown. This practice entailed biodiversity, as the coffee plants were shaded by overhanging fruit and other shade trees. These shade trees were also the winter home of as many as 150 migratory species of songbirds. Because of demand and the encouragement of U.S. governmental aid, many growers turn their coffee plantations into "sun plantations," destroying the overhanging trees and reducing land use to monoculture. Further, sun-grown coffee requires heavy doses of fertilizers, pesticides, and other chemicals. It also increases erosion on steep hillsides where coffee is grown.[17] The consumption of coffee from growers that engage in these practices is thus destroying habitat for migratory songbirds that previously wintered in the shade trees that sheltered coffee bushes. Without labeling requirements, coffee consumers will not know about the direct causal link between their coffee consumption and the destruction of songbird habitat. A spokesperson for Starbucks, which is currently the largest gourmet coffee chain, said that not only do they not know of a "reliable" source for shade-grown coffee, they are "very concerned about the land in coffee-producing countries," but their "first and foremost concern has to be coffee quality."[18] In the absence of consumer knowledge that a label would provide, it is unlikely that producers will change the harmful consumption practices that are driving the move to sun plantations.

Another issue labeling would address is the issue of harm to animals, including factory farming practices of domesticated animals, loss of habitat and the resulting threat to wild species, species harm such as that which resulted from DDT use and destroyed peregrine falcon eggs, and genetically altered animals. Although it may seem absurd to label a package of meat with information about animal suffering and harm to the animal when the ultimate harm has obviously already transpired, the consumer currently has no way of knowing the practices and costs (including economic and environmental) involved in bringing meat to that point. Consider hog farming, factory style. Hogs are kept in buildings, on steel grates, over their own waste and breathing in the gases, never seeing sunlight, rolling in mud, or able to be next to their mothers, except through bars where they can nurse. In order to speed up their development and weight gain, they are fed a high-protein diet with numerous additives. Pigs cannot absorb everything that is in the food, so their feces is laced with heavy metals, including zinc and copper, from the food, which then pollutes wherever the feces is dumped. One hog produces approximately eight times the amount of waste per day of one adult human. This waste is stored in cesspools, euphemistically called lagoons by corporate owners, that stink, leak, and overflow. One such overflow

resulted when heavy rains led to a spill of feces, urine, and afterbirth twice the size of the Exxon Valdez oil spill that poured into the countryside in North Carolina. This spill wiped out "virtually all aquatic life in the 17-mile stretch between Richlands and Jacksonville and left a stench for days."[19] Ninety percent of the pork consumed in this country comes from this type of factory farming, although only 10 percent of the "farmers" raising hogs practice factory farming.[20]

There are so many layers of harm involved that this topic alone is quite unruly and, in large part, beyond the scope of this paper. There is harm to the animals that suffer in the factory farms from the gases and the painful steel grates that injure their hooves. There is corporate displacement of family farms. There is environmental harm from waste laced with heavy metals. Workers in these facilities also have extreme health problems, from respiratory ills to fatigue. To but an informed few, these issues are not apparent.

Thus, when purchasing a shrink-wrapped, brightly labeled package of pork sausage or bacon, the consumer is not faced with any costs other than the price tag. An environmental label would put the consumer's direct connection to funding these harms in full view.

One final issue that I will address, although by no means the final issue of harm,[21] is genetically altered products, especially transgenic gene expression in plants. Flounder genes have been put in tomatoes, chicken genes in potatoes, and tobacco genes in lettuce. Soybeans have also been genetically altered, including the addition of Brazil nut genes.[22] Yet none of these changes are disclosed to the consumer. There is significant global mobilization regarding labeling products that are genetically altered, and this appears to be a promising fight for labeling advocates.[23]

We know that genetically altered crops are biologically active and that they can transfer their genes to wild relatives. There is no way to predict or control what effect this gene transfer will or could have in the eco-system. The wild cousins of potatoes in Peru are at risk. Crops that are genetically altered in order to have greater resistance to pesticides[24] can transfer that trait and lead to what is called a "super weed" that will have even greater resistance and pose a threat to our food sources. All the while, our monoculture agricultural practices have already reduced genetic diversity irreversibly.[25] Extinction of plant species is permanent, and threats from genetically altered crops risk further extinctions. There has been no public debate about whether we *should* be doing this. There has been no discussion about whether consumers wanted genetically altered crops. Consumers were not consulted, or at a minimum, even informed about such practices. Consider a similar case, the use of bovine growth hormone (BGH, also known as BHT) in dairy cows. Consumers have not even been allowed to be informed about the use of BGH in the dairy products they consume.[26] Monsanto's (and others') lobbying efforts resulted in the defeat of the consumer cry for labeling BGH products.

Monsanto not only is an environmental recidivist in its unethical actions regarding our environment, but repeatedly thwarts the public's right to know about Monsanto products that the public is exposed to and is consuming. Monsanto's most recent foray into control of our food source involves the 'control of plant gene expression,' a.k.a. 'The Terminator.'[27] The Terminator is "actually three genes incorporated into a plant. Two come from bacteria; they prevent a mature plant's seeds from manufacturing a protein needed to germinate."[28] The Terminator is meant to prevent farmers from saving seeds and to force them to instead purchase new seeds each year. As Harry Collins, Vice President of Delta and Pine Co. (which with the USDA developed the Terminator that Monsanto was in the process of acquiring) states, "The centuries old practice of farmer saved seed is really a gross disadvantage to third world farmers who inadvertently become locked into obsolete varieties because of their taking the 'easy roads' and not planting newer, more productive varieties."[29]

The full implications of this quote are beyond the scope of this paper; however, it serves well to illustrate the many levels of arrogance and ethnocentrism operating in the development of this transgenic "product." Most important are the risks involved. Transgenic crops can spread their traits. As Collins stated, the control of plant gene expression "will have broad applications in self-pollinated varietal crops."[30] Although the patent description claims that "non-transgenic plants (and transgenic plants that do not contain an expressing coat protein gene) cannot be infected by this virus" (the Terminator), because of genetic transfer and pollination transfer of genetic material, the risk exists. Further, harm and risk of harm from ingestion of seeds and by-products of plants exposed to the Terminator are unknown. Without a label, you will not know. An environmental label would immediately inform the consumer of all of the above issues.

Consumer Informed Consent

Consumers need to be informed about the types of issues I envision in an environmental label for three main reasons. First, consumption contributes to many harms. Second, consumer autonomy is violated in the absence of the information that would be provided by the labels. Third, the information available in scattered sources is not accessible to the average person, and even if this information is amassed, it is insufficient to inform the consumer of existing harms.

Consumption and Harms

First, consumption is environmentally costly and contributes to many undisclosed and unforeseen harms. Many of these consumption-related harms could ideally be avoided, or at least minimized, either through different production methods or a lower consumption rate. When made aware of harms, especially when the harms are made salient to consumer consciences, consumer habits do change, boycotts are instigated, and production is eventually responsive (unfortunately due most often to legal or economic pressure and not attention to ethical duty). Our lifestyles are incredibly environmentally destructive with no correlative accountability, either from production or by consumers. In order for consumer accountability to be achieved, people must have access to knowledge of harms and be able to act on that knowledge. The following examples illustrate how knowledge of harms can be instrumental in a consumption change.

Although eating beef from any source (given all current ranching/farming methods) contributes to and fuels environmental harm, including soil erosion and high water and energy costs, eating beef from rainforest cattle fueled particular practices and environmental destruction that, once made aware, many people considered unacceptable.[31] Slash and burn deforestation and destruction of the rainforests, erosion, increased malaria, displacement of indigenous peoples, and many other harms are all inextricably connected with rainforest cattle ranching. Public linkage of McDonald's to rainforest beef led to its having to refrain from using rainforest beef and explicitly state this policy change. However, in the absence of a reliable label, there is no way for the consumer to know where his or her beef was produced. Although rainforest beef did not receive anywhere near the amount of press coverage devoted to the prurient details of President Clinton's affairs, or O.J. Simpson's criminal and civil trials, the moderate information made available about rainforest beef did have an impact. Further, two related labeling issues, sweatshops partially run by child labor and "mad cow" disease, were very much in the media in the mid- to late 1990s, and the latter issue resulted in a significant stock market ripple (and a subsequent unsuccessful lawsuit from the Cattleman's Association) after Oprah Winfrey aired an episode of her popular talk show on the topic.

Not only do we contribute to environmental harms from consumption, but without knowledge of what is in our food and other consumer goods, we cannot know what we are literally consuming (ingesting) or have been exposed to from products. As we become more knowledgeable about how pesticides persist in the environment, bioaccumulate, and affect us and the environment overall, it becomes quite clear that we are in need of further scientific and "kitchen table"[32] data. Regarding our use of pesticides, it is not possible to predict the full spectrum of potential harmful effects, nor to even test for whatever predictions we can envision, as it is not possible to replicate real-world situations in laboratories. Thus, people and the environment overall are the laboratories where harmful effects (which cannot be sufficiently tested for before release) manifest.

One principle that, if followed, would avoid much of the harm is the precautionary principle. The precautionary principle places the burden of showing that a product will not harm the environment or human health on those wishing to introduce it, and is the principle behind testing required by the Food and Drug Administration, as well as environmental impact statements. It states that in the absence of certainty caution should be the guiding principle. However, the precautionary principle is widely disregarded and difficult to follow, as many of the harmful effects can be of a cumulative or synergistic nature and do not manifest for generations.

Synergistic effects are those that result from the interaction of two or more substances, practices, etc. A recent example of a synergistic effect that has been widely publicized is the harm that is risked from taking ibuprofen or acetaminophen and drinking more than two alcoholic beverages a day. Considering that consumption of alcohol can result in a headache, the risk of this synergistic effect by an ignorant consumer is quite high. Whereas synergistic effects that involve two substances interacting are *perhaps* testable, *Chemical Abstract* lists more than 5.3 million chemicals. In addition, there are approximately 70,000 synthetic chemicals in commercial production, with more than 1,000 new ones added annually. Twenty-five thousand of these chemicals are produced in large quantities.[33] Many of these commercially produced chemicals have multiple modes of action, creating many complications in performing any testing procedure.[34] The difficulty in identifying which chemicals need to be studied and by what testing methods presents an overwhelming problem for any accurate estimate of risks. More pointedly, *it is not possible* to perform risk analyses on the synergistic effects of the number of synthetic chemicals produced. However, knowing what is in or has been used to make a product will enable consumers to begin to put together information about synergistic and cumulative harms.

Consumer Autonomy

Another advantage of environmental labeling would be the contribution to consumer autonomy. Our present market myth is that informed consumers purchase products based on knowledge of the product and desire and within certain economic constraints. We cannot claim to have an informed consumer, if, at the least, she is purchasing a product with a list of ingredients that does not include the pesticide residues that are in that product. An environmental label would require full disclosure of all known, actual ingredients. The call to disclose such information is not without precedent, as there has been legislation directed at providing consumers with this type of information or, alternatively, preventing the use of harmful substances. The Delaney clause of the 1958 federal Food, Drug and Cosmetic Act prohibited or limited the existence of (known) cancer-causing chemicals in food. However, the recent gutting of the Delaney clause via the misleadingly named Food Quality and Protection Act[35] reduced consumer protection because it raised the legal limits on pesticide traces found in food[36] and resulted in less available consumer information, as it changed how pesticides are registered. Any substantive notion and actualization of consumer autonomy is not possible without disclosure of known information about products he consumes. Any substantive notion and actualization of consumer consent to risks from using a product is not possible without disclosure of known information about those risks. An environmental label would begin to address these issues and provide necessary (although not sufficient) information for consumers to exercise autonomy.

Information Now Available

There is information now available concerning environmental harms as discussed above, as well as human health risks, and a myriad of other issues concerning the costs of consumption. However, the information must generally be sought out by the consumer and is not readily available. Further, the information available is often incomplete, and sufficient testing regarding harms and the risk of harms has not been carried out. In the absence of a labeling requirement as I envision environmental labels, there is little to no manufacturer incentive to acquire the information, either through more testing or through a concerted effort to accumulate, disclose, and/or assimilate the information available. Consumers have neither the time to amass this information nor the expertise to comprehend some of the data or to test for potential harm. This burden belongs on those involved in the production of consumer goods, for they are the ones most clearly benefiting from the production, have the most knowledge of resources used, have the most control over resources used, and bear the ethical duty that the precautionary principle imports.

An environmental label is one way that the above issues and concerns can begin to be addressed. A label is convenient, promotes the exercise of consumer autonomy, provides part of the information necessary for obtaining consumer consent, and is a visible tool for educating consumers about the costs of consumption. The existing ecolabels discussed above are insufficient to convey the above information, both because they are not required and thus only appear sporadically, and because they are granted to what are considered "good" or less environmentally harmful products. Further, this "stamp of approval" gives power to others to decide what level is good enough, what harms are important, and what information will be disseminated to the consumer.

Environmental Labels: My Model

Each stage of production and consumption, *from the cradle to the grave*, needs to be examined in order to determine the real costs of the products we consume. This is similar to a life cycle analysis (LCA).[37] The first part of an LCA is to perform a life cycle inventory that takes into account all inputs throughout the manufacturing process, including everything used to make the product as well as by-products and subsequent transportation of the goods. Although we can also use a manufacturer's toxics release inventory (TRI) to obtain data on the end pollutants associated with manufacturing of a particular product, including those discharged into the environment, recycled, and transferred to other sites, we do not presently have a full accounting from the cradle to the grave.[38]

Once a thorough examination of the costs takes place, this information needs to be disclosed to the consumer via a form of environmental labeling. There are a few types of this label that I envision. The possible types include a label on the product, on the shelf, in a pamphlet, or in a computer that can be read with bar code access. The first type, on the product, is desirable for many reasons. If a label is on the product, immediate information will be available and the information will be available after the product is purchased. It is important that the label on the product not be in the form of the existing ecolabels, which convey a "stamp of approval" and a "green light" for consumption. Rather, an environmental label on the product would provide a visual cue and reminder of the *costs* of the product, a goal of environmental labeling. The label could be in many different forms, both as an icon and as written information.

Existing nutrition labels provide one model. Nutrition labels have prescribed categories that, although not exhaustive of nutrition issues, provide basic information and usually a phone number for access to further information. An environmental label could contain environmental categories similar in nature to the categories on nutrition labels. For example, like the fat grams category on the nutrition label, pesticide parts per million used in production or traces in the product could be disclosed in the environmental label. In addition to this existing written information, an icon that warns the consumer, like the thermometers on salsas and sauces, would be beneficial as a quick reference. This could have a higher level for items with higher environmental costs, or it could be the glass of toxic sludge mentioned earlier—the fuller the glass, the more environmentally costly the product.

Another form the label could take would be information placed on the shelf where the product is displayed. Currently on shelves we have information on prices, cost per ounce, and product numbers. In addition to this type of information, in car parts sections there are booklets attached to the shelf so the consumer can look up the relevant information for the part needed. A similar type of booklet could exist for environmental product information. Consumers could look up the product and obtain information about a number of environmental issues, from energy resources utilized, to pesticides used, to toxic exposures to workers, and so on.

Another form environmental labeling could take is to use the bar code to access environmental information. The consumer could take the product to a scanner near the product, scan the bar code, and obtain detailed information from a computer database. The advantage of this method is that the label would not be limited by the size of the product, and the consumer could access information based on interest or topic.

Whatever form the label takes, I envision an "ideal" label that will provide full disclosure of all (known) environmental costs. While working toward that ideal proposed, I propose a minimum standard for acceptable environmental labels. First, I will address the ideal label.

The ideal environmental label would provide full disclosure, much like a complete ingredients list, of all the environmental costs and harms that went into making the product. This would include the issues highlighted above and many others, including disclosure of cases of environmental racism[39] in conjunction with the product or its waste.

There are significant problems with providing ideal, full disclosure. Although the LCA and TRI mentioned above would supply crucial data, there is often disagreement about how to interpret data, and researchers can arrive at significantly disparate numerical ratings and conclusions.[40] Further, things such as solid waste generated and the amount of chemicals used can be fairly reliably measured, but the harms that result from certain emissions may be difficult to impossible to accurately measure.[41]

In light of these daunting impediments to the ideal, why mention it or attempt to defend it? This is a fair enough objection, but it could be raised against a great number of things, and my philosophy students often lodge this charge against ethics in general. The ideal is meant to serve as a goal and a check on the tendency to "lower the bar" that would certainly take place as corporations complain about the difficulty in providing the information that would allow consumers authentic autonomy. Although we might never arrive at the full disclosure the ideal label would require, it should remain the final goal.

As I write this, assuming that we can approach the ideal form, I am well aware of the overwhelming amount of information that would be on such a label. However, we cannot claim to be informed consumers without knowing the real costs and ingredients in products. Recent disclosure of known harmful effects for prescription and over-the-counter drugs is also rather overwhelming and is, additionally, too long to fit on the container. Yet neither of these points argues against consumers being informed. Just because it may be inconvenient, or depressing, or lengthy to do so does not argue against informing one of harms and costs. We do not refrain from telling a patient the risks associated with an operation because it may be overwhelming, nor do we shorten the consent form because it may be longer than the scar from the operation. Ideally, we would expect no less regarding consumer products.

One last point regarding the ideal label. As some consumers are illiterate, or may not be able to comprehend a written label, an ideal label would have both a written label and an icon with a quick reference to the level of harm. The icon would be a visual reminder (it could also be a raised Braille icon) so that the purpose behind labeling could not be easily ignored.

At a minimum environmental labels should have an icon and further access to information on the shelf and/or via a bar code scanner. This approach ensures that consumers who want information can obtain it and would cover a limited number of categories that have been agreed upon as the most important. The bar code would provide access to *known* information, while not imposing the bigger burden on manufacturers to find out information that an ideal label would require. However, in order to provide full consumer autonomy, full disclosure would need to remain a goal, and labels would need to reflect the ongoing process of uncovering and disseminating that information….

Though there are costs associated with the type of label I envision, it is clear that the costs of ignorance, continued harms, and continued risk of further harm outweigh the costs and inconvenience of an environmental label.

Questions

1. Why does Collins-Chobanian distinguish her model for environmental labels from models like the Energy Star or other "positive" labels? In your answer, describe each type of label and provide her environmental ethics argument. Do you agree that labels should inform rather than make us "feel good" about our purchases?

2. What are the five stages of informed consent? Why should consumers be fully informed about what they are consuming?

3. Would you heed such an environmental label and either eschew the product or lower your consumption rate of a product due to its environmental costs? Do you think that the general public would reduce or eliminate consumption based on such a label? Why or why not?

Notes

1. *Journal of Social Philosophy* 32, no. 3 (Fall 2001): 334–56. Copyright 2001 Blackwell Publishers. [Edited.]

2. Center for Investigative Reporting and Bill Moyers, *Global Dumping Ground: The International Traffic in Hazardous Waste* (Washington, D.C.: Seven Locks, 1990), 6.

3. My idea for an environmental label grew out of teaching applied ethics courses and my own frustration at how much information exists

concerning the harm from many products, none of which is available in a convenient form for consumers. Often when I teach about an issue such as factory hog farming, my students exclaim that they didn't know about the issue, wish that they had known, and claim that now that they know, they will no longer buy certain products. Although we have existing nutrition facts labels, and some existing 'ecolabels,' no label as I envision environmental labels exists.

4. See Theo Colborn, Dianne Dumanoski, and John Peterson Myers, *Our Stolen Future* (New York: Penguin Books, 1996), 40, for a discussion of how exposure to pesticides at much lower levels (parts per trillion, one million times lower than parts per million) can lead to significant, harmful results. Colborn et al. liken exposure at the level of parts per trillion to that of a train, 660 cars or 6 miles long, each full of water, with one tiny drop disseminated throughout the entire train.

5. For discussions of environmental labels as 'ecolabels' see Julie W. Lynch, "Environmental Labels: A New Policy Strategy," *Forum for Applied Research and Public Policy* 12, no. 1 (Spring 1997): 121–23; and Amy Lynn Salzhauer, "Obstacles and Opportunities for a Consumer Ecolabel," *Environment* 33, no. 9 (November 1991): 10–37.

6. www.bmu.de/ordner/J2_E.HTM

7. www.ecomarkt.nl/keurmerk/ecolabel.html (Stichting Milieu Wijzer), 1995.

8. The recent push for labor labels that resulted from media coverage of human rights issues of abuse and child labor issues in textile and clothing sweatshops is another related example of consumer labeling. Union labels, another consumer label, have been in existence for a long time.

9. The 'circle of poison' is the name for a particular phenomenon that occurs with pesticides. Although one country may ban the use of some pesticides, another may not, and imports from the country that does not ban the use end up on the tables of those that do. Further, although one country may ban the use of a pesticide, it may still allow for production and export of that pesticide,

again allowing for the banned pesticide to enter via products. In addition, the workers and communities in the country that does not ban use are exposed and put at risk of harm.

10. See "Toxic Effects of Pesticides: Experimental and Clinical Data" and "Short- and Long-Term Health Effects of Pesticides: Epidemiological Data," in World Health Organization, *Public Health Impact of Pesticides Used in Agriculture* (Geneva: World Health Organization, 1990), 33–61.

11. See Geoffrey C. Saign, *Green Essentials* (San Francisco: Mercury House, 1994), 306.

12. Through increased pest resistance and chemical ineffectiveness, crop losses have now measurably increased, even with the use of pesticides.

13. Recent legislation in Florida ensures farmworkers' right to have water while working. Adequate hydration had previously been denied to the workers as they did not have the right to drink water while working, nor were they provided with sufficient breaks to remain hydrated.

14. Pesticides are also an issue in wine, not just from the grapes, but from pesticides used to treat wood used to build the cellars in France. See Frank J. Prial, "Sommelier, What's That Smell?" *New York Times,* January 13, 1999, p. B11.

15. Although I realize that the plastic "jewel boxes" now used to package compact disks are also quite problematic and still utilized with staggering environmental costs, the diminishing of harm is still a sound utilitarian starting point.

16. Smithsonian Migratory Bird Center statistics cited in Heather Dewar, "Thirst for Coffee Linked to Loss of Bird Habitat: Growers Cut Trees to Perk up Yield," *Arizona Republic,* February 2, 1997, p. A26.

17. Ibid.

18. Ibid. Perhaps not at all ironic is the fact that shade-grown coffee, often organically grown, has fewer, sweeter berries that taste better and brings a higher market price, and the plants' lifespan is 25 percent longer.

19. Michael Satchell, "Hog Heaven—and Hell: Pig Farming Has Gone High Tech, and That's

Creating New Pollution Woes," *U.S. News & World Report,* January 22, 1996, p. 55.

20. An additional point is that the corporate hog farm is displacing the traditional family farm, by taking advantage of laws enacted to protect the family farmer. Further, the family farm is not anywhere near as intense an operation and the waste is dispersed, posing nowhere near the environmental harms.

21. Hybrid plant species also pose enormous environmental problems, as they require more pesticides, fertilizers, and water.

22. People with allergies to Brazil nuts have had allergic reactions to altered soybeans. As nut allergies can be fatal, labeling this type of genetic manipulation is a matter of life and death.

23. The Department of Agriculture's 1998 proposal to allow food that has been genetically altered, irradiated, and treated with sewage sludge to be included under an "organic" label met with unprecedented resistance. See Bill Lambrecht, "Agriculture Department Gets 150,000 Negative Responses to Proposal on Organic Foods," *St. Louis Post-Dispatch,* May 1, 1998; and Bill Lambrecht/Associated Press, "'Organic' Label Will Exclude Irradiation, Other Food Processes," *St. Louis Post-Dispatch,* May 9, 1998. Regarding transgenic issues, see Don Corrigan, "Area Residents Take to Streets for Food Labeling," *Webster/Kirkwood Times,* February 12, 1999, www.timesnewspapers.com; Neil Buckley; "Move on Gene-Modified Food," *Financial Times,* London Edition, July 25, 1997; Marian Burros, "Trying to Get Labels on Genetically Altered Food," *New York Times,* May 21, 1997, p. C3; Barnaby J. Feder, "Biotechnology Company to Join Those Urging Labels on Genetically Altered Products," *New York Times,* February 24, 1997; Marc Lappe and Britt Bailey, "Labeling," in *Against the Grain: Biotechnology and the Corporate Takeover of Your Food* (Monroe, Maine: Common Courage Press, 1998), 119–31 (this chapter has a partial industry response to and argument against labeling); Ray Moseley, "Brit Mad-Cow Fear Replaced by Gene-Altered Food Scare," *Arizona Republic,* February 28, 1999, p. A15; and all of the following by Bill Lambrecht of the *St. Louis Post-Dispatch,* available online at www.postnet.com: "Monsanto Softens Its Stance on Labeling in Europe: It Says Disclosures on Gene-Altered Food Are OK There, but Not in the U.S.," March 15, 1998; "Growers Want to Stem Use of 'Organic' Label: They Oppose U.S. Plan to Allow It on Genetically Modified Foods," March 26, 1998; "French Are Wary of Monsanto Super Seeds," June 28, 1998; "World Recoils at Monsanto's Brave New Crops," December 27, 1998; "Talks Collapse on Rules for Genetic Crops," February 25, 1999; "U.S. Helps Block Global Rules on Genetically Modified Products," February 26, 1999.

24. One of the "justifications" provided by genetic engineering firms was that genetically altered plants would need less pesticides once "natural pesticides" from other plants were spliced in. However, what has become clear is that pesticide-resistant traits have instead been intentionally spliced in so that the crop can withstand greater doses of pesticides made necessary by the resistance of pests to existing pesticide usage.

25. See Deane Curtin, "Making Peace with the Earth: Indigenous Agriculture and the Green Revolution," *Environmental Ethics* 17, no. 1 (1995).

26. Vermont did require that dairy products from BGH cows be labeled on the shelf—with a blue label—but not on the product itself.

27. U.S. Patent 5,723,765, awarded March 3, 1998, to the USDA and Delta and Pine Land Co. See "Monsanto Sez [*sic*]: This Isn't Too Different from Hybrid Crops Which Don't Reproduce," *Guardian,* April 15, 1998; Harry Collins, "New Technology and Modernizing World Agriculture," http://ds.dial.pipex.com/ukfg/UKabc/gaiam4; and Bill Lambrecht, "'Terminator' Genes Renders Seeds [*sic*] Sterile: Farmers No Longer Could Save Them for Next Year; U.S. Government Helped Develop It," April 19, 1998, and "Critics Vilify New Seed Technology That Monsanto May Soon Control: 'Terminator'

Would Prevent Saving of Seeds by Making Them Sterile," *St. Louis Post-Dispatch,* November 1, 1998.

28. Bill Lambrecht, "Critics Vilify New Seed Technology."

29. Harry Collins, "New Technology."

30. Ibid.

31. See Frances Moore Lappe, *Diet for a Small Planet* (New York: Ballantine Books, 1982), 9–11; and Jeremy Rifkin, *Beyond Beef: The Rise and Fall of the Cattle Culture* (New York: Dutton, 1992), 153.

32. Kitchen table data are those that come from discussions across the kitchen table. Here, families and friends, often women in particular, discuss health and other problems noticed (or alternatively health benefits) and begin to put together causal data concerning when the problem was noticed, what product was being used or where an exposure might have occurred, etc. This is an invaluable and untapped resource of empirical data. If such details were available via a type of environmental label, this would provide additional information and strengthen the understanding of causal connections gleaned from everyday experience.

33. Committee on Chemical Environmental Mutagens, *Identifying and Estimating the Genetic Impact of Chemical Mutagens* (Washington, D.C.: National Academy Press, 1983).

34. See K. Sankaranarayanan, "Estimation of Genetic Risks of Exposure to Chemical Mutagens: Relevance of Data on Spontaneous Mutations and of Experience with Ionizing Radiation," *Mutation Research,* no. 304 (1994): 139–58.

35. The Food Quality Protection Act was signed into law by President Clinton on August 3, 1996, after receiving no opposition in the House and the Senate. Higher levels of pesticides have been recorded on produce since the act was passed. Although these levels exceed federal health guidelines, they are now legal. See Stevenson Swanson, "Pesticides on Fruit High—but Legal," *Arizona Republic,* February 19, 1999, p. A1.

36. The rationale for raising these limits was that current scientific testing can provide us with information of very minute traces of pesticides in products. It is assumed that at this level, these substances are of no substantive risk. However, even if this might be the case for an isolated exposure to a substance, it cannot be assumed to be the case considering the nature of cumulative and synergistic harms. See also note 4.

37. See Salzhauer, "Obstacles and Opportunity," 13–14, for a full discussion of LCA.

38. See Shelley A. Hearne, "Tracking Toxics: Chemical Use and the Public's 'Right-to-Know,'" *Environment* 38, no. 6 (July/August 1996): 4–34. Hearne argues for an extension of the TRI to include "six throughput measures" to better report pollution, as well as to potentially prevent future pollution.

39. Environmental racism is the intentional targeting of communities of color for point-source generation of, storage of, and sites for hazardous waste, as well as disparate treatment of communities of color regarding environmental cleanup, Superfund status, and enforcement of environmental laws. The acknowledgment of environmental racism led to the environmental justice movement. See *Confronting Environmental Racism: Voices from the Grassroots,* ed. Robert D. Bullard (Boston: South End, 1993); *Unequal Protection: Environmental Justice and Communities of Color,* ed. Robert D. Bullard (San Francisco: Sierra Club Books, 1994); *Faces of Environmental Racism: Confronting Issues of Global Justice,* ed. Laura Westra and Peter Wenz (Lanham, Md.: Rowman & Littlefield, 1995); *Chicano Culture, Ecology, Politics: Subversive Kin,* ed. Devon Pena (Tucson: University of Arizona Press, 1998); *The Struggle for Ecological Democracy: Environmental Justice Movements in the United States,* ed. Daniel Faber (New York: Guilford, 1998); *The State of Native America: Genocide, Colonization, and Resistance,* ed. M. Annette Jaimes (Boston: South End, 1992); Peter H. Eichstaedt, *If You Poison Us: Uranium and Native Americans* (Santa Fe, N. Mex.: Red Crane, 1994); Donald A. Grinde, Jr.,

and Bruce E. Johansen, *Ecocide of Native America: Environmental Destruction of Indian Lands and Peoples* (Santa Fe, N. Mex.: Clear Light, 1992); Ward Churchill, *Struggle for the Land: Indigenous Resistance to Genocide, Ecocide, and Expropriation in Contemporary North America* (Monroe, Maine: Common Courage, 1993); and Shari Collins-Chobanian, "Environmental Racism, American Indians, and Monitored Retrievable Storage Sites for Radioactive Waste," in *Applied Ethics: A Multicultural Approach,* ed. Larry May, Shari Collins-Chobanian, and Kai Wong (Englewood Cliffs, N.J.: Prentice-Hall, 1998), 160–69.

40. For examples see Christopher Flavin, "The Heat Is On: The Greenhouse Effect," in *Worldwatch Reader,* ed. Lester Brown (New York: Norton, 1991); and Dixy Lee Ray and Louis Guzzo, "The Greenhouse Effect: Hype and Hysteria," and "The Blessings of Pesticides," in *Trashing the Planet* (Washington, D.C.: Regnery Gateway, 1990).

41. See Salzhauer, "Obstacles and Opportunities," 13, for more discussion of the difficulty in providing full disclosure.

4. Beyond Extractivism:
Confronting the Climate Denier Within[1]

Naomi Klein

THIS SELECTION FROM NAOMI Klein's 2014 book *This Changes Everything* begins with the example of Nauru, a small island ravaged by colonization and extraction. Extractivism is the practice of depleting natural resources in a nonreciprocal relationship between humans and the Earth. Klein (b. 1970) argues that human extractivism of fossil fuels has not resulted in the assumed result of control of nature; rather, the cumulative effects of fossil-fuel extraction and use have resulted in climate change. She implies that our failure to live within environmental limits has made us all Nauruans.

The best thing about the Earth is if you poke holes in it oil and gas comes out.
                    —Republican US Congressman Steve Stockman, 2013[2]

The open veins of Latin America are still bleeding.
                    —Bolivian Indigenous leader Nilda Rojas Huanca, 2014[3]

It is our predicament that we live in a finite world, and yet we behave as if it were infinite. Steady exponential material growth with no limits on resource consumption and population is the dominant conceptual model used by today's decision makers. This is an approximation of reality that is no longer accurate and [has] started to break down.
                    —Global systems analyst Rodrigo Castro and colleagues, paper
                    presented at a scientific modeling conference, 2014[4]

FOR THE PAST FEW years, the island of Nauru has been on a health kick. The concrete walls of public buildings are covered in murals urging regular exercise and healthy eating, and warning against the danger of diabetes. Young people are asking their grandparents how to fish, a lost skill. But there is a problem. As Nerida-Ann Steshia Hubert, who works at a diabetes center on the island, explains, life spans on Nauru are short, in part because of an epidemic of the disease. "The older folks are passing away early and we're losing a lot of the knowledge with them. It's like a race against time—trying to get the knowledge from them before they die."[5]

For decades, this tiny, isolated South Pacific island, just twenty-one square kilometers and home to ten thousand people, was held up as a model for the world—a developing country that was doing everything right. In the early 1960s, the Australian government, whose troops seized control of Nauru from the Germans in 1914, was so proud of its protectorate that it made promotional videos showing the Micronesians in starched white Bermuda shorts, obediently following lessons in English-speaking schools, settling their disputes in British-style courts, and shopping for modern conveniences in well-stocked grocery stores.[6]

During the 1970s and 1980s, after Nauru had earned independence, the island was periodically featured in press reports as a place of almost obscene riches, much as Dubai is invoked today. An Associated Press article from 1985 reported that Nauruans had "the world's highest per capita gross national product ... higher even than Persian Gulf oil Sheikdoms." Everyone had free health care, housing, and education; homes were kept cool with air-conditioning; and residents zoomed around their tiny island—it took twenty minutes to make the entire loop—in brand-new cars and motorcycles. A police chief famously bought himself a yellow Lamborghini. "When I was young," recalls Steshia Hubert, "we would go to parties where people would throw thousands of dollars on the babies. Extravagant parties—first, sixteenth, eighteenth, twenty-first, and fiftieth birthdays.... They would come with gifts like cars, pillows stuffed with hundred-dollar bills—for one-year-old babies!"[7]

All of Nauru's monetary wealth derived from an odd geological fact. For hundreds of thousands of years, when the island was nothing but a cluster of coral reefs protruding from the waves, Nauru was a popular pit stop for migrating birds, who dropped by to feast on the shellfish and mollusks. Gradually, the bird poop built up between the coral towers and spires, eventually hardening to form a rocky landmass. The rock was then covered over in topsoil and dense forest, creating a tropical oasis of coconut

palms, tranquil beaches, and thatched huts so beatific that the first European visitors dubbed the island Pleasant Isle.[8]

For thousands of years, Nauruans lived on the surface of their island, sustaining themselves on fish and black noddy birds. That began to change when a colonial officer picked up a rock that was later discovered to be made of almost pure phosphate of lime, a valuable agricultural fertilizer. A German–British firm began mining, later replaced by a British–Australian–New Zealand venture.[9] Nauru started developing at record speed—the catch was that it was, simultaneously, committing suicide.

By the 1960s, Nauru still looked pleasant enough when approached from the sea, but it was a mirage. Behind the narrow fringe of coconut palms circling the coast lay a ravaged interior. Seen from above, the forest and topsoil of the oval island were being voraciously stripped away; the phosphate mined down to the island's sharply protruding bones, leaving behind a forest of ghostly coral totems. With the center now uninhabitable and largely infertile except for some minor scrubby vegetation, life on Nauru unfolded along the thin coastal strip, where the homes and civic structures were located.[10]

Nauru's successive waves of colonizers—whose economic emissaries ground up the phosphate rock into fine dust, then shipped it on ocean liners to fertilize soil in Australia and New Zealand—had a simple plan for the country: they would keep mining phosphate until the island was an empty shell. "When the phosphate supply is exhausted in thirty to forty years' time, the experts predict that the estimated population will not be able to live on this pleasant little island," a Nauruan council member said, rather stiffly, in a sixties-era black-and-white video produced by the Australian government. But not to worry, the film's narrator explained: "Preparations are being made now for the future of the Nauruan people. Australia has offered them a permanent home within her own shores.... Their prospects are bright; their future is secure."[11]

Nauru, in other words, was developed to disappear, designed by the Australian government and the extractive companies that controlled its fate as a disposable country. It's not that they had anything against the place, no genocidal intent per se. It's just that one dead island that few even knew existed seemed like an acceptable sacrifice to make in the name of the progress represented by industrial agriculture.

When the Nauruans themselves took control of their country in 1968, they had hopes of reversing these plans. Toward that end, they put a large chunk of their mining revenues into a trust fund that they invested in what seemed like stable real estate ventures in Australia and Hawaii. The goal was to live off the fund's proceeds while winding down phosphate mining and beginning to rehabilitate their island's ecology—a costly task, but perhaps not impossible.[12]

The plan failed. Nauru's government received catastrophically bad investment advice, and the country's mining wealth was squandered. Meanwhile, Nauru continued to disappear, its white powdery innards loaded onto boats as the mining continued unabated. Meanwhile, decades of easy money had taken a predictable toll on Nauruans' life and culture. Politics was rife with corruption, drunk driving was a leading cause of death, average life expectancy was dismally low, and Nauru earned the dubious honor of being featured on a US news show as "the fattest place on Earth" (half the adult population suffers from type 2 diabetes, the result of a diet comprised almost exclusively of imported processed food). "During the golden era when the royalties were rolling in, we didn't cook, we ate in restaurants," recalls Steshia Hubert, a health care worker. And even if the Nauruans

had wanted to eat differently, it would have been hard: with so much of the island a latticework of deep dark holes, growing enough fresh produce to feed the population was pretty much impossible. A bitterly ironic infertility for an island whose main export was agricultural fertilizer.[13]

By the 1990s, Nauru was so desperate for foreign currency that it pursued some distinctly shady get-rich-quick schemes. Aided greatly by the wave of financial deregulation unleashed in this period, the island became a prime money-laundering haven. For a time in the late 1990s, Nauru was the titular "home" to roughly four hundred phantom banks that were utterly unencumbered by monitoring, oversight, taxes, and regulation. Nauru-registered shell banks were particularly popular among Russian gangsters, who reportedly laundered a staggering $70 billion of dirty money through the island nation (to put that in perspective, Nauru's entire GDP is $72 million, according to most recent figures). Giving the country partial credit for the collapse of the Russian economy, a *New York Times Magazine* piece in 2000 pronounced that "amid the recent proliferation of money-laundering centers that experts estimate has ballooned into a $5 trillion shadow economy, Nauru is Public Enemy #1."[14]

These schemes have since caught up with Nauru too, and now the country faces a double bankruptcy: with 90 per cent of the island depleted from mining, it faces ecological bankruptcy; with a debt of at least $800 million, Nauru faces financial bankruptcy as well. But these are not Nauru's only problems. It now turns out that the island nation is highly vulnerable to a crisis it had virtually no hand in creating: climate change and the drought, ocean acidification, and rising waters it brings. Sea levels around Nauru have been steadily climbing by about 5 millimeters per year since 1993, and much more could be on the way if current trends continue. Intensified droughts are already causing severe freshwater shortages.[15]

A decade ago, Australian philosopher and professor of sustainability Glenn Albrecht set out to coin a term to capture the particular form of psychological distress that sets in when the homelands that we love and from which we take comfort are radically altered by extraction and industrialization, rendering them alienating and unfamiliar. He settled on "solastalgia," with its evocations of solace, destruction, and pain, and defined the new word to mean, "the homesickness you have when you are still at home." He explained that although this particular form of unease was once principally familiar to people who lived in sacrifice zones—lands decimated by open pit mining, for instance, or clear-cut logging—it was fast becoming a universal human experience, with climate change creating a "new abnormal" wherever we happen to live. "As bad as local and regional negative transformation is, it is the big picture, the Whole Earth, which is now a home under assault. A feeling of global dread asserts itself as the planet heats and our climate gets more hostile and unpredictable," he writes.[16]

Some places are unlucky enough to experience both local and global solastalgia simultaneously. Speaking to the 1997 UN climate conference that adopted the Kyoto Protocol, Nauru's then-president Kinza Clodumar described the collective claustrophobia that had gripped his country: "We are trapped, a wasteland at our back, and to our front a terrifying, rising flood of biblical proportions."[17] Few places on earth embody the suicidal results of building our economies on polluting extraction more graphically than Nauru. Thanks to its mining of phosphate, Nauru has spent the last century disappearing from the inside out; now, thanks to our collective mining of fossil fuels, it is disappearing from the outside in.

In a 2007 cable about Nauru, made public by WikiLeaks, an unnamed US official summed up his government's analysis of what went wrong on the island: "Nauru simply spent extravagantly, never worrying about tomorrow."[18] Fair enough, but that diagnosis is hardly unique to Nauru; our entire culture is extravagantly drawing down finite resources, never worrying about tomorrow. For a couple of hundred years we have been telling ourselves that we can dig the midnight black remains of other life forms out of the bowels of the earth, burn them in massive quantities, and that the airborne particles and gases released into the atmosphere—because we can't see them—will have no effect whatsoever. Or if they do, we humans, brilliant as we are, will just invent our way out of whatever mess we have made.

And we tell ourselves all kinds of similarly implausible no-consequences stories all the time, about how we can ravage the world and suffer no adverse effects. Indeed we are always surprised when it works out otherwise. We extract and do not replenish and wonder why the fish have disappeared and the soil requires ever more "inputs" (like phosphate) to stay fertile. We occupy countries and arm their militias and then wonder why they hate us. We drive down wages, ship jobs overseas, destroy worker protections, hollow out local economies, then wonder why people can't afford to shop as much as they used to. We offer those failed shoppers subprime mortgages instead of steady jobs and then wonder why no one foresaw that a system built on bad debts would collapse.

At every stage our actions are marked by a lack of respect for the powers we are unleashing—a certainty, or at least a hope, that the nature we have turned to garbage, and the people we have treated like garbage, will not come back to haunt us. And Nauru knows all about this too, because in the past decade it has become a dumping ground of another sort. In an effort to raise much needed revenue, it agreed to house an offshore refugee detention center for the government of Australia. In what has become known as "the Pacific Solution," Australian navy and customs ships intercept boats of migrants and immediately fly them three thousand kilometers to Nauru (as well as to several other Pacific islands). Once on Nauru, the migrants—most from Afghanistan, Sri Lanka, Iraq, Iran, and Pakistan—are crammed into a rat-infested guarded camp made up of rows of crowded, stiflingly hot tents. The island imprisonment can last up to five years, with the migrants in a state of constant limbo about their status, something the Australian government hopes will serve as a deterrent to future refugees.[19]

The Australian and Nauruan governments have gone to great lengths to limit information on camp conditions and have prevented journalists who make the long journey to the island from seeing where migrants are being housed. But the truth is leaking out nonetheless: grainy video of prisoners chanting "We are not animals"; reports of mass hunger strikes and suicide attempts; horrifying photographs of refugees who had sewn their own mouths shut, using paper clips as needles; an image of a man who had badly mutilated his neck in a failed hanging attempt. There are also images of toddlers playing in the dirt and huddling with their parents under tent flaps for shade (originally the camp had housed only adult males, but now hundreds of women and children have been sent there too). In June 2013, the Australian government finally allowed a BBC crew into the camp in order to show off its brand-new barracks—but that PR attempt was completely upstaged one month later by the news that a prisoner riot had almost completely destroyed the new facility, leaving several prisoners injured.[20]

Amnesty International has called the camp on Nauru "cruel" and "degrading," and a 2013 report by the United Nations High Commissioner for Refugees concluded that those conditions, "coupled with the protracted period spent there by some asylum-seekers, raise serious issues about their compatibility with international human rights law, including the prohibition against torture and cruel, inhuman or degrading treatment." Then, in March 2014, a former Salvation Army employee named Mark Isaacs, who had been stationed at the camp, published a tell-all memoir titled The Undesirables. He wrote about men who had survived wars and treacherous voyages losing all will to live on Nauru, with one man resorting to swallowing cleaning fluids, another driven mad and barking like a dog. Isaacs likened the camp to "death factories," and said in an interview that it is about "taking resilient men and grinding them into the dust." On an island that itself was systematically ground to dust, it's a harrowing image. As harrowing as enlisting the people who could very well be the climate refugees of tomorrow to play warden to the political and economic refugees of today.[21]

Reviewing the island's painful history, it strikes me that so much of what has gone wrong on Nauru—and goes on still—has to do with its location, frequently described as "the middle of nowhere" or, in the words of a 1921 National Geographic dispatch, "perhaps the most remote territory in the world," a tiny dot "in lonely seas." The nation's remoteness made it a convenient trash can—a place to turn the land into trash, to launder dirty money, to disappear unwanted people, and now a place that may be allowed to disappear altogether.[22]

This is our relationship to much that we cannot easily see and it is a big part of what makes carbon pollution such a stubborn problem: we can't see it, so we don't really believe it exists. Ours is a culture of disavowal, of simultaneously knowing and not knowing—the illusion of proximity coupled with the reality of distance is the trick perfected by the fossil-fueled global market. So we both know and don't know who makes our goods, who cleans up after us, where our waste disappears to—whether it's our sewage or electronics or our carbon emissions.

But what Nauru's fate tells us is that there is no middle of nowhere, nowhere that doesn't "count"—and that nothing ever truly disappears. On some level we all know this, that we are part of a swirling web of connections. Yet we are trapped in linear narratives that tell us the opposite: that we can expand infinitely, that there will always be more space to absorb our waste, more resources to fuel our wants, more people to abuse.

These days, Nauru is in a near constant state of political crisis, with fresh corruption scandals perpetually threatening to bring down the government, and sometimes succeeding. Given the wrong visited upon the nation, the island's leaders would be well within their rights to point fingers outward—at their former colonial masters who flayed them, at the investors who fleeced them, and at the rich countries whose emissions now threaten to drown them. And some do. But several of Nauru's leaders have also chosen to do something else: to hold up their country as a kind of warning to a warming world.

In *The New York Times* in 2011, for instance, then-president Marcus Stephen wrote that Nauru provides "an indispensable cautionary tale about life in a place with hard ecological limits." It shows, he claimed, "what can happen when a country runs out of options. The world is headed down a similar path with the relentless burning of coal and oil, which is altering the planet's climate, melting ice caps, making oceans more acidic and edging us ever closer to a day when no one will be able to take clean water, fertile soil or abundant food for granted." In other

words, Nauru isn't the only one digging itself to death; we all are.[23]

But the lesson Nauru has to teach is not only about the dangers of fossil fuel emissions. It is about the mentality that allowed so many of us, and our ancestors, to believe that we could relate to the earth with such violence in the first place—to dig and drill out the substances we desired while thinking little of the trash left behind, whether in the land and water where the extraction takes place, or in the atmosphere, once the extracted material is burned. This carelessness is at the core of an economic model some political scientists call "extractivism," a term originally used to describe economies based on removing ever more raw materials from the earth, usually for export to traditional colonial powers, where "value" was added. And it's a habit of thought that goes a long way toward explaining why an economic model based on endless growth ever seemed viable in the first place. Though developed under capitalism, governments across the ideological spectrum now embrace this resource-depleting model as a road to development, and it is this logic that climate change calls profoundly into question.

Extractivism is a nonreciprocal, dominance-based relationship with the earth, one purely of taking. It is the opposite of stewardship, which involves taking but also taking care that regeneration and future life continue. Extractivism is the mentality of the mountaintop remover and the old-growth clear-cutter. It is the reduction of life into objects for the use of others, giving them no integrity or value of their own—turning living complex ecosystems into "natural resources," mountains into "overburden" (as the mining industry terms the forests, rocks, and streams that get in the way of its bulldozers). It is also the reduction of human beings either into labor to be brutally extracted, pushed beyond limits, or, alternatively, into social burden, problems to be locked out at borders and locked away in prisons or reservations. In an extractivist economy, the interconnections among these various objectified components of life are ignored; the consequences of severing them are of no concern.

Extractivism is also directly connected to the notion of sacrifice zones—places that, to their extractors, somehow don't count and therefore can be poisoned, drained, or otherwise destroyed, for the supposed greater good of economic progress. This toxic idea has always been intimately tied to imperialism, with disposable peripheries being harnessed to feed a glittering center, and it is bound up too with notions of racial superiority, because in order to have sacrifice zones, you need to have people and cultures who count so little that they are considered deserving of sacrifice. Extractivism ran rampant under colonialism because relating to the world as a frontier of conquest—rather than as home—fosters this particular brand of irresponsibility. The colonial mind nurtures the belief that there is always somewhere else to go to and exploit once the current site of extraction has been exhausted.

These ideas predate industrial-scale extraction of fossil fuels. And yet the ability to harness the power of coal to power factories and ships is what, more than any single other factor, enabled these dangerous ideas to conquer the world. It's a history worth exploring in more depth, because it goes a long way toward explaining how the climate crisis challenges not only capitalism but the underlying civilizational narratives about endless growth and progress within which we are all, in one way or another, still trapped.

The Ultimate Extractivist Relationship

If the modern-day extractive economy has a patron saint, the honor should probably go to Francis Bacon [1561–1626]. The English

philosopher, scientist, and statesman is credited with convincing Britain's elites to abandon, once and for all, pagan notions of the earth as a life-giving mother figure to whom we owe respect and reverence (and more than a little fear) and accept the role as her dungeon master. "For you have but to follow and as it were hound nature in her wanderings," Bacon wrote in *De Augmentis Scientiarum* in 1623, "and you will be able, when you like, to lead and drive her afterwards to the same place again.... Neither ought a man to make scruple of entering and penetrating into these holes and corners, when the inquisition of truth is his sole object."[24] (Not surprisingly, feminist scholars have filled volumes analyzing the ex-Lord Chancellor's metaphor choices.)

These ideas of a completely knowable and controllable earth animated not only the Scientific Revolution but, critically, the colonial project as well, which sent ships crisscrossing the globe to poke and prod and bring the secrets, and wealth, back to their respective crowns. The mood of human invincibility that governed this epoch was neatly encapsulated in the words of clergyman and philosopher William Derham [1657–1735] in his 1713 book *Physico-Theology*: "We can, if need be, ransack the whole globe, penetrate into the bowels of the earth, descend to the bottom of the deep, travel to the farthest regions of this world, to acquire wealth."[25]

And yet despite this bravado, throughout the 1700s, the twin projects of colonialism and industrialization were still constrained by nature on several key fronts. Ships carrying both slaves and the raw materials they harvested could sail only when winds were favorable, which could lead to long delays in the supply chain. The factories that turned those raw materials into finished products were powered by huge water wheels. They needed to be located next to waterfalls or rapids which made them dependent on the flow and levels of rivers. As with high or low winds at sea, an especially dry or wet spell meant that working hours in the textile, flour, and sugar mills had to be adjusted accordingly—a mounting annoyance as markets expanded and became more global.

Many water-powered factories were, by necessity, spread out around the countryside, near bodies of fast-moving water. As the Industrial Revolution matured and workers in the mills started to strike and even riot for better wages and conditions, this decentralization made factory owners highly vulnerable, since quickly finding replacement workers in rural areas was difficult.

Beginning in 1776, a Scottish engineer named James Watt [1736–1819] perfected and manufactured a power source that offered solutions to all these vulnerabilities. Lawyer and historian Barbara Freese describes Watt's steam engine as "perhaps the most important invention in the creation of the modern world"—and with good reason.[26] By adding a separate condenser, air pump, and later a rotary mechanism to an older model, Watt was able to make the coal-fired steam engine vastly more powerful and adaptable than its predecessors. In contrast, the new machines could power a broad range of industrial operations, including, eventually, boats.

For the first couple of decades, the new engine was a tough sell. Water power, after all, had a lot going for it compared with coal. For one thing, it was free, while coal needed to be continually re-purchased. And contrary to the widespread belief that the steam engine provided more energy than water wheels, the two were actually comparable, with the larger wheels packing several times more horsepower than their coal-powered rivals. Water wheels also operated more smoothly, with fewer technical breakdowns, so long as the water was flowing. "The transition from water to steam in the British cotton industry did not occur because water was scarce, less powerful, or more expensive than steam," writes Swedish coal expert Andreas Malm. "To the contrary, steam gained supremacy *in spite of water being abundant, at least as powerful, and decidedly cheaper.*"[27]

As Britain's urban population ballooned, two factors tipped the balance in favor of the steam engine. The first was the new machine's insulation from nature's fluctuations: unlike water wheels, steam engines worked at the same rate all the time, so long as there was coal to feed them and the machinery wasn't broken. The flow rates of rivers were of no concern. Steam engines also worked anywhere, regardless of the geography, which meant that factory owners could shift production from more remote areas to cities like London, Manchester, and Lancaster, where there were gluts of willing industrial workers, making it far easier to fire troublemakers and put down strikes. As an 1832 article written by a British economist explained, "The invention of the steam-engine has relieved us from the necessity of building factories in inconvenient situations merely for the sake of a waterfall." Or as one of Watt's early biographers put it, the generation of power "will no longer depend, as heretofore, on the most inconstant of natural causes—on atmospheric influences."[28]

Similarly, when Watt's engine was installed in a boat, ship crews were liberated from having to adapt their journeys to the winds, a development that rapidly accelerated the colonial project and the ability of European powers to easily annex countries in distant lands. As the Earl of Liverpool put it in a public meeting to memorialize James Watt in 1824, "Be the winds friendly or be they contrary, the power of the Steam Engine overcomes all difficulties.... Let the wind blow from whatever quarter it may, let the destination of our force be to whatever part of the world it may, you have the power and the means, by the Steam Engine, of applying that force at the proper time and in the proper manner."[29] Not until the advent of electronic trading would commerce feel itself so liberated from the constraints of living on a planet bound by geography and governed by the elements.

Unlike the energy it replaced, power from fossil fuel always required sacrifice zones—whether in the black lungs of the coal miners or the poisoned waterways surrounding the mines. But these prices were seen as worth paying in exchange for coal's intoxicating promise of freedom from the physical world—a freedom that unleashed industrial capitalism's full force to dominate both workers and other cultures. With their portable energy creator, the industrialists and colonists of the 1800s could now go wherever labor was cheapest and most exploitable, and wherever resources were most plentiful and valuable. As the author of a steam engine manual wrote in the mid-1830s, "Its mighty services are always at our command, whether in winter or in summer, by day or by night—it knows of no intermission but what our wishes dictate."[30] Coal represented, in short, total domination, of both nature and other people, the full realization of Bacon's dream at last. "Nature can be conquered," Watt reportedly said, "if we can but find her weak side."[31]

Little wonder then that the introduction of Watt's steam engine coincided with explosive levels of growth in British manufacturing, such that in the eighty years between 1760 and 1840, the country went from importing 2.5 million pounds of raw cotton to importing 366 million pounds of raw cotton, a genuine revolution made possible by the potent and brutal combination of coal at home and slave labor abroad.[32]

This recipe produced more than just new consumer products. In *Ecological Economics*,

Herman Daly and Joshua Farley point out that Adam Smith published *The Wealth of Nations* in 1776—the same year that Watt produced his first commercial steam engine. "It is no coincidence," they write, "that the market economy and fossil fuel economy emerged at essentially the exact same time.... New technologies and vast amounts of fossil energy allowed unprecedented production of consumer goods. The need for new markets for these mass-produced consumer goods and new sources of raw material played a role in colonialism and the pursuit of empire. The market economy evolved as an efficient way of allocating such goods, and stimulating the production of even more."[33] Just as colonialism needed coal to fulfill its dream of total domination, the deluge of products made possible by both coal and colonialism needed modern capitalism.

The promise of liberation from nature that Watt was selling in those early days continues to be the great power of fossil fuels. That power is what allows today's multinationals to scour the globe for the cheapest, most exploitable workforce, with natural features and events that once appeared as obstacles—vast oceans, treacherous landscapes, seasonal fluctuations—no longer even registering as minor annoyances. Or so it seemed for a time.

★ ★ ★

It is often said that Mother Nature bats last, and this has been poignantly the case for some of the men who were most possessed by the ambition of conquering her. A perhaps apocryphal story surrounds the death of Francis Bacon: in an attempt to test his hypothesis that frozen meat could be prevented from rotting, he traipsed around in chilly weather stuffing a chicken full of snow. As a result, it is said, the philosopher caught pneumonia, which eventually led to his demise.[34] Despite some controversy, the anecdote survives for its seeming poetic justice: a man who thought nature could be bent to his will died from simple exposure to the cold.

A similar story of comeuppance appears to be unfolding for the human race as a whole. Ralph Waldo Emerson called coal "a portable climate"—and it has been a smash success, carrying countless advantages, from longer life spans to hundreds of millions freed from hard labor.[35] And yet precisely because our bodies are so effectively separated from our geographies, we who have access to this privilege have proven ourselves far too capable of ignoring the fact that we aren't just changing our personal climate but the entire planet's climate as well, warming not just the indoors but the outdoors too. And yet the warming is no less real for our failure to pay attention.

The harnessing of fossil fuel power seemed, for a couple of centuries at least, to have freed large parts of humanity from the need to be in constant dialogue with nature, having to adjust its plans, ambitions, and schedules to natural fluctuations and topographies. Coal and oil, precisely because they were fossilized, seemed entirely possessable forms of energy. They did not behave independently—not like wind, or water, or, for that matter, workers. Just as Watt's engine promised, once purchased, they produced power wherever and whenever their owners wished—the ultimate nonreciprocal relationship.

But what we have learned from atmospheric science is that the give-and-take, call-and-response that is the essence of all relationships in nature was not eliminated with fossil fuels, it was merely delayed, all the while gaining force and velocity. Now the cumulative effect of those centuries of burned carbon is in the process of unleashing the most ferocious natural tempers of all.

As a result, the illusion of total power and control Watt and his cohorts once peddled has given way to the reality of near total powerlessness and loss of control in the face of such spectacular forces as Hurricane Sandy and Typhoon Haiyan. Which is just one of the reasons climate change is so deeply frightening. Because to confront this crisis truthfully is to confront ourselves—to reckon, as our ancestors did, with our vulnerability to the elements that make up both the planet and our bodies. It is to accept (even embrace) being but one porous part of the world, rather than its master or machinist, as Bacon long ago promised. There can be great well-being in that realization of interconnection, pleasure too. But we should not underestimate the depth of the civilizational challenge that this relationship represents. As Australian political scientist Clive Hamilton puts it, facing these truths about climate change "means recognizing that the power relation between humans and the earth is the reverse of the one we have assumed for three centuries."[36] ...

Some Warnings, Unheeded

There is one other group that might have provided a challenge to Western culture's disastrous view of nature as a bottomless vending machine. That group, of course, is the environmental movement, the network of organizations that exists to protect the natural world from being devoured by human activity. And yet the movement has not played this role, at least not in a sustained and coherent manner.

In part, that has to do with the movement's unusually elite history, particularly in North America. When conservationism emerged as a powerful force in the late nineteenth and early twentieth centuries, it was primarily about men of privilege who enjoyed fishing, hunting, camping, and hiking and who recognized that many of their favorite wilderness spots were under threat from the rapid expansion of industrialization. For the most part, these men did not call into question the frenetic economic project that was devouring natural landscapes all over the continent—they simply wanted to make sure that some particularly spectacular pockets were set aside for their recreation and aesthetic appreciation. Like the Christian missionaries who traveled with traders and soldiers, most early preservationists saw their work as a civilizing addendum to the colonial and industrial projects—not as a challenge to them. Writing in 1914, Bronx Zoo director William Temple Hornaday summed up this ethos, urging American educators to "take up their share of the white man's burden" and help to "preserve the wild life of our country."[37]

This task was accomplished not with disruptive protests, which would have been unseemly for a movement so entrenched in the upper stratum of society. Instead, it was achieved through quiet lobbying, with well-bred men appealing to the noblesse oblige of other men of their class to save a cherished area by turning it into a national or state park, or a private family preserve—often at the direct expense of Indigenous people who lost access to these lands as hunting and fishing grounds.

There were those in the movement, however, who saw in the threats to their country's most beautiful places signs of a deeper cultural crisis. For instance, John Muir [1838–1914], the great naturalist writer who helped found the Sierra Club in 1892, excoriated the industrialists who dammed wild rivers and drowned beautiful valleys. To him they were heathens—"devotees of ravaging commercialism" who "instead of lifting their eyes to the God of the mountains, lift them to the Almighty Dollar."[38]

He was not the only heretic. A strain of radicalism drove some of the early Western ecological thinkers to argue for doing more than protecting isolated landscapes. Though frequently unacknowledged, these thinkers often drew heavily on Eastern beliefs about the interconnectedness of all life, as well as on Native American cosmologies that see all living creatures as our "relations."

In the mid-1800s, Henry David Thoreau [1817–62] wrote that, "The earth I tread on is not a dead, inert mass. It is a body, has a spirit, is organic, and fluid to the influence of its spirit, and to whatever particle of that spirit is in me."[39] This was a straight repudiation of Francis Bacon's casting of the earth as an inert machine whose mysteries could be mastered by the human mind. And almost a century after Thoreau, Aldo Leopold [1887–1948], whose book *A Sand County Almanac* [1949] was the touchstone for a second wave of environmentalists, similarly called for an ethic that "enlarges the boundaries of the community to include soils, waters, plants, and animals" and that recognizes "the individual is a member of a community of interdependent parts." A "land ethic," as he called it, "changes the role of *Homo sapiens* from conqueror of the land-community to plain member and citizen of it. It implies respect for his fellow-members, and also respect for the community as such."[40]

These ideas were hugely influential in the evolution of ecological thought, but unattached to populist movements, they posed little threat to galloping industrialization. The dominant worldview continued to see humans as a conquering army, subduing and mechanizing the natural world. Even so, by the 1930s, with socialism on the rise around the world, the more conservative elements of the growing environmental movement sought to distance themselves from Leopold's "radical" suggestion that nature had an inherent value beyond its utility to man. If watersheds and old-growth forests had a "right to continued existence," as Leopold argued (a preview of the "rights of nature" debates that would emerge several decades later), then an owner's right to do what he wished with his land could be called into question. In 1935, Jay Norwood "Ding" Darling [1876–1962], who would later help found the National Wildlife Federation, wrote to Leopold warning him, "I can't get away from the idea that you are getting us out into water over our depth by your new philosophy of wildlife environment. The end of that road leads to socialization of property."[41]

By the time Rachel Carson [1907–64] published *Silent Spring* in 1962, the attempts to turn nature into a mere cog in the American industrial machine had grown so aggressive, so overtly militaristic, that it was no longer possible to pretend that combining capitalism with conservation was simply a matter of protecting a few pockets of green. Carson's book boiled over with righteous condemnations of a chemical industry that used aerial bombardment to wipe out insects, thoughtlessly endangering human and animal life in the process. The marine biologist-turned-social-critic painted a vivid picture of the arrogant "control men" who, enthralled with "a bright new toy," hurled poisons "against the fabric of life."[42]

Carson's focus was DDT, but for her the problem was not a particular chemical; it was a logic. "The 'control of nature,'" Carson wrote, "is a phrase conceived in arrogance, born of the Neanderthal age of biology and philosophy, when it was supposed that nature exists for the convenience of man.... It is our alarming misfortune that so primitive a science has armed itself with the most modern and terrible weapons, and that in turning them against the insects it has also turned them against the earth."[43]

Carson's writing inspired a new, much more radical generation of environmentalists to see themselves as part of a fragile planetary ecosystem rather than as its engineers or mechanics, giving birth to the field of Ecological Economics. It was in this context that the underlying logic of extractivism—that

there would always be more earth for us to consume—began to be forcefully challenged within the mainstream. The pinnacle of this debate came in 1972 when the Club of Rome published *The Limits to Growth*, a runaway best-seller that used early computer models to predict that if natural systems continued to be depleted at their current rate, humanity would overshoot the planet's carrying capacity by the middle of the twenty-first century. Saving a few beautiful mountain ranges wouldn't be enough to get us out of this fix; the logic of growth itself needed to be confronted.

As author Christian Parenti observed recently of the book's lasting influence, "*Limits* combined the glamour of Big Science—powerful MIT computers and support from the Smithsonian Institution—with a focus on the interconnectedness of things, which fit perfectly with the new countercultural zeitgeist." And though some of the book's projections have not held up over time—the authors underestimated, for instance, the capacity of profit incentives and innovative technologies to unlock new reserves of finite resources—*Limits* was right about the most important limit of all. On "the limits of natural 'sinks,' or the Earth's ability to absorb pollution," Parenti writes, "the catastrophically bleak vision of *Limits* is playing out as totally correct. We may find new inputs—more oil or chromium—or invent substitutes, but we have not produced or discovered more natural sinks. The Earth's capacity to absorb the filthy byproducts of global capitalism's voracious metabolism is maxing out. That warning has always been the most powerful part of *The Limits to Growth*."[44]

And yet in the most powerful parts of the environmental movement, in the key decades during which we have been confronting the climate threat, these voices of warning have gone unheeded. The movement did not reckon with limits of growth in an economic system built on maximizing profits, it instead tried to prove that saving the planet could be a great new business opportunity.

The reasons for this political timidity have plenty to do with the themes already discussed: the power and allure of free market logic that usurped so much intellectual life in the late 1980s and 1990s, including large parts of the conservation movement. But this persistent unwillingness to follow science to its conclusions also speaks to the power of the cultural narrative that tells us that humans are ultimately in control of the earth, and not the other way around. This is the same narrative that assures us that, however bad things get, we are going to be saved at the last minute—whether by the market, by philanthropic billionaires, or by technological wizards—or best of all, by all three at the same time. And while we wait, we keep digging in deeper.

Only when we dispense with these various forms of magical thinking will we be ready to leave extractivism behind and build the societies we need within the boundaries we have—a world with no sacrifice zones, no new Naurus.

Questions

1. What is the story of Nauru? How does Nauru serve as a cautionary tale for us all? Will we heed such tales? Why or why not?

2. Klein argues that we have not harnessed nature with our extractivist methods of fossil fuels, or freed ourselves from natural constraints, but rather we are experiencing dire consequences of climate change. Trace the history she provides to illustrate this phenomenon.

3. Klein considers the notion that we will be saved at the last minute—"by the market, by philanthropic billionaires, or by technological wizards"—to be "magical thinking." Briefly explain why she asserts that this magical thinking will not save us, and take a position on whether you agree.

Notes

1. Naomi Klein, *This Changes Everything* (New York: Simon and Schuster, 2014).

2. Steve Stockman, Twitter post, March 21, 2013, 2:33 p.m. ET, https://twitter.com.

3. Ben Dangl, "Miners Just Took 43 Police Officers Hostage in Bolivia," *Vice*, April 3, 2014.

4. Rodrigo Castro et al., "Human-Nature Interaction in World Modeling with Modelica," prepared for the Proceedings of the 10th International Modelica Conference, March 10–12, 2014, http://www.ep.liu.se.

5. Personal interview with Nerida-Ann Steshia Hubert, March 30, 2012.

6. Hermann Joseph Hiery, *The Neglected War: The German South Pacific and the Influence of World War I* (Honolulu: U of Hawai'i P, 1995), 116–25, 241; "Nauru," New Zealand Ministry of Foreign Affairs and Trade, updated December 9, 2013, http://wwww.mfat.govt.nz; "Nauru" (video), NFSA Australia, NFSA Films.

7. Charles J. Hanley, "Tiny Pacific Isle's Citizens Rich, Fat and Happy—Thanks to the Birds," Associated Press, March 31, 1985; Steshia Hubert interview, March 30, 2012.

8. "Country Profile and National Anthem," Permanent Mission of the Republic of Nauru to the

United Nations, United Nations, http://www. un.int; Jack Hitt, "The Billion-Dollar Shack," *New York Times Magazine*, December 10, 2000.

9. Hiery, *The Neglected War*, 116–25, 241; "Nauru," New Zealand Ministry of Foreign Affairs and Trade.

10. Hitt, "The Billion-Dollar Shack"; David Kendall, "Doomed Island," *Alternatives Journal*, January 2009.

11. "Nauru" (video), NFSA Films.

12. Philip Shenon, "A Pacific Island Is Stripped of Everything," *New York Times*, December 10, 1995.

13. Hitt, "The Billion-Dollar Shack"; Robert Matau, "Road Deaths Force Nauru to Review Traffic Laws," *Islands Business*, July 10, 2013; "The Fattest Place on Earth" (video), *Nightline*, ABC, January 3, 2011; Steshia Hubert interview, March 30, 2012.

14. Hitt, "The Billion-Dollar Shack"; "Nauru," Country Profile, U.N. Data, http://data.un.org.

15. "Nauru," Overview, Rand McNally, http:// education.randmcnally.com; Tony Thomas, "The Naughty Nation of Nauru," *The Quadrant*, January/February 2013; Andrew Kaierua et al., "Nauru," in *Climate Change in the Pacific, Scientific Assessment and New Research, Volume 2: Country Reports*, Australian Bureau of Meteorology and CSIRO, 2011, pp. 134, 140; "Fresh Water Supplies a Continual Challenge to the Region," Applied Geoscience and Technology Division, Secretariat of the Pacific Community, press release, January 18, 2011.

16. Glenn Albrecht, "The Age of Solastalgia," *The Conversation*, August 7, 2012.

17. Kendall, "Doomed Island."

18. "Nauru: Phosphate Roller Coaster; Elections with Tough Love Theme," August 13, 2007, via WikiLeaks, http://www.wikileaks.org.

19. Nick Bryant, "Will New Nauru Asylum Centre Deliver Pacific Solution?" BBC News, June 20, 2013; Rob Taylor, "Ruling Clouds Future of Australia Detention Center," *Wall Street Journal*, January 30, 2014; "Nauru Camp a Human Rights Catastrophe with No End in Sight," Amnesty

International, press release, November 23, 2012; "What We Found on Nauru," Amnesty International, December 17, 2012; "Hundreds Continue 11-Day Nauru Hunger Strike," ABC News (Australia), November 12, 2012.

20. Bryant, "Will New Nauru Asylum Centre Deliver Pacific Solution?"; Oliver Laughland, "Nauru Immigration Detention Centre-Exclusive Pictures," *Guardian*, December 6, 2013; "Hundreds Continue 11-Day Nauru Hunger Strike," ABC News (Australia); "Police Attend Full-Scale Riot at Asylum Seeker Detention Centre on Nauru," ABC News (Australia), July 20, 2013.

21. "Nauru Camp a Human Rights Catastrophe with No End in Sight," Amnesty International, press release, November 23, 2012; "UNHCR Monitoring Visit to the Republic of Nauru, 7 to 9 October 2013," United Nations High Commissioner for Refugees, November 26, 2013; Mark Isaacs, *The Undesirables* (Richmond, Victoria: Hardie Grant Books, 2014), 99; Deborah Snow, "Asylum Seekers: Nothing to Lose, Desperation on Nauru," *Sydney Morning Herald*, March 15, 2014.

22. "The Middle of Nowhere," *This American Life*, December 5, 2003, http://www.thisamericanlife. org; Mitra Mobasherat and Ben Brumfield, "Riot on a Tiny Island Highlights Australia Shutting a Door on Asylum," CNN, July 20, 2013; Rosamond Dobson Rhone, "Nauru, the Richest Island in the South Seas," *National Geographic* 40 (1921): 571, 585.

23. Marcus Stephen, "On Nauru, a Sinking Feeling," *New York Times*, July 18, 2011.

24. Francis Bacon, *De Dignitate et Augmentis Scientiarum, Works*, ed. James Spedding, Robert Leslie Ellis, and Douglas Devon Heath, Vol. 4 (London: Longmans Green, 1870), 296.

25. William Derham, *Physico-Theology: or, A Demonstration of the Being and Attributes of God, from His Works of Creation* (London: Printed for Robinson and Roberts, 1768), 110.

26. Barbara Freese, *Coal: A Human History* (New York: Penguin, 2004), 44.

27. Emphasis in original. Many of the sources in this recounting were originally cited in Andreas Malm, "The Origins of Fossil Capital: From Water to Steam in the British Cotton Industry," *Historical Materialism* 21 (2013): 31.

28. J.R. McCulloch [unsigned], "Babbage on Machinery and Manufactures," *Edinburgh Review* 56 (January 1833): 313–32; François Arago, *Historical Eloge of James Watt*, trans. James Patrick Muirhead (London: J. Murray, 1839), 150.

29. C.H. Turner, *Proceedings of the Public Meeting Held at Freemasons' Hall, on the 18th June, 1824, for Erecting a Monument to the* Late *James Watt* (London: J. Murray, 1824), pp. 3–4, as cited in Andreas Malm, "Steam: Nineteenth-Century Mechanization and the Power of Capital," in *Ecology and Power: Struggles over Land and Material Resources* in *the Past, Present, and Future*, ed. Alf Hornborg, Brett Clark, and Kenneth Hermele (London: Routledge, 2013), 119.

30. M.A. Alderson, *An Essay on the Nature and Application of Steam: With an Historical Notice of the Rise and Progressive Improvement of the Steam-Engine* (London: Sherwood, Gilbert and Piper, 1834), 44.

31. Asa Briggs, *The Power of Steam: An Illustrated History of the World's Steam Age* (Chicago: U of Chicago P, 1982), 72.

32. Jackson J. Spielvogel, *Western Civilization: A Brief History, Volume II: Since 1500*, 8th ed. (Boston: Wadsworth, 2014), 445.

33. Herman E. Daly and Joshua Farley, *Ecological Economics: Principles and Applications* (Washington, DC: Island P, 2011), 10.

34. Rebecca Newberger Goldstein, "What's in a Name? Rivalries and the Birth of Modern Science," in Seeing *Further: The Story of Science, Discovery, and the Genius of the Royal Society*, ed. Bill Bryson (London: Royal Society, 2010), 120.

35. Ralph Waldo Emerson, *The Conduct of Life* (New York: Thomas Y. Crowell, 1903), 70.

36. Clive Hamilton, "The Ethical Foundations of Climate Engineering," in *Climate Change Geoengineering: Philosophical Perspectives, Legal Issues, and Governance Frameworks*, ed. Wil C.G. Burns and Andrew L. Strauss (New York: Cambridge UP, 2013), 58.

37. William T. Hornaday, *Wild Life Conservation in Theory and Practice* (New Haven: Yale UP, 1914), v–vi.

38. "Who Was John Muir?" Sierra Club, http://www.sierraclub.org; John Muir, *The Yosemite* (New York: Century, 1912), 261–62.

39. "In the morning I bathe my intellect in the stupendous and cosmogonal philosophy of the Bhagvat Geeta," wrote Thoreau in *Walden* of the famous Indian scripture. He continued, "I lay down the book and go to my well for water and lo! there I meet the servant of the Brahmin, priest of Brahma and Vishnu and Indra, who still sits in his temple on the Ganges reading the Vedas, or dwells at the root of a tree with his crust and water jug…. The pure Walden water is mingled with the sacred water of the Ganges."

40. Bradford Torrey, ed., *The Writings of Henry David Thoreau: Journal, September 16, 1851–April 30, 1852* (New York: Houghton Mifflin, 1906), 165; Aldo Leopold, *A Sand County Almanac* (Oxford: Oxford UP, 1949), 171; FOOTNOTE: Henry David Thoreau, *Walden* (New York: Thomas Y. Crowell, 1910), 393–94.

41. Leopold, *A Sand County Almanac*, 171; Jay N. Darling to Aldo Leopold, November 20, 1935, Aldo Leopold Archives, University of Wisconsin Digital Collections.

42. Rachel Carson, *Silent Spring* (New York: Houghton Mifflin, 1962), 57, 68, 297.

43. Ibid, 297.

44. Christian Parenti, "'The Limits to Growth': A Book That Launched a Movement," *The Nation*, December 5, 2012.

5. Involuntary Simplicity: Changing Dysfunctional Habits of Consumption[1]

Guy Claxton

GUY CLAXTON (B. 1947) argues that the root of dysfunctional consumption is really a psychological issue. He quotes Ervin László (b. 1932) on the change needed: "Coping with mankind's current predicament calls for inner changes, for a human and humanistic revolution mobilizing new values and aspirations, backed by new levels of personal commitment and political will." Likening consumption to addiction, and consumers to addicts, he profiles consumers as "comfort-addicts" whose world view links their self-identity so closely to material comfort and preferences that to deny a preference is seen as a threat to existence: "One's sense of self, and self-worth, came to depend on possession and consumption." Claxton doesn't advocate external solutions; rather, he advocates "mindfulness," a term from Buddhist scripture. Mindfulness requires presence, reflection, and awareness that lead us to uncover our underlying presuppositions that form beliefs and values. From that point, Claxton is short on details. However, he does illuminate an answer to the citizen-consumer gap. The answer is that it is not enough to provide facts, rational arguments, and willpower. People's psychological beliefs need to change.

When our ruling passion is no longer survival it becomes comfort. To someone whose passion *is* survival our preoccupation with comfort is ignoble and trivial; there is no way it can be justified. It can't even be understood.

—Nicholas Freeling, *A City Solitary*

IN NON-ABUNDANT SOCIETIES, where the prerogative of survival leaves little room for choice, people's patterns of consumption are predominantly dictated by the nature of their circumstances. When there is little to eat, how one acts is largely determined by agricultural or ecological forces beyond individual control. But in the affluent countries of the North, what people consume, what they waste, what long and short-term considerations are or are not taken into account in making consumption decisions—these betray the powerful influence of the cultural and individual assumptions and beliefs that are resident in people's minds. And if dysfunctional habits of consumption are driven by psychological factors, then a satisfactory solution is not going to be found in either technological innovation or in ecopolitical reorganisation, but in the liberation of individuals, in their millions, from the sway of an unconsciously self-destructive worldview.

This obvious starting-point for any discussion about ways of averting further ecological catastrophes is summed up by Laszlo (1989):

> There are hardly any world problems that cannot be traced to human agency and which could not be overcome by appropriate changes in human behaviour. The root cause even of physical and ecological problems are the inner constraints on our vision and values.... Living on the threshold of a new age, we squabble among ourselves to acquire or retain the privileges of bygone times. We cast about for innovative ways to satisfy obsolete values. We manage individual crises while heading towards collective catastrophes. We contemplate changing almost anything on this earth except ourselves.... A new insight must dawn on people: you do not solve world problems by applying technological fixes within the framework of narrowly self-centered values and short-sighted national institutions. Coping with mankind's current predicament calls for inner changes, for a human and humanistic revolution mobilizing new values and aspirations, backed by new levels of personal commitment and political will. (pp. 46–7)

Voluntary Simplicity

Those who have seen that this individual process of *reprioritisation* is the nub of the problem have tended to take two routes. One involves making explicit the tacit dysfunctional beliefs that have driven heedless overconsumption and waste (as Laszlo does), in the hope that "making the unconscious conscious" (in Freud's famous phrase) will do the trick. The other relies more on extolling the virtues of "voluntary simplicity." Elgin (1981), who

coined the phrase, has argued irrefutably *why* changes in personal lifestyle are vital for planetary well-being, and has persuasively shown how such changes can be construed not as sacrifice but as a joyous reorientation of life away from "having" and towards "being" (c.f. Fromm, 1978). "To live more frugally on the material side of life is to be enabled to live more abundantly on the psychological and spiritual side of life" (Elgin, ibid). And he offers in his book plenty of good, practical advice, not just about what we should be doing, but about how to get started and put it into effect. He has recently (Elgin, 1992) returned to the theme, and the mixture is as before: scary facts and prognostications acting as the "stick"; glowing exhortations about the joys of frugality to provide the "carrot"; and tips as to how to do it.

Yet while the spirit, as a result of reflecting on these considerations, may, for many people, be willing, the flesh remains often and indubitably weak. In this area of personal lifestyle, as in many others such as dieting or giving up smoking, to *know* what to do, to *agree* that it is a good idea, even to *want* to change, seem over and over again to be insufficient. A new course of action is enthusiastically embraced, but somehow, as T. S. Eliot (1962) said in "The Hollow Men," "between the idea and the reality, between intention and the act, falls the Shadow." That which is adopted *voluntarily* has, it seems, little power to resist being shouldered aside by a deeper impulse that remains involuntary. The vital tactical question, then, in considering any attempt to save humankind from itself, focuses not on information or exhortation, but on the resilience of habits and beliefs that are "embodied," in the face of contrary principles that are "espoused." One *wants,* and one *wants not to want*; the problem is how to translate the *wanting not to want* into *not wanting.*

To see how to enable oneself to change it is

necessary to understand the psychology of addiction, for people's involuntary rejection of their "better natures" can be seen as reflecting an addiction to luxury, or comfort, that relies on the psychological (though not of course the same physiological) dynamics as that of heroin addicts, whose need may require them, in the heat of the moment, continually to over-ride their aversion to lying to, and stealing from, those they love. In the long run it may be no less destructive—to the sustainability of the planet, if not to individual well-being—to be unable to give up flushing the toilet after every visit, or to drop the attachment to being able to pop into town on a whim, which creates the addiction to the second car. For neither the drug addict nor the comfort addict is the combination of *voluntary* effort—"will-power"—self-talk and guilt adequate to the task.

Traps

This problem arises when the dysfunctional habit is locked in place by an underlying system of belief which determines, to a significant extent, a person's worldview. Such a belief system is called by Stolzenberg (1984) a "trap," which he defines as:

> a closed system of attitudes, beliefs and habits of thought for which one can give an objective demonstration that certain of the beliefs are incorrect, and in which certain of the attitudes and habits of thought prevent this from being recognised.

Such a system constitutes, in effect, one's vantage point; while the system is operating "upstream" of perception, its assumptions are built in to the "reality" that is experienced, and its constituents are not visible, and not open to question. One might say that the word-processing program that is currently installed on my computer is a "trap" in the same sense. Its instructions and subroutines are nowhere to be seen; yet they determine absolutely the "reality" that appears on the screen in front of me. Unless I become aware (as in fact I am) that the "belief system" embodied by WordPerfect 5.1 is simply one amongst many, and that there are many alternative "realities" that my laptop is potentially capable of revealing to me, then I am "trapped" into confusing the view according to WordPerfect with the way things "really" (i.e. inevitably, unquestionably) are. It is possible (as I am about to do) to type, in WordPerfect, a "heretical" statement like "I wish I could be working in Microsoft Word; it's so much better." But whatever I type *within* WordPerfect can have absolutely no effect on the program itself.

Just so, when the mind habitually runs a particular belief system, and when that belief system is instrumental in creating (editing, selecting, interpreting) *experience*, then everything that happens can only be understood in terms of the presuppositions of the system—or it cannot be understood at all. As the programmers say, "it does not compute." To quote Stolzenberg (ibid.) again:

> A belief system has this one distinguishing feature: all acts of observation, judgment etc., are performed solely from the particular standpoint of the system itself. Therefore, once any belief or operating principle has been accepted, that is, is seen as "being so," any argument for not accepting it will be rejected unless it can be shown that there is something "wrong" with it from the standpoint of the system itself.... And any such demonstration would collapse as soon as it had been given because its force would depend upon the correctness of the very methodology that has just been found to be incorrect.

When an outside observer is in a position to see that such a system contains an incorrect belief and also that no proof of its incorrectness can be given in terms of the system itself, then he is in a position to say that this system has become a trap. In such a situation, the outside observer will see those within as being dogmatic, while those on the inside will see the observer as someone who refuses to accept what is "obviously so." And, in fact, both will be right. (pp. 269, 272)

The Trap of Competitive Needs

We might argue that comfort-addicts are in exactly this situation. Their view of the world embodies a nest of assumptions that link together identity, preference and material comfort in such a way that denial of preference is experienced as a mortal blow to personal efficacy, and discomfort is experienced as a threat to physical survival. Xenos (1989), for example, shows how Europeans' "normal" experience of themselves—and their experience of themselves as "normal"—was shifted, in the eighteenth century, by the rise of manufacturing industry and the invention of fashion, towards a constant state of relativised need or scarcity. One's sense of self, and self-worth, came to depend on possession and consumption. As fashions changed, so those one aspired to be like threatened to pull further away, while the hot breath of those one was striving *not* to be like could perpetually be felt on the back of one's neck.

Needs that are conceived to be naturally based, such as needs for food, shelter, sex, etc., can be approached discretely…. But when these needs become intertwined with a fluid, ever-changing social world of emulation and conspicuous consumption, they become transformed into an indiscrete desire constantly shifting its focus from one unpossessed object to another.

Among the social needs constitutive of modern commercial societies are those of recognition and prestige, and even if some of them run up against absolute limits to their satisfaction, others, particularly those tied to fashion, are capable of apparently infinite expansion. Thus the boundlessness of desire is realised in the proliferation of social needs. For us, the denizens of this world of desire, it is no longer a question of episodic insufficiency; out of our affluence we have created a social world of scarcity. (Xenos, ibid., pp. 5, 10)

Put simply, "individual consumerism" has become a cornerstone of modern Northern/ Western identity, so that living in a spiral of escalating affluence is no longer experienced as a fortunate option, but as a matter of absolute necessity. This belief installs consumption at the heart of human identity, as a core trait that is now not the servant, but the master, of survival. The idea of *not* being able to continue to consume in the style, and at the rate, that has been prescribed, therefore, can *only* be experienced as loss, sacrifice and threat, because the perceptual apparatus has been programmed to see that way.

This is true even when the conscious, voluntary mind is espousing alternative values and dispositions. One can *try* to cut down consumption, but if underneath the intention to live frugally there is the buried belief that "I shop; therefore I am," the commitment to the conscious intention will be fragile and half-hearted, and can only manifest as a "gesture" that may placate the espoused belief while, on a deeper level, validating the embodied belief. I *know* I should be buying recycled toilet paper, but somehow, when I get home from the supermarket, I find, almost to my surprise, that yet again it is the softer, whiter product that I have actually bought.

Whilst the underlying trap is in place, the attempt to live frugally is bound to be experienced, however faintly, as *painful*, as a deprivation of what is "needed," and as soon as this occurs, the system as a whole seeks to rectify the situation. The lack of comfort or of choice becomes an itch that demands scratching; and because the "motive" is still in place, there are no good-enough grounds for resisting the urge to "scratch." The Buddhist monk Nanavira Thera (1987) uses again the analogy of the drug addict:

> If (the addict) decides that he must give up his addiction to the drug (it is too expensive; it is ruining his reputation or his career; it is undermining his health; and so on) he will make the decision only when he is in a fit state to consider the matter, that is to say *when he is drugged;* and it is from this (for him, *normal*) point of view that he will envisage the future. But as soon as the addict puts his decision into effect and stops taking the drug he ceases to be "normal," and decisions taken when he was normal now appear in quite a different light—and this will include his decision to stop taking the drug. *Either,* then, he abandons his decision as invalid ("How could I possibly have decided to do such a thing? I must have been off my head.") and returns to his drug-taking, *or* (though he approves the decision) he feels it urgently necessary to return to the state in which he originally took the decision (which was when he was drugged) *in order to make the decision seem valid again.* In both cases the result is the same—a return to the drug. And so long as the addict takes his "normal" drugged state for granted at its face value—i.e. *as* normal—the same thing will happen whenever he tries to give up

his addiction. (pp. 205–6)

The foregoing discussion has tried to make clear that any espousal of "voluntary simplicity" is doomed if it is overlaid on an embodied belief system to which it is antithetical. It follows that encouraging people to see voluntary simplicity as a "good idea," and offering them advice as to how to put it in to practice, is a waste of time if, for the vast majority of the audience, the underlying addiction is not treated. But how is this to be done? How can one truly experience the value of simplicity, when one's experience itself is the product of a belief in the necessity of luxury?

Getting Out of Jail

There are a number of possible methods for escaping from the trap. One is to *require* people to behave in a way that respects ecological values. If they are prevented from retreating into the familiar, sensible, normal, comfortable way, when the going gets tough, and are forced to put up with the withdrawal symptoms (to "go cold turkey"), without any apparent hope of returning to "the good (bad) old days," then a shift in underlying assumptions and priorities can take place which makes it possible for the value of simplicity to be experienced and appreciated. The problems and risks with this ecodictatorial solution are, however, too numerous and too obvious to make it either a viable or a sensible option.

Another strategy is to engage a different motivation, so that the discomfort of acting *as if* one were un-trapped is made worth bearing. Like the first method, the idea is to arrange things so that people will for a sustained period act in line with the espoused belief rather than the embodied one. As the benefit of the new way of acting cannot be experienced to begin with, and therefore cannot act as the *reward* for putting up with the disruption and discomfort, some *other* form of reward can be used to keep the new behaviour going while it "takes root."

These rewards may be either positive or negative, and there are risks associated with each. Lepper and Greene (1975), in their studies of the so-called "undermining effect," have shown that when people are positively reinforced for doing something that they themselves would have voluntarily undertaken anyway, the habit can be "appropriated" by the extrinsic reinforcement, and when the reward stops, the original motivation is now no longer strong enough to keep the behaviour going. So giving people money back on returnable bottles, to encourage them to recycle, is a self-limiting expedient if it turns out that as soon as you stop the cash everybody stops recycling. This of course is why Elgin and others have emphasised that the simplification of lifestyles should be "voluntary." The use of negative reinforcement—punishment—on the other hand, tend towards the eco-fascist option, which we have already discarded.

A third option is to create a special context within which the value of a simplified lifestyle can be experienced; a context within which people's purpose or activity is framed in such a way that the materialistic trap is weakened or unactivated. On a camping holiday, or a meditation retreat, for example, one's expectations and habits of consumption may be radically different from those that are compulsive within the normal routines of life. The problem with this is that there is often little or no carry-over from one context to the other. We seem to be constructed psychologically in such a way that we can happily manifest different priorities in different contexts without feeling obliged to achieve any reconciliation (e.g. Lave, 1988). As Sheldrake (1990) has pointed out, many people sense no contradiction between working all week for a multinational oil company or a merchant bank, and on Friday evening dashing down the M4 in the Range Rover to a country home where the pin-stripe is immediately exchanged for working jeans, and Nature is celebrated, respected (and occasionally, without any felt contradictions, shot) for a couple of days.

This analysis of the causes of resistance to lifestyle changes makes the role of "self-help" and "support" groups very clear. Normal relationships, and the normal routines or life, readily reinforce both each other *and* the beliefs that underpin normal habits of consumption. But the power of *example* and *support,* in the suspension of this package of self-fulfilling, mutually-reinforcing life structures, is formidable, and certainly much greater than rational assent or individual resolve. Religious communities have long known the value of congregation and of *sangha* (Rahula, 1967), but in the lay world this kind of support has often been seen as a comforting *addition* to other strategies for life change, rather than as one of the few strategies that actually addresses the heart of the psychological difficulty.

The final approach to making voluntary simplicity a reality which I shall discuss here is the cultivation of *mindfulness,* a term which Elgin (1981) has borrowed from Buddhist scripture. I have argued elsewhere (Claxton, 1994) that sharpening awareness of the immediate present is a prerequisite for the uncovering of tacit presuppositions. It is only an acquired (and therefore reversible) habit of perceptual imprecision that allows these unrecognised assumptions to be continually dissolved in the process whereby experience is fabricated. We can "leap to conclusions," and mistake those conclusions for "reality," only if we do not see that "leaping to conclusions" is what we are doing. By attending precisely to the minute detail of experience, the nest of assumptions that link identity, security and consumption can be brought to light—not just in an intellectual fashion, but within the realm of spontaneous perceptions and dispositions.

Conclusions

The main conclusion of this analysis, then, is that those who wish to promote what they see as healthier lifestyles, and more sustainable patterns of consumption, must acknowledge that giving information, advice and encouragement have to be seen as just one component of a much wider strategy. To write your book, and then stand back in puzzled confusion while the mass of enthusiastic readers continue much as before, is only possible given an ignorance of the depth of the psychological challenge which a change of lifestyle poses. To become either angry, despondent or exhausted are the reactions of one who has grievously underestimated the magnitude and subtlety of the problem.

The second conclusion is that the practical wisdom that is often associated with spiritual traditions such as Buddhism is "wise" not because it relies on a particular theology, but because it understands the psychological dynamics of inertia, denial and self-deception, and is designed to engage with the issue at the requisite depth (see Fox, 1990). The Three Jewels of Buddhism—Buddha, Dharma and Sangha—represent the power of inspiration and living example, the power of mindfulness, and the power of supportive friendship, respectively. Advocacy of "voluntary simplicity," or any other significant lifestyle change, which does not understand that what is required is not *just* a change of habits, but that these habits are the visible tip of a massive and intricate belief system, is bound to increase frustration, guilt, hostility, and thereby to generate heat and friction—in the manner of one who releases the clutch, only to depress simultaneously the accelerator and the brake—but not much motion.

Questions

1. To address the consumer-versus-citizen split, Claxton argues for a form of integrity that results from "habits and beliefs that are 'embodied.'" Integrity results when "wanting not to want" (the values expressed as a citizen) is translated into "not wanting" (when the value is expressed in the behavior). Explain what this means, the difference between "wanting not to want" and "not wanting."

2. Claxton distinguishes between internal and external change, arguing that external is ineffective. Do you agree that external changes are ineffective (such as rationing, making some products illegal, and so forth)? Why or why not?

3. Given consumers' addiction to consumption, do you think that they will be moved to "mindfulness" to change? Why or why not?

References

Claxton, G. L. 1994 *Noises from the Darkroom: The Science and Mystery of the Mind*. London, Harper-Collins/Aquarian Press.

Elgin, D. 1981 *Voluntary Simplicity: Toward a Way of Life That Is Outwardly Simple, Inwardly Rich*. New York, Morrow.

Elgin, D. 1992 "Ecological Living and the New American Challenge." *Elmwood Quarterly* 8(1): 11–12.

Eliot, T. S. 1962 *Selected Poems*. London, Faber & Faber.

Fox, W. 1990 *Toward a Transpersonal Ecology*. London and Boston, Shambhala.

Fromm, E. 1978 *To Have or to Be*. London, Cape.

Laszlo, E. 1989 *The Inner Limits of Mankind*. London, One-world Publications.

Lave, J. 1988 *Cognition in Practice*. Cambridge, Cambridge University Press.

Lepper, M., and Green, D. 1975 "Turning Play into Work," *Journal of Personality and Social Psychology* 31: 479–86.

Nanavira Thera. 1987 *Clearing the Path*. Colombo, Sri Lanka, Path Press.

Rahula, W. 1967 *What the Buddha Taught*. London, Gordon Fraser.

Sheldrake, R. 1990 *The Rebirth of Nature*. London, Century.

Stolzenberg, G. 1984 "Can an Inquiry into the Foundations of Mathematics Tell Us Anything Interesting about Mind?" in *The Invented Reality*, edited by P. Watzlawick. New York, W. W. Norton.

Note

1. Guy Claxton, "Involuntary Simplicity: Changing Dysfunctional Habits of Consumption," *Environmental Values* 3, no. 1 (1994): 71–78.

Chapter 8: Challenges to Business as Usual

Introduction

"I have spent over a year talking with whistleblowers.... Of the dozen with whom I have worked most closely, all but one lost not just his or her job, but his or her career. Eight lost their homes, and seven lost their families.... Most whistleblowers suffer from alcoholism and depression at some point in the years that follow blowing the whistle."[1]

"Everyone has the right to a standard of living adequate for the health and well-being of himself and his family, including food, clothing, housing and medical care and necessary social services, and the right to security in the event of unemployment, sickness, disability, widowhood, old age or other lack of livelihood in circumstances beyond his control."[2]

ONE WAY TO CHALLENGE business as usual is to "whistleblow." Whistleblowing is one method of exposing harms and calling for accountability within a system. A whistleblower is one who "blows the whistle" on a harmful, unethical, and/or illegal practice from within a firm where the whistleblower works. A whistleblower acts in the public interest, not in self-interest. Whistleblowing is meant as a last resort, to sound an alarm of clear and present danger, to warn those at risk. Whistleblowing has been all too often seen as the action of a disloyal colleague and employee. Regardless of whether the whistleblower had tried to resolve the issue internally, or had exposed a real danger to the public, or had even saved the firm money because they exposed an issue that would cost the firm, whistleblowers are almost always retaliated against for their actions.

One of the main reasons whistleblowers are retaliated against, and perhaps why this retaliation is tolerated, is that they are perceived to be disloyal. Whistleblowers are portrayed as disloyal to colleagues and/or the firm. However, legitimate whistleblowers are following the law and protecting the greater public interest, to which they are in fact *loyal*. As citizens, we are members of our communities before we are members of a firm, and it is only because of communities, and the broader public, that firms can even exist. Firms exist to provide goods and services, not to violate the law, place communities at risk, or lie to the public. Whistleblowers are therefore loyal to exactly those to whom we would argue they *should* be loyal. They are, at great risk to themselves, protecting those who do not have the information to protect themselves. First, they are acting in accordance with Kant's categorical imperative; that is, they universalize the action in question by seeing how it affects everyone. Second, they are acting to maximize overall good, and minimize harm, that is, consistent with utilitarian ethics.

An important question is why loyalty is *owed* to a firm, as an ethical duty. This is especially true in the days of downsizing, country-hopping, forced retirement, employment at will,[3] workplace surveillance, bodily fluid testing, and numerous other practices for the purposes of ensuring the firm's ability to maximize profit and maintain control over workers. As is clear in many case studies throughout this anthology, in the absence of contractual or legal protection, there are no guarantees that employees are protected from toxins, paid living wages, provided with health care or retirement pensions, or given numerous other minimal human needs. Firms provide a paycheck in exchange for labor. If a firm provides more than a paycheck, that in no way justifies expecting silence (and calling this "loyalty") from employees in the face of illegal and unethical activities.

There are some forms of protection and compensation for whistleblowers. The first form of whistleblower protection is under the Occupational Safety and Health Administration (OSHA). OSHA administers whistleblower protections under certain laws, including the *OSH Act* of 1970, the *Asbestos Hazard Emergency Response Act*, the *Toxic Substances Control Act*, and the *Federal Water Pollution Control Act*.[4] However, to obtain OSHA protection, the whistleblower must blow the whistle on a violation of one of these laws. Certain occupations may also have whistleblower protection, such as railroad workers. Under the Code of Federal Regulations, Title 49, Volume 4, Part 225.2.a.1, "The railroad shall provide 'whistle blower' protection to any person subject to this policy."[5] The policy is to ensure "complete and accurate reporting of all accidents, incidents, injuries, and occupational illnesses arising from the operation of the railroad."[6]

Significant compensation for a whistleblower is provided under the Federal False Claims Act 1986's *qui tam* provision. *Qui tam* is short for a Latin phrase that refers to "he who brings the action for the king as well as for himself."[7] Under the *qui tam* provision, whistleblowers who bring forth evidence of their firm's defrauding the US government are entitled to between 25 and 30 per cent of the amount recovered, as well as any costs, including attorneys' fees, that were incurred while defending themselves or bringing the claim forth. If, during the investigation, the employer retaliates against the employee, the Act has provisions for the employee to be rehired, given twice the amount of lost pay, as well as other damages the court may see fit. However, unless the whistleblower has brought forth a claim that involves defrauding the federal government, this act does not apply to them.

One way in which a whistleblower is able to withstand the scrutiny is through integrity. In "The Meaning of Integrity," Robert C. Solomon defines integrity as "wholeness," including wholeness of the person (not separate selves) and the person's being a part of the larger community, society, and humanity.[8] Solomon argues that a clean conscience and doing one's duty (best understood in the Kantian sense), as defined by his or her role or position, are essential to integrity. If, Solomon writes, a boss requires an employee to do something unethical or illegal, the boss lacks integrity.

Solomon writes that when the self is fragmented within society and community, the result is an "individual," and for Solomon this is another example of one who lacks integrity (integrity is both internal and external). Solomon writes that the individual is a creation of Europe in the 1000s and 1100s and has become extremely important to capitalism and consumerism. Solomon states that what many consider an individual in the United States is seen as a sociopath in Japan and other societies. Indeed, he argues, we obtain our identities from our communities, and often in work, there is no such thing as an atomistic individual. The whistleblower is acting with integrity in recognizing that *necessary* connection to the community.

While whistleblowing is an important check on the harms within a system, it remains a challenge from within and has not yet served a transformative role in preventing harm. Challenging the system from without happens when a group of businesses, activists, scientists, and citizens form a network invested in transformation to "the green economy." Recognizing that our current economic systems, as well as current models of globalization, do not bring wealth but rather provide "illth,"[9] green economists seek to make economics the servant and not the master.

Two key principles are informative in defining the green economy. First, a firm must be socially responsible, and second, the firm's practices must be (authentically) environmentally sustainable.[10] Examples of firms already engaged in green economy practices include organic farmers, renewable energy firms, some socially responsible investment funds, and the examples that David Korten lists in his essay in this chapter. The firms "are proving that it is possible to create an economy that, unlike the current one, won't generate inequality and environmental destruction."[11]

There exist many models for redressing the harmful and standard practices illustrated throughout this anthology. These models include those presented in the anthology itself, such as those that either are, or could be derived from, the *United Nations Universal Declaration of Human Rights*; the *United Nations Declaration of Human Rights Principles and Responsibilities for Transnational Corporations and Other Business Enterprises*; stakeholder theory; holding key personnel criminally responsible; revoking the charter; Kant's categorical imperative; sustainable development practices; the land ethic; the Occupational Safety & Health Administration's ability to enforce the OSH Act; whistleblowing; reduced consumption; and many others. Perhaps we have reached, both nationally and globally, a point where we are finally unwilling to continue to support and participate in practices driven by greed, practices that result in all forms of harm to humans, and increasing environmental destruction. If so, then perhaps we are not too late.

Notes

1. C. Fred Alford, "Whistleblowers and the Narrative of Ethics," *Journal of Social Philosophy* 32, no. 3 (Fall 2001): 403.

2. *The United Nations Universal Declaration of Human Rights*, Article 25.

3. Employment at will means that an employer, in the absence of an employee having contractual protection, legal protection, or a union protection, can hire, fire, demote, promote, or refuse to promote at will—no reason must be provided. Many states have employment at will and refer to it as the "right to work," a misleading term, and emphasize the "right to work without being

required to join a union." Note the inconsistency of employment at will with "merit."

4. See the U.S. Department of Labor, Section 11 of the Occupational Safety and Health Act of 1970, www.osha.gov.

5. See the Code of Federal Regulations, Title 49, Vol. 4, Parts 200 to 399, revised October 1, 1998, the U.S. Government Printing Office.

6. 49CFR225.33 (1).

7. See Gregory C. Smith, "The *Qui Tam* Provision of the Federal False Claims Act," www.fwlaw.com/quitam.

8. Robert Solomon, *A Better Way to Think about Business* (New York: Oxford University Press, 1999).

9. Brian Milani, *Designing the Green Economy: The Postindustrial Alternative to Corporate Globalization* (Lanham, MD: Rowman & Littlefield, 2001).

10. "Green Festival Will Boost the Growing Alternative Exonomy," *Quarterly Newsletter of Global Exchange*, 51 (Summer 2002), www.globalexchange.org.

11. Ibid., 5.

I.   Whistleblowing and Leaks[1]

Sissela Bok

IN THIS ESSAY, SISSELA BOK (b. 1934) identifies whistleblowers as those who "sound an alarm from within the very organization in which they work," an alarm about the firm's action that threatens the public interest. Bok discusses three major moral conflicts that would-be whistleblowers must resolve prior to blowing the whistle. The first conflict that must be resolved is whether speaking out is in the public interest. The second is between loyalties—to one's colleagues and firm versus to one's community and those at risk. The third conflict to resolve is whether the facts support speaking out, and how the whistleblower will handle retaliation that is all too often a result. Once a whistleblower has resolved the conflicts, Bok provides three requirements (which parallel the conflicts) that justify whistleblowing.

The first requirement is, again, to be accurate in dissent and ensure that the issue is in the public interest. The second is to minimize the breach of loyalty in the act of speaking out by exhausting internal avenues before going public. This requirement has exceptions, including if the firm is so corrupt that the information will not be addressed or if there is not time due to the nature of the harm. One does not owe loyalty to one's firm and colleagues if the action in question is morally wrong or violates the public's interest. The final requirement is to openly make the charge and to provide accurate data. Whistleblowing is intended as a last resort, an urgent call that is to obtain the public's interest and motivate a response for a clear and present danger. Bok urges potential whistleblowers to consult within the organization before blowing the whistle.

Revelation from Within

All that pollution up at Mølledal—all that reeking waste from the mill—it's seeped into the pipes feeding from the pump-room; and the same damn poisonous slop's been draining out on the beach as well. I've investigated the facts as scrupulously as possible. There's irrefutable proof of the presence of decayed organic matter in the water—millions of bacteria. It's positively injurious to health, for either internal or external use. Ah, what a blessing it is to feel that you've done some service for your home town and your fellow citizens.

Dr. Thomas Stockman, in Henrik Ibsen,
An Enemy of the People, Act I

SUCH WAS DR. STOCKMAN'S elation, in Ibsen's play, after having written a report on the contamination of the town's newly installed mineral baths. As the spa's medical director, he took it for granted that everyone would be eager to learn why so many who had come to the baths for health purposes the previous summer had been taken ill; and he assumed that the board of directors and the taxpayers would gladly pay for the extensive repairs that he recommended. By the fifth act of the play, he had been labeled an "enemy of the people" at a public meeting, lost his position as the spa's medical director, and suffered through the stoning of his house by an angry crowd. But he held his ground: "Should I let myself be whipped from the field by public opinion and the solid majority and other such barbarities? No thank you!"[2]

"Whistleblower" is a recent label for those who, like Dr. Stockman, make revelations meant to call attention to negligence, abuses, or dangers that threaten the public interest. They sound an alarm based on their expertise or inside knowledge, often from within the very organization in which they work. With as much resonance as they can muster, they strive to breach secrecy, or else arouse an apathetic public to dangers everyone knows about but does not fully acknowledge.[3]

Few whistleblowers, however, share Dr. Stockman's initial belief that it will be enough to make their message public, and that people who learn of the danger will hasten to counter it. Most know, rather, that their alarms pose a threat to anyone who benefits from the ongoing practice and that their own careers and livelihood may be at risk. The lawyer who breaches confidentiality in reporting bribery by corporate clients knows the risk, as does the nurse who reports on slovenly patient care in a hospital, the engineer who discloses safety defects in the braking systems of a fleet of new rapid-transit vehicles, or the industrial worker who speaks out about hazardous chemicals seeping into a playground near the factory dump ...

Blowing the Whistle

The alarm of the whistleblower is meant to disrupt the status quo: to pierce the background noise, perhaps the false harmony, or the imposed silence of "business as usual." Three elements, each jarring, and triply jarring when conjoined, lend acts of whistleblowing special urgency and bitterness: dissent, breach of loyalty, and accusation.[4]

Like all *dissent*, first of all, whistleblowing makes public a disagreement with an authority or a majority view. But whereas dissent can arise from all forms of disagreement with, say, religious dogma or government policy or court decisions, whistleblowing has the narrower aim of casting light on negligence or abuse, of alerting the public to a risk and of assigning responsibility for that risk.

It is important, in this respect, to see the shadings between the revelations of neglect and abuse which are central to whistleblowing, and dissent on grounds of policy. In practice, however, the two often come together. Coercive regimes or employers may regard dissent of any form as evidence of abuse or of corruption that calls for public exposure. And in all societies, persons may blow the whistle on abuses in order to signal policy dissent. Thus Daniel Ellsberg, in making his revelations about government deceit and manipulation in the Pentagon Papers, obviously aimed not only to expose misconduct and assign responsibility but also to influence the nation's policy toward Southeast Asia.

In the second place, the message of the whistleblower is seen as a *breach of loyalty* because it comes from within. The whistleblower, though he is neither referee nor coach, blows the whistle on his own team. His insider's position carries with it certain obligations to colleagues and clients. He may have signed a promise of confidentiality or a loyalty oath. When he steps out of routine channels to level accusations, he is going against these obligations. Loyalty to colleagues and to clients comes to be pitted against concern for the public interest and for those who may be injured unless someone speaks out. Because the whistleblower criticizes from within, his act differs from muckraking and other forms of exposure by outsiders. Their acts may arouse anger, but not the sense of betrayal that whistleblowers so often encounter.

The conflict is strongest for those who take their responsibilities to the public seriously, yet have close bonds of collegiality and of duty to clients as well. They know the price of betrayal. They know, too, how organizations protect and enlarge the area of what is concealed, as failures multiply and vested interests encroach. And they are aware that they violate, by speaking out, not only loyalty but usually hierarchy as well.

It is the third element of *accusation*, of calling a "foul" from within, that arouses the strongest reactions on the part of the hierarchy. The charge may be one of unethical or unlawful conduct on the part of colleagues or superiors. Explicitly or implicitly, it singles out specific groups or persons as responsible: as those who knew or should have known what was wrong and what the dangers were, and who had the capacity to make different choices. If no one could be held thus responsible—as in the case of an impending avalanche or a volcanic eruption—the warning would not constitute whistleblowing. At times the whistleblower's greatest effort is expended on trying to show that someone *is* responsible for danger or suffering: that the collapse of a building, the derailment of a train, or a famine that the public may have attributed to bad luck or natural causes was in reality brought about by specific individuals, and that they can be held responsible, perhaps made to repair the damage or at least to avoid compounding it ...

Individual Moral Choice

What questions might individuals consider, as they wonder whether to sound an alarm? How might they articulate the problem they see, and weigh its seriousness before deciding whether or not to reveal it? Can they make sure that their choice is the right one? And what about the choices confronting journalists or others asked to serve as intermediaries?

In thinking about these questions, it helps to keep in mind the three elements mentioned earlier: dissent, breach of loyalty, and accusation. They impose certain requirements: of judgment and accuracy in dissent, of exploring alternative ways to cope with improprieties that minimize the breach of loyalty, and of fairness in accusation. The judgment expressed by whistleblowers concerns a problem that should matter to the public. Certain outrages are so blatant, and certain dangers so great, that all who are in a position to warn of them have a *prima facie* obligation to do so. Conversely, other problems are so minor that to blow the whistle would be a disproportionate response. And still others are so hard to pin down that whistleblowing is premature. In between lie a great many of the problems troubling whistleblowers. Consider, for example, the following situation:

An attorney for a large company manufacturing medical supplies begins to suspect that some of the machinery sold by the company to hospitals for use in kidney dialysis is unsafe, and that management has made attempts to influence federal regulatory personnel to overlook these deficiencies.

The attorney brings these matters up with a junior executive, who assures her that he will look into the matter, and convey them to the chief executive if necessary. When she questions him a few weeks later, however, he tells her that all the problems have been taken care of, but offers no evidence, and seems irritated at her desire to learn exactly where the issues stand. She does not know how much further she can press her concern without jeopardizing her position in the firm.

The lawyer in this case has reason to be troubled, but does not yet possess sufficient evidence to blow the whistle. She is far from being as sure of her case as was Ibsen's Dr. Stockman, who had received laboratory analyses of the water used in the town spa or as the engineers in the BART case, whose professional expertise allowed them to evaluate the risks of the faulty braking system. Dr. Stockman and the engineers would be justified in assuming that they had an obligation to draw attention to the dangers they saw, and that anyone who shared their knowledge would be wrong to remain silent or to suppress evidence of the danger. But if the attorney blew the whistle about her company's sales of machinery to hospitals merely on the basis of her suspicions, she would be doing so prematurely. At the same time, the risks to hospital patients from the machinery, should she prove correct in her suspicions, are sufficiently great so that she has good reason to seek help in looking into the problem, to feel complicitous if she chooses to do nothing, and to take action if she verifies her suspicions.

Her difficulty is shared by many who suspect, without being sure, that their companies are concealing the defective or dangerous nature of their products—automobiles that are firetraps, for instance, or canned foods with carcinogenic additives. They may sense that merely to acknowledge that they don't know for sure is too often a weak excuse for inaction, but recognize also that the destructive power of adverse publicity can be great. If the warning turns out to have been inaccurate, it may take a long time to undo the damage to individuals and organizations. As a result, potential whistleblowers must first try to specify the degree to which there is genuine impropriety, and consider how imminent and how serious the threat is which they perceive.

If the facts turn out to warrant disclosure, and if the would-be whistleblower has decided to act upon them in spite of the possibilities of reprisal, then how can the second element—breach of loyalty—be overcome or minimized? Here, as in the Pentagon Papers case, the problem is one of which set of loyalties to uphold. Several professional codes of ethics, such as those of engineers and public servants, facilitate such a choice at least in theory, by requiring that loyalty to the public interest should override allegiance to colleagues, employers, or clients whenever there is a genuine conflict. Accordingly, those who have assumed a professional responsibility to serve the public interest—as had both Dr. Stockman in Ibsen's play and the engineers in the BART case—have a special obligation not to remain silent about dangers to the public.

Before deciding whether to speak out publicly, however, it is important for them to consider whether the existing avenues for change within the organization have been sufficiently explored. By turning first to insiders for help, one can often uphold both sets of loyalties and settle the problem without going outside the organization. The engineers in the BART case clearly tried to resolve the problem they saw in this manner, and only reluctantly allowed it to come to public attention as a last resort. Dr. Stockman, on the other hand, acted much more impetuously and with little concern for discretion. Before the directors of the mineral baths had even received his report, he talked freely about it, and welcomed a journalist's request to publicize the matter. While he had every reason to try to remedy the danger he had discovered, he was not justified in the methods he chose; on the contrary, they were singularly unlikely to bring about corrective action.

It *is* disloyal to colleagues and employers, as

well as a waste of time for the public, to sound the loudest alarm first. Whistleblowing has to remain a last alternative because of its destructive side effects. It must be chosen only when other alternatives have been considered and rejected. They may be rejected if they simply do not apply to the problem at hand, or when there is not time to go through routine channels, or when the institution is so corrupt or coercive that steps will be taken to silence the whistleblower should he try the regular channels first.

What weight should an oath or a promise of silence have in the conflict of loyalties? There is no doubt that one sworn to silence is under a stronger obligation because of the oath he has taken, unless it was obtained under duress or through deceit, or else binds him to something in itself wrong or unlawful. In taking an oath, one assumes specific obligations beyond those assumed in accepting employment. But even such an oath can be overridden when the public interest at issue is sufficiently strong. The fact that one has promised silence is no excuse for complicity in covering up a crime or violating the public trust.

The third element in whistleblowing—accusation—is strongest whenever efforts to correct a problem without going outside the organization have failed, or seem likely to fail. Such an outcome is especially likely whenever those in charge take part in the questionable practices, or have too much at stake in maintaining them. The following story relates the difficulties one government employee experienced in trying to decide whether to go public with accusations against superiors in his agency:

As a construction inspector for a federal agency, John Samuels (not his real name) had personal knowledge of shoddy and deficient construction practices by private contractors. He knew his superiors received free vacations and entertainment, had their homes remodeled, found jobs for their relatives—all

courtesy of a private contractor. These superiors later approved a multimillion no-bid contract with the same "generous" firm.

Samuels also had evidence that other firms were hiring nonunion laborers at a low wage while receiving substantially higher payments from the government for labor costs. A former superior, unaware of an office dictaphone, had incautiously instructed Samuels on how to accept bribes for overlooking sub-par performance.

As he prepared to volunteer this information to various members of Congress, he became tense and uneasy. His family was scared and the fears were valid. It might cost Samuels thousands of dollars to protect his job. Those who had freely provided him with information would probably recant or withdraw their friendship. A number of people might object to his using a disctaphone to gather information. His agency would start covering up and vent its collective wrath upon him. As for reporters and writers, they would gather for a few days, then move on to the next story. He would be left without a job, with fewer friends, with massive battles looming, and without the financial means of fighting them. Samuels decided to remain silent.[5]

Samuels could be sure of his facts, and fairly sure that it would not help to explore avenues within the agency in trying to remedy the situation. But was the method he envisaged—of volunteering his information to members of Congress and to the press—the one most likely to do so, and to provide a fair hearing for those he was charging with corruption and crime? Could he have gone first to the police? If he had been concerned to proceed in the fairest possible manner, he should at least have considered alternative methods of investigating and reporting the abuses he had witnessed.

These abuses were clearly such as to warrant attention. At other times, potential whistleblowers must also ask themselves whether their message, however accurate, is one to which the public is entitled in the first place or whether it infringes on personal and private matters that no one should invade. Here, the very notion of what is in the public interest is at issue: allegations regarding an official's unusual sexual or religious practices may well appeal to the public's interest without therefore being relevant to "the public interest." Those who regard such private matters as threats to the public voice their own religious and political prejudices in the language of accusation. Such a danger is never stronger than when the accusation is delivered surreptitiously; the anonymous allegations made during the McCarthy period regarding political beliefs and associations often injured persons who did not even know their accusers or the exact nature of the charges.

In fairness to those criticized, openly accepted responsibility for blowing the whistle should therefore be preferred to the secret denunciation or the leaked rumor—the more so, the more derogatory and accusatory the information. What is openly stated can be more easily checked, its source's motives challenged, and the underlying information examined. Those under attack may otherwise be hard put to it to defend themselves against nameless adversaries. Often they do not even know that they are threatened until it is too late to respond.

The choice between open and surreptitious revelation from within is admittedly less easy for the persons who intend to make them. Leaking information anonymously is safer, and can be kept up indefinitely; the whistleblower, on the contrary, shoots his bolt by going public. At the same time, those who leak know that their message may be taken less seriously, precisely because its source remains concealed. And because these messages go through several intermediaries before they appear in print, they may undergo changes along the way. At times, they are so adulterated that they lose their point altogether.

Journalists and other intermediaries must make choices of their own with respect to a leaked message. Should they use it at all, even if they doubt its accuracy? Should they pass it on verbatim or interpret it? Or should they seek to "plug" the leak? Newspaper and television bureaus receive innumerable leaks but act on only some of them. Unless the information is accompanied by indications of how the evidence can be checked, the source's anonymity, however safe, diminishes the value of the message.

In order to assure transmission of their message, yet be safe from retaliation, leakers often resort to a compromise: by making themselves known to a journalist or other intermediary, they make it possible to verify their credibility; by asking that their identity be concealed, they still protect themselves from the consequences they fear.

If anonymous sources can point to independent evidence of genuine risk or wrongdoing, the need for them to step forward is reduced and their motives are less important. For this reason, the toll-free numbers that citizens can use to report on government fraud, tax evasion, or police abuse serve an important purpose in protecting critics both from inside and from outside an organization. Without such evidence, accusations openly made by identifiable persons are preferable. The open charge is fairer to the accused, and allows listeners to weigh the motives and the trustworthiness of the whistleblowers.

Must the whistleblower who speaks out openly also resign? Only if staying on means being forced to participate in the objectionable activity, and thus to take on partial responsibility for its consequences. Otherwise, there should be no burden on whistleblowers to resign in voicing their alarm. In principle, at least, it is often their duty to speak out, and their positions ought not thereby to be at issue. In practice, however, they know that retaliation, forced departure, perhaps blacklisting, may be sufficient risks at times so that it may be wise to resign before sounding the alarm: to resign in protest, or to leave quietly, secure another post, and only then blow the whistle.[6] In each case, those who speak out can then do so with the authority and knowledge of insiders, but without their vulnerability.

It is not easy to weigh all these factors, nor to compensate for the degree of bias, rationalization, and denial that inevitably influences one's judgment. By speaking out, whistleblowers may spark a re-examination of these forces among colleagues and others who had ignored or learned to live with shoddy or corrupt practices. Because they have this power to dramatize moral conflict, would-be whistleblowers have a special responsibility to ask themselves about biases in deciding whether or not to speak out: a desire for self-defense in a difficult bureaucratic situation perhaps, or unrealistic expectations regarding the likely effects of speaking out.[7]

As they weigh the reasons for sounding the alarm, or on the contrary for remaining silent, they may find it helpful to ask about the legitimacy of the rationale for collective secrecy in the particular problem they face. If they are wondering whether or not to blow the whistle on the unnecessary surgery they have witnessed, for example, or on the manufacture of unsafe machinery, what weight should they place on claims to professional confidentiality or corporate secrecy?

Reducing bias and error in moral choice often requires consultation, even open debate; such methods force us to articulate the arguments at stake and to challenge privately held assumptions. But choices about whether or not to blow the whistle present special problems for such consultation. On the one hand, once whistleblowers sound their alarm publicly, their judgment will be subjected to open scrutiny; they will have to articulate their reasons for speaking out and substantiate their charges. On the other hand, it will then be too late to retract their charges should they turn out to have been unfounded.

For those who are concerned about a situation within their organization, it is therefore preferable to seek advice *before* deciding either to go public or to remain silent. But the more corrupt the circumstances, the more dangerous it may be to consult colleagues, and the more likely it is that those responsible for the abuse or neglect will destroy the evidence linking them to it. And yet, with no one to consult, the would-be whistleblowers themselves may have a biased view of the state of affairs; they may see corruption and conspiracy where none exists, and choose not to consult others when in fact it would have been not only safe but advantageous to do so ...

Questions

1. What are the three routes Bok provides that the whistleblower may take? What are the benefits and risks of each?

2. Bok's criteria that justify whistleblowing require the potential whistleblower to first sufficiently try the internal avenue (unless it is clear that the firm is corrupt). What are two ethical advantages to this criterion?

3. Bok condemns Dr. Stockman's route to whistleblow about the town's toxic water. Why? Do you agree?

Notes

1. From Sissela Bok, Chapter XIV of *Secrets: On the Ethics of Concealment and Revelation* (New York: Pantheon Books, 1989).

2. Henrik Ibsen, *An Enemy of the People* (1882), in *Henrik Ibsen: The Complete Major Prose Plays*, trans. and ed. Rolf Fjelde (New York: New American Library, 1965), pp. 281–386; passage quoted on p. 384.

3. I draw, for this chapter, on my earlier essays on whistleblowing: "Whistleblowing and Professional Responsibilities," in Daniel Callahan and Sissela Bok, eds., *Ethics Teaching in Higher Education* (New York: Plenum Press, 1980), pp. 277–95 (reprinted, slightly altered, in *New York University Education Quarterly* II (Summer 1980):2–10; "Blowing the Whistle," in Joel Fleishman, Lance Liebman, and Mark Moore, eds., *Public Duties: The Moral Obligations of Officials* (Cambridge, Mass.: Harvard University Press, 1981), pp. 204–21.

4. Consider the differences and the overlap between whistleblowing and civil disobedience with respect to these three elements. First, whistleblowing resembles civil disobedience in its openness and its intent to act in the public interest. But the dissent in whistleblowing, unlike that in civil disobedience, usually does not represent a breach of law; it is, on the contrary, protected by the right of free speech and often encouraged in codes of ethics and other statements of principle. Second, whistleblowing violates loyalty, since it dissents from within and breaches secrecy, whereas civil disobedience need not and can as easily challenge from without. Whistleblowing, finally, accuses specific Individuals, whereas civil disobedience need not. A combination of the two occurs, for instance, when former CIA agents publish books to alert the public about what they regard as unlawful and dangerous practices, and in so doing openly violate, and thereby test, the oath of secrecy that they have sworn.

5. This case is adapted from [Louis Clark, "The Sound of Professional Suicide," *The Barrister* 5 (Summer 1978):10.]

6. On resignation in protest, see Albert Hirschman, *Exit, Voice, and Loyalty* (Cambridge, Mass.: Harvard University Press, 1970); Brian Barry, in a review of Hirschman's book in *British Journal of Political Science* 4 (1974):79–104, has pointed out that "exit" and "voice" are not alternatives but independent variations that may occur separately or together. Both leaking and whistleblowing represent "voice." They can be undertaken while staying on at work, or before one's voluntary exit, or simultaneously with it, or after it; they can also have the consequence of involuntary or forced "exit" through dismissal or being "frozen out" even though retained at work. See also Edward Weisband and Thomas M. Franck, *Resignation in Protest* (New York: Viking Press, 1975); James Thomson, "Getting Out and Speaking Out," *Foreign Policy*, no. 13 (Winter 1973–1974), pp. 49–69; Joel L. Fleishman and Bruce L. Payne, *Ethical Dilemmas and the Education of Policymakers* (Hastings-on-Hudson, N.Y.: Hastings Center, 1980).

7. If, for example, a government employee stands to make large profits from a book exposing the iniquities in his agency, there is danger that he might slant his report in order to cause more of a sensation. Sometimes a warning is so clearly justifiable and substantiated that it carries weight no matter what the motives of the speaker. But scandal can pay; and the whistleblower's motives ought ideally to be above suspicion, for his own sake as well as for the sake of the respect he desires for his warning. Personal gain from speaking out increases the need to check the accuracy of the speaker.

2. Whistleblowers and the Narrative of Ethics[1]

C. Fred Alford

C. FRED ALFORD (B. 1947) details the consequences whistleblowers suffer after whistleblowing. Alford spent over 120 hours listening to people who comprise a support group for whistleblowers. One of his first observations is that these whistleblowers spoke in the following terms: "I did it because I had to ... because I had no other choice ... because I couldn't live with myself if I hadn't done anything ... I have to look at myself in the mirror every morning." Comparing whistleblowers and "rescuers" that helped Jews in Nazi Germany, Alford teases out the ethical threads of a whistleblower's conscience. The whistleblowers Alford studied did not view themselves as altruistic but rather unlucky for being in the place at the time of knowing the risky action(s) of the firm. They report not really having had a choice once they clearly saw the aggressors and victims, and they had to choose loyalty to one group.

Another aspect Alford observes is that whistleblowers are not easily able to "double." In the context of an employee, doubling is having two distinct sets of morals and duties that do not overlap, and the individual does not feel any contradictory issues or guilt with this. Whistleblowers are able to imagine the consequences of the action in question; they have a sense of the urgency of the moment, can identify with the victim, and do not double. Furthermore, Alford urges, they take the role of the pariah (that choiceless choice) and take their own actions in the world very seriously, illustrating excellence of character and virtues. It seems that whistleblowers have been properly socialized, in keeping with Mill's identification of oneself with the greater good, and while they feel compelled to "do the right thing" and expose harm to others, it really is a choice against doubling. Whistleblowers refuse to double by being a loving parent at home, a caring member of the church or community, and then turning that off when they cross the threshold of employment. Another term for this is integrity.

WHAT IF WE DEVELOPED an ethical theory based on the narratives of people widely regarded as ethical? This would be an inductive ethical theory, built from the ground up—not the ground that justifies ethics, just the ground of human experience. The first step would be to ask ethical people about their experiences. "Why did you do it?" would be an important question, but perhaps not the most important one. More important would be to figure out what type of world the ethical actor inhabits. "What kind of world do you inhabit so that this is who you became through your actions?" would be the ideal question, if anyone could answer it.

This approach has been tried, sometimes in conjunction with an ambitious theoretical project, the statements of moral people being used to support this or that ethical theory. What if we could avoid this temptation, stringently refusing to regard ethical narratives as evidence for this or that theory? What if we let the ethical person's story be the ethical theory, an ethical theory in narrative form? This is particularly attractive when the ethical person is trying to explain his acts to him- or herself. It is also particularly dangerous, the opportunity for the deception of self and other especially high.

There are other risks. One is the naturalistic fallacy, the derivation of ought from is. We may avoid this risk if we recognize that the description of what good people do does not make it good, nor does it automatically recommend it to others. Goodness is at least in part a prior moral judgment, not just a conclusion from watching good people, even though these people and their acts may cause us to change our views according to what Rawls calls reflective equilibrium. Detailed consideration of action widely regarded as ethical, including the "why" behind it, may cause us to revise our principles.

I conclude by comparing the way whistleblowers talk about their experiences with the way Hannah Arendt talks about thought and thinking. They are similar. According to Arendt, the key moral failure of Adolf Eichmann, desk murderer of millions, is that he was thoughtless. I turn to Arendt not to prove that she is right, or that whistleblowers are, but to show that whistleblowers are indeed talking about ethics, and not something else, such as the structure of meaningful narrative.

Whistleblowers and Rescuers

Whistleblowers are, I believe, a good example of people who have acted ethically, whose stories could help us build an ethical theory from the ground up. One advantage of choosing whistleblowers for study is that their actions take place in complex organizations, in situations of ambiguity and lack of moral clarity. Their actions, in other words, take place in the real world. Whistleblowers are no saints, and their situations sometimes lack the moral crystal clarity of rescuers of the Jews during the Holocaust, another group to which I shall refer.

The term "whistleblower" refers to those who speak out against illegal or unethical practices within the organizations they work for. Speaking out may involve going public, or it may just involve going to the boss's boss. The practices about which they speak out must involve harm to others, not just the whistleblower. To speak out against racial or sexual discrimination against oneself is admirable, but it is not by itself whistleblowing.

I have spent over a year talking with whistleblowers, including more than eighty hours with a group of a dozen whistleblowers. All have acted morally at risk to themselves. I say this not only on the basis of what they said to me, but on the basis of my research into their cases, many of which are in the public record. Most have paid a heavy price.

Of the dozen with whom I have worked most closely, all but one lost not just his or her job, but his or her career. Eight lost their homes, and seven lost their families. Their cases drag on for years, putting a tremendous strain upon a marriage. Most whistleblowers suffer from alcoholism and depression at some point in the years that follow blowing the whistle. The average whistleblower is a fifty-five year old engineer who now sells computers at Radio Shack. Divorced and in debt to his lawyer, he lives in a one-bedroom rented apartment and does not have a retirement plan.

At several points I will compare whistleblowers with rescuers of Jews during the Holocaust—not because they are the same: rescuers risked their lives, and those of their families; whistleblowers risk their livelihoods. It is the difference that intrigues. Whatever the risks, rescuers are able to form mammalian attachments with those they rescue. Whistleblowers are deprived of even this satisfaction; perhaps they do not even seek it. Surely this must be an interesting and important difference.

An additional advantage of comparing whistleblowers with rescuers is that the ethics of rescuers have been subject to extensive and sophisticated study. It will be useful to draw upon this literature in thinking about whistleblowers, not because this literature has it right, but because even an imperfect literature can be the subject of fruitful encounter.

The Altruistic Personality of Rescuers

Consider *The Altruistic Personality*, by Samuel and Pearl Oliner, the most well-known and ambitious account of rescuers. The Oliners tell a lovely story. The rescuer comes from a close family, in which discipline is based on reasoning, not physical punishment. Parents set high moral standards. "Out of such benevolent experiences, children learn to trust those around them." Attachment rather than status is the basic value, and rescuers are open to the world. Acting on this openness, they become confident in their abilities to affect the world. Although rescuers' values are expressed as principles, they are experienced viscerally as care, attachment, and "extensivity": being present in the world with others, extended to it. The decision to care for others in need was in effect made in childhood,

which is why rescuers are so quick to act when called upon. Most make their decision to help within minutes.

In contrast, the bystander, who saw but did not act, comes from a family with weak attachments. Discipline was based on punishment. Family values center on the self and social convention. Relationships with others are guarded and based on exchange. "Insecure in their families, such individuals move yet further along the constricted continuum in their relationships with others." Insulation and detachment from victims are the standard response to crisis.[2]

One trouble with the Oliners' story is that it is based on the thinnest of evidence. Thirty-two percent of rescuers and 39 percent of bystanders received physical punishment. Or so they said, forty years after the Holocaust. On this distinction a whole story is built. Similarly, even if rescuers were twice as likely to mention parents' values, this still leaves 56 percent of rescuers who did not, a majority. Seventy-eight percent of rescuers had supportive and close parental homes, compared with 55 percent (still a majority) of nonrescuers.

These are among the strongest distinctions, no better and generally worse than that which led Stanley Milgram to wonder at the weakness of his correlations in his famous study, *Obedience to Authority*. Ordering "teachers" to deliver what they believed were painful electrical shocks to learners, he found no very convincing social-psychological correlations with disobedience, not even the teachers' scores on Lawrence Kohlberg's famous test of stages of moral development.[3]

Almost as interesting as the rescuers are those who stand just off stage, the subject of implicit criticism. One is Kant, the Oliners taking their stand with Carol Gilligan against those who posit universal morals and internalized rules as the basis of morality.[4] Another backstage bystander is Theodor Adorno and his colleagues who wrote *The Authoritarian Personality*.[5] In their account, morality stems from a strong ego, able to stand alone against society, able to remember its commitment to universal values even when society has lost its head. For Gilligan, on the other hand, morality stems from attachment to others and the care and concern that goes with it. Morality is not an act of the strong, isolated individual, but the related one.

The Oliners are telling the story of their ideal person, not the autonomous individual, but the caring one, whose strength stems from relatedness, not a successful resolution of the Oedipus conflict. In so doing they are taking sides in an important contemporary argument about morality, Gilligan versus Kant, or to put it as simply as possible, care versus universal rules.

Depending upon how I asked the question to the whistleblowers, I could evoke responses that fit either Gilligan or Kant. This is something to worry about. Nor was it necessary to set the answer up in a heavy-handed way in order to influence the response. Simply preceding the question with five minutes of talking about universals, such as discussing whether every person has equal rights in every situation, produced a context in which most whistleblowers would respond in terms of universals when asked why they did it. But if I preceded the question with five minutes of talking about care and concern for others, then most whistleblowers would answer in those terms when asked why they did it.

Consider the question that leads the authors of the single largest whistleblower study to date to conclude that "whistleblowers held slightly more universalistic values than non-whistleblowers." That question is "Should decisions be made on a case by case basis?"[6] Slightly more whistleblowers say no, but it is not clear to what they are saying no. The

authors are not so much setting up a response as generating answers to a question so ambiguous as to support any conclusion about whistleblowing.[7]

Just Listening to What Whistleblowers Say

There is another way to do research, a way that does not prejudice the answers, at least not in the same way: just listen. That is what I have done with the whistleblowers. Ninety percent of my time has been spent just listening to what they say among themselves. Only occasionally did I arrange to meet a whistleblower for a private interview.

The approach of just listening takes a long time, more than eighty hours with a dozen whistleblowers, almost half that time with a dozen more. Most of the listening took place at a support group for whistleblowers, the rest at a country retreat for stressed-out whistleblowers. Occasionally (once or twice in a three-hour session) I would ask a whistleblower to clarify his or her point, saying simply, "Could you expand on that point a little bit?" Sometimes they would, and sometimes they would not. They were not talking with me. I was present at their sufferance. They were talking with each other. Among the most interesting discussions occurred when an old whistleblower was inducting a new whistleblower into the fraternity, into the role of whistleblower.

My approach did not solve all problems in research. One might argue that my relative silence allowed the whistleblowers to project all sorts of expectations onto me. Occasionally they seemed to think that I understood them better than they understood themselves. But if I was the subject of their projections, these were nonetheless *their* projections.

When talking among themselves, whistleblowers talk in terms of a moral theory that is not well represented among the schools. "I did it because I had to ... because I had no other choice ... because I couldn't live with myself if I hadn't done anything ... because it was speak up or stroke out ... What else could I do? I have to look at myself in the mirror every morning?" This is what whistleblowers say (the comments of several strung together here to form a single quote).

How to regard this almost universal answer, as common among whistleblowers as it is among rescuers of the Jews?[8] Is it really an answer, or is it preliminary to the real answer, the inarticulate preface? The answer certainly seems to have the quality of a tautology. "I did it because I had to." I have come to believe that this is the answer. It is not preliminary to something else. As Wittgenstein says, the trick is to know when to stop, in this case, when to stop asking "why?"[9]

Taking whistleblowers' simple answer seriously does not result in a simple explanation. On the contrary, it results in an elaborate explanation. It means that one must be hesitant about invoking explanatory entities such as a strong conscience or superego that presumably lies behind the deceptively simple reality. Eva Fogelman, for example, invokes the "innermost core of a person" as an explanation of why rescuers did it, when all she means are things that people said about themselves that seemed to be consistent over time. Even about this Fogelman had to assume that her subjects were not creating a false and artificial consistency by emphasizing some things and deemphasizing others.[10]

In order to make sense of choiceless choices, we need not posit an unconscious that makes unconscious choices, though existential psychoanalysts such as Binswanger have had some success with this approach.[11] We need only abandon the idea of a master narrative, and with it, that of a master storyteller. Instead, we must consider that one part of the self tells the other part, and then they take turns.

"I told myself I couldn't live with myself if I didn't do something." This is how most whistleblower narratives begin, one part of the self talking about another. "I had to speak up or stroke out. That was my choice." The story the self tells itself is that it really had no choice: one part couldn't live if the other didn't act.

How Whistleblowers Explain Their Acts to Themselves

How do whistleblowers explain the experience of choiceless choice to themselves? Four stories they tell seem especially relevant. In all four stories the whistleblower is both subject and object, the storyteller and the one the story is about. In all four the storyteller is more than a little chagrined at the intransigence of his subject, himself. Together these stories go some way to explaining the experience of choiceless choice, not just to me, but to the whistleblowers themselves.

Though I give only one example to support each story, I heard a version of each story from at least half a dozen whistleblowers. Not every whistleblower offered his or her story as an explicit attempt to explain his or her experience of choiceless choice. I am reporting on conversations among whistleblowers, and like all conversations they jump around a bit. Nevertheless, I believe this was almost always the implicit context. Not just "why did I do it," but "how did I get myself into a situation where this was all I could do?"

The narrative structure is always the same, a conversation of voices within the whistleblower, the voice that compelled explaining to the voice that acted why it had no choice. In explaining this to him- or herself, the whistleblower is trying to come to terms with an experience of compulsion that seems more like freedom, liberation from an impossible situation. But a strange and frightening freedom it is, one that can seize a person and not let go until it has destroyed just about everything the whistleblower values: career, home, family. How to live with this kind of person who is oneself is the subtext of most of these narratives.

Metalepsis

There is one more voice to consider, that of the theorist, myself. Following each story I elaborate upon its relevance, treating it not just as an answer to the individual whistleblower's question "Why did I do it?" but as part of an ethical theory that begins but does not end with this question. Mine is a "passing theory," a term drawn from Donald Davidson via Richard Rorty. So is Arendt's account of thinking, to which I turn at the end.[12] The term "passing theory" suggests the way in which speakers of different languages come to understand each other in passing, almost as if they were ships in the night.

In the language of narrative studies, mine is a metalepsis, the intrusion of one storyline into another. My voice is a theoretical voice, but that is primarily a question of style. My voice is no more or less authoritative, it has no greater epistemic status, than the stories it is about. I say this not out of modesty, but out of methodology. I would not want to be seen as doing what I have criticized others for doing, using narrative to support a theory.

Metalepsis may pose problems. When one of the languages is theoretical, the requirements of passing become more complex. If the goal is communication, not merely the subsumption of experience by theory, the theoretical language must not redefine the experience of the one who is being studied in terms the subject would no longer recognize—if, that is, the subject were acquainted with the basic terms and concepts of the theory: not "would the subject agree?" but "would the informed subject find the theory to be an account, however flawed, of his act, and not that of another person, or force of nature?"

The subject's experience is not an empirical indicator, nor is it a signpost to a mechanism of some kind, such as a guilty conscience. The purpose of the theoretical language is not to reduce the subject's experience to the status of evidence for this or that theory. The theoretical language sees the narrator's story as part of a larger story whose narrative world is more encompassing, but not alien. It is something like the difference between my story and the story of my people, a term so broad it can cover anything from my family to my species. Rather than describe this principle further, it will be more useful to exemplify it. In trying to exemplify it I believe I am respecting not just a good epistemological principle, but a good moral one as well.

An Imagination for Consequences

"I am afflicted by my imagination for consequences" is how Tom put it. Tom blew the whistle on the Department of Energy's failure to clean up properly an abandoned research site. "I just couldn't stop imagining what would happen if children climbed over the fence and played in the radioactive dust."

"What about your colleagues?" asked another whistleblower. "Were they too scared to protest?"

"I don't think so," the engineer replied. "They just didn't think about it. Site protection was not our responsibility. It really wasn't my job. My job was just to shut [the old reactor] down. I just couldn't stop thinking about it. My boss said to keep my mind on my job. He meant don't think about what you are doing. I did, and I lost my job."

Tom is currently delivering pizza. He sounds

ashamed, as though he has failed in some way. If he could have just kept his mind on his job, he would have done fine. He seems to feel he is a prisoner of his almost visceral connection to the long-term consequences of his acts.

Arendt writes about the "enlargement of the mind," as Kant calls it. "To think with the enlarged mentality—that means you train your imagination to go visiting."[13]

Only in Tom's case it sounds as though his imagination is training him. What academics frequently regard as virtuous, such as an enlarged mentality, the whistleblower often experiences as a burden, an inability to do otherwise. The academic names the virtue, but the whistleblower pays the price.

If whistleblowers are connected in an almost visceral way with the consequences of their acts, this does not mean that they are connected in an almost visceral way with those who are affected by them. Tom's concern for the children who might play in the dust is unusual. Most do not talk about the others they are serving except in the most general terms, such as "the public." In this regard they are different from rescuers.

Consider how Philip Hallie writes about Magda Trocmé, a rescuer of Jews who spoke about "covering" those Jews she cared for. "When you cover people, you are allowing their own heat to warm their bodies under that blanket or sweater; you are not intruding on those bodies.... In this image of covering lies the essence of Magda's way of caring for others."[14] There is a mammalian connection with another for the rescuer that is lacking for the whistleblower, a lived connection to another person.

Martin Buber wrote that empathy is like a bridge, thrown "from self-being to self-being across the abyss of dread of the universe."[15] For whistleblowers, one end of this bridge must generally be supported by an imaginary abutment.

This is no small difference. It means that the rescuer is acting in accordance with our mammalian human nature. The rescuer may be going against the larger group, but he or she is forming an attachment with another, perhaps the basic human (actually, mammalian) act.[16] It is no accident that rescuers use a lot of skin talk, their relationship with the victim a type of "skinship," a term coined by anthropologists.

One rescuer put it this way. "When I came home, I looked at my skin. You see I looked and I said [to myself], 'Of course we are the same!'"[17] Like whistleblowers, rescuers speak in several voices. Unlike whistleblowers, one of these voices is often talking skin talk.

Whistleblowers' attachments are different, more abstract. They are acting against an aspect of human nature, which tells us something important about "human nature." It too is only one voice, albeit a powerful one:

Regardless of circumstances, chimpanzees, monkeys, and humans cannot readily exit the group to which they belong. The double meaning of "belonging to" says it all: they are part of and possessed by the group.[18]

In such groups, the modal strategy is the alliance: two against one. "Many primates excel at this: their main tool for internal competition is the alliance of two parties against a third."[19] Even rescuers employ this strategy, the rescuer and his or her charge against the world. The whistleblower risks less, but he or she generally risks it alone.

One might argue that although whistleblowers are not connected to those they benefit, the structure of their imagination for consequences is nonetheless the structure of all empathy: taking up in one's imagination the place of the other. Certainly this is true, but it is not simply true, as discussed below under "Identification with the Victim."

A Sense of the Historical Moment

"It was just my moral bad luck to be there at the right time," said Joe. "Or should I say the wrong time? Most people are not faced with being asked to lie to the Feds. I knew at that moment I was going to be part of history."

He was, though it was not history that made the newspapers, just another case of Medicare fraud. But it was history nonetheless. It need not have been. Had Joe been unaware of his historical moment, it might have passed him by. He was waiting for it.

"You sound like you were just waiting to pounce," said another whistleblower.

"No, not pounce. Act. I come from a large family, and each of my brothers and sisters made something of themselves. Suddenly I knew it was my turn. It just didn't make me rich."

It cost Joe his job, but he is lucky. So far it has not cost him his house or family. Though he never got his job back, he was vindicated. His boss eventually went to jail.

"What do you mean by moral bad luck?" I asked.

"If any of my brothers or sisters had been in the same situation they'd have done the same thing. But they weren't. It was my bad luck to be the one to have to pay the price."

Joe was asked to lie about how well his organization was serving its disabled clients. He might have talked about them and their needs. Instead he talked about himself, his moment in history.

Like Tom, Joe is attached not so much to others as to his acts. His acts are his children. Acts grow up, leave home, live their own lives, get married and bring forth other acts, but for children and grandchildren alike the whistleblower is forever responsible. Perhaps whistleblowers' acts are like children in another sense as well: someone to keep them company in the world. Not other people, but

a chain of acts, serves as the bridge across the abyss of dread to which Buber refers.

Identification with the Victim

"I'd been a part of management for years. They were my friends, we watched each other's kids grow up. But when I finally figured out what they ... no I don't mean they, I mean we. When I finally figured out what we were doing to the poor people who were our clients, I couldn't even go out for a drink with them anymore. Management was my world, I didn't even know our clients' names, but I had to choose. Only it wasn't really a choice, you know, more like an ultimatum I gave myself."

Anna Freud wrote about "identification with the aggressor," as she called it.[20] An early stage in the development of conscience, identification with the aggressor occurs not just when we are scared of others, but when we cannot bear their censure. We internalize the criticism, but rather than directing it at ourselves we turn it outward, becoming the critic because we cannot bear the criticism. Moral maturity is reached, says Anna Freud, when we become able to turn this criticism back against ourselves.

That's Freud! Sigmund or Anna, it makes little difference.[21] For both, conscience is the aggression we would have visited against others turned back on ourselves. I do not know if this is true, but I have promised not to posit entities and mechanisms as explanations, so I will not pursue the point, introducing it only to note the possibility nowhere discussed by either Freud, "identification with the victim." Only I introduce it not as mechanism, but as choiceless choice.

Somewhere along the way we have to choose. When push comes to shove, are we going to throw in our lot with the executioner or the victim? With power or its victims? Hannah Arendt divides the world into parvenus and pariahs. Which shall we choose to be? Shall we assimilate ourselves to authority or to those who suffer its injustice? What if this choice were the basis of all morality?

To be sure, the world is not always divided so starkly. What marks a historical moment is that suddenly it is, and we have to choose, suddenly to find that we have already made the choice a thousand times before in similar, less dramatic situations, even if we did not know it at the time. This is what Iris Murdoch means when she says "at crucial moments of choice most of the business of choosing is already over."[22] We have chosen by how we have lived our lives up until this point. Then our lives choose for us. Aristotle (in book 2 of the *Nicomachean Ethics*) had a similar idea. He called it character, *ethos,* the term that comes down to us as ethics.

It is the power of the Milgram experiment to have created a world in which there were only two choices: identification with the aggressor or identification with the victim. Milgram has, in other words, created a historical moment. Few imagined that when forced to choose so starkly, most would choose to side with the aggressor, even when they could hear the cries of the victim. Perhaps it is fear of being substituted for the victim that leads so many to side with the aggressor, a fear reinforced by the structure of the experiment itself. Each "teacher" believed he had a fifty-fifty chance of being the victim. There but for the grace of Odds go I.

Until this point I have suggested that whistleblowers are not primarily motivated by empathy, their "skinship," with the victim. Am I not now suggesting they are? Not necessarily. Whistleblowers identify with the victim by making the victim's fight their own. It does not matter that in many cases the whistleblower does not know the actual victim. On the contrary, that just makes it easier! Identification with the victim may be defined

not as empathy with the sufferer, but as resistance to the aggressor, refusal to ally oneself with the aggressor, as the quotation that opens this section makes clear.[23]

This need not be the case. Tom, the whistleblower who speaks about his imagination for consequences, combines empathy with resistance. My point is not logical, or even psychological, but empirical. As most whistleblowers talk about it, their identification with the victim takes the form of a refusal to align themselves with the aggressor, coupled with an inability not to choose sides. In good measure this inability stems from a reluctance or incapacity to double.

Not Very Good at Doubling

"When I came home at night, I was supposed to love and care about my family," said Jane. "And I did. When I went to work in the morning I was supposed to regard everyone else's family as expendable. After a while I just couldn't do it anymore."

"Why'd it take you ten years?" asked another whistleblower.

"I don't know. I think I just got used to living in two different worlds. Then somehow I just couldn't anymore."

The whistleblower is not very good at "doubling," as Robert Jay Lifton calls it.[24] Lifton introduced the concept in order to explain how the Nazi doctors he interviewed could torture their "patients." Doubling occurs when a part of the self comes to act autonomously, as though part of the self were authorized to act for the self entire. It is through doubling that we are able to ignore our ethical qualms at work because our work self temporarily speaks for our whole self. Doubling occurs when the voices that speak to us no longer speak to each other, as when the voice of the family self no longer hears the voice of the work self, and vice versa.

One businessman, not a whistleblower, put it this way. "What is right in the corporation is not what is right in a man's home or in his church. What is right in the corporation is what the guy above you wants from you. That's what morality is in the corporation."[25]

The businessman tells a tale in which three selves have trouble talking with each other because they inhabit worlds in which different moral languages are spoken. There is an implicit master narrator, the one who tells the tale of the other isolated narrators, but the master narrator is a shadowy presence. He is an observer, perhaps even a mourner of their lost unity that never was, but he is no integrator. Because there is a shadowy master narrator, one would have to say the man's doubling (actually, tripling) is not complete, though it would be more accurate, and certainly more in accord with Lifton's thinking, to say that he has doubled but not split. The man retains awareness of other selves with other stories, but each is sequestered.

It would be possible to elaborate the concept of doubling further, as Lifton does, but it does not seem necessary. What is important is that something like doubling seems a requirement of modern life. From Kant to Max Weber to Jürgen Habermas, modern life is defined in terms of its separation into spheres of value, as they are sometimes called: science, religion and morality, and art. Unproblematic, even liberating in the abstract, this division becomes immensely problematic when organization and bureaucracy become one of these spheres, a type of pseudoscience.

This is precisely what the critique of instrumental reason, as the Frankfurt School calls it, is all about, its explanation of the Holocaust. It is what Habermas's project is concerned with, the colonization of the lifeworld, as he calls it, by strategic and instrumental action. Here too is Zygmunt Bauman's explanation not just of the Holocaust, but of modern life.

All social organization, says Bauman in *Modernity and the Holocaust,*

> consists in subjecting the conduct of its units to either instrumental or procedural criteria of evaluation. More importantly still, it consists in delegalizing all other criteria, and first and foremost such standards as may render behaviour of units resilient to uniformizing pressures and thus autonomous vis-a-vis the collective purpose of the organization (which, from the organizational point of view, makes them unpredictable and potentially de-stabilizing).... All social organization consists therefore in neutralizing the disruptive and deregulating impact of moral behavior.[26]

All social organization, in other words, speaks with a single voice, that of instrumental reason.

Doubling is a sophisticated emotional and cognitive act, one that whistleblowers are unable or unwilling to perform. In this regard, they are dysfunctional actors in modern society. One might even call them pariahs.

Thought and Being

Hannah Arendt, who once described her philosophical method as telling stories, tells a story about thinking. It is an ethical passing theory, articulating rather than subsuming the way whistleblowers, as well as other moral actors, talk about their experiences. Nowhere fully articulated in her work, what I call her passing theory is implicit in her first book (not published until almost twenty years later), a historical biography called *Rahel Varnhagen: The Life of a Jewish Woman,* and explicit only in her last, the posthumously published *The Life of the Mind.* ("Explicit" here does not mean "fully developed.")

Arendt went to see the trial of Adolf

Eichmann expecting to see the face of radical evil. What she saw was something far different, what she called the banality of evil, marked above all by thoughtlessness: "The longer one listened to him, the more obvious it became that his inability to speak was closely connected with an inability to *think*, namely to think from the standpoint of somebody else."[27]

Elsewhere Arendt characterizes thinking in terms of its ability to distance us from others, and it may seem that she is contradicting herself. The contradiction is mitigated when one considers that what she means by taking someone else's standpoint is not so much empathy as taking one's imaginative stance from the midst of a world that includes others. It is the failure to do this that marks the parvenu. With this term she includes all who sacrifice their knowledge of reality for the sake of fitting into society.

Thoughtlessness is the parvenu's sacrifice of reality. "Along with reality, truth had to be sacrificed; truth became whatever society says is true."[28] Life becomes what Vaclav Havel calls "living within a lie." People don't believe in what they are doing, but they act as if they do. The result not only confirms the system but gives it an unreal and reified quality, resulting in the ironic detachment that characterizes so many contemporary characters. More than half the whistleblowers I spoke with talked about their former colleagues using terms like zombies, sleepwalkers, or the living dead. It is, I believe, this phenomenon they were referring to.

Thoughtlessness is monologic: it engages in dialogue neither with others nor with oneself. Thoughtlessness seems to be a way of not having to choose between the roles of parvenu and pariah, as though one did not have to choose between identification with the aggressor or the victim. Thoughtlessness is the pretense that it does not matter what

one does, for one is not really doing anything real or important. Thoughtlessness is the willful unawareness of the existence of historical moments.

To be thoughtful is to be a pariah, though that is not enough. One must, says Arendt, become a conscious pariah, which means accepting not only one's marginal status, but also the responsibility that goes with it. The pariah must "relinquish once and for all the prerogatives of the *schlemihl*, cut loose from the world of fancy and illusion ... and come to grips with the world of men and women."[29] The pariah must, in other words, think and act on the knowledge he or she has obtained by virtue of living on the margins. He or she must seize the historical moment.

Thought is a dialogue with oneself, in which parts of oneself are free to represent others, "free" because freedom of thought means being able to imagine oneself as actor in the larger world, a world marked above all by plurality. Thought is imagination that is still bound to the world. In this regard, thought is distinct from introspection, in which "thinking becomes limitless because it is no longer molested by anything exterior."[30] Thought is introspection that is willing to be molested by reality, indeed to engage in internal dialogue with the assailant.

Thought is "training your imagination to visiting," as Arendt puts it, as good a synonym as any for what Tom called "an imagination for consequences."[31] When we let our imagination go visiting we engage in an internal dialogue with the wayfarer, taking that part of ourselves that has seen a larger world into account in what we say to ourselves. There is an element of empathy, of making other people's standpoints "present to [one's mind]," but it is far from identification with them, but more like knowledge by acquaintance. Sometimes Arendt called this perspective "common sense," by which she meant a sense of what we have in common. At other times she emphasized the plurality of viewpoints. Common sense is plural.

Arendt quotes Socrates on why it is better to suffer an injustice than inflict one: "It would be better for me that my lyre or chorus I directed should be out of tune and that multitudes of men should disagree with me than that I, being one, should be out of harmony with myself, and contradict me" (*Gorgias,* 482c). If I inflict an injustice, I must live with the unjust one forever. If I suffer an injustice, I need only live with the consequences of another's injustice.

It is, I believe, the dread of having to live forever with someone whom one despises that most motivates whistleblowers. This is the source of the terrible compulsion behind choiceless choice. It is, I believe, the dread of isolation from others that motivates many who do not blow the whistle. What it is not is a question of *Selbstdenken*, or "being one." About this Socrates is misleading. Then again, Socrates was always misleading on this point, assuming the unity of the self ("no one does wrong knowingly" makes sense only if the self is one) even when Plato insisted on dividing the self into reason, spirit and desire. But then again, was not Plato's Socrates always a character in an internal dialogue of Plato's?

Not unity, but a conversation among the parts, is key, what Plato called the soundless dialogue (*eme emautô*) between me and myself (*Theaetetus,* 189e; *Sophist,* 263e). It is actually Hippias who remains one when he goes home alone, because "he does not seek to keep himself company" (*Hippias Major,* 304d). Hippias uses others as Socrates would use himself. This does not necessarily make Socrates happier. When Socrates goes home alone he must listen to the other fellow who is waiting there for him, his internal partner. If Socrates has done something that is shameful, his internal partner will not let him rest

in peace. "Later times have given the fellow who awaits Socrates in his home the name of 'conscience,'"[32] says Arendt.

The mark of thought is that the parts converse, the part that went visiting talking to the part that stayed home. The mark of doubling is that the parts of the self live independent lives, never talking to each other about what they are doing. The self who is waiting at home never talks with the self who went to work. It was Jane's inability to do this, her inability not to engage in a conversation between the self who cared for her family and the self who was supposed to regard other families as expendable, that led her to blow the whistle, though perhaps the term "forced her" would be more accurate. Certainly it would be a more accurate description of how she experiences her life.

It is Arendt's almost desperate hope that a thoughtful person's ability to be dissatisfied with the self he or she is living with, as Socrates was often dissatisfied, and as Jane was, might serve as an antidote to evil, and a source of goodness.[33] During what Arendt calls "boundary situations" and "special emergencies," the internal dialogue becomes impossible to continue unless the thoughtful one acts in the world to bring the selves back into a friendly relationship.

By "boundary situation," Arendt means something similar to what I mean by a sense of the historical moment. It is an experience of "something immanent which already points to transcendence, and which, if we respond to it, will result in our *becoming the Existenz we potentially are.*"[34] Earlier I said the ideal question to ask whistleblowers would be "What kind of world do you inhabit so that this is who you became through your actions?" Here is the outline of an answer: it is a world in which one must sometimes say no in order to be, almost regardless of the price.

This is, of course, precisely what the

whistleblower means when he or she says, "I couldn't live with myself if I didn't do something." It is the universal answer, given by almost every whistleblower and almost every rescuer of Jews during the Holocaust. It is the meaning of choiceless choice, the Socratic meaning, as long as one does not overemphasize oneness. "I couldn't live with myself if I didn't do something" is not hyperbole. It is the simple truth, reflecting a not so simple relationship between self, and world, though we should probably throw in a few more selves and worlds for good measure.

Here of course is the problem. Arendt writes as if there are only two selves. "Socratic two-in-one heals the solitariness of thought; its inherent duality points to the infinite plurality which is the law of the earth."[35] Although it may be true that two is closer to plurality than one is to two, there is no reason to assume that the self remains two when the world is many. Today many become thoughtless because there are too many voices in their heads, too many "friends" waiting at home to tell them what to do. So we go home and shut the little mental door to keep them at bay.

Arendt's account is still modeled on conscience, the little voice that says no. In the postmodern world the problem is often not too few voices for a dialogue, but too many. Arendt suppresses the plurality of voices because for her conscience, "to know with and by myself," is based on contradiction. Contradiction is in turn the organon of the Kantian categorical imperative: act only on that maxim through which you can at the same time will that it should become a universal law. Without contradiction, the categorical imperative would offer no guidance, nor would any other principle. Arendt does make the good point that we find logical contradiction compelling only because we find its psychological correlate disturbing, but she assumes a homology.[36] What if this homology

is not built in but is itself a cultural construct? Then there will be dozens of voices waiting for us when we get home, and to whom shall we listen to tell us whom to listen to?

The problem, of course (though this is not really the place to go into it), is that Arendt's pluralism has gone far beyond Kant's. In one respect, Arendt's account of morality is Kant's account of aesthetic judgment, in which an enlarged sense of taste is the standard. "The larger the realm in which the enlightened individual is able to move, from standpoint to standpoint, the more 'general' will be his thinking."[37] By enlarged, Kant means so cosmopolitan that all enlightened people would agree. A person who describes something as beautiful, says Kant, insists that everyone ought to give the object in question his approval.[38] This is not, needless to say, how many moderns (to say nothing of postmoderns) would interpret plurality.

There is an underlying assumption of not just commonality, but universality, in Kant's account from which Arendt borrows in order to make a rough equation between common sense and conscience. But, Arendt borrows from Kant within the framework of her own thought, which is far more pluralistic than his, a framework in which common sense means something quite different and far less categorical.

The result is that when Arendt talks about thinking, she can only mean the thoughts of particular people at particular times and places. This is why I have found it useful to reverse Arendt, so to speak, focusing not on thought, but on the actual ways in which a group of men and women widely regarded as ethical experience their world. What makes my account different from Arendt's is not that I refer to narrative whereas she refers to thought. There is no such thing as thought, only the narratives of thinkers. Most ethical theory is concerned with the narratives of professional thinkers. I have focused on the amateurs, the ones who have paid the price.

Almost all the whistleblowers I interviewed are middle-aged citizens of the predecessor culture, one in which there were fewer voices. It would be good to figure out how to foster these men and women. It would be sad to discover that their existence depends upon cultural inheritances, such as the tattered legacy of the Enlightenment, that are impossible to repair. Minerva's owl flies at dusk. But there are lots of little kingdoms in the twilight, lots of little spaces and places in which men and women like these might be fostered and protected. Trouble is, for them to make a difference they must be fostered but not protected.

Morality Is Not about Morality

An imagination for consequences, a sense of the historical moment, identification with the victim, and a reluctance to double are the categories by which whistleblowers explain their choiceless choices to themselves. These categories nest nicely within Arendt's account of thinking as a dialogue with oneself, in which parts of oneself are encouraged to go visiting. To have demonstrated only this, however, would be little more than an academic exercise.

What the convergence reveals is that morality not only depends upon, but is, a set of virtues not always recognized as moral virtues. Allowing one's imagination to go visiting, taking one's actions in the world with deadly seriousness, taking up the role of the pariah, cultivating a dialogue with oneself: these are excellences of character not always associated with morality. Yet when we look at a group of men and women who have risked much to do what they believe is right, these are the attributes we see. Or rather, these are the attributes they see in themselves, the attributes they associate with their acts.

Not empathy, not an adherence to universal principles, not an ethic of care and concern, but a type of seriousness about themselves and the world is at the center of their explanations. Theirs is a seriousness that is not hostile to imagination but part of it, similar to what Arendt calls thought—similar, but not identical.

There is an unreflected quality to the ethical act, giving it the quality of a compulsion, that the term thinking does not quite capture. Arendt turns to thinking, one suspects, because the notion of an ethical compulsion fits so poorly with the legacy of the Enlightenment. It is, however, not given that in choosing ethically we find our greatest freedom or dignity. That instead may reside in being, even when this being feels not like freedom but necessity.

Questions

1. How do identifying with the victim and imagination for consequences combine to impel a whistleblower to come forward?

2. What is the "choiceless choice" whistleblowers face? How does this carry a witness forward into a whistleblower?

3. What is doubling? How do whistleblowers refuse to double? Why is this another term for integrity?

Notes

1. C. Fred Alford, "Whistleblowers and the Narrative of Ethics," *Journal of Social Philosophy* 32, no. 3 (Fall 2001): 402–18. Copyright 2001 Blackwell Publishers.

2. Samuel Oliner and Pearl Oliner, *The Altruistic Personality: Rescuers of Jews in Nazi Germany* (New York: Free, 1988), 251–52. I consider the Oliners' study, and whistleblowing in general, in more detail in *Whistleblowers: Broken Lives and Organizational Power* (Ithaca, N.Y.: Cornell University Press, 2001).

3. Stanley Milgram, *Obedience to Authority* (New York: Harper and Row, 1974), 205.

4. Carol Gilligan, *In a Different Voice: Psychological Theory and Women's Development* (Cambridge: Harvard University Press, 1982).

5. T. Adorno, E. Frenkel-Brunswick, D. J. Levinson, and R. N. Sanford, *The Authoritarian Personality* (New York: Harper, 1950).

6. Joyce Rothschild and Terance Miethe, *Keeping Organizations True to Their Purposes: The Role of Whistleblowing in Organizational Accountability and Effectiveness.* Final Report to the Aspen Institute, Aspen, Colo., 1996.

7. It is not at all clear what most researchers mean by "universalistic." For example, when Monroe writes that rescuers all give universalistic explanations, she means that rescuers say they would have given shelter to anyone who asked them, not just Jews. See Kristen Monroe, *The Heart of Altruism* (Princeton, N.J.: Princeton University Press, 1996), 198–200. One might as well call this a "particularistic explanation": any particular individual who came before them would receive shelter. Oliner and Oliner use the term "consistently universalistic orientation" in an identical way: those who helped Jews say they would have helped anyone (*Altruistic Personality,* 166–67).

    This confusion about universalism is important for two reasons. First, it is part of the myth of the rescuer as ideal human being, the term "universal" serving a double duty to indicate one who acts on principle while caring for all humans, the rescuer transformed into a loving Kantian (an oxymoron?) who does not reject care. Second, it prevents us from seeing that people who act in ways that we intuitively recognize as remarkably good do not act in accord with familiar and popular philosophical accounts of goodness.

8. Monroe, *Heart of Altruism,* 210, 234.

9. Ludwig Wittgenstein, *Tractatus Logico-Philosophicus,* trans. F. P. Ramsey and C. K. Ogden (London: Routledge and Kegan Paul, 1992), part 7.

10. Eva Fogelman, *Conscience and Courage: Rescuers of Jews during the Holocaust* (New York: Doubleday, 1994), xviii.

11. Ludwig Binswanger, *Being in the World: Selected Papers of Ludwig Bingswanger,* ed. with an introduction by Jacob Needleman (London: Souvenir, 1975).

12. Richard Rorty, *Contingency, Irony, and Solidarity* (Cambridge: Cambridge University Press, 1989), 14.

13. Hannah Arendt, *The Life of the Mind* (one-volume edition) (New York: Harcourt Brace, 1978), part 3, 257.

14. Philip Hallie, *Lest Innocent Blood Be Shed: The Story of the Village of Le Chambon* (New York: Harper and Row, 1979), 65.

15. Martin Buber, *Between Man and Man,* repr. ed., trans. R. G. Smith (New York: MacMillan, 1965), 175.

16. Frans De Waal, *Good Natured: The Origins of Right and Wrong in Humans and Other Animals* (Cambridge: Harvard University Press, 1996), 174.

17. Fogelman, *Conscience and Courage,* 262.

18. De Waal, *Good Natured,* 169.

19. Ibid., 172.

20. Anna Freud, *The Ego and the Mechanisms of Defense,* rev. ed. (Vol. 2 of *The Writings of Anna Freud*) (New York: International Universities Press, 1966), 109–21.

21. Sigmund Freud, *Civilization and Its Discontents,* trans. J. Strachey (New York: W.W. Norton, [1929] 1961), 83–96.

22. Iris Murdoch, *The Sovereignty of Good over Other Concepts* (Cambridge: Cambridge University Press, 1967), 21.

23. Several studies of rescuers designate a subcategory of rescuer who acts not primarily out of care and concern, but out of resistance to hated authority. See Fogelman, *Conscience and Courage,* 118. Most whistleblowers seem to fit this general category, though one must be careful in separating care and concern from hatred of aggression, cruelty, and destructiveness. "Nice" emotions like care and concern do not necessarily have nice sources, nor should they.

24. Robert Jay Lifton, *The Nazi Doctors: Medical Killing and the Psychology of Genocide* (New York: Basic, 1986), 418–29.

25. Robert Jackall, *Moral Mazes* (New York: Oxford University Press, 1988), 6.

26. Zygmunt Bauman, *Modernity and the Holocaust* (Ithaca, N.Y.: Cornell University Press, 1989), 213–15.

27. Hannah Arendt, *Eichmann in Jerusalem: A Report on the Banality of Evil,* rev. and enl. ed. (New York: Harcourt Brace Jovanovich, 1964), 287.

28. Hanna Pitkin, *The Attack of the Blob: Hannah Arendt's Concept of the Social* (Chicago: University of Chicago Press, 1998), 26.

29. Hannah Arendt, *The Jew as Pariah,* ed. R. Feldman (New York: Grove, 1978), 77.

30. Hannah Arendt, *Rahel Varnhagen: The Life of a Jewish Woman,* trans. R. Winston and C. Winston (New York: Harcourt Brace Jovanovich, 1974), 10.

31. Arendt, *Life of the Mind,* part 3, 257.

32. Ibid., part 1, 190.

33. Ibid., 5.

34. Ibid., 192. The internal quotes are from Karl Jaspers.

35. Ibid., 187.

36. Ibid., 186–88.

37. Ibid., part 3, 258.

38. Kant, *Critique of Judgment,* trans. J. C. Meredith (Oxford: Oxford University Press, 1973), bk. 1, sec. 1, para. 55.

3. Economies for Life[1]

David C. Korten

DAVID KORTEN (B. 1937) states, "Most people are now aware that rule by global corporations and financial speculators engaged in the single-minded pursuit of money is destroying communities, cultures, and natural systems everywhere on the planet." Korten calls this the "suicide economy." He points out that the limited liability corporations, those that we allow to concentrate power without limits and operate for the "benefit" of stockholders who neither know about, nor hold responsibility for, the firm's actions, are the corporations that harm workers and communities and pollute the environment. This situation is behavior that we would otherwise call sociopathic or criminal.

Korten proposes living economies in which business is locally based, "human-scale," owned by the stakeholders, and accountable to the laws enacted within democracies. In living economies, people have greater autonomy and more stable employment and are invested in both the enterprise and the community. Much of this change would result from owners being held responsible for the full costs of their production, and real costs of products would be reflected in "full-cost pricing." Korten concludes that this is not an unobtainable ideal because many of the elements needed to transition to a living economy are in place. He provides numerous examples, including not-for-profit business, independent businesses including farmers' markets, community banks, and the independent media, and he reminds us that these types of business already make up most businesses and therefore provide "most jobs."

THE LANGUAGE OF ECONOMIC dysfunction has become so common that when I use the term "the global suicide economy" in my talks, I rarely need to elaborate. Most people are now aware that rule by global corporations and financial speculators engaged in the single-minded pursuit of money is destroying communities, cultures, and natural systems everywhere on the planet. Until recently, however, most people responded with polite but resigned skepticism to my message that economic transformation is possible.

Now, with the revelations of high-profile corporate fraud and corruption, I sense a dramatic change. While the political power brokers talk of new rules and penalties to restore confidence in financial markets, members of religious orders and congregations, community groups, city officials, business people, and young activists are talking about the possibility of far greater changes—of creating truly new economies. They speak of real wealth as a sense of belonging, contribution, beauty, joy, relationship, and spiritual connection. They share their dreams of a world of locally rooted living economies that meet the material needs of all people everywhere, while providing meaning, building community, and connecting us to a place on the Earth.

Many are acting to make their dreams a reality. In late 2001, the Social Ventures Network, an alliance of socially committed entrepreneurs, responded to this upsurge in civic innovation by launching a new nationwide initiative—the Business Alliance for Local Living Economies—to encourage, strengthen, and facilitate the interlinking of these initiatives with the aim of creating a cohesive national movement.

The suicide economy is a product of human choices motivated by a love of money. It is within our means to make different choices motivated by a love of life. We have created a suicide economy based on absentee ownership, monopoly, and the concentration of power delinked from obligations to people or place. Now we must create living economies based on locally rooted ownership and deeply held American ideals of equity, democracy, markets, and personal responsibility.

In the place of a suicide economy devoted to maximizing returns to money, we can create living economies devoted to meeting the basic needs of people. In the place of a suicide economy in which the powerful reap the profits and the rest bear the cost, we can create a system of living economies in which decisions are made by those who will bear the consequences.

In the place of the suicide economy's global trading system designed to allow the wealthy few to control the resources and dominate the markets of the many, we can create living economy trade through which each community exchanges those things it produces in surplus for those it cannot reasonably produce at home on terms that support living

wage jobs and high environmental standards everywhere.

Under a system of relatively self-reliant local living economies, communities and nations will not find themselves pitted against one another for jobs, markets, and resources. In the absence of such competition, the free sharing of information, knowledge, and technology will become natural, to the mutual benefit of all.

Locally Owned, Human-Scale Enterprises

Living economies are made up of human-scale enterprises locally owned by people who have a direct stake in the many impacts associated with the enterprise. A firm owned by workers, community members, customers, and/or suppliers who directly bear the consequences of its actions is more likely to provide:

- Employees with safe, meaningful, family-wage jobs.
- Customers with useful, safe, high-quality products.
- Suppliers with steady markets and fair dealing.
- Communities with a healthy social and natural environment.

One of my favorite prototypes of a living economy enterprise is Philadelphia's White Dog Cafe. (See *YES!* Spring 2001.) Founder, owner, and proprietor Judy Wicks buys most of her food from local organic farmers, serves only meat from humanely raised animals, pays her workers a living wage, devotes 10 percent of profits to local charity, and has mobilized other Philadelphia restaurants to join in rebuilding the local food production and distribution system. Wicks is also a former board chair of the Social Ventures Network and a founder of the newly formed Business Alliance for Local Living Economies.[2]

Living economy enterprises may be organized as partnerships; individual or family-owned business; consumer- or producer-owned cooperatives; community corporations; or companies privately owned by workers, other community members, or social investors. They may be for-profit or nonprofit.

There is no place in living economies, however, for publicly traded, limited liability corporations, the organizational centerpiece of the suicide economy. This corporate form is legally structured to allow virtually unlimited concentration of power to the exclusive financial benefit of absentee shareholders who have no knowledge of, or liability for, the social and environmental consequences of the actions taken on their behalf. It is a legally sanctioned invitation to benefit from behavior that otherwise would be considered sociopathic—even criminal.

Life-Serving Rules

In the suicide economy, the success of an enterprise is measured by the financial return to its investors. The corporate media cheer when stock prices rise, increasing investor wealth, but sound the alarm when wages rise. Information on the price of a corporation's stock is available on a minute-by-minute basis, but information on its social and environmental impacts is rarely disclosed.

Rule-making in the suicide economy focuses on enforcing contracts, providing incentives for investors, and protecting the rights of property owners. Government intervention to protect workers, the environment, and consumers is denounced by corporate elites as an infringement of market freedom. Trade agreements like NAFTA and institutions like the World Trade Organization open countries to unbridled competition for investment and jobs that creates a race to the bottom in terms of labor, health, social, and environmental standards.

When Mr. Bush spoke to Wall Street bankers on July 9 on the subject of corporate accountability, his remarks centered on restoring investor confidence by increasing financial integrity and transparency. He made no mention of corporate accountability to workers, communities, the environment, or any other larger public interest. Follow closely the policy debates between Republicans and Democrats on financial fraud, and you will find they center on the competing private financial interests of managers and shareholders—with Republicans generally favoring the corporate managers and Democrats favoring the Wall Street financiers.

The primary purpose of a true market economy, however, is not to make money for the rich and powerful. When Adam Smith conceptualized the idea of the market economy in his classic *The Wealth of Nations*, he had in mind economies that allocate human and material resources justly and sustainably to meet the self-defined needs of people and community.

In order to allocate justly and sustainably, a market economy requires enforceable rules. Because markets respond only to the needs of those with money to pay, there must be rules to assure an equitable distribution of income. Because markets respond to prices, a just and sustainable allocation of resources depends on public regulation and user fees to assure that market prices internalize the true cost of a product or service—including the social and environmental costs otherwise borne by the public. Public oversight is also needed to assure that common heritage resources essential to the survival and well-being of all—like land and water—are protected and equitably shared.

When enterprises are locally rooted, human-scale, owned by stakeholders, and held accountable to the rule of law by democratically elected governments, there is a natural

415

incentive for all concerned to take human and community needs and interests into account. When income and ownership are equitably distributed, justice is served and political democracy is strong. When workers are owners, the conflict between labor and capital disappears. When needs are met locally by locally owned enterprises, people have greater control over their lives, money is recycled in the community rather than leaking off into the global financial casino, jobs are more secure, economies are more stable, and there are the means and the incentives to protect the environment and to build the relationships of mutual trust and responsibility that are the foundation of community.

Quality of Life

Our quality of life would be stunningly different if we based economic decisions on life values rather than purely financial values—a natural choice if owners had to live with the non-financial consequences of their decisions.

Full-cost pricing of energy, materials, and land use could expose the real inefficiencies of factory farming, conventional construction, and urban sprawl and make life-serving alternatives comparatively cost-effective. Much of our food could be grown fresh on local family farms without toxic chemicals, and processed nearby. Organic wastes could be composted and recycled back into the soil. Environmentally efficient buildings designed for their specific micro environment and constructed of local materials could radically reduce energy consumption. Much of our remaining energy needs could be supplied locally from wind and solar sources. Local wastes could be recycled to provide materials and energy for other local businesses.

Compact communities could bring work, shopping, and recreation nearer to our residences—thus saving energy and commuting time, reducing CO2 emissions and dependence on imported oil, and freeing time for family and community activities. Land now devoted to roads and parking could be converted to bike lanes, trails, and parks.

By reducing waste and unnecessary use of energy and other resources, we in America could reduce our need to expropriate the resources of other countries. We could quit allocating a major portion of our national treasure to the large military required to secure our access to those resources. The world's poor would regain access to the resources that are rightfully theirs to improve their own lives—and the threat of terrorism would be greatly reduced. The elimination of global corporations with their massive overhead, inflated executive compensation packages, and myopic focus on short-term profits would free still more resources. Together these savings could provide workers with family wages and finance first-rate education, health care, and community services for all.

We would expect to see the effects of living economy institutions ripple out across the social landscape. With ample living wage jobs, educational opportunities, and essential services, crime rates would drop, and prison and other criminal justice costs would fall.

An economy that responds to rather than creates demand diverts fewer resources to advertising. Fewer ads mean less visual pollution and wasteful consumerism, an improved sense of self-worth, and still more resources freed up to be converted into shorter work weeks and more leisure time. We would work less and live more. Our lives would be freer and richer. Our environment would be cleaner and healthier. A world no longer divided between obscenely rich and desperately poor would know more peace and less violence, more love and less hate, more hope and less fear. The Earth could heal and provide a home for our children for generations to come.

Awakening Majority

The ideal of a living economy might seem an impossible dream, except for the fact that so many of its elements are already in place. There are millions of for- and not-for-profit enterprises and public initiatives around the world aligned with the values and organizational principles of living economies. They include local independent businesses of all sorts from bookstores to bakeries, land trusts, local organic farms, farmers' markets, community-supported agriculture initiatives, restaurants specializing in locally grown organic produce, community banks, local currencies, buy-local campaigns, suppliers of fair-traded coffee, independent media, and many more. Indeed, independent, human-scale businesses are by far the majority of all businesses, provide most jobs, create nearly all new jobs, and are the source of most innovation.

It is clear that living economies are a viable alternative to the suicide economy. Nonetheless, the suicide economy continues to dominate our economic, political, social, and cultural lives. So how do we get from a few million living enterprises that are struggling to survive at the fringes of the global suicide economy to a healthy planetary system of thriving living economies? The answer is, "We grow it into being."

No one planned the suicide economy. It is what organizational consultant Margaret Wheatley calls an "emergent system." Those responsible for corporate interests grew it into being through their day-to-day effort to increase profits and market share. Step by step over the last several hundred years, they reshaped politics, the legal system, and modern culture to create the interlocking systems of interests and mutual obligations of what has become a suicide economy.

The complex, self-reinforcing dynamics of an emergent system make it virtually impossible to transform from within. Those who attempt to do so are almost invariably marginalized or expelled. When environmental writer Carl Frankel set out to write the book *In Earth's Company* on corporate environmentalism, he looked for true environmental champions within the corporate world. He found three. By the time his book was published, all three had been fired.

An emergent system that no longer serves can be displaced only by a more powerful emergent system. According to Wheatley, "This means that the work of change is to start over, to organize new local efforts, connect them to each other, and know that their values and practices can emerge as something even stronger."

This insight is critical to the work ahead. The most promising approach to ridding our societies of the pathological culture and institutions of the suicide economy is to displace them—an idea that at first seems hopelessly naive. Consider, however, that the institutions of the suicide economy are animated by our life energy. They have only the power that we each yield to them. Each time we choose where we shop, work, and invest, we can redirect our life energy from the suicide economy to the emergent living economy.

Choosing living economy enterprises may appear more expensive. Organic produce may cost more than non-organic; a bar of soap may cost more at a local store than at a big chain. That greater expense disappears, however, when we factor in such benefits of the living economy as improved health, caring communities, shorter commutes, meaningful work, cleaner air and water, free time, economic security, and hope for our children's future. Employment in a smaller enterprise may pay less, but be more secure.

When top mutual funds were returning 20 to 50 percent a year, putting money in a community bank that pays 4 or 5 percent seemed an expensive choice. In a period of market decline, however, an insured CD with a community bank that makes loans to local businesses begins to look like a smart, as well as ethical, choice.

Making It Happen

Those interested in helping to grow a living economy in their own community might start with a few simple questions. What do local people and businesses regularly buy that is or could be supplied locally by socially and environmentally responsible independent enterprises? Which existing local businesses are trying to practice living economy values? In what sectors are they clustered? Are there collaborative efforts aligned with living economy values already underway? The answers will point to promising opportunities.

Food is often a logical place to start. Everyone needs and cares about food, and food can be grown almost everywhere, is freshest and most wholesome when local, and is our most intimate connection to the land. In many communities, a farmers' market or a restaurant serving locally produced organic foods provides a focal point for organizing. In some communities, clusters of businesses devoted to energy conservation, environmental construction, and the local production of solar, wind, and mini-hydro power are forming living economy webs devoted to advancing local energy independence.

Many groups are working to create the financial infrastructure for living economies. Some are creating interest-free local currencies that encourage and facilitate transactions among local people and enterprises. Others are establishing community banks dedicated to financing local enterprises. The ShoreBank is one of my favorite examples of a living-economy financial institution. The bank is privately owned by a number of

individual investors, foundations, and nonprofit organizations dedicated to its social and environmental mission. It finances enterprises and projects that provide jobs, contribute to environmental health, upgrade low- and moderate-income rental housing units, create affordable home ownership opportunities, and develop and staff day-care centers and job-training programs. (See "A Founder of the Next Economy," *YES!* Fall 1999.)

A number of groups are developing a "fair trade" infrastructure that seeks to improve the conditions of low-income producers of coffee, handicrafts, and other goods. Still others are mobilizing political action to eliminate public subsidies, tax rebates, sweetheart contracts, regulatory exemptions, and giveaways of public resources on which the profits of otherwise inefficient corporate monoliths often depend, and to put in place new rules that favor local independent businesses, stakeholder ownership, living-wage employers, and environmental responsibility....

Countless local living-economy initiatives are being launched all across America and around the world, including some by former corporate employees who have chosen to walk away from the suicide economy to start new businesses aligned with their values. The greater the number and diversity of such initiatives, the more rapidly the web of an emergent planetary system of local living economies can grow, and the more readily each of us can redirect our life energy toward living economies in our shopping, employment, and investment choices.

Corporate scandals, a faltering economy, and stock-market declines have dealt a serious blow to the legitimacy of the suicide economy and the big corporations that dominate our lives. Thousands of people are already spreading the message that there is a life-serving alternative that we can grow into being. As suggested by the case examples from Appalachia and Argentina presented in this issue of *YES!,* living economy initiatives flourish most readily under the conditions of economic adversity that dramatically expose the suicide economy's false promises of instant, effortless wealth. The United States may be entering such a period. While the ruling elites occupy themselves with seeking to restore faith in the pathological institutions on which their power and privilege were built, the rest of us can embrace this moment of economic failure as an historic opportunity. Through our individual and collective choices, we can grow into being the economic institutions, relationships, and culture of a just, sustainable, and compassionate world of living economies that work for all.

How would we live?

When challenged to think of a world of living economies free of publicly traded corporations many people ask:

How would we earn our living?

For all their economic power, the number of jobs provided by global corporations relative to the world's workforce is small. The 200 largest corporations in the world employ less than 1 percent of the global work force although they account for about 30 percent of global economic activity. Between 1983 and 1999 the number of people they employ grew by 14 percent while their profits grew over 360 percent. Most job growth comes from local independent businesses.

Who would produce our food?

Smaller independently managed farms using environmentally sound agricultural practices are far more productive and efficient in the use of scarce land than are corporate factory farms. A 1992 US Agricultural Census shows that, based on total output per unit area, small farms produce over ten times more dollar output per acre than do the largest farms. The intercropping methods used by small farms guarantee more biodiversity and do less environmental damage than do large scale monoculture crops. Localizing food production means fresher, more nutritious food, more jobs, major energy savings, and a healthier environment.

How would drug research be financed?

Most basic research on new drug treatments is already funded with public money. Eighty-five percent of the research contributing to the top five selling drugs of 1995 was conducted by US taxpayer-funded researchers and foreign academic studies. Marketing, advertising, and administrative costs for the top nine drug companies totaled $45 billion in 2001; research and development expenditures totaled $19 billion.

How would we finance retirement?

Contrary to the claims of those who would profit from the privatization of Social Security, the elderly can't eat stock bubbles; they need food, shelter, clothing, and medical and personal services that someone must produce. Living economies might feature intergenerational living arrangements with cooperative community facilities for child and elder care along with a system of social insurance much like the current social security system.

Who would build our airplanes?

There will be far less need for air travel in a world of local living economies. Where there is need for the production of large, complex pieces of technology, they can be produced by publicly or worker-owned companies, or in facilities owned by cooperatives of the independent businesses that provide component parts and services.

Questions

1. Korten proposes a path to the living economy, a path outside of the system, because those who try to change the system from within are either ostracized or removed. How do living economy businesses play a part in realizing that economy?

2. Korten advocates displacing the suicide economy's institutions and culture through support of living economy businesses when making purchases, and through beginning in your own community to understand local examples of food and energy supply and the businesses that are already formed or forming living economy webs. In what ways can these businesses form a living economy?

3. Korten clarifies our choice: We can either follow the ruling elite who are invested in further propping up the system that has brought us scandal, economic insecurity, and environmental destruction, or we can see it as an opportunity to transform the system into an economy that provides a "just, sustainable, and compassionate world of living economies that work for all." Given the vulnerabilities made apparent in the suicide economy with the onset of Covid-19, how would you advocate transforming the post-Covid-19 economy into a living economy?

Notes

1. Reprinted from *Yes! A Journal of Positive Futures* 23 (Fall 2002). P.O. Box 10818, Bainbridge Island, Wash. 98110. Subscriptions: 800/937-4451 Website: www.yesmagazine.org. [Edited.]

2. The Business Alliance for Local Living Economies (BALLE) was launched in 2001 by the San Francisco-based Social Ventures Network. By mid-2002, BALLE had signed on 17 regional chapters, which are encouraging people to buy from, work for, and otherwise support locally owned, values-based enterprises. BALLE chapters also facilitate business-to-business relationships among firms committed to living economy values. Information on BALLE is available at www.livingeconomies.org.

Permissions Acknowledgments

Alford, C. Fred. "Whistleblowers and the Narrative of Ethics." *Journal of Social Philosophy* 32.3 (Fall 2001): 402–18. Copyright © 2001 Blackwell Publishers. Reprinted by permission of John Wiley & Sons, Inc. conveyed through Copyright Clearance Center, Inc.

Beck, Valentin and Bernd Ladwig. "Ethical Consumerism: Veganism." *WIREs Climate Change* (2021) 12:e689. Reprinted by permission of John Wiley & Sons, Inc. conveyed through Copyright Clearance Center, Inc. https://doi.org/10.1002/wcc.689

Benatar, David. Chapter 6: "Affirmative Action," from *The Second Sexism: Discrimination Against Men and Boys.* Copyright © 2012, Wiley-Blackwell, an imprint of John Wiley & Sons, Inc. pp. 213–25, 234–38 [excerpted]. Reprinted by permission of John Wiley & Sons, Inc. conveyed through Copyright Clearance Center, Inc.

Bok, Sissela. Excerpted from *Secrets: On the Ethics of Concealment and Revelation.* Copyright © 1983, 1989 by Sissela Bok. pp. 210–11, 213–15, 219–25 [edited]. Used by permission of Pantheon Books, an imprint of the Knopf Doubleday Publishing Group, a division of Penguin Random House LLC. All rights reserved.

Claxton, Guy. "Involuntary Simplicity: Changing Dysfunctional Habits of Consumption." *Environmental Values* 3.1 (February 1994): 71–81. Reprinted by permission of The White Horse Press, conveyed through Copyright Clearance Center, Inc. https://doi.org/10.3197/096327194776679791

Crouch, Martha L. "Biotechnology Is Not Compatible with Sustainable Agriculture." *Journal of Agricultural and Environmental Ethics* 8.2 (1995):

98–111. Copyright © 1969 Kluwer Academic Publishers. Reprinted by permission of Springer Nature, conveyed through Copyright Clearance Center, Inc. https://doi.org/10.1007/BF02251874

Danaher, John and Sven Nyholm. "Automation, Work and the Achievement Gap." *AI and Ethics,* (2021): 227–37. https://doi.org/10.1007/s43681-020-00028-x. Used under license CC BY 4.0 http://creativecommons.org/licenses/by/4.0/

Darley, John M. "How Corporations Socialize Individuals into Evildoing." *Codes of Conduct: Behavioral Research into Business Ethics,* edited by David M. Messick and Ann E. Tenbrunsel. pp. 13–43 [edited]. Copyright © 1996 Russell Sage Foundation. Reprinted by permission of the Russell Sage Foundation, conveyed through Copyright Clearance Center, Inc.

Deitch, Elizabeth A., Adam Barsky, Rebecca M. Butz, Suzanne Chan, Arthur P. Brief, and Jill C. Bradley. "Subtle Yet Significant: The Existence and Impact of Everyday Racial Discrimination in the Workplace." *Human Relations,* 56.11 (2003): 1299–1324. Reprinted by permission of SAGE Publishing, conveyed through Copyright Clearance Center, Inc.

Donaldson, Thomas. "Moral Minimums for Multinationals." *Ethics & International Affairs,* Vol. 3 (1989): 163–82. Copyright © 1989 Carnegie Council for Ethics in International Affairs. Reprinted by permission of Cambridge University Press, conveyed through Copyright Clearance Center, Inc. doi:10.1111/j.1747-7093.1989.tb00217.x

Friedman, Milton. "The Social Responsibility of Business Is to Increase Its Profits," from *The New York Times,* September 13, 1970. Copyright ©

Fulcher, Patrice A. Excerpted from "Hustle and Flow: Prison Privatization Fueling the Prison Industrial Complex." *Washburn Law Journal*, 51.3 (2012): 589–617 [edited]. Reproduced courtesy of the Washburn Law Journal.

Galbraith, John Kenneth. "How Much Should a Country Consume?," from *Perspectives on Conservation: Essays on America's Natural Resources*, edited by Henry Jarett, RFF Press, an imprint of Earthscan Routledge Books. Copyright © 1958, 2011. Reproduced by permission of Taylor and Francis Group, LLC, a division of Informa plc, conveyed through Copyright Clearance Center, Inc.

Goodland, Robert. "The Case that the World Has Reached Limits." *Population, Technology, and Lifestyles*, eds. Robert Goodland, Herman E. Daly, and Salah El Serafy. Copyright © 1992 Island Press. Reproduced by permission of Island Press, Washington, DC.

Jaggar, Alison M. Excerpted from "Is Globalization Good for Women?" *Comparative Literature* 53.4 (2001): 298–314 [edited]. Reproduced by permission of the author. https://doi.org/10.1215/-53-4-298

Klein, Naomi. Chapter 5, "Beyond Extractivism: Confronting the Climate Denier Within," from *This Changes Everything: Capitalism vs. the Climate*. Alfred A. Knopf Canada, 2014. Copyright © 2014 by Naomi Klein. pp. 161–75, 183–87 [excerpted]. Reprinted in Canada by permission of Vintage Canada/Alfred A. Knopf Canada, a division of Penguin Random House Canada Limited. All rights reserved. Any third-party use of this material, outside of this publication, is prohibited. Interested parties must apply directly to Penguin Random House Canada Limited for permission. Reprinted in the US by permission of Simon & Schuster, Inc. All rights reserved.

Korten, David C. "Economies for Life." *Yes! A Journal of Positive Futures*, Issue 23 (Fall 2002): 13–17 [edited]. Reprinted by permission of Yes! Magazine.

Leopold, Aldo. "The Land Ethic," from *A Sand County Almanac: And Sketches Here and There*. Copyright © 1949, 1977 by Oxford University Press, Inc. pp.190–213. Reprinted by permission of Oxford University Press, conveyed through PLSclear.

Najjar, Fauzi. "The Arabs, Islam and Globalization." *Middle East Policy*, 12.3 (Fall 2005): 91–106 [edited]. Reprinted by permission of John Wiley & Sons, Inc. conveyed through Copyright Clearance Center, Inc. https://doi.org/10.1111/j.1061-1924.2005.00215.x

Nalick, Michael, Matthew Josefy, Asghar Zardkoohi, and Leonard Bierman. Excerpted from "Corporate Sociopolitical Involvement: A Reflection of Whose Preferences?" *Academy of Management Perspectives*, 30.4 (6 October 2016): 384–91, 397–403 [edited]. Copyright © 2016 Academy of Management Perspectives. Republished by permission of the Academy of Management (NY), conveyed through Copyright Clearance Center, Inc. https://doi.org/10.5465/amp.2015.0033

Peña, Devon G. Excerpted from Part 4, Chapter 9: "Promised Land or Wasteland?" *The Terror of the Machine: Technology, Work, Gender, and Ecology on the U.S.–Mexico Border*, published by CMAS Books. pp. 325–31 [edited]. Copyright © 1997 by the Center for Mexican American Studies, University of Texas at Austin. Reproduced by permission of CMAS.

Ponting, Clive. Chapter 10, "Creating the Third World," from *A Green History of the World: The Environment and the Collapse of Great Civilization*. Copyright © Clive Ponting, 1991. pp. 194–223 [edited]. Reprinted by permission of St. Martin's Press LLC.

Shiva, Vandana. Excerpted from Chapter One, *Staying Alive: Women, Ecology and Development*, published by North Atlantic Books. Copyright © 1999, 2010, 2016 by Vandana Shiva. Reprinted by permission of the publisher.

Singer, Peter. "What Should a Billionaire Give—And What Should You?," from *The New York Times Magazine*, December 17, 2006. Copyright ©

2006 The New York Times Company. All rights reserved. Used under license.

Steele, Shelby. "Affirmative Action: The Price of Preference," from *The Content of Our Character: A New Vision of Race in America*, reprinted by HarperPerennial, by arrangement with St. Martin's Press. Copyright © 1990 by Shelby Steele. pp. 111–26. Reprinted in the UK and Commonwealth by permission of the Carol Mann Agency on behalf of the author. Reprinted elsewhere by permission of St. Martin's Press LLC.

The publisher has made every attempt to locate all copyright holders of the articles published in this text and would be grateful for information that would allow correction of any errors or omissions in subsequent editions of the work.

This book is made of paper from well-managed FSC® - certified forests, recycled materials, and other controlled sources.